IMPORTANT

HERE IS YOUR REGISTRATION CODE TO ACCESS MCGRAW-HILL PREMIUM CONTENT AND MCGRAW-HILL ONLINE RESOURCES

For key premium online resources you need THIS CODE to gain access. Once the code is entered, you will be able to use the web resources for the length of your course.

Access is provided only if you have purchased a new book.

If the registration code is missing from this book, the registration screen on our website, and within your WebCT or Blackboard course will tell you how to obtain your new code. Your registration code can be used only once to establish access. It is not transferable.

To gain access to these online resources

1. **USE** your web browser to go to: **www.mhhe.com/fahey7e**

2. **CLICK** on "First Time User"

3. **ENTER** the Registration Code printed on the tear-off bookmark on the right

4. After you have entered your registration code, click on "Register"

5. **FOLLOW** the instructions to setup your personal UserID and Password

6. **WRITE** your UserID and Password down for future reference. Keep it in a safe place.

If your course is using WebCT or Blackboard, you'll be able to use this code to access the McGraw-Hill content within your instructor's online course.

To gain access to the McGraw-Hill content in your instructor's WebCT or Blackboard course simply log into the course with the user ID and Password provided by your instructor. Enter the registration code exactly as it appears to the right when prompted by the system. You will only need to use this code the first time you click on McGraw-Hill content.

These instructions are specifically for student access. Instructors are not required to register via the above instructions.

The McGraw-Hill Companies

McGraw Hill | Higher Education

Thank you, and welcome to your McGraw-Hill Online Resources.

ISBN-13: 978-0-07-302990-0
ISBN-10: 0-07-302990-4 t/a
Fahey - Fit & Well: Core Concepts and
Labs in Physical Fitness and Wellness, 7/e

Selected Material from

Fit& Well

Core Concepts and Labs in Physical Fitness and Wellness

Seventh Edition

Thomas D. Fahey
California State University, Chico

Paul M. Insel
Stanford University

Walton T. Roth
Stanford University

 **Custom Publishing**

Boston   Burr Ridge, IL   Dubuque, IA   New York   San Francisco   St. Louis
Bangkok   Bogotá   Caracas   Lisbon   London   Madrid   Mexico City   Milan
New Delhi   Seoul   Singapore   Sydney   Taipei   Toronto

The McGraw·Hill Companies

Selected Material from
Fit & Well
Core Concepts and Labs in Physical Fitness and Wellness
Seventh Edition

This book is a McGraw-Hill Custom Publishing textbook and contains select material from *Fit and Well: Core Concepts and Labs in Physical Fitness and Wellness*, Seventh Edition by Thomas D. Fahey, Paul M. Insel, and Walton T. Roth. Copyright © 2007, 2005, 2003, 2001, and 1999 by The McGraw-Hill Companies, Inc. Reprinted with permission of the publisher. Many custom published texts are modified versions or adaptations of our best-selling textbooks. Some adaptations are printed in black and white to keep prices at a minimum, while others are in color.

1 2 3 4 5 6 7 8 9 0 MER MER 0 9 8 7 6

ISBN-13: 978-0-07-331364-1
ISBN-10: 0-07-331364-5

Editor: Michael Hemmer
Production Editor: Nina Meyer
Printer/Binder: Mercury Print Productions

Brief Contents

Contents

7   Putting Together a Complete Fitness Program   199

8   Nutrition   227

9 Weight Management 281

10 Stress 311

V̇W BEHAVIOR CHANGE WORKBOOK ACTIVITIES

V̇W LABORATORY ACTIVITIES

Preface

For today's fitness-conscious student, *Fit and Well* combines the best of two worlds. In the area of physical fitness, *Fit and Well* offers expert knowledge based on the latest findings in exercise physiology and sports medicine, along with tools for self-assessment and guidelines for becoming fit. In the area of wellness, it offers accurate, current information on today's most important health-related topics and issues, again with self-tests and guidelines for achieving wellness. To create this book, we have drawn on our combined expertise and experience in exercise physiology, athletic training, personal health, scientific research, and teaching.

OUR AIMS

Our aims in writing this book can be stated simply:

- To show students that becoming fit and well greatly improves the quality of their lives
- To show students how they can become fit and well
- To motivate students to make healthy choices and to provide them with tools for change

The first of these aims means helping students see how their lives can be enhanced by a fit and well lifestyle. This book offers convincing evidence of a simple truth: To look and feel our best, to protect ourselves from degenerative diseases, and to enjoy the highest quality of life, we need to place fitness and wellness among our top priorities. *Fit and Well* makes clear both the imprudence of our modern, sedentary lifestyle and the benefits of a wellness lifestyle.

Our second aim is to give students the tools and information they need to become fit and well. This book provides students with everything they need to create personalized fitness programs, including instructions for fitness tests, explanations of the components of fitness and guidelines for developing them, descriptions and illustrations of exercises, sample programs, and more. In addition, *Fit and Well* provides accurate, up-to-date, scientifically based information about other key topics in wellness, including nutrition, weight management, stress, cardiovascular health, cancer, drugs, alcohol, STDs, and a multitude of others.

In providing this material, we have pooled our efforts. Thomas Fahey has contributed his knowledge as an exercise physiologist, teacher, and author of numerous exercise science textbooks. Paul M. Insel and Walton T. Roth have contributed their knowledge of current topics in health as the authors of the leading personal health textbook, *Core Concepts in Health*.

Because we know this expert knowledge can be overwhelming, we have balanced the coverage of complex topics with student-friendly features designed to make the book accessible. Written in a straightforward, easy-to-read style and presented in a colorful, open format, *Fit and Well* invites the student to read, learn, and remember. Boxes, labs, tables, figures, artwork, photographs, and other features add interest to the text and highlight areas of special importance.

Our third aim is to involve students in taking responsibility for their health. *Fit and Well* makes use of interactive features to get students thinking about their current levels of physical fitness and wellness. We offer students assessment tools and laboratory activities to evaluate themselves in terms of each component of physical fitness and each major wellness area, ranging from cardiorespiratory endurance and muscular strength to heart disease, cancer, and STDs.

We also show students how they can make difficult lifestyle changes by using the principles of behavior change. Chapter 1 contains a step-by-step description of this simple but powerful tool for change. The chapter not only explains the five-step process but also offers a wealth of tips for ensuring success. Behavior management aids, including personal contracts, behavior checklists, and self-tests, appear throughout the book. *Fit and Well's* combined emphasis on self-assessment, self-development in each area of wellness, and behavior change ensures that students are inspired to become fit and well and also have the tools to do so.

When students use these tools to make significant lifestyle changes, they begin to realize that they are in charge of their health—and their lives. From this realization comes a sense of competence and personal power. Perhaps our overriding aim in writing *Fit and Well* is to convey the fact that virtually everyone has the ability to understand, monitor, and make changes in his or her levels of fitness and wellness. By making healthy choices from an early age, individuals may minimize the amount of professional medical care they will ever require. Our hope is that *Fit and Well* will help people make this exciting discovery: that they have the power to shape their future.

CONTENT AND ORGANIZATION OF THE SEVENTH EDITION

The basic content of *Fit and Well* remains unchanged in the seventh edition. Chapter 1 provides an introduction to fitness and wellness and explains the principles of behavior change. Chapters 2–7 focus on the various areas of fitness. Chapter 2 provides an overview, discussing the components of fitness, the principles of physical training, and the factors involved in designing a well-rounded, personalized exercise program. Chapter 3 provides basic information on how the cardiorespiratory system functions, how the body produces energy for exercise, and how individuals can create successful cardiorespiratory fitness programs. Chapters 4, 5, and 6 look at muscular strength and endurance, flexibility and low-back health, and body composition, respectively. Chapter 7 puts it all together, describing the nature of a complete program that develops all the components of fitness. This chapter also includes complete sample exercise programs.

Chapters 8, 9, and 10 treat three key areas of wellness promotion: nutrition, weight management, and stress management, respectively. It is in these areas that individuals have some of the greatest opportunities for positive change. Chapters 11 and 12 focus on two of the most important reasons for making lifestyle changes: cardiovascular disease and cancer. Students learn the basic mechanisms of these diseases, how they are related to lifestyle, and what individuals can do to prevent them. Chapters 13 and 14 focus on other important wellness issues: addictive behaviors, including the use and abuse of tobacco, alcohol, and other drugs (Chapter 13) and sexually transmitted diseases (Chapter 14). Finally, Chapter 15 looks at four additional wellness topics: interpersonal relationships, aging, the health care system, and environmental health.

For the seventh edition, each chapter was carefully reviewed, revised, and updated. The latest information from scientific and wellness-related research is incorporated in the text, and newly emerging topics are discussed. The following list gives a sample of some of the new and updated material included in the seventh edition of *Fit and Well*:

- Research on links between lifestyle and quality of life
- 2005 Dietary Guidelines for Americans and the USDA MyPyramid food guidance system
- Physical activity guidelines from the USDA, Surgeon General, ACSM, WHO, and other organizations
- Fitness training recommendations from the 2006 edition of ACSM's *Guidelines for Exercise Training and Prescription*
- Core muscle fitness and training with stability balls, resistance bands, and Pilates exercises
- Use of pedometers to track and increase activity levels
- Health problems associated with overweight and obesity, and popular approaches to weight loss (diets, supplements, prescription medications, and surgery)
- Trans fat labeling requirements
- Food safety
- Gender differences in cardiovascular disease
- Tobacco cessation products

- Performance aids and dietary supplement safety and labeling issues
- Body image and eating disorders
- Preventing and managing low-back pain
- Nutrition for athletes
- Diabetes and pre-diabetes
- College stressors and coping methods
- CVD and cancer testing and treatment recommendations
- Binge drinking and alcohol emergencies
- Ecstasy, GHB, and other club drugs
- Spiritual wellness
- Complementary and alternative medicine
- Health fraud and quackery
- Safety and emergency preparedness

Research in the areas of health and wellness is ongoing, with new discoveries, advances, trends, and theories reported nearly every week. For this reason, no wellness book can claim to have the final word on every topic. Yet, within these limits, *Fit and Well* does present the latest available information and scientific thinking on important wellness topics. Taken together, the chapters of the book provide students with a complete, up-to-date guide to maximizing their well-being, now and throughout their lives.

WW To help students obtain the most current wellness information, each chapter in the seventh edition is also closely tied to the Web site developed as a companion to the text. Boxes, illustrations, tables, labs, terms, and sections of text marked with the World Wide Web icon have corresponding links and activities on the *Fit and Well* Online Learning Center (www.mhhe.com/fahey).

FEATURES OF THE SEVENTH EDITION

This edition of *Fit and Well* builds on the features that attracted and held our readers' interest in previous editions. These features are designed to help students increase their understanding of the key concepts of wellness and to make better use of the book.

Laboratory Activities

To help students apply the principles of fitness and wellness to their lives, *Fit and Well* includes **laboratory activities** for classroom use. These hands-on activities give students the opportunity to assess their current level of fitness and wellness, to create plans for changing their lifestyle to reach wellness, and to monitor their progress. They can assess their daily physical activity, for example, or their level of cardiorespiratory endurance; they can design a program to improve muscular strength or meet weight-loss goals; they can explore their risk of developing cardiovascular disease or cancer; and they can examine their attitudes and behaviors in relation to alcohol use and STDs. Many labs end with a Using Your Results section, which guides students in evaluating their scores, setting goals for change, and moving forward. Labs are found at the end of each chapter; they are perforated for easy removal.

The laboratory activities are also found in an interactive format on the *Fit and Well* Online Learning Center. For a complete list of laboratory activities, see p. x in the table of contents.

Illustrated Exercise Sections

To ensure that students understand how to perform important exercises and stretches, *Fit and Well* includes three **illustrated exercise sections**, one in Chapter 4 and two in Chapter 5. The section in Chapter 4 covers exercises for developing muscular strength and endurance, as performed both with free weights and on weight machines. One section in Chapter 5 presents stretches for flexibility, and the other presents exercises to stretch and strengthen the lower back. Each exercise is illustrated with one or more full-color photographs showing proper technique.

Digital video clips of the exercises from the text and key lab activities are found on the *Fit and Well* Online Learning Center. Look for the video icon in the text to find out when to look online for corresponding video clips.

Sample Programs

To help students get started, Chapter 7 offers seven complete **sample programs** designed to develop overall fitness. The programs are built around four popular cardiorespiratory endurance activities: walking/jogging/running, bicycling, swimming, and in-line skating. Each program includes detailed information and guidelines on equipment and technique; target intensity, duration, and frequency; calorie cost of the activity; record keeping; and adjustments to make as fitness improves. They also include strength training and stretching exercises. The chapter also includes general guidelines for putting together a personal fitness program: setting goals; selecting activities; setting targets for intensity, duration, and frequency; maintaining a commitment; and recording and assessing progress.

Boxes

Boxes are used in *Fit and Well* to explore a wide range of current topics in greater detail than is possible in the text itself. Boxes fall into five different categories, each marked with a special icon and label.

 Take Charge boxes distill from the text the practical advice students need to apply information to their lives. By referring to these boxes, students can easily find information about such topics as becoming more active, rehabilitating athletic injuries, exercising in hot weather, adding whole-grain foods to the diet, judging serving sizes, helping a friend who has an eating disorder, managing anger, dealing with an alcohol emergency, enhancing support in interpersonal relationships, and many others.

Critical Consumer boxes are designed to help students develop and apply critical thinking skills, thereby enabling them to make sound choices related to health and well-being. Critical Consumer boxes provide specific guidelines for choosing a fitness center and exercise footwear and equipment; for evaluating health information, diet pills and aids, supplements, and smoking cessation products; and for using food labels and dietary supplement labels to make informed dietary choices.

Dimensions of Diversity boxes focus on the important theme of diversity. Most wellness issues are universal; we all need to exercise and eat well, for example. However, certain differences among people—based on gender, educational attainment, socioeconomic status, ethnicity, age, and other factors—do have important implications for wellness. Dimensions of Diversity boxes give students opportunities to identify special wellness concerns that affect them because of who they are, as individuals or as members of a group. Topics of Dimensions of Diversity boxes include fitness for people with disabilities, gender differences in the effects of smoking, gender and ethnic differences in body image, ethnic foods, and the relationship between poverty and cancer.

 Wellness Connection boxes highlight important links among the different dimensions of wellness—physical, emotional, social/interpersonal, intellectual, spiritual, and environmental—and emphasize that all the dimensions must be developed for an individual to achieve optimal health and well-being. Topics include the effects of exercise on mental functioning, paths to spiritual wellness, expressive writing, hostility and heart disease, coping with cancer, and the benefits of volunteering.

In Focus boxes highlight current topics and issues of particular interest to students. These boxes focus on such topics as the importance of lifestyle for young adults, exercise safety, exercise machines versus free weights, diabetes, fitness and fatness, popular diets, glycemic index, the benefits of quitting smoking, and many others.

Vital Statistics

Vital Statistics tables and figures highlight important facts and figures in an accessible format. From tables and figures marked with the Vital Statistics label, students learn about such matters as the leading causes of death for Americans and the factors that play a part in each cause; the relationship between lifestyle and quality of life; public health achievements of the twentieth century; drug use in the

United States; the effects of binge drinking on college students; routes of HIV infection; and a wealth of other information. For students who learn best when material is displayed graphically or numerically, Vital Statistics tables and figures offer a way to grasp information quickly and directly.

Common Questions Answered

Sections called **Common Questions Answered** appear at the ends of Chapters 2–14. In these student-friendly sections, the answers to frequently asked questions are presented in easy-to-understand terms. Included are such questions as, Do I need more protein in my diet when I train with weights? How can I safely increase exercise intensity? What is core strength training? Is stretching the same as warming up? How can I tell if I'm allergic to a food? and, Does drinking coffee help an intoxicated person sober up more quickly? Answers to additional questions can be found on the Online Learning Center.

Motivation for Change

Motivation for Change sections provide strategies for beginning a behavior change program and maintaining healthy new habits over time. Motivation for Change strategies focus on such key aspects of behavior change as building self-efficacy, finding role models and social support, overcoming obstacles and lapses, changing environmental cues, giving rewards, and tracking program progress. These sections appear at appropriate points throughout each chapter.

Tips for Today

Chapter-ending **Tips for Today** sections provide a brief distillation of the major message of each chapter, followed by suggestions for a few simple things that students can try right away. Tips for Today are designed to encourage students and to build their confidence by giving them easy steps they can take immediately to improve their wellness.

Quick-Reference Appendixes

Included at the end of the book are four appendixes containing vital information in an easy-to-use format. **Appendix A, Injury Prevention and Personal Safety,** is a reference guide to preventing common injuries, whether at home, at work, at play, or on the road. It also provides information on emergency preparedness and on giving emergency care when someone else's life is in danger.

Appendix B, Nutritional Content of Common Foods, allows students to assess their daily diet in terms of 11 nutrient categories, including protein, fat, saturated fat, fiber, cholesterol, and sodium. **Appendix C, Nutritional Content of Popular Items from Fast-Food Restaurants,** provides a breakdown of the nutritional content of commonly ordered menu items at popular fast-food restaurants.

Appendix D, Monitoring Your Progress, is a log that enables students to record and summarize the results of the assessment tests they complete as part of the laboratory activities. With space for preprogram and postprogram assessment results, the log provides an easy way to track the progress of a behavior change program.

Built-in Behavior Change Workbook

The built-in **Behavior Change Workbook** contains 15 separate activities that complement the lifestyle management model presented in Chapter 1. The workbook guides students in developing a successful program by walking them through each of the steps of behavior change—from choosing a target behavior to completing and signing a contract. It also includes activities to help students overcome common obstacles to behavior change. The workbook is also found on the Online Learning Center.

OTHER FEATURES AND LEARNING AIDS

At the beginning of each chapter, under the heading **Looking Ahead,** five or six statements preview the main points of the chapter for the student and serve as learning objectives. Each chapter also opens with **Test Your Knowledge**—three multiple-choice and true-false questions, with answers. These self-quizzes facilitate learning by emphasizing key points, highlighting common misconceptions, and sparking debate. Within each chapter, important terms appear in boldface type and are defined on the same or facing page of text in a **running glossary,** helping students handle new vocabulary.

Other features and learning aids are found at the end of each chapter. **Chapter summaries** offer students a concise review and a way to make sure they have grasped the most important concepts in the chapter. **For Further Exploration** sections offer suggestions for using the free student supplements that accompany the text—the Online Learning Center and the Daily Fitness and Nutrition Journal—to build fitness and wellness. These sections also list recommended books, newsletters, organizations, hotlines, and Web sites.

For more on the features of the book, refer to the illustrated **User's Guide to *Fit and Well,*** found on pp. xvii–xx.

TEACHING TOOLS

Available with the seventh edition of *Fit and Well* is a comprehensive package of supplementary materials designed to enhance teaching and learning.

Instructor's Resource CD-ROM (ISBN 0-07-302983-1)

The Instructor's Resource CD-ROM combines major electronic resources offered with the seventh edition of *Fit and Well.*

- The **Course Integrator Guide** includes learning objectives, extended chapter outlines, lists of additional resources, and many other teaching tools. It also describes all the print and electronic supplements available with the text and shows how to integrate them into lectures and assignments for each chapter. For the seventh edition, the guide was prepared by Julie Lombardi, Millersville University.

- One hundred **Additional Laboratory Activities** supplement the labs that are included in the text. These additional labs are also available to students on the Online Learning Center.

- The **test bank** includes more than 1500 true-false, multiple-choice, and essay questions. The questions are available as Word files and with the **EZ Test computerized testing software.** EZ Test provides a powerful, easy-to-use test maker to create printed quizzes and exams. For secure online testing, exams created in EZ Test can be exported to WebCT, Blackboard, PageOut, and EZ Test Online. EZ Test comes with a Quick Start Guide, and, once the program is installed, users have access to a User's Manual and Flash tutorials. Additional help is available online at www.mhhe.com/eztest.

- The **PowerPoint slides,** expanded for the seventh edition, provide a lecture tool that you can alter or expand to meet the needs of your course. The slides include key lecture points and images from the text and other sources. For the seventh edition, the PowerPoint presentations were created by Andrew Shim, Indiana University of Pennsylvania. As an aid for instructors who wish to create their own presentations, a complete **image bank,** including all the illustrations from the text, is also available on the Instructor's CD-ROM.

Printed versions of key supplements—the Course Integrator Guide, Additional Labs, and test bank—are also available (ISBN 0-07-302982-3). The printed supplements are loose-leaf and three-hole-punched, ready to be placed in a binder.

Resource Presentation Manager DVD-ROM (ISBN 0-07-302986-6)

This DVD-ROM is a presentation tool of videos correlated to *Fit and Well.* It is designed to help you demonstrate proper training techniques, engage students in class discussions, and promote critical thinking about fitness and wellness topics. The video library contains demonstrations of many strength training and flexibility exercises as well as student interviews and historical health videos on nutrition, body image, stress, and many other topics. Videos can be viewed from the DVD-ROM, saved to a playlist for later viewing, or downloaded to a computer. For many clips, an Instructor's Guide is available with objectives, pre-viewing critical thinking questions, and suggested follow-up discussion questions.

Primis Online www.mhhe.com/primis/online

Primis Online is a database-driven publishing system that allows instructors to create customized textbooks, lab manuals, or readers for their courses directly from the Primis Web site. The custom text can be delivered in print or electronic (eBook) form. A Primis eBook is a digital version of the customized text sold directly to students as a file downloadable to their computer or accessed online by password. *Fit and Well* can be customized using Primis Online.

Digital Solutions

The *Fit and Well* **Online Learning Center** (www.mhhe .com/fahey) provides many resources for both instructors and students. Instructor tools include downloadable versions of the Course Integrator Guide and the PowerPoint slides, links to professional resources, and a guide to using the Internet. For students, there are learning objectives, self-quizzes and glossary flashcards for review, interactive Internet activities, video clips of correct training techniques, and extensive links. The Online Learning Center also includes many tools for wellness behavior change, including interactive versions of the Behavior Change Workbook as well as lab activities from the text and additional labs from the Course Integrator Guide. Through the Online Learning Center, students can also access **PowerWeb** (www.dushkin.com/online) resources, including articles on key wellness topics, study tips, and a daily news feed.

The **Online Lab and Assessment Workbook,** developed in collaboration with Quia™, offers an electronic version of labs, assessments, and quizzes compiled from the text and its main supplements. This online supplement provides students with interactive labs and assessments, self-scoring quizzes, and instant feedback. Benefits for instructors include a grade book that automatically scores, tracks, and records students' results; it also offers instructors the opportunity to review individual and class performance and customize activities for their course. To find out more about the Quia™ Online Lab and Assessment Workbook, including how you can package it with *Fit and Well,* contact your local sales representative.

Classroom Performance System (CPS) brings interactivity into the classroom or lecture hall. CPS is a wireless response system that gives instructors and students immediate feedback from the entire class. Each student uses a wireless response pad similar to a television remote to instantly respond to polling or quiz questions. Contact your local sales representative for more information about using CPS with *Fit and Well.*

PageOut (www.pageout.net) is a free, easy-to-use program that enables instructors to quickly develop Web sites for their courses. PageOut can be used to create a course home page, an instructor home page, an interactive syllabus that can be linked to elements in the Online

Learning Center, Web links, online discussion areas, an online grade book, and much more. Instructors can combine Online Learning Center resources with popular **course-management systems.** The McGraw-Hill Instructor Advantage program offers access to a complete online teaching Web site called the Knowledge Gateway, toll-free phone support, and unlimited e-mail support directly from WebCT and Blackboard. Instructors who use 500 or more copies of a text can enroll in the Instructor Advantage Plus program, which provides on-campus, hands-on training from a certified platform specialist.

For more information about McGraw-Hill's digital resources, including how to obtain passwords for PageOut and PowerWeb, contact your local representative and visit McGraw-Hill online (www. mhhe.com/solutions).

Student Resources Available with *Fit and Well*

In addition to the materials on the Online Learning Center, there are many resources available with *Fit and Well* designed to help students learn and apply key concepts.

- The **Daily Fitness and Nutrition Journal** (ISBN 0-07-302988-2) is a handy booklet that guides students in planning and tracking their fitness programs. It also helps students assess their current diet and make appropriate changes. It is packaged free with each new copy of the text.

- The **Health and Fitness Pedometer** (ISBN 0-07-320933-3) can be packaged with copies of the text. It allows students to count their daily steps and track their level of physical activity.

- **NutritionCalc Plus** (ISBN 0-07-319532-4) is a dietary analysis program with an easy-to-use interface that allows users to track their nutrient and food group intakes, energy expenditures, and weight control goals. It generates a variety of reports and graphs for analysis, including comparisons with the Dietary Reference Intakes. The ESHA database includes thousands of ethnic foods, supplements, fast foods, and convenience foods; users can also add foods to the database. NutritionCalc Plus is available on CD-ROM (Windows only) or in an Internet version.

- **HealthQuest 4.2** (ISBN 0-07-295117-6) is an interactive CD-ROM that helps students explore their wellness behavior. It includes tutorials, assessments, and behavior change guidance in such key areas as stress, fitness, nutrition, communicable diseases, cardiovascular disease, cancer, tobacco, alcohol, and other drugs.

Additional supplements and many packaging options are available; check with your local sales representative.

A NOTE OF THANKS

Fit and Well has benefited from the thoughtful commentary, expert knowledge, and helpful suggestions of many people. We are deeply grateful for their participation in the project.

Academic Reviewers of the Seventh Edition

Kym Y. Atwood, University of West Florida
John Burgess, Suffolk Community College, Grant Campus
Ronnie Carda, University of Wisconsin–Madison
Ronald H. Cox, Miami University
Karen K. Dennis, Illinois State University
Steve Frierman, Hofstra University
Jeffrey T. Godin, Fitchburg State College
Charlie Goehl, Elmhurst College
Ronnie R. Harris, Jacksonville State University
Ryan Hubbard, California State University, Los Angeles
Andrew G. Jameson, University of Mississippi
Joe L. Jones, Cameron University
William B. Karper, University of North Carolina at Greensboro
Catherine E. King, Floyd College
Vincent E. Mumford, University of Central Florida
Hikaru Murata, Missouri Western State College
Daniel A. Pray, Shoreline Community College
Nicholas Ratamess, College of New Jersey
Susan T. Saylor, Shelton State Community College
Benjamin J. Staupe, Rock Valley College
Virginia L. Trummer, University of Texas at San Antonio
Lydia Vanderford, Clayton College and State University
Matthew S. Wiggins, Murray State University
Jennifer Yee, Creighton University
Ben Zhou, California State University, Dominguez Hills

Special thanks are due to Rich Schroeder, DeAnza College, for hosting the photo and video shoots for several editions and to the many students at DeAnza College and California State University, Chico, who have participated in these shoots. Special thanks also go to Gary Ligouri at North Dakota State University and to the NDSU students who participated in the special fitness and wellness focus groups. We are also grateful to the *Fit and Well* book team, without whose efforts the book could not have been published. Special thanks to Chris Johnson, sponsoring editor; Kirstan Price, developmental editor; Julia Ersery, developmental editor for technology; Sarah Hill, editorial assistant; Pam Cooper, marketing manager; Brett Coker, production editor; Randy Hurst, production supervisor; Violeta Díaz, design manager; Robin Mouat, art manager; Brian J. Pecko, manager, photo research; and Marty Granahan, permissions editor.

Thomas D. Fahey
Paul M. Insel
Walton T. Roth

A User's Guide to *Fit and Well*

Are you looking for ways to improve your lifestyle and become fit and well? Do you need help finding reliable wellness resources online? Would you like to boost your grade? *Fit and Well* can help you do all this and much more!

LABORATORY ACTIVITIES

These hands-on self-assessments help you determine your current level of wellness and create plans for making positive changes in your lifestyle. Lab activities are included at the end of every chapter on easy-to-use perforated pages.

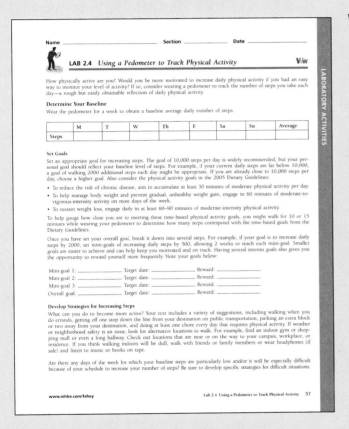

Vw *FIT AND WELL* ONLINE LEARNING CENTER (www.mhhe.com/fahey)

Look for the World Wide Web icon throughout the text. Elements marked with the icon have corresponding activities and links on the *Fit and Well* Online Learning Center. The lab activities can be found online in an interactive format.

TAKE CHARGE BOXES

Take Charge boxes, found throughout the text, provide practical advice that you can apply to your everyday life.

TIPS FOR TODAY

Tips for Today sections, found at the end of each chapter, provide a brief summary of the major message of the chapter, followed by suggestions for a few easy steps you can try right away to improve your level of wellness.

MOTIVATION FOR CHANGE

Motivation for Change sections provide strategies for beginning a behavior change program and maintaining new healthy habits over time.

RUNNING GLOSSARY

Important terms appear in boldface type in the text and are defined in a running glossary on the same or facing page. A pronunciation guide to the glossary terms is found on the Online Learning Center.

CRITICAL CONSUMER BOXES

Critical Consumer boxes help you develop and apply critical thinking skills so you can make sound choices related to wellness. Additional resources for each Critical Consumer topic are found on the *Fit and Well* Online Learning Center.

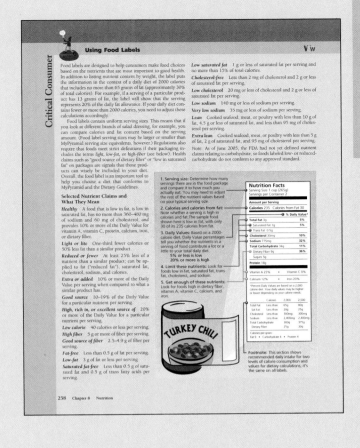

BEHAVIOR CHANGE WORKBOOK

The Behavior Change Workbook takes you step-by-step through the process of behavior change. It helps you target a specific behavior, set goals, create a plan, and overcome common obstacles to change. The Workbook is available in an interactive format on the Online Learning Center, and a printed copy is included in the full and alternate editions of the text.

Behavior Change Workbook

This workbook is designed to take you step by step through a behavioral change program. The first eight activities in the workbook will help you develop a successful plan—beginning with choosing a target behavior, moving through the planning steps described in Chapter 1, and completing and signing a behavior change contract. The final seven activities will help you work through common obstacles to behavior change and maximize your program's chances of success.

Part 1 Developing a Plan for Behavior Change and Completing a Contract

1. Choosing a Target Behavior
2. Gathering Information About Your Target Behavior
3. Monitoring Your Current Patterns of Behavior
4. Setting Goals
5. Examining Your Attitudes About Your Target Behavior
6. Choosing Rewards
7. Breaking Behavior Chains
8. Completing a Contract for Behavior Change

Part 2 Overcoming Obstacles to Behavior Change

9. Building Motivation and Commitment
10. Managing Your Time Successfully
11. Developing Realistic Self-Talk
12. Involving the People Around You
13. Dealing with Feelings
14. Overcoming Peer Pressure: Communicating Assertively
15. Maintaining Your Program over Time

ACTIVITY 1 CHOOSING A TARGET BEHAVIOR

Use your knowledge of yourself and the results of Lab 1.2 (Lifestyle Evaluation) to identify five behaviors that you could change to improve your level of wellness. Examples of target behaviors include smoking cigarettes, not exercising regularly, eating candy bars every night, not getting enough sleep, getting drunk frequently on weekends, and not wearing a safety belt when driving or riding in a car. List your five behaviors below.

1. _____
2. _____
3. _____
4. _____
5. _____

For successful behavior change, it's best to focus on one behavior at a time. Review your list of behaviors and select one to start with. Choose a behavior that is important to you and that you are strongly motivated to change. If this will be your first attempt at behavior change, start with a simple change, such as wearing your bicycle helmet regularly, before tackling a more difficult change, such as quitting smoking. Circle the behavior on your list that you've chosen to start with; this will be your target behavior throughout this workbook.

W-1

SAMPLE EXERCISE PROGRAMS

Illustrated exercise programs in Chapters 4 and 5 show proper technique for exercises and stretches that develop muscular strength and endurance, flexibility, and low-back health; video clips of the exercises can be found on the Online Learning Center. The complete sample fitness programs in Chapter 7 are built around popular endurance activities such as walking, jogging, cycling, and swimming.

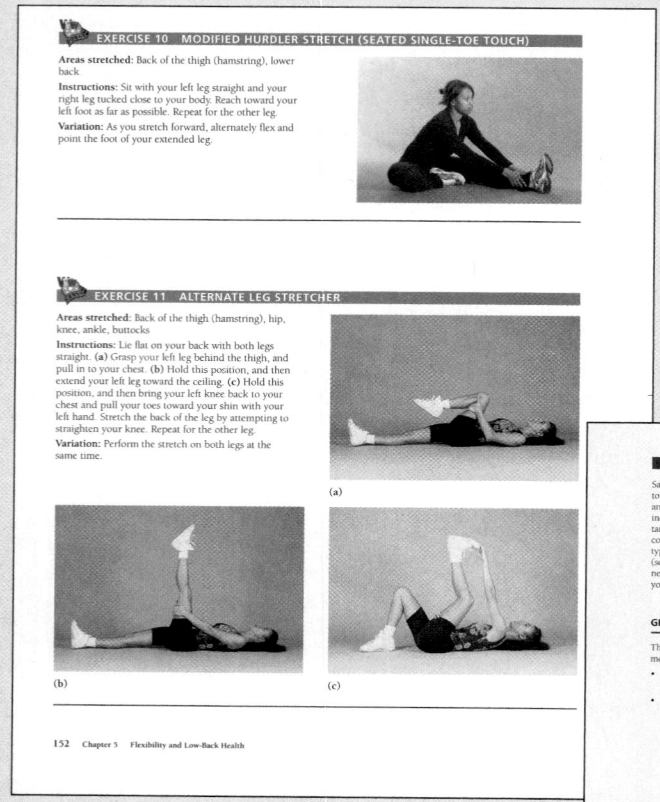

EXERCISE 10 MODIFIED HURDLER STRETCH (SEATED SINGLE-TOE TOUCH)

Areas stretched: Back of the thigh (hamstring), lower back

Instructions: Sit with your left leg straight and your right leg tucked close to your body. Reach toward your left foot as far as possible. Repeat for the other leg.

Variation: As you stretch forward, alternately flex and point the foot of your extended leg.

EXERCISE 11 ALTERNATE LEG STRETCHER

Areas stretched: Back of the thigh (hamstring), hip, knee, ankle, buttocks

Instructions: Lie flat on your back with both legs straight. **(a)** Grasp your left leg behind the thigh, and pull in to your chest. **(b)** Hold this position, and then extend your left leg toward the ceiling. **(c)** Hold this position, and then bring your left knee back to your chest and pull your toes toward your shin with your left hand. Stretch the back of the leg by attempting to straighten your knee. Repeat for the other leg.

Variation: Perform the stretch on both legs at the same time.

(a)

(b)

(c)

152 Chapter 5 Flexibility and Low-Back Health

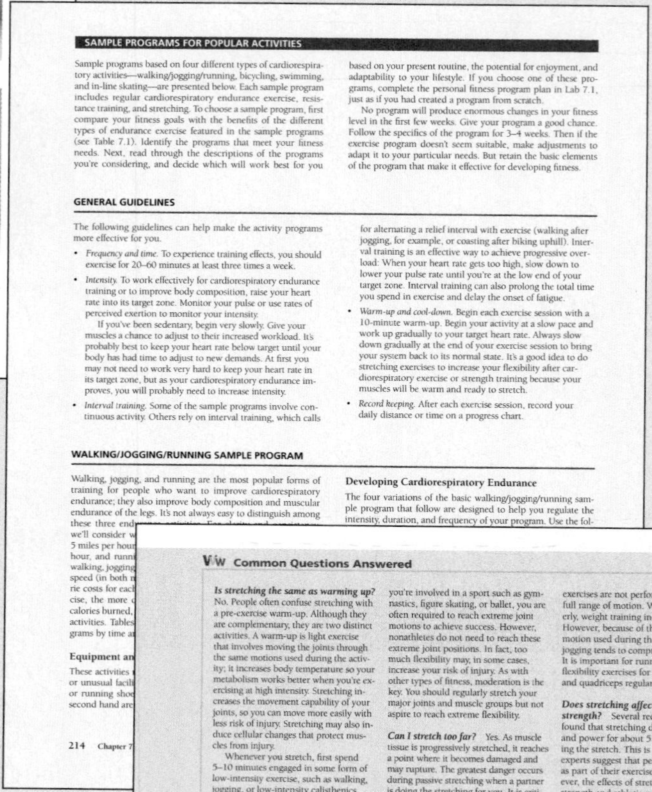

SAMPLE PROGRAMS FOR POPULAR ACTIVITIES

Sample programs based on four different types of cardiorespiratory activities—walking/jogging/running, bicycling, swimming, and in-line skating—are presented below. Each sample program includes regular cardiorespiratory endurance exercise, resistance training, and stretching. To choose a sample program, first compare your fitness goals with the benefits of the different types of endurance exercise featured in the sample programs (see Table 7.1). Identify the programs that meet your fitness needs. Next, read through the descriptions of the programs you're considering, and decide which will work best for you based on your present routine, the potential for enjoyment, and adaptability to your lifestyle. If you choose one of these programs, complete the personal fitness program plan in Lab 7.1, just as if you had created a program from scratch.

No program will produce enormous changes in your fitness level in the first few weeks. Give your program a good chance. Follow the specifics of the program for 3–4 weeks. Then if the exercise program doesn't seem suitable, make adjustments to adapt it to your particular needs. But retain the basic elements of the program that make it effective for developing fitness.

GENERAL GUIDELINES

The following guidelines can help make the activity programs more effective for you.

- *Frequency and time.* To experience training effects, you should exercise for 20–60 minutes at least three times a week.
- *Intensity.* To work effectively for cardiorespiratory endurance training or to improve body composition, raise your heart rate into its target zone. Monitor your pulse or use rates of perceived exertion to monitor your intensity.
  If you've been sedentary, begin very slowly. Give your muscles a chance to adjust to their increased workload. It's probably best to keep your heart rate below target until your body has had time to adjust to new demands. At first you may not need to work very hard to keep your heart rate in its target zone, but as your cardiorespiratory endurance improves, you will probably need to increase intensity.
- *Interval training.* Some of the sample programs involve continuous activity. Others rely on interval training, which calls for alternating a relief interval with exercise (walking after jogging, for example, or coasting after biking uphill). Interval training is an effective way to achieve progressive overload: When your heart rate gets too high, slow down to lower your pulse rate until you're at the low end of your target zone. Interval training can also prolong the total time you spend in exercise and delay the onset of fatigue.
- *Warm-up and cool-down.* Begin each exercise session with a 10-minute warm-up. Begin your activity at a slow pace and work up gradually to your target heart rate. Always slow down gradually at the end of your exercise session to bring your system back to its normal state. It's a good idea to do stretching exercises to increase your flexibility after cardiorespiratory exercise or strength training because your muscles will be warm and ready to stretch.
- *Record keeping.* After each exercise session, record your daily distance or time on a progress chart.

WALKING/JOGGING/RUNNING SAMPLE PROGRAM

Walking, jogging, and running are the most popular forms of training for people who want to improve cardiorespiratory endurance; they also improve body composition and muscular endurance of the legs. It's not always easy to distinguish among these three end...

Developing Cardiorespiratory Endurance

The four variations of the basic walking/jogging/running sample program that follow are designed to help you regulate the intensity, duration, and frequency of your program. Use the fol-

214 Chapter 7

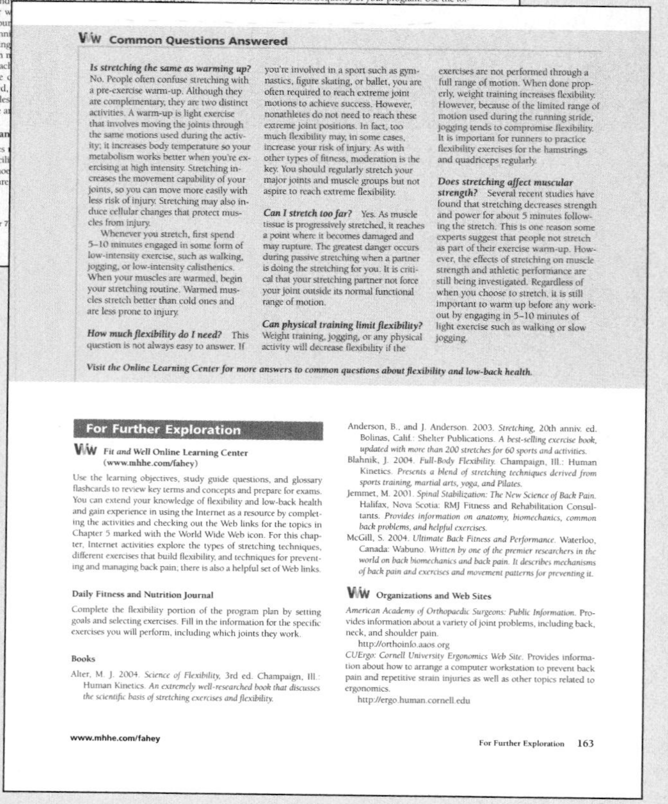

Common Questions Answered

Is stretching the same as warming up? No. People often confuse stretching with a pre-exercise warm-up. Although they are complementary, they are two distinct activities. A warm-up is light exercise that involves moving the joints through the same motions used during the activity; it increases body temperature so your metabolism works better when you're exercising at high intensity. Stretching increases the movement capability of your joints, so you can move more easily with less risk of injury. Stretching may also induce cellular changes that protect muscles from injury.

Whenever you stretch, first spend 5–10 minutes engaged in some form of low-intensity exercise, such as walking, jogging, or low-intensity calisthenics. When your muscles are warmed, begin your stretching routine. Warmed muscles stretch better than cold ones and are less prone to injury.

How much flexibility do I need? This question is not always easy to answer. If you're involved in a sport such as gymnastics, figure skating, or ballet, you are often required to reach extreme joint motions to achieve success. However, nonathletes do not need to reach these extreme joint positions. In fact, too much flexibility may, in some cases, increase your risk of injury. As with other types of fitness, moderation is the key. You should regularly stretch your major joints and muscle groups but not aspire to reach extreme flexibility.

Can I stretch too far? Yes. As muscle tissue is progressively stretched, it reaches a point where it becomes damaged and may rupture. The greatest danger occurs during passive stretching when a partner is doing the stretching for you. It is critical that your stretching partner not force your joint outside its normal functional range of motion.

Can physical training limit flexibility? Weight training, jogging, or any physical activity will decrease flexibility if the exercises are not performed through a full range of motion. When done properly, weight training increases flexibility. However, because of the limited range of motion used during the running stride, jogging tends to compromise flexibility. It is important for runners to practice flexibility exercises for the hamstrings and quadriceps regularly.

Does stretching affect muscular strength? Several recent studies have found that stretching decreases strength and power for about 5 minutes following the stretch. This is one reason some experts suggest that people not stretch as part of their exercise warm-up. However, the effects of stretching on muscle strength and athletic performance are still being investigated. Regardless of when you choose to stretch, it is still important to warm up before any workout by engaging in 5–10 minutes of light exercise such as walking or slow jogging.

Visit the Online Learning Center for more answers to common questions about flexibility and low-back health.

For Further Exploration

Fit and Well Online Learning Center (www.mhhe.com/fahey)

Use the learning objectives, study guide questions, and glossary flashcards to review key terms and concepts and prepare for exams. You can extend your knowledge of flexibility and low-back health and gain experience in using the Internet as a resource by completing the activities and checking out the Web links for the topics in Chapter 5 marked with the World Wide Web icon. For this chapter, Internet activities explore the types of stretching techniques, different exercises that build flexibility, and techniques for preventing and managing back pain; there is also a helpful set of Web links.

Daily Fitness and Nutrition Journal

Complete the flexibility portion of the program plan by setting goals and selecting exercises. Fill in the information for the specific exercises you will perform, including which joints they work.

Books

Alter, M. J. 2004. *Science of Flexibility*, 3rd ed. Champaign, Ill.: Human Kinetics. *An extremely well-researched book that discusses the scientific basis of stretching exercises and flexibility.*

Anderson, B., and J. Anderson. 2003. *Stretching*, 20th anniv. ed. Bolinas, Calif.: Shelter Publications. *A best-selling exercise book, updated with more than 200 stretches for 60 sports and activities.*

Blahnik, J. 2004. *Full-Body Flexibility*. Champaign, Ill.: Human Kinetics. *Presents a blend of stretching techniques derived from sports training, martial arts, yoga, and Pilates.*

Jemmet, M. 2001. *Spinal Stabilization: The New Science of Back Pain*. Halifax, Nova Scotia: RMJ Fitness and Rehabilitation Consultants. *Provides information on anatomy, biomechanics, common back problems, and helpful exercises.*

McGill, S. 2004. *Ultimate Back Fitness and Performance*. Waterloo, Canada: Wabuno. *Written by one of the premier researchers in the world on back biomechanics and back pain. It describes mechanisms of back pain and exercises and movement patterns for preventing it.*

Organizations and Web Sites

American Academy of Orthopaedic Surgeons: Public Information. Provides information about a variety of joint problems, including back, neck, and shoulder pain.
http://orthoinfo.aaos.org

CUErgo: Cornell University Ergonomics Web Site. Provides information about how to arrange a computer workstation to prevent back pain and repetitive strain injuries as well as other topics related to ergonomics.
http://ergo.human.cornell.edu

www.mhhe.com/fahey

For Further Exploration 163

FOR FURTHER EXPLORATION

For Further Exploration sections at the end of each chapter describe books, newsletters, organizations, hotlines, and Web sites that you can turn to for additional advice and information. These sections also suggest ways to use the free tools available with *Fit and Well:*

- The Daily Fitness and Nutrition Journal gives you an easy way to plan and track a fitness program and a program for dietary improvement.
- The *Fit and Well* Online Learning Center (www.mhhe.com/fahey) provides interactive study guide questions, learning objectives, chapter outlines, glossary flashcards, Internet activities, answers to common fitness questions, links, and other useful study aids.

Looking **AHEAD**

After reading this chapter, you should be able to

- Describe the dimensions of wellness
- Identify the major health problems in the United States today, and discuss their causes
- Describe the behaviors that are part of a fit and well lifestyle
- Explain the steps in creating a behavior management plan to change a wellness-related behavior
- Discuss the available sources of wellness information and how to think critically about them

1

Introduction to Wellness, Fitness, and Lifestyle Management

Test Your Knowledge

1. **Which of the following lifestyle factors is the leading preventable cause of death for Americans?**
   a. excess alcohol consumption
   b. cigarette smoking
   c. obesity

2. **More than two-thirds of all college students make which of the following positive lifestyle choices?**
   a. using safety belts
   b. not drinking and driving
   c. eating two or fewer high-fat foods per day
   d. not smoking cigarettes

3. **Only 50% of health-related Web sites are nonpromotional and based on scientific information.**
   True or false?

ANSWERS

1. B. Smoking causes about 435,000 deaths per year; obesity is responsible for more than 100,000; and alcohol, as many as 85,000.

2. ALL FOUR. However, the majority of students do not exercise regularly, do not wear bicycle helmets, and eat few fruits and vegetables. There are many areas in which college students can change their behavior to improve their health.

3. FALSE. The number is closer to 35%. Most health-related Web sites sell products and/or are not based on scientific information.

ViW *Fit and Well* **Online Learning Center**   www.mhhe.com/fahey

Visit the *Fit and Well* Online Learning Center for study aids, online labs, additional information about wellness, links, Internet activities that explore the importance of a wellness lifestyle, and much more.

A first-year college student resolves to meet the challenge of making new friends. A long-sedentary senior starts riding her bike to school every day instead of taking the bus. A busy part-time student organizes a group of coworkers to help plant trees in a blighted inner-city neighborhood. What do these people have in common? Each is striving for optimal health and well-being. Not satisfied to be merely free of major illness, these individuals want more. They want to live life actively, energetically, and fully, in a state of optimal personal, interpersonal, and environmental well-being. They have taken charge of their health and are on the path to wellness.

WELLNESS: THE NEW HEALTH GOAL

Wellness is an expanded idea of health. In the past, many people thought of health as being just the absence of physical disease. But wellness transcends this concept of health, as when individuals with serious illnesses or disabilities rise above their physical or mental limitations to live rich, meaningful, vital lives. Some aspects of health are determined by your genes, your age, and other factors that may be beyond your control. But true wellness is largely determined by the decisions you make about how to live your life. In this book, we will use the terms *health* and *wellness* interchangeably to mean the ability to live life fully—with vitality and meaning.

The Dimensions of Wellness

No matter what your age or health status, you can optimize your health in each of the following six interrelated dimensions. Wellness in any dimension is not a static goal but a dynamic process of change and growth (Figure 1.1).

Physical Wellness Optimal physical health requires eating well, exercising, avoiding harmful habits, making responsible decisions about sex, learning about and recognizing the symptoms of diseases, getting regular medical and dental checkups, and taking steps to prevent injuries at home, on the road, and on the job. The habits you develop and the decisions you make today will largely determine not only how many years you will live, but the quality of your life during those years.

Emotional Wellness Optimism, trust, self-esteem, self-acceptance, self-confidence, self-control, satisfying relationships, and an ability to share feelings are just some of the qualities and aspects of emotional wellness. Emotional wellness is a dynamic state that fluctuates with your physical, intellectual, spiritual, interpersonal and social, and environmental wellness. Maintaining emotional wellness requires monitoring and exploring your thoughts and feelings, identifying obstacles to emotional well-being, and finding solutions to emotional problems, with the help of a therapist if necessary.

Intellectual Wellness The hallmarks of intellectual health include an openness to new ideas, a capacity to question and think critically, and the motivation to master new skills, as well as a sense of humor, creativity, and curiosity. An active mind is essential to wellness; it detects problems, finds solutions, and directs behavior. People who enjoy intellectual wellness never stop learning. They seek out and relish new experiences and challenges.

Spiritual Wellness To enjoy spiritual health is to possess a set of guiding beliefs, principles, or values that give meaning and purpose to your life, especially during difficult times. Spiritual wellness involves the capacity for love, compassion, forgiveness, altruism, joy, and fulfillment. It is an antidote to cynicism, anger, fear, anxiety, self-absorption, and pessimism. Spirituality transcends the individual and can be a common bond among people. Organized religions help many people develop spiritual health, while many others find meaning and purpose in their lives on their own—through nature, art, meditation, political action, or good works.

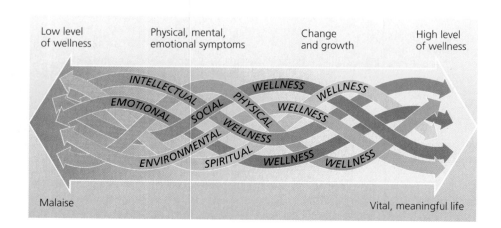

Figure 1.1 The wellness continuum.
Wellness is composed of six interrelated dimensions, all of which must be developed in order to achieve overall wellness.

With wellness comes health and vitality throughout the life span.

Interpersonal and Social Wellness Satisfying relationships are basic to both physical and emotional health. We need to have mutually loving, supportive people in our lives. Developing interpersonal wellness means learning good communication skills, developing the capacity for intimacy, and cultivating a support network of caring friends and/or family members. Social wellness requires participating in and contributing to your community, country, and world.

Environmental, or Planetary, Wellness Increasingly, personal health depends on the health of the planet—from the safety of the food supply to the degree of violence in a society. Other examples of environmental threats to health are ultraviolet radiation in sunlight, air and water pollution, lead in old house paint, and second-hand tobacco smoke in indoor air. Wellness requires learning about and protecting yourself against such hazards—and doing what you can to reduce or eliminate them, either on your own or with others.

The six dimensions of wellness interact continuously, influencing and being influenced by one another. For example, spiritual wellness is associated with social skills, which can help build interpersonal relationships, which are in turn linked to physical wellness and a longer life expectancy. The self-esteem that comes with emotional

wellness is associated with increased physical activity and healthier eating habits, which support physical wellness. Individually and collectively, the wellness dimensions are associated with increased quality and quantity of life. Maintaining good health is a dynamic process, and increasing your level of wellness in one area of life often influences many others. For example, regular exercise (developing the physical dimension of wellness) can increase feelings of well-being and self-esteem (emotional wellness), which in turn can increase feelings of confidence in social interactions and achievements at work or school (interpersonal and social wellness). Some of the key links among different dimensions of wellness are highlighted in this text in boxes labeled Wellness Connection.

To help discover what wellness means to you and where you currently fall on the wellness continuum, complete Lab 1.1.

New Opportunities, New Responsibilities

Wellness is a relatively recent concept. A century ago, people considered themselves lucky just to survive to adulthood (Figure 1.2, p. 4). A child born in 1900, for example, could expect to live only about 47 years. Many people died as a result of common **infectious diseases** (pneumonia, tuberculosis, diarrhea) and poor environmental conditions (unrefrigerated food, poor sanitation, air and water pollution). However, since 1900, the average life expectancy has nearly doubled, thanks largely to the development of vaccines and antibiotics to prevent and fight infectious diseases and to public health campaigns to improve environmental conditions.

But a different set of diseases has emerged as our major health threat, and heart disease, cancer, and stroke are the three leading causes of death for Americans today (Table 1.1, p. 5). Treating these and other **chronic diseases** is enormously expensive and extremely difficult. The best treatment for these diseases is prevention—people having a greater awareness about their own health and about taking care of their bodies.

The good news is that people do have some control over whether they develop cardiovascular disease (CVD),

Terms

wellness Optimal health and vitality, encompassing physical, emotional, intellectual, spiritual, interpersonal and social, and environmental well-being.

infectious disease A disease that is communicable from one person to another; caused by invading microorganisms such as bacteria and viruses.

chronic disease A disease that develops and continues over a long period of time; usually caused by a variety of factors, including lifestyle factors.

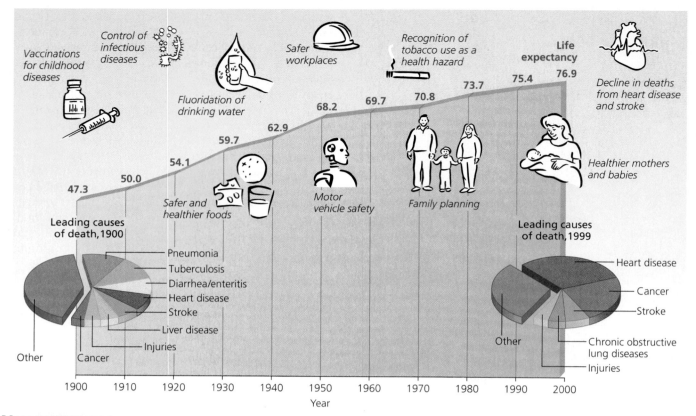

Vaccinations for childhood diseases

Control of infectious diseases

Fluoridation of drinking water

Safer and healthier foods

Safer workplaces

Motor vehicle safety

Recognition of tobacco use as a health hazard

Family planning

Life expectancy

Decline in deaths from heart disease and stroke

Healthier mothers and babies

47.3   50.0   54.1   59.7   62.9   68.2   69.7   70.8   73.7   75.4   76.9

Leading causes of death, 1900

- Pneumonia
- Tuberculosis
- Diarrhea/enteritis
- Heart disease
- Stroke
- Liver disease
- Injuries

Other   Cancer

Leading causes of death, 1999

- Heart disease
- Cancer
- Stroke
- Chronic obstructive lung diseases
- Injuries

Other

1900 1910 1920 1930 1940 1950 1960 1970 1980 1990 2000

Year

VITAL STATISTICS

Figure 1.2 Public health achievements of the twentieth century.   During the twentieth century, public health achievements greatly improved the quality of life for Americans, and life expectancy rose from 47 years to 77 years. A dramatic shift in the leading causes of death also occurred, with deaths from infectious diseases declining from more than 33% of all deaths to just 2.2%. Heart disease, cancer, and stroke are now responsible for more than 50% of all deaths among Americans.   SOURCES: National Center for Health Statistics. 2005. *Health, United States, 2005, with Chartbook on Trends in the Health of Americans.* Hyattsville, Md.: National Center for Health Statistics; Centers for Disease Control and Prevention. 1999. Ten great public health achievements—United States, 1900–1999. *Morbidity and Mortality Weekly Report* 48(50): 1141.

cancer, and other chronic diseases. People make choices every day that either increase or decrease their risks for these diseases—lifestyle choices involving such behaviors as exercise, diet, smoking, and drinking. When researchers look at the lifestyle factors that contribute to death in the United States (see the last column in Table 1.1 and Table 1.2), it becomes clear that individuals can profoundly influence their own health risks. Smoking is the leading preventable cause of death among Americans, followed by poor diet and inactivity. Wellness cannot be prescribed; physicians and other health care professionals can provide information, advice, and encouragement—but the rest is up to each of us.

This chapter provides an overview of a lifestyle that contributes to wellness and describes a method that can help you make lasting changes in your life to promote good health. The chapters that follow provide more detailed information about physical activity, healthy eating habits, and other components of a wellness lifestyle. The book as a whole is designed to be used to help you take charge of your behavior and improve the quality of your life—to become fit and well.

National Wellness Goals

You may think of health and wellness as personal concerns, goals that you strive for on your own for your own benefit. But the U.S. government also has a vital interest in the health of all Americans. A healthy population is the nation's greatest resource, the source of its vigor and wealth. Poor health, in contrast, drains the nation's resources and raises national health care costs. As the embodiment of our society's values, the federal government also has a humane interest in people's health.

The U.S. government's national Healthy People initiative seeks to prevent unnecessary disease and disability and to achieve a better quality of life for all Americans. Healthy People reports, published first in 1980 and revised every decade, set national health goals based on 10-year agendas. Each report includes both broad goals

Table 1.1   Leading Causes of Death in the United States

Rank	Cause of Death	Number of Deaths	Percent of Total Deaths	Female/Male Ratio*	Lifestyle Factors
1	Heart disease	684,462	28.0	51/49	D I S A
2	Cancer**	554,643	22.7	48/52	D I S A
3	Stroke	157,803	6.5	61/39	S
4	Chronic lower respiratory diseases	126,128	5.2	51/49	I S A
5	Unintentional injuries (accidents)	105,695	4.3	35/65	D I S
6	Diabetes mellitus	73,965	3.0	53/47	S
7	Influenza and pneumonia	64,847	2.7	56/44	
8	Alzheimer's disease	63,343	2.6	71/29	
9	Kidney disease	42,536	1.7	52/48	D I S A
10	Septicemia (systemic blood infection)	34,243	1.4	56/44	A
11	Intentional self-harm (suicide)	30,642	1.3	20/80	A
12	Chronic liver disease and cirrhosis	27,201	1.1	36/64	A
13	Hypertension (high blood pressure)	21,841	0.9	62/38	D I S A
14	Parkinson's disease	17,898	0.7	43/57	
15	Pneumonia due to aspiration	17,457	0.7	50/50	
	All causes	2,443,930			

Key

D   Cause of death in which diet plays a part

I   Cause of death in which an inactive lifestyle plays a part

S   Cause of death in which smoking plays a part

A   Cause of death in which excessive alcohol consumption plays a part

Note: Although not among the overall top 15 causes of death, homicide (17,096 deaths) and HIV/AIDS (13,544 deaths) are major killers; both are among the 10 leading causes of death among Americans age 15–44.

*Ratio of females to males who died of each cause. For example, about the same number of women and men died of heart disease, but only about half as many women as men died of unintentional injuries and four times as many men as women committed suicide.

**Among people under age 85, cancer is the leading cause of death. Decreased rates of smoking have reduced deaths from both heart disease and cancer, but among ex-smokers, heart disease risk declines more quickly and to a greater degree than cancer risk.

SOURCES: National Center for Health Statistics. 2005. Deaths: Preliminary data for 2003. *National Vital Statistics Report* 53(15); Jemal, A., et al. 2005. Cancer Statistics, 2005. *CA: A Cancer Journal for Clinicians* 55(1) 10–30.

and specific targets in many different areas of wellness. The latest report, *Healthy People 2010,* proposes two broad national goals:

- *Increase quality and years of healthy life.* The life expectancy of Americans has increased significantly in the past century; however, people can expect poor health to limit their activities and cause distress during the last 15% of their lives (Figure 1.3, p. 6). Health-related quality of life calls for a full range of functional capacity to enable people to work, play, and maintain satisfying relationships.

- *Eliminate health disparities among Americans.* Many health problems today disproportionately affect certain American populations (see the box "Wellness Issues for Diverse Populations" on p. 7). *Healthy People 2010* calls for eliminating disparities in health status, health risks, and use of preventive services among all population groups within the next decade.

Examples of individual health promotion objectives from *Healthy People 2010,* as well as estimates of how we are tracking toward the goals, appear in Table 1.3 (p. 7).

The objectives are tied closely to the wellness lifestyle described in this chapter. The principal topics covered in this book parallel the priority concerns of the Healthy People initiative, and the approach of *Fit and Well* is based on the initiative's premise that personal responsibility is a key to achieving wellness.

Behaviors That Contribute to Wellness

A lifestyle based on good choices and healthy behaviors maximizes the quality of life. It helps people avoid disease, remain strong and fit, and maintain their physical and mental health as long as they live. Figure 1.4 (p. 8) highlights the results of just a few of the research studies that have found clear links between lifestyle behaviors and the risk of developing and dying from chronic disease. The most important behaviors and habits are introduced briefly here and described in detail in later chapters.

Be Physically Active   The human body is designed to work best when it is active. It readily adapts to nearly any

Table 1.2 — Actual Causes of Death Among Americans

	Number of Deaths Per Year	Percent of Total Deaths Per Year
Tobacco	435,000	18.1
Obesity*	112,000	4.6
Alcohol consumption	85,000	3.5
Microbial agents	75,000	3.1
Toxic agents	55,000	2.3
Motor vehicles	43,000	1.8
Firearms	29,000	1.2
Sexual behavior	20,000	0.8
Illicit drug use	17,000	0.7

Note: Actual causes of death are defined as lifestyle and environmental factors that contribute to the leading killers of Americans. Microbial agents include bacterial and viral infections like influenza and pneumonia; toxic agents include environmental pollutants and chemical agents such as asbestos.

*The number of deaths due to obesity is an area of ongoing controversy and research. Recent estimates have ranged from 112,000 to 365,000.

SOURCES: Centers for Disease Control and Prevention. 2005. *Frequently Asked Questions About Calculating Obesity-Related Risk* (http://www.cdc.gov/od/oc/media/pressrel/r050614.htm; retrieved June 28, 2005). Mokdad, A. H., et al. 2005. Correction: Actual causes of death in the United States, 2000. *Journal of the American Medical Association* 293(3): 293–294. Mokdad, A. H., et al. 2004. Actual causes of death in the United States, 2000. *Journal of the American Medical Association* 291(10): 1238–1245.

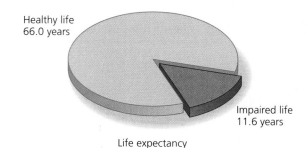

Figure 1.3 Quantity of life versus quality of life. Years of healthy life as a proportion of life expectancy in the U.S. population. SOURCES: National Center for Health Statistics. 2005. Deaths: preliminary data for 2003. *National Vital Statistics Reports* 53(15). National Center for Health Statistics. 2001. *Healthy People 2000 Final Review.* Hyattsville, Md.: Public Health Service.

level of activity and exertion; in fact, **physical fitness** is defined as a set of physical attributes that allow the body to respond or adapt to the demands and stress of physical effort. The more we ask of our bodies—our muscles, bones, heart, lungs-—the stronger and more fit they become. However, the reverse is also true: The less we ask of them, the less they can do. When our bodies are not kept active, they begin to deteriorate. Bones lose their density, joints stiffen, muscles become weak, and cellular energy systems begin to degenerate. To be truly well, human beings must be active. Unfortunately, a sedentary lifestyle is common among Americans today: More than 60% of Americans are not regularly physically active, and about 25% are not active at all.

The benefits of physical activity are both physical and mental, immediate and long term (Figure 1.5, p. 9). In the short term, being physically fit makes it easier to do everyday tasks, such as lifting; it provides reserve strength for emergencies; and it helps people look and feel good. In the long term, being physically fit confers protection against chronic diseases and lowers the risk of dying prematurely. Physically active individuals are less likely to develop or die from heart disease, respiratory disease, high blood pressure, cancer, osteoporosis, and type 2 diabetes (the most common form of diabetes). Their cardiorespiratory systems tend to resemble those of people 10 or more years younger than themselves. As they get older, they may be able to avoid weight gain, muscle and bone loss, fatigue, and other problems associated with aging. With healthy hearts, strong muscles, lean bodies, and a repertoire of physical skills they can call on for recreation and enjoyment, fit people can maintain their physical and mental well-being throughout their lives.

Choose a Healthy Diet In addition to being sedentary, many Americans have a diet that is too high in calories, unhealthy fats, and added sugars, and too low in fiber, complex carbohydrates, fruits, and vegetables. This diet is linked to a number of chronic diseases, including heart disease, stroke, high blood pressure, type 2 diabetes, and certain kinds of cancer. It has been estimated that as many as 15% of deaths in the United States can be attributed to poor diet combined with lack of exercise. A healthy diet promotes wellness in both the short and long term. It provides necessary nutrients and sufficient energy without also providing too much of the dietary substances linked to diseases.

Maintain a Healthy Body Weight Overweight and obesity are associated with a number of disabling and potentially fatal conditions and diseases, including heart disease, cancer, and type 2 diabetes. In 2005, researchers estimated that obesity kills between 112,000 and 365,000 Americans each year and is responsible for more than $75 billion in direct medical costs annually. Healthy body weight is an important part of wellness— but short-term dieting is not part of a fit and well lifestyle.

Terms

physical fitness A set of physical attributes that allow the body to respond or adapt to the demands and stress of physical effort.

When it comes to striving for wellness, most differences among people are insignificant. We all need to exercise, eat well, and manage stress. We need to know how to protect ourselves from heart disease, cancer, sexually transmitted diseases, and injuries.

But some of our differences—differences among us both as individuals and as members of groups—do have implications for wellness. Some of us, for example, have grown up with eating habits that increase our risk of obesity or heart disease. Some of us have inherited predispositions for certain health problems, such as osteoporosis or high cholesterol levels. These health-related differences among individuals and groups can be biological—determined genetically—or cultural—acquired as patterns of behavior through daily interactions with our family, community, and society. Many health conditions are a function of biology and culture combined.

When we talk about wellness issues as they relate to diverse populations, we face two related dangers. The first is the danger of stereotyping, of talking about people as groups rather than as individuals. The second is that of overgeneralizing, of ignoring the extensive biological and cultural diversity that exists among people who may be grouped together because of their gender, socioeconomic status, or ethnicity. Every person is an individual with her or his own unique genetic endowment as well as unique experiences in life. However, many of these influences are shared with others of similar genetic and cultural backgrounds. Information about group similarities relating to wellness issues can be useful; for example, it can alert people to areas that may be of special concern for them and their families.

Wellness-related differences among groups can be identified and described along several different dimensions, including the following:

- *Gender.* Men and women have different life expectancies and different incidences of many diseases, including heart disease, cancer, and osteoporosis. Men have higher rates of death from injuries, suicide, and homicide; women are at greater risk for Alzheimer's disease and for depression. Men and women also differ in body composition and certain aspects of physical performance.

- *Ethnicity.* A genetic predisposition for a particular health problem can be linked to ethnicity as a result of each ethnic group's relatively distinct history. Diabetes is more prevalent among individuals of Native American or Latino heritage, for example, and African Americans have higher rates of hypertension. Ethnic groups may also vary in other ways that relate to wellness: traditional diets; patterns of family and interpersonal relationships; and attitudes toward using tobacco, alcohol, and other drugs, to name just a few.

- *Income and education.* Inequalities in income and education are closely related and underlie many of the health disparities among Americans. People with low incomes and less education have higher rates of injury and many diseases, are more likely to engage in unhealthy behaviors such as smoking, and have less access to health care services. Poverty and low educational attainment are far more important predictors of poor health than any ethnic factor.

These are just some of the "dimensions of diversity"—differences among people and groups that are associated with different wellness concerns. Other factors, too, such as age, geographic location, sexual orientation, and disability, can present challenges as an individual strives for wellness. In this book, topics and issues relating to wellness that affect different American populations are given special consideration in boxes labeled Dimensions of Diversity. These discussions are designed to deepen our understanding of the concepts of wellness and vitality in the context of ever-growing diversity in the population.

Table 1.3   Selected *Healthy People 2010* Objectives

Objective	Estimate of Current Status (%)	Goal (%)
Increase the proportion of people age 18 and older who engage regularly in moderate physical activity.	32	50
Increase the proportion of people age 2 and older who consume at least 3 daily servings of vegetables, with at least one-third being dark-green or orange vegetables.	3	50
Increase the prevalence of healthy weight among people age 20 and older.	34	60
Reduce the proportion of adults 18 and older who use cigarettes.	22	12
Reduce the proportion of college students reporting binge drinking during the past 2 weeks.	39	20
Increase the proportion of adults who take protective measures to reduce the risk of skin cancer (sunscreens, sun-protective clothing, and so on).	58	75
Increase the use of safety belts by motor vehicle occupants.	75	92
Increase the number of residences with a functioning smoke alarm on every floor.	87	100
Increase the proportion of persons with health insurance.	83	100

SOURCE: National Center for Health Statistics. 2004. *DATA 2010: The Healthy People 2010 Database, November 2004 Edition* (http://wonder.cdc.gov/data2010/obj.htm; retrieved October 27, 2005).

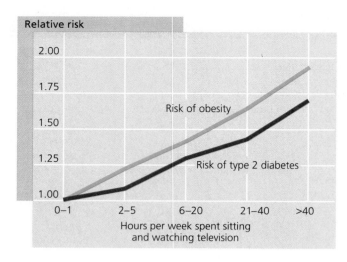

(a) Sedentary lifestyle and risk of obesity and type 2 diabetes

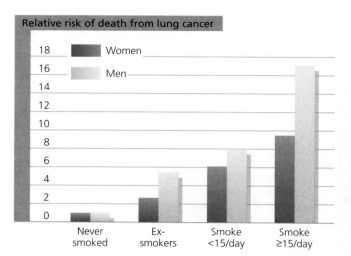

(b) Cigarette smoking status and risk of death from lung cancer

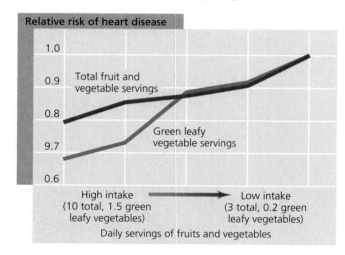

(c) Fruit and vegetable intake and risk of heart disease

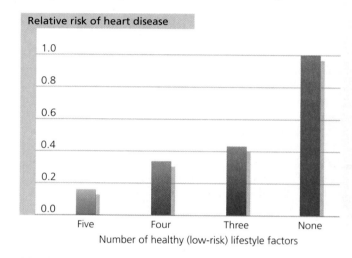

(d) Lifestyle factors and risk of heart disease

Figure 1.4   Lifestyle and risk of chronic disease.   The research results shown above are just a few recent findings linking lifestyle behaviors to rates of disease and death. They indicate that (a) people who spend more time watching television are more likely to be obese and to develop type 2 diabetes; (b) people who smoke are much more likely to die of lung cancer than people who have never smoked or who have quit; (c) people who consume diets rich in fruits and vegetables, particularly green leafy vegetables, reduce their risk of heart disease; and (d) people who engage in a combination of healthy lifestyle behaviors have an 82% lower risk of heart disease than those who do not engage in such behaviors. The five lifestyle factors examined in this study were participation in regular physical activity, avoidance of smoking, maintenance of a healthy diet, body weight, and level of alcohol consumption.   SOURCES: (a) Hu, F. B., et al. 2003. Television watching and other sedentary behaviors in relation to risk of obesity and type 2 diabetes mellitus in women. *Journal of the American Medical Association* 289(14): 1785–1791. (b) Prescott, E., et al. 1998. Mortality in women and men in relation to smoking. *International Epidemiological Association* 27: 27–32. (c) Joshipura, K. J., et al. 2001. The effect of fruit and vegetable intake on risk for coronary heart disease. *Annals of Internal Medicine* 134: 1106–1114. (d) Stampfer, M. J., et al. 2000. Primary prevention of coronary heart disease in women through diet and lifestyle. *New England Journal of Medicine* 343(1): 16–22.

Maintaining a healthy body weight requires a lifelong commitment to regular exercise, a healthy diet, and effective stress management.

Manage Stress Effectively   Many people cope with stress by eating, drinking, or smoking too much. Others don't deal with it at all. In the short term, inappro-priate stress management can lead to fatigue, sleep disturbances, and other unpleasant symptoms. Over longer periods of time, poor management of stress can lead to less efficient functioning of the immune system and increased susceptibility to disease. There *are* effective ways to handle stress, and learning to incorporate them into daily life is an important part of a fit and well lifestyle.

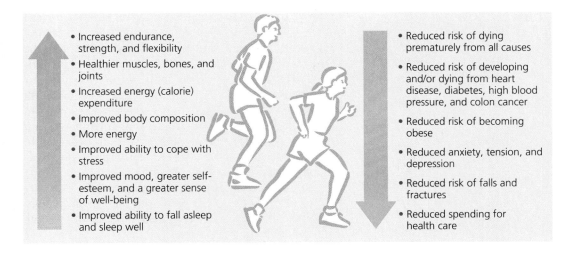

- Increased endurance, strength, and flexibility
- Healthier muscles, bones, and joints
- Increased energy (calorie) expenditure
- Improved body composition
- More energy
- Improved ability to cope with stress
- Improved mood, greater self-esteem, and a greater sense of well-being
- Improved ability to fall asleep and sleep well

- Reduced risk of dying prematurely from all causes
- Reduced risk of developing and/or dying from heart disease, diabetes, high blood pressure, and colon cancer
- Reduced risk of becoming obese
- Reduced anxiety, tension, and depression
- Reduced risk of falls and fractures
- Reduced spending for health care

Figure 1.5   Benefits of regular physical activity.

Avoid Tobacco and Drug Use and Limit Alcohol Consumption   Tobacco use is associated with 8 of the top 10 causes of death in the United States; it kills about 435,000 Americans each year, more than any other behavioral or environmental factor. A hundred years ago, before cigarette smoking was widespread, lung cancer was considered a rare disease. Today, with nearly 25% of the American population smoking, lung cancer is the most common cause of cancer death among both men and women and one of the leading causes of death overall. The direct medical costs of smoking exceed $75 billion per year in the United States; the cost of lost productivity exceeds $90 billion per year.

Excessive alcohol consumption is linked to 6 of the top 10 causes of death and results in about 85,000 deaths a year in the United States. Alcohol or drug intoxication is an especially notable factor in the death and disability of young people, particularly through **unintentional injuries** (such as drownings and car crashes caused by drunken driving) and violence. Unintentional injuries, homicide, and suicide are the top three leading causes of death for 15- to 34-year-olds; in this age group, the mortality rate for males is more than twice that for females.

Protect Yourself from Disease and Injury   The most effective way of dealing with disease and injury is to prevent them. Many of the lifestyle strategies discussed here—being physically active, managing body weight, and so on—help protect you against chronic illnesses. In addition, you can take specific steps to avoid infectious diseases, particularly those that are sexually transmitted. These diseases are preventable through responsible sexual behavior, another component of a fit and well lifestyle.

Unintentional injuries are the leading cause of death for people age 45 and under, but they, too, can be prevented. Learning and adopting safe, responsible behaviors is also part of a fit and well lifestyle.

Other important behaviors in a fit and well lifestyle include developing meaningful relationships, planning ahead for successful aging, becoming knowledgeable about the health care system, and acting responsibly in relation to the environment. Lab 1.2 will help you evaluate your behaviors as they relate to wellness.

The Role of Other Factors in Wellness

Of course, behavior isn't the only factor involved in good health. Heredity, the environment, and access to adequate health care are other important influences. These factors can interact in ways that raise or lower the quality of a person's life and the risk of developing particular diseases. For example, a sedentary lifestyle combined with a genetic predisposition for diabetes can greatly increase a person's risk for developing the disease. If this person also lacks adequate health care, he or she is much more likely to suffer dangerous complications from diabetes and to have a lower quality of life.

But in many cases, behavior can tip the balance toward health even if heredity or environment is a negative factor. Breast cancer, for example, can run in families, but it is also associated with overweight and a sedentary lifestyle. A woman with a family history of breast cancer is less likely to die from the disease if she controls her weight, exercises, performs regular breast self-exams, and consults with her physician about mammograms. By learning about her family history and taking action, this woman can influence the effects of heredity on her health.

REACHING WELLNESS THROUGH LIFESTYLE MANAGEMENT

Your life may not resemble the picture drawn here of a fit and well lifestyle at all. You probably have a number of healthy habits and some others that place your health at risk. Taking steps toward a wellness lifestyle may at first seem like too much work, but, as you make progress, it gets easier. At first, you'll be rewarded with a greater sense of control over your life, a feeling of empowerment, higher self-esteem, and more joy. These benefits will encourage you to make further improvements. Over time, you'll come to know what wellness feels like—more energy, greater vitality; deeper feelings of curiosity, interest, and enjoyment; and a higher quality of life.

This section introduces the general process of behavior change and highlights the decisions and challenges you'll face at each stage. For additional advice, work through the activities in the Behavior Change Workbook located at the end of the text and on the Online Learning Center.

Getting Serious About Your Health

Before you can start changing a wellness-related behavior, you have to know that the behavior is problematic and that you *can* change it. To make good decisions, you need information about relevant topics and issues, including what resources are available to help you change.

Terms

target behavior An isolated behavior selected as the object for a behavior change program.

Examining Your Current Health Habits Have you considered how your current lifestyle is affecting your health today and how it will affect your health in the future? Do you know which of your current habits enhance your health and which detract from it? Begin your journey toward wellness with self-assessment: Think about your own behavior, complete the self-assessment in Lab 1.2, and talk with friends and family members about what they've noticed about your lifestyle and your health. Challenge any unrealistically optimistic attitudes or ideas you may hold. For example, "To protect my health, I don't need to worry about quitting smoking until I'm 40 years old," or "Being overweight won't put *me* at risk for diabetes." Health risks are very real, and health habits throughout life are important.

Many people start to consider changing a behavior when they get help from others. An observation from a friend, family member, or physician can help you see yourself as others do and may get you thinking about your behavior in a new way. For example, Jason has been getting a lot of stomachaches lately. His girlfriend, Anna, notices other changes as well and suggests that the stress of classes plus a part-time job and serving as president of the school radio station might be causing some of Jason's problems. Jason never thought much about trying to control the stressors in his life, but with encouragement from Anna he starts noticing what events trigger stress for him.

Landmark events such as a birthday, the birth of a child, or the death of someone close to you, can get you thinking about behavior change. New information can also help you get started. As you read this text, you may find yourself reevaluating some of your wellness-related behaviors. This could be a great opportunity to make healthful changes that will stay with you for the rest of your life.

Choosing a Target Behavior To maximize your chances of success, don't try to change all your problem behaviors at once—start exercising, quit smoking, give up high-fat foods, avoid drugs, get more sleep. Working on just one behavior will make high demands on your energy. Concentrate on one behavior that you want to change, your **target behavior,** and work on it systematically. Start with something simple, like snacking on candy between afternoon classes or always driving to a particular class instead of walking or biking.

Obtaining Information About Your Target Behavior Once you've chosen a target behavior, you need to find out more about it. You need to know its risks and benefits for you—both now and in the future. How is your target behavior affecting your level of wellness today? What diseases or conditions does this behavior place you at risk for? What effect would changing your behavior have on your health? As a starting point, use material from this text and from the resources listed in the For Further Exploration section at the end of each chapter;

General Strategies

A key first step in sharpening your critical thinking skills is to look carefully at your sources of wellness information. Critical thinking involves knowing where and how to find relevant information, how to separate fact from opinion, how to recognize faulty reasoning, how to evaluate information, and how to assess the credibility of sources.

- *Go to the original source.* Media reports often simplify the results of medical research. Find out for yourself what a study really reported, and determine whether it was based on good science. What type of study was it? Was it published in a recognized medical journal? Was it an animal study or did it involve people? Did the study include a large number of people? What did the authors of the study actually report in their findings? (You'll find additional strategies for evaluating research studies in Chapter 11.)

- *Watch for misleading language.* Reports that feature "breakthroughs" or "dramatic proof" are probably hype. Some studies will find that a behavior "contributes to" or is "associated with" an outcome; this does not imply a proven cause-and-effect relationship.

- *Distinguish between research reports and public health advice.* If a study finds a link between a particular vitamin and cancer, that should not necessarily lead you to change your behavior. But if the Surgeon General or the American Cancer Society advises you to eat less trans fat or quit smoking, you can assume that many studies point in this direction and that this is advice you should follow.

- *Remember that anecdotes are not facts.* Sometimes we do get helpful health information from our friends and family. But just because your cousin Bertha lost 10 pounds on Dr. Amazing's new protein diet doesn't mean it's a safe, effective way for you to lose weight. Before you make a big change in your lifestyle, verify the information with your physician or other reliable sources.

- *Be skeptical and use your common sense.* If a report seems too good to be true, it probably is. Be especially wary of information contained in advertisements. The goal of an ad is to sell you something, to create a feeling of need for a product where no real need exists.

- *Make choices that are right for you.* Your roommate swears by swimming; you prefer aerobics. Your sister takes a yoga class to help her manage stress; your brother unwinds by walking in the woods. Friends and family members can be a great source of ideas and inspiration, but each of us needs to find a wellness lifestyle that works for us.

Internet Resources

Evaluating health information from online sources poses special challenges; when reviewing a health-related Web site, ask the following questions:

- *What is the source of the information? Who is the author or sponsor of the Web page?* Web sites maintained by government agencies, professional associations, or established academic or medical institutions are likely to present trustworthy information. Many other groups and individuals post accurate information, but it is important to look at the qualifications of the people who are behind the site. (Check the home page or click on an "about us" or "who we are" link.)

- *How often is the site updated?* Look for sites that are updated frequently. Also check the "last modified" date of any specific Web page on a site.

- *What is the purpose of the page? Does the site promote particular products or procedures? Are there obvious reasons for bias?* Be wary of information from sites that sell specific products, use testimonials as evidence, appear to have a social or political agenda, or ask for money.

- *What do other sources say about a topic?* Be cautious of claims or information that appear at only one site or come from a chat room, bulletin board, or blog.

- *Does the site conform to any set of guidelines or criteria for quality and accuracy?* Look for sites that identify themselves as conforming to some code or set of principles, such as those set forth by the Health on the Net Foundation or the American Medical Association. These codes include criteria such as use of information from respected sources and disclosure of the site's sponsors.

---

refer to the box "Evaluating Sources of Health Information" for additional guidelines.

Finding Outside Help   Have you identified a particularly challenging target behavior or mood, something like alcohol addiction, binge eating, or depression, that interferes with your ability to function or places you at a serious health risk? Outside help is often needed to change behaviors or conditions that may be too deeply rooted or too serious for a self-management approach. If this is the case, don't be stopped by the seriousness of the problem—there are many resources available to help you solve it. On campus, the student health center or

campus counseling center can provide assistance. To locate community resources, consult the yellow pages, your physician, your local health department, or the United Way.

Building Motivation to Change

Knowledge is a necessary ingredient for behavior change, but it isn't usually enough to make people act. Millions of people smoke or have sedentary lifestyles, for example, even though they know it's bad for their health. This is particularly true of young adults, who may not be motivated to change because they feel well despite engaging in unhealthy

Take a good look at the next group of college students you see. Chances are, they all look pretty healthy. But if you could look inside their cells and vital organs, you would see that the external appearance of health can be deceiving. Some students would have noticeable layers of fat and scar tissue lining blood vessels, including the crucial arteries that supply blood to the heart and brain. You can safely predict that a number of these students will have heart attacks or strokes when they hit middle age. Nearly all the students would have microscopic evidence of sun damage on their skin, and a few would have the early cellular changes associated with skin cancer.

If you could train your super vision on their skeletons, you would detect that some students have weaker, thinner bones—not noticeable to them now but likely to result in osteoporosis and the potential for serious fractures later in life. In some students, you would also detect something slightly amiss in the balance of sugar and insulin in their blood and tissue. Students in this group are more likely to later develop diabetes.

You might think that this group of college students—with so many impending health problems—is unusual, but, unfortunately, these students are similar to the majority of young adults in the United States. Most apparently healthy young people harbor early signs of serious chronic diseases that will become obvious later in life. However, the good news is that if you

make some changes now in your daily habits, you can prevent or delay the onset of nearly all of these common diseases.

What does it take to stave off the typical illnesses of middle and old age? As described in the section on behaviors that contribute to wellness, the answer is less complicated than you might have thought. Lifestyle choices you make daily throughout your life can make a tremendous difference. You can choose to be a nonsmoker, to eat a healthy diet, to keep your weight under control, to wear sunscreen and protective clothing when out in the sun, and so on. If you are successful in following the guidelines for wellness behaviors most of the time, your odds for a long and vigorous life will increase dramatically.

Unfortunately, knowing what we should do to protect our health in later years is often not enough to get us to change our habits. Most of us need a more immediate payoff to get motivated. So consider all the reasons why healthy behaviors are a plus for you today as well as for your future self. For example, if you've felt tired and blue lately, being physically active is almost certain to provide you with an infusion of energy and feelings of well-being. Keeping fit will also allow you to fully enjoy your favorite activities. If you love to ski, remember that if you are in shape when you hit the slopes, you will ski better, have more fun, experience less fatigue and soreness, and be less likely to get injured. What if you want to take a hike in the

mountains or learn to windsurf? Being regularly active will make it much more likely that these experiences will be exhilarating rather than merely exhausting. Everyday chores, such as hauling your books around, cleaning, and carrying groceries or children, are much easier if you are active. Life's daily activities are more satisfying when you have the strength, energy, and confidence to handle them with ease.

Think about what might motivate you to make healthy changes in your life. Have you seen the quality of life of members of your family affected by chronic diseases? Knowing that a particular disease runs in your family can help guide your priorities and motivate you to make healthy changes. You might also find motivation from thinking about the benefits for your loved ones. Consider the examples of a pregnant smoker who is finally able to quit for good when she becomes aware that smoking is harmful to her baby, and a couch potato who becomes inspired to increase his activity level in order to keep up with his kids.

Don't feel overwhelmed by the description of a wellness lifestyle and think that you must change all your bad habits at once or overhaul your lifestyle completely. Studies show that even small improvements in your lifestyle can make a big difference in your health. Start by making a few positive changes. Your efforts will be rewarded—you'll feel better now, and you will continue to reap the benefits throughout your life.

behaviors (see the box "Lifestyle Matters for Young Adults"). To succeed at behavior change, you need strong motivation.

Examining the Pros and Cons of Change

Health behaviors have short-term and long-term benefits and costs. For example, in the short term, an inactive lifestyle allows more time to watch TV and hang out with friends but leaves a person less able to participate in recreational activities. In the long term, it increases risk of heart disease, cancer, stroke, and premature death. For successful behavior change, you must believe that the benefits of changing outweigh the costs.

Do a careful analysis of the short-term and long-term benefits and costs of continuing your current (target) behavior and of changing to a new, healthier, behavior. Focus on the effects that are most meaningful to you, in-

cluding those that are tied to your personal identity and values. For example, if you see yourself as an active person who is a good role model for others, then adopting behaviors such as regular physical activity and getting adequate sleep would support your personal identity. If you value independence and control over your life, then quitting smoking would be consistent with your values and goals. To complete your analysis, ask friends and family members about the effects of your behavior on them. For example, a younger sister may tell you that your smoking habit influenced her decision to take up smoking.

Pay special attention to the short-term benefits of behavior change, as these can be an important motivating force. Although some people are motivated by long-term goals, such as avoiding a disease that may hit them in 30 years, most are more likely to be moved to action by shorter-term, more personal, goals. Feeling better, doing better in school, improving at a sport, reducing stress, and increasing self-esteem are common short-term benefits of health behavior change. Many wellness behaviors are associated with immediate improvements in quality of life. For example, surveys of Americans have found that nonsmokers feel healthy and full of energy more days each month than do smokers, and they report fewer days of sadness and troubled sleep; the same is true when physically active people are compared with sedentary people. Over time, these types of differences add up to a substantially greater quality of life for people who engage in healthy behaviors.

You can further strengthen your motivation by raising your consciousness about your problem behavior. This will enable you to focus on the negatives of the behavior and imagine the consequences if you don't make a change. At the same time, you can visualize the positive results of changing your behavior. Ask yourself, What do I want for myself, now and in the future?

For example, Ruby has never worried much about her smoking because the problems associated with it seem so far away. But lately she's noticed her performance on the volleyball team isn't as good as it used to be. Over the summer she visited her aunt, who has chronic emphysema from smoking and can barely leave her bed. Ruby knows she wants to have children and a career as a teacher someday, and seeing her aunt makes her wonder if her smoking habit could make it difficult for her to reach these goals. She starts to wonder whether her smoking habit is worth the short- and long-term sacrifices.

Social pressures can also increase the motivation to make changes. In Ruby's case, anti-smoking ordinances make it impossible for her to smoke in her dorm and in many public places. The inconvenience of finding a place to smoke—and pressure from her roommate, who doesn't like the smoky smell of Ruby's clothes in their room—add to Ruby's motivation to quit.

Boosting Self-Efficacy

When you start thinking about changing a health behavior, a big factor in your eventual success is whether you have confidence in yourself and in your ability to change. **Self-efficacy** refers to your belief in your ability to successfully take action and perform a specific task. Strategies for boosting self-efficacy include developing an internal locus of control, using visualization and self-talk, and obtaining encouragement from supportive people.

LOCUS OF CONTROL Who do you believe is controlling your life? Is it your parents, friends, or school? Is it "fate"? Or is it you? **Locus of control** refers to the figurative "place" a person designates as the source of responsibility for the events in his or her life. People who believe they are in control of their own lives are said to have an internal locus of control. Those who believe that factors beyond their control—heredity, friends and family, the environment, fate, luck, or other outside forces—are more important in determining the events of their lives are said to have an external locus of control.

For lifestyle management, an internal locus of control is an advantage because it reinforces motivation and commitment. An external locus of control can sabotage efforts to change behavior. For example, if you believe you are destined to die of breast cancer because your mother died from the disease, you may view monthly breast self-exams and regular checkups as a waste of time. In contrast, if you believe you can take action to reduce your hereditary risk of breast cancer, you will be motivated to follow guidelines for early detection of the disease.

If you find yourself attributing too much influence to outside forces, gather more information about your wellness-related behaviors. List all the ways that making lifestyle changes will improve your health. If you believe you'll succeed, and if you recognize and accept that you are in charge of your life, you're on your way to wellness.

VISUALIZATION AND SELF-TALK One of the best ways to boost your confidence and self-efficacy is to visualize yourself successfully engaging in a new, healthier behavior. Imagine yourself going for a regular after-dinner walk or choosing healthier snacks. Also visualize yourself enjoying all the short-term and long-term benefits that your lifestyle change will bring. Create a new self-image: What will you and your life be like when you become a regular exerciser or a healthy eater?

You can also use self-talk, the internal dialogue you carry on with yourself, to increase your confidence in your ability to change. Counter any self-defeating patterns of thought with more positive or realistic thoughts: "I am a strong, capable person, and I can maintain my commitment to change." Refer to Chapter 10 for more on self-talk.

ROLE MODELS AND OTHER SUPPORTIVE INDIVIDUALS Social support can make a big difference in your level of motivation and your chances of success. Perhaps you know people who have reached the goal you are striving for; they could be role models or mentors for you, providing information and support for your efforts. Gain strength from their experiences, and tell yourself, "If they can do it, so can I." In addition, find a buddy who wants to make the same changes you do and who can take an active role in your behavior change program. For example, an exercise buddy can provide companionship and encouragement for times when you might be tempted to skip your workout.

Terms

self-efficacy The belief in one's ability to take action and perform a specific behavior.

locus of control The figurative "place" a person designates as the source of responsibility for the events in his or her life.

Identifying and Overcoming Key Barriers to Change

Don't let past failures at behavior change discourage you; they can be a great source of information you can use to boost your chances of future success. Make a list of the problems and challenges you faced in any previous behavior change attempts; to this, add the short-term costs of behavior change that you identified in your analysis of the pros and cons of change. Once you've listed these key barriers to change, develop a practical plan for overcoming each one. For example, if you always smoke when you're with certain friends, practice in advance how you will turn down the next cigarette you are offered.

Self-talk can also help overcome barriers. Make behavior change a priority in your life and plan to commit the necessary time and effort. Ask yourself, How much time and energy will behavior change *really* require? Isn't the effort worth the short- and long-term benefits?

Enhancing Your Readiness to Change

The transtheoretical, or "stages of change," model has been shown to be an effective approach to lifestyle self-management. According to this model, you move through distinct stages as you work to change your target behavior. Starting at the wrong stage or moving too quickly through the stages can reduce the likelihood that you'll succeed in changing your behavior. Read the descriptions of the stages below to determine at what stage you find yourself for the target behavior you've selected. To move forward in the cycle of change, try the techniques and strategies in the box "Tips for Moving Forward in the Cycle of Behavior Change." You may find it helpful to work through the strategies for all the stages. You'll find additional suggestions for successful behavior change in the next section of the chapter.

Precontemplation: No Intention of Changing Behavior

People at this stage do not intend to change their behavior. They may be unaware of the risks associated with their behavior, or they may deny that their behavior will have any serious consequences for them. They may have tried unsuccessfully to change in the past and may now feel demoralized and think the situation is hopeless. They may also blame other people or external factors for their problems. People in the precontemplation stage believe that there are more reasons or more important reasons not to change than there are reasons to change.

Contemplation: Intending to Take Action Within 6 Months

People at this stage are aware that they have a problem and have started to think and learn about it. They acknowledge the benefits that behavior change will have for them but are also very aware of the costs of changing—to be successful, people must believe that the benefits of change outweigh the costs. People in the contemplation stage wonder about possible courses of action but may feel unsure of how to proceed. There may also be specific barriers to change that appear too difficult to overcome.

Preparation: Planning to Take Action Within a Month

People at this stage plan to take action within a month or may already have begun to make small changes in their behavior. They may be engaging in their new, healthier, behavior but not yet regularly or consistently. They may have created a plan for change but may be uncertain or anxious about the possibility of successful behavior change.

Action: Outwardly Changing Behavior

During the action stage, people outwardly modify their behavior and their environment. The action stage usually requires the greatest commitment of time and energy, and people in this stage are at risk for reverting to old, unhealthy, patterns of behavior.

Maintenance: Successful Behavior Change for 6 Months or More

People at this stage have maintained their new, healthier, lifestyle for at least 6 months. Lapses may have occurred, but people in maintenance have been successful in quickly reestablishing the desired behavior. The maintenance stage typically lasts from 6 months to about 5 years or longer.

Termination

For some behaviors, such as addictions, a person may reach the sixth and final stage of termination. People at this stage have exited the cycle of change and are no longer tempted to lapse back into their old behavior. They have a new self-image and total self-efficacy with regard to their target behavior.

Lapses are a natural part of the process at all stages of change. Many people lapse and must recycle through earlier stages, although most don't go back to the first stage. If you lapse, use what you learn about yourself and the process of change to help you in your next attempt.

Precontemplation

• Raise your awareness of your target behavior and its effects on you and others. Research the ways it affects you now and how it may affect you in the future.

• Examine the defense mechanisms you use to resist change; examples include denying the consequences of your behavior and rationalizing your reasons for not changing. Develop a strategy for overcoming each of your key mental defenses. For example, "I don't exercise because I don't have time—*but* I could reduce my TV time by 30 minutes a day and go for a walk instead." Or, "I currently eat fast food every day because there are no healthier lunch options on campus—*but* I could pack up a sandwich and fruit in the morning and bring it with me for lunch." Work to recognize the difference between true barriers to your effort to change and the excuses you create to resist change.

• Talk to friends and family members about your interest in behavior change. The people around you may be very aware of your target behavior and may have insights into how you typically rationalize your choices.

• Identify relevant campus and community resources—for example, an exercise class offered by the physical education department or a stop-smoking or stress-management workshop offered by the student health center.

Contemplation

• Begin keeping a written record of your target behavior and the circumstances surrounding it to help you learn more about the behavior and to use when you begin to plan the specifics of your behavior change program.

• Complete a cost-benefit analysis of the pros and cons of your target behavior and of changing it. Examine both the present and the future in your analysis. Don't forget to include factors tied to your self-image, to how you feel about yourself, and to how your behavior affects others. Does your current behavior support your image of yourself as a responsible, healthy person? If not, can you continue to feel good about yourself if you don't change?

• Identify key barriers to change, and find options, alternatives, and strategies that can be used to overcome these barriers.

• Engage your emotions through such strategies as imagining what your life might be like if you were not to change, watching movies related to your target behavior, and reviewing certain effects of your behavior—for example, look at the residue left by cigarette smoke blown or tobacco juice spit into a white handkerchief, have someone videotape you while you are drunk or hungover and watch the tape, make a pile of the amount of candy or junk food you eat in a month, etc.

• Boost self-efficacy and begin to create a new self-image by imagining yourself and your life after you change your target behavior. Identify strategies that helped you make positive changes in the past; link your current effort to past successes.

• Think before you act, and avoid reflex behaviors. Ask yourself why you are engaging in your target behavior.

• Enlist the help of friends and family members to identify the causes and consequences of your target behavior.

Preparation

• Create a specific plan for change that includes a start date, realistic goals, rewards, and information on exactly how you will go about changing your behavior (see the section on creating a personalized plan). Make sure you have all the information and equipment called for in your plan.

• Make change a priority in your life, and commit the necessary time and effort to change. Create and sign a contract.

• Practice visualization and self-talk to prepare yourself for the change you'll be making. Imagine yourself in challenging situations—surrounded by smoking friends when you are trying to quit or invited for a late-night pizza when you are trying to cut back on snacking—and mentally prepare yourself for appropriate action.

• Try your desired behavior for a day or a week; even a brief period of success will help boost self-efficacy.

• Tell the people in your life about the change you'll be making. Ask for help, specifying both dos and don'ts.

Action

• Monitor your behavior and your program's progress.

• Make changes in your environment that will discourage your target behavior and encourage healthier responses. Plan ahead to help overcome difficult situations.

• Find alternatives for your target behavior. For example, if you typically overeat or binge drink to manage stress, substitute a walk or a relaxation technique for the target behavior. Work on developing an internal locus of control and an appropriate degree of assertiveness—believe that you can control your own behavior and help shape your environment.

• Give yourself the rewards you named in your contract as well as plenty of self-praise. Keep a positive attitude about yourself and the change you are attempting. Manage your stress level, and don't let yourself get overwhelmed. Focus on the benefits you've already obtained from your new behavior.

• Involve the people around you. Arrange with someone to join your program as a buddy and/or find a role model who has already made the change you are working toward and who can provide both inspiration and practical advice.

• Don't get discouraged if your program is difficult or if you experience brief lapses—the action stage typically lasts for at least several months. Real change is difficult.

Maintenance

• Continue with all the positive strategies you used in earlier stages—monitor your behavior with a journal, manage your environment, and practice realistic self-talk.

• Be prepared for complications and lapses, but don't let a slip set you back. As you continue on with your program, your confidence and self-efficacy will increase, and you'll be less likely to slip. But don't let continued success allow you to forget about the negative aspects of your original (target) behavior and the effort required to change it.

• Act as a role model and help someone else make a positive lifestyle change.

SOURCES: Marcus, B. H., and L. H. Forsyth. 2003. *Motivating People to Be Physically Active.* Champaign, Ill.: Human Kinetics. Sarafino, E. P. 2001. *Behavior Modification: Understanding Principles of Behavior Change.* Mountain View, Calif.: Mayfield. Centers for Disease Control and Prevention, Division of Nutrition and Physical Activity. 1999. *Promoting Physical Activity: A Guide for Community Action.* Champaign, Ill.: Human Kinetics. Prochaska, J. O., J. C. Norcross, and C. C. DiClemente. 1994. *Changing for Good: A Revolutionary Six-Stage Program for Overcoming Bad Habits and Moving Your Life Positively Forward.* New York: Avon Books.

Date	November 5				Day	M	TU	W	TH	F	SA	SU	

Time of day	M/S	Food eaten	Cals.	H	Where did you eat?	What else were you doing?	How did someone else influence you?	What made you want to eat what you did?	Emotions and feelings?	Thoughts and concerns?
7:30	M	1 C Crispix cereal 1/2 C skim milk coffee, black 1 C orange juice	110 40 — 120	3	home	reading newspaper	alone	I always eat cereal in the morning	a little keyed up & worried	thinking about quiz in class today
10:30	S	1 apple	90	1	hall outside classroom	studying	alone	felt tired & wanted to wake up	tired	worried about next class
12:30	M	1 C chili 1 roll 1 pat butter 1 orange 2 oatmeal cookies 1 soda	290 120 35 60 120 150	2	campus food court	talking	eating w/ friends; we decided to eat at the food court	wanted to be part of group	excited and happy	interested in hearing everyone's plans for the weekend
	M/S = Meal or snack				H = Hunger rating (0–3)					

Figure 1.6 Sample health journal entries.   Visit the Online Learning Center for examples of health journal formats focusing on other target behaviors.

Developing Skills for Change: Creating a Personalized Plan

Once you are committed to making a change, it's time to put together a plan of action. Your key to success is a well-thought-out plan that sets goals, anticipates problems, and includes rewards.

1. Monitor Your Behavior and Gather Data

Begin by keeping careful records of the behavior you wish to change (your target behavior) and the circumstances surrounding it. Keep these records in a health journal or a paper or electronic notebook. Sample blank journal logs for a variety of target behaviors can be found on the Online Learning Center. Track the details of your behavior along with observations and comments. Note exactly what the activity was, when and where it happened, what you were doing, and what your feelings were at the time (see the sample journal in Figure 1.6 and Activity 3 in the Behavior Change Workbook at the end of the text). If your goal is to start an exercise program, use your journal to track your daily activities to determine how best to make time for your workouts. Keep your journal for a week or two to get some solid information about the behavior you want to change.

2. Analyze the Data and Identify Patterns

After you have collected data on the behavior, analyze the data to identify patterns. When are you most likely to overeat? What events trigger your appetite? Perhaps you are especially hungry at midmorning or when you put off eating dinner until 9:00. Perhaps you overindulge in food and drink when you go to a particular restaurant or when you're with certain friends. Note the connections between your feelings and such external cues as time of day, location, situation, and the actions of others around you. Do you always have a cigarette when you read the newspaper? Do you bite your fingernails when you study?

3. Set Realistic, Specific, and Measurable Goals

Don't set an impossibly difficult overall goal for your program—going from a sedentary lifestyle to running a marathon within 2 months, for example. Working toward more realistic, achievable goals will greatly increase your chances of success. Your goal should also be specific and measurable, something you can easily track. Instead of a vague goal such as improving eating habits or being more physically active, set a specific target—eating 9 servings of fruits and vegetables each day or walking or biking for 30 minutes at least 5 days per week.

It's a good idea to break your ultimate goal down into a few small steps. Your plan will seem less overwhelming and more manageable, increasing the chances that you'll stick to it. You'll also build in more opportunities to reward yourself (discussed in step 4), as well as milestones you can use to measure your progress. If you've been sedentary but plan to start a physical activity program, begin by taking 10- to 15-minute walks a few times a week. If you plan to increase your fruit and vegetable consumption from 3 to 7 servings per day, break your program into four steps, beginning with increasing from 3 to 4 servings per day. Take easier steps first and work up to harder steps. With each small success, you'll build your confidence and self-efficacy.

For some programs or circumstances, it may be better to focus your program on something other than outcome goals. For example, if you are in one of the early stages of change for your target behavior, setting challenging outcome goals like 60 minutes of daily physical activity or quitting smoking may be premature. The overall goal of your first change program might be to move from the precontemplation to the preparation stage of change, and your program mini-goals might be to work through specific strategies for various stages—spending 2 hours researching your target behavior or completing a detailed cost-benefit analysis, for example. Weight-loss programs can also benefit from goals that promote the development of healthy habits because specific body weight targets can take a long time to achieve and can lead to an unhealthy emphasis on weight rather than on the behaviors needed to achieve and maintain a healthy body weight. For example, a program might focus on setting weekly minutes of physical activity, or reducing portion sizes or the number of late-night snacks, rather than on achieving a specific body weight. (Additional examples of behavior change goals appear in later chapters.)

4. Devise a Strategy or Plan of Action

Next, you need to develop specific strategies and techniques that will support your day-to-day efforts at behavior change.

OBTAIN INFORMATION AND SUPPLIES Identify campus and community resources that can provide practical help—for example, a stop-smoking course or a walking club. Take any necessary preparatory steps, such as signing up for a stress-management workshop or purchasing walking shoes, nicotine replacement patches, or a special calendar to track your progress.

MODIFY YOUR ENVIRONMENT You can be more effective in changing behavior if you control the environmental cues that provoke it. This might mean not having cigarettes or certain foods or drinks in the house, not going to parties where you're tempted to overindulge, or not spending time with particular people, at least for a while. Use the data you collected in your health journal to identify patterns. If you always get a candy bar at a certain vending machine, change your route so you don't pass by it. If you always end up taking a coffee break and chatting with friends when you go to the library to study, choose a different place to study, such as your room. Finding alternatives to or substitutes for your target behavior is a key part of a successful plan for change.

It's also helpful to control other behaviors or habits that are linked to the target behavior. You may give in to an urge to eat when you have a beer (alcohol increases the appetite) or watch TV. Try substituting other activities for habits that are linked with your target behavior, such as exercising to music instead of plopping down in front of the TV. Or put an exercise bicycle in front of the set and burn calories while watching your favorite show.

Your environment contains powerful cues for both positive and negative lifestyle choices. Identifying and using the healthier options available to you throughout the day is a key part of a successful behavior change program.

You can change the cues in your environment so they trigger the new behavior you want instead of the old one. Tape a picture of a cyclist speeding down a hill on your TV screen. Leave your exercise shoes in plain view. Put a chart of your progress in a special place at home to make your goals highly visible and inspire you to keep going.

See Activity 7 in the Behavior Change Workbook for a detailed example of how to develop strategies to break the chain of events surrounding a target behavior.

REWARD YOURSELF Another powerful way to affect your target behavior is to set up a reward system that will reinforce your efforts. Most people find it difficult to change long-standing habits for rewards they can't see right away. Giving yourself instant, real rewards for good behavior along the way provides positive reinforcement that will help you stick with a plan to change your behavior.

Carefully plan your reward payoffs and what they will be. In most cases, rewards should be collected when you reach specific objectives or subgoals in your plan. For example, you might treat yourself to a movie after a week of avoiding extra snacks. Don't forget to reward yourself for good behavior that is consistent and persistent—such as simply sticking with your program week after week. Decide on a reward after you reach a certain goal or mark off the sixth week or month of a valiant effort. Write it down in your health journal and remember it as you follow your plan—especially when the going gets rough. If you don't think you can successfully manage your own reward system, ask someone to help; a friend can act as your reward "bank" and administer rewards according to your plan.

Make a list of your activities and favorite events to use as rewards. They should be special, inexpensive, and preferably unrelated to food or alcohol. You might treat yourself to a concert, a ball game, a new CD, a long-distance phone call to a friend, a day off from studying, or a long hike in the woods—whatever is rewarding to you.

INVOLVE THE PEOPLE AROUND YOU Rewards and support can also come from family and friends. Tell them about your plan and ask for their help. Encourage them to be active, interested participants. To help friends and family members respond appropriately, you may want to create a specific list of dos and don'ts. For example, ask them to support you when you set aside time to go running or avoid second helpings at Thanksgiving dinner.

PLAN AHEAD FOR CHALLENGING SITUATIONS Take time out now to list situations and people that have the potential to derail your program and to develop possible coping mechanisms. For example, if you think you'll have trouble exercising during finals week, schedule short bouts of physical activity as stress-reducing study breaks. If a visit to a friend who smokes is likely to tempt you to lapse, plan to bring nicotine patches and chewing gum along with you on your visit.

5. Make a Personal Contract A serious personal contract—one that commits you to your word—can result in a higher chance of follow-through than a casual, offhand promise. Your contract can help prevent procrastination by specifying the important dates and can also serve as a reminder of your personal commitment to change. Your contract should include a statement of your goal and your commitment to reaching it. Include details of your plan: the date you'll begin, the steps you'll use to measure your progress, the concrete strategies you've developed for promoting change, and the date you expect to reach your final goal. Have someone—preferably someone who will be actively helping you with your program—sign your contract as a witness.

A Sample Behavior Change Plan Let's take the example of Michael, who wants to improve his diet. By monitoring his eating habits in his health journal for several weeks, he gets a good sense of his typical diet—what he eats and where he eats it. Through self-assessment and investigation, he discovers that he currently consumes only about one serving of fruit per week, much less than the recommended three to five servings per day. He also finds out that fruit is a major source of fiber, vitamins, minerals, and other substances important for good health. He sets the target of eating three servings of fruit per day as the overall goal for his behavior change plan. Then Michael develops a specific plan for change that involves several changes in his behavior and his environment, which he describes in a contract that commits him to reaching his goal (Figure 1.7). Additional sample plans and contracts for other target behaviors can be found on the *Fit and Well* Online Learning Center.

A beautiful setting and a friendly companion help make exercise a satisfying and pleasurable experience. Choosing the right activity and doing it the right way are important elements in a successful behavior change program.

Putting Your Plan into Action

The starting date has arrived, and you are ready to put your plan into action. This stage requires commitment, the resolve to stick with the plan no matter what temptations you encounter. Remember all the reasons you have to make the change—and remember that *you* are the boss. Use all your strategies to make your plan work. Make sure your environment is change-friendly, and obtain as much support and encouragement from others as possible. Keep track of your progress in your health journal, and give yourself regular rewards. And don't forget to give yourself a pat on the back—congratulate yourself, notice how much better you look or feel, and feel good about how far you've come and how you've gained control of your behavior.

Staying with It

As you continue with your program, don't be surprised when you run up against obstacles; they're inevitable. In fact, it's a good idea to expect problems and give yourself time to step back, see how you're doing, and make some changes before going on. If your program is grinding to a halt, identify what is blocking your progress. It may come from one of these sources.

Social Influences Take a hard look at the reactions of the people you're counting on, and see if they're really

My Personal Contract for Eating Three Servings of Fruit per Day

I agree to increase my consumption of fruit from one serving per week to three servings per day. I will begin my program on __10/5__ and plan to reach my final goal by __12/7__. I have divided my program into three parts, with three separate goals. For each step in my program, I will give myself the reward listed.

1. I will begin to have a serving of fruit with breakfast on __10/5__.
   (Reward: __baseball game__)
2. I will begin to have a serving of fruit with lunch on __10/26__.
   (Reward: __music CD__)
3. I will begin to substitute fruit juice for soda for one snack each day on __11/16__.
   (Reward: __concert__)

My plan for increasing fruit consumption includes the following strategies:
1. Keeping my refrigerator stocked with easy-to-carry fruit and fruit juice.
2. Packing fruit in my book backpack every day.
3. Placing reminders to buy, carry, and eat fruit in my room, backpack, and wallet.
4. Buying lunch at a place that serves fruit or fruit juice.

I understand that it is important for me to make a strong personal effort to make the change in my behavior. I sign this contract as an indication of my personal commitment to reach my goal.

Michael Cook 9/28

Witness: *Katie Lim* 9/28

Figure 1.7 A sample behavior change contract.

supporting you. If they come up short, connect and network with others who will be more supportive.

A related trap is trying to get your friends or family members to change *their* behaviors. The decision to make a major behavior change is something people come to only after intensive self-examination. You may be able to influence someone by tactfully providing facts or support, but that's all. Focus on yourself. If you succeed, you may become a role model for others.

Levels of Motivation and Commitment

You won't make real progress until an inner drive leads you to the stage of change at which you are ready to make a personal commitment to the goal. If commitment is your problem, you may need to wait until the behavior you're dealing with makes your life more unhappy or unhealthy; then your desire to change it will be stronger. Or you may find that changing your goal will inspire you to keep going. For more ideas, refer to the box "Motivation Boosters" and to Activity 9 in the Behavior Change Workbook.

Choice of Techniques and Level of Effort   If your plan is not working as well as you thought it would, make changes where you're having the most trouble. If you've lagged on your running schedule, for example, maybe it's because you don't like running. An aerobics class might suit you better. There are many ways to move toward your goal. Or you may not be trying hard enough. You do have to push toward your goal. If it were easy, you wouldn't need a plan.

Stress Barrier   If you've hit a wall in your program, look at the sources of stress in your life. If the stress is temporary, such as catching a cold or having a term paper due, you may want to wait until it passes before strengthening your efforts. If the stress is ongoing, find healthy ways to manage it, such as taking a half-hour walk after lunch or beginning a yoga class. You may even want to make stress management your highest priority for behavior change (see Chapter 10).

Procrastinating, Rationalizing, and Blaming   Try to detect the games you might be playing with yourself so that you can stop them. If you're procrastinating ("It's Friday already; I might as well wait until Monday to begin"), break your plan down into still smaller steps that you can accomplish one day at a time. If you're rationalizing or making excuses ("I wanted to go swimming today, but I wouldn't have had time to wash my hair afterward"), remember that when you "win" by deceiving yourself, it's not much of a victory. If you're wasting time blaming yourself or others ("Everyone in that class talks so much that I don't get a chance to speak"), recognize that blaming is a way of taking your focus off the real problem and denying responsibility for your actions. Try refocusing by taking a positive attitude and renewing your determination to succeed.

MOTIVATION FOR CHANGE!   Behavior change is like many other challenges you'll encounter at school and work—it requires that you develop certain skills. Just as when you take a course in an unfamiliar subject, you shouldn't expect that you'll master everything in your behavior change program quickly and with ease or that you'll achieve perfection. But with consistent effort, you can build your skills and achieve your goals. Think of any obstacles or difficult situations you encounter during your behavior change program as challenges to your skills that will require effort to address but that are within your ability to manage. Thinking of behavior change in this way will help you tolerate mistakes and lapses, remain motivated, and see your behavior change program as an opportunity for personal growth and improvement.

Motivation Boosters

- Write down the potential benefits of the change. If you want to lose weight, your list might include increased ease of movement, energy, and self-confidence.

- Now write down the costs of not changing.

- Frequently visualize yourself achieving your goal and enjoying its benefits. If you want to manage time more effectively, picture yourself as a confident, organized person who systematically tackles important tasks and sets aside time each day for relaxation, exercise, and friends.

- Discount obstacles to change. Counter thoughts such as "I'll never have time to exercise" with thoughts such as "Lots of other people have done it and so can I."

- Bombard yourself with propaganda. Take a class dealing with the change you want to make. Read books and watch talk shows on the subject. Post motivational phrases or pictures on your refrigerator or over your desk. Talk to people who have already made the change you want to make.

- Build up your confidence. Remind yourself of other goals you've achieved. At the end of each day, mentally review your good decisions and actions. See yourself as a capable person, one who is in charge of his or her health.

- Create choices. You will be more likely to exercise every day if you have two or three types of exercise to choose from and more likely to quit smoking if you've identified more than one way to distract yourself when you crave a cigarette. Get ideas from people who have been successful and adapt some of their strategies to suit you.

- If you slip, keep trying. Research suggests that four out of five people will experience some degree of backsliding when they try to change a behavior. Only one in four succeeds the first time around. If you retain your commitment to change even when you lapse, you are still farther along the path to change than before you made the commitment.

Being Fit and Well for Life

Your first attempts at making behavior changes may never go beyond the project stage. Those that do may not all succeed. But as you experience some success, you'll start to have more positive feelings about yourself. You may discover new physical activities and sports you enjoy; you may encounter new situations and meet new people. Perhaps you'll surprise yourself by accomplishing things you didn't think were possible—breaking a long-standing nicotine habit, competing in a race, climbing a mountain, developing a lean, muscular body. Most of all, you'll discover the feeling of empowerment that comes from taking charge of your health (see the box "Signs of Wellness"). Being healthy takes extra effort, but the paybacks in energy and vitality are priceless.

Once you've started, don't stop. Assume that health improvement is forever. Take on the easier problems first, and then use what you learn to tackle more difficult problems later. Periodically review what you've accomplished to make sure you don't fall into old habits. And keep informed about the latest health news and trends. Research is constantly providing new information that directly affects daily choices and habits.

This book will introduce you to the main components of a fit and well lifestyle, show you how to assess your current health status, and help you put together a program that will lead to wellness. You can't control every aspect of your health—there are too many unknowns in life for that to be possible. But you can create a lifestyle that minimizes your health risks and maximizes your enjoyment of life and well-being. You can take charge of your health in a dramatic and meaningful way. *Fit and Well* will show you how.

You are in charge of your health. Many of the decisions you make every day have an impact on the quality of your life, both now and in the future. By making positive choices, large and small, you help ensure a lifetime of wellness.

Right now you can

- Go for a 15-minute walk.

- Have an orange, a nectarine, or a plum for a snack.

- Call a friend and arrange for a time to catch up with each other.

- Start thinking about whether you have a health behavior you'd like to change. If you do, consider the elements of a behavior change strategy. For example,
  - Begin a mental list of the pros and cons of the behavior.
  - Create a format for a log to monitor your target behavior.
  - Think of someone who can support you in your attempts to make a behavior change and talk to that person about your plan.

SUMMARY

- Wellness is the ability to live life fully, with vitality and meaning. Wellness is dynamic and multidimensional; it incorporates physical, emotional, intellectual, spiritual, interpersonal and social, and environmental dimensions.

- People today have greater control over and greater responsibility for their health than ever before.

- Behaviors that promote wellness include being physically active; choosing a healthy diet; maintaining a healthy

1. The persistent presence of a support network.)

2. Chronic positive expectations; the tendency to frame events in a constructive light.

3. Episodic outbreaks of joyful, happy experiences.

4. A sense of spiritual involvement.

5. A tendency to adapt to changing conditions.

6. Rapid response and recovery of stress response systems to repeated challenges.

7. An increased appetite for physical activity.

8. A tendency to identify and communicate feelings.

9. Repeated episodes of gratitude and generosity.

10. A persistent sense of humor.

SOURCE: Ten warning signs of good health. 1996. *Mind/Body Health Newsletter* 5(1).

body weight; managing stress effectively; avoiding use of tobacco and limiting alcohol use; and protecting yourself from disease and injury.

- Although heredity, environment, and health care all play roles in wellness and disease, behavior can mitigate their effects.

- To make lifestyle changes, you need information about yourself, your health habits, and resources available to help you change.

- You can increase your motivation for behavior change by examining the benefits and costs of change, boosting self-efficacy, and identifying and overcoming key barriers to change.

- The stages of change model describes six stages that people may move through as they try to change their behavior: precontemplation, contemplation, preparation, action, maintenance, and termination.

- A specific plan for change can be developed by (1) collecting data on your behavior and recording it in a journal; (2) analyzing the recorded data; (3) setting specific goals; (4) devising strategies for obtaining information, modifying the environment, rewarding yourself, involving others, and planning ahead; and (5) making a personal contract.

- To start and maintain a behavior change program you need commitment, a well-developed and manageable plan, social support, and strong stress-management techniques. It is also important to monitor the progress of your program, revising it as necessary.

For Further Exploration

VVW *Fit and Well* **Online Learning Center (www.mhhe.com/fahey)**

Visit the *Fit and Well* Online Learning Center and familiarize yourself with the resources available at the site. You can use the learning objectives, study guide questions, and glossary flashcards to review key terms and concepts for this chapter and prepare for exams. You can extend your knowledge of wellness and gain experience in using the Internet as a resource by completing the activities and checking out the Web links for the topics in Chapter 1 marked with the World Wide Web icon. For this chapter, there are activities relating to *Healthy People 2010* objectives, online assessments, and evaluation of online resources; there are Web links for the Vital Statistics tables and figures, the Critical Consumer box, and the chapter as a whole. Behavior change resources and tools include an online version of the Behavior Change Workbook, sample logs for a variety of target behaviors, and sample behavior change plans. There are also additional self-assessments focusing on the stages of change, occupational wellness, family history, and other aspects of wellness and behavior change.

Daily Fitness and Nutrition Journal

Have you chosen a target behavior related to physical activity or diet? If so, begin reviewing the behavior change planning and monitoring tools available in the log. If you've chosen a target behavior in another area, the fitness and nutrition examples can provide a good model for the type of program plan and log you should create for your behavior change program. Visit the Online Learning Center for some blank sample logs that you can print and use.

Books

Komaroff, A. L., ed. 2005. *Harvard Medical School Family Health Guide.* New York: Free Press. *Provides consumer-oriented advice for the prevention and treatment of common health concerns.*

Prochaska, J. O., J. C. Norcross, and C. C. DiClemente. 1994. *Changing for Good: The Revolutionary Program That Explains the Six Stages of Change and Teaches You How to Free Yourself from Bad Habits.* New York: Morrow. *Outlines the authors' model of behavior change and offers suggestions and advice for each stage of change.*

Smith P. B., M. MacFarlane, and E. Kalnitsky. 2002. *The Complete Idiot's Guide to Wellness.* Indianapolis, In.: Alpha Books. *A concise guide to healthy habits, including physical activity, nutrition, and stress management.*

Newsletters

Consumer Reports on Health (800-234-2188; http://www.ConsumerReportsonHealth.org)

Harvard Health Letter (877-649-9457; http://www.health.harvard.edu)

Harvard Men's Health Watch (877-649-9457)

Harvard Women's Health Watch (800-829-5921)

Mayo Clinic Health Letter (866-516-4974)

University of California at Berkeley Wellness Letter (800-829-9170; http://www.wellnessletter.com)

Organizations, Hotlines, and Web Sites

The Internet addresses (also called uniform resource locators, or URLs) listed here were accurate at the time of publication. Up-to-date links to these and many other wellness-oriented Web sites are provided on the links page of the *Fit and Well* Online Learning Center (http://www.mhhe.com/fahey).

Centers for Disease Control and Prevention. Provides a wide variety of health information.
> 800-311-3435
> http://www.cdc.gov

Many other government sites provide health-related materials:
> *Federal Trade Commission:* http://www.ftc.gov
> *First Gov for Consumers—Health:* http://www.consumer.gov/health.htm
> *National Institutes of Health:* http://www.nih.gov
> *National Library of Medicine, MedlinePlus:* http://www.medlineplus.gov

Go Ask Alice. Sponsored by the Columbia University Health Service, this site provides answers to student questions about stress, sexuality, fitness, and many other wellness topics.
> http://www.goaskalice.columbia.edu

Healthfinder. A gateway to online publications, Web sites, support and self-help groups, and agencies and organizations that produce reliable health information.
> http://www.healthfinder.gov

Healthy People 2010. Provides information on Healthy People objectives and priority areas.
> http://www.healthypeople.gov

MedlinePlus: Evaluating Health Information. Provides background information and links to sites with guidelines for finding and evaluating health information on the Web.
> http://www.nlm.nih.gov/medlineplus/evaluatinghealthinformation.html

National Health Information Center (NHIC). Puts consumers in touch with the organizations that are best able to provide answers to health-related questions.
> 800-336-4797
> http://www.health.gov/nhic

National Women's Health Information Center. Provides information and answers to frequently asked questions.
> 800-994-WOMAN
> http://womenshealth.gov

Student Counseling Virtual Pamphlet Collection. Provides links to more than 400 pamphlets produced by different student counseling centers; topics include relationships, family issues, substance abuse, anger management, and study skills.
> http://www.dr-bob.org/vpc

World Health Organization (WHO). Provides information about WHO activities and about many health topics and issues affecting people around the world.
> http://www.who.int

The following are just a few of the many sites that provide consumer-oriented information on a variety of health issues:
> *Family Doctor.Org:* http://www.familydoctor.org
> *InteliHealth:* http://www.intelihealth.com
> *Mayo Clinic:* http://www.mayoclinic.com
> *WebMD:* http://webmd.com

The following sites provide daily health news updates:
> *CNN Health:* http://www.cnn.com/health
> *MedlinePlus News:* http://www.nlm.nih.gov/medlineplus/newsbydate.html
> *Yahoo Health News:* http://dailynews.yahoo.com/h/hl

Selected Bibliography

American Cancer Society. 2005. *Cancer Facts and Figures 2005.* Atlanta: American Cancer Society.

American Heart Association. 2005. *2005 Heart and Stroke Statistical Update.* Dallas, Tex.: American Heart Association.

Calle, E. E., et al. 2003. Overweight, obesity, and mortality from cancer in a prospectively studied cohort of U.S. adults. *New England Journal of Medicine* 348(17): 1625–1638.

Centers for Disease Control and Prevention. 2005. Annual smoking-attributable mortality, years of potential life lost, and productivity losses—United States, 1997–2001. *Morbidity and Mortality Weekly Report* 54(5): 113–117.

Centers for Disease Control and Prevention. 2005. Racial/ethnic and socioeconomic disparities in multiple risk factors for heart disease and stroke, United States, 2003. *Morbidity and Mortality Weekly Report* 54(5): 113–117.

Centers for Disease Control and Prevention. 2005. Trends in leisure-time physical inactivity by age, sex, and race/ethnicity—United States, 1994–2004. *Morbidity and Mortality Weekly Report* 54(39): 991–994.

Centers for Disease Control and Prevention. 2004. Health behaviors of adults, 1999–2001. *Vital and Health Statistics* 10(219).

Centers for Disease Control and Prevention. 2003. Prevalence of diabetes and impaired fasting glucose in adults. *Morbidity and Mortality Weekly Report* 52(35): 833–837.

Centers for Disease Control and Prevention. 2003. Prevalence of physical activity, including lifestyle activities among adults. *Morbidity and Mortality Weekly Report* 52(32): 764–769.

Centers for Disease Control and Prevention, Division of Nutrition and Physical Activity. 1999. *Promoting Physical Activity: A Guide for Community Action.* Champaign, Ill.: Human Kinetics.

Douglas, K. A., et al. 1997. Results from the 1995 National College Health Risk Behavior Survey. *Journal of American College Health* 46(2): 55–56.

Flegal, K. M., et al. 2005. Excess deaths associated with underweight, overweight, and obesity. *Journal of the American Medical Association* 293(15): 1861–1867.

Gallagher, K. I., and J. M. Jakicic. 2002. Overcoming barriers to effective exercise programming. *ACSM's Health and Fitness Journal,* November/December.

Glanz, K., F. M. Lewis, and B. K. Rimer, eds. 1997. *Health Behavior and Health Education: Theory, Research, and Practice,* 2nd ed. San Francisco: Jossey-Bass.

Marcus, B. H., and L. H. Forsyth. 2003. *Motivating People to Be Physically Active.* Champaign, Ill.: Human Kinetics.

Mokdad, A. H., et al. 2005. Correction: Actual causes of death in the United States, 2000. *Journal of the American Medical Association* 293(3): 293–294.

Muller, A. 2002. Education, income inequality, and mortality: A multiple regression analysis. *British Medical Journal* 324(7328): 23–25.

National Center for Health Statistics. 2005. *Health, United States, 2005.* Hyattsville, Md.: Public Health Service.

Ortlepp, J. R., et al. 2003. Relation of body mass index, physical fitness, and the cardiovascular risk profile in 3217 young normal weight men with an apparently optimal lifestyle. *International Journal of Obesity and Related Metabolic Disorders* 27(8): 979–982.

Slater, M. D., and D. E. Zimmerman. 2002. Characteristics of health-related Web sites identified by common Internet portals. *Journal of the American Medical Association* 288(3): 316–317.

Stampfer, M. J., et al. 2000. Primary prevention of coronary heart disease in women through diet and lifestyle. *New England Journal of Medicine* 343(1): 16–22.

U.S. Department of Health and Human Services. 2000. *Healthy People 2010,* 2nd ed. Washington, D.C.: DHHS.

World Health Organization. 2001. *What Is the WHO Definition of Health?* (http://www.who.int/aboutwho/en/qal.htm; retrieved July 26, 2001).

LAB 1.1 *Your Wellness Profile*

Consider how your lifestyle, attitudes, and characteristics relate to each of the six dimensions of wellness. Fill in your strengths for each dimension (examples of strengths are listed with each dimension). Once you've completed your lists, choose what you believe are your five most important strengths and circle them.

Physical wellness: To maintain overall physical health and engage in appropriate physical activity (e.g., stamina, strength, flexibility, healthy body composition).

_____

_____

_____

Emotional wellness: To have a positive self-concept, deal constructively with your feelings, and develop positive qualities (e.g., optimism, trust, self-confidence, determination, persistence, dedication).

_____

_____

_____

Intellectual wellness: To pursue and retain knowledge, think critically about issues, make sound decisions, identify problems, and find solutions (e.g., common sense, creativity, curiosity).

_____

_____

_____

Spiritual wellness: To develop a set of beliefs, principles, or values that gives meaning or purpose to one's life; to develop faith in something beyond oneself (e.g., religious faith, service to others).

_____

_____

_____

Interpersonal/social wellness: To develop and maintain meaningful relationships with a network of friends and family members, and to contribute to the community (e.g., friendly, good-natured, compassionate, supportive, good listener).

_____

_____

_____

Environmental wellness: To protect yourself from environmental hazards, and to minimize the negative impact of your behavior on the environment (e.g., carpooling, recycling).

_____

_____

_____

Next, think about where you fall on the wellness continuum for each of the dimensions of wellness. Indicate your placement for each—physical, emotional, intellectual, spiritual, interpersonal/social, and environmental—by placing Xs on the continuum below.

Low level of wellness	Physical, psychological, emotional symptoms	Change and growth	High level of wellness

Based on both your current lifestyle and your goals for the future, what do you think your placement on the wellness continuum will be in 10 years? What new health behaviors would you have to adopt to achieve your goals? Which of your current behaviors would you need to change to maintain or improve your level of wellness in the future?

Does the description of wellness given in this chapter encompass everything you believe is part of wellness for you? Write your own definition of wellness, and include any additional dimensions that are important to you. Then rate your level of wellness based on your own definition.

the ability to be able to do all the things you'd like to w/ ease, have fun, stay healthy, avoid unhealthy habits, avoid diseases the best you can.

Using Your Results

How did you score? Are you satisfied with your current level of wellness—overall and in each dimension? In which dimension(s) would you most like to increase your level of wellness?

What should you do next? As you consider possible target behaviors for a behavior change program, choose things that will maintain or increase your level of wellness in one of the dimensions you listed as an area of concern. Remember to consider health behaviors such as smoking or eating a high-fat diet that may threaten your level of wellness in the future. Below, list several possible target behaviors and the wellness dimensions that they influence.

For additional guidance in choosing a target behavior, complete the lifestyle self-assessment in Lab 1.2.

LAB 1.2 *Lifestyle Evaluation*

VWw

How does your current lifestyle compare with the lifestyle recommended for wellness? For each question, choose the answer that best describes your behavior; then add up your score for each section.

	Almost Always	Sometimes	Never

Exercise/Fitness

1. I engage in moderate exercise, such as brisk walking or swimming, for 20–60 minutes, three to five times a week.　　4　①　0
2. I do exercises to develop muscular strength and endurance at least twice a week.　　2　①　0
3. I spend some of my leisure time participating in individual, family, or team activities, such as gardening, bowling, or softball.　　2　①　0
4. I maintain a healthy body weight, avoiding overweight and underweight.　　②　1　0

Exercise/Fitness Score: _____ 5 _____

Nutrition

1. I eat a variety of foods each day, including seven or more servings of fruits and/or vegetables.　　3　①—⓪
2. I limit the amount of total fat and saturated and trans fat in my diet.　　3　①　0
3. I avoid skipping meals.　　2　①　0
4. I limit the amount of salt and sugar I eat.　　2　①　0

Nutrition Score: _____ 4 _____

Tobacco Use

If you never use tobacco, enter a score of 10 for this section and go to the next section.
1. I avoid using tobacco.　　2　1　⓪
2. I smoke only low-tar-and-nicotine cigarettes, or I smoke a pipe or cigars, or I use smokeless tobacco.　　2　1　⓪

Tobacco Use Score: _____ 0 _____

Alcohol and Drugs

1. I avoid alcohol, or I drink no more than one (women) or two (men) drinks a day.　　4　①　⑩
2. I avoid using alcohol or other drugs as a way of handling stressful situations or the problems in my life.　　2　①　0
3. I am careful not to drink alcohol when taking medications (such as cold or allergy medications) or when pregnant.　　2　①　0
4. I read and follow the label directions when using prescribed and over-the-counter drugs.　　2　1　⓪

Alcohol and Drugs Score: _____ 3 _____

Emotional Health

1. I enjoy being a student, and I have a job or do other work that I enjoy.　　②　1　0
2. I find it easy to relax and express my feelings freely.　　②　1　0
3. I manage stress well.　　2　①　0
4. I have close friends, relatives, or others whom I can talk to about personal matters and call on for help when needed.　　2　①　0
5. I participate in group activities (such as community or church organizations) or hobbies that I enjoy.　　2　①　0

Emotional Health Score: _____ 7 _____

Safety

1. I wear a safety belt while riding in a car.   (2) 1 0
2. I avoid driving while under the influence of alcohol or other drugs.   2 (1) 0
3. I obey traffic rules and the speed limit when driving.   2 (1) 0
4. I read and follow instructions on the labels of potentially harmful products or substances, such as household cleaners, poisons, and electrical appliances.   (2) 1 0
5. I avoid smoking in bed.   (2) 1 0

Safety Score: _____ 7

Disease Prevention

1. I know the warning signs of cancer, heart attack, and stroke.   2 (1) 0
2. I avoid overexposure to the sun and use sunscreen.   (2) 1 (0)
3. I get recommended medical screening tests (such as blood pressure and cholesterol checks and Pap tests), immunizations, and booster shots.   2 1 (0)
4. I practice monthly skin and breast/testicle self-exams.   2 1 (0)
5. I am not sexually active *or* I have sex with only one mutually faithful, uninfected partner *or* I always engage in safer sex (using condoms), *and* I do not share needles to inject drugs.   (2) 1 0

Disease Prevention Score: _____ 3

Scores of 9 and 10 Excellent! Your answers show that you are aware of the importance of this area to your health. More important, you are putting your knowledge to work for you by practicing good health habits. As long as you continue to do so, this area should not pose a serious health risk.

Scores of 6 to 8 Your health practices in this area are good, but there is room for improvement.

Scores of 3 to 5 Your health risks are showing.

Scores of 0 to 2 You may be taking serious and unnecessary risks with your health.

Using Your Results

How did you score? In which areas did you score the lowest? Are you satisfied with your scores in each area? In which areas would you most like to improve your scores?

tobacco, Alcohol & Drug, disease prevention.

What should you do next? To improve your scores, look closely at any item to which you answered "sometimes" or "never." Identify and list at least three possible targets for a health behavior change program. (If you are aware of other risky health behaviors you currently engage in, but which were not covered by this assessment, you may include those in your list.) For each item on your list, identify your current "stage of change" and one strategy you could adopt to move forward (see pp. 14–16). Possible strategies might be obtaining information about the behavior, completing an analysis of the pros and cons of change, or beginning a written record.

Behavior	Stage	Strategy
1. _____	_____	_____
2. _____	_____	_____
3. _____	_____	_____

SOURCE: Adapted from *Healthstyle: A Self-Test,* developed by the U.S. Public Health Service. The behaviors covered in this test are recommended for most Americans, but some may not apply to people with certain chronic diseases or disabilities or to pregnant women, who may require special advice from their physician.

2

Looking AHEAD

After reading this chapter, you should be able to

- Describe how much physical activity is recommended for developing health and fitness
- Identify the components of physical fitness and how each component affects wellness
- Explain the goal of physical training and the basic principles of training
- Describe the principles involved in designing a well-rounded exercise program
- Discuss the steps that can be taken to make an exercise program safe, effective, and successful

Principles of Physical Fitness

Test Your Knowledge

1. **To improve your health, you must exercise for at least 30 minutes straight, 5 or more days per week.**
   True or false?

2. **Among American adults, about what percentage of trips of less than 1 mile long are made by walking?**
   a. 15%
   b. 25%
   c. 50%

3. **If all inactive American adults became physically active, the savings in direct costs for medical care would be about _____ per year.**
   a. $75 million
   b. $7.5 billion
   c. $75 billion

ANSWERS

1. FALSE. Experts recommend about 30 minutes of moderate physical activity on most days of the week, but activity can be done in short bouts—10-minute sessions, for example—spread out over the course of the day.

2. A. The vast majority of short trips are made in automobiles. On average, Americans spend 100 minutes per day driving and 170 minutes per day watching television. Most people have many opportunities to incorporate more moderate physical activity into their daily routine.

3. C. People who engage in regular physical activity make fewer physician visits, use less medication, and have fewer hospital stays than physically inactive people.

VW *Fit and Well* **Online Learning Center**   www.mhhe.com/fahey

Visit the *Fit and Well* Online Learning Center for study aids, online labs, additional information about physical activity, links, Internet activities that explore the importance of physical activity, consumer resources, and much more.

A ny list of the benefits of physical activity is impressive. A physically active lifestyle helps you generate more energy, control your weight, manage stress, and boost your immune system. It provides psychological and emotional benefits, contributing to your sense of competence and well-being. It offers protection against heart disease, diabetes, high blood pressure, depression, anxiety, osteoporosis, some types of cancer, and even premature death. Exercise increases your physical capacity so that you are better able to meet the challenges of daily life with energy and vigor. Although people vary greatly in the levels of physical fitness and performance they can ultimately achieve, the benefits of regular physical activity are available to everyone. (For more on the benefits of exercise, see the box "Exercise and Total Wellness.")

This chapter provides an overview of physical fitness. It explains how lifestyle physical activity and more formal exercise programs contribute to wellness. It describes the components of fitness, the basic principles of physical training, and the essential elements of a well-rounded exercise program. Chapters 3–6 provide an in-depth look at each of the elements of a fitness program; Chapter 7 will help you put all these elements together into a complete, personalized program.

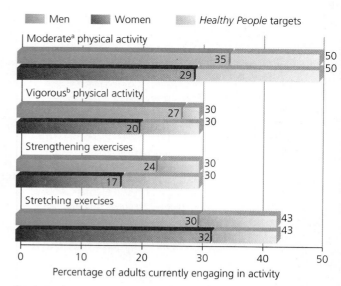

Figure 2.1   Current levels of physical activity among American adults.   SOURCE: National Center for Health Statistics. 2004. *DATA2010: The Healthy People 2010 Database* (http://wonder.cdc.gov/data2010; retrieved January 1, 2005).

PHYSICAL ACTIVITY AND EXERCISE FOR HEALTH AND FITNESS

Despite the many benefits of an active lifestyle, levels of physical activity have declined in recent years and remain low for all populations of Americans (Figure 2.1). According to the Centers for Disease Control and Prevention (CDC), more than 55% of U.S. adults do not engage in recommended amounts of physical activity; 25% are not active at all. In the summer of 1996, the U.S. Surgeon General published *Physical Activity and Health,* a landmark report designed to reverse these trends and get Americans moving. Here is a summary of its findings:

- People of all ages benefit from regular physical activity.

- People can obtain significant health benefits by including a moderate amount of physical activity on most, if not all, days of the week. Through a modest increase in daily activity, most Americans can improve their health and quality of life.

- Additional health benefits can be gained through greater amounts of physical activity. People who can maintain a regular regimen of more vigorous or longer-duration activity are likely to obtain even greater benefits.

Why aren't more Americans active? Possible barriers include lack of time and resources, social and environmental influences, and—most important—lack of motivation and commitment (see Lab 2.3 for more on barriers).

Some people also fear serious injury. Although physical activity does carry some risks, the risks of inactivity are far greater. Evidence is growing that for most Americans, simply becoming more physically active may be the single most important lifestyle change for promoting health and well-being.

MOTIVATION FOR CHANGE!   Habit helps us conserve mental and physical energy as we go through our daily lives, but it also blinds us to areas we could change. Make a list of 10 ways you can incorporate more physical activity into your life by changing a habit, such as walking instead of riding the bus, taking the stairs in a certain building instead of the elevator, and so on. Be specific about both the habits you choose and your strategies for changing them. Then put one strategy into action. For example, if you always park in the closest spot to your classroom or office, find a different area or lot to park in—one that would require you to walk for 5 minutes to reach your destination. Post reminders for the first week or two until your new parking strategy has become a habit and you park in the new spot without thinking. Use your success at making one simple change to counter negative self-talk about a lack of opportunities for physical activity and to motivate you to make other healthy changes in your habits.

Hundreds of studies show that exercise gives people both a longer life and a healthier life. Most of us want to live longer and avoid heart disease, cancer, and other chronic diseases, but many people choose to be active for other reasons. Some get a kick out of hitting a game-winning cross-court backhand, backpacking through a wilderness area, or completing a difficult skateboard move. Others enjoy the friends they make at the gym, on the tennis court, or on the walking trail; the way their fitness program gives them more energy; or the satisfaction they get from walking farther, running faster, or lifting more weight.

Samantha is a single 28-year-old junior executive from Boston who has a busy work and social schedule. Her fast-paced life makes it essential that she stay in shape. She attends an exercise class at a health club three times a week and lifts weights after the class. "The gym is an oasis in my incredibly busy day. I finish my exercise class refreshed and invigorated. I feel healthy, and I like the way my clothes fit. Being fit gives me the energy and self-confidence I need to compete in the business world. It's given my social life a boost, too."

Max is a 22-year-old college student who lives in Salt Lake City and loves to ski. "I came to Salt Lake because the surrounding mountains have the best snow in the world. I love the feeling of plunging down a steep chute and feeling the fresh powder surround me. The solitude and the beauty of the mountains are a spiritual experience for me. I stay in shape and eat right so that I can better enjoy the high I get from skiing."

Nora is a 42-year-old mother of three children who lives in a small town outside Austin, Texas. She gets plenty of physical activity in her daily routine, which includes biking to her part-time job and helping out with after-school youth programs at the local community center. However, her passion is throwing the javelin in Masters track and field competitions. "I developed a love for the sport in college. I enjoy the competition and striving to improve in a very difficult event. I have friends all over the world who share my passion. I like testing myself in competition—when I win or perform up to my personal best, the feeling is indescribable."

Bill is an 18-year-old college student at a small Midwest college who loves to run. "I run almost every day to forget my problems and relieve stress. Going away to college has been a big shock—I've gone from being part of a tight family to being on my own. Running helps me sort things out. I get lost in myself while I run through the woods and fields around the college. I do some of my best and most creative thinking when I run. I can't imagine my life without running."

The benefits of exercise go far beyond its disease-preventive effects. The enjoyment you get from physical activity enriches your life and makes you a more complete person.

Physical Activity on a Continuum

Physical activity can be defined as any body movement carried out by the skeletal muscles and requiring energy. Different types of physical activity can be arranged on a continuum based on the amount of energy they require. Quick, easy movements such as standing up or walking down a hallway require little energy or effort; more intense, sustained activities such as cycling 5 miles or running in a race require considerably more.

Exercise refers to a subset of physical activity—planned, structured, repetitive movement of the body designed specifically to improve or maintain physical fitness. As discussed in Chapter 1, physical fitness is a set of physical attributes that allows the body to respond or adapt to the demands and stress of physical effort—to perform moderate-to-vigorous levels of physical activity without becoming overly tired. Levels of fitness depend on such physiological factors as the heart's ability to pump blood and the size of muscle fibers. To develop fitness, a person must perform enough physical activity to stress the body and cause long-term physiological changes. Only exercise will significantly improve fitness. Knowing this is important for setting goals and developing a program.

Lifestyle Physical Activity for Health Promotion

The latest version of the Dietary Guidelines for Americans, issued jointly in 2005 by the U.S. Department of Health and Human Services and the U.S. Department of Agriculture, includes specific recommendations for physical activity to improve health. The Guidelines recommend that all adults engage in at least 30 minutes of moderate-intensity physical activity, beyond usual activity, at work or home on most days of the week. This level of activity can promote health and psychological well-being: It lowers the risk of high blood pressure, stroke, heart disease, type 2 diabetes, colon cancer, and osteoporosis, and it reduces feelings of mild-to-moderate depression and anxiety. This recommendation is consistent with earlier recommendations from the Surgeon General, CDC, and American College of Sports Medicine.

What exactly is moderate physical activity? Activities such as brisk walking, dancing, swimming, cycling, and yard work can all count toward the daily total. The Surgeon General's report defines a moderate amount of activity as roughly the amount of activity required to use 150 calories of energy a day. The same amount of activity

Terms

physical activity Any body movement carried out by the skeletal muscles and requiring energy.

exercise Planned, structured, repetitive movement of the body designed to improve or maintain physical fitness.

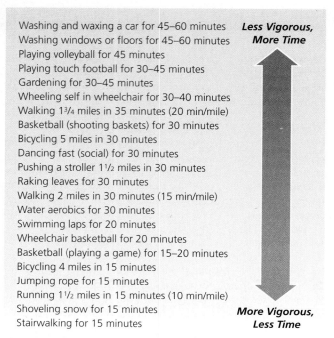

Washing and waxing a car for 45–60 minutes
Washing windows or floors for 45–60 minutes
Playing volleyball for 45 minutes
Playing touch football for 30–45 minutes
Gardening for 30–45 minutes
Wheeling self in wheelchair for 30–40 minutes
Walking 1¾ miles in 35 minutes (20 min/mile)
Basketball (shooting baskets) for 30 minutes
Bicycling 5 miles in 30 minutes
Dancing fast (social) for 30 minutes
Pushing a stroller 1½ miles in 30 minutes
Raking leaves for 30 minutes
Walking 2 miles in 30 minutes (15 min/mile)
Water aerobics for 30 minutes
Swimming laps for 20 minutes
Wheelchair basketball for 20 minutes
Basketball (playing a game) for 15–20 minutes
Bicycling 4 miles in 15 minutes
Jumping rope for 15 minutes
Running 1½ miles in 15 minutes (10 min/mile)
Shoveling snow for 15 minutes
Stairwalking for 15 minutes

Less Vigorous, More Time

More Vigorous, Less Time

Figure 2.2 Examples of moderate amounts of physical activity.
A moderate amount is roughly equivalent to physical activity that uses approximately 150 calories of energy a day, or 1000 calories a week. Some activities can be performed at various intensities; the suggested durations correspond to expected intensity of effort.
SOURCE: Department of Health and Human Services. 1996. *Physical Activity and Health: A Report of the Surgeon General.* Atlanta, Ga.: DHHS.

can be obtained in longer sessions of lower-intensity activity as in shorter sessions of more strenuous activity. For example, 30 minutes of brisk walking is the equivalent of 15 minutes of running or shoveling snow. See Figure 2.2 for examples of activities equivalent to about 30 minutes of moderate physical activity.

In the lifestyle approach to physical activity, people can choose activities that they find enjoyable and that fit into their daily routine; everyday tasks at school, work, and home can be structured to contribute to the daily activity total (see the box "Making Time for Physical Activity"). The daily total of lifestyle activity can be accumulated in multiple short bouts—for example, two 10-minute bicycle rides to and from class and a brisk 15-minute walk to the post office. In addition to moderate-intensity physical activity, the Surgeon General's report recommends that people perform resistance training (exercising against an opposing force such as a weight) at least twice a week to build and maintain muscular strength.

By increasing lifestyle physical activity to 30 minutes per day, people can expect to significantly improve their health and well-being. If all the Americans who are now completely sedentary were to adopt a more active lifestyle, there would be enormous benefit to the public's health and to individual well-being. Such a program may not, however, significantly increase physical fitness. A

program of 30 minutes of lifestyle activity per day may also not be enough activity for some people to achieve and maintain a healthy body weight.

Lifestyle Physical Activity for Health Promotion and Weight Management Since the publication of the physical activity guidelines from the CDC/ACSM and Surgeon General, other organizations have released physical activity recommendations that focus on specific health concerns (Table 2.1, p. 32). Because more than 60% of U.S. adults are overweight, guidelines that focus on weight management are of particular interest. The guidelines from the Institute of Medicine, the 2005 Dietary Guidelines for Americans, and the World Health Organization/FAO Expert Report—all of which focus on weight control in addition to general health promotion—set higher daily goals for physical activity than the Surgeon General's report.

These guidelines do not conflict with those from the Surgeon General, but they do have a different emphasis. They recognize that for people who need to lose weight and maintain weight loss, 30 minutes per day of physical activity may not be enough—and so they recommend 45–90 or more minutes per day of physical activity. For example, the Dietary Guidelines recommend 60 minutes of daily physical activity to manage body weight and prevent unhealthy weight gain and 60 to 90 minutes of daily activity to sustain weight loss. The different recommendations may seem confusing and contradictory, but all major health organizations have the same message: People can improve their health by becoming more active.

Exercise Programs to Develop Physical Fitness The Surgeon General's report and Dietary Guidelines for Americans also summarize the benefits of more formal exercise programs. They conclude that people can obtain even greater health benefits by increasing the duration and intensity of activity. Thus, a person who engages in a structured, formal exercise program designed to measurably improve physical fitness will obtain even greater improvements in quality of life and greater reductions in disease and mortality risk. The American College of Sports Medicine has issued separate guidelines for creating a formal exercise program that will develop physical fitness. These guidelines are described in detail later in this chapter.

How Much Physical Activity Is Enough?

Some experts feel that people get most of the health benefits of an exercise program simply by becoming more active over the course of the day; the amount of activity needed depends on an individual's health status and goals. Other experts feel that the activity goal set by the lifestyle approach is too low; they argue that people should exercise long enough and intensely enough to

"Too little time" is a common excuse for not being physically active. Learning to manage your time successfully is crucial if you are to maintain a wellness lifestyle. You can begin by keeping a record of how you are currently spending your time; in your health journal, use a grid broken into blocks of 15, 20, or 30 minutes to track your daily activities. Then analyze your record: List each type of activity and the total time you engaged in it on a given day—for example, sleeping, 7 hours; eating, 1.5 hours; studying, 3 hours; and so on. Take a close look at your list of activities and prioritize them according to how important they are to you, from essential to somewhat important to not important at all.

Based on the priorities you set, make changes in your daily schedule by subtracting time from some activities in order to make time for physical activity. Look particularly carefully at your leisure time activities and your methods of transportation; these are areas where it is easy to build in physical activity. Make changes using a system of trade-offs. For example, you may choose to reduce the total amount of time you spend playing computer games, listening to the radio, and chatting on the telephone in order to make time for an after-dinner bike ride or walk with a friend. You may decide to watch 10 fewer minutes of television in the morning in order to change your 5-minute drive to class into a 15-minute walk. In making these kinds of changes in your schedule, don't feel that you have to miss out on anything you enjoy. You can get more from less time by focusing on what you are doing and by combining activities.

The following are just a few ways to incorporate more physical activity into your daily routine:

- Take the stairs instead of the elevator or escalator.
- Walk to the mailbox, post office, store, bank, or library whenever possible.

- Park your car a mile or even just a few blocks from your destination, and walk briskly.
- Do at least one chore every day that requires physical activity: wash the windows or your car, clean your room or house, mow the lawn, rake the leaves.
- Take study or work breaks to avoid sitting for more than 30 minutes at a time. Get up and walk around the library, your office, or your home or dorm; go up and down a flight of stairs.
- Stretch when you stand in line or watch TV.
- When you take public transportation, get off one stop down the line and walk to your destination.
- Go dancing instead of to a movie.
- Walk to visit a neighbor or friend rather than calling him or her on the phone. Go for a walk while you chat.
- Put your remote controls in storage; when you want to change TV or radio stations, get up and do it by hand.
- Take the dog for a walk (or an extra walk) every day.
- Play actively with children or go for a walk pushing a stroller.
- If weather or neighborhood safety rule out walking outside, look for alternate locations—an indoor track, enclosed shopping mall, or even a long hallway. Look for locations near or on the way to your campus, workplace, or residence.
- Remember, being busy isn't the same as being active. Seize every opportunity to get up and walk around. Move more and sit less.

Visit the U.S. Department of Health and Human Performance's Small Step Web site (www.smallstep.gov) for more ideas.

---

improve their body's capacity for exercise—that is, to improve physical fitness. More research is needed to clarify the health effects of different amounts of lifestyle physical activity, of moderate-intensity versus high-intensity exercise, and of continuous versus intermittent exercise. However, there is probably truth in both of these positions.

Regular physical activity, regardless of intensity, makes you healthier and can help protect you from many chronic diseases. However, exercising at low intensities does little to improve physical fitness. Although you get many of the health benefits of exercise by simply being more active, you obtain even more benefits when you are physically fit. In addition to long-term health benefits, fitness also significantly contributes to quality of life. Fitness can give you freedom—freedom to move your body the way you want. Fit people have more energy and better body control. They can enjoy a more active lifestyle—cycling, hiking, skiing, and so on—than their more sedentary counterparts. Even if you don't like sports, you need physical energy and stamina in your daily life and for many nonsport

leisure activities—visiting museums, playing with children, gardening, and so on.

Where does this leave you? Most experts agree that some physical activity is better than none, but that more—as long as it does not result in injury—is better than some. To set a personal goal for physical activity and exercise, consider your current activity level, your health status, and your goals. At the very least, strive to become more active and meet the goal set by the Surgeon General's report of using about 150 calories a day in physical activity—the equivalent of about 30 minutes of moderate-intensity activity. Choose to be active whenever you can. If weight management is a concern for you, begin by achieving the goal of 30 minutes of activity per day and then look to raise your activity level further, to 45–90 minutes per day or more. For even better health and well-being, participate in a structured exercise program that develops physical fitness. Any increase in physical activity will contribute to your health and well-being, now and in the future.

Next, let's take a closer look at the components of physical fitness and the basic principles of fitness training.

Table 2.1 Summary of Physical Activity Recommendations from Selected Leading Health Organizations

Organization	Recommendation	Purpose
Centers for Disease Control and Prevention/ American College of Sports Medicine	A minimum of 30 minutes per day of moderate activity on most days of the week (*The American College of Sports Medicine has separate guidelines for exercise programs to develop fitness; see pp. 39–40 and Table 2.2.*)	Health promotion and prevention of chronic disease
U.S. Surgeon General: Report on Physical Activity and Health	A minimum of 150 calories per day expended in moderate physical activity (the equivalent of about 30 minutes of brisk walking); resistance training twice a week	Health promotion and prevention of chronic disease
U.S. Department of Health and Human Services and U.S. Department of Agriculture: 2005 Dietary Guidelines for Americans	30 minutes of moderate-intensity exercise on most days of the week	Reduce the risk of chronic disease
	60 minutes of moderate-to-vigorous-intensity exercise on most days of the week	Manage body weight and prevent unhealthy weight gain
	60–90 minutes of moderate-intensity exercise per day	Sustain weight loss
Institute of Medicine, National Academies	At least 60 minutes of moderate physical activity per day	Health promotion, prevention of chronic disease, and weight control
International Association for the Study of Obesity	45–60 minutes of moderate physical activity per day	Prevention of weight gain
	60–90 minutes of moderate physical activity per day	Maintenance of weight loss
World Health Organization	At least 60 minutes of moderate physical activity per day	Health promotion, prevention of chronic disease, and weight control
American Academy of Orthopaedic Surgeons*	30 minutes of moderate physical activity per day, appropriate for specific condition and designed by a physician; seek advice if pain is severe	Health promotion and symptom relief in people with muscle, bone, or joint pain (back pain, osteoporosis, arthritis, and so on)
American College of Obstetrics and Gynecology*	30 minutes or more of moderate exercise on most, if not all days of the week; previously inactive women or those with complications should consult a physician before beginning activity	Promotion of a healthy pregnancy and postpartum recovery; prevention of gestational diabetes and excessive weight gain during pregnancy
American Diabetes Association*	Surgeon General's recommendations are appropriate for most people, but all levels of activity are possible if blood sugar is well-controlled; avoid exercise when blood sugar is above 250 mg/dl and ingest carbohydrates prior to exercise when blood sugar is below 100 mg/dl	Health promotion; prevention of cardiovascular disease; assistance with control of diabetes
American Heart Association*	At least 30 minutes (or 150 calories) of moderate exercise per day	Health promotion; prevention of cardiovascular disease

*See Chapter 7 for additional activity and exercise guidelines for people with special health concerns.

SOURCE: See "Selected Bibliography" for complete citations for all recommendations.

MOTIVATION FOR CHANGE! Would you be more motivated to try to increase daily physical activity if you had an easy way to monitor your level of activity? If so, consider wearing a pedometer to track the number of steps you take each day—a rough but easily obtainable reflection of daily physical activity. Wear the pedometer for a week to obtain a baseline average daily number of steps, and then set an appropriate goal—for example, walking 2000 additional steps each day or increasing daily steps to 10,000. Record your daily steps in a prominent location to monitor your progress and boost your motivation. Lab 2.4 includes additional advice on using a pedometer to monitor physical activity.

HEALTH-RELATED COMPONENTS OF PHYSICAL FITNESS

Physical fitness has many components, some related to general health and others related more specifically to particular sports or activities. The five components of fitness most important for health are cardiorespiratory endurance, muscular strength, muscular endurance, flexibility, and body composition. **Health-related fitness** contributes to your capacity to enjoy life, helps your body withstand physical and psychological challenges, and protects you from chronic disease.

Cardiorespiratory Endurance

Cardiorespiratory endurance is the ability to perform prolonged, large-muscle, dynamic exercise at moderate-to-high levels of intensity. It depends on such factors as the ability of the lungs to deliver oxygen from the environment to the bloodstream, the heart's capacity to pump blood, the ability of the nervous system and blood vessels to regulate blood flow, and the capability of the body's chemical systems to use oxygen and process fuels for exercise.

When levels of cardiorespiratory fitness are low, the heart has to work very hard during normal daily activities and may not be able to work hard enough to sustain high-intensity physical activity in an emergency. As cardiorespiratory fitness improves, the heart begins to function more efficiently. It doesn't have to work as hard at rest or during low levels of exercise. The heart pumps more blood per heartbeat, resting heart rate slows, blood volume increases, blood supply to the tissues improves, the body is better able to cool itself, and resting blood pressure decreases. A healthy heart can better withstand the strains of everyday life, the stress of occasional emergencies, and the wear and tear of time. Endurance training also improves the functioning of the chemical systems, particularly in the muscles and liver, thereby enhancing the body's ability to use energy supplied by food and to do more exercise with less effort from the oxygen transport system.

Cardiorespiratory endurance is a central component of health-related fitness because the functioning of the heart and lungs is so essential to overall good health. A person can't live very long or very well without a healthy heart. Low levels of cardiorespiratory fitness are linked with heart disease, the leading cause of death in the United States. In addition to protecting against heart disease, cardiorespiratory fitness also reduces the risk of type 2 diabetes, colon cancer, stroke, depression, and anxiety. A moderate level of cardiorespiratory fitness can even help compensate for certain health risks, including excess body fat: People who are lean but who have low cardiorespiratory fitness have been found to have higher death rates than people with higher levels of body fat who are otherwise fit. Cardiorespiratory endurance exercise further benefits quality of life by improving self-image, mood, cognitive functioning, and the ability to manage stress. Exercising to improve cardiorespiratory endurance also provides opportunities to have fun and to socialize.

Muscular Strength

Muscular strength is the amount of force a muscle can produce with a single maximum effort. It depends on such factors as the size of muscle cells and the ability of nerves to activate muscle cells. Strong muscles are important for the smooth and easy performance of everyday activities, such as carrying groceries, lifting boxes, and climbing stairs, as well as for emergency situations. They help keep the skeleton in proper alignment, preventing

Cardiorespiratory endurance is a key component of health-related fitness. These participants in a group endurance class are conditioning their hearts and lungs as well as gaining many other health benefits.

back and leg pain and providing the support necessary for good posture. Muscular strength has obvious importance in recreational activities. Strong people can hit a tennis ball harder, kick a soccer ball farther, and ride a bicycle uphill more easily. Muscle tissue is an important element of overall body composition. Greater muscle mass means a higher rate of **metabolism** and faster energy use. Training to build muscular strength can also help people manage stress and boost their self-confidence.

Maintaining strength and muscle mass is vital for healthy aging. Older people tend to lose both number and size of muscle cells—a condition called sarcopenia.

Terms

health-related fitness Physical capacities that contribute to health: cardiorespiratory endurance, muscular strength, muscular endurance, flexibility, and body composition.

cardiorespiratory endurance The ability of the body to perform prolonged, large-muscle, dynamic exercise at moderate-to-high levels of intensity.

muscular strength The amount of force a muscle can produce with a single maximum effort.

metabolism The sum of all the vital processes by which food energy and nutrients are made available to and used by the body.

Many of the muscle cells that remain become slower, and some become nonfunctional because they lose their attachment to the nervous system. Strength training helps maintain muscle mass and function and possibly helps decrease the risk of osteoporosis (bone loss) in older people, which greatly enhances their quality of life and prevents life-threatening injuries.

Muscular Endurance

Muscular endurance is the ability to resist fatigue and sustain a given level of muscle tension—that is, to hold a muscle contraction for a long period of time or to contract a muscle over and over again. It depends on such factors as the size of muscle cells, the ability of muscles to store fuel, and the blood supply to muscles. Muscular endurance is important for good posture and for injury prevention. For example, if abdominal and back muscles can't hold the spine correctly, the chances of low-back pain and back injury are increased. Good muscular endurance in the trunk muscles is more important than muscular strength for preventing back pain. Muscular endurance helps people cope with the physical demands of everyday life and enhances performance in sports and work. It is also important for most leisure and fitness activities.

Flexibility

Flexibility is the ability to move the joints through their full range of motion. It depends on joint structure, the length and elasticity of connective tissue, and nervous system activity. Flexible, pain-free joints are important for good health and well-being. Inactivity causes the joints to become stiffer with age. Stiffness often causes older people to assume unnatural body postures that can stress joints and muscles. Stretching exercises can help ensure a healthy range of motion for all major joints.

Terms

VIW

muscular endurance The ability of a muscle or group of muscles to remain contracted or to contract repeatedly for a long period of time.

flexibility The range of motion in a joint or group of joints, flexibility is related to muscle length.

body composition The proportion of fat and fat-free mass (muscle, bone, and water) in the body.

fat-free mass The nonfat component of the human body, consisting of skeletal muscle, bone, and water.

skill-related fitness Physical capacities that contribute to performance in a sport or activity: speed, power, agility, balance, coordination, and reaction time.

physical training The performance of different types of activities that cause the body to adapt and improve its level of fitness.

specificity The training principle that the body adapts to the particular type and amount of stress placed on it.

Body Composition

Body composition refers to the proportion of fat and **fat-free mass** (muscle, bone, and water) in the body. Healthy body composition involves a high proportion of fat-free mass and an acceptably low level of body fat, adjusted for age and gender. A person with excessive body fat—especially when excess fat is located in the abdomen—is more likely to experience a variety of health problems, including heart disease, insulin resistance, high blood pressure, stroke, joint problems, type 2 diabetes, gallbladder disease, blood vessel inflammation, some types of cancer, and back pain.

The best way to lose fat is through a lifestyle that includes a sensible diet and exercise. The best way to add muscle mass is through resistance training, also known as strength training or, when weights are used, weight training. Large changes in body composition aren't necessary to improve health; even a small increase in physical activity and a small decrease in body fat can lead to substantial health improvements. As described earlier, cardiorespiratory fitness may be more important than body composition in determining overall health status.

Skill-Related Components of Fitness

In addition to the five health-related components of physical fitness, the ability to perform a particular sport or activity may depend on **skill-related fitness** components such as the following:

- *Speed:* The ability to perform a movement in a short period of time.
- *Power:* The ability to exert force rapidly, based on a combination of strength and speed.
- *Agility:* The ability to change the position of the body quickly and accurately.
- *Balance:* The ability to maintain equilibrium while moving or while stationary.
- *Coordination:* The ability to perform motor tasks accurately and smoothly using body movements and the senses.
- *Reaction and movement time:* The ability to respond and react quickly to a stimulus.

Skill-related fitness tends to be sport-specific and is best developed through practice. For example, the speed, coordination, and agility needed to play basketball can be developed by playing basketball. Some fitness experts downplay sports participation because some sports don't contribute to all the health-related components of physical fitness. However, engaging in sports is fun and can help you build fitness and contribute to other areas of wellness. You can get immense satisfaction from hitting a well-executed cross-court backhand in tennis, climbing a challenging rock wall, hitting the green from 150 yards

Physical fitness and athletic achievement are not limited to the able-bodied. People with disabilities can also attain high levels of fitness and performance, as shown by the elite athletes who compete in the Paralympics. The premier event for athletes with disabilities, the Paralympics are held in the same year and city as the Olympics. The performance of these skilled athletes makes it clear that people with disabilities can be active, healthy, and extraordinarily fit; just like able-bodied athletes, athletes with disabilities strive for excellence and can serve as role models.

Currently, some 54 million Americans are estimated to have chronic, significant disabilities. Some disabilities are the result of injury, such as spinal cord injuries sustained in car crashes. Other disabilities result from illness, such as the blindness that sometimes occurs as a complication of diabetes or the joint stiffness that accompanies arthritis. And some disabilities are present at birth, as in the case of congenital limb deformities or cerebral palsy.

Exercise and physical activity are as important for people with disabilities as for able-bodied individuals—if not *more* important. Being active helps prevent sec-

ondary conditions that may result from prolonged inactivity, such as circulatory or muscular problems. It provides an emotional boost that helps support a positive attitude as well as opportunities to make new friends, increase self-confidence, and gain a sense of accomplishment. Currently, about 22% of people with disabilities engage in regular moderate activity.

People with disabilities don't have to be elite athletes to participate in sports and lead an active life. Some health clubs and fitness centers offer activities and events geared for people of all ages and types of disabilities. They may have modified aerobics classes, special weight training machines, classes involving mild exercise in warm water, and other activities adapted for people with disabilities. Popular sports and recreational activities include adapted horseback riding, golf, swimming, and skiing. Competitive sports are also available—for example, there are wheelchair versions of billiards, tennis, hockey, and basketball, as well as sports for people with hearing, visual, or mental impairments. For those who prefer to get their exercise at home, special videos are available geared to individuals who

use wheelchairs or who have arthritis, hearing impairments, or many other disabilities.

If you have a disability and want to be more active, check with your physician about what's appropriate for you. Call your local community center, YMCA/YWCA, independent living center, or fitness center to locate potential facilities; look for a facility with experienced personnel and appropriate adaptive equipment. For specialized videos, check with hospitals and health associations that are geared to specific disabilities, such as the Arthritis Foundation. Remember that no matter what your level of ability or disability, it's possible to make physical activity an integral part of your life.

SOURCES: National Center for Health Statistics. 2004. *DATA2010: The Healthy People 2010 Database: November 2004 Edition* (http://wonder.cdc .gov/data2010; retrieved October 27, 2005). National Center on Physical Activity and Disability. 2000. *White Paper: Spinal Cord Injury and Fitness.* Chicago: National Center on Physical Activity and Disability. U.S. Department of Health and Human Services. 1996. *Physical Activity and Health: A Report of the Surgeon General.* Atlanta, Ga.: DHHS.

out in golf, or spiking a ball past an opponent in volleyball. Sports can be an important and fun part of an active wellness lifestyle.

PRINCIPLES OF PHYSICAL TRAINING: ADAPTATION TO STRESS

The human body is very adaptable. The greater the demands made on it, the more it adjusts to meet those demands. Over time, immediate, short-term adjustments translate into long-term changes and improvements. When breathing and heart rate increase during exercise, for example, the heart gradually develops the ability to pump more blood with each beat. Then, during exercise, it doesn't have to beat as fast to meet the cells' demands for oxygen. The goal of **physical training** is to produce these long-term changes and improvements in the body's functioning. Although people differ in the maximum levels of physical fitness and performance they can achieve through training, the wellness benefits of exercise are available to everyone (see the box "Fitness and Disability").

Particular types and amounts of exercise are most effective in developing the various components of fitness. To put together an effective exercise program, a person should first understand the basic principles of physical training. Important principles are specificity, progressive overload, reversibility, and individual differences. All of these rest on the larger principle of adaptation.

Specificity—Adapting to Type of Training

To develop a particular fitness component, exercises must be performed that are specifically designed for that component. This is the principle of **specificity.** Weight training, for example, develops muscular strength but is less effective for developing cardiorespiratory endurance or flexibility. Specificity also applies to the skill-related fitness components—to improve at tennis, you must practice tennis—and to the different parts of the body—to develop stronger arms, you must exercise your arms. A well-rounded exercise program includes exercises geared to each component of fitness, to different parts of the body, and to specific activities or sports.

Progressive Overload—Adapting to Amount of Training and the FITT Principle

The body adapts to the demands of exercise by improving its functioning. When the amount of exercise (also called overload or stress) is progressively increased, fitness continues to improve. This is the principle of **progressive overload.**

The amount of overload is very important. Too little exercise will have no effect on fitness (although it may improve health); too much may cause injury and problems with the body's immune system and hormone levels. The point at which exercise becomes excessive is highly individual—it occurs at a much higher level in an Olympic athlete than in a sedentary person. For every type of exercise, there is a training threshold at which fitness benefits begin to occur, a zone within which maximum fitness benefits occur, and an upper limit of safe training. The amount of exercise needed depends on the individual's current level of fitness, his or her fitness goals, and the component being developed. A novice, for example, might experience fitness benefits from jogging a mile in 10 minutes, but this level of exercise would cause no physical adaptations in a trained distance runner. Beginners should start at the lower end of the fitness benefit zone; fitter individuals will make more rapid gains by exercising at the higher end of the fitness benefit zone. Progression is critical—fitness increases only if the volume and intensity of workouts increase. Exercising at the same intensity every training session will maintain fitness but will not increase it, because the training stress is below the threshold to produce adaptation.

The amount of overload needed to maintain or improve a particular level of fitness for a particular fitness component is determined through four dimensions, represented by the acronym FITT:

- *Frequency*—how often
- *Intensity*—how hard
- *Time*—how long (duration)
- *Type*—mode of activity

Some experts use the acronym FITTE, where the *E* stands for enjoyment—a key component of a successful, long-term fitness program.

Frequency Developing fitness requires regular exercise. Optimum exercise frequency, expressed in number of days per week, varies with the component being developed and the individual's fitness goals. For most people, a frequency of 3–5 days per week for cardiorespiratory endurance exercise and 2 or more days per week for resistance and flexibility training is appropriate for a general fitness program.

An important consideration in determining appropriate exercise frequency is recovery time, which is also

When stressed by the demands of lifting more than the usual amount of weight, the body responds by building muscular strength and endurance. To safely and effectively develop strength, this exerciser must overload her muscles with enough weight to improve her body's functioning but not so much weight that she becomes injured.

highly individual and depends on factors such as training experience, age, and intensity of training. For example, 24 hours of rest between highly intensive workouts that involve heavy weights or fast track sprints is not enough recovery time for safe and effective training; intense workouts need to be spaced out during the week to allow sufficient recovery time. On the other hand, you can exercise every day if your program consists of moderate-intensity walking or cycling. Learn to "listen to your body" to obtain a sufficient amount of rest between workouts. Chapters 3–5 provide more detailed information about training techniques and recovery periods for workouts focused on different fitness components.

Intensity Fitness benefits occur when a person exercises harder than his or her normal level of activity. The appropriate exercise intensity varies with each fitness component. To develop cardiorespiratory endurance, for example, a person must raise his or her heart rate above normal; to develop muscular strength, a person must lift a heavier weight than normal; to develop flexibility, a person must stretch muscles beyond their normal length.

Time (Duration) Fitness benefits occur when you exercise for an extended period of time. For cardiorespiratory endurance exercise, 20–60 minutes is recommended; exercise can take place in a single session or in several sessions of 10 or more minutes. The greater the intensity of exercise, the less time needed to obtain fitness benefits. For high-intensity exercise, such as running, 20–30 minutes is appropriate. For moderate-intensity exercise, such as walking, 45–60 minutes may be needed. High-intensity exercise poses a greater risk of injury than low-intensity exercise, so if you are a nonathletic adult, it's probably best to emphasize low-to-moderate-intensity activity of longer duration.

To build muscular strength, muscular endurance, and flexibility, similar amounts of time are advisable, but these exercises are more commonly organized in terms of a specific number of repetitions of particular exercises. For resistance training, for example, a recommended program includes 1 or more sets of 8–12 repetitions of 8–10 different exercises that work the major muscle groups.

Type (Mode of Activity) The type of exercise in which you should engage varies with each fitness component and with your personal fitness goals. To develop cardiorespiratory endurance, you need to engage in continuous activities involving large-muscle groups—walking, jogging, cycling, or swimming, for example. Resistive exercises develop muscular strength and endurance, while stretching exercises build flexibility. The frequency, intensity, and time, or duration, of the exercise will be different for each type of activity. See pp. 39–40 for more on choosing appropriate activities for your fitness program.

Reversibility—Adapting to a Reduction in Training

Fitness is a reversible adaptation. The body adjusts to lower levels of physical activity the same way it adjusts to higher levels. This is the principle of **reversibility.** When a person stops exercising, up to 50% of fitness improvements are lost within 2 months. However, not all fitness levels reverse at the same rate. Strength fitness is very resilient, so a person can maintain strength fitness by doing resistive exercise as infrequently as once a week. On the other hand, cardiovascular and cellular fitness reverse themselves more quickly—sometimes within just a few days or weeks. Thus, if a training schedule must be curtailed temporarily, fitness improvements are best maintained if exercise intensity is kept constant and frequency and/or duration is reduced.

Individual Differences—Limits on Adaptability

Anyone watching the Olympics, a professional football game, or a tennis championship match can readily see that, from a physical standpoint, we are not all created equal. There are large individual differences in our ability to improve fitness, achieve a desirable body composition, perform and learn sports skills. Some people are able to run longer distances, or lift more weight, or kick a soccer ball more skillfully than others will ever be able to, no matter how much they train. Each person responds to training at different rates; a program that works for one person may not be right for another person. There are limits on the adaptability—the potential for improvement—of any human body. The body's ability to transport and use oxygen, for example, can be improved by only about 15–30% through training. An endurance athlete must therefore inherit a large metabolic capacity in order to reach competitive performance levels. In the past few years, scientists have identified specific genes that influence body fat, strength, and endurance.

However, a person doesn't have to be an Olympic sprinter to experience health benefits from running. Physical training improves fitness regardless of heredity. For the average person, the body's adaptability is enough to achieve reasonable fitness goals.

DESIGNING YOUR OWN EXERCISE PROGRAM

Physical training works best when you have a plan. A plan helps you make gradual but steady progress toward your goals. Once you've determined that exercise is safe for you, planning for physical fitness consists of assessing how fit you are now, determining where you want to be, and choosing the right activities to help you get there. These activities are discussed next, along with some general guidelines for training.

Medical Clearance

People of any age who are not at high risk for serious health problems can safely exercise at a moderate intensity (60% or less of maximum heart rate) without a prior medical evaluation (see Chapter 3 for a discussion of maximum heart rate). Likewise, if you are male and under 40 or female and under 50 and in good health, exercise is probably safe for you. If you do not fit into these age groups or have health problems—especially high blood pressure, heart disease, muscle or joint problems, or obesity—see your physician before starting a vigorous

Terms

progressive overload The training principle that placing increasing amounts of stress on the body causes adaptations that improve fitness.

reversibility The training principle that fitness improvements are lost when demands on the body are lowered.

Is Exercise Safe?

Participating in exercise and sports is usually a wonderful experience that improves wellness in both the short and long term. In rare instances, however, vigorous exertion is associated with sudden death. It may seem difficult to understand that although regular exercise protects people from heart disease, it also increases the risk of sudden death.

What causes sudden death during or immediately following exercise? Congenital heart defects (heart abnormalities present at birth) are the most common cause of exercise-related sudden death in people under 35. In nearly all other cases, coronary artery disease is responsible. In this condition, fat and other substances build up in the arteries that supply blood to the heart. Death can result if an artery becomes blocked or if the heart's rhythm and pumping action are disrupted. Exercise, particularly intense exercise, may trigger a heart attack in someone with underlying heart disease. (In the very rare cases of death among young athletes, the cause may be a congenital or genetic cardiovascular disorder rather than coronary artery disease.)

What is the risk of dying suddenly during exercise? A study of jogging deaths in Rhode Island found that there was one death per 396,000 hours of jogging, or about one death per 7620 joggers per year—an extremely low risk for each individual jogger. Another study of men involved in a variety of physical activities found one death per 1.51 million hours of exercise. This 12-year study of more than 21,000 men found that those who didn't exercise vigorously were 74 times more likely to die suddenly from cardiac arrest during or shortly after exercise. It is also important to note that people are much safer exercising than engaging in many other common activities, including driving a car.

Although quite small, the risk does exist and may lead some people to wonder why exercise is considered such an important part of a wellness lifestyle. Exercise causes many positive changes in the body—in healthy people as well as those with heart disease—that more than make up for the slightly increased short-term risk of sudden death. Training slows or reverses the fatty buildup in arteries and helps protect people from deadly heart rhythm abnormalities. People who exercise regularly have an overall risk of sudden death only about two-thirds that of nonexercisers. Active people who stop exercising can expect their heart attack risk to increase by 300%.

Who is most at risk for sudden death during exercise? Obviously, someone with underlying coronary artery disease is at greater risk than someone who is free from the condition. However, many cases of heart disease may go undiagnosed. The riskiest scenario may be when a middle-aged or older individual suddenly begins participating in a vigorous sport or activity after a long period of a sedentary lifestyle. This finding provides strong evidence for the recommendation that people increase their level of physical activity gradually and engage in regular, rather than sporadic, activity.

For the vast majority of people, exercise is a safe and effective way to increase both life expectancy and quality of life. If you decide you don't want to exercise, you might want to see your physician to determine if you can resist the deadly effects of a sedentary lifestyle.

SOURCES: Thompson, P. D. 2001. Cardiovascular risks of exercise. *Physician and Sportsmedicine* 29(4). Albert, C. M., et al. 2000. Trigger of sudden death from cardiac causes by vigorous exertion. *New England Journal of Medicine* 343(19): 1355–1361.

---

exercise program. The Canadian Society for Exercise Physiology has developed the Physical Activity Readiness Questionnaire (PAR-Q) to help evaluate exercise safety; it is included in Lab 2.1. Completing it should alert you to any potential problems you may have. If a physician isn't sure whether exercise is safe for you, she or he may recommend an **exercise stress test** or a **graded exercise test (GXT)** to see whether you show symptoms of heart disease during exercise. For most people, however, it's far safer to exercise than to remain sedentary. For more information, see the box "Is Exercise Safe?".

Assessment

The first step in creating a successful fitness program is to assess your current level of physical activity and fitness for each of the five health-related fitness components. The results of the assessment tests will help you set specific fitness goals and plan your fitness program. Lab 2.2 gives you the opportunity to assess your current overall level of activity and determine if it is appropriate. Assessment tests in Chapters 3, 4, 5, and 6 will help you evaluate your cardiorespiratory endurance, muscular strength, muscular endurance, flexibility, and body composition.

Setting Goals

The ultimate general goal of every health-related fitness program is the same—wellness that lasts a lifetime. Whatever your specific goals, they must be important enough to you to keep you motivated. Most sports psychologists believe that setting and achieving goals is the most effective way to stay motivated about exercise. Exercising for yourself, rather than for the impression you think you'll make on others, is more likely to lead to long-lasting commitment. After you complete the assessment tests in Chapters 3–6, you will be able to set goals directly related to each fitness component, such as working toward a 3-mile jog or doing 20 push-ups. First, though, think carefully about your overall goals, and be clear about why you are starting a program.

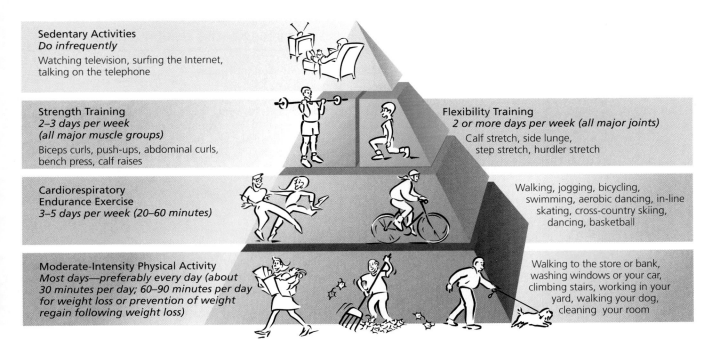

Figure 2.3   Physical activity pyramid.   This physical activity pyramid shows the component of a balanced fitness program and emphasizes the importance of daily moderate-intensity physical activity. If you are currently sedentary, gradually increase the amount of moderate-intensity physical activity in your life. If you are already moderately active, begin a formal exercise program that includes cardiorespiratory endurance exercise, flexibility training, and strength training to help you develop all the health-related components of fitness.

Choosing Activities for a Balanced Program

An ideal fitness program combines a physically active lifestyle with a systematic exercise program to develop and maintain physical fitness. This overall program is shown in the physical activity pyramid in Figure 2.3. If you are currently sedentary, your goal is to focus on activities at the bottom of the pyramid and gradually increase the amount of moderate-intensity physical activity in your daily life. Appropriate activities include brisk walking, climbing stairs, yard work, and washing your car. You don't have to exercise vigorously, but you should experience a moderate increase in your heart and breathing rates. As described earlier, your activity time can be broken up into small blocks over the course of a day.

The next two levels of the pyramid illustrate parts of a formal exercise program. The principles of this program are consistent with those of the American College of Sports Medicine (ACSM), the professional organization for people involved in sports medicine and exercise science. The ACSM has established guidelines for creating an exercise program that will develop physical fitness (Table 2.2, p. 40). A balanced program includes activities to develop all the health-related components of fitness.

- *Cardiorespiratory endurance* is developed by continuous rhythmic movements of large-muscle groups in activities such as walking, jogging, cycling, swimming, and aerobic dance and other forms of group exercise.

Choose activities that you enjoy and that are convenient. Other popular choices are in-line skating, dancing, and backpacking. Start-and-stop activities such as tennis, racquetball, and soccer can also develop endurance if one's skill level is sufficient to enable periods of continuous play. Training for cardiorespiratory endurance is discussed in Chapter 3.

- *Muscular strength and endurance* can be developed through resistance training—training with weights or performing calisthenic exercises such as push-ups and curl-ups. Training for muscular strength and endurance is discussed in Chapter 4.

- *Flexibility* is developed by stretching the major muscle groups, regularly and with proper technique. Flexibility is discussed in Chapter 5.

- *Healthy body composition* can be developed through a sensible diet and a program of regular exercise. Endurance exercise is best for reducing body fat; resistance

Terms

exercise stress test A test usually administered on a treadmill or cycle ergometer that involves analysis of the changes in electrical activity in the heart from an electrocardiogram (EKG or ECG) taken during exercise. Used to determine if any heart disease is present and to assess current fitness level.

graded exercise test (GXT) An exercise test that starts at an easy intensity and progresses to maximum capacity.

Table 2.2   Exercise Recommendations for Fitness Development in Healthy Adults

Exercise to Develop and Maintain Cardiorespiratory Endurance and Body Composition

Frequency of training	3–5 days per week.
Intensity of training	55/65–90% of maximum heart rate or 40/50–85% of heart rate reserve or maximum oxygen uptake reserve.* The lower intensity values (55–64% of maximum heart rate and 40–49% of heart rate reserve) are most applicable to individuals who are quite unfit. For average individuals, intensities of 70–85% of maximum heart rate or 60–80% of heart rate reserve are appropriate.
Time (duration) of training	20–60 total minutes of continuous or intermittent (in sessions lasting 10 or more minutes) aerobic activity. Duration is dependent on the intensity of activity; thus, low-intensity activity should be conducted over a longer period of time (30 minutes or more). Low-to-moderate-intensity activity of longer duration is recommended for nonathletic adults.
Type (mode) of activity	Any activity that uses large-muscle groups, can be maintained continuously, and is rhythmic and aerobic in nature—for example, walking-hiking, running-jogging, cycling-bicycling, cross-country skiing, aerobic dance and other forms of group exercise, rope skipping, rowing, stair climbing, swimming, skating, and endurance game activities.

Exercise to Develop and Maintain Muscular Strength and Endurance, Flexibility, and Body Composition

Resistance training	One set of 8–10 exercises that condition the major muscle groups should be performed 2–3 nonconsecutive days per week. Most people should complete 8–12 repetitions of each exercise to the point of fatigue; practicing other repetition ranges (for example, 3–5 or 12–15) also builds strength and endurance; for older and frailer people (approximately 50–60 and older), 10–15 repetitions with a lighter weight may be more appropriate. Multiple-set regimens will provide greater benefits if time allows. Any mode of exercise that is comfortable throughout the full range of motion is appropriate (for example, free weights, bands, or machines).
Flexibility training	Static stretches should be performed for the major muscle groups at least 2–3 days per week, ideally 5–7 days per week. Stretch to the point of tightness, holding each stretch for 15–30 seconds; perform 2–4 repetitions of each stretch.

*Instructions for calculating target heart rate intensity for cardiorespiratory endurance exercise are presented in Chapter 3.

SOURCE: Adapted from American College of Sports Medicine. 2006. *ACSM's Guidelines for Exercise Testing and Prescription*, 7th ed. Philadelphia: Lippincott Williams & Wilkins.

---

training builds muscle mass, which, to a small extent, helps increase metabolism. Body composition is discussed in Chapter 6.

There are as many different fitness programs as there are individuals. Consider the following examples:

• Maggie's life revolves around sports. She's been on softball teams and swim teams, and now she's on her college varsity soccer team. She follows a rigorous exercise regimen established by her soccer coach. Afternoon soccer practice begins with warm-ups, drills, and practice in specific skills, and it ends with a scrimmage and then a jog around the soccer field. Games are every Saturday. Maggie likes team sports, but she also enjoys exercising alone, so she goes on long bicycle rides whenever she can fit them in. She can't imagine what it would be like not to be active every day.

• Maria is a busy young mother of twins. To keep in shape, she joined a health club with a weight room, exercise classes, and child care. Three mornings a week, she takes the twins to the club and attends the 7:00

"wake-up" low-impact aerobics class. The instructor leads the class through warm-ups; a 20-minute aerobic workout; exercises for the arms, abdomen, buttocks, and legs; stretches; and a relaxation exercise. Maria is exhilarated and ready for the rest of the day before 9:00 A.M.

• Tom is an engineering student with a lot of studying to do and an active social life as well. For exercise, he plays tennis three times a week. He likes to head for the courts around 6:00 P.M., when most people are eating dinner. He warms up for 10 minutes by practicing his forehand and backhand against a backboard and then plays a hard, fast game with his regular partner for 45 minutes to an hour. Afterward, he does some stretching exercises while his muscles are still warm and then cools down with an easy 5-minute walk. Then he showers and gets ready for dinner. Twice a week he works out at the gym, with particular attention to keeping his arms strong and his shoulders limber. On Saturday nights, he goes dancing with friends.

• Ruben started a new job as a financial adviser in a large city. He spends 3 hours a day commuting on the train and has a new family, so he has no time for a

	Lifestyle physical activity	Moderate exercise program	Vigorous exercise program
Description	Moderate physical activity—an amount of activity that uses about 150 calories per day	Cardiorespiratory endurance exercise (20–60 minutes, 3–5 days per week); strength training (2–3 days per week) and stretching exercises (2 or more days per week)	Cardiorespiratory endurance exercise (20–60 minutes, 3–5 days per week); interval training; strength training (3–4 days per week); and stretching exercises (5–7 days per week)
Sample activities or program	*One of the following:* • Walking to and from work, 15 minutes each way • Cycling to and from class, 10 minutes each way • Yard work for 30 minutes • Dancing (fast) for 30 minutes • Playing basketball for 20 minutes	• Jogging for 30 minutes, 3 days per week • Weight training, 1 set of 8 exercises, 2 days per week • Stretching exercises, 3 days per week	• Running for 45 minutes, 3 days per week • Intervals: running 400 m at high effort, 4 sets, 2 days per week • Weight training, 3 sets of 10 exercises, 3 days per week • Stretching exercises, 6 days per week
Health and fitness benefits	Better blood cholesterol levels, reduced body fat, better control of blood pressure, improved metabolic health, and enhanced glucose metabolism; improved quality of life; reduced risk of some chronic diseases Greater amounts of activity can help prevent weight gain and promote weight loss	All the benefits of lifestyle physical activity, plus improved physical fitness (increased cardiorespiratory endurance, muscular strength and endurance, and flexibility) and even greater improvements in health and quality of life and reductions in chronic disease risk	All the benefits of lifestyle physical activity and a moderate exercise program, with greater increases in fitness and somewhat greater reductions in chronic disease risk Participating in a vigorous exercise program may increase risk of injury and overtraining

Figure 2.4 **Health and fitness benefits of different amounts of physical activity and exercise.**

structured exercise program. However, he manages to stay active during his busy workweek by engaging in short bouts of physical activity. He parks some distance from the train station and walks briskly to and from his car—15 minutes each way. At work, he takes the stairs to his sixth-floor office. During several breaks throughout the day, he does isometric exercises and stretches; these breaks help him maintain fitness and reduce the physical and mental stress of his high-pressure, sedentary job. Twice a week, he does calisthenic exercises at home in the evening, and he goes for a brisk 30-minute walk with his family on Saturday mornings.

• Kadija is a paraplegic who uses a wheelchair for mobility. She considers herself a sports fanatic. She plays wheelchair basketball two nights a week and stays in shape by training on the arm ergometer and lifting weights at the gym three days a week. During the spring, she enjoys competing in track and field. Her favorite event is the 400-meter race. She also enjoys water skiing in the summertime. She has not let her disability keep her from exercising regularly or being physically fit.

Each of these people has worked an adequate or more-than-adequate fitness program into a busy daily routine. Chapter 7 contains guidelines to help you choose activities and put together a complete exercise program that

suits your goals and preferences. (Refer to Figure 2.4 for a summary of the health and fitness benefits of different levels of physical activity.)

What about the tip of the activity pyramid? Although sedentary activities are often unavoidable—attending class, studying, working in an office, and so on—many people choose inactivity over activity during their leisure time. Change sedentary patterns by becoming more active whenever you can. Move more and sit less.

MOTIVATION FOR CHANGE!   Your school and community may present challenges to making healthy lifestyle choices, but they also have resources that can help you. Find out what local resources are "available" and will support your efforts at change. For example, go to your school's physical education office and ask for a comprehensive listing of all the exercise and fitness facilities and courses available on your campus. Obtain the same information about facilities and classes in your neighborhood, including those offered by the city or county recreation department. What fitness facilities and/or courses fit your goals, schedule, preferences, and budget? If you can't find a local program or facility to fit your needs, check out the programs available through the President's Challenge (http://www.presidentschallenge.org).

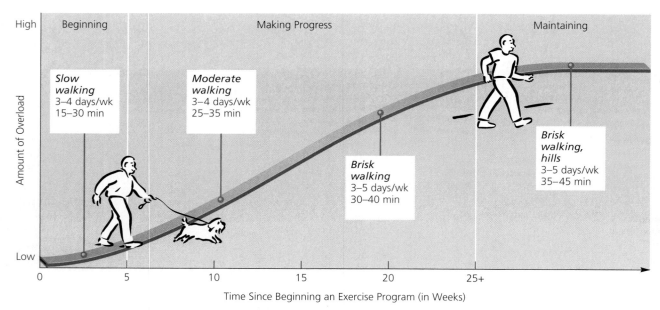

Figure 2.5 Progression of an exercise program. This figure shows how the amount of overload is increased gradually over time in a sample walking program. Regardless of the activity chosen, it is important that an exercise program begin slowly and progress gradually. Once a person achieves the desired level of fitness, she or he can maintain it by exercising 3 to 5 days a week. SOURCE: Progression data from American College of Sports Medicine. 2006. *ACSM's Guidelines for Exercise Testing and Prescription,* 7th ed. Philadelphia: Lippincott Williams & Wilkins.

Guidelines for Training

The following guidelines will make your exercise program more effective and successful.

Train the Way You Want Your Body to Change
Stress your body such that it adapts in the desired direction. To have a more muscular build, lift weights. To be more flexible, do stretching exercises. To improve performance in a particular sport, practice that sport or the movements used in it.

Train Regularly
Consistency is the key to improving fitness. Fitness improvements are lost if too much time is allowed to pass between exercise sessions.

Start Slowly, and Get in Shape Gradually
An exercise program can be divided into three phases: the beginning phase, during which the body adjusts to the new type and level of activity; the progress phase, during which fitness is increased; and the maintenance phase, in which the targeted level of fitness is maintained over the long term (Figure 2.5). When beginning a program, start slowly to give your body time to adapt to the stress of exercise. Choose activities carefully according to your fitness status—if you have been sedentary or are overweight, try an activity such as walking or swimming that won't jar the body or strain the joints.

As you progress, increase duration and frequency before increasing intensity. If you train too much or too intensely, you are more likely to suffer injuries or become

overtrained, a condition characterized by lack of energy, aching muscles and joints, and decreased physical performance. Injuries and overtraining slow down an exercise program and impede motivation. The goal is not to get in shape as quickly as possible but to gradually become and remain physically fit.

Warm Up Before Exercise
Warming up can decrease your chances of injury by helping your body gradually progress from rest to activity. A good warm-up can increase muscle temperature, reduce joint stiffness, bathe the joint surfaces in lubricating fluid, and increase blood flow to the muscles, including—very important—the heart. Some studies suggest that warming up may also reduce the risk of injury, enhance muscle metabolism, and mentally prepare a person for a workout.

A warm-up should include low-intensity, whole-body movements similar to those used in the activity that will follow. For example, runners may walk and jog slowly prior to running at full-speed. A tennis player might hit forehands and backhands at a low intensity before playing a vigorous set of tennis. It is important to note that a warm-up is not the same thing as a stretching workout. For safety and effectiveness, it is best to stretch *after* an endurance or strength training workout, when muscles are warm—and not as part of a warm-up. (Appropriate and effective warm-ups are discussed in greater detail in Chapters 3–5.)

Cool Down After Exercise
During exercise, as much as 90% of circulating blood is directed to the muscles and skin, up from as little as 20% during rest. If you

suddenly stop moving after exercise, the amount of blood returning to your heart and brain may be insufficient, and you may experience dizziness, a drop in blood pressure, or other problems. Cooling down at the end of a workout helps safely restore circulation to its normal resting condition. So don't sit or lie down or jump into the shower after exercise without cooling down first. Cool down by continuing to move at a slow pace—walking, for example—for 5–10 minutes, as your heart and breathing rate slowly return to normal. At the end of the cool-down period, do stretching exercises while your muscles are still warm. Cool down longer after intense exercise sessions.

Exercise Safely   Physical activity can cause injury or even death if you don't consider safety. Wear a helmet when rock climbing, skiing, or riding a bike, and wear eye protectors when playing racquetball or squash. Walk or run with a partner in a park or on a deserted track. Wear bright clothing when exercising on public streets. When cycling, remember to give cars plenty of leeway, even when you have the right of way; in a collision, a car will sustain less damage than a bicycle or your unprotected body. Train within your capacity because overloading your muscles and joints can lead to serious injury. Use good-quality equipment and keep it in good repair. Report broken gym equipment to the health club manager. (See Appendix A for more information on personal safety.)

Listen to Your Body, and Get Adequate Rest
Rest can be as important as exercise for improving fitness. Fitness reflects an adaptation to the stress of exercise. Building fitness involves a series of exercise stresses, recuperation, and adaptation leading to improved fitness, followed by further stresses. Build rest into your training program, and don't exercise if it doesn't feel right. Sometimes you need a few days of rest to recover enough to train with the intensity required for improving fitness. On the other hand, you can't train sporadically either. If you listen to your body and it always tells you to rest, you won't make any progress.

Cycle the Volume and Intensity of Your Workouts   To add enjoyment and variety to your program, and to further improve fitness, don't train at the same intensity during every workout. Some days train intensely and other days train lightly. Proper management of the level of workout intensity is a key to improved physical fitness. Use cycle training, also known as periodization, to provide enough recovery for intense training: Because you trained lightly one workout, you can train harder the next. However, take care to increase the volume and intensity of your program gradually—never more than 10% per week.

Vary Your Activities   Change your exercise program from time to time to keep things fresh and help

develop a higher degree of fitness. The body adapts quickly to an exercise stress, such as walking, cycling, or swimming. Gains in fitness in a particular activity become more difficult with time. Varying the kinds of exercises in your program allows you to adapt to many types of exercise and develops fitness in a variety of activities. Changing activities may also help reduce your risk of injury.

Try varying the type of training you do during different times of the year. During the summer, you might emphasize conditioning by jogging, playing basketball, and doing high-volume strength training exercises. During the fall, you might emphasize resistance training using more weights and fewer repetitions, gradually introducing more cardiovascular exercise into your program. In the spring, you might try a variety of activities, continue weight training, and get in great shape for the summer.

Try Training with a Partner   Training partners can motivate and encourage each other through hard spots and help each other develop proper exercise techniques. Training with a partner can make exercising seem easier and more fun. It can also help you keep motivated and on track. For example, you may find it easy to hit the snooze button and skip a planned solo 20-minute morning walk. But would you stay in bed if you knew a friend was waiting for you? A commitment to a friend is a powerful motivator.

Train Your Mind   This is one of the most difficult skills to acquire, but it is critical for achieving and maintaining fitness. Becoming fit requires commitment, discipline, and patience. These qualities come from understanding the importance of exercise and having clear and reachable goals. Use the lifestyle management techniques discussed in Chapter 1 to keep your program on track. Believe in yourself and your potential—and you *will* achieve your goals!

Fuel Your Activity Appropriately   Good nutrition, including rehydration and resynthesis of liver and muscle carbohydrate stores, is part of optimal recuperation from exercise. Eat enough calories to support your exercise program without gaining body fat. Many studies show that consuming carbohydrates and protein before or after exercise promotes restoration of stored fuels so that you can exercise intensely again shortly. Nutrition for exercise is discussed in greater detail in Chapters 3 and 8.

Terms

overtraining   A condition caused by training too much or too intensely, characterized by lack of energy, decreased physical performance, fatigue, depression, aching muscles and joints, and susceptibility to injury.

Have Fun   You are more likely to stick with an exercise program if it's fun. Choose a variety of activities that you enjoy. Some people like to play competitive sports, such as tennis, golf, or volleyball. Competition can boost motivation, but remember: Sports are competitive but training for fitness is not. Other people like more solitary activities, such as jogging, walking, or swimming. Still others like high-skill individual sports, such as skiing, surfing, or skateboarding. Many activities can help you get fit, so choose the ones you enjoy. You can also boost your enjoyment and build your social support network by exercising with friends and family.

Track Your Progress   Monitoring the progress of your program can help keep you motivated and on track. Depending on the activities you've included in your program, you may track different measures of your program—minutes of jogging, miles of cycling, laps of swimming, number of push-ups, amount of weight lifted, and so on. If your program is focused on increasing daily physical activity, consider using an inexpensive pedometer to monitor the number of steps you take each day (see Lab 2.4 for more information on setting goals and monitoring activity using a pedometer). Specific examples of program monitoring can be found in the labs for Chapters 3, 4, and 5 and in the Daily Fitness and Nutrition Journal.

Keep Your Exercise Program in Perspective

As important as physical fitness is, it is only part of a well-rounded life. You have to have time for work and school, family and friends, relaxation and hobbies. Some people become overinvolved in exercise and neglect other parts of their lives. They think of themselves as runners, dancers, swimmers, or triathletes rather than as people who participate in those activities. Balance and moderation are the key ingredients of a fit and well life.

Tips for Today

Physical activity and exercise offer benefits in nearly every area of wellness, helping you generate energy, manage stress, improve your mood, and, of course, become physically stronger and healthier. Even a low-to-moderate level of activity provides valuable health benefits. The important thing is to get moving!

Right now you can

- Go outside and take a brisk 15-minute walk.

- Look at your calendar for the rest of the week and write in some physical activity—such as walking, running, biking, skating, swimming, hiking, or playing Frisbee—on as many days as you can. Schedule the activity for a specific time and stick to it.

- Call a friend and invite her or him to start planning a regular exercise program with you.

SUMMARY

- Exercising daily in moderation contributes substantially to good health. Even without a formal, vigorous exercise program, you can get many of the same health benefits by becoming more physically active.

- If you are already active, you benefit even more by increasing the intensity or duration of your activities.

- The five components of physical fitness most important for health are cardiorespiratory endurance, muscular strength, muscular endurance, flexibility, and body composition.

- Physical training is the process of producing long-term improvements in the body's functioning through exercise. All training is based on the fact that the body adapts to physical stress.

- According to the principle of specificity, bodies change specifically in response to the type of training received.

- Bodies also adapt to progressive overload. Therefore, when you progressively increase the frequency, intensity, and time (duration) of the right type of exercise, you become increasingly fit.

- Bodies adjust to lower levels of activity by losing fitness, a principle known as reversibility. To counter the effects of reversibility it's important to keep training at the same intensity, even if you have to reduce the number or length of sessions.

- According to the principle of individual differences, people vary in the maximum level of fitness they can achieve.

- When designing an exercise program, determine if medical clearance is needed, assess your current level of fitness, set realistic goals, and choose activities that develop all components of fitness.

- In addition, train regularly, get in shape gradually, warm up and cool down, maintain a structured but flexible program, exercise safely, consider training with a partner, train your mind, have fun, and keep exercise in perspective.

For Further Exploration

ViW   *Fit and Well* Online Learning Center
(www.mhhe.com/fahey)

Use the learning objectives, study guide questions, and glossary flashcards to review key terms and concepts and prepare for exams. You can extend your knowledge of physical activity and gain experience in using the Internet as a resource by completing the activities and checking out the Web links for the topics in Chapter 2 marked with the World Wide Web icon. For this chapter, Internet activities explore common fitness terms, your current level of fitness, and a variety of physical activities that you can incorporate into your life; there are Web links for the Vital Statistics figure, the Critical Consumer box on fitness centers, and the chapter as a whole.

Daily Fitness and Nutrition Journal

Start completing the fitness program planning portion of the log by beginning an analysis of the costs and benefits of increasing physical

Where can I work out? Identify accessible and pleasant places to work out. For running, find a field or park with a soft surface. For swimming, find a pool that's open at times convenient for you. For cycling, find an area with minimal traffic and air pollution. Make sure the location is safe and convenient. If you join a health club or fitness center, follow the guidelines in the box "Choosing a Fitness Center," on p. 47.

Where can I get help and advice about exercise? Because fitness is essential to a wellness lifestyle, you need to learn as much as you can about exercise. One of the best places to get help is an exercise class. There, expert instructors can help you learn the basics of training and answer your questions. Make sure the instructor is certified by a recognized professional organization and/or has formal training in exercise physiology. Read articles by credible experts in fitness magazines. Because of competition among publications, many of these magazines include articles by leading experts in exercise science written at a layperson's level.

A qualified personal trainer can also be helpful in getting you started in an exercise program or a new form of training. Make sure this person has proper qualifications, such as a college degree in exercise physiology or physical education or ACSM, National Strength and Conditioning Association (NSCA), or American Council on Exercise (ACE) certification. Don't seek out a person for advice simply because he or she looks fit. UCLA researchers recently found that 60% of the personal trainers in their study couldn't pass a basic exam on training methods, exercise physiology, or biomechanics. Even some trainers with more than 5 years experience couldn't pass the test. Trainers who performed best had college degrees in exercise physiology, physical education, or physical therapy. So choose your trainer carefully and don't get caught up with fads.

How can I fit a workout into my day? Good time management is an important skill in creating and maintaining an exercise program. Choose a regular time to exercise, preferably the same time every day. Don't tell yourself you'll exercise "sometime during the day" when you have free time—that free time may never come. Schedule your workout, and make it a priority. Include alternative plans in your program to account for circumstances like bad weather or vacations.

You don't have to work on all fitness components in the same exercise session. The important thing is to have a regular schedule. (You'll have the chance to develop strategies for successful time management in the Behavior Change Workbook at the end of the text.)

What should my fitness goals be? For a successful program, it is a good idea to have both general, long-term goals and more specific, short-term goals. Begin by thinking about your general overall goals—the benefits you want to obtain by increasing your activity level and/or beginning a formal exercise program. Examples of long-term goals include reducing your risk of chronic diseases like heart disease and diabetes, improving your mood, increasing your energy level, developing a more positive attitude and self-image, maintaining a healthy body weight, and improving the fit of your clothes. Choose goals that are important to you.

To help shape your fitness program, you need to also set specific, short-term goals based on measurable factors. These specific goals should be an extension of your overall goals—what specific changes to your current activity and exercise habits are needed to achieve your general goals. You need information about your current levels of physical activity and physical fitness in order to set appropriate goals.

The labs in this chapter will help you determine your physical activity level—for example, how many minutes per day you engage in moderate or vigorous activity or how many daily steps you take. Using this information, you can set goals for lifestyle physical activity to help you meet your overall goals. For example, if your general long-term goals are to reduce the risk of chronic disease and

prevent weight gain, the Dietary Guidelines recommend 60 minutes of moderate physical activity daily. If you currently engage in 30 minutes of moderate activity daily, then your behavior change goal would be to add 30 additional minutes of daily physical activity (or an equivalent number of additional daily steps—about 3500 to 4000); your time frame for the change might be 8–12 weeks.

Labs in Chapters 3–6 provide opportunities to specifically assess your fitness status for all the health-related components of fitness (cardiorespiratory endurance, muscular strength, muscular endurance, flexibility, body composition). The results of these assessments can guide you in setting specific fitness goals. For instance, if the labs in Chapter 4 indicate that you have good muscular strength and endurance in your lower body but poor strength and endurance in your upper body, then setting a specific goal for improving upper-body muscle fitness would be an appropriate goal—increasing the number of push-ups you can do from 22 to 30, for example. Chapters 3–6 include additional advice for setting appropriate goals.

Some experts suggest you further evaluate fitness goals using the SMART acronym; that is, make sure that your goals are

- Specific
- Measurable
- Attainable
- Realistic
- Time-frame specific

Once you start your behavior change program, you may discover that your goals aren't quite appropriate—perhaps you were overly optimistic, or maybe you set the bar too low. There are limits to the amount of fitness you can achieve, but within the limits of your genes and health status, you can make significant improvements in fitness. Adjust your goals as needed.

Do I need to join a gym or buy exercise equipment in order to build fitness? No. There are many ways to increase physical activity and boost physical fitness without spending money on a gym membership or equipment.

Activities like walking, stretching, and calisthenics can be practiced by anyone at no cost. There are also many low-cost options, such as small hand weights, stability balls, and jump ropes. Exercising at home is convenient and private—characteristics that you may value. On the other hand, you may prefer to train at a gym because of the variety of exercise options and equipment and because it offers the opportunity to train with others. If you like the idea of training in a gym, look for inexpensive options. For example, your school or employer may offer free or low-cost gym memberships.

Should I follow my exercise program if I'm sick? If you have a mild head cold or feel one coming on, it is probably OK to exercise moderately. Just begin slowly and see how you feel. However, if you have symptoms of a more serious illness—fever, swollen glands, nausea, extreme tiredness, muscle aches—wait until you have fully recovered before resuming your exercise program. Continuing to exercise while suffering from an illness more serious than a cold can compromise your recovery and may even be dangerous.

Visit the Online Learning Center for more answers to common questions about fitness.

activity, setting some general fitness goals, and thinking about your current activity and exercise habits. If you need to track your daily activities in order to identify ways to incorporate more lifestyle physical activity into your day, visit the Online Learning Center for some blank sample logs that you can print and use; also refer to the time-management section (Activity 10) in the Behavior Change Workbook.

Books

American College of Sports Medicine. 2003. *ACSM Fitness Book*, 3rd ed. Champaign, Ill.: Human Kinetics. *Provides a step-by-step approach to becoming more active and developing a fitness program.*

American College of Sports Medicine. 2006. *ACSM's Guidelines for Exercise Testing and Prescription*, 7th ed. Philadelphia: Lippincott Williams & Wilkins. *Includes the ACSM guidelines for safety of exercising, a basic discussion of exercise physiology, and information about fitness testing and prescription.*

Department of Health and Human Services. 1996. *Physical Activity and Health: A Report of the Surgeon General*. Atlanta, Ga.: DHHS (also available online: http://www.cdc.gov/nccdphp/sgr/sgr.htm). *Summarizes evidence for the benefits of physical activity and makes recommendations.*

Earle, R. W., and T. R. Baechle, eds. 2004. *NSCA's Essentials of Personal Training*. Champaign, Ill.: Human Kinetics. *Comprehensive discussions of fitness testing, exercise and disease, nutrition and physical performance, and exercise prescription.*

Journals

ACSM Health and Fitness Journal (401 West Michigan Street, Indianapolis, IN 46202; http://www.acsm-healthfitness.org)

Physician and Sportsmedicine (4530 W. 77th Street, Minneapolis, MN 55435; many of the articles are also available online at http://www.physsportsmed.com)

V:W Organizations, Hotlines, and Web Sites

American Alliance for Health, Physical Education, Recreation, and Dance (AAHPERD). A professional organization dedicated to promoting quality health and physical education programs.
800-213-7193
http://www.aahperd.org

American College of Sports Medicine (ACSM). The principal professional organization for sports medicine and exercise science. Provides brochures, publications, and audio- and videotapes.
317-637-9200
http://www.acsm.org

American Council on Exercise (ACE). Promotes exercise and fitness; the Web site features fact sheets on many consumer topics, including choosing shoes, cross-training, and steroids.
800-825-3636
http://www.acefitness.org

American Heart Association: Just Move. Provides practical advice for people of all fitness levels plus an online fitness diary.
http://www.justmove.org

Canada's Physical Activity Guide. Offers many suggestions for incorporating physical activity into everyday life.
http://www.hc-sc.gc.ca/hl-vs/physactiv/index_e.html

CDC Physical Activity Information. Provides information on the benefits of physical activity and suggestions for incorporating moderate physical activity into daily life.
http://www.cdc.gov/nccdphp/dnpa/

Disabled Sports USA. Provides sports and recreation services to people with physical or mobility disorders.
http://www.dsusa.org

International Health, Racquet, and Sportsclub Association (IHRSA): Health Clubs. Provides guidelines for choosing a health or fitness facility and links to clubs that belong to IHRSA.
http://www.healthclubs.com

MedlinePlus: Exercise and Physical Fitness. Provides links to news and reliable information about fitness and exercise from government agencies and professional associations.
http://www.nlm.nih.gov/medlineplus/
exercisephysicalfitness.html

President's Council on Physical Fitness and Sports (PCPFS). Provides information on PCPFS programs and publications, including fitness guides and fact sheets.
http://www.fitness.gov
http://www.presidentschallenge.org

SmallStep.Gov. Provides resources for increasing activity and improving diet through small changes in daily habits.
http://www.smallstep.gov

The following provide links to sites with information on a wide variety of activities and fitness issues; evaluate commercial sites carefully.

Critical Consumer

Fitness centers can provide you with many benefits—motivation and companionship are among the most important. A fitness center may also offer expert instruction and supervision as well as access to better equipment than you could afford on your own. If you're thinking of joining a fitness center, here are some guidelines to help you choose a club that's right for you.

Convenience

• Look for an established facility that's within 10–15 minutes of your home or work. If it's farther away, your chances of sticking to an exercise regimen start to diminish.

• Check out the facility's hours, then visit it at the time you would normally exercise. Is there adequate parking? Will you have easy access to the equipment and exercise classes you want at that time?

• If needed, ask about childcare or youth programs. What services are available, and how are they supervised?

Atmosphere

• Look around to see if there are other members who are your age and at about your fitness level. Some clubs may cater to a certain age group or lifestyle—for example, hard-core bodybuilders.)

• If you like to exercise to music, make sure you like the music played there, both its type and volume.

• Observe how the members dress. Will you fit in, or will you be uncomfortable?

• Observe the staff. Are they easy to identify? Are they friendly and helpful?

• Check to see that the facility is clean, including showers and lockers. Make sure the facility is climate controlled, well ventilated, and well lit.

Safety

• Find out if the facility offers some type of preactivity screening as well as basic fitness testing that includes cardiovascular screening.

• Determine if there is emergency equipment such as automated external defibrillators (AEDs) on the premises and if personnel are trained in CPR. AEDs can help someone with cardiac arrest.

• Ask if at least one staff member on each shift is trained in first aid.

• Find out if the club has an emergency plan in case a member has a heart attack or serious injury (many clubs do not).

Trained Personnel

• Determine if the personal trainers and fitness instructors are certified by a recognized professional association such as the American College of Sports Medicine (ACSM), National Strength and Conditioning Association (NSCA), or American Council on Exercise (ACE). All personal trainers are not equal—more than 100 organizations certify trainers and few of these require much formal training. Trainers with college degrees in exercise physiology or physical education are usually the most knowledgeable.

• Find out if the club has a trained exercise physiologist on staff, someone with a degree in exercise physiology, kinesiology, or exercise science. If the facility offers nutritional counseling, it should employ someone who is a registered dietitian (R.D.) or who has other formal training.

• Ask how much experience the instructors have. Clubs may employ people because they were good athletes or look fit; by themselves, these are not good reasons to hire someone. Ideally, trainers should have both academic preparation and practical experience.

Cost

• Buy only what you need and can afford. If you want to use only workout equipment, you may not need a club that has racquetball courts and saunas.

• Check the contract. Choose the one that covers the shortest period of time possible, especially if it's your first fitness club experience. Don't feel pressured to sign a long-term contract.

• Make sure the contract permits you to extend your membership if you have a prolonged illness or go on vacation.

• Try out the club. Ask for a free trial workout, or a 1-day pass, or an inexpensive 1- or 2-week trial membership.

• Find out whether there is an extra charge for the particular services you want. Get any special offers in writing.

Effectiveness

• Tour the facility. Does it offer what the brochure says it does? Does it offer the activities and equipment you want?

• Check the equipment. A good club will have treadmills, bikes, stair-climbers, resistance machines, and weights. Make sure these machines are up-to-date and well maintained.

• Find out if new members get a formal orientation and instruction on how to safely use the equipment. Will a staff member help you develop a program that is appropriate for your current fitness level and goals?

• Make sure the facility is certified. Look for the displayed names American College of Sports Medicine (ACSM), American Council on Exercise (ACE), Aerobics and Fitness Association of America (AFAA), or International Health, Racquet, and Sportsclub Association (IHRSA).

• Don't get cheated. Check with your Better Business Bureau or Consumer Affairs office to see if others have complained.

Fitness Partner Connection Jumpsite: http//www.primusweb.com/
fitnesspartner

NetSweat: The Internet's Fitness Resource: http//www.netsweat.com

Yahoo!Fitness: dir.yahoo.com/Health/Fitness

Selected Bibliography

American Academy of Orthopaedic Surgeons. 2002. *Prevent Injuries America: Sports Injuries and Baby Boomers* (http://orthoinfo.aaos.org/fact/prev_report.cfm?Thread_ID=147&category=Prevention; retrieved April 7, 2004).

American College of Sports Medicine. 2006. *ACSM's Guidelines for Exercise Testing and Prescription.* Philadelphia: Lippincott Williams & Wilkins.

American College of Sports Medicine. 2006. *ACSM's Resource Manual for Guidelines for Exercise Testing and Prescription,* 5th ed. Philadelphia: Lippincott Williams & Wilkins.

American College of Sports Medicine. 1998. The recommended quantity and quality of exercise for developing and maintaining cardiorespiratory and muscular fitness, and flexibility in healthy adults. ACSM position paper. *Medicine and Science in Sports and Exercise* 30(6): 975–991.

American College of Obstetrics and Gynecology Committee on Obstetric Practice. 2002. Exercise during pregnancy and the postpartum period. Committee Opinion No. 267. *International Journal of Gynaecology and Obstetrics* 77:79–81.

American Diabetes Association. 2003. Physical activity/exercise and diabetes mellitus. *Diabetes Care* 26:S73–S77.

American Heart Association. 2003. Exercise and physical activity in the prevention and treatment of atherosclerotic cardiovascular disease. *Circulation* 107:3109–3116.

Byers, T., et al. 2002. American Cancer Society guidelines on nutrition and physical activity for cancer prevention: Reducing the risk of cancer with healthy food choices and physical activity. *CA: A Cancer Journal for Clinicians* 52(2): 92–119.

Centers for Disease Control and Prevention. 2005. Trends in leisure-time physical inactivity by age, sex, and race/ethnicity—United States, 1994–2004. *Morbidity and Mortality Weekly Report* 54(39): 991–994.

Centers for Disease Control and Prevention. 2001. *Lower Direct Medical Costs Associated with Physical Activity* (http://www.cdc.gov/nccdphp/ndpa/pr-cost.htm; retrieved October 9, 2001).

Department of Health and Human Services. 1996. *Physical Activity and Health: A Report of the Surgeon General.* Atlanta, Ga.: DHHS.

Dong, L., G. Block, and S. Mandel. 2004. Activities contributing to total energy expenditure in the United States: Results from the NHAPS Study. *International Journal of Behavioral Nutrition and Physical Activity* 1(4).

Exercise for health: How much exercise is enough? ACSM works with others to avoid misunderstanding. 2003. *ACSM Fit Society Page,* Winter.

Garman, J. F., et al. 2004. Occurrence of exercise dependence in a college-aged population. *Journal of American College Health* 52(5): 221–228.

Greaney, M. L., et al. 2004. What older adults find useful for maintaining healthy eating and exercise habits. *Journal of Nutrition for the Elderly* 24: 19–35.

Hu, F. B. 2003. Sedentary lifestyle and risk of obesity and type 2 diabetes. *Lipids* 38(2): 103–108.

Institutes of Medicine, National Academies. 2002. *Dietary Reference Intakes for Energy, Carbohydrate, Fiber, Fat, Fatty Acids, Cholesterol, Protein, and Amino Acids.* Washington, D.C.: National Academy Press.

Is easy-does-it exercise enough? 2004. *Consumer Reports on Health,* February.

Kruger, J., et al. 2005. Physical activity profiles of U.S. adults trying to lose weight: NHIS 1998. *Medicine and Science in Sports and Exercise* 37: 364–368.

Le Masurier, G. 2005. Walkee talkee: Answers to pedometer FAQs. *ACSM Fit Society Page,* Spring.

Lee, I. 2003. Physical activity in women: How much is good enough? *Journal of the American Medical Association* 290(10): 1377–1379.

Lucas, J. W., J. S. Schiller, and V. Benson. 2004. Summary health statistics for U.S. adults: National Health Interview Survey, 2001. *Vital Health Statistics* 10: 1–134.

Lustyk, M. K., et al. 2004. Physical activity and quality of life: Assessing the influence of activity frequency, intensity, volume, and motives. *Behavioral Medicine* 30: 124–131.

Malek, M. H., et al. 2002. Importance of health science education for personal fitness trainers. *Journal of Strength and Conditioning Research* 16: 19–24.

Pate, R. R., et al. 1995. Physical activity and public health: A recommendation from the Centers for Disease Control and Prevention and the American College of Sports Medicine. *Journal of the American Medical Association* 273: 402–407.

President's Council on Physical Fitness and Sports. 2000. Definitions: Health, fitness, and physical activity. *Research Digest* 3(9).

Schoenborn, C. A., et al. 2004. Health behaviors of adults: United States, 1999–2001. *Vital Health Statistics* 10: 1–79.

Swain, D. P. 2005. Moderate or vigorous intensity exercise: Which is better for improving aerobic fitness? *Preventive Cardiology* 8: 55–58.

Vanhees, L., et al. 2005. How to assess physical activity? How to assess physical fitness? *European Journal of Cardiovascular Prevention and Rehabilitation* 12: 102–114.

World Health Organization/FAO Expert Consultation. 2003. *Diet, Nutrition and the Prevention of Chronic Diseases.* WHO Technical Report Series 916. Geneva: World Health Organization.

LAB 2.1 *Safety of Exercise Participation*

Physical Activity Readiness
Questionnaire - PAR-Q
(revised 2002)

PAR-Q & YOU

(A Questionnaire for People Aged 15 to 69)

Regular physical activity is fun and healthy, and increasingly more people are starting to become more active every day. Being more active is very safe for most people. However, some people should check with their doctor before they start becoming much more physically active.

If you are planning to become much more physically active than you are now, start by answering the seven questions in the box below. If you are between the ages of 15 and 69, the PAR-Q will tell you if you should check with your doctor before you start. If you are over 69 years of age, and you are not used to being very active, check with your doctor.

Common sense is your best guide when you answer these questions. Please read the questions carefully and answer each one honestly: check YES or NO.

YES	NO		
☐	☐	1.	Has your doctor ever said that you have a heart condition <u>and</u> that you should only do physical activity recommended by a doctor?
☐	☐	2.	Do you feel pain in your chest when you do physical activity?
☐	☐	3.	In the past month, have you had chest pain when you were not doing physical activity?
☐	☐	4.	Do you lose your balance because of dizziness or do you ever lose consciousness?
☐	☐	5.	Do you have a bone or joint problem (for example, back, knee or hip) that could be made worse by a change in your physical activity?
☐	☐	6.	Is your doctor currently prescribing drugs (for example, water pills) for your blood pressure or heart condition?
☐	☐	7.	Do you know of <u>any other reason</u> why you should not do physical activity?

If you answered

YES to one or more questions

Talk with your doctor by phone or in person BEFORE you start becoming much more physically active or BEFORE you have a fitness appraisal. Tell your doctor about the PAR-Q and which questions you answered YES.

- You may be able to do any activity you want — as long as you start slowly and build up gradually. Or, you may need to restrict your activities to those which are safe for you. Talk with your doctor about the kinds of activities you wish to participate in and follow his/her advice.
- Find out which community programs are safe and helpful for you.

NO to all questions

If you answered NO honestly to <u>all</u> PAR-Q questions, you can be reasonably sure that you can:
- start becoming much more physically active — begin slowly and build up gradually. This is the safest and easiest way to go.
- take part in a fitness appraisal — this is an excellent way to determine your basic fitness so that you can plan the best way for you to live actively. It is also highly recommended that you have your blood pressure evaluated. If your reading is over 144/94, talk with your doctor before you start becoming much more physically active.

DELAY BECOMING MUCH MORE ACTIVE:
- if you are not feeling well because of a temporary illness such as a cold or a fever — wait until you feel better; or
- if you are or may be pregnant — talk to your doctor before you start becoming more active.

PLEASE NOTE: If your health changes so that you then answer YES to any of the above questions, tell your fitness or health professional. Ask whether you should change your physical activity plan.

<u>Informed Use of the PAR-Q</u>: The Canadian Society for Exercise Physiology, Health Canada, and their agents assume no liability for persons who undertake physical activity, and if in doubt after completing this questionnaire, consult your doctor prior to physical activity.

No changes permitted. You are encouraged to photocopy the PAR-Q but only if you use the entire form.

NOTE: If the PAR-Q is being given to a person before he or she participates in a physical activity program or a fitness appraisal, this section may be used for legal or administrative purposes.

"I have read, understood and completed this questionnaire. Any questions I had were answered to my full satisfaction."

NAME _____

SIGNATURE _____   DATE _____

SIGNATURE OF PARENT _____   WITNESS _____
or GUARDIAN (for participants under the age of majority)

Note: This physical activity clearance is valid for a maximum of 12 months from the date it is completed and becomes invalid if your condition changes so that you would answer YES to any of the seven questions.

 © Canadian Society for Exercise Physiology   Supported by: Health Canada   Santé Canada

Part II   General Health Profile

To help further assess the safety of exercise for you, complete as much of this health profile as possible.

General Information

Age: _____   Total cholesterol: _____   Blood pressure: _____ / _____

Height: _____   HDL: _____   Triglycerides: _____

Weight: _____   LDL: _____   Blood glucose level: _____

Are you currently trying to _____ gain or _____ lose weight? (check one if appropriate)

Medical Conditions/Treatments

Check any of the following that apply to you and add any other conditions that might affect your ability to exercise safely.

_____ heart disease   _____ depression, anxiety, or another   _____ other injury or joint problem: _____

_____ lung disease   psychological disorder   _____ substance abuse problem

_____ diabetes   _____ eating disorder   _____ other: _____

_____ allergies   _____ back pain   _____ other: _____

_____ asthma   _____ arthritis   _____ other: _____

_____ Do you have a family history of cardiovascular disease (CVD) (a parent, sibling, or child who had a heart attack or stroke before age 55 for men or 65 for women)?

List any medications or supplements you are taking or any medical treatments you are undergoing. Include the name of the substance or treatment and its purpose. Include both prescription and over-the-counter drugs and supplements.

_____   _____

_____   _____

Lifestyle Information

Check any of the following that is true for you, and fill in the requested information.

✔ I usually eat high-fat foods (fatty meats, cheese, fried foods, butter, full-fat dairy products) every day.

✔ I consume fewer than 5 servings of fruits and vegetables on most days.

✔ I smoke cigarettes or use other tobacco products. If true, describe your use of tobacco (type and frequency): _____

✔ I regularly drink alcohol. If true, describe your typical weekly consumption pattern: _____

✔ I often feel as if I need more sleep. (I need about _8_ hours per day; I get about _6_ hours per day.)

✔ I feel as though stress has adversely affected my level of wellness during the past year.

Describe your current activity pattern. What types of moderate physical activity do you engage in on a daily basis? Are you involved in a formal exercise program or do you regularly participate in sports or recreational activities?

_____

_____

Using Your Results

How did you score? Did the PAR-Q indicate that exercise is likely to be safe for you? Is there anything in your health profile that you think may affect your ability to exercise safely? Have you had any problems with exercise in the past?

What should you do next? If the assessments in this lab indicate that you should see your physician before beginning an exercise program, or if you have any questions about the safety of exercise for you, make an appointment to talk with your health care provider to address your concerns.

LAB 2.2 *Your Physical Activity Profile*

Complete this lab to assess your overall level of activity on a typical day. The amount of time you spend on sleep and on light, moderate, and vigorous activity should total 24 hours. To complete the chart below, fill in your activities and the amount of time you spend on each one; in addition, keep track of the number of flights of stairs you climb. Classify each activity as light, moderate, or vigorous according to the following guidelines:

Light activities—most sitting and standing activities: Attending class; studying; using a computer; watching TV; listening to music; talking on the phone; eating meals; walking slowly; driving; most child-care activities; light housework such as ironing, cooking, dusting, vacuuming; light yard work or home repair such as pruning, weeding, plumbing; office work, sales, or another occupational activity involving sitting or standing and movement of little more than hands.

Moderate activities—breathing rate increases but comfortable conversation is possible: Walking moderately or briskly; cycling moderately; active play with children or pushing a stroller; moderate housework such as scrubbing floors, washing windows; moderate yard work or home repair such as planting, raking, painting, wallpapering; hand-washing a car; waiting tables, washing dishes, or another occupational activity involving extended periods of moderate effort; social dancing; fitness activities requiring moderate effort such as low-impact aerobic dance, Frisbee, recreational swimming, hitting a punching bag.

Vigorous activities—too out of breath to talk easily: Walking briskly uphill; heavy housework such as moving furniture or carrying heavy items upstairs; vigorous yard work or home activities such as shoveling snow, trimming trees, hand-sawing; heavy construction work or digging; fitness activities requiring vigorous effort, such as jogging or running, high-impact aerobic dance; circuit weight training, swimming laps, most competitive sports.

Activity	Duration	Classification

Number of flights of stairs: _____ flights

Physical Activity Summary (should total 24 hours)

Sleep: _____ hours   Number of flights of stairs: _____ flights

Light activity: _____ hours

Moderate activity: _____ hours

Vigorous activity: _____ hours

Using Your Results

How did you score? Are you at all surprised by the amount of time you spend in light, moderate, and vigorous activity? Do you spend at least 30 minutes each day—the recommended minimum—in moderate or vigorous activity? Are you satisfied with the amount of moderate and vigorous physical activity in your daily life? Is it appropriate for your health status and goals?

What should you do next? Enter the results of this lab in the Preprogram Assessment column in Appendix D. If you want to increase the amount of moderate or vigorous physical activity in your life, begin by analyzing the amount of time in each intensity category according to the type of activity:

	Light activity (hours)	Moderate activity (hours)	Vigorous activity (hours)
Home and child-care activities			
School- or job-related activities			
Transportation-related activities			
Leisure activities			
Exercise/sport activities			

How much of your time in transportation-related activities and leisure activities is classified as light activity? Transportation and leisure activities are often the areas where it is easiest to substitute moderate activities for light activities. Examples include walking or biking rather than driving for short errands and going for a walk with a friend rather than chatting on the phone; see p. 31 for additional suggestions. Below, identify three strategies for boosting physical activity in your daily life.

1. _____

2. _____

3. _____

Can you also identify additional opportunities to climb stairs each day?

Begin to adopt the strategies you've identified to increase physical activity. After several weeks of a program to become more physically active, do this lab again, and enter the results in the Postprogram Assessment column of Appendix D. How do the results compare?

SOURCE: Activity classifications from CDC Division of Nutrition and Physical Activity. 1999. *Promoting Physical Activity: A Guide for Community Action.* Champaign, Ill.: Human Kinetics.

LAB 2.3 *Overcoming Barriers to Being Active*

Barriers to Being Active Quiz

Directions: Listed below are reasons that people give to describe why they do not get as much physical activity as they think they should. Please read each statement and indicate how likely you are to say each of the following statements.

How likely are you to say this?	Very likely	Somewhat likely	Somewhat unlikely	Very unlikely
1. My day is so busy now, I just don't think I can make the time to include physical activity in my regular schedule.	3	2	①	0
2. None of my family members or friends like to do anything active, so I don't have a chance to exercise.	3	2	1	⓪
3. I'm just too tired after work to get any exercise.	3	②	1	0
4. I've been thinking about getting more exercise, but I just can't seem to get started.	③	2	1	0
5. I'm getting older so exercise can be risky.	3	2	1	⓪
6. I don't get enough exercise because I have never learned the skills for any sport.	3	2	1	⓪
7. I don't have access to jogging trails, swimming pools, bike paths, etc.	3	2	①	0
8. Physical activity takes too much time away from other commitments—like work, family, etc.	3	2	1	⓪
9. I'm embarrassed about how I will look when I exercise with others.	3	2	1	⓪
10. I don't get enough sleep as it is. I just couldn't get up early or stay up late to get some exercise.	3	②	1	0
11. It's easier for me to find excuses not to exercise than to go out and do something.	3	②	1	0
12. I know of too many people who have hurt themselves by overdoing it with exercise.	3	2	1	⓪
13. I really can't see learning a new sport at my age.	3	2	1	⓪
14. It's just too expensive. You have to take a class or join a club or buy the right equipment.	3	2	1	⓪
15. My free times during the day are too short to include exercise.	③	2	1	0
16. My usual social activities with family or friends do not include physical activity.	③	2	1	0
17. I'm too tired during the week and I need the weekend to catch up on my rest.	③	2	1	0

How likely are you to say this?	Very likely	Somewhat likely	Somewhat unlikely	Very unlikely
18. I want to get more exercise, but I just can't seem to make myself stick to anything.	③	2	1	0
19. I'm afraid I might injure myself or have a heart attack.	3	2	1	⓪
20. I'm not good enough at any physical activity to make it fun.	3	2	1	⓪
21. If we had exercise facilities and showers at work, then I would be more likely to exercise.	3	2	1	⓪

Scoring

- Enter the circled numbers in the spaces provided, putting the number for statement 1 on line 1, statement 2 on line 2, and so on.

- Add the three scores on each line. Your barriers to physical activity fall into one or more of seven categories: lack of time, social influence, lack of energy, lack of willpower, fear of injury, lack of skill, and lack of resources. A score of 5 or above in any category shows that this is an important barrier for you to overcome.

$$\underline{\hspace{1cm}} + \underline{\hspace{1cm}} + \underline{\hspace{1cm}} = \underline{\hspace{3cm}}$$
$$\quad 1 \qquad 8 \qquad 15 \qquad \text{Lack of time}$$

$$\underline{\hspace{1cm}} + \underline{\hspace{1cm}} + \underline{\hspace{1cm}} = \underline{\hspace{3cm}}$$
$$\quad 2 \qquad 9 \qquad 16 \qquad \text{Social influence}$$

$$\underline{\hspace{1cm}} + \underline{\hspace{1cm}} + \underline{\hspace{1cm}} = \underline{\hspace{3cm}}$$
$$\quad 3 \qquad 10 \qquad 17 \qquad \text{Lack of energy}$$

$$\underline{\hspace{1cm}} + \underline{\hspace{1cm}} + \underline{\hspace{1cm}} = \underline{\hspace{3cm}}$$
$$\quad 4 \qquad 11 \qquad 18 \qquad \text{Lack of willpower}$$

$$\underline{\hspace{1cm}} + \underline{\hspace{1cm}} + \underline{\hspace{1cm}} = \underline{\hspace{3cm}}$$
$$\quad 5 \qquad 12 \qquad 19 \qquad \text{Fear of injury}$$

$$\underline{\hspace{1cm}} + \underline{\hspace{1cm}} + \underline{\hspace{1cm}} = \underline{\hspace{3cm}}$$
$$\quad 6 \qquad 13 \qquad 20 \qquad \text{Lack of skill}$$

$$\underline{\hspace{1cm}} + \underline{\hspace{1cm}} + \underline{\hspace{1cm}} = \underline{\hspace{3cm}}$$
$$\quad 7 \qquad 14 \qquad 21 \qquad \text{Lack of resources}$$

Using Your Results

How did you score? How many key barriers did you identify? Are they what you expected?

What should you do next? For your key barriers, try the strategies listed on the following pages and/or develop additional strategies that work for you. Check off any strategy that you try.

Suggestions for Overcoming Physical Activity Barriers

Lack of time

_____ Identify available time slots. Monitor your daily activities for 1 week. Identify at least three 30-minute time slots you could use for physical activity.

_____ Add physical activity to your daily routine. For example, walk or ride your bike to work or shopping, organize social activities around physical activity, walk the dog, exercise while you watch TV, park farther from your destination, etc.

_____ Make time for physical activity. For example, walk, jog, or swim during your lunch hour, or take fitness breaks instead of coffee breaks.

_____ Select activities requiring minimal time, such as walking, jogging, stair climbing.

_____ Other: _____

Social influence

_____ Explain your interest in physical activity to friends and family. Ask them to support your efforts.

_____ Invite friends and family members to exercise with you. Plan social activities involving exercise.

_____ Develop new friendships with physically active people. Join a group, such as the YMCA or a hiking club.

_____ Other: _____

Lack of energy

_____ Schedule physical activity for times in the day or week when you feel energetic.

_____ Convince yourself that if you give it a chance, exercise will increase your energy level; then, try it.

_____ Other: _____

Lack of willpower

_____ Plan ahead. Make physical activity a regular part of your daily or weekly schedule and write it on your calendar.

_____ Invite a friend to exercise with you on a regular basis and write it on _both_ your calendars.

_____ Join an exercise group or class.

_____ Other: _____

Fear of injury

_____ Learn how to warm up and cool down to prevent injury.

_____ Learn how to exercise appropriately considering your age, fitness level, skill level, and health status.

_____ Choose activities involving minimal risk.

_____ Other: _____

Lack of skill

_____ Select activities requiring no new skills, such as walking, jogging, or stair-climbing.

_____ Exercise with friends who are at the same skill level as you are.

_____ Find a friend who is willing to teach you some new skills.

_____ Take a class to develop new skills.

_____ Other: _____

Lack of resources

_____ Select activities that require minimal facilities or equipment, such as walking, jogging, jumping rope, or calisthenics.

_____ Identify inexpensive, convenient resources available in your community (community education programs, park and recreation programs, worksite programs, etc.).

_____ Other: _____

Are any of the following additional barriers important for you? If so, try some of the strategies listed here or invent your own.

Weather conditions

_____ Develop a set of regular activities that are always available regardless of weather (indoor cycling, aerobic dance, indoor swimming, calisthenics, stair climbing, rope skipping, mall walking, dancing, gymnasium games, etc.).

_____ Look on outdoor activities that depend on weather conditions (cross-country skiing, outdoor swimming, outdoor tennis, etc.) as "bonuses"—extra activities possible when weather and circumstances permit.

_____ Other: _____

Travel

_____ Put a jump rope in your suitcase and jump rope.

_____ Walk the halls and climb the stairs in hotels.

_____ Stay in places with swimming pools or exercise facilities.

_____ Join the YMCA or YWCA (ask about reciprocal membership agreement).

_____ Visit the local shopping mall and walk for half an hour or more.

_____ Bring a small tape recorder and your favorite aerobic exercise tape.

_____ Other: _____

Family obligations

_____ Trade babysitting time with a friend, neighbor, or family member who also has small children.

_____ Exercise _with_ the kids—go for a walk together, play tag or other running games, get an aerobic dance or exercise tape for kids (there are several on the market) and exercise together. You can spend time together and still get your exercise.

_____ Hire a babysitter and look at the cost as a worthwhile investment in your physical and mental health.

_____ Jump rope, do calisthenics, ride a stationary bicycle, or use other home gymnasium equipment while the kids watch TV or when they are sleeping.

_____ Try to exercise when the kids are not around (e.g., during school hours or their nap time).

_____ Other: _____

Retirement years

_____ Look on your retirement as an opportunity to become more active instead of less. Spend more time gardening, walking the dog, and playing with your grandchildren. Children with short legs and grandparents with slower gaits are often great walking partners.

_____ Learn a new skill you've always been interested in, such as ballroom dancing, square dancing, or swimming.

_____ Now that you have the time, make regular physical activity a part of every day. Go for a walk every morning or every evening before dinner. Treat yourself to an exercycle and ride every day during a favorite TV show.

_____ Other: _____

SOURCE: CDC Division of Nutrition and Physical Activity. 1999. _Promoting Physical Activity: A Guide for Community Action._ Champaign, Ill.: Human Kinetics.

LAB 2.4 *Using a Pedometer to Track Physical Activity*

How physically active are you? Would you be more motivated to increase daily physical activity if you had an easy way to monitor your level of activity? If so, consider wearing a pedometer to track the number of steps you take each day—a rough but easily obtainable reflection of daily physical activity.

Determine Your Baseline

Wear the pedometer for a week to obtain a baseline average daily number of steps.

	M	T	W	Th	F	Sa	Su	Average
Steps								

Set Goals

Set an appropriate goal for increasing steps. The goal of 10,000 steps per day is widely recommended, but your personal goal should reflect your baseline level of steps. For example, if your current daily steps are far below 10,000, a goal of walking 2000 additional steps each day might be appropriate. If you are already close to 10,000 steps per day, choose a higher goal. Also consider the physical activity goals in the 2005 Dietary Guidelines:

- To reduce the risk of chronic disease, aim to accumulate at least 30 minutes of moderate physical activity per day.
- To help manage body weight and prevent gradual, unhealthy weight gain, engage in 60 minutes of moderate-to-vigorous-intensity activity on most days of the week.
- To sustain weight loss, engage daily in at least 60–90 minutes of moderate-intensity physical activity.

To help gauge how close you are to meeting these time-based physical activity goals, you might walk for 10 or 15 minutes while wearing your pedometer to determine how many steps correspond with the time-based goals from the Dietary Guidelines.

Once you have set your overall goal, break it down into several steps. For example, if your goal is to increase daily steps by 2000, set mini-goals of increasing daily steps by 500, allowing 2 weeks to reach each mini-goal. Smaller goals are easier to achieve and can help keep you motivated and on track. Having several interim goals also gives you the opportunity to reward yourself more frequently. Note your goals below:

Mini-goal 1: _____ Target date: _____ Reward: _____

Mini-goal 2: _____ Target date: _____ Reward: _____

Mini-goal 3: _____ Target date: _____ Reward: _____

Overall goal: _____ Target date: _____ Reward: _____

Develop Strategies for Increasing Steps

What can you do to become more active? Your text includes a variety of suggestions, including walking when you do errands, getting off one stop down the line from your destination on public transportation, parking an extra block or two away from your destination, and doing at least one chore every day that requires physical activity. If weather or neighborhood safety is an issue, look for alternative locations to walk. For example, find an indoor gym or shopping mall or even a long hallway. Check out locations that are near or on the way to your campus, workplace, or residence. If you think walking indoors will be dull, walk with friends or family members or wear headphones (if safe) and listen to music or books on tape.

Are there any days of the week for which your baseline steps are particularly low and/or it will be especially difficult because of your schedule to increase your number of steps? Be sure to develop specific strategies for difficult situations.

Below, list at least five strategies for increasing daily steps:

Track Your Progress

Based on the goals you set, fill in your goal portion of the progress chart with your target average daily steps for each week. Then wear your pedometer every day and note your total daily steps. Track your progress toward each mini-goal and your final goal. Every few weeks, stop and evaluate your progress. If needed, adjust your plan and develop additional strategies for increasing steps. In addition to the chart in this worksheet, you might also want to graph your daily steps to provide a visual reminder of how you are progressing toward your goals. Make as many copies of this chart as you need.

Week	Goal	M	Tu	W	Th	F	Sa	Su	Average
1									
2									
3									
4									

Progress Checkup

How close are you to meeting your goal? How do you feel about your program and your progress?

If needed, describe changes to your plan and additional strategies for increasing steps:

Week	Goal	M	Tu	W	Th	F	Sa	Su	Average
5									
6									
7									
8									

Progress Checkup

How close are you to meeting your goal? How do you feel about your program and your progress?

If needed, describe changes to your plan and additional strategies for increasing steps:

Week	Goal	M	Tu	W	Th	F	Sa	Su	Average
9									
10									
11									
12									

Progress Checkup

How close are you to meeting your goal? How do you feel about your program and your progress?

If needed, describe changes to your plan and additional strategies for increasing steps:

Looking **AHEAD**

After reading this chapter, you should be able to

- Describe how the body produces the energy it needs for exercise
- List the major effects and benefits of cardiorespiratory endurance exercise
- Explain how cardiorespiratory endurance is measured and assessed
- Describe how frequency, intensity, time (duration), and type of exercise affect the development of cardiorespiratory endurance
- Explain the best ways to prevent and treat common exercise injuries

Cardiorespiratory Endurance

Test Your **Knowledge**

1. **Compared to sedentary people, those who engage in regular moderate endurance exercise are likely to**
   a. have fewer colds.
   b. be less anxious and depressed.
   c. fall asleep more quickly and sleep better.
   d. be more alert and creative.

2. **About what percentage of home exercise equipment purchased in the past five years is still in use?**
   a. 25%
   b. 50%
   c. 75%

3. **During an effective 30-minute cardiorespiratory endurance workout, you should lose 1–2 pounds.**
   True or false?

ANSWERS

1. ALL FOUR. Endurance exercise has many immediate benefits that affect all the dimensions of wellness and improve overall quality of life.

2. A. Before you buy a piece of equipment, make sure that it will help you achieve your fitness goals, that you enjoy using it regularly, and that it functions as promised.

3. FALSE. Any weight loss during an exercise session is due to fluid loss that needs to be replaced to prevent dehydration and enhance performance. It is best to drink enough during exercise to match fluid loss in sweat (usually about 6–12 ounces every 15–20 minutes of exercise); weigh yourself before and after a workout to check if you are drinking enough.

VW *Fit and Well* **Online Learning Center**   www.mhhe.com/fahey

Visit the *Fit and Well* Online Learning Center for study aids, online labs, additional information about cardiorespiratory endurance, links, Internet activities that explore the development of cardiorespiratory fitness, consumer resources, and much more.

C ardiorespiratory endurance—the ability of the body to perform prolonged, large-muscle, dynamic exercise at moderate-to-high levels of intensity—is a key health-related component of fitness. As explained in Chapter 2, a healthy cardiorespiratory system is essential to high levels of fitness and wellness.

This chapter reviews the short- and long-term effects and benefits of cardiorespiratory endurance exercise. It then describes several tests that are commonly used to assess cardiorespiratory fitness. Finally, it provides guidelines for creating your own cardiorespiratory endurance program, one that is geared to your current level of fitness and built around activities you enjoy.

BASIC PHYSIOLOGY OF CARDIORESPIRATORY ENDURANCE EXERCISE

A basic understanding of the body processes involved in cardiorespiratory endurance exercise can help you design a safe and effective fitness program. In this section, we'll take a brief look at how the cardiorespiratory system functions and how the body produces the energy it needs to respond to the challenge of physical activity.

The Cardiorespiratory System

The cardiorespiratory system picks up and transports oxygen, nutrients, and other key substances to the organs and tissues that need them; it also picks up waste products and carries them to where they can be used or expelled. The cardiorespiratory system consists of the heart, the blood vessels, and the respiratory system (Figure 3.1).

The Heart   The heart is a four-chambered, fist-sized muscle located just beneath the ribs under the sternum (breastbone). Its role is to pump oxygen-poor blood to the lungs and oxygenated (oxygen-rich) blood to the rest of the body. Blood actually travels through two separate circulatory systems: The right side of the heart pumps blood to the lungs in what is called **pulmonary circulation,** and the left side pumps blood through the rest of the body in **systemic circulation.**

Waste-carrying, oxygen-poor blood enters the right upper chamber, or **atrium,** of the heart through the **venae cavae,** the largest veins in the body (Figure 3.2). As the right atrium fills, it contracts and pumps blood into the right lower chamber, or **ventricle,** which, when it contracts, pumps blood through the pulmonary artery into the lungs. There, blood picks up oxygen and discards carbon dioxide. Cleaned, oxygenated blood then flows from the lungs through the pulmonary veins into the left atrium. As this chamber fills, it contracts and pumps

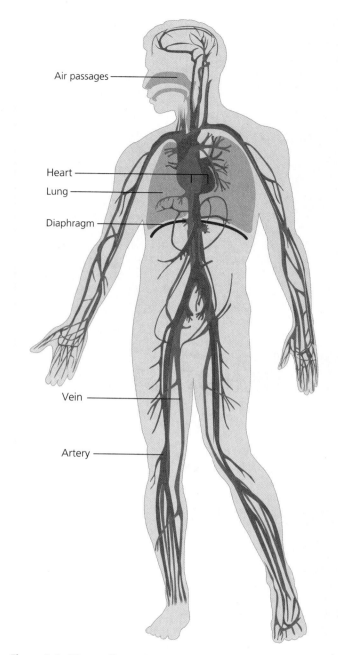

Figure 3.1   The cardiorespiratory system.

blood into the powerful left ventricle, which pumps it through the **aorta,** the body's largest artery, to be fed into the rest of the body's blood vessels.

The period of the heart's contraction is called **systole;** the period of relaxation is called **diastole.** During systole, the atria contract first, pumping blood into the ventricles; a fraction of a second later, the ventricles contract, pumping blood to the lungs and the body. During diastole, blood flows into the heart. **Blood pressure,** the force exerted by blood on the walls of the blood vessels, is created by the pumping action of the heart; blood pressure is greater during systole than

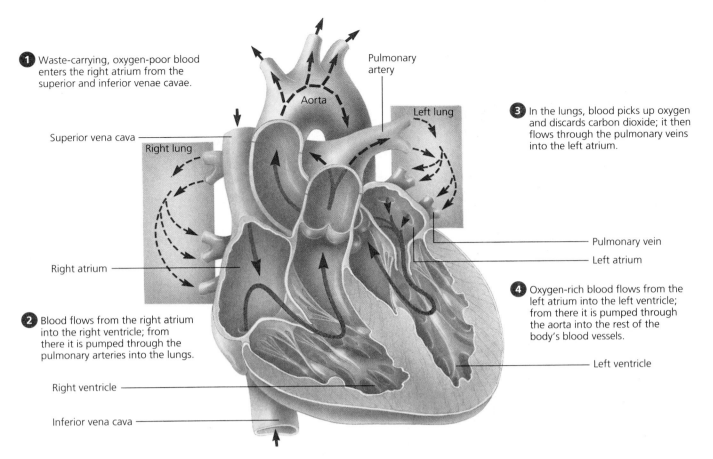

1 Waste-carrying, oxygen-poor blood enters the right atrium from the superior and inferior venae cavae.

Pulmonary artery

Aorta

Left lung

3 In the lungs, blood picks up oxygen and discards carbon dioxide; it then flows through the pulmonary veins into the left atrium.

Superior vena cava

Right lung

Right atrium

Pulmonary vein

Left atrium

4 Oxygen-rich blood flows from the left atrium into the left ventricle; from there it is pumped through the aorta into the rest of the body's blood vessels.

2 Blood flows from the right atrium into the right ventricle; from there it is pumped through the pulmonary arteries into the lungs.

Right ventricle

Left ventricle

Inferior vena cava

Figure 3.2   Circulation in the heart.

during diastole. A person weighing 150 pounds has about 5 quarts of blood, which are circulated about once every minute.

The heartbeat—the split-second sequence of contractions of the heart's four chambers—is controlled by nerve impulses. These signals originate in a bundle of specialized cells in the right atrium called the pacemaker or sinoatrial (SA) node. Unless it is speeded up or slowed down by the brain in response to such stimuli as danger or the tissues' need for more oxygen, the heart produces nerve impulses at a steady rate.

The Blood Vessels   Blood vessels are classified by size and function. **Veins** carry blood to the heart; **arteries** carry it away from the heart. Veins have thin walls, but arteries have thick elastic walls that enable them to expand and relax with the volume of blood being pumped through them. After leaving the heart, the aorta branches into smaller and smaller vessels. The smallest arteries branch still further into **capillaries,** tiny vessels only one cell thick. The capillaries deliver oxygen and nutrient-rich blood to the tissues and pass on oxygen-poor, waste-carrying blood. From the capillaries, this blood empties into small veins (venules) and then into larger veins that return it to the heart to repeat the cycle.

Terms

pulmonary circulation The part of the circulatory system that moves blood between the heart and the lungs; controlled by the right side of the heart.

systemic circulation The part of the circulatory system that moves blood between the heart and the rest of the body; controlled by the left side of the heart.

atria The two upper chambers of the heart in which blood collects before passing to the ventricles; also called *auricles.*

venae cavae The large veins through which blood is returned to the right atrium of the heart.

ventricles The two lower chambers of the heart from which blood flows through arteries to the lungs and other parts of the body.

aorta The large artery that receives blood from the left ventricle and distributes it to the body.

systole Contraction of the heart.

diastole Relaxation of the heart.

blood pressure The force exerted by the blood on the walls of the blood vessels; created by the pumping action of the heart. Blood pressure increases during systole and decreases during diastole.

veins Vessels that carry blood to the heart.

arteries Vessels that carry blood away from the heart.

capillaries Very small blood vessels that distribute blood to all parts of the body.

Blood pumped through the heart doesn't reach the cells of the heart, so the organ has its own network of arteries, veins, and capillaries. Two large vessels, the right and left coronary arteries, branch off the aorta and supply the heart muscle with oxygenated blood. Blockage of a coronary artery is a leading cause of heart attacks (see Chapter 11).

The Respiratory System The **respiratory system** supplies oxygen to the body and carries off carbon dioxide, a waste product of body processes. Air passes in and out of the lungs as a result of pressure changes brought about by the contraction and relaxation of the diaphragm and rib muscles; the lungs expand and contract about 12–20 times a minute. As air is inhaled, it passes through the nasal passages, the throat, larynx, trachea (windpipe), and bronchi into the lungs. The lungs consist of many branching tubes that end in tiny, thin-walled air sacs called **alveoli.**

Carbon dioxide and oxygen are exchanged between alveoli and capillaries in the lungs. Carbon dioxide passes from blood cells into the alveoli, where it is carried up and out of the lungs (exhaled). Oxygen from inhaled air is passed from the alveoli into blood cells; these oxygen-rich blood cells then return to the heart and are pumped throughout the body. Oxygen is an important component of the body's energy-producing system, so the cardiorespiratory system's ability to pick up and deliver oxygen is critical for the functioning of the body.

The Cardiorespiratory System at Rest and During Exercise At rest and during light activity, the cardiorespiratory system functions at a fairly steady pace. Your heart beats at a rate of about 50–90 beats per minute, and you take about 12–20 breaths per minute. A typical resting blood pressure in a healthy adult, measured in millimeters of mercury, is 110 systolic and 70 diastolic (110/70); as described earlier, blood pressure is higher when the heart contracts (systole) than when the heart relaxes (diastole).

During exercise, the demands on the cardiorespiratory system increase. Body cells, particularly working muscles, need to obtain more oxygen and fuel and to eliminate more waste products. In order to meet this increased demand, your heart rate increases, up to 170–210 beats per minute during intense exercise; the heart also pumps out more blood with each beat (stroke volume). The combination of faster heart rate and greater stroke volume means the heart pumps and circulates more blood per minute—a **cardiac output** of 20 or more quarts per minute, compared to about 5 quarts per minute at rest. Blood flow also changes: At rest, about 15–20% of blood is distributed to the skeletal muscles; during exercise, as much as 85–90% may be delivered to working muscles. Systolic blood pressure increases, while diastolic pressure holds steady or declines slightly; a typical exercise blood pressure might be 175/65. To oxygenate this increased blood flow, you will take deeper breaths and breathe more

quickly, up to 40–60 breaths per minute. All of these changes are controlled and coordinated by special centers in the brain, which use the nervous system and chemical messengers to control the process.

Later in this chapter you'll learn more about the short- and long-term effects of exercise on the body.

Energy Production

Metabolism is the sum of all the chemical processes necessary to maintain the body. Energy is required to fuel vital body functions—to build and break down tissue, contract muscles, conduct nerve impulses, regulate body temperature, and so on. The rate at which your body uses energy—its metabolic rate—depends on your level of activity. At rest, you have a low metabolic rate; if you stand up and begin to walk, your metabolic rate increases. If you jog, your metabolic rate may increase more than 800% above its resting level. Olympic-caliber distance runners can increase their metabolic rate by a whopping 2000% or more.

Energy from Food The body converts chemical energy from food into substances that cells can use as fuel. These fuels can be used immediately or stored for later use. The body's ability to store fuel is critical, because if all the energy from food were released immediately, much of it would be wasted.

The three classes of energy-containing nutrients in food are carbohydrates, fats, and proteins. During digestion, most carbohydrates are broken down into the simple sugar **glucose.** Some glucose remains circulating in the blood ("blood sugar"), where it can be used as a quick source of fuel to produce energy. Glucose may also be converted to **glycogen** and stored in the liver, muscles, and kidneys. If glycogen stores are full and the body's immediate need for energy is met, the remaining glucose is converted to fat and stored in the body's fatty tissues. Excess energy from dietary fat is also stored as body fat. Protein in the diet is used primarily to build new tissue, but it can be broken down for energy or incorporated into fat stores. Glucose, glycogen, and fat are important fuels for the production of energy in the cells; protein is a significant energy source only when other fuels are lacking. (See Chapter 8 for more on the roles of carbohydrate, fat, and protein in the body.)

ATP: The Energy "Currency" of Cells The basic form of energy used by cells is **adenosine triphosphate,** or **ATP.** When a cell needs energy, it breaks down ATP, a process that releases energy in the only form the cell can use directly. Cells store a small amount of ATP; when they need more, they create it through chemical reactions that utilize the body's stored fuels—glucose, glycogen, and fat. When you exercise, your cells need to produce more energy. Consequently, your body mobilizes its stores of fuel to increase ATP production.

| Table 3.1 | Characteristics of the Body's Energy Systems |

	Energy System*		
	Immediate	**Nonoxidative**	**Oxidative**
Duration of activity for which system predominates	0–10 seconds	10 seconds–2 minutes	>2 minutes
Intensity of activity for which system predominates	High	High	Low to moderately high
Rate of ATP production	Immediate, very rapid	Rapid	Slower, but prolonged
Fuel	Adenosine triphosphate (ATP), creatine phosphate (CP)	Muscle stores of glycogen and glucose	Body stores of glycogen, glucose, fat, and protein
Oxygen used?	No	No	Yes
Sample activities	Weight lifting, picking up a bag of groceries	400-meter run, running up several flights of stairs	1500-meter run, 30-minute walk, standing in line for a long time

*For most activities, all three systems contribute to energy production; the duration and intensity of the activity determine which system predominates.

SOURCE: Adapted from Brooks, G. A., et. al. 2005. *Exercise Physiology: Human Bioenergetics and its Applications,* 4th ed. New York: McGraw-Hill. Copyright © 2005 The McGraw-Hill Companies. Reproduced with permission of The McGraw-Hill Companies.

Exercise and the Three Energy Systems

The muscles in your body use three energy systems to create ATP and fuel cellular activity. These systems use different fuels and chemical processes and perform different, specific functions during exercise (Table 3.1). The three energy systems work together during all forms of exercise, but one or two are dominant depending on the duration and intensity of activity.

The Immediate Energy System
The **immediate ("explosive") energy system** provides energy rapidly but for only a short period of time. It is used to fuel activities that last for about 10 or fewer seconds—examples in sports include weight lifting and shot-putting; examples in daily life include rising from a chair or picking up a bag of groceries. The components of this energy system include existing cellular ATP stores and creatine phosphate (CP), a chemical that cells can use to make ATP. CP levels are depleted rapidly during exercise, so the maximum capacity of this energy system is reached within a few seconds. Cells must then switch to the other energy systems to restore levels of ATP and CP. (Without adequate ATP, muscles will stiffen and become unusable.)

The Nonoxidative Energy System
The **nonoxidative (anaerobic) energy system** is used at the start of an exercise session and for high-intensity activities lasting for about 10 seconds to 2 minutes, such as the 400-meter run. During daily activities, this system may be called on to help you run to catch a bus or dash up several flights of

stairs. The nonoxidative energy system creates ATP by breaking down glucose and glycogen. This system doesn't require oxygen, which is why it is sometimes referred to as the **anaerobic** system. The capacity of this system to produce energy is limited, but it can generate a great deal

Terms

respiratory system The lungs, air passages, and breathing muscles; supplies oxygen to the body and carries off carbon dioxide.

alveoli Tiny air sacs in the lungs through whose walls gases such as oxygen and carbon dioxide diffuse in and out of blood.

cardiac output The amount of blood pumped by the heart each minute; a function of heart rate and stroke volume (the amount of blood pumped during each beat).

glucose A simple sugar that circulates in the blood and can be used by cells to fuel adenosine triphosphate (ATP) production.

glycogen A complex carbohydrate stored principally in the liver and skeletal muscles; the major fuel source during most forms of intense exercise. Glycogen is the storage form of glucose.

adenosine triphosphate (ATP) Energy source for cellular processes.

immediate ("explosive") energy system Energy system that supplies energy to muscle cells through the breakdown of cellular stores of ATP and creatine phosphate (CP).

nonoxidative (anaerobic) energy system Energy system that supplies energy to muscle cells through the breakdown of muscle stores of glucose and glycogen; also called the *anaerobic system* or the *lactic acid system* because chemical reactions take place without oxygen and produce lactic acid.

anaerobic Occurring in the absence of oxygen.

of ATP in a short period of time. For this reason, it is the most important energy system for very intense exercise.

There are two key limiting factors for the nonoxidative energy system. First, the body's supply of glucose and glycogen is limited. If these are depleted, a person may experience fatigue and dizziness, and judgment may be impaired. (The brain and nervous system rely on carbohydrates as fuel and must have a continuous supply to function properly.) Second, the nonoxidative system results in the production of **lactic acid.** Although lactic acid is an important fuel for the body, it releases substances called hydrogen ions that are thought to interfere with metabolism and muscle contraction, thereby causing fatigue. During heavy exercise, such as sprinting, the body produces large amounts of lactic acid and hydrogen ions, and muscles become fatigued rapidly. Fortunately, exercise training increases the body's ability to cope with these substances.

The Oxidative Energy System The **oxidative (aerobic) energy system** is used during any physical activity that lasts longer than about 2 minutes, such as distance running, swimming, hiking, or even standing in line for a long time. The oxidative system requires oxygen to generate ATP, which is why it is considered an **aerobic** system. The oxidative system cannot produce energy as quickly as the other two systems, but it can supply energy for much longer periods of time. It provides energy during most daily activities.

In the oxidative energy system, ATP production takes place in cellular structures called **mitochondria.** Because mitochondria can use carbohydrates (glucose and glycogen) or fats to produce ATP, the body's stores of fuel for this system are much greater than those for the other two energy systems. The actual fuel used depends on the intensity and duration of exercise and on the fitness status of the individual. Carbohydrates are favored during more intense exercise (over 65% of maximum capacity);

fats, for mild, low-intensity activities. During a prolonged exercise session, carbohydrates are the predominant fuel at the start of the workout, but fat utilization increases over time. Fit individuals use a greater proportion of fat as fuel because increased fitness allows people to do activities at lower intensities. This is an important adaptation because glycogen depletion is one of the limiting factors for the oxidative energy system. Thus, by being able to use more fat as fuel, a fit individual can exercise for a longer time before glycogen is depleted and muscles become fatigued.

Oxygen is another limiting factor. The oxygen requirement of this energy system is proportional to the intensity of exercise—as intensity increases, so does oxygen consumption. There is a limit to the body's ability to increase the transport and use of oxygen; this limit is referred to as **maximal oxygen consumption,** or $\dot{V}O_{2max}$. $\dot{V}O_{2max}$ is influenced by genetics, fitness status (power-generating capacity and fatigue resistance), gender, and age. It depends on many factors, including the capacity of blood to carry oxygen, the rate at which oxygen is transported to the tissues, and the amount of oxygen that cells extract from the blood. $\dot{V}O_{2max}$ determines how intensely a person can perform endurance exercise and for how long, and it is considered the best overall measure of the capacity of the cardiorespiratory system. (The assessment tests described later in the chapter are designed to help you predict your $\dot{V}O_{2max}$).

The Energy Systems in Combination Your body typically uses all three energy systems when you exercise. The intensity and duration of the activity determine which system predominates. For example, when you play tennis, you use the immediate energy system when hitting the ball, but you replenish cellular energy stores using the nonoxidative and oxidative systems. When cycling, the oxidative system predominates. However, if you must suddenly exercise intensely—ride up a steep hill, for example—the other systems become important because the oxidative system is unable to supply ATP fast enough to sustain high-intensity effort.

Physical Fitness and Energy Production Physically fit people can increase their metabolic rate substantially, generating the energy needed for powerful or sustained exercise. People who are not fit cannot respond to exercise in the same way. Their bodies are less capable of delivering oxygen and fuel to exercising muscles; they can't burn as many calories during or after exercise; and they are less able to cope with lactic acid and other substances produced during intense physical activity that contribute to fatigue. Because of this, they become fatigued more rapidly—their legs hurt and they breathe heavily walking up a flight of stairs, for example. Regular physical training can substantially improve the body's ability to produce energy and meet the challenges of increased physical activity.

Terms

lactic acid A metabolic acid resulting from the metabolism of glucose and glycogen; an important source of fuel for many tissues of the body, its accumulation may produce fatigue.

oxidative (aerobic) energy system Energy system that supplies energy to cells through the breakdown of glucose, glycogen, fats, and amino acids; also called the *aerobic system* because chemical reactions require oxygen.

aerobic Dependent on the presence of oxygen.

mitochondria Intracellular structures containing enzymes used in the chemical reactions that convert the energy in food to a form the body can use.

maximal oxygen consumption ($\dot{V}O_{2max}$) The highest rate of oxygen consumption an individual is capable of during maximum physical effort, reflecting the body's ability to transport and use oxygen; measured in milliliters used per minute per kilogram of body weight.

For many sports, one energy system will be most important. For weight lifters, for example, it is the immediate energy system; for sprinters, the nonoxidative system; and for endurance runners, the oxidative system. In designing an exercise program, focus on the energy system most important to your goals. Because improving the functioning of the cardiorespiratory system is critical to overall wellness, endurance exercise that utilizes the oxidative energy system—activities performed at moderate-to-high intensities for a prolonged duration—is a key component of any health-related fitness program.

BENEFITS OF CARDIORESPIRATORY ENDURANCE EXERCISE

Cardiorespiratory endurance exercise helps the body become more efficient and better able to cope with physical challenges. It also lowers risk for many chronic diseases. Let's take a closer look at the physiological adaptations and long-term benefits of regular endurance exercise.

Improved Cardiorespiratory Functioning

At rest, a healthy cardiorespiratory system has little difficulty keeping pace with the body's need for oxygen, fuel, and waste removal. During exercise, however, demands on the system increase dramatically as the metabolic rate goes up. The principal cardiorespiratory responses to exercise include the following:

- Increased cardiac output and blood pressure. More blood is pumped by the heart each minute because both heart rate and stroke volume (the amount of blood pumped with each beat) go up. Increased cardiac output and blood pressure speed the delivery of oxygen and fuel and the removal of waste products.

- Increased ventilation (rate and depth of breathing).

- Increased blood flow to active skeletal muscles and to the heart; constant or slightly increased blood flow to the brain. The body controls blood pressure and blood flow by adjusting cardiac output and regulating the size of the blood vessels feeding different tissues.

- Increased blood flow to the skin and increased sweating. The chemical reactions that produce energy for exercise release heat, which must be dissipated to maintain a safe body temperature.

- Improved function of the cells lining the blood vessels (the endothelium), resulting in better blood flow and blood pressure control. These cells release the chemical nitric oxide, which affects energy level, blood pressure, sexual health, and breathing control.

- Decreased blood flow to the stomach, intestines, liver, and kidneys, resulting in reduced activity in the gastrointestinal tract and reduced urine output.

Exercise offers both long-term health benefits and immediate pleasures. Many popular sports and activities develop cardiorespiratory endurance.

All of these changes help the body respond to the challenge of exercise in the short term. When performed regularly, endurance exercise also causes more permanent adaptations. It improves the functioning of the heart, the ability of the cardiorespiratory system to carry oxygen to the body's tissues, and the capacity of the cells to take up and use oxygen. These improvements reduce the effort required to carry out everyday activities and make the body better able to respond to physical challenges.

Endurance training enhances the health of the heart by maintaining or increasing its blood and oxygen supply, decreasing work and oxygen demand of the heart, and increasing the function of the heart muscle. The trained heart is more efficient and subject to less stress. It pumps more blood per beat, so heart rate is lower at rest and during exercise. The resting heart rate of a fit person is often 10–20 beats per minute lower than that of an unfit person; this translates into as many as 10 million fewer beats in the course of 1 year. Improved heart efficiency results because endurance training improves heart contraction strength, increases heart cavity size (in young adults), and increases blood volume so that the heart pushes more blood into the circulation system during each of its contractions. Training also tends to reduce blood pressure, so the heart does not have to work as hard when it contracts.

Improved Cellular Metabolism

Regular endurance exercise also improves metabolism at the cellular level. It increases the number of capillaries in the muscles so that they can be supplied with more oxygen and fuel and can more quickly eliminate waste products. Greater capillary density helps heal injuries more quickly and reduces muscle aches. Endurance exercise also trains the muscles to make the most of available oxygen and fuel so that they work more efficiently. Exercise increases the size and number of mitochondria in muscle cells, thereby increasing the energy capacity of the cells. Endurance training also helps in energy production by preventing glycogen depletion and increasing the muscles' ability to use lactic acid and fat as fuels.

Fitness programs that best develop metabolic efficiency include both long-duration, moderately intense endurance exercise and brief periods of more intense effort. For example, climbing a small hill while jogging or cycling introduces the kind of intense exercise that leads to more efficient use of lactic acid and fats.

Regular exercise may also help protect your cells from chemical damage. Many scientists believe that aging and some chronic diseases are linked to cellular damage caused by **free radicals.** Training activates antioxidant enzymes that prevent free radical damage to cell structures, thereby enhancing health. (See Chapter 8 for more on free radicals and antioxidants.) Training also improves the functional stability of cells and tissues by improving the regulation of salts and fluids in the cells. This is particularly important in the heart, where instability can lead to cardiac arrest and death.

Reduced Risk of Chronic Disease

Regular endurance exercise lowers your risk of many chronic, disabling diseases. It can also help people with those diseases improve their health (see the box "Benefits of Exercise for Older Adults"). The most significant health benefits occur when someone who is sedentary becomes moderately active.

Terms

free radicals Highly reactive compounds that can damage cells by taking electrons from key cellular components such as DNA or the cell membrane; produced by normal metabolic processes and through exposure to environmental factors, including sunlight.

cardiovascular disease (CVD) Disease of the heart and blood vessels.

coronary heart disease (CHD) Heart disease caused by the buildup of fatty deposits on the arteries that supply oxygen to the heart; also called *coronary artery disease (CAD)*.

lipoproteins Substances in blood, classified according to size, density, and chemical composition, that transport fats.

Cardiovascular Disease A sedentary lifestyle is one of the six major controllable risk factors for **cardiovascular disease (CVD).** CVD is a general category that encompasses several major diseases of the heart and blood vessels, including **coronary heart disease (CHD),** the most common form of CVD; stroke; and high blood pressure (see Chapter 11). The other primary factors are smoking, unhealthy cholesterol levels, high blood pressure, diabetes, and obesity. People who are sedentary have CVD death rates significantly higher than those of fit individuals. CVD usually begins to develop in childhood and adolescence; it progresses slowly over many years before producing any symptoms. Adopting healthy habits while young can help many people prevent or delay a heart attack or other serious form of CVD.

Endurance exercise has a positive effect on levels of fats in the blood. High concentrations of blood fats such as cholesterol and triglycerides are linked to cardiovascular disease because they contribute to the formation of fatty deposits on the lining of arteries. If one of the coronary arteries, which supply oxygenated blood to the heart, becomes blocked by such a deposit, the result is a heart attack; blockage of a cerebral artery can cause a stroke.

Cholesterol is carried in the blood by **lipoproteins,** which are classified according to size and density. Cholesterol carried by low-density lipoproteins (LDLs) tends to stick to the walls of arteries. High-density lipoproteins (HDLs), on the other hand, pick up excess cholesterol in the bloodstream and carry it back to the liver for excretion from the body. High LDL levels and low HDL levels are associated with a high risk of CVD. Low LDL levels and high HDL levels are associated with lower risk. More information about cholesterol and heart disease is provided in Chapter 11. For our purposes in this chapter, it is important to know only that endurance exercise influences blood fat levels in a positive way—by increasing HDL and decreasing triglycerides (and possibly LDL)—thereby reducing the risk of CVD.

Regular exercise tends to reduce high blood pressure, a contributing factor in diseases such as CHD, stroke, kidney failure, and blindness. It further reduces the risk of CHD by enhancing the function of the cells that line the arteries (endothelial cells) and reducing inflammation. It also helps prevent obesity and type 2 diabetes, both of which contribute to CVD.

Cancer Some studies have shown a relationship between increased physical activity and a reduction in a person's risk of all types of cancer, but these findings are not conclusive. Exercise reduces the risk of colon cancer and may reduce the risk of cancers of the breast and reproductive organs in women. Exercise may decrease the risk of colon cancer by speeding the movement of food through the gastrointestinal tract (quickly eliminating potential carcinogens), enhancing immune function, and reducing blood fats. The protective mechanism in the

Research has shown that most aspects of physiological functioning peak when people are about 30 years old and then decline at a rate of about 0.5–1.0% a year. This decline in physical capacity is characterized by a decrease in maximal oxygen consumption, cardiac output, muscular strength, fat-free mass, joint mobility, and other factors. However, regular exercise can substantially alter the rate of decline in functional status, and it is associated with both longevity and improved quality of life.

Regular endurance exercise can improve maximal oxygen consumption in older people by up to 15–30%—the same degree of improvement seen in younger people. In fact, studies have shown that Masters athletes in their 70s have $\dot{V}O_{2max}$ values equivalent to those of sedentary 20-year-olds: At any age, endurance training can improve cardiorespiratory functioning, cellular metabolism, body composition, and psychological and emotional well-being. Older people who exercise regularly have better balance and greater bone density and are less likely than their sedentary peers to suffer injuries as a result of falls. Regular endurance training also substantially reduces the risk of many chronic and disabling diseases including heart disease, cancer, diabetes, osteoporosis, and dementia.

Other forms of exercise training are also beneficial for older adults. Resistance training is a safe and effective way to build strength and fat-free mass and can help people remain independent as they age. Lifting weights has also been shown to boost spirits in older people, perhaps because improvements in strength appear quickly and are easily applied to everyday tasks such as climbing stairs and carrying groceries. Flexibility exercises can improve the range of motion in joints and also help people maintain functional independence as they age.

Life expectancy in the United States has increased dramatically over the past century, and about 70% of Americans now live to at least age 70. A lifetime of regular exercise is one of the best age-proofing strategies available; however, it's never too late to start. Even in people over 80, beginning an exercise program can improve physical functioning and quality of life. Most older adults are able to participate in a program that includes moderate walking and strengthening and stretching exercises, and modified programs can be created for people with chronic conditions and other special health concerns (see Chapter 7). The wellness benefits of exercise are available to people of all ages and levels of ability.

SOURCES: Brooks, G. A., et al. 2005. *Exercise Physiology: Human Bioenergetics and Its Applications*, 4th ed. New York: McGraw-Hill. American College of Sports Medicine. 2006. *ACSM's Resource Manual for Guidelines for Exercise Testing and Prescription*, 5th ed. Philadelphia: Lippincott Williams & Wilkins.

case of reproductive system cancers is less clear, but it may be related to levels of female hormones. Physical activity during the high school and college years may be particularly important for preventing breast cancer later in life. Regular physical activity may also reduce the risk of pancreatic cancer and prostate cancer.

Type 2 Diabetes   Regular exercise helps prevent the development of type 2 diabetes, the most common form of diabetes. Exercise metabolizes (burns) excess sugar and makes cells more sensitive to the hormone insulin, which is involved in the regulation of blood sugar levels. Obesity is a key risk factor for diabetes, and exercise helps keep body fat at healthy levels. But even without fat loss, exercise improves control of blood sugar levels in many people with diabetes, and physical activity is an important part of treatment. (See Chapter 6 for more on diabetes and insulin resistance.)

Osteoporosis   A special benefit of exercise, especially for women, is protection against osteoporosis, a disease that results in loss of bone density and poor bone strength. Weight-bearing exercise helps build bone during the teens and twenties. People with denser bones can better endure the bone loss that occurs with aging. With stronger bones and muscles and better balance, fit people are less likely to experience debilitating falls and bone fractures. (See Chapter 8 for more on osteoporosis.)

Deaths from All Causes   Physically fit people have a reduced risk of dying from all causes, with the greatest benefits found for people with the highest levels of fitness (see Figure 3.3 for the results of one study). Poor fitness is a good predictor of premature death and is as important a risk factor as smoking, high blood pressure, obesity, and diabetes.

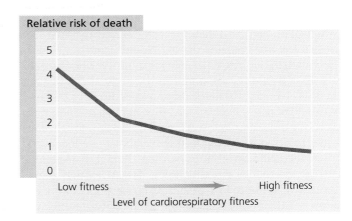

Figure 3.3   Cardiorespiratory fitness and risk of death.   People with high levels of cardiorespiratory fitness have a substantially lower risk of death than unfit individuals.   SOURCE: Myers, J., et al. 2002. Exercise capacity and mortality among men referred for exercise testing. *New England Journal of Medicine* 346 (11): 793–801.

Benefits of Cardiorespiratory Endurance Exercise   **67**

Although much of the discussion of the benefits of exercise focuses on improvements to physical wellness, many people discover that the best reason to become and stay active is the boost that regular exercise provides to the nonphysical dimensions of wellness. The following are just some of the effects of regular physical activity.

- *Reduced anxiety.* Exercise reduces symptoms of anxiety such as worry and self-doubt both in people who are anxious most of the time (trait anxiety) and in people who become anxious in response to a particular experience (state anxiety). Exercise is associated with a lower risk for panic attacks, generalized anxiety disorder, and social anxiety disorder.

- *Reduced depression and improved mood.* Exercise relieves feelings of sadness and hopelessness and can be as effective as psychotherapy in treating mild-to-moderate cases of depression. Exercise improves mood and increases feelings of well-being in both depressed and non-depressed people.

- *Improved sleep.* Regular physical activity helps people fall asleep more easily; it also improves the quality of sleep, making it more restful.

- *Reduced stress.* Exercise reduces the body's overall response to all forms of stressors and helps people deal more effectively with the stress they do experience.

- *Enhanced self-esteem, self-confidence, and self-efficacy.* Exercise can boost self-esteem and self-confidence by providing opportunities for people to succeed and excel; it also improves body image (see Chapters 6 and 9). Sticking with an exercise program increases people's belief in their ability to be active, thereby boosting self-efficacy.

- *Enhanced creativity and intellectual functioning.* In studies of college students, physically active students score higher on tests of creativity than sedentary students. Exercise improves alertness and memory in the short term, and, over time, exercise helps maintain reaction time, short-term memory, and nonverbal reasoning skills.

- *Improved work productivity.* Workers' quality of work, time-management abilities, and mental and interpersonal performance have been found to be better on days they exercise.

- *Increased opportunities for social interaction.* Exercise provides many opportunities for positive interaction with others.

How does exercise cause all these positive changes? A variety of mechanisms has been proposed. Physical activity stimulates the thought and emotion centers of the brain, producing improvements in mood and cognitive functioning. It increases alpha brain-wave activity, which is associated with a highly relaxed state. Exercise stimulates the release of chemicals such as **endorphins,** which may suppress fatigue, decrease pain, and produce euphoria; and phenylethylamine, which may boost energy, mood, and attention. Exercise decreases the secretion of hormones triggered by emotional stress and alters the levels of many other **neurotransmitters,** including serotonin, a brain chemical linked to mood.

Exercise also provides a distraction from stressful stimuli and an emotional outlet for feelings of stress, hostility, and aggression. It relaxes and warms the body, which may improve both mood and sleep. And exercise is a fun way to spend time!

The message from all this research is that exercise is a critical factor in developing all the dimensions of wellness. A lifetime of physical activity can leave you with a healthier body and a sharper, happier, more creative mind.

Better Control of Body Fat

Too much body fat is linked to a variety of health problems, including CVD, cancer, and type 2 diabetes. Healthy body composition can be difficult to achieve and maintain because a diet that contains all essential nutrients can be relatively high in calories, especially for someone who is sedentary. Excess calories are stored in the body as fat. Regular exercise increases daily calorie expenditure so that a healthy diet is less likely to lead to weight gain. Endurance exercise burns calories directly and, if intense enough, continues to do so by raising resting metabolic rate for several hours following an exercise session. A higher metabolic rate means that it is easier for a person to maintain a healthy weight or to lose weight. Exercise alone cannot ensure a healthy body composition, however; as described in Chapters 6 and 9, you will lose more weight more rapidly and keep it off longer if you decrease your calorie intake as well as boost your calorie expenditure through exercise.

Endurance exercise can also help maintain or increase metabolic rate slightly by helping people maintain a high proportion of fat-free mass. Strength training, discussed in Chapter 4, is even more effective at building muscle mass than endurance training. (Energy balance and the role of exercise in improving body composition are discussed in detail in Chapter 6.) Even if regular exercise doesn't lead to significant changes in body composition, it is still extremely beneficial for wellness and has been found to help compensate for the harmful health effects of excess body fat. People with excess body fat can significantly improve health and well-being by including moderate physical activity in their daily routine.

Improved Immune Function

Exercise can have either positive or negative effects on the immune system, the physiological processes that protect us from disease. Moderate endurance exercise boosts immune function, whereas overtraining (excessive training) depresses it. Physically fit people get fewer colds and upper respiratory tract infections than people who are not fit. Exercise affects immune function by influencing levels

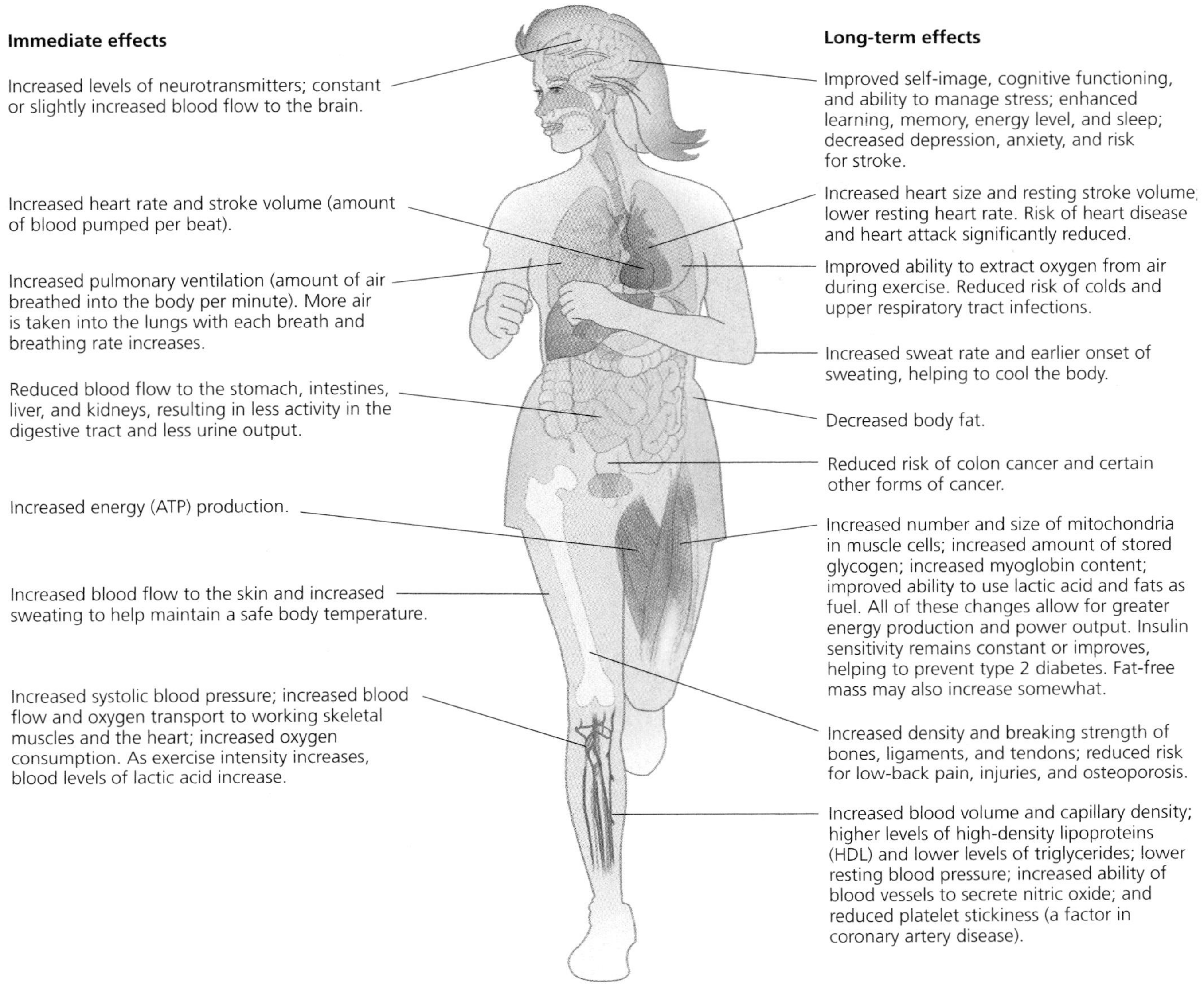

Immediate effects

Increased levels of neurotransmitters; constant or slightly increased blood flow to the brain.

Increased heart rate and stroke volume (amount of blood pumped per beat).

Increased pulmonary ventilation (amount of air breathed into the body per minute). More air is taken into the lungs with each breath and breathing rate increases.

Reduced blood flow to the stomach, intestines, liver, and kidneys, resulting in less activity in the digestive tract and less urine output.

Increased energy (ATP) production.

Increased blood flow to the skin and increased sweating to help maintain a safe body temperature.

Increased systolic blood pressure; increased blood flow and oxygen transport to working skeletal muscles and the heart; increased oxygen consumption. As exercise intensity increases, blood levels of lactic acid increase.

Long-term effects

Improved self-image, cognitive functioning, and ability to manage stress; enhanced learning, memory, energy level, and sleep; decreased depression, anxiety, and risk for stroke.

Increased heart size and resting stroke volume, lower resting heart rate. Risk of heart disease and heart attack significantly reduced.

Improved ability to extract oxygen from air during exercise. Reduced risk of colds and upper respiratory tract infections.

Increased sweat rate and earlier onset of sweating, helping to cool the body.

Decreased body fat.

Reduced risk of colon cancer and certain other forms of cancer.

Increased number and size of mitochondria in muscle cells; increased amount of stored glycogen; increased myoglobin content; improved ability to use lactic acid and fats as fuel. All of these changes allow for greater energy production and power output. Insulin sensitivity remains constant or improves, helping to prevent type 2 diabetes. Fat-free mass may also increase somewhat.

Increased density and breaking strength of bones, ligaments, and tendons; reduced risk for low-back pain, injuries, and osteoporosis.

Increased blood volume and capillary density; higher levels of high-density lipoproteins (HDL) and lower levels of triglycerides; lower resting blood pressure; increased ability of blood vessels to secrete nitric oxide; and reduced platelet stickiness (a factor in coronary artery disease).

Figure 3.4   Immediate and long-term effects of regular cardiorespiratory endurance exercise.   When endurance exercise is performed regularly, short-term changes in the body develop into more permanent adaptations; these include improved ability to exercise, reduced risk of many chronic diseases, and improved psychological and emotional well-being.

of specialized cells and chemicals involved in the immune response. In addition to regular moderate exercise, the immune system can be strengthened by eating a well-balanced diet, managing stress, and getting 7–8 hours of sleep every night.

Improved Psychological and Emotional Well-Being

Most people who participate in regular endurance exercise experience social, psychological, and emotional benefits. Performing physical activities provides proof of skill mastery and self-control, thus enhancing self-image. Recreational sports provide an opportunity to socialize, have

fun, and strive to excel. Endurance exercise lessens anxiety, depression, stress, anger, and hostility, thereby improving mood and boosting cardiovascular health. Regular exercise also improves sleep. For more on the wellness benefits of regular endurance exercise, see the box "Exercise and the Mind." Refer to Figure 3.4 for a summary of specific

Terms

endorphins Substances resembling morphine that are secreted by the brain and that decrease pain, suppress fatigue, and produce euphoria.

neurotransmitters Brain chemicals that transmit nerve impulses.

physiological benefits of cardiorespiratory endurance exercise. As cardiorespiratory fitness is developed, these benefits translate into both physical and emotional well-being and a much lower risk of chronic disease.

> MOTIVATION FOR CHANGE! Make a list of five benefits of endurance exercise that are particularly meaningful to you—reducing your risk of diabetes, for example, or being able to hike with friends. Put the list in a prominent location—on your mirror or refrigerator, for example—and use it as a motivational tool for beginning and maintaining your fitness program.

ASSESSING CARDIORESPIRATORY FITNESS

The body's ability to maintain a level of exertion (exercise) for an extended period of time is a direct reflection of cardiorespiratory fitness. It is determined by the body's ability to take up, distribute, and use oxygen during physical activity. As explained earlier, the best quantitative measure of cardiorespiratory endurance is maximal oxygen consumption, expressed as $\dot{V}O_{2max}$, the amount of oxygen the body uses when a person reaches maximum ability to supply oxygen during exercise (measured in milliliters of oxygen used per minute for each kilogram of body weight). Maximal oxygen consumption can be measured precisely in an exercise physiology laboratory through analysis of the air a person inhales and exhales when exercising to a level of exhaustion (maximum intensity). This procedure can be expensive and time-consuming, making it impractical for the average person.

Assessment Tests

Fortunately, several simple assessment tests provide reasonably good estimates of maximal oxygen consumption (within ±10–15% of the results of a laboratory test). Three methods are described here and presented in Lab 3.1: a 1-mile walk test, a 3-minute step test, and a 1.5-mile run-walk test. To assess yourself, choose one among these methods based on your access to equipment, your current physical condition, and your own preference. Don't take any of these tests without checking with your physician if you are ill or have any of the risk factors for exercise discussed in Chapter 2 and Lab 2.1. Table 3.2 lists the fitness prerequisites and cautions recommended for each test.

- *The 1-Mile Walk Test.* The 1-mile walk test estimates your level of cardiorespiratory fitness (maximal oxygen consumption) based on the amount of time it takes you to complete 1 mile of brisk walking and your exercise heart rate at the end of your walk. A fast time and a low heart rate indicate a high level of cardiorespiratory endurance.

- *The 3-Minute Step Test.* The rate at which the pulse returns to normal after exercise is also a good measure of cardiorespiratory capacity; heart rate remains lower and recovers faster in people who are more physically fit. For the step test, you step continually at a steady rate and then monitor your heart rate during recovery.

- *The 1.5-Mile Run-Walk Test.* Oxygen consumption increases with speed in distance running, so a fast time on this test indicates high maximal oxygen consumption.

Additional assessments for cardiorespiratory fitness can be found on the *Fit and Well* Online Learning Center; these include cycle ergometer and swimming tests and a distance test for people who use wheelchairs.

Table 3.2	Fitness Prerequisites and Cautions for the Cardiorespiratory Endurance Assessment Tests

Note: The conditions for exercise safety given in Chapter 2 apply to all fitness assessment tests. If you answered yes to any question on the PAR-Q in Lab 2.1, see your physician before taking any assessment test. If you experience any unusual symptoms while taking a test, stop exercising and discuss your condition with your instructor.

Test	Fitness Prerequisites/Cautions
1-mile walk test	Recommended for anyone who meets the criteria for safe exercise. Can be used by individuals who cannot perform other tests because of low fitness level or injury.
3-minute step test	If you suffer from joint problems in your ankles, knees, or hips or you are significantly overweight, check with your physician before taking this test. People with balance problems or for whom a fall would be particularly dangerous, including older adults and pregnant women, should use special caution or avoid this test.
1.5-mile run-walk test	Recommended for people who are healthy and at least moderately active. If you have been sedentary, you should participate in a 4- to 8-week walk-run program before taking the test. Don't take this test in extremely hot or cold weather if you aren't used to exercising under those conditions.

A pulse count can be used to determine exercise heart rate. The pulse can be taken at the carotid artery in the neck (left) or at the radial artery in the wrist (right).

Monitoring Your Heart Rate

Each time your heart beats, it pumps blood into your arteries; this surge of blood causes a pulse that you can feel by holding your fingers against an artery. Counting your pulse to determine your exercise heart rate is a key part of most assessment tests for maximal oxygen consumption. Heart rate can also be used to monitor exercise intensity during a workout. (Intensity is described in more detail in the next section.)

The two most common sites for monitoring heart rate are the carotid artery in the neck and the radial artery in the wrist. To take your pulse, press your index and middle fingers gently on the correct site. You may have to shift position several times to find the best place to feel your pulse. Don't use your thumb to check your pulse; it has a pulse of its own that can confuse your count. Be careful not to push too hard, particularly when taking your pulse in the carotid artery (strong pressure on this artery may cause a reflex that slows the heart rate).

Heart rates are usually assessed in beats per minute (bpm). But counting your pulse for an entire minute isn't practical when you're exercising. And because heart rate slows rapidly when you stop exercising, it can give inaccu-

rate results. It's best to do a shorter count—10 seconds—and then multiply the result by 6 to get your heart rate in beats per minute.

Interpreting Your Score

Once you've completed one or more of the assessment tests, use the table under "Rating Your Cardiovascular Fitness" at the end of Lab 3.1 to determine your current level of cardiorespiratory fitness. As you interpret your score, remember that field tests of cardiorespiratory fitness are not precise scientific measurements and do have up to a 10–15% margin of error.

You can use the assessment tests to monitor the progress of your fitness program by retesting yourself from time to time. Always compare scores for the *same* test: Your scores on different tests may vary considerably because of differences in skill and motivation and weaknesses in the tests themselves.

DEVELOPING A CARDIORESPIRATORY ENDURANCE PROGRAM

Cardiorespiratory endurance exercises are best for developing the type of fitness associated with good health, so they should serve as the focus of your exercise program. To create a successful endurance exercise program, you must set realistic goals; set your starting frequency, intensity, and time (duration) of exercise at appropriate levels; choose suitable activities; remember to warm up and cool down; and adjust your program as your fitness improves.

MOTIVATION FOR CHANGE!   Are you having trouble getting started on a fitness program? Do you want to exercise more but find you just can't fit it into your day? Listen carefully to what you're telling yourself, perhaps by writing down your self-talk about exercise for a few days. Are you rationalizing, making excuses, procrastinating, or avoiding responsibility for your choices? For example, "I'm too busy with my classes this semester to fit exercise into my schedule," or "Right now I want to spend all my free time with my new girlfriend/boyfriend," or "I'll try to start running once the weather gets warmer." Can you think of ways to counter these statements and change your exercise habits? For example, "I see a lot of other busy people who are exercising, and I can probably do it too"; "I could ask a friend to go for a hike in the hills with me"; "I can use the exercise equipment at the gym until the weather warms up." Remember that when you make excuses, the only one who loses is you.

Setting Goals

You can use the results of cardiorespiratory fitness assessment tests to set a specific oxygen consumption goal for your cardiorespiratory endurance program. Your goal should be high enough to ensure a healthy cardiorespiratory system, but not so high that it will be impossible to achieve. Scores in the fair and good ranges for maximal oxygen consumption suggest good fitness; scores in the excellent and superior ranges indicate a high standard of physical performance.

Through endurance training, an individual may be able to improve maximal oxygen consumption ($\dot{V}O_{2max}$) by about 10–30%. The amount of improvement possible depends on age, health status, and initial fitness level; people who start at a very low fitness level can improve by a greater percentage than elite athletes because the latter are already at a much higher fitness level, a level that may approach their genetic physical limits. If you are tracking $\dot{V}O_{2max}$ using the field tests described in this chapter, you may be able to increase your score by more than 30% due to improvements in other physical factors, such as muscle power, which can affect your performance on the tests.

Another physical factor you can track to monitor progress is resting heart rate—your heart rate at complete rest, measured in the morning before you get out of bed and move around. Resting heart rate may decrease by as much as 10–15 beats per minute in response to endurance training. Changes in resting heart rate may be noticeable after only about 4–6 weeks of training.

You may want to set other types of goals for your fitness program. For example, if you walk, jog, or cycle as part of your fitness program, you may want to set a time or distance goal—working up to walking 5 miles in one session, completing a 4-mile run in 28 minutes, or cycling a total of 35 miles per week. A more modest goal might be to achieve the Surgeon General's minimum activity level of doing at least 30 minutes of moderate activity on most days. Although it's best to base your program on measurable goals, you may also want to set more qualitative goals, such as becoming more energetic, sleeping better, and improving the fit of your clothes.

Terms

Vw

target heart rate zone The range of heart rates that should be reached and maintained during cardiorespiratory endurance exercise to obtain training effects.

heart rate reserve The difference between maximum heart rate and resting heart rate; used in one method for calculating target heart rate range.

ratings of perceived exertion (RPE) A system of monitoring exercise intensity based on assigning a number to the subjective perception of target intensity.

Applying the FITT Equation

As described in Chapter 2, you can use the acronym FITT to remember key parameters of your fitness program: frequency, intensity, time (duration), and type of activity.

Frequency of Training   To build cardiorespiratory endurance, you should exercise 3–5 days per week. Beginners should start with 3 and work up to 5 days per week. Training more than 5 days per week can lead to injury and isn't necessary for the typical person on an exercise program designed to promote wellness. (It is safe to do moderate-intensity activity such as walking and gardening every day.) Training fewer than 3 days per week makes it difficult to improve your fitness (unless exercise intensity is very high) or to use exercise to lose weight. In addition, you risk injury because your body never gets a chance to fully adapt to regular exercise training.

Intensity of Training   Intensity is the most important factor in achieving training effects. You must exercise intensely enough to stress your body so that fitness improves. Two main methods of monitoring exercise intensity are described below; choose the method that works best for you. Be sure to make adjustments in your intensity levels for environmental or individual factors. For example, on a hot and humid day or on your first day back to your program after an illness, you should decrease your intensity level.

TARGET HEART RATE ZONE   One of the best ways to monitor the intensity of cardiorespiratory endurance exercise is to measure your heart rate. It isn't necessary to exercise at your maximum heart rate to improve maximal oxygen consumption. Fitness adaptations occur at lower heart rates with a much lower risk of injury.

According to the American College of Sports Medicine, your **target heart rate zone**—rates at which you should exercise to experience cardiorespiratory benefits—is between 65% and 90% of your maximum heart rate. To calculate your target heart rate zone, follow these steps:

1. Estimate your maximum heart rate (MHR) by subtracting your age from 220, or have it measured precisely by undergoing an exercise stress test in a doctor's office, hospital, or sports medicine lab. (Note: The formula to estimate maximum heart rate carries an error of about ±10–15 beats per minute and can be very inaccurate for some people, particularly older adults and young children. If your exercise heart rate seems inaccurate—that is, exercise within your target zone seems either too easy or too difficult—then use the perceived exertion method described in the next section or have your maximum heart rate measured precisely.)

2. Multiply your MHR by 65% and 90% to calculate your target heart rate zone. (Note: Very unfit people should use 55% of MHR for their training threshold.)

For example, a 19-year-old would calculate her target heart rate zone as follows:

MHR = 220 − 19 = 201

65% training intensity = 0.65 × 201 = 131 bpm

90% training intensity = 0.90 × 201 = 181 bpm

To gain fitness benefits, the young woman in our example would have to exercise at an intensity that raises her heart rate to between 131 and 181 bpm.

An alternative method for calculating target heart rate range uses **heart rate reserve,** the difference between maximum heart rate and resting heart rate. Using this method, target heart rate is equal to resting heart rate plus between 50% (40% for very unfit people) and 85% of heart rate reserve. Although some people (particularly those with very low levels of fitness) will obtain more accurate results using this more complex method, both methods provide reasonable estimates of an appropriate target heart rate zone. Formulas for both methods of calculating target heart rate are given in Lab 3.2.

If you have been sedentary, start by exercising at the lower end of your target heart rate range (65% of maximum heart rate or 50% of heart rate reserve) for at least 4–6 weeks. Fast and significant gains in maximal oxygen consumption can be made by exercising closer to the top of the range, but you may increase your risk of injury and overtraining. You *can* achieve significant health benefits by exercising at the bottom of your target range, so don't feel pressured into exercising at an unnecessarily intense level. If you exercise at a lower intensity, you can increase the duration or frequency of training to obtain as much benefit to your health, as long as you are above the 65% training threshold. (For people with a very low initial level of fitness, a lower training intensity, 55–64% of maximum heart rate or 40–49% of heart rate reserve, may be sufficient to achieve improvements in maximal oxygen consumption, especially at the start of an exercise program. Intensities of 70–85% of maximum heart rate are appropriate for average individuals.)

By monitoring your heart rate, you will always know if you are working hard enough to improve, not hard enough, or too hard. As your program progresses and your fitness improves, you will need to jog, cycle, or walk faster in order to reach your target heart rate zone. To monitor your heart rate during exercise, count your pulse while you're still moving or immediately after you stop exercising. Count beats for 10 seconds, and then multiply that number by 6 to see if your heart rate is in your target zone. If the young woman in our example were aiming for 144 bpm, she would want a 10-second count of 24 beats. Target heart rate ranges and 10-second

| Table 3.3 | Target Heart Rate Range and 10-Second Counts |

Age (years)	Target Heart Rate Range (bpm)*	10-Second Count (beats)*
20–24	127–180	21–30
25–29	124–176	20–29
30–34	121–171	20–28
35–59	118–167	19–27
40–44	114–162	19–27
45–49	111–158	18–26
50–54	108–153	18–25
55–59	105–149	17–24
60–64	101–144	16–24
65+	97–140	16–23

*Target heart rates lower than those shown here are appropriate for individuals with a very low initial level of fitness. Ranges are based on the following formula: Target heart rate = 0.65 to 0.90 of maximum heart rate, assuming maximum heart rate = 220 − age. The heart rate range values shown here correspond to RPE values of about 12–18.

counts based on the maximum heart rate formula are shown in Table 3.3.

RATINGS OF PERCEIVED EXERTION Another way to monitor intensity is to monitor your perceived level of exertion. Repeated pulse counting during exercise can become a nuisance if it interferes with the activity. As your exercise program progresses, you will probably become familiar with the amount of exertion required to raise your heart rate to target levels. In other words, you will know how you feel when you have exercised intensely enough. If this is the case, you can use the scale of **ratings of perceived exertion (RPE)** shown in Figure 3.5 to monitor the intensity of your exercise session without checking your pulse.

To use the RPE scale, select a rating that corresponds to your subjective perception of how hard you are exercising when you are training in your target heart rate zone. If your target zone is about 135–155 bpm, exercise intensely enough to raise your heart rate to that level, and then associate a rating—for example, "somewhat hard" or "hard" (14 or 15)—with how hard you feel you are working. To reach and maintain intensity in future workouts, exercise hard enough to reach what you feel is the same level of exertion. You should periodically check your RPE against your target heart rate zone to make sure it's correct. RPE is an accurate means of monitoring exercise intensity, and you may find it easier and more convenient than pulse counting.

TALK TEST Another easy method of monitoring exercise exertion—in particular, to prevent overly intense exercise—is the *talk test.* Although your breathing rate will increase during cardiorespiratory endurance exercise, you should not work out so intensely that you

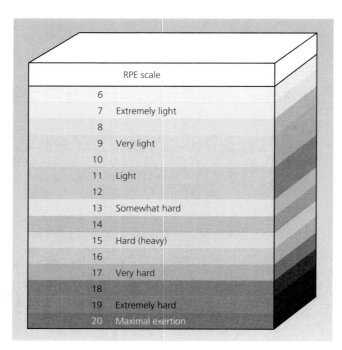

RPE scale

6	
7	Extremely light
8	
9	Very light
10	
11	Light
12	
13	Somewhat hard
14	
15	Hard (heavy)
16	
17	Very hard
18	
19	Extremely hard
20	Maximal exertion

Figure 3.5 Ratings of perceived exertion (RPE). Experienced exercisers may use this subjective scale to estimate how near they are to their target heart rate zone. The scale was developed in the 1950s by Swedish exercise physiologist Gunnar Borg and is also known as the Borg scale. SOURCE: *Psychology from Research to Practice* (1978), ed. H. L. Pick. Kluwer Academic/Plenum Publishing Corporation. With kind permission of Springer Science and Business Media and the author.

cannot speak comfortably. The talk test has been shown to be an effective gauge of intensity for many different types of activities.

Time (Duration) of Training A total duration of 20–60 minutes is recommended; exercise can take place in a single session or in multiple sessions lasting 10 or more minutes. The total duration of exercise depends on its intensity. To improve cardiorespiratory endurance during a low-to-moderate-intensity activity such as walking or slow swimming, you should exercise for 45–60 minutes. For high-intensity exercise performed at the top of your target heart rate zone, a duration of 20 minutes is sufficient. Some studies have shown that 5–10 minutes of extremely intense exercise (greater than 90% of maximal oxygen consumption) improves cardiorespiratory endurance. However, training at this intensity, particularly during high-impact activities, increases the risk of injury. Also, because of the discomfort of high-intensity exercise, you are more

Terms

synovial fluid Fluid produced within many joints that provides lubrication and nutrients for the joints.

likely to discontinue your exercise program. Longer-duration, low-to-moderate-intensity activities generally result in more gradual gains in maximal oxygen consumption. In planning your program, start with less vigorous activities and gradually increase intensity.

Type of Activity Cardiorespiratory endurance exercises include activities that involve the rhythmic use of large-muscle groups for an extended period of time, such as jogging, walking, cycling, aerobic dancing and other forms of group exercise, cross-country skiing, and swimming. Start-and-stop sports, such as tennis and racquetball, also qualify, as long as you have enough skill to play continuously and intensely enough to raise your heart rate to target levels.

Having fun is a strong motivator; select a physical activity that you enjoy, and it will be easier to stay with your program. Exercising with a friend can also be helpful as a motivator. Consider whether you prefer competitive or individual sports, or whether starting something new would be best. Other important considerations are access to facilities, expense, equipment, and the time required to achieve an adequate skill level and workout (see the box "Evaluating Home Exercise Equipment").

Warming Up and Cooling Down

It's important to warm up before every session of cardiorespiratory endurance exercise and to cool down afterward. Because the body's muscles work better when their temperature is slightly above resting level, warming up enhances performance and decreases the chance of injury. It gives the body time to redirect blood to active muscles and the heart time to adapt to increased demands. Warming up also helps spread **synovial fluid** throughout the joints, which helps protect their surfaces from injury.

As mentioned in Chapter 2, a warm-up session should include low-intensity movements similar to those in the activity that will follow. Low-intensity movements include walking slowly before beginning a brisk walk, hitting forehands and backhands before a tennis match, and running a 12-minute mile before progressing to an 8-minute one. An active warm-up of 5–10 minutes is adequate for most types of exercise. However, warm-up time will depend on your level of fitness, experience, and individual preferences.

Some people like to include stretching exercises in their warm-up. If you like to stretch before exercising, experts recommend that you stretch after the active part of your warm-up, when your body temperature has been elevated (see Chapter 5). Studies have found that stretching prior to exercise can decrease performance, so some experts even recommend that stretching be done *after* a workout.

Cooling down after exercise is important for returning the body to a nonexercising state. A cool-down

Cardiorespiratory endurance can be developed without special equipment or facilities, but if you choose to use fitness equipment, quality is an important factor. Good equipment can enhance your enjoyment of your fitness program and decrease your risk of injury. Before considering any piece of equipment, ask yourself the following questions:

• *Will the equipment help me achieve my fitness goals?* Make sure the piece of equipment you're considering works your target fitness components. Don't be fooled by outrageous advertising claims, and be sure to check the fine print of any advertisement. Exercise is not "easy" or "effortless," and it is impossible for any equipment to make you lose fat in a particular area (spot reduce). The Federal Trade Commission provides good general advice for people shopping for exercise equipment (http://www.ftc.gov).

• *Will I really use the equipment regularly?* Before you invest money in a piece of equipment, try it out for a time at a fitness center or health club. Make sure it is something you can use safely and comfortably over the long term.

• *Is the equipment well made?* Before you buy, do some research. Ask coaches and fitness instructors, and check consumer publications. If you intend to push the equipment to the limit, look for a heavy-duty model.

• *Is the equipment easy to use?* You will be more likely to use a piece of equipment regularly if it is easy to set up and use. Any instructions should be easy to follow.

• *Do I have room for the equipment?* A good treadmill or home gym may be large and require significant space to use and store. Make sure you have a place to use it that is pleasant and well ventilated and where any noise produced by the equipment will not be a problem.

• *Can I afford a quality piece of equipment?* Shop around to find the best deal; try discount stores, specialty shops, and catalogs. However, be aware of deals that seem too good to be true; an exceptionally low price may indicate poor quality. In addition, get the details on warranties, guarantees, and return policies before you buy.

The following are among the most popular types of home exercise equipment:

Treadmills: Some studies of exercise equipment have found that treadmills are the best type of home exercise equipment for developing fitness and burning calories and are more likely to be used consistently. Choose a motorized treadmill with a platform or surface that is large enough to fit your stride, stable enough to accommodate your weight, and cushioned enough to absorb the impact of your feet. The handrails should be able to support your weight if you lose your balance.

Stationary cycles: Try both upright and recumbent (reclining) models to see which type suits you best. Check to make sure the seat and handlebars of the cycle can be adjusted to comfortably fit your height and leg extension. Look for a model whose resistance can be changed easily.

Cross-country ski machines: Although learning to coordinate the movements needed to use a cross-country ski machine may take time, this type of equipment typically provides a full-body workout. Look for a model that allows separate adjustment of the lower-body sliding footpads and the upper-body rope-and-pulley device.

Stair climbers and elliptical trainers: Check to be sure that you can work the pedals securely and smoothly while maintaining good posture; machines with independent foot action usually allow a more natural rhythm. For greater durability, choose a machine with hydraulic rather than airfilled shock absorbers.

Another key piece of equipment for many fitness activities and sports is proper footwear; refer to Chapter 7 for advice on shopping for athletic shoes.

---

helps maintain blood flow to the heart and brain and redirects blood from working muscles to other areas of the body; it helps prevent a large drop in blood pressure, dizziness, and other potential cardiovascular complications. A cool-down, consisting of 5–10 minutes of reduced activity, should follow every workout to allow heart rate, breathing, and circulation to return to normal. Decrease the intensity of exercise gradually during your cool-down. For example, following a running workout, begin your cool-down by jogging at half speed for 30 seconds to a minute; then do several minutes of walking, reducing your speed slowly. A good rule of thumb is to cool down at least until your heart rate drops below 100 beats per minute. Doing stretching exercises at the end of a workout is an excellent strategy: Your muscles are warm, allowing you to stretch farther with less risk of injury; in addition, there is no danger of decreased performance.

The general pattern of a safe and successful workout for cardiorespiratory fitness is illustrated in Figure 3.6.

Building Cardiorespiratory Fitness

Building fitness is as much an art as a science. Your rate of progress will depend on your age, health status, initial level of fitness, and motivation. Your fitness improves when you overload your body. However, you must increase the intensity, frequency, and duration of exercise carefully to avoid injury and overtraining.

For the initial phase of your program, which may last anywhere from 3 to 6 weeks, exercise at the low end of your target heart rate zone. Begin with a frequency of

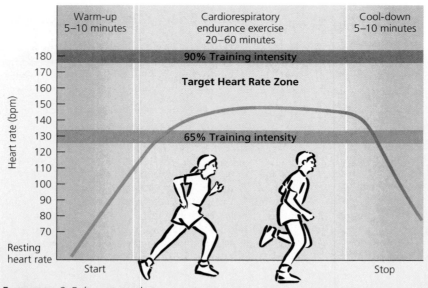

| Warm-up 5–10 minutes | Cardiorespiratory endurance exercise 20–60 minutes | Cool-down 5–10 minutes |

Figure 3.6 The FITT principle for a cardiorespiratory endurance workout. Longer-duration exercise at lower intensities can often be as beneficial for promoting health as shorter-duration, high-intensity exercise.

Frequency: 3–5 days per week

Intensity: 55/65–90% of maximum heart rate, 40/50–85% of heart rate reserve plus resting heart rate, or an RPE rating of about 12–18 (lower intensities—55–64% of maximum heart rate and 40–49% of heart rate reserve—are applicable to people who are quite unfit; for average individuals, intensities of 70–85% of maximum heart rate are appropriate)

Time (duration): 20–60 minutes (one session or multiple sessions lasting 10 or more minutes)

Type of activity: Cardiorespiratory endurance exercises, such as walking, jogging, biking, swimming, cross-country skiing, and rope skipping

3–4 days per week, and choose a duration appropriate for your fitness level: 12–15 minutes if you are very unfit, 20 minutes if you are sedentary but otherwise healthy, and 30–40 minutes if you are an experienced exerciser. Use this phase of your program to allow both your body and your schedule to adjust to your new exercise routine. Once you can exercise at the upper levels of frequency (4–5 days per week) and duration (30–40 minutes) without excessive fatigue or muscle soreness, you are ready to progress.

The next phase of your program is the improvement phase, lasting from 4 to 6 months. During this phase, slowly and gradually increase the amount of overload until you reach your target level of fitness (see the sample training progression in Table 3.4). Take care not to increase overload too quickly. It is usually best to avoid increasing intensity and duration during the same session or all three training variables in 1 week. Increasing duration in increments of 5–10 minutes every 2–3 weeks is usually appropriate. Signs of a too rapid progression in overload include muscle aches and pains, lack of usual interest in exercise, extreme fatigue, and inability to complete a workout. Keep an exercise log or training diary to help monitor your workouts and progress.

Maintaining Cardiorespiratory Fitness

You will not improve your fitness indefinitely. The more fit you become, the harder you have to work to improve. There are limits to the level of fitness you can achieve, and if you increase intensity and duration indefinitely, you are likely to become injured or overtrained. After a progression phase of 4–6 months, you may reach your goal of an acceptable level of fitness. You can then maintain fitness by continuing to exercise at the same intensity at least 3 nonconsecutive days every week. If you stop exercising, you lose your gains in fitness fairly rapidly. If you take time off for any reason, start your program again at a lower level and rebuild your fitness in a slow and systematic way.

When you reach the maintenance phase, you may want to set new goals for your program and make some adjustments to maintain your motivation. Adding variety to your program can be a helpful strategy. Engaging in multiple types of endurance activities, an approach known as **cross-training,** can help boost enjoyment and prevent some types of injuries. For example, someone who has been jogging 5 days a week may change her program so that she jogs 3 days a week, plays tennis 1 day a week, and goes for a bike ride 1 day a week.

Table 3.4	Sample Progression for an Endurance Program		
Stage/Week	Frequency (days/ week)	Intensity* (beats/ minute)	Time (duration in minutes)
Initial stage			
1	3	120–130	15–20
2	3	120–130	20–25
3	4	130–145	20–25
4	4	130–145	25–30
Improvement stage			
5–7	3–4	145–160	25–30
8–10	3–4	145–160	30–35
11–13	3–4	150–165	30–35
14–16	4–5	150–165	30–35
17–20	4–5	160–180	35–40
21–24	4–5	160–180	35–40
Maintenance stage			
25+	3–5	160–180	20–60

*The target heart rates shown here are based on calculations for a healthy 20-year-old with a resting heart rate of 60 beats per minute; the program progresses from an initial target heart rate of 50% to a maintenance range of 70–85% of heart rate reserve.

SOURCE: Adapted from American College of Sports Medicine, 2006. *ACSM's Guidelines for Exercise Testing and Prescription,* 7th ed. Philadelphia: Lippincott Williams & Wilkins. Reprinted with permission from the publisher.

MOTIVATION FOR CHANGE! Studies of college students have found that social support is a key factor influencing whether students exercise. Do your friends and family members actively support your fitness goals and program? If not, enlist their help and encouragement—it can make a big difference.

EXERCISE SAFETY AND INJURY PREVENTION

Exercising safely in a variety of environmental conditions and preventing muscle and joint injuries are two important challenges for people who engage in cardiorespiratory endurance exercise. This section provides basic exercise safety guidelines that can be applied to a variety of fitness activities; visit the Online Learning Center for more detailed information about the prevention and care of exercise injuries and safe exercise in challenging environmental conditions. Chapters 4 and 5 include additional advice specific to strength training and flexibility training.

Hot Weather and Heat Stress

Human beings depend on a relatively constant body temperature to survive. An increase (or decrease) of just a few degrees in body temperature can quickly lead to distress and even death. Exercise safety in a high-temperature environment depends on the body's ability to dissipate heat and maintain blood flow to active muscles. Heat from exercise is released through evaporation of sweat, which cools the skin and the blood circulating near the surface of the body. The hotter the weather, the more water the body loses through sweat; the more humid the weather, the less efficient the sweating mechanism is at lowering body temperature. If you lose too much water or if your body temperature rises too high, you may suffer from heat stress. People with a low level of fitness are at greater risk for problems associated with heat stress, which can include dehydration, heat cramps, heat exhaustion, and life-threatening heatstroke.

Dehydration Your body needs water to carry out many chemical reactions and to regulate body temperature. Sweating during exercise depletes your body's water supply and can lead to **dehydration** if fluids aren't replaced. Although dehydration is most common in hot weather, it can occur in even comfortable temperatures if fluid intake is insufficient.

Dehydration increases body temperature and decreases sweat rate, plasma volume, cardiac output, maximal oxygen consumption, exercise capacity, muscular strength, and stores of liver glycogen. You may begin to feel thirsty when you have a fluid deficit of about 1% of total body weight. In people who play sports such as football and tennis or who engage in distance running, fluid deficits of up to 5% are quite common. At this level of dehydration, people feel uncomfortable and may alternate between fatigue and restlessness. At higher levels of fluid deficit, loss of coordination, delirium, and death can occur.

Drinking fluids before and during exercise is important to prevent dehydration and enhance performance. Thirst receptors in the brain make you want to drink fluids, but during heavy or prolonged exercise or exercise in hot weather, thirst alone isn't a good indication of how much you need to drink. As a rule of thumb, drink at least 2 cups (16 ounces) of fluid 2 hours before exercise and then drink enough during exercise to

Terms

cross-training Alternating two or more activities to improve a single component of fitness (for example, walking 2 days per week and swimming 2 days per week to build cardiorespiratory endurance).

dehydration Excessive loss of body fluid.

To prevent dehydration and enhance performance, consume an adequate amount of fluid before and during exercise.

match fluid loss in sweat. Drink at least 1 cup of fluid for every 20–30 minutes of exercise, more in hot weather or if you sweat heavily. To determine if you're drinking enough fluid, weigh yourself before and after an exercise session—any weight loss is due to fluid loss that needs to be replaced.

There have been rare instances of athletes consuming too much water and developing hyponatremia, a condition characterized by lung congestion, muscle weakness, and nervous system problems. Hyponatremia may result from drinking too much water, too few electrolytes, or both; it is usually associated with water consumption during or after more than 4–6 hours of prolonged stressful exercise. Following the fluid guidelines presented here, including consumption of sports drinks containing electrolytes during long exercise sessions, can help prevent hyponatremia. A postexercise weight check can also help identify overconsumption of fluids—if you gain weight during a workout, you have probably consumed too much fluid.

Bring a water bottle when you exercise so you can replace your fluids when they're being depleted. For exercise sessions lasting less than 60–90 minutes, cool water is an excellent fluid replacement. For longer workouts, you might want to choose a sports drink that contains water and small amounts of electrolytes (sodium, potassium, and magnesium) and simple carbohydrates ("sugar," usually in the form of sucrose, glucose, or glucose polymers). Electrolytes, which are lost from the body in sweat, are important because they help regulate the balance of fluids in body cells and the bloodstream. The carbohydrates in typical sports drinks are rapidly digestible and can thus help maintain blood glucose levels. Choose a beverage with no more than 8 grams of simple carbohydrate per 100 milliliters. See Chapter 8 for more on diet and fluid recommendations for active people.

Heat Cramps Involuntary cramping and spasms in the muscle groups used during exercise are sometimes called **heat cramps.** While depletion of sodium and potassium from the muscles is involved with the problem, the primary cause for cramps is muscle fatigue. Children are particularly susceptible to heat cramps, but the condition can also occur in adults, even those who are fit. The best treatment for heat cramps is a combination of gentle stretching, replacement of fluid and electrolytes, and rest.

Heat Exhaustion Symptoms of **heat exhaustion** include a rapid and weak pulse, low blood pressure, faintness, profuse sweating, and, in some cases, psychological disorientation; core body temperature may be normal or slightly elevated. Heat exhaustion occurs when an insufficient amount of blood returns to the heart because so much of the body's blood volume is being directed to working muscles (for exercise) and to the skin (for cooling). Treatment for heat exhaustion includes resting in a cool area and drinking fluids. An affected individual should rest for the remainder of the day and drink plenty of fluids for the next 24 hours.

Heatstroke **Heatstroke** is a major medical emergency involving the failure of the brain's temperature regulatory center. The body does not sweat enough, and body temperature rises dramatically to extremely dangerous levels. In addition to high body temperature, symptoms can include hot skin (dry or sweaty), very high or very low blood pressure, confusion, erratic behavior, and loss of consciousness. A heatstroke victim should be cooled as rapidly as possible and immediately transported to a hospital.

Several deaths in professional sports occurred when athletes exercised intensely in hot conditions while taking supplements containing such stimulants as caffeine and ephedra. These deaths have not been positively linked to supplement use, but any supplement that can affect body temperature, fluid balance, or blood pressure is potentially risky when combined with intense exercise. (See Chapter 4 for more on supplements.)

Following a few simple principles can minimize the problems associated with exercising in the heat. To help alert people about weather conditions that could increase the risk of heat illness, the U.S. Weather Service developed the **heat index**—a measure that incorporates both temperature and relative humidity. For example, a temperature of 95 degrees combined with a relative humidity of 50% has a heat index of 107. Prolonged exposure or physical activity when the heat index is 80–90 can cause fatigue; at a heat index of 90 or above, heat cramps, heat exhaustion, and heatstroke become more likely. Reduce and avoid exercise when the heat index is 90 or above. A complete chart of heat index values can be found on the *Fit and Well* Online Learning Center. Local heat index information is available from the National Weather Service (http://www.weather.gov). Additional strategies to help avoid the risk of heat illness include the following:

- Be in good physical condition. Exercise training can help the body adapt to heat by increasing the sweat rate.

- Use caution when exercising in extreme heat or humidity (over 80°F and/or 60% humidity).

- Slow exercise or add rest breaks to maintain your prescribed target heart rate; as you become acclimatized, you can gradually increase intensity and duration.

- Exercise in the early morning or evening, when temperatures are lowest.

- Do not use supplements containing stimulants, such as ephedra, because they can promote heat illnesses.

- Drink 2 cups of fluids 2 hours before you begin exercising, and drink 4–8 ounces of fluid every 10–15 minutes during exercise (more frequently during high-intensity activities). Plan for regular water breaks. For an exercise session lasting longer than 60–90 minutes, choose a sports beverage that is cold (8–13°C; 46–55°F), low in sugar (less than 8 grams per 100 milliliters), and contains a small amount of electrolytes.

- During a period of hot weather, weigh yourself every day before exercising. If your weight has decreased by 3% or more from the previous day, don't exercise without first rehydrating.

- Avoid supplements and beverages containing stimulants like ephedra and caffeine when exercising in the heat. Do not use salt pills.

- Wear clothing that breathes, allowing air to circulate and cool the body. Wearing white or light colors will help by reflecting, rather than absorbing, heat. A hat can help keep direct sun off your face. Do not wear rubber, plastic, or other nonporous clothing. "Sauna suits" cause loss of body water, not fat, and don't improve body composition.

- Rest frequently in the shade.

- Slow down or stop if you begin to feel uncomfortable. Watch for the signs of heat disorders listed below; if they occur, act appropriately.

Problem	Symptoms	Treatment
Heat cramps	Muscle cramps, usually in the muscles most used during exercise.	Stop exercising, drink fluids, and massage or stretch cramped muscles.
Heat exhaustion	Weakness, dizziness, headache, rapid pulse, profuse sweating, pale face, normal or slightly elevated temperature.	Cool the body: Stop exercising, get out of the heat, remove excess clothing, drink cold fluids, and apply cool and/or damp towels to the body.
Heatstroke	Hot, flushed skin (may be dry or sweaty), red face, chills, shivering, disorientation, erratic behavior, high body temperature, unconsciousness, convulsions.	*Get immediate medical attention,* and try to lower body temperature. Get out of the heat, remove excess clothing, drink cold fluids, and apply cool and/or damp towels to the body or immerse it in cold water.

Preventing Heat Problems   To avoid heat-related problems, use caution when exercising in hot and humid weather. Watch for the signals of heat stress, regardless of the weather, and follow the tips in the box "Exercise in Hot Weather."

Cold Weather

In extremely cold conditions, problems can result if a person's body temperature drops or if particular parts of the body are exposed. If the body's ability to warm itself through shivering or exercise can't keep pace with heat loss, the core body temperature begins to drop. This condition, known as **hypothermia**, depresses the

Terms

heat cramps Sudden development of muscle spasms and pain associated with intense exercise in hot weather.

heat exhaustion Heat illness related to dehydration resulting from exertion in hot weather.

heatstroke A severe and often fatal heat illness produced by exposure to very high temperatures, especially when combined with intense exercise; characterized by significantly elevated core body temperature.

heat index A measure of how hot it feels; the temperature that would have the same heating effect on a person as a given combination of temperature and relative humidity.

hypothermia Low body temperature due to exposure to cold conditions.

central nervous system, resulting in sleepiness and a lower metabolic rate. As metabolic rate drops, body temperature declines even further, and coma and death can result. **Frostbite**—the freezing of body tissues—is another potential danger of exercise in extremely cold conditions. Frostbite most commonly occurs in exposed body parts like earlobes, fingers, and toes, and it can cause permanent circulatory damage. Hypothermia and frostbite both require immediate medical treatment.

What can you do to exercise safely in cold conditions? First of all, don't stay out in very cold temperatures for too long. Take both the temperature and the wind into account when planning your exercise session. Frostbite within 30 minutes is possible in calm conditions when the temperature is colder than $-5°F$ or in windy conditions (30 mph) if the temperature is below 10°F. **Wind chill** values that reflect both the temperature and the wind speed are available as part of a local weather forecast and from the National Weather Service (http://www.weather.gov); a complete wind chill chart is available on the *Fit and Well* Online Learning Center.

Appropriate clothing provides insulation and helps trap warm air next to the skin. Dress in layers so you can remove them as you warm up and put them back on if you get cold. A substantial amount of heat loss comes from the head and neck, so keep these areas covered. In subfreezing temperatures, protect the areas of your body most susceptible to frostbite—fingers, toes, ears, nose, and cheeks—with warm socks, mittens or gloves, and a cap, hood, or ski mask. Wear clothing that breathes and will wick moisture away from your skin to avoid being cooled or overheated by trapped perspiration. Many types of comfortable, lightweight clothing that provide good insulation are available. It's also important to warm up thoroughly and to drink plenty of fluids.

Poor Air Quality

Air pollution can decrease exercise performance and negatively affect health, particularly if you have respiratory problems such as asthma, bronchitis, or emphysema, or if you smoke. The effects of smog are worse during exercise

than at rest because air enters the lungs faster. Polluted air may also contain carbon monoxide, which displaces oxygen in the blood and reduces the amount of oxygen available to working muscles. Symptoms of poor air quality include eye and throat irritations, difficulty breathing, and possibly headache and malaise.

Do not exercise outdoors during a smog alert or if air quality is very poor. If you have any type of cardiorespiratory difficulty, you should also avoid exertion outdoors when air quality is poor. You can avoid some smog and air pollution by exercising in indoor facilities, in parks, near water (riverbanks, lakeshores, and ocean beaches), or in residential areas with less traffic (areas with stop-and-go traffic will have lower air quality than areas where traffic moves quickly). Air quality is also usually better in the early morning and late evening, before and after the commute hours.

Exercise Injuries

Even the most careful physically active person can suffer an injury. Most injuries are annoying rather than serious or permanent. However, an injury that isn't cared for properly can escalate into a chronic problem, sometimes serious enough to permanently curtail the activity. It's important to learn how to deal with injuries so they don't derail your fitness program. Strategies for the care of common exercise injuries and discomforts appear in Table 3.5; some general guidelines are given below.

When to Call a Physician   Some injuries require medical attention. Consult a physician for head and eye injuries, possible ligament injuries, broken bones, and internal disorders such as chest pain, fainting, elevated body temperature, and intolerance to hot weather. Also seek medical attention for ostensibly minor injuries that do not get better within a reasonable amount of time. You may need to modify your exercise program for a few weeks to allow an injury to heal.

Managing Minor Exercise Injuries   For minor cuts and scrapes, stop the bleeding and clean the wound. Treat injuries to soft tissue (muscles and joints) with the R-I-C-E principle: rest, ice, compression, and elevation. Immediately following the injury, rest the affected area and apply ice. Elevate the affected part of the body, and compress it with an elastic bandage to minimize swelling. Apply ice regularly for 36–48 hours after an injury occurs or until all the swelling is gone. (Don't leave ice on one spot for more than 20 minutes.) The day after the injury, some experts recommend also taking an over-the-counter medication such as aspirin, ibuprofen, or naproxen to decrease inflammation.

Don't apply heat to an injury at first, because heat draws blood to the area and increases swelling. After the

Table 3.5   Care of Common Exercise Injuries and Discomforts

Injury	Symptoms	Treatment
Blister	Accumulation of fluid in one spot under the skin	Don't pop or drain it unless it interferes too much with your daily activities. If it does pop, clean the area with antiseptic and cover with a bandage. Do not remove the skin covering the blister.
Bruise (contusion)	Pain, swelling, and discoloration	R-I-C-E: rest, ice, compression, elevation.
Fractures and dislocations	Pain, swelling, tenderness, loss of function, and deformity	Seek medical attention, immobilize the affected area, and apply cold.
Joint sprain	Pain, tenderness, swelling, discoloration, and loss of function	R-I-C-E. Apply heat when swelling has disappeared. Stretch and strengthen affected area.
Muscle cramp	Painful, spasmodic muscle contractions	Gently stretch for 15–30 seconds at a time and/or massage the cramped area. Drink fluids and increase dietary salt intake if exercising in hot weather.
Muscle soreness or stiffness	Pain and tenderness in the affected muscle	Stretch the affected muscle gently; exercise at a low intensity; apply heat. Nonsteroidal anti-inflammatory drugs, such as ibuprofen, help some people.
Muscle strain	Pain, tenderness, swelling, and loss of strength in the affected muscle	R-I-C-E; apply heat when swelling has disappeared. Stretch and strengthen the affected area.
Shin splints	Pain and tenderness on the front of the lower leg; sometimes also pain in the calf muscle	Rest; apply ice to the affected area several times a day and before exercise; wrap with tape for support. Stretch and strengthen muscles in the lower legs. Purchase good-quality footwear and run on soft surfaces.
Side stitch	Pain on the side of the abdomen	Stretch the arm on the affected side as high as possible; if that doesn't help, try bending forward while tightening the abdominal muscles.
Tendinitis	Pain, swelling, and tenderness of the affected area	R-I-C-E; apply heat when swelling has disappeared. Stretch and strengthen the affected area.

swelling has subsided, apply either moist heat (hot towels, heat packs, warm water immersion) or dry heat (heating pads) to speed up healing.

To rehabilitate your body, follow the steps listed in the box "Rehabilitation Following a Minor Athletic Injury."

Preventing Injuries   The best method for dealing with exercise injuries is to prevent them. If you choose activities for your program carefully and follow the training guidelines described here and in Chapter 2, you should be able to avoid most types of injuries. Important guidelines for preventing athletic injuries include the following:

- Train regularly and stay in condition.
- Gradually increase the intensity, duration, or frequency of your workouts.
- Avoid or minimize high-impact activities; alternate them with low-impact activities.
- Get proper rest between exercise sessions.
- Drink plenty of fluids.
- Warm up thoroughly before you exercise and cool down afterward.
- Achieve and maintain a good level of flexibility.
- Use proper body mechanics when lifting objects or executing sports skills.
- Don't exercise when you are ill or overtrained.
- Use proper equipment, particularly shoes, and choose an appropriate exercise surface. If you exercise on a grass field, soft track, or wooden floor, you are less likely to be injured than on concrete or a hard track.
- Don't return to your normal exercise program until any athletic injuries have healed. Restart your program at a lower intensity and gradually increase the amount of overload.

1. Reduce the initial inflammation using the R-I-C-E principle:

Rest: Stop using the injured area as soon as you experience pain. Avoid any activity that causes pain.

Ice: Apply ice to the injured area to reduce swelling and alleviate pain. Apply ice immediately for 10–20 minutes and repeat every few hours until the swelling disappears. Let the injured part return to normal temperature between icings, and do not apply ice to one area for more than 20 minutes. An easy method for applying ice is to freeze water in a paper cup, peel some of the paper away, and rub the exposed ice on the injured area. If the injured area is large, you can surround it with several bags of crushed ice or ice cubes, or bags of frozen vegetables. Place a thin towel between the bag and your skin. If you use a cold gel pack, limit application time to 10 minutes.

Compression: Wrap the injured area firmly with an elastic or compression bandage between icings. If the area starts throbbing or begins to change color, the bandage may be wrapped too tightly. Do not sleep with the wrap on.

Elevation: Raise the injured area above heart level to decrease the blood supply and reduce swelling. Use pillows, books, or a low chair or stool to raise the injured area.

2. After 36–48 hours, apply heat *if the swelling has completely disappeared.* Immerse the affected area in warm water or apply warm compresses, a hot water bottle, or a heating pad. As soon as it's comfortable, begin moving the affected joints slowly. If you feel pain, or if the injured area begins to swell again, reduce the amount of movement. Continue stretching and moving the affected area until you have regained normal range of motion.

3. Gradually begin exercising the injured area to build strength and endurance. Depending on the type of injury, weight training, walking, and resistance training with a partner can all be effective.

4. Gradually reintroduce the stress of an activity until you can return to full intensity. Don't progress too rapidly or you'll reinjure yourself. Before returning to full exercise participation, you should have a full range of motion in your joints, normal strength and balance among your muscles, normal coordinated patterns of movement (with no injury compensation movements, such as limping), and little or no pain.

Good cardiorespiratory fitness is essential for a long and healthy life. It also provides many immediate benefits that span all the dimensions of wellness—improved mood, better sleep, greater creativity, and fewer colds, to name just a few. The good news is that you don't have to be an elite athlete to enjoy these benefits. Regular, moderate exercise, even in short bouts spread through the day, can build and maintain cardiorespiratory fitness.

Right now you can

- Do a short bout of endurance exercise: 10–15 minutes of walking, jogging, cycling, or another endurance activity.

- If you have physical activity planned for later in the day, drink some fluids now to make sure you are fully hydrated for your workout.

- Consider the exercise equipment, including shoes, you currently have on hand. If you'll need new equipment to begin your program, check the phone book, campus store, Internet, and other resources to start gathering the information you'll need to get the best equipment you can afford.

- Think of someone you know who engages in regular endurance exercise. Call or e-mail that person and ask what strategies she or he uses to find time for exercise and to stay motivated.

SUMMARY

- The cardiorespiratory system consists of the heart, blood vessels, and respiratory system; it picks up and transports oxygen, nutrients, and waste products.

- The body takes chemical energy from food and uses it to produce ATP and fuel cellular activities. ATP is stored in the body's cells as the basic form of energy.

- During exercise, the body supplies ATP and fuels cellular activities by combining three energy systems: immediate, for short periods of energy; nonoxidative (anaerobic), for intense activity; and oxidative (aerobic), for prolonged activity. Which energy system predominates depends on the duration and intensity of the activity.

- Cardiorespiratory endurance exercise improves cardiorespiratory functioning and cellular metabolism; it reduces the risk of chronic diseases such as heart disease, cancer, type 2 diabetes, obesity, and osteoporosis; and it improves immune function and psychological and emotional well-being.

- Cardiorespiratory fitness is measured by seeing how well the cardiorespiratory system transports and uses oxygen. The upper limit of this measure is called maximal oxygen consumption, or $\dot{V}O_{2max}$.

- $\dot{V}O_{2max}$ can be measured precisely in a laboratory, or it can be estimated reasonably well through less expensive assessment tests.

What kind of clothing should I wear during exercise? Exercise clothing should be comfortable, let you move freely, and allow your body to cool itself. Avoid clothing that constricts normal blood flow or is made from nylon or rubberized fabrics that prevent evaporation of perspiration. Cotton is an excellent material for facilitating the evaporation of sweat. If you sweat heavily when you exercise and find that too much moisture accumulates in cotton clothing, try fabrics containing synthetic materials such as polypropylene that wick moisture away from the skin. Socks made with moisture-wicking compounds may be particularly helpful for people whose feet sweat heavily.

A sports bra is a key piece of clothing for women. A good sports bra should be made of a breathable fabric to allow for evaporation of sweat; it should fit well and have comfortable seams and closures. Try on several styles and sizes to see what fits best, and try the jump test to make sure the bra will provide enough support for your activities. Find a bra that emphasizes function and not fashion.

Do I need a special diet for my endurance exercise program? No. For most people, a nutritionally balanced diet contains all the energy and nutrients needed to sustain an exercise program. Don't waste your money on unnecessary vitamins, minerals, and protein supplements. (Chapter 8 has information about putting together a healthy diet.)

Should I use a heart rate monitor to keep track of exercise intensity? Electronic heart rate monitors, which are relatively accurate and inexpensive, can help you stay within your target heart rate range. Heart rate monitors function by detecting the pulse in your finger or hand or by measuring the electrical activity of your heart through a belt you wear around your chest. In general, the belt models are most accurate; some of the more expensive belt models can download heart rate information to your home computer. If very close tracking of heart rate is important in your program, you may find a monitor to be helpful. However, other measures of exercise intensity also work well, including pulse taking, RPE, and the talk test.

Will interval training develop cardiorespiratory endurance (CRE)? Interval training refers to short bouts of high-intensity exercise alternated with short periods of rest or light activity. Interval training can be practiced during many different types of activities and at different levels of intensity. For example, increasing walking pace from 3.5 miles per hour to 4.5 miles per hour for several 5-minute periods during a 45-minute walk is an example of interval training. Another example would be a 400-meter run followed by a 200-meter walk, with the cycle repeated two to ten times.

You will develop CRE more quickly doing interval training because your workout incorporates bouts of higher intensity activity. You may be able to continue your workout for a longer period because the high-intensity intervals are brief enough to avoid fatigue from lactic acid build-up. Interval training may also allow you to burn more calories during an exercise session compared with a workout of the same length that doesn't include the intervals of higher intensity activity. However, intervals are also more uncomfortable and increase your risk of injury and overtraining. Don't perform interval training more than 2–3 days per week.

How can I safely increase exercise intensity to build fitness? For both athletes and nonathletes, it is extremely important to increase intensity very gradually and to rest between exercise sessions. If you train too hard and/or don't rest enough, you are more likely to be injured—and be discouraged from continuing with your fitness program. For endurance training, overload techniques such as interval training and wind sprints can help you build fitness quickly but also pose a greater risk of injury or overtraining. Start off with a few high-intensity bouts of exercise and build up gradually. Don't practice interval training or wind sprints more than 2–3 days per week unless you have a high fitness level.

Increase intensity or duration by about 1–3% in a single workout; rest the following day and then do your typical workout. Repeat the more difficult workout after another day of rest. Adjust your progress according to how you feel. You can't increase fitness in a few days. Be patient—with gradual increases in intensity and plenty of rest between workouts, you will be able to move to a higher level of fitness without injury.

If I plan to include both cardiorespiratory endurance training and strength training in a single workout, which should I do first? It depends on your goals. If the primary goal of your fitness program is conditioning your cardiorespiratory system, then do your endurance workout first. If your fitness program is focused on large gains in strength and you plan to lift relatively heavy weights, then do your strength training workout first. You are likely to make the most rapid gains in fitness in whichever activity you engage in first, when you are fresh.

Is there such a thing as proper fitness walking technique? Yes. Most of us have a natural way of walking that we practice with no thought. But efficient fitness walking technique may differ slightly from your slower-paced walking technique, and a check of walking form may help boost walking efficiency and reduce the risk of injury. Consider having a friend watch you walk and compare your walking form to the following guidelines:

- Keep your head up and eyes looking ahead.

- Relax the muscles of your face, shoulders, and hands; don't clench your fists.

- Keep your arms near your sides, with elbows bent at about 90 degrees. Arms should swing freely from the shoulders forward and back; they should not cross in front of the body during the forward swing.

- Hold your chest up and tuck your hips slightly forward to help maintain an upright posture. Lean forward very slightly from the waist.

- Move and lift the upper leg naturally from the hip; swing the lower leg forward.

- As you step forward, your heel should land firmly on the ground first, followed by the ball of the foot. Push off from the ball of the foot and toes. Take care not to over- or understride; if your walking movement feels awkward, try slightly shortening or lengthening your stride.

Is it all right to participate in cardiorespiratory endurance exercise while menstruating? Yes. There is no evidence that exercise during menstruation is unhealthy or that it has negative effects on performance. If you have headaches, backaches, and abdominal pain during menstruation, you may not feel like exercising; for some women, exercise helps relieve these symptoms. Listen to your body, and exercise at whatever intensity is comfortable for you.

What causes muscle cramps and what can I do about them? Muscle cramps are caused by local muscle fatigue that triggers the nervous system to overstimulate the muscles. Until recently, muscle cramps were thought to be caused by dehydration or salt depletion in the muscles, but scientists have found little evidence for this. Muscle cramps can occur during or after exercise performed either in heat or in cold. You can prevent cramps by improving your fitness and making sure you consume enough fluid and electrolytes during exercise and in your diet (low intake of fluid and electrolytes contributes to fatigue). When cramps do occur, gently stretch the cramping muscle for 15–30 seconds. Do not overstretch the cramping muscle because this can lead to serious injury.

Will high altitude affect my ability to exercise? At high altitudes (above 1500 meters or about 4900 feet) there is less oxygen available in the air than at lower altitudes. High altitude doesn't affect anaerobic exercise, such as stretching and weight lifting, but it does affect aerobic activities—that is, any type of cardiovascular endurance exercise—because the heart and lungs have to work harder, even when the body is at rest, to deliver enough oxygen to body cells. The increased cardiovascular strain of exercise reduces endurance. To play it safe when at high altitudes, avoid heavy exercise—at least for the first few days—and drink plenty of water. And don't expect to reach your normal lower altitude exercise capacity.

I'm concerned about my safety when I go for a jog or walk. What can I do to make sure that my training sessions are safe and enjoyable? A person exercising alone in the park can be a tempting target for criminals. Don't exercise alone. You are much safer training in a group or with a partner. Another alternative is to take an exercise class. Classes are fun and much safer than exercising by yourself. If you must train alone, try to exercise where there are plenty of people. A good bet is the local high school or college track.

Make sure you're wearing proper safety equipment. If you're riding a bike, wear a helmet. If you're playing racquetball or handball, wear eye protectors. Don't go in-line skating unless you're wearing the proper pads and protective equipment. If you are jogging at night, wear reflective clothing that can be seen easily.

Refer to Appendix A for more on personal safety.

Visit the Online Learning Center for more answers to common questions about endurance training.

- To have a successful exercise program, set realistic goals; choose suitable activities; begin slowly; always warm up and cool down; and, as fitness improves, exercise more often, longer, and/or harder.

- Intensity of training can be measured through target heart rate zone and ratings of perceived exertion.

- With careful attention to fluid intake, clothing, duration of exercise, and exercise intensity, endurance training can be safe in hot and cold weather conditions.

- Serious injuries require medical attention. Application of the R-I-C-E principle (rest, ice, compression, elevation) is appropriate for treating many types of muscle or joint injuries.

For Further Exploration

VW *Fit and Well* Online Learning Center (www.mhhe.com/fahey)

Use the learning objectives, study guide questions, and glossary flashcards to review key terms and concepts and prepare for exams.

You can extend your knowledge of cardiorespiratory endurance and gain experience in using the Internet as a resource by completing the activities and checking out the Web links for the topics in Chapter 3 marked with the World Wide Web icon. For this chapter, Internet activities explore the benefits of endurance exercise, target heart rate zone, and activities to improve cardiorespiratory fitness; there are Web links for the Critical Consumer box on exercise equipment and the chapter as a whole. You'll also find additional cardiorespiratory endurance self-assessments, including a non-exercise test, a swimming test, a timed run-walk test, a cycle ergometer test, and a test for people who use wheelchairs.

Daily Fitness and Nutrition Journal

Complete the cardiorespiratory endurance portion of the program plan by setting goals and selecting activities that will build endurance. Also calculate and record your current resting heart rate and your target heart rate zone or RPE value.

Books

American College of Sports Medicine. 2003. *ACSM Fitness Book.* 3rd ed. Champaign, Ill.: Human Kinetics. *Includes fitness* assessment tests and advice on creating a complete fitness program.

Barough, N. 2004. *Walking for Fitness.* New York: DK. *Provides advice on putting together a walking program that matches your fitness goals.*

Beim, G., and R. Winter. 2003. *The Female Athlete's Body Book: How to Prevent and Treat Sports Injuries in Women and Girls.* New York: McGraw-Hill/Contemporary. *Provides detailed information on the prevention and treatment of athletic injuries in women and girls.*

Brennfleck, J. 2002. *Sports Injuries Sourcebook.* Detroit, Mich.: Omnigraphics. *Provides information about the prevention and care of exercise injuries, with specific sections on different age groups and popular activities.*

Hewitt, B., ed. 2005. *New Cyclist Handbook.* Emmaus, Penn.: Rodale. *Includes information on buying and caring for a bicycle as well as on increasing fitness.*

Juba, K. 2002. *Swimming for Fitness.* New York: Lyons Press. *Provides step-by-step instructions for setting up a swimming fitness program, including advice on technique and avoiding injury and overtraining.*

National Institute on Aging. 2003. *Fitness Over Fifty: An Exercise Guide from the National Institute on Aging.* Long Island City, N.Y.: Hatherleigh Press. *Includes information on a safe and effective fitness program.*

Nieman, D. C. 2007. *Exercise Testing and Prescription: A Health-Related Approach,* 6th ed. New York: McGraw-Hill. *A comprehensive discussion of the effect of exercise and exercise testing and prescription.*

Noakes, T. 2003. *Lore of Running.* 4th ed. Champaign, Ill.: Human Kinetics. *Provides detailed information on physiology, training, racing, and injury prevention.*

Pryor, E., and M. Kraines. 2000. *Keep Moving! Fitness through Aerobics and Step,* 4th ed. Mountain View, Calif.: Mayfield. *The fitness principles and techniques every aerobic dancer should know.*

Ｗｗ Organizations and Web Sites

American Academy of Orthopaedic Surgeons. Provides fact sheets on many fitness and sports topics, including how to begin a program, how to choose equipment, and how to prevent and treat many types of injuries.

http://orthoinfo.aaos.org

American Heart Association. Provides information on cardiovascular health and disease, including the role of exercise in maintaining heart health and exercise tips for people of all ages.

800-AHA-USA1

http://www.americanheart.org

http://www.justmove.org

Dr. Pribut's Running Injuries Page. Provides information about running and many types of running injuries.

http://www.drpribut.com/sports/spsport.html

Federal Trade Commission: Consumer Protection—Diet, Health, and Fitness. Provides several brochures with consumer advice about purchasing exercise equipment.

http://www.ftc.gov/bcp/menu-health.htm

Franklin Institute Science Museum/The Heart: An Online Exploration. An online museum exhibit with information on the structure and function of the heart, blood vessels, and respiratory system.

http://www.fi.edu/biosci/heart.html

MedlinePlus: Exercise and Physical Fitness. Provides links to news and reliable information about fitness from government agencies and professional associations.

http://www.nlm.nih.gov/medlineplus/exercisephysicalfitness.html

Physician and Sportsmedicine. Provides many articles with easy-to-understand advice about exercise injuries.

http://www.physsportsmed.com

Runner's World Online. Contains a wide variety of information about running, including tips for beginning runners, advice about training, and a shoe buyer's guide.

http://www.runnersworld.com

University of Florida: Keeping Fit. Provides useful information about fitness in a question-and-answer format; an extensive set of links is also provided.

http://hermes.hhp.ufl.edu/keepingfit

Women's Sports Foundation. Provides information and links about training and about many specific sports activities.

http://www.womenssportsfoundation.org/cgi-bin/iowa/

Yahoo/Recreation. Contains links to many sites with practical advice on many sports and activities.

http://dir.yahoo.com/recreation/sports

See also the listings in Chapters 2 and 11.

Selected Bibliography

Achten, J., and A. E. Jeukendrup. 2003. Heart rate monitoring: Applications and limitations. *Sports Medicine* 33:517–538.

American Academy of Orthopaedic Surgeons. 2001. *Selecting Home Exercise Equipment* (http://orthoinfo.aaos.org/fact/thr_report.cfm; retrieved October 17, 2001).

American College of Sports Medicine. 2006. *ACSM's Guidelines for Exercise Testing and Prescription,* 7th ed. Philadelphia: Lippincott Williams & Wilkins.

American College of Sports Medicine. 2006. *ACSM's Resource Manual for Guidelines for Exercise Testing and Prescription,* 5th ed. Philadelphia: Lippincott Williams & Wilkins.

American College of Sports Medicine. 2005. *Study: Workers More Productive after Exercise* (http://www.acsm.org/publications/newsreleases2005/AM_WorkerProductivity.htm; retrieved June 30, 2005).

Brooks, G. A., et al. 2005. *Exercise Physiology: Human Bioenergetics and Its Applications,* 4th ed. New York: McGraw-Hill.

Carnethon, M. R., et al. 2005. A longitudinal study of physical activity and heart rate recovery: CARDIA, 1987–1993. *Medicine and Science in Sports and Exercise* 37:606–612.

Carroll, J. F., and C. K. Kyser. 2002. Exercise training in obesity lowers blood pressure independent of weight change. *Medicine and Science in Sports and Exercise* 34(4): 596–601.

Cheuvront, S. N., I. R. Carter, and M. N. Sawka. 2003. Fluid balance and endurance exercise performance. *Current Sports Medicine Reports* 2:202–208.

Colcombe, S. J., et al. 2004. Cardiovascular fitness, cortical plasticity, and aging. *Proceedings of the National Academy of Sciences* 101(9): 3316–3321.

Coris, E. E., A. M. Ramirez, and D. J. Van Durme. 2004. Heat illness in athletes: A dangerous combination of heat, humidity, and exercise. *Sports Medicine* 34(1): 9–16.

Duscha, B. D., et al. 2005. Effects of exercise training amount and intensity on peak oxygen consumption in middle-age men and women at risk for cardiovascular disease. *Chest* 128(4): 2788–2793.

Friedenreich, C. M., et al. 2004. Case-control study of lifetime total physical activity and prostate cancer risk. *American Journal of Epidemiology* 159(8): 740–749.

Gleeson, M., D. C. Nieman, and B. K. Pedersen. 2004. Exercise, nutrition, and immune function. *Journal of Sports Science* 22(1): 115–125.

Goodwin, R. D. 2003. Association between physical activity and mental disorders among adults in the United States. *Preventive Medicine* 36(6): 698–703.

Hew-Butler, T., et al. 2005. Consensus statement of the 1st International Exercise-Associated Hyponatremia Consensus Development Conference,

Cape Town, South Africa, 2005. *Clinical Journal of Sports Medicine* 15(4): 208–213.

Hu, F. B., et al. 2004. Adiposity compared with physical activity in predicting mortality among women. *New England Journal of Medicine* 351(26):2694–2703.

Humpel, N., N. Owen, and E. Leslie. 2002. Environmental factors associated with adults' participation in physical activity. A review. *American Journal of Preventive Medicine* 22(3): 188–199.

Interval training: More benefit, less fatigue. 2005. *Consumer Reports,* May.

John, E. M., P. L. Horn-Ross, and J. Koo. 2004. Lifetime physical activity and breast cancer risk in a multiethnic population. *Cancer Epidemiology, Biomarkers, and Prevention* 12(11 Pt. 1): 1143–1152.

Karavatas, S. G., and K. Tavakol. 2005. Concurrent validity of Borg's rating of perceived exertion in African-American young adults, employing heart rate as the standard. *Internet Journal of Allied Health Sciences and Practice* 3 (January).

Ketelhut, R. G., I. W. Franz, and J. Scholze. 2004. Regular exercise as an effective approach in antihypertensive therapy. *Medicine and Science in Sports and Exercise* 36(1): 4–8.

Keteyian, S. J., and I. Kolokouri. 2001. Guidelines for selecting home exercise equipment. *ACSM's Fit Society Page,* January/February.

Kondo, N., et al. 2005. Association of inflammatory marker and highly sensitive C-reactive protein with aerobic exercise capacity, maximum oxygen uptake and insulin resistance in healthy middle-aged volunteers. *Circulation Journal* 69:452–457.

Kriska, A. M., et al. 2003. Physical activity, obesity, and the incidence of Type 2 diabetes in a high-risk population. *American Journal of Epidemiology* 158(7): 669–675.

Lambert, C. P., and W. J. Evans. 2005. Adaptations to aerobic and resistance exercise in the elderly. *Reviews in Endocrine and Metabolic Disorders* 6:137–143.

Laughlin, M. H. 2004. Joseph B. Wolfe Memorial Lecture. Physical activity in prevention and treatment of coronary disease: The battle line is in exercise vascular cell biology. *Medicine and Science in Sports and Exercise* 36:352–362.

Lee, C. D., A. R. Folsom, and S. N. Blair. 2003. Physical activity and stroke risk: A meta-analysis. *Stroke* 34(10): 2475–2481.

Luebbers, P. E. 2005. Running and walking form. *ACSM Fit Society Page,* Summer.

National Weather Service. 2003. *Extreme Heat: Heat Index* (http://www.crh.noaa.gov/arx/heatindex.html; retrieved October 31, 2003).

Nieman, D. C. 2005. Can exercise help me sleep better? *ACSM's Health & Fitness Journal* 9(3): 6.

Noakes, T. D. 2003. Over consumption of fluids by athletes. *British Medical Journal* 327:113–114.

Nurmi-Lawton, J. A., et al. 2004. Evidence of sustained skeletal benefits from impact-loading exercise in young females. *Journal of Bone and Mineral Research* 19(2): 314–322.

PBS Healthweek. 2001. *Home Exercise Equipment* (http://www.pbs.org/healthweek/featurep4_339.htm; retrieved October 18, 2001).

Persinger, R., et al. 2004. Consistency of the talk test for exercise prescription. *Medicine and Science in Sports and Exercise* 36(9): 1632–1636.

Peterson, J. A. 2005. 10 common mistakes made by individuals who engage in aerobic exercises. *ACSM's Health & Fitness Journal* 9(3): 44.

Scott, S. 2005. Combating depression with exercise. *ACSM's Health & Fitness Journal* 9(4): 31.

Slattery, M. L. 2004. Physical activity and colorectal cancer. *Sports Medicine* 34(4): 239–252.

Slentz, C. A., et al. 2005. Inactivity, exercise, and visceral fat. STRRIDE: A randomized, controlled study of exercise intensity and amount. *Journal of Applied Physiology* 99(4): 1613–1618.

Swain, D. P. 2005. Moderate or vigorous intensity exercise: Which is better for improving aerobic fitness? *Preventive Cardiology* 8:55–58.

Sykes K., L. L. Choo, and M. Cotterrell. 2004. Accumulating aerobic exercise for effective weight control. *Journal of the Royal Society of Health* 124:24–28.

Verghese, J., et al. 2003. Leisure activities and the risk of dementia in the elderly. *New England Journal of Medicine* 348(25): 2508–2516.

LAB 3.1   *Assessing Your Current Level of Cardiorespiratory Endurance*   **WW**

Before taking any of the cardiorespiratory endurance assessment tests, refer to the fitness prerequisites and cautions given in Table 3.2. Choose one of the following three tests presented in this lab:

- 1-mile walk test
- 3-minute step test
- 1.5-mile run-walk test

For best results, don't exercise strenuously or consume caffeine the day of the test, and don't smoke or eat a heavy meal within about 3 hours of the test.

The 1-Mile Walk Test

Equipment

1. A track or course that provides a measurement of 1 mile
2. A stopwatch, clock, or watch with a second hand
3. A weight scale

Preparation

Measure your body weight (in pounds) before taking the test.

Body weight: _____ lb

Instructions

1. Warm up before taking the test. Do some walking, easy jogging, or calisthenics and some stretching exercises.
2. Cover the 1-mile course as quickly as possible. Walk at a pace that is brisk but comfortable. You must raise your heart rate above 120 beats per minute (bpm).
3. As soon as you complete the distance, note your time and take your pulse for 10 seconds.

   Walking time: _____ min _____ sec

   10-second pulse count: _____ beats
4. Cool down after the test by walking slowly for several minutes.

Determining Maximal Oxygen Consumption

1. Convert your 10-second pulse count into a value for exercise heart rate by multiplying it by 6.

   Exercise heart rate: $\underset{\text{10-sec pulse count}}{\underline{\qquad\qquad}} \times 6 =$ _____ bpm

2. Convert your walking time from minutes and seconds to a decimal figure. For example, a time of 14 minutes and 45 seconds would be 14 + (45/60), or 14.75 minutes.

   Walking time: _____ min + (_____ sec ÷ 60 sec/min) = _____ min
3. Insert values for your age, gender, weight, walking time, and exercise heart rate in the following equation, where

   W = your weight (in pounds)

   A = your age (in years)

   G = your gender (male = 1; female = 0)

   T = your time to complete the 1-mile course (in minutes)

   H = your exercise heart rate (in beats per minute)

   $\dot{V}O_{2max} = 132.853 - (0.0769 \times W) - (0.3877 \times A) + (6.315 \times G) - (3.2649 \times T) - (0.1565 \times H)$

For example, a 20-year-old, 190-pound male with a time of 14.75 minutes and an exercise heart rate of 152 bpm would calculate maximal oxygen consumption as follows:

$$\dot{V}O_{2max} = 132.853 - (0.0769 \times 190) - (0.3877 \times 20) + (6.315 \times 1) - (3.2649 \times 14.75) - (0.1565 \times 152)$$
$$= 45 \ ml/kg/min$$

$$\dot{V}O_{2max} = 132.853 - (0.0769 \times \underline{\hspace{2cm}}) - (0.3877 \times \underline{\hspace{2cm}}) + (6.315 \times \underline{\hspace{2cm}})$$
$$\text{weight (lb)} \qquad \text{age (years)} \qquad \text{gender}$$

$$- (3.2649 \times \underline{\hspace{2cm}}) - (0.1565 \times \underline{\hspace{2cm}}) = \underline{\hspace{1cm}} ml/kg/min$$
$$\text{walking time (min)} \qquad \text{exercise heart rate (bpm)}$$

4. Copy this value for $\dot{V}O_{2max}$ into the appropriate place in the chart on the final page of this lab.

The 3-Minute Step Test

Equipment

1. A step, bench, or bleacher step that is 16.25 inches from ground level
2. A stopwatch, clock, or watch with a second hand
3. A metronome

Preparation

Practice stepping up onto and down from the step before you begin the test. Each step has four beats: up-up-down-down. Males should perform the test with the metronome set for a rate of 96 beats per minute, or 24 steps per minute. Females should set the metronome at 88 beats per minute, or 22 steps per minute.

Instructions

1. Warm up before taking the test. Do some walking, easy jogging, and stretching exercises.
2. Set the metronome at the proper rate. Your instructor or a partner can call out starting and stopping times; otherwise, have a clock or watch within easy viewing during the test.
3. Begin the test and continue to step at the correct pace for 3 minutes.
4. Stop after 3 minutes. Remain standing and count your pulse for the 15-second period from 5 to 20 seconds into recovery.

    15-second pulse count: _____ beats
5. Cool down after the test by walking slowly for several minutes.

Determining Maximal Oxygen Consumption

1. Convert your 15-second pulse count to a value for recovery heart rate by multiplying by 4.

    Recovery heart rate: $\underline{\hspace{2cm}} \times 4 = \underline{\hspace{1.5cm}} bpm$
    $\text{15-sec pulse count}$

2. Insert your recovery heart rate in the equation below, where

    H = recovery heart rate (in beats per minute)
    Males: $\dot{V}O_{2max} = 111.33 - (0.42 \times H)$
    Females: $\dot{V}O_{2max} = 65.81 - (0.1847 \times H)$

    For example, a man with a recovery heart rate of 162 bpm would calculate maximal oxygen consumption as follows:

    $$\dot{V}O_{2max} = 111.33 - (0.42 \times 162) = 43 \ ml/kg/min$$

    Males: $\dot{V}O_{2max} = 111.33 - (0.42 \times \underline{\hspace{3cm}}) = \underline{\hspace{1.5cm}} ml/kg/min$
    $\text{recovery heart rate (bpm)}$

    Females: $\dot{V}O_{2max} = 65.81 - (0.1847 \times \underline{\hspace{3cm}}) = \underline{\hspace{1.5cm}} ml/kg/min$
    $\text{recovery heart rate (bpm)}$

3. Copy this value for $\dot{V}O_{2max}$ into the appropriate place in the chart on the final page of this lab.

The 1.5-Mile Run-Walk Test

Equipment

1. A running track or course that is flat and provides exact measurements of up to 1.5 miles
2. A stopwatch, clock, or watch with a second hand

Preparation

You may want to practice pacing yourself prior to taking the test to avoid going too fast at the start and becoming prematurely fatigued. Allow yourself a day or two to recover from your practice run before taking the test.

Instructions

1. Warm up before taking the test. Do some walking, easy jogging, and stretching exercises.
2. Try to cover the distance as fast as possible without overexerting yourself. If possible, monitor your own time, or have someone call out your time at various intervals of the test to determine whether your pace is correct.
3. Record the amount of time, in minutes and seconds, it takes you to complete the 1.5-mile distance.
   Running-walking time: _____ min _____ sec
4. Cool down after the test by walking or jogging slowly for about 5 minutes.

Determining Maximal Oxygen Consumption

1. Convert your running time from minutes and seconds to a decimal figure. For example, a time of 14 minutes and 25 seconds would be $14 + (25/60)$, or 14.4 minutes.
   Running-walking time: _____ min + (_____ sec ÷ 60 sec/min) = _____ min
2. Insert your running time into the equation below, where

   T = running time (in minutes)
   $\dot{V}O_{2max} = (483 \div T) + 3.5$

   For example, a person who completes 1.5 miles in 14.4 minutes would calculate maximal oxygen consumption as follows:
   $\dot{V}O_{2max} = (483 \div 14.4) + 3.5 = 37 \text{ ml/kg/min}$

   $\dot{V}O_{2max} = (483 \div \underset{\text{run-walk time (min)}}{\underline{\hspace{2cm}}}) + 3.5 = \underline{\hspace{2cm}} \text{ ml/kg/min}$

3. Copy this value for $\dot{V}O_{2max}$ into the appropriate place in the chart on the final page of this lab.

Rating Your Cardiovascular Fitness

Record your $\dot{V}O_{2max}$ score(s) and the corresponding fitness rating from the table below.

Women	Very Poor	Poor	Fair	Good	Excellent	Superior
Age: 18–29	Below 31.6	31.6–35.4	35.5–39.4	39.5–43.9	44.0–50.1	Above 50.1
30–39	Below 29.9	29.9–33.7	33.8–36.7	36.8–40.9	41.0–46.8	Above 46.8
40–49	Below 28.0	28.0–31.5	31.6–35.0	35.1–38.8	38.9–45.1	Above 45.1
50–59	Below 25.5	25.5–28.6	28.7–31.3	31.4–35.1	35.2–39.8	Above 39.8
60–69	Below 23.7	23.7–26.5	26.6–29.0	29.1–32.2	32.3–36.8	Above 36.8
Men						
Age: 18–29	Below 38.1	38.1–42.1	42.2–45.6	45.7–51.0	51.1–56.1	Above 56.1
30–39	Below 36.7	36.7–40.9	41.0–44.3	44.4–48.8	48.9–54.2	Above 54.2
40–49	Below 34.6	34.6–38.3	38.4–42.3	42.4–46.7	46.8–52.8	Above 52.8
50–59	Below 31.1	31.1–35.1	35.2–38.2	38.3–43.2	43.3–49.6	Above 49.6
60–69	Below 27.4	27.4–31.3	31.4–34.9	35.0–39.4	39.5–46.0	Above 46.0

SOURCE: Ratings based on norms from The Cooper Institute of Aerobic Research, Dallas, Texas; from *The Physical Fitness Specialist Manual*, Revised 2002. Used with permission.

	$\dot{V}O_{2max}$	Cardiovascular Fitness Rating
1-mile walk test		
3-minute step test		
1.5-mile run-walk test		

Using Your Results

How did you score? Are you surprised by your rating for cardiovascular fitness? Are you satisfied with your current rating?

If you're not satisfied, set a realistic goal for improvement:_____

Are you satisfied with your current level of cardiovascular fitness as evidenced in your daily life—your ability to walk, run, bicycle, climb stairs, do yard work, engage in recreational activities?

If you're not satisfied, set some realistic goals for improvement, such as completing a 5K run or 25-mile bike ride:

What should you do next? Enter the results of this lab in the Preprogram Assessment column in Appendix D. If you've set goals for improvement, begin planning your cardiorespiratory endurance exercise program by completing the plan in Lab 3.2. After several weeks of your program, complete this lab again, and enter the results in the Postprogram Assessment column of Appendix D. How do the results compare? (Remember, it's best to compare $\dot{V}O_{2max}$ scores for the same test.)

SOURCES: Kline, G. M., et al. 1987. Estimation of $\dot{V}O_{2max}$ from a one-mile track walk, gender, age, and body weight. *Medicine and Science in Sports and Exercise* 19(3): 253–259. McArdle, W. D., F. I. Katch, and V. L. Katch. 1991. *Exercise Physiology: Energy, Nutrition, and Human Performance.* Philadelphia: Lea and Febiger, pp. 225–226. Brooks, G. A., and T. D. Fahey. 1987. *Fundamentals of Human Performance.* New York: Macmillan.

LAB 3.2 *Developing an Exercise Program for Cardiorespiratory Endurance* WW

1. **Goals.** List goals for your cardiorespiratory endurance exercise program. Your goals can be specific or general, short or long term. In the first section, include specific, measurable goals that you can use to track the progress of your fitness program. These goals might be things like raising your cardiorespiratory fitness rating from fair to good or swimming laps for 30 minutes without resting. In the second section, include long-term and more qualitative goals, such as improving self-confidence and reducing your risk for chronic disease.

Specific Goals: Current Status   Final Goals

_____   _____

_____   _____

_____   _____

Other goals: _____

_____

2. **Type of Activities.** Choose one or more endurance activities for your program. These can include any activity that uses large-muscle groups, can be maintained continuously, and is rhythmic and aerobic in nature. Examples include walking, jogging, cycling, group exercise such as aerobic dance, rowing, rope skipping, stair-climbing, cross-country skiing, swimming, skating, and endurance game activities such as soccer and tennis. Choose activities that are both convenient and enjoyable. Fill in the activity names on the program plan.

3. **Frequency.** On the program plan, fill in how often you plan to participate in each activity; the ACSM recommends participating in cardiorespiratory endurance exercise 3–5 days per week.

Program Plan

| Type of Activity | Frequency (check ✓) | | | | | | | Intensity (bpm or RPE) | Time (min) |
	M	T	W	Th	F	Sa	Su		

4. **Intensity.** Determine your exercise intensity using one of the following methods, and enter it on the program plan. Begin your program at a lower intensity and slowly increase intensity as your fitness improves, so select a range of intensities for your program.

   a. Target heart rate zone: Calculate target heart rate zone in beats per minute and then calculate the corresponding 10-second exercise count by dividing the total count by 6. For example, the 10-second exercise counts corresponding to a target heart rate zone of 122–180 bpm would be 20–30 beats.

   Maximum heart rate: $220 - \underset{\text{age (years)}}{\underline{\hspace{2cm}}} = \underline{\hspace{2cm}}$ bpm

Maximum Heart Rate Method

65% training intensity $= \underset{\text{maximum heart rate}}{\underline{\hspace{3cm}}}$ bpm $\times\ 0.65 = \underline{\hspace{2cm}}$ bpm

90% training intensity $= \underset{\text{maximum heart rate}}{\underline{\hspace{3cm}}}$ bpm $\times\ 0.90 = \underline{\hspace{2cm}}$ bpm

Target heart rate zone $= \underline{\hspace{2cm}}$ to $\underline{\hspace{2cm}}$ bpm   **10-second count** $= \underline{\hspace{2cm}}$ to $\underline{\hspace{2cm}}$

Heart Rate Reserve Method

Resting heart rate: _____ bpm (taken after 10 minutes of complete rest)

Heart rate reserve = $\underset{\text{maximum heart rate}}{\underline{\hspace{2cm}}}$ bpm − $\underset{\text{resting heart rate}}{\underline{\hspace{2cm}}}$ bpm = _____ bpm

50% training intensity = ($\underset{\text{heart rate reserve}}{\underline{\hspace{2cm}}}$ bpm × 0.50) + $\underset{\text{resting heart rate}}{\underline{\hspace{2cm}}}$ bpm = _____ bpm

85% training intensity = ($\underset{\text{heart rate reserve}}{\underline{\hspace{2cm}}}$ bpm × 0.85) + $\underset{\text{resting heart rate}}{\underline{\hspace{2cm}}}$ bpm = _____ bpm

Target heart rate zone = _____ to _____ bpm   10-second count = _____ to _____

b. Ratings of perceived exertion (RPE): If you prefer, determine an RPE value that corresponds to your target heart rate range (see p. 73 and Figure 3.5).

5. **Time (Duration).** A total time of 20–60 minutes is recommended; your duration of exercise will vary with intensity. For developing cardiorespiratory endurance, higher-intensity activities can be performed for a shorter duration; lower intensities require a longer duration. Enter a duration (or a range of duration) on the program plan.

6. **Monitoring Your Program.** Complete a log like the one below to monitor your program and track your progress. Note the date on top, and fill in the intensity and time (duration) for each workout. If you prefer, you can also track other variables such as distance. For example, if your cardiorespiratory endurance program includes walking and swimming, you may want to track miles walked and yards swum in addition to the duration of each exercise session. For more extensive sets of logs, refer to the Daily Fitness and Nutrition Journal that accompanies your text.

Activity/Date													
1	Intensity												
	Time												
	Distance												
2	Intensity												
	Time												
	Distance												
3	Intensity												
	Time												
	Distance												
4	Intensity												
	Time												
	Distance												

7. **Making Progress.** Follow the guidelines in the chapter and Table 3.4 to slowly increase the amount of overload in your program. Continue keeping a log, and periodically evaluate your progress.

Progress Checkup: Week _____ of program

Goals: Original Status   Current Status

_____   _____

_____   _____

_____   _____

List each activity in your program and describe how satisfied you are with the activity and with your overall progress. List any problems you've encountered or any unexpected costs or benefits of your fitness program so far.

After reading this chapter, you should be able to

- Describe the basic physiology of muscles and how strength training affects muscles
- Define muscular strength and endurance and describe how they relate to wellness
- Explain how muscular strength and endurance can be assessed
- Apply the FITT principle to create a safe and successful strength training program
- Describe the effects of supplements and drugs that are marketed to active people and athletes
- Explain how to safely perform common strength training exercises using free weights and weight machines

4

Muscular Strength and Endurance

Test Your Knowledge

1. **For women, weight training typically results in which of the following?**
   a. bulky muscles
   b. significant increases in body weight
   c. improved body image

2. **To maximize strength gains, it is a good idea to hold your breath as you lift a weight.**
   True or false?

3. **Regular strength training is associated with which of the following benefits?**
   a. denser bones
   b. reduced risk of heart disease
   c. improved body composition
   d. higher grades

ANSWERS

1. C. Because the vast majority of women have low levels of testosterone, they do not develop large muscles or gain significant amounts of weight in response to a moderate weight training program. Men have higher levels of testosterone, so they can build large muscles more easily.

2. FALSE. Holding one's breath while lifting weights, called the Valsalva maneuver, can significantly (and possibly dangerously) elevate blood pressure; it also reduces blood flow to the heart and may cause faintness. You should breathe smoothly and normally while weight training. Some experts recommend that you exhale during the most difficult part of each exercise (the "sticking point").

3. ALL FOUR. Regular strength training has many benefits for lifetime wellness for both men and women.

ViW *Fit and Well* **Online Learning Center**   www.mhhe.com/fahey

Visit the *Fit and Well* Online Learning Center for study aids, online labs, additional information about muscular strength and endurance, links, Internet activities that explore the development of a strength training program, consumer resources, and much more.

Exercise experts have long emphasized the importance of cardiovascular fitness. Other physical fitness factors, such as muscle strength and flexibility, were mentioned almost as an afterthought. As more was learned about how the body responds to exercise, however, it became obvious that these other factors are vital to health, wellness, and overall quality of life. Muscles make up more than 40% of your body mass. You depend on them for movement, and, because of their mass, they are the site of a large portion of the energy reactions (metabolism) that take place in your body. Strong, well-developed muscles help you perform daily activities with greater ease, protect you from injury, and enhance your well-being in other ways.

As described in Chapter 2, **muscular strength** is the ability to generate force during a maximal effort; **muscular endurance** is the ability to resist fatigue while holding or repeating a muscular contraction. This chapter explains the benefits of strength training (also called resistance training) and describes methods of assessing muscular strength and endurance. It then explains the basics of weight training and provides guidelines for setting up your own strength training program.

BASIC MUSCLE PHYSIOLOGY AND THE EFFECTS OF STRENGTH TRAINING

Muscles move the body and enable it to exert force because they move the skeleton. When a muscle contracts (shortens), it moves a bone by pulling on the tendon that attaches the muscle to the bone. Muscles consist of individual muscle cells, or **muscle fibers,** connected in bundles (Figure 4.1). A single muscle is made up of many bundles of muscle fibers and is covered by layers of connective tissue that hold the fibers together. Muscle fibers, in turn, are made up of smaller units called **myofibrils.** Under a magnifying glass or a microscope, skeletal muscle fibers have a striped appearance due to the presence of actin and myosin, the two main proteins of contraction and the principal components of the myofibrils. A muscle contraction is triggered by nerve impulses that cause the release of calcium in the muscle; actin combines with myosin and ATP to produce force.

Strength training causes the size of individual muscle fibers to increase by increasing the number of myofibrils. Larger muscle fibers mean a larger and stronger muscle. The development of large muscle fibers is called **hypertrophy;** inactivity causes **atrophy,** the reversal of this process. In some species, muscles can increase in size through a separate process called **hyperplasia,** which involves an increase in the number of muscle fibers rather than the size of muscle fibers. In humans, hyperplasia is not thought to play a significant role in determining muscle size.

Muscle fibers are classified as slow-twitch or fast-twitch fibers according to their strength, speed of contraction, and energy source. **Slow-twitch fibers** are relatively fatigue-resistant, but they don't contract as rapidly or strongly as fast-twitch fibers. The principal energy system that fuels slow-twitch fibers is aerobic (oxidative). **Fast-twitch fibers** contract more rapidly and forcefully than slow-twitch fibers but fatigue more quickly. Although oxygen is important in the energy system that fuels fast-twitch fibers, they rely more on anaerobic (nonoxidative) metabolism than do slow-twitch fibers (see Chapter 3 for a discussion of energy systems).

Most muscles contain a mixture of slow-twitch and fast-twitch fibers. The proportion of the types of fibers varies significantly among different muscles and different

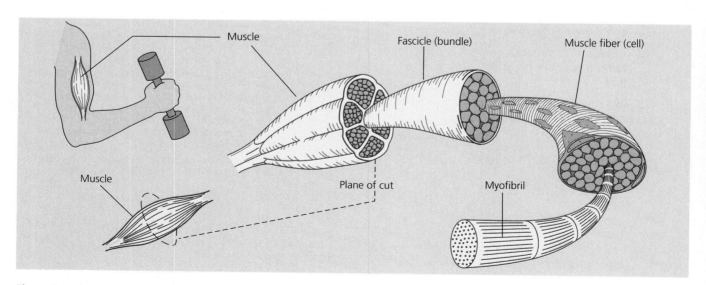

Figure 4.1 Components of skeletal muscle tissue.

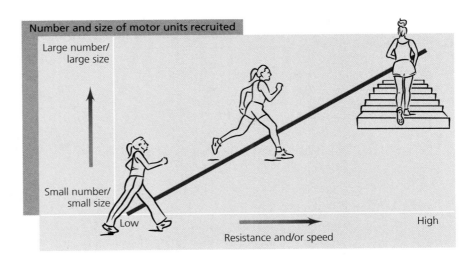

Figure 4.2 Motor unit recruitment during muscle contraction. The number and size of motor units recruited for muscle contraction depends on the load (amount of resistance) and the speed of the movement. For light resistance, a small number of small motor units, made up primarily of slow-twitch fibers, are recruited. To move against heavy resistance or to move a light object very fast, a large number of motor units are recruited, including both small and large motor units. Large motor units contain a high proportion of fast-twitch fibers.

individuals, and that proportion is largely fixed at birth, although fibers can contract faster or slower following a period of training or a period of inactivity. The type of fiber that acts during a particular activity depends on the type of work required. Endurance activities like jogging tend to use slow-twitch fibers, whereas strength and **power** activities like sprinting use fast-twitch fibers. Strength training can increase the size and strength of both fast-twitch and slow-twitch fibers, although fast-twitch fibers are preferentially increased.

To exert force, the body recruits one or more motor units to contract. A **motor unit** is made up of a nerve connected to a number of muscle fibers. The number of muscle fibers in a motor unit varies from two to hundreds. Small motor units contain slow-twitch fibers, while large motor units contain fast-twitch fibers. When a motor nerve calls on its fibers to contract, all fibers contract to their full capacity. The number of motor units recruited depends on the amount of strength required: When a person picks up a small weight, he or she uses fewer and smaller motor units than when picking up a large weight (Figure 4.2). Strength training improves the body's ability to recruit motor units—a phenomenon called muscle learning—which increases strength even before muscle size increases.

In summary, strength training increases muscle strength because it increases the size of muscle fibers and improves the body's ability to call on motor units to exert force. The physiological changes and benefits that result from strength training are summarized in Table 4.1.

BENEFITS OF MUSCULAR STRENGTH AND ENDURANCE

Enhanced muscular strength and endurance can lead to improvements in the areas of performance, injury prevention, body composition, self-image, lifetime muscle and bone health, and chronic disease prevention.

Improved Performance of Physical Activities

A person with a moderate-to-high level of muscular strength and endurance can perform everyday tasks—such as climbing stairs and carrying books or groceries—with ease. Muscular strength and endurance are also important in recreational activities: People with poor muscle strength tire more easily and are less effective in activities like hiking, skiing, and playing tennis. Increased strength can enhance your enjoyment of recreational sports by making it possible to achieve high levels of performance and to handle advanced techniques. Strength training also results in modest improvements in maximal oxygen consumption.

Terms

muscular strength The amount of force a muscle can produce with a single maximum effort.

muscular endurance The ability of a muscle or group of muscles to remain contracted (sustain a level of muscular force) or to contract repeatedly.

muscle fiber A single muscle cell, usually classified according to strength, speed of contraction, and energy source.

myofibrils Protein structures that make up muscle fibers.

hypertrophy An increase in the size of a muscle fiber, usually stimulated by muscular overload.

atrophy A decrease in the size of muscle cells.

hyperplasia An increase in the number of muscle cells.

slow-twitch fibers Red muscle fibers that are fatigue-resistant but have a slow contraction speed and a lower capacity for tension; usually recruited for endurance activities.

fast-twitch fibers White muscle fibers that contract rapidly and forcefully but fatigue quickly; usually recruited for actions requiring strength and power.

power The ability to exert force rapidly.

motor unit A motor nerve (one that initiates movement) connected to one or more muscle fibers.

Table 4.1	Physiological Changes and Benefits from Strength Training
Change	**Benefits**
Increased muscle mass*	Increased muscular strength Improved body composition Higher rate of metabolism Toned, healthy-looking muscles
Increased utilization of motor units during muscle contractions	Increased muscular strength and power
Improved coordination of motor units	Increased muscular strength and power
Increased strength of tendons, ligaments, and bones	Lower risk of injury to these tissues
Increased storage of fuel in muscles	Increased resistance to muscle fatigue
Increased size of fast-twitch muscle fibers (from a high-resistance program)	Increased muscular strength and power
Increased size of slow-twitch muscle fibers (from a high-repetition program)	Increased muscular endurance
Increased blood supply to muscles (from a high-repetition program)	Increased delivery of oxygen and nutrients Increased elimination of wastes
Biochemical improvements (for example, increased sensitivity to insulin)	Enhanced metabolic health
Improved blood fat levels	Reduced risk of heart disease

*Due to genetic and hormonal differences, men will build more muscle mass than women, but both genders make about the same percent gains in strength through a good program.

Injury Prevention

Increased muscle strength and endurance provides protection against injury because it helps people maintain good posture and appropriate body mechanics when carrying out everyday activities like walking, lifting, and carrying. Good muscle strength and, particularly, endurance in the abdomen, hips, lower back, and legs support the back in proper alignment and help prevent low-back pain, which afflicts more than 85% of Americans at some time in their lives. (Prevention of low-back pain is discussed in Chapter 5.) Training for muscular strength and endurance also makes the **tendons, ligaments,** and cartilage cells stronger and less susceptible to injury. Resistance exercise prevents injuries best when the strength training program is gradual, progressive, and builds all the major muscle groups.

Improved Body Composition

As Chapter 2 explained, healthy body composition means that the body has a high proportion of fat-free mass (primarily composed of muscle) and a relatively small proportion of fat. Strength training improves body composition by increasing muscle mass, thereby tipping the body composition ratio toward fat-free mass and away from fat. Building muscle mass through strength training also helps with losing fat because metabolic rate is related to muscle mass: The more muscle mass, the higher the metabolic rate. A high metabolic rate means that a nutritionally sound diet coupled with regular exercise will not lead to an increase in body fat. Strength training can boost resting metabolic rate by 0–15%, depending on how hard

you train. Resistance exercise also increases muscle temperature, which in turn slightly increases the rate at which you burn calories over the hours following a weight training session.

Enhanced Self-Image and Quality of Life

Strength training leads to an enhanced self-image by providing stronger, firmer-looking muscles and a toned, healthy-looking body. Men tend to build larger, stronger muscles. Women tend to lose inches, increase strength, and develop greater muscle definition. The larger muscles in men combine with high levels of the hormone **testosterone** for a strong tissue-building effect; see the box "Gender Differences in Muscular Strength." Strength training improves body image in both men and women.

Because strength training involves measurable objectives (pounds lifted, repetitions accomplished), a person can easily recognize improved performance, leading to greater self-confidence and self-esteem. It's especially satisfying to work on improving one's personal record. Strength training also improves quality of life by increasing energy, preventing injuries, and making daily activities easier and more enjoyable.

Improved Muscle and Bone Health with Aging

Research has shown that good muscle strength helps people live healthier lives. A lifelong program of regular strength training prevents muscle and nerve degeneration that can compromise the quality of life and increase

Men are generally stronger than women because they typically have larger bodies overall and a larger proportion of their total body mass is made up of muscle. But when strength is expressed per unit of cross-sectional area of muscle tissue, men are only 1–2% stronger than women in the upper body and about equal to women in the lower body. (Men have a larger proportion of muscle tissue in the upper body, so it's easier for them to build upper-body strength than it is for women.) Individual muscle fibers are larger in men, but the metabolism of cells within those fibers is the same in both sexes.

Two factors that help explain these disparities are testosterone levels and the speed of nervous control of muscle. Testosterone is responsible for the development of secondary sex characteristics in males (facial hair, deep voice, and so forth). Testosterone also promotes the growth of muscle tissue in both males and females. Testosterone levels are about 5–10 times higher in men than in women, so men tend to have larger muscles. Also, because

the male nervous system can activate muscles faster, men tend to have more power.

Some women are concerned that they will develop large muscles from strength training. Because of hormonal differences, most women do not develop big muscles unless they train intensely over many years or take anabolic steroids. Women do gain muscle and improve body composition through strength training, but they don't develop bulky muscles or gain significant amounts of weight: A study of average women who weight trained 2–3 days per week for 8 weeks found that the women gained about 1.75 pounds of muscle and lost about 3.5 pounds of fat.

Losing muscle over time is a much greater health concern for women than small gains in muscle weight in response to strength training, especially because any gains in muscle weight are typically more than balanced with loss of fat weight. Both men and women lose muscle mass and power as they age, but because men start out with more muscle when they are young and don't lose power as

quickly, older women tend to have greater impairment of muscle function than older men. This may partially account for the higher incidence of life-threatening falls in older women.

The bottom line is that both men and women can increase strength through strength training. Women may not be able to lift as much weight as men, but pound for pound of muscle, they have nearly the same capacity to gain strength as men. The lifetime wellness benefits of strength training are available to everyone. Strength training is particularly beneficial for women because it helps prevent bone and muscle loss with aging and maintains fat-free weight during weight control programs.

SOURCES: Fahey, T. D. 2006. *Weight Training for Men and Women,* 6th ed. New York: McGraw-Hill. IDEA. 2001. *Fitness Tip—Why Women Need Weight Training* (http://www.ideafit.com/ftwomen.htm; retrieved October 22, 2002). Krivickas, L. S., et al. 2001. Age and gender-related differences in maximum shortening velocity of skeletal muscle fibers. *American Journal of Physical Medicine and Rehabilitation* 80:447–455.

the risk of hip fractures and other potentially life-threatening injuries. In the general population, people begin to lose muscle mass after age 30, a condition called *sarcopenia.* At first they may notice that they can't play sports as well as they could in high school. After more years of inactivity and strength loss, people may have trouble performing even the simple movements of daily life—getting out of a bathtub or automobile, walking up a flight of stairs, or doing yard work. By age 75 about 25% of men and 75% of women can't lift more than 10 pounds. Although aging contributes to decreased strength, inactivity causes most of the loss. Poor strength makes it much more likely that a person will be injured during everyday activities.

As a person ages, motor nerves can become disconnected from the portion of muscle they control. Muscle physiologists estimate that by age 70, 15% of the motor nerves in most people are no longer connected to muscle tissue. Aging and inactivity also cause muscles to become slower and therefore less able to perform quick, powerful movements. Strength training helps maintain motor nerve connections and the quickness of muscles.

Osteoporosis is common in people over age 55, particularly postmenopausal women. Osteoporosis leads to

fractures that can be life-threatening. Hormonal changes from aging account for much of the bone loss that occurs, but lack of bone stress due to inactivity and a poor diet are contributing factors. Strength training can lessen bone loss even if it is taken up later in life, and if practiced regularly, strength training can even build bone mass in post-menopausal women and older men. Increased muscle strength can also help prevent falls, which are a major cause of injury in people with osteoporosis. (Additional strategies for preventing osteoporosis are described in Chapter 8.)

Terms

tendon A tough band of fibrous tissue that connects a muscle to a bone or other body part and transmits the force exerted by the muscle.

ligament A tough band of tissue that connects the ends of bones to other bones or supports organs in place.

testosterone The principal male hormone, responsible for the development of secondary sex characteristics and important in increasing muscle size.

Prevention and Management of Chronic Disease

Strength training helps in the prevention and management of several major chronic diseases. Strength training improves glucose metabolism, an important factor in the prevention of the most common form of diabetes (type 2 diabetes). As described earlier, it also boosts bone mineral density, helping to prevent osteoporosis and associated bone fractures. Strength training also modifies risk factors for cardiovascular disease. Regular strength training is associated with small increases in maximal oxygen consumption, decreased systolic and diastolic blood pressures, and, in some people, positive changes in blood fat levels (increased HDL cholesterol and decreased LDL cholesterol). Improvements in body composition and glucose metabolism are also beneficial for cardiovascular health.

Strength training is important for a healthy heart and is appropriate for many people with heart disease. In addition to reducing the coronary heart disease risk factors just described, stronger muscles reduce the demand on the heart during ordinary daily activities such as lifting and carrying objects. The benefits of resistive exercise to the heart are so strong that the American Heart Association recommends that healthy adults and many low-risk cardiac patients do strength training 2–3 days per week. Resistance training is not appropriate for people with some types of heart disease.

MOTIVATION FOR CHANGE! Make a list of five benefits of muscular strength and endurance that are particularly meaningful to you—reducing your risk of back pain, for example, or improving your tennis game. Post the list in a prominent location and use it as a motivational tool for beginning and maintaining your strength training program.

Terms

Vlw

repetition maximum (RM) The maximum amount of resistance that can be moved a specified number of times; 1 RM is the maximum weight that can be lifted once. 5 RM is the maximum weight that can be lifted five times.

repetitions The number of times an exercise is performed during one set.

static (isometric) exercise Exercise involving a muscle contraction without a change in the length of the muscle.

dynamic (isotonic) exercise Exercise involving a muscle contraction with a change in the length of the muscle.

concentric muscle contraction An isotonic contraction in which the muscle gets shorter as it contracts.

eccentric muscle contraction An isotonic contraction in which the muscle lengthens as it contracts; also called a *pliometric contraction*.

ASSESSING MUSCULAR STRENGTH AND ENDURANCE

Muscular strength and muscular endurance are distinct but related components of fitness. Muscular strength, the maximum amount of force a muscle can produce in a single effort, is usually assessed by measuring the maximum amount of weight a person can lift one time. This single maximal movement is referred to as a **repetition maximum (RM).** You can assess the strength of your major muscle groups by taking the one-repetition maximum (1 RM) tests for the bench press and the leg press. You can measure 1 RM directly or estimate it by doing multiple repetitions with a submaximal (lighter) weight. It is best to train for at least several weeks before attempting a direct 1 RM test; once you have a baseline value, you can retest after 6–12 weeks to check your progress. Refer to Lab 4.1 for guidelines on taking these tests. Instructions for assessing grip strength using a dynamometer are also included in Lab 4.1. For more accurate results, avoid any strenuous weight training for 48 hours beforehand.

Muscular endurance is the ability of a muscle to exert a submaximal force repeatedly or continuously over time. This ability depends on muscular strength because a certain amount of strength is required for any muscle movement. Muscular endurance is usually assessed by counting the maximum number of **repetitions** of a muscular contraction a person can do (such as in push-ups) or the maximum amount of time a person can hold a muscular contraction (such as in the flexed-arm hang). You can test the muscular endurance of major muscle groups in your body by taking the curl-up test and the push-up test. Refer to Lab 4.2 for complete instructions on taking these assessment tests.

Record your results and your fitness rating from the assessment tests in Labs 4.1 and 4.2. If the results show that improvement is needed, a weight training program will enable you to make rapid gains in muscular strength and endurance.

CREATING A SUCCESSFUL STRENGTH TRAINING PROGRAM

Strength training develops muscular strength and endurance in the same way that endurance exercise develops cardiovascular fitness: When the muscles are stressed by a greater load than they are used to, they adapt and improve their function. The type of adaptation that occurs depends on the type of stress applied. To get the most out of your strength training program, design it to achieve maximum fitness benefits with minimum risk of injury. Before you begin, seriously consider the type and amount of training that's right for you.

Left: A concentric contraction: The biceps muscle shortens as the arm lifts a weight toward the shoulder. **Right:** An eccentric contraction: The biceps muscle lengthens as the arm lowers a weight toward the thigh.

 ## Static Versus Dynamic Strength Training Exercises

Strength training exercises are generally classified as static or dynamic. Each involves a different way of using and strengthening muscles.

Static Exercise Also called **isometric** exercise, **static exercise** involves a muscle contraction without a change in the length of the muscle or the angle in the joint on which the muscle acts. To perform an isometric exercise, a person can use an immovable object like a wall to provide resistance, or just tighten a muscle while remaining still (for example, tightening the abdominal muscles while sitting at a desk). In isometrics, the muscle contracts, but there is no movement.

Isometric exercises aren't as widely used as isotonic exercises because they don't develop strength throughout a joint's entire range of motion. However, static exercises are useful in strengthening muscles after an injury or surgery, when movement of the affected joint could delay healing. Isometrics are also used to overcome weak points in an individual's range of motion. Statically strengthening a muscle at its weakest point will allow more weight to be lifted with that muscle during dynamic exercise. Certain types of calisthenics and Pilates exercises (described in more detail later in the chapter) also involve static contractions. For maximum strength gains, hold the isometric contraction maximally for 6 seconds; do 5–10 repetitions.

Dynamic Exercise Also called **isotonic** exercise, **dynamic exercise** involves a muscle contraction with a change in the length of the muscle. (Isotonic means "same tension," which does not accurately describe the way muscles contract, but the term is widely used to describe dynamic exercises.) Dynamic exercises are the most popular type of exercises for increasing muscle strength and seem to be most valuable for developing strength that can be transferred to other forms of physical activity. They can be performed with weight machines, free weights, or a person's own body weight (as in sit-ups or push-ups).

There are two kinds of dynamic muscle contractions: concentric and eccentric. A **concentric muscle contraction** occurs when the muscle applies enough force to overcome resistance and shortens as it contracts. An **eccentric muscle contraction** (also called a pliometric contraction) occurs when the resistance is greater than the force applied by the muscle and the muscle lengthens as it contracts. For example, in an arm curl, the biceps muscle works concentrically as the weight is raised toward the shoulder and eccentrically as the weight is lowered.

Two of the most common dynamic exercise techniques are constant resistance exercise and variable resistance exercise. Constant resistance exercise uses a constant load (weight) throughout a joint's entire range of motion. Training with free weights is a form of constant resistance exercise. A problem with this technique is that, because of differences in leverage, there are points in a joint's range of motion where the muscle controlling the movement is stronger and points where it is weaker. The amount of weight a person can lift is limited by the weakest point in the range. In variable resistance exercise, the load is changed to provide maximum load throughout the entire range of motion. This form of exercise uses machines that place more stress on muscles at the end of the range of motion, where a person has better leverage and is capable of exerting more force. The Nautilus pull-over machine is an example of a variable resistance exercise machine. Constant and variable resistance exercises are both extremely effective for building strength and endurance.

Four other kinds of isotonic techniques, used mainly by athletes for training and rehabilitation, are eccentric loading, plyometrics, speed loading, and isokinetics.

• **Eccentric (pliometric) loading** involves placing a load on a muscle as it lengthens. The muscle contracts eccentrically in order to control the weight. Eccentric loading is practiced during most types of resistance training. For example, you are performing an eccentric movement as you lower the weight to your chest during a bench press in preparation for the active movement. You can also perform exercises designed specifically to overload muscle eccentrically, a technique called negatives.

• **Plyometrics** is the sudden eccentric loading and stretching of muscles followed by a forceful concentric contraction. An example would be the action of the lower-body muscles when jumping from a bench to the ground and then jumping back onto the bench. This type of exercise is used to develop explosive strength; it also helps build and maintain bone density.

• **Speed loading** involves moving a weight as rapidly as possible in an attempt to approach the speeds used in movements like throwing a softball or sprinting. In the bench press, for example, speed loading might involve doing 5 repetitions as fast as possible using a weight that is half the maximum load you can lift. You can gauge your progress by timing how fast you can perform the repetitions.

• **Isokinetic** exercise involves exerting force at a constant speed against an equal force exerted by a special strength training machine. The isokinetic machine

provides variable resistance at different points in the joint's range of motion, matching the effort applied by the individual, while keeping the speed of the movement constant. In other words, the force exerted by the individual at any point in the range of motion is resisted by an equal force from the isokinetic machine. Isokinetic exercises are excellent for building strength and endurance, but the equipment is expensive and less commonly available than other kinds of weight machines.

Comparing the Different Types of Exercise

Static exercises require no equipment, so they can be done virtually anywhere. They build strength rapidly and are useful for rehabilitating injured joints. On the other hand, they have to be performed at several different angles for each joint to improve strength throughout the joint's entire range of motion. Dynamic exercises can be performed without equipment (calisthenics) or with equipment (weight training). They are excellent for building strength and endurance, and they tend to build strength through a joint's full range of motion.

Most people develop muscular strength and endurance using dynamic exercises. Ultimately, the type of exercise a person chooses depends on individual goals, preferences, and access to equipment.

Weight Machines Versus Free Weights

Your muscles will get stronger if you make them work against a resistance. Resistance can be provided by free weights, by your own body weight, or by sophisticated exercise machines. Weight machines are preferred by many people because they are safe, convenient, and easy to use. You just set the resistance (usually by placing a pin in the weight stack), sit down at the machine, and start working. Machines make it easy to isolate and work specific muscles. You don't need a **spotter**, someone who stands by to assist when free weights are used, and you don't have to worry about dropping a weight on yourself.

Free weights require more care, balance, and coordination to use, but they strengthen your body in ways that are more adaptable to real life. They are also more popular with athletes for developing explosive strength for sports. Unless you are training seriously for a sport that requires a great deal of strength, training on machines is probably safer, more convenient, and just as effective as training with free weights. However, you can increase strength with either weight machines or free weights. Information listed in the box "Exercise Machines Versus Free Weights" can help you make a decision about which equipment you may prefer.

Terms

eccentric (pliometric) loading Loading the muscle while it is lengthening; sometimes called *negatives*.

plyometrics Rapid stretching of a muscle group that is undergoing eccentric stress (the muscle is exerting force while it lengthens), followed by a rapid concentric contraction.

speed loading Moving a load as rapidly as possible.

isokinetic The application of force at a constant speed against an equal force.

spotter A person who assists with a weight training exercise done with free weights.

Exercise Machines

Advantages

- Safe and convenient
- Don't require spotters
- Don't require lifter to balance bar
- Provide variable resistance
- Require less skill
- Make it easy to move from one exercise to the next
- Allow easy isolation of muscles and muscle groups
- Support back (on many machines)

Disadvantages

- Limited availability
- Inappropriate for performing dynamic movements
- Allow a limited number of exercises
- Train muscles rather than movements
- Minimal stress is placed on the core stabilizing muscles (those in the torso)

Free Weights

Advantages

- Allow dynamic movements
- Allow the user to develop control of the weights
- Allow a greater variety of exercises
- Widely available; inexpensive and convenient for home use
- Many exercises train core stabilizing muscles
- Better for building power
- Truer to real-life situations; strength transfers to daily activities

Disadvantages

- Not as safe
- Require spotters
- Require more skill
- Cause more blisters and calluses

Other Training Methods and Types of Equipment

Remember, you don't need a fitness center or expensive equipment to strength train. If you prefer to train at home and/or like low-cost equipment alternatives, consider the following.

Resistance Bands   Resistance or exercise bands are elastic strips or tubes of rubber material that are inexpensive, lightweight, and portable. They are available in a variety of styles and levels of resistance; some are sold with instructional guides or DVDs, and classes may be offered at fitness centers. Many free weights exercises can be adapted for resistance bands. For example, you can do biceps curls by standing on the center of the band and holding one end of the band in each hand; resistance is provided when you try to stretch the band further to perform the curl. Special guidelines for using resistance bands safely include examining them regularly for flaws and tears and taking care to avoid snapping the bands. Keeping a firm grip on the bands may require wrapping or looping the band; some people find bands with pre-formed handles easier to grasp.

Exercise (Stability) Balls   The exercise or stability ball is an extra-large inflatable ball. It was originally developed for use in physical therapy but has become a popular piece of exercise equipment for use in the home or gym. It can be used to work the entire body, but it is particularly effective for working the so-called stability muscles ("the core") in the abdomen, chest, and back—muscles that are important for preventing back problems. The ball's instability forces the exerciser to use the stability muscles to balance the body—even when a person simply sits on the ball. Moves such as crunches have been found to be more effective when they are performed with an exercise ball.

When choosing a ball, check that your thighs are parallel to the ground when you sit on it; if you are a beginner or have back problems, choose a larger ball so that your thighs are at an angle, with hips higher than knees. Beginners should use caution until they feel comfortable with the movements and take care to avoid poor form due to fatigue. Although stability ball exercises are generally safe, use of poor technique can cause the ball to move or roll rapidly and cause falls. It is a good idea to take a class or obtain help from a trainer to learn proper technique and create an effective stability program.

Pilates   Pilates (*pil LAH teez*) was developed by German gymnast and boxer George Pilates early in the twentieth century. It often involves the use of specially designed resistance training devices, although some classes feature just mat or floor work. Pilates focuses on strengthening and stretching the core muscles in the back, abdomen, and buttocks to create a solid base of support for whole-body movement; the emphasis is on concentration, control, movement flow, and breathing. Mat exercises can be done at home, but because there are hundreds of Pilates exercises, some of them strenuous, it is best to begin with some qualified instruction. The Pilates Method Alliance (www.pilatesmethodalliance.com) offers advice on finding a qualified teacher.

Resistance for strength training can be provided by many different techniques and types of equipment. Shown here are resistance bands (top), a stability ball (center), and a Pilates mat exercise that uses body weight for resistance.

No-Equipment Calisthenics Resistance can be provided by your own body weight. Exercises such as sit-ups, push-ups, squats, step-ups, heel raises, chair dips, and lunges can be done anywhere.

Examples of strength training programs using these techniques can be found on the *Fit and Well* Online Learning Center; the Web resources include video clips showing several different types of exercises using resistance bands and stability balls.

Applying the FITT Principle: Selecting Exercises and Putting Together a Program

A complete weight training program works all the major muscle groups. It usually takes about 8–10 different exercises to get a complete workout. Use the FITT principle—frequency, intensity, time, and type—to set the parameters of your program.

Frequency of Exercise For general fitness, the American College of Sports Medicine recommends a frequency of 2–3 nonconsecutive days per week for weight training. Allow your muscles at least 1 day of rest between workouts; if you train too often, your muscles won't be able to work at a high enough intensity to improve their fitness, and soreness and injury are more likely to result. If you enjoy weight training and would like to train more often, try working different muscle groups on alternate days—a training plan called a split routine. For example, work your arms and upper body one day, work your lower body the next day, and then return to upper-body exercises on the third day.

Intensity of Exercise: Amount of Resistance
The amount of weight (resistance) you lift in weight training exercises is equivalent to intensity in cardiorespiratory endurance training. It determines the way your body will adapt to weight training and how quickly these adaptations will occur. Choose weights based on your current level of muscular fitness and your fitness goals. To build strength rapidly, you should lift weights as heavy as 80% of your maximum capacity (1 RM). If you're more interested in building endurance, choose a lighter weight (perhaps 40–60% of 1 RM) and do more repetitions. For example, if your maximum capacity for the leg press is 160 pounds, you might lift 130 pounds to build strength and 80 pounds to build endurance. For a general fitness program to develop both strength and endurance, choose a weight in the middle of this range, perhaps 70% of 1 RM. Or you can create a program that includes both higher-intensity exercise (80% of 1 RM for 8–10 repetitions) and lower-intensity exercise (60% of 1 RM for 15–20 repetitions); this routine will develop both fast-twitch and slow-twitch muscle fibers.

Women should not use light weights or resistance in an effort to prevent developing bulky muscles. Resistive exercise helps women gain muscle and lose fat. Muscle is less dense than fat, so weight training and similar exercises will not produce excess bulk. As discussed, testosterone levels largely determine increases in muscle size during strength training. College-age women have only about one-fifth the testosterone of college-age men.

Because it can be tedious and time-consuming to continually reassess your maximum capacity for each exercise, you might find it easier to choose a weight based on the number of repetitions of an exercise you can perform with a given resistance.

Time of Exercise: Repetitions and Sets

To improve fitness, you must do enough repetitions of each exercise to fatigue your muscles. The number of repetitions needed to cause fatigue depends on the amount of resistance: the heavier the weight, the fewer repetitions to reach fatigue. In general, a heavy weight and a low number of repetitions (1–5) build strength and overload primarily fast-twitch fibers, whereas a light weight and a high number of repetitions (15–20) build endurance and overload primarily slow-twitch fibers (Figure 4.3). For a general fitness program to build both strength and endurance, try to do about 8–12 repetitions of each exercise; a few exercises, such as abdominal crunches and calf raises, may require more. Choose a weight heavy enough to fatigue your muscles but light enough for you to complete the repetitions with good form. To avoid risk of injury, older (approximately age 50–60 and above) and frailer people should perform more repetitions (10–15) using a lighter weight.

In weight training, a **set** refers to a group of repetitions of an exercise followed by a rest period. For developing strength and endurance for general fitness, you can make gains doing a single set of each exercise, provided you use enough resistance to fatigue your muscles. (You should just barely be able to complete the 8–12 repetitions—using good form—for each exercise.) Doing more than 1 set of each exercise will increase strength development, and most serious weight trainers do at least 3 sets of each exercise (see the section "More Advanced Strength Training Programs" for guidelines on more advanced programs).

If you perform more than 1 set of an exercise, you need to rest long enough between sets to allow your muscles to work at a high enough intensity to increase fitness. The length of the rest interval depends on the amount of resistance. In a program to develop a combination of strength and endurance for wellness, a rest period of 1–3 minutes between sets is appropriate; if you are lifting heavier loads to build maximum strength, rest 3–5 minutes between sets. You can save time in your workouts if you alternate sets of different exercises. Each muscle group can rest between sets while you work on other muscles.

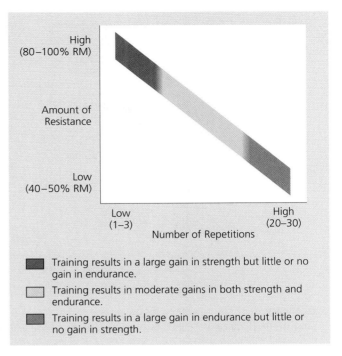

Figure 4.3 **Training for strength versus training for endurance.**

Overtraining—doing more exercise than your body can recover from—can occur in response to heavy resistance training. Possible signs of overtraining include lack of progress or decreased performance, chronic fatigue, decreased coordination, and chronic muscle soreness. The best remedy for overtraining is rest: Add more days of recovery between workouts. With extra rest, chances are you'll be refreshed and ready to train again. Adding variety to your program, discussed later in the chapter, can also help with overtraining from resistance exercise.

Type or Mode of Exercise

For overall fitness, you need to include exercises for your neck, upper back, shoulders, arms, chest, abdomen, lower back, thighs, buttocks, and calves—about 8–10 exercises in all. If you are also training for a particular sport, include exercises to strengthen the muscles important for optimal performance *and* the muscles most likely to be injured. A weight training program for general fitness is presented later in this chapter, on pp. 115–126.

It is important to balance exercises between **agonist** and **antagonist** muscle groups. (When a muscle

Terms

set A group of repetitions followed by a rest period.

agonist A muscle in a state of contraction, opposed by the action of another muscle, its *antagonist*.

antagonist A muscle that opposes the action of another muscle, its *agonist*.

Figure 4.4 The FITT principle for a strength training workout.

Warm-up 5–10 minutes	Strength training exercises for major muscle groups (8–10 exercises)		Cool-down 5–10 minutes
	Sample program		
	Exercise	*Muscle group developed*	
	Bench press	Chest, shoulders, triceps	
	Pull-ups	Lats, biceps	
	Shoulder press	Shoulders, trapezius, triceps	
	Upright rowing	Deltoids, trapezius	
	Biceps curls	Biceps	
	Lateral raises	Shoulders	
	Squats	Gluteals, quadriceps	
	Heel raises	Calves	
	Abdominal curls	Abdominals	
	Spine extensions	Low- and mid-back spine extensors	
Start	Side bridges	Obliques, quadratus lumborum	*Stop*

Frequency: 2–3 nonconsecutive days per week

Intensity/Resistance: Weights heavy enough to cause muscle fatigue when exercises are performed with good form for the selected number of repetitions

Time: Repetitions: 8–12 of each exercise (10–15 with a lower weight for people over age 50–60); **Sets:** 1 (doing more than 1 set per exercise may result in faster and greater strength gains)

Type of activity: 8–10 strength training exercises that focus on major muscle groups

contracts, it is known as the agonist; the opposing muscle, which must relax and stretch to allow contraction by the agonist, is known as the antagonist.) Whenever you do an exercise that moves a joint in one direction, also select an exercise that works the joint in the opposite direction. For example, if you do knee extensions to develop the muscles on the front of your thighs, also do leg curls to develop the antagonistic muscles on the back of your thighs.

The order of exercises can also be important. Do exercises for large-muscle groups or for more than one joint before you do exercises that use small-muscle groups or single joints. This allows for more effective overload of the larger, more powerful muscle groups. Small-muscle groups fatigue more easily than larger ones, and small-muscle fatigue limits your capacity to overload large-muscle groups. For example, lateral raises, which work the shoulder muscles, should be performed after bench presses, which work the chest and arms in addition to the shoulders. If you fatigue your shoulder muscles by doing lateral raises first, you won't be able to lift as much weight and effectively fatigue all the key muscle groups used during the bench press. Also, order exercises so that you work agonist and antagonist muscle groups in sequence, one after the other. For example, follow biceps curls, which work the biceps, with triceps extensions, which exercise the triceps—the antagonist muscle to the biceps.

The Warm-Up and Cool-Down

As with cardiorespiratory endurance exercise, you should warm up before every weight training session and cool down afterward (Figure 4.4). You should do both a general warm-up—several minutes of walking or easy jogging—and a warm-up for the weight training exercises you plan to perform. For example, if you plan to do 1 or more sets of 10 repetitions of bench presses with 125 pounds, you might do 1 set of 10 repetitions with 50 pounds as a warm-up. Do similar warm-up exercises for each exercise in your program.

To cool down after weight training, relax for 5–10 minutes after your workout. Although this is controversial, a few studies have suggested that including a period of postexercise stretching may help prevent muscle soreness; warmed-up muscles and joints make this a particularly good time to work on flexibility.

Getting Started and Making Progress

The first few sessions of weight training should be devoted to learning the exercises. You need to learn the movements, and your nervous system needs to practice communicating with your muscles so you can develop strength effectively. To start, choose a weight that you can move easily through 8–12 repetitions, and do only 1 set of each exercise. Gradually add weight and (if you want)

Exercise/Date		9/14	9/16	9/18	9/21	9/23	9/25	9/28	9/30	10/2	10/5	10/7	10/9	10/12	10/14	10/16
Bench press	Wt.	45	45	45	50	50	50	60	60	60	60	65	65	70	70	70
	Sets	1	1	1	1	1	1	1	1	1	1	1	1	1	1	1
	Reps.	10	12	12	10	12	12	10	9	12	12	12	12	9	9	10
Pull-ups (assisted)	Wt.	–	–	–	–	–	–	–	–	–	–	–	–	–	–	–
	Sets	1	1	1	1	1	1	1	1	1	1	1	1	1	1	1
	Reps.	5	5	5	6	6	6	7	7	7	8	8	8	9	9	10
Shoulder press	Wt.	20	20	20	25	25	25	30	30	30	30	30	30	35	35	35
	Sets	1	1	1	1	1	1	1	1	1	1	1	1	1	1	1
	Reps.	10	12	12	10	12	12	8	10	9	10	12	12	10	10	10
Upright rowing	Wt.	5	5	10	10	10	10	12	12	12	12	15	15	15	15	15
	Sets	1	1	1	1	1	1	1	1	1	1	1	1	1	1	1
	Reps.	12	12	8	10	11	12	9	10	12	12	8	8	8	9	10
Biceps curls	Wt.	15	15	15	20	20	20	25	25	25	25	25	25	30	30	30
	Sets	1	1	1	1	1	1	1	1	1	1	1	1	1	1	1
	Reps.	10	10	10	10	12	12	8	10	10	10	12	12	9	10	12
Lateral raise	Wt.	5	5	5	5	5	5	7.5	7.5	7.5	7.5	7.5	7.5	10	10	10
	Sets	1	1	1	1	1	1	1	1	1	1	1	1	1	1	1
	Reps.	8	8	10	10	12	12	8	10	10	10	12	12	8	8	9
Squats	Wt.	–	–	–	45	45	45	55	55	55	65	65	65	75	75	75
	Sets	1	1	1	1	1	1	1	1	1	1	1	1	1	1	1
	Reps.	10	12	15	8	12	12	8	12	12	10	13	12	8	10	10
Heel raises	Wt.	–	–	–	45	45	45	55	55	55	65	65	65	75	75	75
	Sets	1	1	1	1	1	1	1	1	1	1	1	1	1	1	1
	Reps.	15	15	15	8	12	12	10	12	12	10	12	12	10	9	12
Abdominal curls	Wt.	–	–	–	–	–	–	–	–	–	–	–	–	–	–	–
	Sets	1	1	1	1	1	1	1	1	1	1	1	1	1	1	1
	Reps.	20	20	20	20	20	20	25	25	25	25	25	25	25	25	25
Spine extensions	Wt.	–	–	–	–	–	–	–	–	–	–	–	–	–	–	–
	Sets	1	1	1	1	1	1	1	1	1	1	1	1	1	1	1
	Reps.	5	5	5	8	8	8	10	10	10	10	10	10	11	12	12
Side bridge	Wt.	–	–	–	–	–	–	–	–	–	–	–	–	–	–	–
	Sets	1	1	1	1	1	1	1	1	1	1	1	1	1	1	1
	Seconds	60	60	60	65	65	70	70	70	70	76	75	80	80	80	80

Figure 4.5   A sample workout card for a general fitness strength training program.

sets to your program over the first few weeks until you are doing 1–3 sets of 8–12 repetitions of each exercise.

As you progress, add weight according to the "two-for-two" rule: When you can perform two additional repetitions with a given weight on two consecutive training sessions, increase the load. For example, if your target is to perform 8–10 repetitions per exercise, and you performed 12 repetitions at your previous two workouts, it would be appropriate to increase your load. If adding weight means you can do only 7 or 8 repetitions, stay with that weight until you can again complete more than 12 repetitions per set. If you can do only 4–6 repetitions after adding weight, or if you can't maintain good form, you've added too much and should take some off. Knowing how much resistance to add and when to add it is as much an art as a science. You can add more resistance in large-muscle exercises, such as squats and bench presses, than you can in small-muscle exercises, such as curls. For example, when you can complete more than 12 repetitions of squats with good form, you may be able to add 10–20 pounds of additional resistance; for curls, on the other hand, you might add only 3–5 pounds. As a general guideline, try increases of approximately 5%, half a pound of additional weight for each 10 pounds you are currently lifting.

You can expect to improve rapidly during the first 6–10 weeks of training: a 10–30% increase in the amount of weight lifted. Gains will then come more slowly. Your rate of improvement will depend on how hard you work and how your body responds to resistance training. There will be individual differences in the rate of improvement. Factors such as age, gender, motivation, and heredity will affect your progress.

Your ultimate goal depends on you. But be sure your goal is realistic. For most people, it is unrealistic to strive for the appearance of bodybuilders and fitness models appearing in magazines; most of these athletes and models are genetically gifted with muscular bodies, and some take dangerous drugs to develop such large, well-defined muscles. After you have achieved the level of strength and muscularity that you want, you can maintain your gains by training 2–3 days per week. You can monitor the progress of your program by recording the amount of resistance and the number of repetitions and sets you perform on a workout card like the one shown in Figure 4.5.

Spotters should be present when a person trains with free weights. If two spotters are used, one spotter should stand at each end of the barbell. If one spotter is present, he or she should stand behind the lifter.

More Advanced Strength Training Programs

The weight training program described in this section—at least 1 set of 8–12 repetitions of 8–10 exercises, performed 2–3 days per week—is sufficient to develop and maintain muscular strength and endurance for general fitness. If you have a different goal, you may need to adjust your program accordingly. As described above, performing more sets of a smaller number of repetitions with a heavier load will cause greater increases in strength. A program designed to build strength might include 3–5 sets of 4–6 repetitions each; the load used should be heavy enough to cause fatigue with the smaller number of repetitions. Rest long enough after a set (3–5 minutes) to allow your muscles to recover and to work intensely during the next set.

Experienced weight trainers often engage in some form of cycle training, also called periodization, in which the exercises, number of sets and repetitions, and intensity are varied within a workout and/or between workouts. For example, you might do a particular exercise more intensely during some sets or on some days than others; you might also vary the exercises you perform for particular muscle groups. Several sample cycle training programs can be found on the *Fit and Well* Online Learning Center. For more detailed information on these more advanced training techniques, consult a strength coach certified by the National Strength and Conditioning Association or another reliable source. If you decide to adopt a more advanced training regimen, start off slowly to give your body a chance to adjust and to minimize the risk of injury.

Weight Training Safety

Injuries do happen in weight training. Maximum physical effort, elaborate machinery, rapid movements, and heavy weights can combine to make the weight room a dangerous place if proper precautions aren't taken. To help ensure that your workouts are safe and productive, follow the guidelines in the box "Safe Weight Training" and the suggestions given below.

Use Proper Lifting Technique Every exercise has a proper technique that is important for obtaining maximum benefits and preventing injury. Your instructor or weight room attendant can help explain the specific techniques for performing different exercises and using different weight machines. Perform exercises smoothly and with good form. The ACSM suggests a moderate rate for each repetition—a 3-second concentric contraction and a 3-second eccentric contraction. Lift or push the weight forcefully during the active phase of the lift and then lower it slowly with control. Perform all lifts through the full range of motion.

Use Spotters and Collars with Free Weights Spotters are necessary when an exercise has potential for danger: A weight that is out of control or falls can cause a serious injury. A spotter can assist you if you cannot complete a lift or if the weight tilts. A spotter can also help you move a weight into position before a lift and provide help or additional resistance during a lift. Spotting requires practice and coordination between the lifter and the spotter(s).

Collars are devices that secure weights to a barbell or dumbbell. Although people lift weights without collars, doing so is dangerous. It is easy to lose your balance or to raise one side of the weight faster than the other. Without collars, the weights on one side of the bar will slip off, and the weights on the opposite side will crash to the floor.

Be Alert for Injuries Report any obvious muscle or joint injuries to your instructor or physician, and stop exercising the affected area. Training with an injured joint or muscle can lead to a more serious injury. Make sure you get the necessary first aid. Even minor injuries heal faster if you use the R-I-C-E principle of treating injuries described in Chapter 3.

General Guidelines

• When beginning a program or trying new exercises or equipment, ask an instructor for help doing exercises safely and with correct technique.

• Lift weights from a stabilized body position; keep weights as close to your body as possible.

• Protect your back by maintaining control of your spine and avoiding dangerous positions. Don't twist your body while lifting.

• Observe proper lifting techniques and good form at all times. If you have to alter your technique to complete a repetition, you are probably lifting too much weight. Don't lift beyond the limits of your strength.

• Don't hold your breath while doing weight training exercises. Holding your breath, called the Valsalva maneuver, causes a decrease in blood returning to the heart and can make you become dizzy and faint. It can also increase blood pressure to dangerous levels. Exhale when exerting the greatest force, and inhale when moving the weight into position for the active phase of the lift. Breathe smoothly and steadily.

• Rest between sets if you perform more than 1 set of each exercise. Fatigue hampers your ability to obtain maximum benefits from your program and is a prime cause of injury. Also allow muscles a full day of rest (48 hours) between workouts.

• Do exercises through a full range of motion, and do stretching exercises after your workout to help prevent tightness.

• Be aware of what's going on around you. Stay away from other people when they're doing exercises, and don't get distracted. If you bump into someone, you could cause an injury.

• Gloves are not mandatory but may prevent calluses on your hands.

• Don't use defective equipment. Be aware of broken collars or bolts, frayed cables, broken chains, or loose cushions. Report equipment damage or malfunctions immediately.

• Don't chew gum when exercising; you could choke on the gum or bite your tongue.

• Always warm up before training and cool down afterward.

• Don't exercise if you're ill, injured, or overtrained. Do not try to work through the pain.

• When returning to training after an illness or layoff, start with lighter weights than you were using before the break in training.

• Don't take dangerous and/or illegal drugs or supplements, such as anabolic steroids, in an attempt to speed the progress of your program. (See pp. 108–112 for more on supplements.)

Free Weights

• Make sure the bar is loaded evenly on both sides and that weights are secured with collars.

• When you pick a weight up from the ground, keep your back straight and your head level or up. Don't bend at the waist with straight legs.

• Lift weights smoothly and slowly; don't jerk them. Control the weight through the entire range of motion. Lifting a weight too fast can increase the force output to dangerous levels.

• Do most of your lifting with your legs. Keep your hips and buttocks tucked in. When doing standing lifts, maintain a good posture so that you protect your back. Feet should be shoulder-width apart, heels and balls of the feet in contact with the floor, and knees slightly bent.

• Don't bounce weights against your body during an exercise.

• When lifting barbells and dumbbells, wrap your thumbs around the bar when gripping it. You can easily drop a weight when using a "thumbless" grip.

Spotting

• Use spotters for free weights exercises in which the bar crosses the face or head (e.g., the bench press), is placed on the back (e.g., squats), or is racked in front of the chest (e.g., overhead press from the rack).

• Spotters should be at least as tall and as strong as the lifter.

• If one spotter is used, the spotter should stand behind the lifter; if two spotters are used, one spotter should stand at each end of the barbell.

• For squats with heavy resistance, use at least three spotters—one behind the lifter (hands near lifter's hips, waist, or torso) and one on each side of the bar. Squatting in a power rack will increase safety during this exercise.

• Spot dumbbell exercises at the forearms, as close to the weights as possible.

• For over-the-face and over-the-head lifts, the spotter should hold the bar with an alternate grip (one palm up and one palm down) inside the lifter's grip.

• When providing a handoff, the spotter should make sure that the lifter has control of the weight before moving away.

• Ensure good communication between spotter and lifter by agreeing on verbal signals before the exercise.

• Spotters should pay attention and be ready to act quickly to assist a person having trouble. Lifters should tell spotters to take the bar if they can no longer contribute to making the lift.

Weight Machines

• Keep away from moving weight stacks. Pay attention when you're changing weights. Someone may jump on the machine ahead of you and begin an exercise while your fingers are close to the weight stack.

• Adjust each machine for your body so that you don't have to work in an awkward position. Lock everything in place before you begin.

• Stay away from moving parts of the machine that could pinch your skin.

• Make sure the machines are clean. Dirty vinyl is a breeding ground for germs that can cause skin diseases. Carry a towel around with you, and place it on the machine where you will sit or lie down.

Many dietary supplements are marketed to athletes and other active people. Few have been proven safe and/or effective, many are expensive, and some are dangerous, illegal, and/or banned by major sports organizations.

Consult a physician if you're having any unusual symptoms during exercise or if you're uncertain whether weight training is a proper activity for you. Conditions such as heart disease and high blood pressure can be aggravated during weight training. Symptoms such as headaches; dizziness; labored breathing; numbness; vision disturbances; and chest, neck, or arm pains should be reported immediately.

A Caution About Supplements and Drugs

Many active people use a wide variety of nutritional supplements and drugs in the quest for improved performance and appearance. Most of these substances are ineffective and expensive, and many are dangerous. A balanced diet should be your primary nutritional strategy. A selective summary of "performance aids" is given in Table 4.2, along with their potential side effects.

Supplements Taken to Increase Muscle Growth The most popular category of supplements are those taken to increase muscle growth. Most of the supplements in this group are controlled substances that require a prescription to obtain through legal means. In addition to health risks, there are serious legal consequences for using them to enhance performance or appearance.

Terms

ₘ

anabolic steroids Synthetic male hormones taken to enhance athletic performance and body composition.

• **Anabolic steroids** are a group of synthetic derivatives of testosterone. People take them in hope of gaining weight and muscle size and improving strength, power, speed, endurance, aggressiveness, and appearance. Despite drug testing, anabolic steroids are taken by some athletes in sports such as bodybuilding, track and field, and football. Some world class athletes play a cat-and-mouse game with athletic drug testing agencies by disguising samples against drug tests or using drugs that can't be detected with current methods. Between 2003 and 2005, a number of world-class and professional athletes tested positive for designer anabolic steroids such as tetrahydrogestrinone (THG) that were specifically formulated to beat the drug tests. The discovery of these drugs led to a U.S. congressional investigation and more stringent anti-doping rules in many sports. Use of anabolic steroids has filtered down to high school students, and about 6% of high school students have used them.

Anabolic steroids increase protein synthesis, which enhances fat-free weight, muscle mass, and strength. Side effects include liver damage and tumors, decreased levels of high-density lipoprotein (good cholesterol), heart disease, depressed sperm and testosterone production, high blood pressure, increased risk of AIDS (through shared needles), depressed immune function, problems with sugar metabolism, psychological disturbances, masculinization in women and children, premature closure of bone growth centers, and an increased risk of cancer. Side effects are greatest in people who take high doses of drugs for prolonged periods.

• Human chorionic gonadotrophin (HCG) is sometimes taken by anabolic steroid users to boost natural testosterone production, which is suppressed by steroids, and to prevent the muscle atrophy common during withdrawal from steroids. Although HCG tends to increase testosterone levels, it sometimes interferes with normal testosterone regulation, which causes additional deterioration in health and well-being. Use of HCG is not recommended and is banned in most sports.

• Growth hormone is used to increase muscle mass and strength. Reports in the news media suggest that, as with anabolic steroids, its general use has filtered down to high school students. Although advances in genetics have made human growth hormone more widely available, it is extremely expensive and has serious side effects. Growth hormone builds muscles, but the few studies on the hormone in humans have shown no beneficial effects on muscle or exercise performance. Prolonged growth hormone administration may result in elevated blood sugar, high insulin levels, carpal tunnel syndrome, heart enlargement, and increased blood fat levels. Prolonged use could also lead to acromegaly, characterized by enlarged bones in the head, face, and hands, as well as diseases of the heart, nerves, bones, and joints.

Table 4.2	Performance Aids Marketed to Weight Trainers		

Substance	Supposed Effects	Actual Effects	Selected Potential Side Effects
Adrenal androgens: DHEA, androstenedione	Increased testosterone, muscle mass, and strength; decreased body fat	Increased testosterone, strength, and fat-free mass and decreased fat in older subjects (more studies needed in younger people)	Gonadal suppression, prostate hypertrophy, breast development in males, masculinization in women and children. Long-term effects unknown
Amino acids	Increased muscle mass	No effects if dietary protein intake is adequate	Minimal side effects; unbalanced amino acid intake can cause problems with protein metabolism
Anabolic steroids	Increased muscle mass, strength, power, psychological aggressiveness, and endurance	Increased strength, power, fat-free mass, and aggression; no effects on endurance	Minor to severe: gonadal suppression, liver disease, acne, breast development in males, masculinization in women and children, heart disease, cancer. Steroids are controlled substances*
Chromium picolinate	Increased muscle mass; decreased body fat, improved blood sugar control	Well-controlled studies show no significant effect on fat-free mass or on body fat	Moderate doses (50–200 μg) appear safe; higher doses may cause DNA damage and other serious effects. Long-term effects unknown
Creatine monohydrate	Increased muscle creatine phosphate, muscle mass, and capacity for high-intensity exercise	Increased muscle mass and performance in some types of high-intensity exercise	Minimal side effects; some reports of muscle cramping and exacerbation of existing kidney problems. Long-term effects unknown
Ephedra	Decreased body fat; increased training intensity due to stimulant effect	Decreased appetite, particularly when taken with caffeine; some evidence for increased training intensity	Abnormal heart rhythms, nervousness, headache, gastrointestinal distress, and heatstroke; 2004 FDA ban challenged in court
Ginseng	Decreased effects of physical and emotional stress; increased oxygen consumption	Most well-controlled studies show no effect on performance	No serious side effects; high doses can cause high blood pressure, nervousness, and insomnia
Growth hormone	Increased muscle mass, strength, and power; decreased body fat	Increased muscle mass and strength; decreased fat mass	Diabetes, acromegaly (disease characterized by increased growth of bones in hands and face), enlarged heart and other organs. An extremely expensive controlled substance*
HMB (beta-hydroxy-beta-methylbutyrate)	Increased strength and muscle mass; decreased body fat	Some studies show increased fat-free mass and decreased fat; more research needed	No reported side effects. Long-term effects unknown
"Metabolic-optimizing" meals for athletes	Increased muscle mass; energy supply; decreased body fat	No proven effects beyond those of balanced meals	No reported side effects; extremely expensive
Protein	Increased muscle mass	No effects if dietary protein intake is adequate	Can be dangerous for people with liver or kidney disease

*Possession of a controlled substance is illegal without a prescription, and physicians are not allowed to prescribe controlled substances for the improvement of athletic performance. In addition, the use of anabolic steroids, growth hormone, or any of several other substances listed in this table is banned for athletic competition.

SOURCES: Brooks, G. A., et al. 2005. *Exercise Physiology: Human Bioenergetics and Its Applications,* 4th ed. New York: McGraw-Hill. Sports-supplement dangers. 2001. *Consumer Reports,* June. Williams, M. H. 1998. *The Ergogenics Edge: Pushing the Limits of Sports Performance.* Champaign, Ill.: Human Kinetics.

- Dehydroepiandrosterone (DHEA) and androstenedione are two relatively weak male hormones produced in the adrenal glands of both men and women. Both are broken down into testosterone. People take these drugs to stimulate muscle growth and aid in weight control. Because they were classified as supplements, they have been widely available in health food stores and supermarkets (see the box "Dietary Supplements: A Consumer Dilemma"). The few studies in humans show that they are of little value in improving athletic performance. These substances have side effects similar to those of anabolic steroids, particularly when taken in high doses. In 2004, the FDA acted to remove androstenedione from the supplement market.

- Insulin is used by the body to help control carbohydrate, fat, and protein metabolism. Some athletes take insulin injections to promote muscle hypertrophy, but its effectiveness in stimulating muscle growth is not known. Insulin supplementation is an extremely dangerous practice because it can cause insulin shock (characterized by extremely low blood sugar), which can lead to unconsciousness and death.

- Insulin-like growth factor (IGF-1) is produced by the pituitary gland and is stimulated by growth hormone. Although IGF-1 is a powerful anabolic agent, its effects in healthy, active people are unknown. Side effects are thought to be similar to those of growth hormone. Long-term use is known to promote cancer.

- Beta-agonists are a type of medication used to treat asthma, including exercise-induced asthma; this family of drugs includes clenbuterol, salmeterol, and terbutaline. Some athletes who do not have asthma take beta-agonists in an attempt to enhance performance. They hope to prevent muscle atrophy, increase fat-free weight, and decrease body fat. Potential side effects include insomnia, heart arrhythmias, anxiety, anorexia, and nausea. More serious effects include heart enlargement, heart attack (particularly if used with steroids), and heart failure.

- Protein, amino acid, and polypeptide supplements are taken to accelerate muscle development, decrease body fat, and stimulate the release of growth hormone. By a wide margin, these products are the most popular supplements taken by active people. Still, there is little scientific proof to support their use, even in athletes on extremely heavy training routines. The protein requirements of these athletes are not much higher than those of sedentary individuals. Also, most athletes take in more than enough protein in their diets. Although there appear to be few side effects from using these products, substituting amino acid or polypeptide supplements for protein-rich food can cause deficiencies in important nutrients, such as iron and the B vitamins.

- So-called metabolic-optimizing meals contain a wide variety of individual supplemental components and are widely used by athletes and active people. Some studies suggest that these meals may increase the hormone concentrations necessary for the development of fitness, but their effects on muscle growth and performance have not been demonstrated.

Supplements Taken to Speed Recovery from Training The primary purpose of taking these agents is to replenish depleted body fuel supplies that are important during exercise and recovery.

- Creatine monohydrate is used in an effort to enhance recovery, power, strength, and muscle size. Creatine monohydrate supplements increase creatine phosphate levels in muscle. As discussed in Chapter 3, creatine phosphate is a critical fuel source in the body. Physicians have used it successfully to treat muscle-wasting diseases. It may also help improve mental function. Several, but not all, studies have shown that creatine monohydrate supplementation improves performance in short-term, high-intensity, repetitive exercise. It may help to enlarge muscles in people who lift weights by allowing them to train harder. On the other hand, a panel of ACSM experts found no evidence that creatine supplements increase the aerobic power of muscle. Creatine may increase water retention in muscles, giving the feeling of increased muscularity without an actual increase in muscle size. Although this supplement appears safe, its long-term effects are unknown, so people should take this substance with caution.

- Chromium picolinate is used to enhance the action of insulin and to improve carbohydrate metabolism. Although a few studies have shown benefits, the efficacy of this supplement is extremely controversial.

- Other substances in this category include carbohydrate beverages that athletes use during and immediately following exercise to help them recover from intense training; these beverages may speed the replenishment of liver and muscle glycogen.

Substances Taken to Increase Training Intensity and Overcome Fatigue Active people often spend many hours a day training, and monotony and fatigue sometimes impede significant improvement. Some people use stimulants to help them increase training intensity and overcome fatigue.

- Amphetamines are sometimes used by athletes to prevent fatigue and to increase confidence and training intensity. These drugs stimulate the nervous system, causing increased arousal, wakefulness, confidence, and the feeling of an enhanced capability to make decisions; they mask fatigue, so users feel energized, but once the drug wears off, depression or fatigue sets in. Because amphetamines can cause extreme confusion, they are of little use in sports requiring rapid decisions. Amphetamines can cause severe neural and psychological effects

"Builds lean muscle fast!" "Burns fat and gives you super energy!" "The most effective muscle-building product ever!" It's only human nature to want to feel, perform, and look as good as possible. But wading through advertising hype can be tricky when you are considering taking a dietary supplement. While drugs and food products undergo stringent government testing, dietary supplements can be freely marketed without testing for safety or effectiveness. There is no guarantee that advertising claims about dietary supplements are accurate or true.

What's the difference between a drug—which must be approved by the Food and Drug Administration (FDA)—and a dietary supplement? In some cases, the only real difference is in how the product is marketed. Some dietary supplements are as potentially dangerous as potent prescription drugs. But because they have a different classification, dietary supplements do not have to prove they are safe and effective before being sold; the FDA can, however, take action against any unsafe supplement product after it reaches the market. This is what occurred in two high-profile cases in 2004 when the FDA acted against popular dietary supplements—androstenedione and ephedra.

The male hormone testosterone is a powerful drug with many adverse effects; it is closely regulated by the FDA. Androstenedione, a hormone converted in the body to testosterone (and estrogen), was widely available without a prescription as a dietary supplement. Andro disrupts the hormonal balance of its users and can increase the risk of heart disease. Teens who take andro are at risk for early closure of bone growth centers, which could limit their adult height. Other potential adverse effects of andro include acne, psychological disturbances, male breast development, baldness, and kidney and liver dysfunction. Advertisements for andro claimed that it would increase muscle size, strength, and performance, but there are actually few good studies of andro's effects on humans; the two best studies showed no significant difference in muscle growth and strength in andro users compared with nonusers. Most medical experts believe that andro is neither safe nor effective—yet it has been used by thousands of athletes, most of whom are unaware of the risks. In 2004, the FDA stated that androstenedione was potentially dangerous and should not be marketed as a supplement; it asked manufacturers to stop selling supplements containing andro.

The controversy over another compound, ephedra, continues despite efforts by the FDA to remove it from sale. Ephedra was a common ingredient of dietary supplements, often touted as an "energy booster" and a "fat burner." Marketed as a natural herbal product and available without a prescription, consumers might assume that ephedra is free from serious side effects. However, the drug can cause severe high blood pressure, heart attacks, strokes, seizures, and heat illness, and it has been linked to a number of deaths. It may be especially risky in users who are dehydrated and/or fatigued or when it is combined with other stimulants such as caffeine. Many sports organizations banned the use of ephedra because of safety concerns, and following the publication of additional studies and reports, the FDA acted to remove ephedra-containing products from the market. The ban has been successfully challenged in court, however, and it is likely that new formulations of supplements will appear containing combinations of other stimulants. Chapter 9 has more information about ephedra and other dietary supplements marketed for weight loss.

Glowing reports about the supposed effects of dietary supplements may sound enticing, but how can you determine if a particular supplement might be helpful? Ask yourself the following questions:

• *Do you really need a supplement at all?* Nutritional authorities agree that most athletes and young adults can obtain all the necessary ingredients for health and top athletic performance by eating a well-balanced diet and training appropriately. There is no dietary supplement that outperforms wholesome food and a good training regimen. Remember, too, that athletic performance and appearance are not life-and-death issues. It's one thing to take a cancer chemotherapy drug with many known adverse effects if there is a reasonable chance that it will save your life. It's another to take a potentially dangerous dietary supplement, which may not even work for you, when your goal is to increase your sports performance.

• *Is the product safe and effective?* The fact that a dietary supplement is available in your local store is no guarantee of safety. As described above, the FDA doesn't regulate supplements in the same way as drugs. The only way to determine if a supplement really works is to perform carefully controlled research on human subjects. Testimonials from individuals who claim to have benefited from the product don't count. Few dietary supplements have undergone careful human testing, so it is difficult to tell which of them may actually work. Reliable resources for information on dietary supplements include the FDA Center for Food Safety and Applied Nutrition (http://www.cfsan.fda.gov/~dms/supplmnt.html) and the Nutritional Supplements for Athletes Web site from Kansas State University (http://www.oznet.ksu.edu/nutrition/supplements.htm).

• *Can you be sure that the specific product is of high quality?* There is no official agency that ensures the quality of dietary supplements. There is no guarantee that a supplement contains the desired ingredient, that dosages are appropriate, that potency is standardized, or that the product is free from contaminants (see Chapter 8 for more information on dietary supplement labeling).

A recent study of 12 over-the-counter brands of supplements containing androstenedione and related steroids found that one brand contained more and eleven brands contained less than the amount stated on the label; in addition, one brand contained a significant amount of a controlled steriod. The International Olympic Committee issued a warning to athletes based on a test of 634 different nutritional supplements: Researchers had found that 15% of the supplements tested contained unlabled substances that would cause an athlete to fail a drug test.

Many dietary supplements are ineffective and/or unsafe, but it is extremely difficult for consumers to get the information they need to make an informed decision. Once you have gathered the best information you can find, consider whether the potential benefits of the supplement appear to outweigh the risks and the cost. When in doubt, it's best to avoid the product. Remember that no supplement eliminates the need for proper training, and no supplement has been shown to be safe and effective in long-term weight loss. A product that is marginally effective, not proven safe, and expensive to boot is probably not worth the money or the risk.

that include aggressiveness, paranoia, hallucinations, compulsive behavior, restlessness, irritability, heart arrhythmias, high blood pressure, and chest pains (see Chapter 13).

• Caffeine, found naturally in many plant species, is a favorite stimulant among many active people. Caffeine stimulates the nervous system and helps increase fat levels in the blood. Although there is some evidence that caffeine may improve endurance, the drug does not appear to enhance short-term maximal exercise capacity. Caffeine increases the incidence of abnormal heart rhythms and insomnia and is addictive. Ephedra, another naturally occurring stimulant, is described in more detail below and in the box on dietary supplements.

Substances Taken to Increase Endurance
Erythropoietin and darbepoetin are related drugs that stimulate the growth of oxygen-carrying red blood cells. These drugs are used to help treat anemia in patients with cancer and kidney disease. Some athletes have taken these drugs in an effort to boost their performance in endurance events. By increasing the production of red blood cells, erythropoietin and darbepoetin enhance oxygen uptake and endurance. However, these supplements are extremely dangerous because they increase blood viscosity (thickness) and can cause potentially fatal blood clots.

Substances Taken to Aid Weight Control
Substances used in weight control include drugs that suppress appetite, drugs that affect metabolic rate, and diuretics to control weight and increase muscle definition.

• Prescription appetite suppressants include diethylpropion and phentermine; these and related drugs can have serious side effects and are not approved for long-term use. Over-the-counter stimulants, including caffeine, phenylpropanolamine (PPA), and ephedra, have sometimes been used for weight control. However, there have been reports of adverse effects from PPA and ephedra, including an increased risk of heart attack or stroke in some people. Because of these risks, the FDA banned PPA in 2000 and ephedra in 2004. (The ephedra ban was reversed by the courts in 2005, but the matter is still in litigation.) An additional concern with over-the-counter supplements is that, due to lack of standardization, labels may not correctly indicate the amount of stimulant in a product. See Chapter 9 for more on diet pills.

• Dinitrophenol (DPN) was prescribed in the 1920s and 1930s for weight loss; it works by releasing food energy as heat. The drug was banned in 1938 because it can cause a dangerous increase in body temperature, leading to heat injury and death. The use of DPN has been reported among some athletes (who obtain it illegally), but the drug is no safer now than it was in the past.

• Diuretics (drugs that promote loss of body fluid) and potassium supplements are sometimes taken by people in an attempt to accentuate muscle definition. Others take potassium supplements to promote fluid retention in their muscle cells, thus increasing muscle size. Athletes may combine these practices with very-low-calorie diets and dehydration in the quest for weight loss and leanness. There is no evidence that these unhealthy practices improve appearance or muscle size. Serious complications have developed from these practices, including muscle cell destruction, low blood pressure, blood chemistry abnormalities, and heart problems.

Supplement and Drug Use by Active People
The variety and combinations of supplements and drugs used by physically active people make it extremely difficult to determine the efficacy of these practices or to predict their side effects. Many medical studies describe catastrophic side effects from use of unsafe drugs and nutritional supplements. Most supplements simply don't work.

Keep in mind that no nutritional supplement or drug will change a weak, untrained person into a strong, fit person. Those changes require regular training that stresses the muscles, heart, lungs, and metabolism and causes the body to adapt. They also require a healthy, balanced diet, as described in Chapter 8. The next section describes weight training exercises that can help you reach your goals.

WEIGHT TRAINING EXERCISES

A general book on fitness and wellness cannot include a detailed description of all weight training exercises. Here we present a basic program for developing muscular strength and endurance for general fitness using free weights and weight machines. Instructions for each exercise are accompanied by photographs and a listing of the muscles being trained. (Figure 4.6 is a diagram of the muscular system.) Table 4.3 on p. 114 lists alternative and additional exercises that can be performed on various machines or with free weights. If you are interested in learning how to do these exercises, ask your instructor or coach for assistance.

If you want to develop strength for a particular activity, your program should contain exercises for general fitness, exercises for the muscle groups most important for the activity, and exercises for muscle groups most often injured. Labs 4.2 and 4.3 will help you assess your current level of muscular endurance and design your own weight training program. Regardless of the goals of your program or the type of equipment you use, your program should be structured so that you obtain maximum results without risking injury. You should train at least 2 days per week, and each exercise session should contain a warm-up, 1 or more sets of 8–12 repetitions of 8–10 exercises, and a period of rest.

Weight training exercises begin on p. 115.

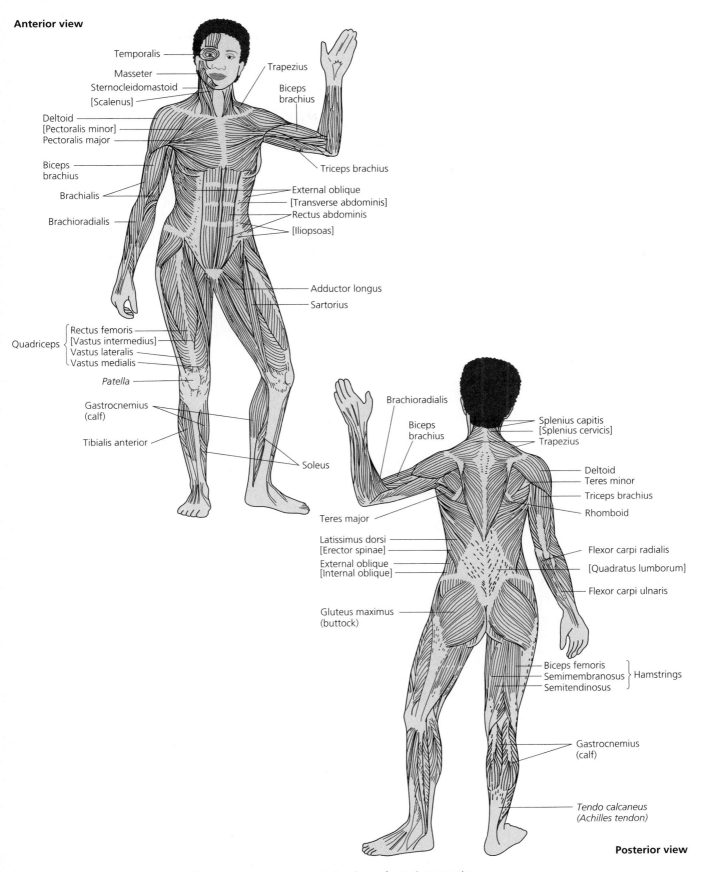

Anterior view

Temporalis
Masseter
Sternocleidomastoid
[Scalenus]
Deltoid
[Pectoralis minor]
Pectoralis major
Biceps brachius
Brachialis
Brachioradialis

Trapezius
Biceps brachius
Triceps brachius
External oblique
[Transverse abdominis]
Rectus abdominis
[Iliopsoas]

Adductor longus
Sartorius

Quadriceps {
Rectus femoris
[Vastus intermedius]
Vastus lateralis
Vastus medialis
Patella

Gastrocnemius (calf)
Tibialis anterior

Soleus

Brachioradialis
Biceps brachius

Teres major

Splenius capitis
[Splenius cervicis]
Trapezius

Deltoid
Teres minor
Triceps brachius
Rhomboid

Latissimus dorsi
[Erector spinae]
External oblique
[Internal oblique]

Gluteus maximus (buttock)

Flexor carpi radialis
[Quadratus lumborum]
Flexor carpi ulnaris

Biceps femoris
Semimembranosus } Hamstrings
Semitendinosus

Gastrocnemius (calf)

Tendo calcaneus (Achilles tendon)

Posterior view

Figure 4.6 The muscular system. The muscle names enclosed in brackets refer to deep muscles.

| Table 4.3 | Weight Training Exercises for Machines and Free Weights |

Company	Legs	Arms	Shoulders and Chest	Torso
Cybex	Hip abduction Hip adduction Leg extension Leg press Leg curl Rotary calf	Arm curl Triceps extension	Chest press Incline press Overhead press	Ab crunch Pull-down Torso rotation
Flex Fitness	Leg extension Leg curl Seated leg press	Biceps Overhead triceps	Deltoid raise Shoulder press Pectoral fly Vertical press 30° Pec contractor	Vertical row Low back Lat flexor Uni-lateral lat Abdominal
Hammer	Abductor Adductor Calf H squat Iso leg curl Iso leg extension Iso lateral leg press Leg curl Leg extension Leg press Seated calf raise	Behind-neck press Bench press Flat back chest Front military press Incline press Iso behind-neck press Iso incline press Iso wide chest Seated bicep Seated triceps	Bench press Flat back chest Iso wide chest Lateral raise Rear deltoid Rotator cuff Seated dip	Behind-neck pull-down Bilateral row Dead lift Front pull-down High row Iso pullover Low row Pullover Row Shrug
Hoist	Leg extension lying leg curl Leg press/calf raise Inner and outer thigh Multi hip	Standing biceps/triceps	Chest press/mid-row Lat pulldown/high row Chin-dip assist Pec fly/rear delt Lateral raise	Chin-dip assist Low back Rotary torso Ab crunch Mid row
Life Machines	Calf raise Leg abduction Leg adduction Leg curl Leg extension Leg press	Biceps curl Triceps extension	Chest press Incline press Lateral raise Pec fly Seated raise Shoulder press	Ab crunch Lat pull-down Low back extension Seated row Shoulder pullover
Nautilus	Calf raise Leg curl Leg extension Leg press	Biceps curl Preacher curl Triceps extension	10-degree chest 50-degree chest Bench press Incline press Lateral raise Military press Seated dip	Abdominal Compound row Hip and back Hip flexion Lat pull-down Pullover Rotary torso
Magnum	Glute/ham Leg abduction Leg adduction Leg curl Leg extension Leg press Multi-hip Seated calf	Arm curl Biangular arm curl Triceps extension Triceps pushdown	Bench press Bilateral chest Lateral raise Pec real delt Shoulder press Vertical bench press	Biangular lat row Cable cross over Lat pull-down Rogers row Rotary back Upper back
Universal Gym	Abductor kick Adductor kick Calf raises (leg press) Knee extension Knee flexion Leg press	Biceps curl Dips Lat pull	Bench press Front raise Incline press Rip-up Shoulder press Upright row	Bent-over row Crunch Lat pull Pullover Pull-up Side bend

Company	Legs	Arms	Shoulders and Chest	Torso
Free weights	Back squat	Barbell curl	Bench press	Abdominal crunch
	Front squat	Dumbbell curl	Decline press	Abdominal sit-ups
	Hack squat	French curl	Dumbbell back raise	Bent-over row
	Leg curl	Preacher curl	Dumbbell flys	Dead lift
	Leg extension		Dumbbell front raise	Incline lever row
	Leg press		Dumbbell lateral raise	Lat pull-down
	Lunges		Incline press	Pullover
	Seated calf		Incline press	Seated row
	Smith machine		Overhead press	Shrug
	Step-ups			Upright row
Exercise bands	Squats	Biceps curls	Chest press	Trunk curl
	Lunges	Triceps extensions	Shoulder press	Reverse crunch
	Hamstring curls		Lateral raise	Sit backs
	Leg abduction		Seated row	Back extensions
	Leg adduction			Lat pull-down
	Kick backs			
Exercises without weights	Squats	Isometric curls	Push-ups	Curl-ups
	Overhead squats	Isometric triceps	Pull-ups	Bicycles
	Lunges	extensions	Handstand press	Knee raises from bar
	Side lunges	Chair dips	against wall	Side bends
	Rear lunges	90° Bent-arm bar hang,		Twists
	Wall sits	supine grip		
	Step-ups			

SOURCE: Adapted from Fahey., T. D., 2004. *Basic Weight Training for Men and Women,* 5th ed. Copyright © 2004 The McGraw-Hill Companies, Inc. Reprinted with permission of The McGraw-Hill Companies, Inc.

WEIGHT TRAINING EXERCISES
Free Weights

EXERCISE 1   BENCH PRESS

Muscles developed: Pectoralis major, triceps, deltoids

Instructions: (a) Lying on a bench on your back with your feet on the floor, grasp the bar with palms upward and hands shoulder-width apart. If the weight is on a rack, move the bar carefully from the supports to a point over the middle of your chest. **(b)** Lower the bar to your chest. Then press it in a straight line to the starting position. If your back arches too much, try doing this exercise with your feet on the bench. **(a)**

(b)

To allow an optimal view of exercise technique, a spotter does not appear in these demonstration photographs; however, spotters should be used for most exercises with free weights. Video clips illustrating spotting technique can be found on the *Fit and Well* Online Learning Center.

Muscles developed: Latissimus dorsi, biceps

Instructions: (a) Begin by grasping the pull-up bar with both hands, palms facing forward and elbows extended fully. **(b)** Pull yourself upward until your chin goes above the bar. Then return to the starting position.

Assisted pull-up: (c) This is done as described above for a pull-up, except that a spotter assists the person by pushing upward at the waist, hips, or legs during exercise.

(a)

(b)

(c)

EXERCISE 3   SHOULDER PRESS (OVERHEAD OR MILITARY PRESS)

Muscles developed: Deltoids, triceps, trapezius

Instructions: This exercise can be done standing or seated, with dumbbells or a barbell. The shoulder press begins with the weight at your chest, preferably on a rack. **(a)** Grasp the weight with your palms facing away from you. **(b)** Push the weight overhead until your arms are extended. Then return to the starting position (weight at chest). Be careful not to arch your back excessively.

If you are a more advanced weight trainer, you can "clean" the weight (lift it from the floor to your chest). The clean should be attempted only after instruction from a knowledgeable coach; otherwise, it can lead to injury.

(a)

(b)

EXERCISE 4   UPRIGHT ROWING

Muscles developed: trapezius, deltoids, and biceps brachius

Instructions: From a standing position with arms extended fully, grasp a barbell with a close grip (hands about 6–12 inches apart) and palms toward the body. Raise the bar to about the level of your collarbone, keeping your elbows above bar level at all times. Return to the starting position.

   This exercise can be done using dumbbells, a weighted bar (shown), or a barbell.

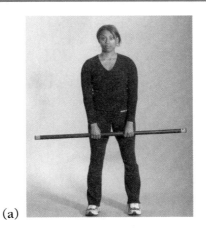

(a)   (b)

EXERCISE 5   BICEPS CURL

Muscles developed: Biceps, brachialis

Instructions: **(a)** From a standing position, grasp the bar with your palms upward and your hands shoulder-width apart. **(b)** Keeping your upper body rigid, flex (bend) your elbows until the bar reaches a level slightly below the collarbone. Return the bar to the starting position.

   The exercise can be done using dumbbells, a curl bar (shown), or a barbell; some people find that using a curl bar places less stress on the wrists.

(a)   (b)

EXERCISE 6   LATERAL RAISE

Muscles developed: Deltoids

Instructions: **(a)** Stand with feet shoulder-width apart and a dumbbell in each hand. Hold the dumbbells parallel to each other. **(b)** With elbows slightly bent, slowly lift both weights until they reach shoulder level. Keep your wrists in a neutral position, in line with your forearms. Return to the starting position.

(a)   (b)

EXERCISE 7 SQUAT

Muscles developed: Quadriceps, gluteus maximus, hamstrings, gastrocnemius

Instructions: If the bar is racked, place the bar on the fleshy part of your upper back and grasp the bar at shoulder width. Keeping your back straight and head level, remove the bar from the rack and take a step back. Stand with feet shoulder-width apart and toes pointed slightly outward. **(a)** Rest the bar on the back of your shoulders, holding it there with hands facing forward. **(b)** Keeping your head up and lower back straight, squat down until your thighs are below parallel with the floor, your back starts to round, *or* your heels come off the floor. Drive upward toward the starting position, keeping your back in a fixed position throughout the exercise.

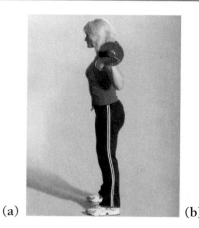 **(a)**
 **(b)**

EXERCISE 8 HEEL RAISE

Muscles developed: Gastrocnemius, soleus

Instructions: Stand with feet shoulder-width apart and toes pointed straight ahead. **(a)** Rest the bar on the back of your shoulders, holding it there with hands facing forward. **(b)** Press down with your toes while lifting your heels. Return to the starting position.

 **(a)**
 **(b)**

EXERCISE 9 CURL-UP OR CRUNCH

Muscles developed: Rectus abdominis, obliques, transverse abdominis

Instructions: **(a)** Lie on your back on the floor with your arms folded across your chest and your feet on the floor or on a bench. **(b)** Curl your trunk up and forward by raising your head and shoulders from the ground. Lower to the starting position. Focus on using your abdominal muscles rather than the muscles in your shoulders, chest, and neck.

This exercise can also be done using an exercise ball (see p. 102). (see p. 102)

(a)

(b)

Muscles developed: Erector spinae, gluteus maximus, hamstrings, deltoids

Instructions: Begin on all fours with your knees below your hips and your hands below your shoulders.

Unilateral spine extension: (a) Extend your right leg to the rear and reach forward with your right arm. Kee neck neutral and your raised arm and leg in line with your torso. Don't arch your back or let your hip or sho Hold this position for 10–30 seconds. Repeat with your left leg and left arm.

Bilateral spine extension: (b) Extend your left leg to the rear and reach forward with your right arm. Keep your neck neutral and your raised arm and leg in line with your torso. Don't arch your back or let your hip or shoulder sag. Hold this position for 10–30 seconds. Repeat with your right leg and left arm.

You can make this exercise more difficult by attaching weights to your ankles and wrists.

(a)

(b)

Muscles developed: Obliques, quadratus lumborum

Instructions: Lie on the floor on your side with your knees bent and your top arm lying alongside your body. Lift your hips so that your weight is supported by your forearm and knee. Hold this position for 10 seconds, breathing normally. Repeat on the other side. Work up to a 60-second hold; perform one or more repetitions on each side.

Variation: You can make the exercise more difficult by keeping your legs straight and supporting yourself with your feet and forearm (see Lab 5.3) or with your feet and hand (with elbow straight). You can also do this exercise on an exercise ball.

EXERCISE 1   BENCH PRESS (CHEST OR VERTICAL PRESS)

Muscles developed: Pectoralis major, anterior deltoids, triceps

Instructions: Sit or lie on the seat or bench, depending on the type of machine and the manufacturer's instructions. Your back, hips, and buttocks should be pressed against the machine pads. Place your feet on the floor or the foot supports. **(a)** Grasp the handles with your palms facing away from you; the handles should be aligned with your armpits. **(b)** Push the bars until your arms are fully extended, but don't lock your elbows. Return to the starting position.

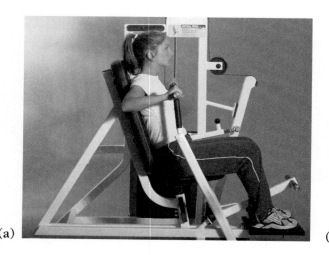

(a)

(b)

EXERCISE 2   LAT PULL

Note: This exercise focuses on the same major muscles as the assisted pull-up; choose an appropriate exercise for your program based on your preferences and equipment availability.

Muscles developed: Latissimus dorsi, biceps

Instructions: Begin in a seated or kneeling position, depending on the type of lat machine and the manufacturer's instructions. **(a)** Grasp the bar of the machine with arms fully extended. **(b)** Slowly pull the weight down until it reaches the top of your chest. Slowly return to the starting position.

(a)

(b)

Muscles developed: Latissimus dorsi, biceps

Instructions: Set the weight according to the amount of assistance you need to complete a set of pull-ups—the heavier the weight, the more assistance provided. **(a)** Stand or kneel on the assist platform, and grasp the pull-up bar with your elbows fully extended and your palms facing away. **(b)** Pull up until your chin goes above the bar and then return to the starting position.

(a)

(b)

EXERCISE 4   OVERHEAD PRESS (SHOULDER PRESS)

Muscles developed: Deltoids, trapezius, triceps

Instructions: Adjust the seat so that your feet are flat on the ground and the hand grips are slightly above your shoulders. **(a)** Sit down, facing away from the machine, and grasp the hand grips with your palms facing forward. **(b)** Press the weight upward until your arms are extended. Return to the starting position.

(a)

(b)

EXERCISE 5 BICEPS CURL

Muscles developed: Biceps, brachialis

Instructions: (a) Adjust the seat so that your back is straight and your arms rest comfortably against the top and side pads. Place your arms on the support cushions and grasp the hand grips with your palms facing up.
(b) Keeping your upper body still, flex (bend) your elbows until the hand grips almost reach your collarbone. Return to the starting position.

(a)

(b)

EXERCISE 6 PULLOVER

Muscles developed: Latissimus dorsi, pectoralis major and minor, triceps, abdominals

Instructions: Adjust the seat so your shoulders are aligned with the cams. Push down on the foot pads with your feet to bring the bar forward until you can place your elbows on the pads. Rest your hands lightly on the bar. If possible, place your feet flat on the floor. (a) To get into the starting position, let your arms go backward as far as possible. (b) Pull your elbows forward until the bar almost touches your abdomen. Return to the starting position.

(a)

(b)

Muscles developed: Deltoids, trapezius

Instructions: (a) Adjust the seat so the pads rest just above your elbows when your upper arms are at your sides, your elbows are bent, and your forearms are parallel to the floor. Lightly grasp the handles. **(b)** Push outward and up with your arms until the pads are at shoulder height. Lead with your elbows rather than trying to lift the bars with your hands. Return to the starting position.

(a)

(b)

Note: This exercise focuses on the same major muscles as the assisted dip; choose an appropriate exercise for your program based on your preferences and equipment availability.

Muscles developed: Triceps

Instructions: (a) Adjust the seat so that your back is straight and your arms rest comfortably against the top and side pads. Place your arms on the support cushions and grasp the hand grips with palms facing inward. **(b)** Keeping your upper body still, extend your elbows as much as possible. Return to the starting position.

(a)

(b)

Muscles developed: Triceps, deltoid, pectoralis major

Instructions: Set the weight according to the amount of assistance you need to complete a set of dips—the heavier the weight, the more assistance provided. **(a)** Stand or kneel on the assist platform with your body between the dip bar. With your elbows fully extended and palms facing your body, support your weight on your hands. **(b)** Lower your body until your upper arms are approximately parallel with the bars. Then push up until you reach the starting position.

(a)

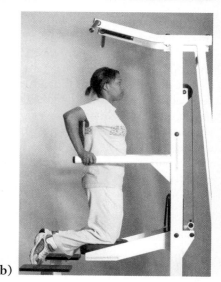
(b)

Muscles developed: Gluteus maximus, quadriceps, hamstrings

Instructions: Sit or lie on the seat or bench, depending on the type of machine and the manufacturer's instructions. Your head, back, hips, and buttocks should be pressed against the machine pads. Loosely grasp the handles at the side of the machine. **(a)** Begin with your feet flat on the foot platform about shoulder-width apart. Extend your legs but do not forcefully lock your knees. **(b)** Slowly lower the weight by bending your knees and flexing your hips until your knees are bent at about a 90-degree angle or your heels start to lift off the foot platform. Keep your lower back flat against the support pad. Then extend your knees and return to the starting position.

(a)

(b)

EXERCISE 11   ABDOMINAL CURL

Muscles developed: Rectus abdominis, internal and external obliques, hip flexors (rectus femoris and iliopsoas muscle group) as stabilizers

Instructions: (a) Adjust the seat so the machine rotates at the level of your navel, the pad rests on your upper chest, and your feet can rest comfortably on the floor. **(b)** Move your trunk forward as far as possible. Return to the starting position.

(a)

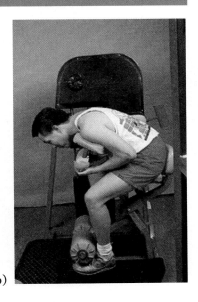

(b)

EXERCISE 12   LEG EXTENSION (KNEE EXTENSION)

Muscles developed: Quadriceps

Instructions: (a) Adjust the seat so that the pads rest comfortably on top of your lower shins. Loosely grasp the handles. **(b)** Extend your knees until they are almost straight. Return to the starting position.

Knee extensions cause kneecap pain in some people. If you have kneecap pain during this exercise, check with an orthopedic specialist before repeating it.

(a)

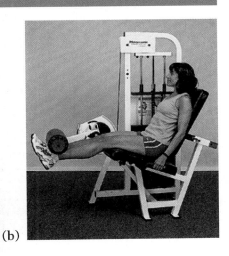

(b)

EXERCISE 13 | PRONE LEG CURL (KNEE FLEXION)

Muscles developed: Hamstrings, gastrocnemius

Instructions: (a) Lie on the front of your body, resting the pads of the machine just below your calf muscles and with your knees just off the edge of the bench. (b) Flex your knees until they approach your buttocks. Return to the starting position.

(a)

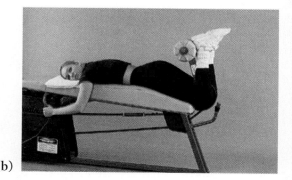

(b)

EXERCISE 14 | HEEL RAISE

Muscles developed: Gastrocnemius, soleus

Instructions: (a) Stand with your head between the pads and one pad on each shoulder. The balls of your feet should be on the platform. Lightly grasp the handles. (b) Press down with your toes while lifting your heels. Return to the starting position. Changing the direction your feet are pointing (straight ahead, inward, and outward) will work different portions of your calf muscles.

(a)

(b)

EXERCISE 15 | LOW-BACK MACHINE (BACK EXTENSIONS)

Muscles developed: Erector spinae, quadratus lumborum

Instructions: (a) Sit on the seat with your upper legs under the thigh-support pads, your back on the back roller pad, and your feet on the platform. (b) Extend backward until your back is straight. Return to the starting position. Try to keep your spine rigid.

(a)

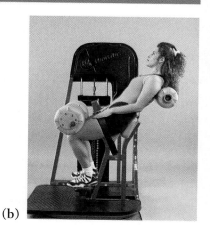

(b)

Good muscular strength and endurance will enhance your quality of life—both now and in the future. You don't need a complicated or heavy training program to improve strength: Just 1 set of 8–12 repetitions of 8–10 exercises, done 2–3 days per week, is enough for general fitness.

Right now you can

- Think of three things you've done in the past 24 hours that would have been easier or more enjoyable if you increased your level of muscular strength and endurance. Examples might be carrying your books, climbing stairs, or playing recreational sports. Begin to visualize improvements in your quality of life that could come from increased muscular strength and endurance.

- Do a set of static (isometric) exercises. If you're sitting, try tightening your abdominal muscles as you press your lower back into the seat or work your arms by placing the palms of your hands on top of your thighs and pressing down. Hold the contraction for 6 seconds and do 5–10 repetitions; don't hold your breath.

- Make an appointment with a trainer at your campus or neighborhood fitness facility. A trainer can help you put together an appropriate weight training program and introduce you to the equipment at the facility.

- Invest in an inexpensive set of free weights, a stability ball, or a resistance band. Then make a regular appointment with yourself to use your new equipment.

SUMMARY

- Hypertrophy, or increased muscle fiber size, occurs when weight training causes the number of myofibrils to increase; total muscle size thereby increases. Strength also increases through muscle learning. Most women do not develop large muscles from weight training.

- Improvements in muscular strength and endurance lead to enhanced physical performance, protection against injury, improved body composition, better self-image, improved muscle and bone health with aging, and reduced risk of chronic disease.

- Muscular strength can be assessed by determining the amount of weight that can be lifted in one repetition of an exercise; muscular endurance can be assessed by determining the number of repetitions of a particular exercise that can be performed.

- Static (isometric) exercises (contraction without movement) are most useful when a person is recovering from an injury or surgery or needs to overcome weak points in a range of motion.

- Dynamic (isotonic) exercises involve contraction that results in movement. The two most common types are constant resistance (free weights) and variable resistance (many weight machines).

- Free weights and weight machines have pluses and minuses for developing fitness, although machines tend to be safer.

- Lifting heavy weights for only a few repetitions helps develop strength. Lifting lighter weights for more repetitions helps develop muscular endurance.

- A strength training program for general fitness includes at least 1 set of 8–12 repetitions (enough to cause fatigue) of 8–10 exercises, along with warm-up and cool-down periods; the program should be carried out 2–3 nonconsecutive days per week.

- Safety guidelines for strength training include using proper technique, using spotters and collars when necessary, and taking care of injuries.

- Supplements or drugs that are promoted as instant or quick "cures" usually don't work and are either dangerous or expensive or both.

For Further Exploration

WW *Fit and Well* Online Learning Center (www.mhhe.com/fahey)

Use the learning objectives, study guide questions, and glossary flashcards to review key terms and concepts and prepare for exams. You can extend your knowledge of muscular strength and endurance and gain experience in using the Internet as a resource by completing the activities and checking out the Web links for the topics in Chapter 4 marked with the World Wide Web icon. For this chapter, Internet activities explore the benefits of muscular strength and endurance, different exercises that build strength, and strategies for evaluating supplements; there are Web links for the Critical Consumer box on dietary supplements and the chapter as a whole.

Daily Fitness and Nutrition Journal

Complete the muscular strength and endurance portion of the program plan by setting goals and selecting exercises. Fill in the information for the specific exercises you will perform, including which muscles they develop, how much resistance you plan to start with, and the number of reps and sets you plan to perform.

Books

Bailes, J., and J. McCloskey. 2005. *When Winning Costs Too Much: Steroids, Supplements, and Scandal in Today's Sports World.* New York: Taylor Trade. *An overview of issues relating to the use of steroids and other performance aids.*

Delavier, F. 2001. *Strength Training Anatomy.* Champaign, Ill.: Human Kinetics. *Includes exercises for all major muscle groups as well as full anatomical pictures of the muscular system. Women's Strength Training Anatomy, a matching volume for women, was published in 2003.*

Fahey, T. D. 2007. *Basic Weight Training for Men and Women,* 6th ed. New York: McGraw-Hill. *A practical guide to developing training programs, using free weights, tailored to individual needs.*

Nelson, M. 2000. *Strong Women Stay Young.* Rev. ed. New York: Bantam Books. *A program of strengthening exercises geared toward first-time exercisers, written by a Tufts University professor.*

Page, P. A. 2005. *Strength Band Training.* Champaign, Ill.: Human Kinetics. *Describes and illustrates more than 100 resistance band exercises, targeting every major muscle group.*

How long must I weight train before I begin to see changes in my body? You will increase strength very rapidly during the early stages of a strength training program, primarily the result of muscle learning (the increased ability of the nervous system to recruit muscle fibers to exert force). Actual changes in muscle size usually begin after about 6–8 weeks of training.

I am concerned about my body composition. Will I gain weight if I do resistance exercises? Your weight probably will not change significantly as a result of a general fitness program: 1 set of 8–12 repetitions of 8–10 exercises. You will tend to increase muscle mass and lose body fat, so your weight will stay about the same. You may notice a change in how your clothes fit, however, because muscle is denser than fat. Men will tend to build larger muscles than women because of the tissue-building effects of testosterone. Increased muscle mass will help you control body fat. Muscle increases your metabolism, which means you burn more calories every day. If you combine resistance exercises with endurance exercises, you will be on your way to developing a healthier body composition. Concentrate on fat loss rather than weight loss.

Do I need more protein in my diet when I train with weights? No. Although there is some evidence that power athletes involved in heavy training have a higher-than-normal protein requirement, there is no reason for most people to consume extra protein. Most Americans take in more protein than they need, so even if there is an increased protein need during heavy training, it is probably supplied by the average diet. Consuming a protein-rich snack before or after training may promote muscle hypertrophy. (See Chapter 8 for more on dietary needs of athletes

and specific recommendations for protein intake.)

What causes muscle soreness the day or two following a weight training workout? The muscle pain you feel a day or two after a heavy weight training workout is caused by injury to the muscle fibers and surrounding connective tissue. Contrary to popular belief, delayed-onset muscle soreness is not caused by lactic acid buildup. Scientists believe that injury to muscle fibers causes inflammation, which in turn causes the release of chemicals that break down part of the muscle tissue and cause pain. After a bout of intense exercise that causes muscle injury and delayed-onset muscle soreness, the muscles produce protective proteins that prevent soreness during future workouts. If you don't work out regularly, you lose these protective proteins and become susceptible to muscle soreness again.

Will strength training improve my sports performance? Strength developed in the weight room does not automatically increase your power in sports such as skiing, tennis, or cycling. Hitting a forehand in tennis and making a turn on skis are precise skills that require coordination between your nervous system and muscles. In skilled people, movements become reflex—you don't think about them when you do them. Increasing strength can disturb this coordination. Only by simultaneously practicing a sport and improving fitness can you expect to become more powerful in the skill. Practice helps you integrate your new strength with your skills, which makes you more powerful. Consequently, you can hit the ball harder in tennis or make more graceful turns on the ski slopes. (Refer to Chapter 2 for more on the concept of specificity of physical training.)

Will I improve faster if I train every day? No. Your muscles need time to recover between training sessions. Doing resistance exercises every day will cause you to become overtrained, which will increase your chance of injury and impede your progress. If you find that your strength training program has reached a plateau, try one of these strategies:

• Train less frequently. If you are currently training the same muscle groups three or more times per week, you may not be allowing your muscles to fully recover from intense workouts.

• Change exercises. Using different exercises for a particular muscle group may stimulate further strength development.

• Vary the load and number of repetitions. Try increasing or decreasing the loads you are using and changing the number of repetitions accordingly.

• Vary the number of sets. If you have been performing 1 set of each exercise, add sets.

• If you are training alone, find a motivated training partner. A partner can encourage you and assist you with difficult lifts, forcing you to work harder.

If I stop weight training, will my muscles turn to fat? No. Fat and muscle are two different kinds of tissue, and one cannot turn into the other. Muscles that aren't used become smaller (atrophy), and body fat may increase if caloric intake exceeds calories burned. Although the result of inactivity may be smaller muscles and more fat, the change is caused by two separate processes.

Should I wear a weight belt when I lift? Until recently, most experts advised people to wear weight belts. However, several studies have shown that weight belts do not prevent back injuries

VW Organizations and Web Sites

American College of Sports Medicine Position Stand: Progression Models in Resistance Training for Healthy Adults. Provides an in-depth look at strategies for setting up a strength training program and making progress based on individual program goals; look for the February 2002 Position Stand.

http://www.acsm-msse.org

and may, in fact, increase the risk of injury by encouraging people to lift more weight than they are capable of lifting with good form. Although wearing a belt may allow you to lift more weight in some lifts, you may not get the full benefit of your program because use of a weight belt reduces the effectiveness of the workout on the muscles that help support your spine.

Do abdominal machines advertised on television really work?

Studies comparing major types of abdominal exercises have found that "ab" machines are less effective than curl-ups and sit-ups for developing the abdominal muscles. There is no advantage to using an abdominal machine as compared to performing crunches—and a machine may cost $50 or more. A 2004 review of abdominal machines by *Consumer Reports* concluded that no infomercial machine was worth the money and suggested that consumers stick to crunches, possibly with an exercise ball for added difficulty.

Can activities such as yoga and taijiquan be used to build muscular strength and endurance?

Both of these forms of exercise involve carefully controlled body movements and precise body positions, so they can help build muscular strength and endurance—although probably not to the degree of traditional weight training exercises.

• Yoga involves a series of physical postures that stretch, strengthen, and relax different parts of the body. Some forms of yoga are much more vigorous than others, but most emphasize breathing, stretching, body awareness, and balance.

• Taijiquan (pronounced *tie jee choo-en*), commonly referred to as "tai chi chuan" or simply "tai chi," is a martial art consisting of a series of slow, fluid, elegant movements that promote relaxation and concentration as well as the development of body awareness, balance, and muscular strength.

To obtain the greatest benefit from these techniques with the least risk of injury, it's best to begin by finding a qualified instructor. See Chapter 10 for more on the use of yoga and taijiquan specifically for stress management.

What is core strength training?

Most body movements involve several joints and many muscles, either as prime movers, assist muscles, stabilizers, or antagonists. The link, and coordination, among these movements is called the kinetic chain. The key to most linked movements is the core, also called the trunk or midsection, consisting of the abdominal muscles, deep lateral stabilizing muscles, and the spinal extensor muscles. The core is critical because it transmits forces between the lower and upper body and helps stabilize the spine. Building strength and endurance in these muscle groups is key to most sports movements, to many activities of daily living, and to a healthy lower back.

What exercises build core strength and endurance? You can build core strength by forcing the trunk muscles to stabilize the spine while standing, sitting, or lying down. Examples of simple, low-tech core strengthening exercises include sitting on an exercise ball and keeping it from falling over and holding a push-up position on your forearms for 15 seconds. Whole-body exercises are particularly effective; examples include curl-ups on an exercise ball, side bridges, spine extensions, squats, and standing bench presses on a crossover pulley. Pilates often focuses on the core muscles. The program of strength and stretching exercises for low-back health presented in Chapter 5 also features many exercises that help build core strength.

What is circuit training?

Circuit training is a system of organizing a series of exercises that are performed consecutively. Exercises for different muscle groups follow each other, providing a well-rounded workout and helping to delay the onset of fatigue. By moving directly from one exercise to the next, you can keep your heart rate in your training zone and so train both your muscles and your cardiorespiratory system.

Circuit training can be done at home using calisthenic exercises and/or exercises with free weights, or circuits can be put together at a fitness center. A circuit may include just strength training exercises or may alternate between weight training machines and cardiorespiratory endurance stations. For example, you may perform a set of bench presses followed by 3 minutes on a treadmill and then a set of shoulder presses. Circuit training can be an effective method for building cardiorespiratory endurance and muscular strength during the same workout. It is important to warm up thoroughly before a circuit training workout and to cool down after. Other safety tips include maintaining proper form for each exercise (not rushing), not lifting beyond the limits of your strength, and keeping your heart rate within your target zone. A sample calisthenics circuit training program is included on the *Fit and Well* Online Learning Center.

Visit the Online Learning Center for more answers to common questions about strength training.

Exercise: A Guide from the National Institute on Aging. Provides practical advice on fitness for seniors; includes animated instructions for specific weight training exercises.
http://weboflife.ksc.nasa.gov/exerciseandaging/toc.html

Georgia State University: Strength Training. Provides information about the benefits of strength training and how to develop a safe and effective program; also includes illustrations of a variety of exercises.
http://www.gsu.edu/~wwwfit/strength.html

Human Anatomy On-line. Provides text, illustrations, and animation about the muscular system, nerve-muscle connections, muscular contraction, and other topics.

http://www.innerbody.com/htm/body.html

Kansas State University: Nutritional Supplements for Athletes. Provides information and links to recent research findings about specific supplements.

http://www.oznet.ksu.edu/nutrition/supplements.htm

National Strength and Conditioning Association. Professional organization that focuses on strength development for fitness and athletic performance.

http://www.nsca-lift.org

Pilates Method Alliance. Provides information about Pilates and about instructor certification; includes a directory of instructors.

http://www.pilatesmethodalliance.com

University of California, San Diego/Muscle Physiology Home Page. Provides an introduction to muscle physiology, including information about types of muscle fibers and energy cycles.

http://muscle.ucsd.edu

University of Michigan/Muscles in Action. Interactive descriptions of muscle movements.

http://www.med.umich.edu/lrc/Hypermuscle/Hyper.html

See also the listings in Chapter 2.

Selected Bibliography

Acacio, B. D., et al. 2004. Pharmacokinetics of dehydroepiandrosterone and its metabolites after long-term daily oral administration to healthy young men. *Fertility and Sterility* 81(3): 595–604.

American College of Sports Medicine. 2006. *ACSM's Guidelines for Exercise Testing and Prescription*. Philadelphia: Lippincott Williams & Wilkins.

American College of Sports Medicine. 2006. *ACSM's Resource Manual for Guidelines for Exercise Testing and Prescription,* 5th ed. Philadelphia: Lippincott Williams & Wilkins.

American College of Sports Medicine. 2005. *News Release: Pilates Research Offers New Information on Popular Technique* (http://www.acsm.org/publications/newsreleases2005/Summit_pilates.htm; retrieved June 30, 2005).

American College of Sports Medicine. 2002. Position Stand: Progression models in resistance training for healthy adults. *Medicine and Science in Sports and Exercise* 34(2): 364–380.

Andersen, L. L., et al. 2005. The effect of resistance training combined with timed ingestion of protein on muscle fiber size and muscle strength. *Metabolism* 54:151–156.

Brooks, G. A., et al. 2005. *Exercise Physiology: Human Bioenergetics and Its Applications*. New York: McGraw-Hill.

Centers for Disease Control and Prevention. 2004. Strength training among adults aged ≥65 years. *Morbidity and Mortality Weekly Report* 53(2): 25–28.

Crews, L. 2005. Mind-body exercise: Yoga and Pilates. *ACSM Fit Society Page,* Spring.

Cronin, J., and B. Crewther. 2004. Training volume and strength and power development. *Journal of Science and Medicine in Sport* 7:144–155.

Cronin, J. B., P. J. McNair, and R. N. Marshall. 2003. Force-velocity analysis of strength-training techniques and load: Implications for training strategy and research. *Journal of Strength and Conditioning Research* 17:148–155.

Cussler E. C., et al. 2003. Weight lifted in strength training predicts bone change in postmenopausal women. *Medicine and Science in Sports and Exercise* 35:10–17.

Earle, R. W., and T. R. Baechle, eds. 2004. *NSCA's Essentials of Personal Training*. Champaign, Ill: Human Kinetics.

Field, A. E., et al. 2005. Exposure to the mass media, body shape concerns, and use of supplements to improve weight and shape among male and female adolescents. *Pediatrics* 116(2): e214–220.

Folland, J. P., et al. 2001. Acute muscle damage as a stimulus for training-induced gains in strength. *Medicine and Science in Sports and Exercise* 33(7): 1200–1205.

Food and Drug Administration. 2004. *Questions and Answers: Androstenedione* (http://cfsan.fda.gov/~androqa.html; retrieved April 8, 2004).

Get on the bandwagon. 2005. *University of California, Berkeley Wellness Letter,* January.

Glowacki, S. P., et al. 2004. Effects of resistance, endurance, and concurrent exercise on training outcomes in men. *Medicine and Science in Sports and Exercise* 36:2119–2127.

Green, G. A., D. H. Catlin, and B. Starcevic. 2001. Analysis of over-the-counter dietary supplements. *Clinical Journal of Sports Medicine* 11(4): 254–259.

Hartgens, F., and H. Kuipers. 2004. Effects of androgenic-anabolic steroids in athletes. *Sports Medicine* 34:513–554.

Ibanez, J., et al. 2005. Twice-weekly progressive resistance training decreases abdominal fat and improves insulin sensitivity in older men with type 2 diabetes. *Diabetes Care* 28:662–667.

Izquierdo, M., et al. 2002. Effects of creatine supplementation on muscle power, endurance, and sprint performance. *Medicine and Science in Sports and Exercise* 34(2): 332–343.

Jurca, R., et al. 2004. Associations of muscle strength and fitness with metabolic syndrome in men. *Medicine and Science in Sports and Exercise* 36:1301–1307.

Kemmler, W. K., et al. 2004. Effects of single- vs. multiple-set resistance training on maximum strength and body composition in trained postmenopausal women. *Journal of Strength and Conditioning Research* 18: 689–694.

Kraemer, W. J., et al. 2004. Changes in muscle hypertrophy in women with periodized resistance training. *Medicine and Science in Sports and Exercise* 36:697–708.

Liu-Ambrose, T., et al. 2004. Resistance and agility training reduce fall risk in women aged 75 to 85 with low bone mass: A 6-month randomized, controlled trial. *Journal of the American Geriatrics Society* 52:657–665.

Magkos, F., and S. A. Kavouras. 2004. Caffeine and ephedrine: Physiological, metabolic and performance-enhancing effects. *Sports Medicine* 34: 871–889.

Peterson, J. A. 2005. 10 common mistakes made while strength training. *ACSM's Health & Fitness Journal* 9(2): 44.

Pollock, M. L., et al. 2000. AHA Science Advisory: Resistance exercise in individuals with and without cardiovascular disease. *Circulation* 101: 828–833.

Sorace, P., and T. LaFontaine, 2005. Resistance training muscle power: Design programs that work! *ACSM's Health & Fitness Journal* 9(2): 6–12.

Thiblin, I., and A. Petersson. 2005. Pharmacoepidemiology of anabolic androgenic steroids: A review. *Fundamental and Clinical Pharmacology* 19:27–44.

Trockel, M. T., M. D. Barnes, and D. L. Eggert. 2000. Health-related variables and academic performance among college students: Implications for sleep and other behaviors. *Journal of American College Health* 49(3): 125–131.

TV exercise devices. 2004. *Consumer Reports,* January.

Willardson, J. M., and L. N. Burkett. 2005. A comparison of 3 different rest intervals on the exercise volume completed during a workout. *Journal of Strength and Conditioning Research* 19:23–26.

LAB 4.1 *Assessing Your Current Level of Muscular Strength*

For best results, don't do any strenuous weight training within 48 hours of any test. Use great caution when completing 1 RM tests; do not take the maximum bench press or leg press test if you have any injuries to your shoulders, elbows, back, hips, or knees. In addition, do not take these tests until you have had at least one month of weight training experience.

The Maximum Bench Press Test

Maximum bench press test.

Equipment

1. Universal Gym Dynamic Variable Resistance machine
2. Weight scale

If free weights are used, the following equipment is needed:

1. Flat bench (with or without racks)
2. Barbell
3. Assorted weight plates, with collars to hold them in place
4. One or two spotters
5. Weight scale

Preparation

Try a few bench presses with a small amount of weight so you can practice your technique, warm up your muscles, and, if you use free weights, coordinate your movements with those of your spotters. Weigh yourself and record the results.

Body weight: _____ lb

Instructions

1. Set the machine for a weight that is lower than the amount you believe you can lift. For free weights, men should begin with a weight about 2/3 of their body weight; women should begin with the weight of just the bar (45 lb).

2. Lie on the bench with your feet firmly on the floor. If you are using a weight machine, grasp the handles with palms away from you; the tops of the handles should be aligned with the tops of your armpits.

   If you are using free weights, grasp the bar slightly wider than shoulder width with your palms away from you. If you have one spotter, she or he should stand directly behind the bench; if you have two spotters, they should stand to the side, one at each end of the barbell. Lower the bar to your chest in preparation for the lift.

3. Push the bars or barbell until your arms are fully extended. Exhale as you lift. If you are using free weights, the weight moves from a low point at the chest to a high point over the chin. Keep your feet firmly on the floor, don't arch your back, and push the weight evenly with your right and left arms. Don't bounce the weight on your chest.

4. Rest for several minutes, then repeat the lift with a heavier weight. It will probably take several attempts to determine the maximum amount of weight you can lift (1 RM).

   1 RM: _____ lb   Check one : _____ Universal _____ Free weights _____ Other

5. If you used free weights, convert your free weights bench press score to an estimated value for 1 RM on the Universal bench press using the appropriate formula:

   Males: Estimated Universal 1 RM = (1.016 × free weights 1 RM _____ lb) + 18.41 = _____ lb

   Females: Estimated Universal 1 RM = (0.848 × free weights 1 RM _____ lb) + 21.37 = _____ lb

Rating Your Bench Press Result

1. Divide your Universal 1 RM value by your body weight.

   1 RM _____ lb ÷ body weight _____ lb = _____

2. Find this ratio in the table to determine your bench press strength rating. Record the rating here and in the chart at the end of this lab.

   Bench press strength rating: _____

Strength Ratings for the Maximum Bench Press Test

Pounds Lifted/Body Weight (lb)

Men	Very Poor	Poor	Fair	Good	Excellent	Superior
Age: Under 20	Below 0.89	0.89–1.05	1.06–1.18	1.19–1.33	1.34–1.75	Above 1.75
20–29	Below 0.88	0.88–0.98	0.99–1.13	1.14–1.31	1.32–1.62	Above 1.62
30–39	Below 0.78	0.78–0.87	0.88–0.97	0.98–1.11	1.12–1.34	Above 1.34
40–49	Below 0.72	0.72–0.79	0.80–0.87	0.88–0.99	1.00–1.19	Above 1.19
50–59	Below 0.63	0.63–0.70	0.71–0.78	0.79–0.89	0.90–1.04	Above 1.04
60 and over	Below 0.57	0.57–0.65	0.66–0.71	0.72–0.81	0.82–0.93	Above 0.93
Women						
Age: Under 20	Below 0.53	0.53–0.57	0.58–0.64	0.65–0.76	0.77–0.87	Above 0.87
20–29	Below 0.51	0.51–0.58	0.59–0.69	0.70–0.79	0.80–1.00	Above 1.00
30–39	Below 0.47	0.47–0.52	0.53–0.59	0.60–0.69	0.70–0.81	Above 0.81
40–49	Below 0.43	0.43–0.49	0.50–0.53	0.54–0.61	0.62–0.76	Above 0.76
50–59	Below 0.39	0.39–0.43	0.44–0.47	0.48–0.54	0.55–0.67	Above 0.67
60 and over	Below 0.38	0.38–0.42	0.43–0.46	0.47–0.53	0.54–0.71	Above 0.71

SOURCE: Based on norms from The Cooper Institute of Aerobic Research, Dallas, Texas; from *The Physical Fitness Specialist Manual,* Revised 2002. Used with permission.

The Maximum Leg Press Test

Equipment

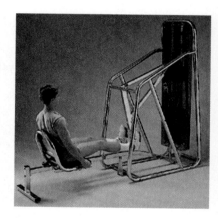

1. Universal Gym Dynamic Variable Resistance leg press machine. (If you're using a Universal Gym leg press with two sets of pedals, use the lower pedals.)
2. Weight scale

The ratings for this test were developed using the Universal Gym Dynamic Variable Resistance machine; results will be somewhat less accurate if the test is performed on another type of machine.

Preparation

Try a few leg presses with the machine set for a small amount of weight so you can practice your technique and warm up your muscles. Weigh yourself and record the results.

Maximum leg press test.

Body weight: _____ lb

Instructions

1. Set the machine for a weight that is lower than the amount you believe you can press.
2. Adjust the seat so that your knees are bent at a 70-degree angle to start.
3. Grasp the side handlebars and push with your legs until your knees are fully extended.
4. Rest for several minutes, then repeat the press with a higher weight setting. It will probably take several attempts to determine the maximum amount of weight you can press.

   1 RM: _____ lb

Rating Your Leg Press Result

1. Divide your 1 RM value by your body weight.

   1 RM _____ lb ÷ body weight _____ lb = _____

2. Find this ratio in the table to determine your leg press strength rating. Record the rating below and in the chart at the end of this lab.

   Leg press strength rating: _____

Strength Ratings for the Maximum Leg Press Test

Pounds Lifted/Body Weight (lb)

Men	Very Poor	Poor	Fair	Good	Excellent	Superior
Age: Under 20	Below 1.70	1.70–1.89	1.90–2.03	2.04–2.27	2.28–2.81	Above 2.81
20–29	Below 1.63	1.63–1.82	1.83–1.96	1.97–2.12	2.13–2.39	Above 2.39
30–39	Below 1.52	1.52–1.64	1.65–1.76	1.77–1.92	1.93–2.19	Above 2.19
40–49	Below 1.44	1.44–1.56	1.57–1.67	1.68–1.81	1.82–2.01	Above 2.01
50–59	Below 1.32	1.32–1.45	1.46–1.57	1.58–1.70	1.71–1.89	Above 1.89
60 and over	Below 1.25	1.25–1.37	1.38–1.48	1.49–1.61	1.62–1.79	Above 1.79
Women						
Age: Under 20	Below 1.22	1.22–1.37	1.38–1.58	1.59–1.70	1.71–1.87	Above 1.87
20–29	Below 1.22	1.22–1.36	1.37–1.49	1.50–1.67	1.68–1.97	Above 1.97
30–39	Below 1.09	1.09–1.20	1.21–1.32	1.33–1.46	1.47–1.67	Above 1.67
40–49	Below 1.02	1.02–1.12	1.13–1.22	1.23–1.36	1.37–1.56	Above 1.56
50–59	Below 0.88	0.88–0.98	0.99–1.09	1.10–1.24	1.25–1.42	Above 1.42
60 and over	Below 0.85	0.85–0.92	0.93–1.03	1.04–1.17	1.18–1.42	Above 1.42

SOURCE: Based on norms from The Cooper Institute of Aerobic Research, Dallas, Texas; from *The Physical Fitness Specialist Manual*, Revised 2002. Used with permission.

Predicting 1 RM from Submaximal Lifts

Values for 1 RM can be predicted by performing multiple repetitions using a submaximal weight. Although less accurate than direct measurement of 1 RM, this method may be safer for some people. To calculate 1 RM using this method, choose a weight with which you can perform about 5 repetitions. Follow the instructions given in the maximum bench press and maximum leg press test descriptions for warming up and performing the lifts—but do as many repetitions as you can using the amount of resistance you have chosen. Enter your resistance and number of repetitions into the formula below to predict your 1 RM on these tests. Then, enter your 1 RM values into the appropriate formula in the maximum bench press and maximum leg press tests to obtain your rating.

Bench press: 1 RM = (resistance _____ lb ÷ 2.2 lb/kg) ÷ (1.0278 − (0.0278 × number of repetitions _____))
= _____ kg × 2.2 lb/kg = _____ lb

Leg press: 1 RM = (resistance _____ lb ÷ 2.2 lb/kg) ÷ (1.0278 − (0.0278 × number of repetitions _____))
= _____ kg × 2.2 lb/kg = _____ lb

SOURCE: Brzycki, M. 1993. Strength testing: Predicting a one-rep max from a reps-to-fatigue. *Journal of Physical Education, Recreation, and Dance* 64:88–90.

Hand Grip Strength Test

Equipment   Grip strength dynamometer

Preparation   If necessary, adjust the hand grip size on the dynamometer into a position that is comfortable for you; then lock the grip in place. The second joint of your fingers should fit snugly under the handle of the dynamometer.

Instructions

1. Stand with the hand to be tested first at your side, away from your body. The dynamometer should be in line with your forearm and held at the level of your thigh. Squeeze the dynamometer as hard as possible without moving your arm; exhale as you squeeze. During the test, don't let the dynamometer touch your body or any other object.

Hand grip strength test.

2. Perform two trials with each hand. Rest for about a minute between trials. Record the scores for each hand to the nearest kilogram.

Right hand: Trial 1: _____ kg   Trial 2: _____ kg   Right hand best trial _____ kg

Left hand: Trial 1: _____ kg   Trial 2: _____ kg   Left hand best trial _____ kg

(Scores on the dynamometer should be given in kilograms. If the dynamometer you are using gives scores in pounds, convert pounds to kilograms by dividing your score by 2.2.)

Rating Your Hand Grip Strength

Refer to the table for a rating of your grip strength. Record the rating below and in the chart at the end of this lab.

Total score (sum of the best trial for each hand) _____ kg   Rating for hand grip strength: _____

Grip Strength* (kg)

Men	Needs Improvement	Fair	Good	Very Good	Excellent
Age: 15–19	Below 84	84–94	95–102	103–112	Above 112
20–29	Below 97	97–105	106–112	113–123	Above 123
30–39	Below 97	97–104	105–112	113–122	Above 122
40–49	Below 94	94–101	102–109	110–118	Above 118
50–59	Below 87	87–95	96–101	102–109	Above 109
60–69	Below 79	79–85	86–92	93–101	Above 101
Women					
Age: 15–19	Below 54	54–58	59–63	64–70	Above 70
20–29	Below 55	55–60	61–64	65–70	Above 70
30–39	Below 56	56–60	61–65	66–72	Above 72
40–49	Below 55	55–58	59–64	65–72	Above 72
50–59	Below 51	51–54	55–58	59–64	Above 64
60–69	Below 48	48–50	51–53	54–59	Above 59

*Combined right and left hand grip strength.

SOURCE: *The Canadian Physical Activity, Fitness & Lifestyle Appraisal: CSEP-Health & Fitness Program's Health-Related Appraisal and Counseling Strategy,* 3rd edition, 2003. Reprinted by permission from the Canadian Society for Exercise Physiology.

Summary of Results

Maximum bench press test: Weight pressed: _____ lb   Rating: _____
Maximum leg press test: Weight pressed: _____ lb   Rating: _____
Hand grip strength test: Total score: _____ kg   Rating: _____
Remember that muscular strength is specific: Your ratings may vary considerably for different parts of your body.

Using Your Results

How did you score? Are you at all surprised by your rating for muscular strength? Are you satisfied with your current rating?

If you're not satisfied, set a realistic goal for improvement: _____
Are you satisfied with your current level of muscular strength as evidenced in your daily life—for example, your ability to lift objects, climb stairs, and engage in sports and recreational activities?

If you're not satisfied, set some realistic goals for improvement:

What should you do next? Enter the results of this lab in the Preprogram Assessment column in Appendix D. If you've set goals for improvement, begin planning your strength training program by completing the plan in Lab 4.3. After several weeks of your program, complete this lab again and enter the results in the Postprogram Assessment column of Appendix D. How do the results compare?

LAB 4.2 *Assessing Your Current Level of Muscular Endurance*

For best results, don't do any strenuous weight training within 48 hours of any test. To assess endurance of the abdominal muscles, perform the curl-up test. To assess endurance of muscles in the upper body, perform the push-up test.

The Curl-Up Test

Equipment

1. Four 6-inch strips of self-stick Velcro or heavy tape
2. Ruler
3. Partner
4. Mat (optional)

Preparation

Affix the strips of Velcro or long strips of tape on the mat or testing surface. Place the strips 3 inches apart.

Instructions

1. Start by lying on your back on the floor or mat, arms straight and by your sides, shoulders relaxed, palms down and on the floor, and fingers straight. Adjust your position so that the longest fingertip of each hand touches the end of the near strip of Velcro or tape. Your knees should be bent about 90 degrees, with your feet about 12–18 inches from your buttocks.

2. To perform a curl-up, flex your spine while sliding your fingers across the floor until the fingertips of each hand reach the second strip of Velcro or tape. Then return to the starting position; the shoulders must be returned to touch the mat between curl-ups, but the head need not touch. Shoulders must remain relaxed throughout the curl-up, and feet and buttocks must stay on the floor. Breathe easily, exhaling during the lift phase of the curl-up; do not hold your breath.

3. Once your partner says "go," perform as many curl-ups as you can at a steady pace with correct form. Your partner counts the curl-ups you perform and calls a stop to the test if she or he notices any incorrect form or drop in your pace.

   Number of curl-ups: _____

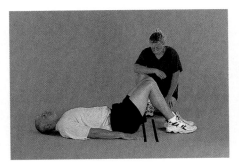

Curl-up test: (a) starting position.

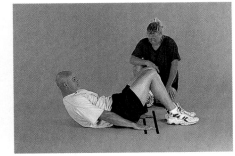

(b) Curl-up.

Rating Your Curl-Up Test Result

Your score is the number of completed curl-ups. Refer to the appropriate portion of the table for a rating of your abdominal muscular endurance. Record your rating below and in the chart at the end of this lab.

Rating: _____

Ratings for the Curl-Up Test

Number of Curl-Ups

Men	Very Poor	Poor	Average	Good	Excellent	Superior
Age: 16–19	Below 48	48–57	58–64	65–74	75–93	Above 93
20–29	Below 46	46–54	55–63	64–74	75–93	Above 93
30–39	Below 40	40–47	48–55	56–64	65–81	Above 81
40–49	Below 38	38–45	46–53	54–62	63–79	Above 79
50–59	Below 36	36–43	44–51	52–60	61–77	Above 77
60–69	Below 33	33–40	41–48	49–57	58–74	Above 74
Women						
Age: 16–19	Below 42	42–50	51–58	59–67	68–84	Above 84
20–29	Below 41	41–51	52–57	58–66	67–83	Above 83
30–39	Below 38	38–47	48–56	57–66	67–85	Above 85
40–49	Below 36	36–45	46–54	55–64	65–83	Above 83
50–59	Below 34	34–43	44–52	53–62	63–81	Above 81
60–69	Below 31	31–40	41–49	50–59	60–78	Above 78

SOURCE: Ratings based on norms calculated from data collected by Robert Lualhati on 4545 college students, 16–80 years of age, at Skyline College, San Bruno, California. Used with permission.

 The Push-Up Test

Equipment: Mat or towel (optional)

Preparation

In this test, you will perform either standard push-ups or modified push-ups, in which you support yourself with your knees. The Cooper Institute developed the ratings for this test with men performing push-ups and women performing modified push-ups. Biologically, males tend to be stronger than females; the modified technique reduces the need for upper-body strength in a test of muscular endurance. Therefore, for an accurate assessment of upper-body endurance, men should perform standard push-ups and women should perform modified push-ups. However, in using push-ups as part of a strength training program, individuals should choose the technique most appropriate for increasing their level of strength and endurance—regardless of gender.

Instructions

1. *For push-ups:* Start in the push-up position with your body supported by your hands and feet. *For modified push-ups:* Start in the modified push-up position with your body supported by your hands and knees. *For both positions,* your arms and your back should be straight and your fingers pointed forward.

(a) Push-up.   (b) Modified push-up.

2. Lower your chest to the floor with your back straight, and then return to the starting position.

3. Perform as many push-ups or modified push-ups as you can without stopping.

   Number of push-ups: _____ or number of modified push-ups: _____

Rating Your Push-Up Test Result

Your score is the number of completed push-ups or modified push-ups. Refer to the appropriate portion of the table for a rating of your upper-body endurance. Record your rating below and in the chart at the end of this lab.

Rating: _____

Ratings for the Push-Up and Modified Push-Up Tests

Men	Number of Push-Ups					
	Very Poor	*Poor*	*Fair*	*Good*	*Excellent*	*Superior*
Age: 18–29	Below 22	22–28	29–36	37–46	47–61	Above 61
30–39	Below 17	17–23	24–29	30–38	39–51	Above 51
40–49	Below 11	11–17	18–23	24–29	30–39	Above 39
50–59	Below 9	9–12	13–18	19–24	25–38	Above 38
60 and over	Below 6	6–9	10–17	18–22	23–27	Above 27

Women	Number of Modified Push-Ups					
	Very Poor	*Poor*	*Fair*	*Good*	*Excellent*	*Superior*
Age: 18–29	Below 17	17–22	23–29	30–35	36–44	Above 44
30–39	Below 11	11–18	19–23	24–30	31–38	Above 38
40–49	Below 6	6–12	13–17	18–23	24–32	Above 32
50–59	Below 6	6–11	12–16	17–20	21–27	Above 27
60 and over	Below 2	2–4	5–11	12–14	15–19	Above 19

SOURCE: Based on norms from The Cooper Institute of Aerobic Research, Dallas, Texas; from *The Physical Fitness Specialist Manual*, Revised 2002. Used with permission.

Summary of Results

Curl-up test: Number of curl-ups: _____ Rating: _____

Push-up test: Number of push-ups: _____ Rating: _____

Remember that muscular endurance is specific: Your ratings may vary considerably for different parts of your body.

Using Your Results

How did you score? Are you at all surprised by your ratings for muscular endurance? Are you satisfied with your current ratings?

If you're not satisfied, set realistic goals for improvement: _____

satisfied with your current level of muscular endurance as evidenced in your daily life—for example, your
ty to carry groceries or your books, hike, and do yard work?

If you're not satisfied, set some realistic goals for improvement:

What should you do next? Enter the results of this lab in the Preprogram Assessment column in Appendix D. If you've
set goals for improvement, begin planning your strength training program by completing the plan in Lab 4.3. After
several weeks of your program, complete this lab again and enter the results in the Postprogram Assessment column
of Appendix D. How do the results compare?

LAB 4.3 *Designing and Monitoring a Strength Training Program* V̇w

1. *Set goals.* List goals for your strength training program. Your goals can be specific or general, short or long term. In the first section, include specific, measurable goals that you can use to track the progress of your fitness program. These goals might be things like raising your upper-body muscular strength rating from fair to good or being able to complete 10 repetitions of a lat pull with 125 pounds of resistance. In the second section, include long-term and more qualitative goals, such as improving self-confidence and reducing your risk for back pain.

Specific Goals: Current Status   Final Goals

_____   _____
_____   _____
_____   _____

Other goals: _____
_____

2. *Choose exercises.* Based on your goals, choose 8–10 exercises to perform during each weight training session. If your goal is general training for wellness, use one of the sample programs in Figure 4.4 (p. 104) and on pp. 115–126. List your exercises and the muscles they develop in the program plan.

3. *Frequency: Choose the number of training sessions per week.* Work out at least 2 nonconsecutive days per week. Indicate the days you will train on your program plan; be sure to include days of rest to allow your body to recover.

4. *Intensity: Choose starting weights.* Experiment with different amounts of weight until you settle on a good starting weight, one that you can lift easily for 10–12 repetitions. As you progress in your program, add more weight. Fill in the starting weight for each exercise on the program plan.

5. *Time: Choose a starting number of sets and repetitions.* Include at least 1 set of 8–12 repetitions of each exercise. (When you add weight, you may have to decrease the number of repetitions slightly until your muscles adapt to the heavier load.) If program is focusing on strength alone, your sets can contain fewer repetitions using a heavier load. If you are over approximately age 50–60, your sets should contain more repetitions (10–15) using a lighter load. Fill in the starting number of sets and repetitions of each exercise on the program plan.

6. *Monitor your progress.* Use the workout card on the next page to monitor your progress and keep track of exercises, weights, sets, and repetitions. (A more extensive series of logs is included in the Daily Fitness and Nutrition Journal.)

Program Plan for Weight Training

Exercise	Muscle(s) Developed	M	T	W	Th	F	Sa	Su	Intensity: Weight (lb)	Repetitions	Sets

The Frequency columns are grouped under the header "Frequency (check ✓)" and the Repetitions/Sets columns under "Time."

WORKOUT CARD FOR _____

Exercise/Date	Wt	Sets	Reps	Wt	Sets	Reps	Wt	Sets	Reps	Wt	Sets	Reps	Wt	Sets	Reps	Wt	Sets	Reps	Wt	Sets	Reps	Wt	Sets	Reps	Wt	Sets	Reps	Wt	Sets	Reps	Wt	Sets	Reps	Wt	Sets	Reps	Wt	Sets	Reps

AHEAD

After reading this chapter, you should be able to

- Describe the potential benefits of flexibility and stretching exercises
- List the factors that affect the flexibility in a joint
- Explain the different types of stretching exercises and how they affect muscles
- Describe the intensity, duration, and frequency of stretching exercises that will develop the most flexibility with the lowest risk of injury
- List safe stretching exercises for major joints
- Describe how low-back pain can be prevented and managed

5

Flexibility and Low-Back Health

Test Your Knowledge

1. **Stretching exercises should be performed**
   a. at the start of a warm-up.
   b. following the active part of a warm-up.
   c. after endurance exercise or strength training.

2. **If you injure your back, it's usually best to rest in bed until the pain is completely gone.**
   True or false?

3. **To gain flexibility, you should stretch until you feel pain.**
   True or false?

ANSWERS

1. B and/or C. It's best to do stretching exercises when your muscles are warm, after either the active part of a warm-up (5–10 minutes of an activity such as walking or easy jogging) or an endurance or strength training workout. If a high-performance workout is your goal, it is best to stretch after exercise because stretching muscles may temporarily reduce their explosive strength.

2. FALSE. Prolonged bed rest may actually worsen back pain. Limit bed rest to a day or less, treat pain and inflammation with cold and then heat, and begin moderate physical activity as soon as possible.

3. FALSE. Stretch to the point of slight tension or mild discomfort, not pain. If you are very sore or sore for more than 24 hours following a stretching workout, you have stretched too intensely.

ViW *Fit and Well* **Online Learning Center**   www.mhhe.com/fahey

Visit the *Fit and Well* Online Learning Center for study aids, online labs, additional information about flexibility and low-back health, links, Internet activities that explore the development of flexibility, and much more.

Flexibility—the ability of a joint to move through its full **range of motion**—is extremely important for general fitness and wellness. The smooth and easy performance of everyday and recreational activities is impossible if flexibility is poor. Flexibility is a highly adaptable physical fitness component. It increases in response to a regular program of stretching exercises and decreases with inactivity. Flexibility is also specific: Good flexibility in one joint doesn't necessarily mean good flexibility in another. Flexibility can be increased through stretching exercises for all major joints.

There are two basic types of flexibility: static and dynamic. Static flexibility refers to the ability to assume and maintain an extended position at one end or point in a joint's range of motion; it is what most people mean by the term *flexibility*. Dynamic flexibility, unlike static flexibility, involves movement; it is the ability to move a joint through its range of motion with little resistance. For example, static shoulder flexibility would determine how far you could extend your arm across the front of your body or out to the side. Dynamic shoulder flexibility would affect your ability to pitch a softball, swing a golf club, or swim the crawl stroke. When gymnasts perform a split on the balance beam, they must have good static flexibility in their legs and hips; to perform a split leap, they must have good dynamic flexibility.

Static flexibility depends on many factors, including the ability to tolerate stretched muscles, the structure of a joint, and the tightness of muscles, tendons, and ligaments that are attached to the joint. Dynamic flexibility depends on static flexibility, but it also involves such factors as strength, coordination, and resistance to movement. Dynamic flexibility can be important for both daily activities and sports. However, because static flexibility is easier to measure and better researched, most assessment tests and stretching programs—including those presented in this chapter—target static flexibility.

This chapter describes the factors that affect flexibility and the benefits of maintaining good flexibility. It provides guidelines for assessing your current level of flexibility and putting together a successful stretching program. It also examines the common problem of low-back pain.

WHAT DETERMINES FLEXIBILITY?

The flexibility of a joint is affected by its structure, by muscle elasticity and length, and by nervous system activity. Some factors—joint structure, for example—can't be changed. Other factors, such as the length of resting muscle fibers, can be changed through exercise; these factors should be the focus of a program to develop flexibility.

Joint Structure

The amount of flexibility in a joint is determined in part by the nature and structure of the joint. Hinge joints such as those in your fingers and knees allow only limited forward and backward movement; they lock when fully extended. Ball-and-socket joints like the hip enable movement in many different directions and have a greater range of motion. Major joints are surrounded by **joint capsules,** semielastic structures that give joints strength and stability but limit movement. Heredity plays a part in joint structure and flexibility; for example, although everyone has a broad range of motion in the ball-and-socket hip joint, not everyone can do a split. Gender may also play a role. Some studies have found that women on average have greater flexibility in certain joints; for example, there are gender differences in the anatomy of the hip joint, leading to greater range of motion among women.

Muscle Elasticity and Length

Soft tissues, including skin, muscles, tendons, and ligaments, also limit the flexibility of a joint. Muscle tissue is the key to developing flexibility because it can be lengthened if it is regularly stretched. As described in Chapter 4, muscles contain proteins that create movement by causing muscles to contract. These contractile proteins can also stretch, and they are involved in the development of flexibility. However, the most important component of muscle tissue related to flexibility is the connective tissue that surrounds and envelops every part of muscle tissue, from individual muscle fibers to entire muscles. Connective tissue provides structure, elasticity, and bulk and makes up about 30% of muscle mass. Two principal types of connective tissue are **collagen,** white fibers that provide structure and support, and **elastin,** yellow fibers that are elastic and flexible. Muscles contain both collagen and elastin, closely intertwined, so muscle tissue exhibits the properties of both types of fibers. A recently discovered structural protein in muscles called **titin** also has elastic properties and contributes to flexibility.

When a muscle is stretched, the wavelike elastin fibers straighten; when the stretch is relieved, they rapidly snap back to their resting position. If gently and regularly stretched, connective tissues may lengthen and flexibility may improve. Without regular stretching, the process reverses: These tissues shorten, resulting in decreased flexibility. Regular stretching may contribute to flexibility by lengthening muscle fibers through the addition of contractile units called sarcomeres.

The stretch characteristics of connective tissue in muscle are important considerations for a stretching program. The amount of stretch a muscle will tolerate is limited, and as the limits of its flexibility are reached, connective tissue becomes more brittle and may rupture if overstretched (Figure 5.1). A safe and effective program

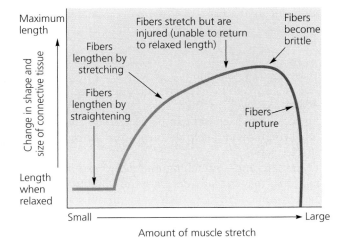

Figure 5.1 **The effect of stretch on connective tissue.**

stretches muscles enough to slightly elongate the tissues but not so much that they are damaged. Research has shown that flexibility is improved best by stretching when muscles are warm (following exercise or the application of heat) and the stretch is applied gradually and conservatively. Sudden, high-stress stretching is less effective and can lead to muscle damage.

Nervous System Activity

Nerves that send information about the muscle and skeletal systems to the nervous system are called *proprioceptors*. When these nerves detect any change in the position or force of muscles and joints, they send signals to the spine and brain, which in turn send signals back to the muscles to coordinate muscle action in ways that protect muscles and tendons from injury. They help control the speed, strength, and coordination of muscle contractions. Two key proprioceptors are **stretch receptors** (muscle spindles), which lie parallel to myofibrils within muscle fibers, and **Golgi tendon organs**, which are embedded in tendons (connect muscles to bones).

When a muscle is stretched (lengthened), stretch receptors detect the amount and rate of the change in muscle length. The stretch receptor sends a signal to the spinal cord, which then sends a signal back to the same muscle, triggering a muscle contraction that resists the change in muscle length. Another signal is sent to the antagonist muscle, causing it to relax, which further facilitates contraction of the stretched muscle. These reflexes occur frequently in active muscles and allow for fine control of muscle length and movement.

Small movements that only slightly stimulate these receptors cause small reflex actions. Rapid, powerful, and sudden changes in muscle length strongly stimulate the receptors and can cause large and powerful reflex muscle contractions. Thus, stretches that involve rapid, bouncy movements can be dangerous and cause injury because

each bounce causes a reflex contraction, and so a muscle might be stretching at the same time it is contracting. Performing a gradual stretch and then holding it allows the stretch receptors to adjust to the new muscle length and to reduce the signals sent to the spine, thereby allowing muscles to lengthen and, over time, improving flexibility.

The Golgi tendon organ protects the muscles from too much tension and can act to reduce the strength of the contraction signaled by the stretch receptors in response to stretching. Like stretch receptors, Golgi tendon organs send signals to the spine about muscle tension and the rate of change of the tension; however, they often cause an opposite response in stretching muscles. In response to tension (stretch) in a muscle, Golgi tendon organ signals are sent to the contracting muscle to inhibit muscle contraction and promote relaxation and lengthening of the muscles and their antagonists (a process called an inverse stretch reflex or reciprocal inhibition). Golgi tendon organ signals promoting muscle relaxation and lengthening are stronger than signals from the stretch receptors promoting muscle contraction. Holding a stretch further facilitates muscle lengthening.

The stretching technique called **proprioceptive neuromuscular facilitation (PNF)**, described on pages 146–147, takes advantage of the inverse stretch reflex to improve flexibility. For example, contracting a muscle prior to stretching it can help allow the muscle to stretch farther. The advanced strength training technique called plyometrics, described in Chapter 4, also takes advantage of the patterns of nervous system action in stretching and contracting muscles.

Terms

flexibility The range of motion in a joint or group of joints.

range of motion The full motion possible in a joint.

joint capsules Semielastic structures, composed primarily of connective tissue, that surround major joints.

soft tissues Tissues of the human body that include skin, fat, linings of internal organs and blood vessels, connective tissues, tendons, ligaments, muscles, and nerves.

collagen White fibers that provide structure and support in connective tissue.

elastin Yellow fibers that make connective tissue flexible.

titin A filament in muscle that helps align proteins that cause muscle contraction; titin has elastic properties and also plays a role in flexibility.

stretch receptors Sense organs in skeletal muscles that initiate a nerve signal to the spinal cord in response to a stretch; a contraction follows.

Golgi tendon organ Proprioceptive organ lying within tendons that recognizes and reacts to changes in muscle tension.

proprioceptive neuromuscular facilitation (PNF) A technique for stretching and strengthening muscles; PNF relies on neuromuscular reflexes to stimulate training effects.

Modifying nervous control through movement and specific exercises is the best way to improve the functional range of motion. Stretching regularly trains all of the proprioceptors to allow greater lengthening of the muscles. Proprioceptors adapt very quickly to stretching (or lack of stretching), so frequent training is beneficial for developing flexibility.

BENEFITS OF FLEXIBILITY AND STRETCHING EXERCISES

Good flexibility provides benefits for the entire musculoskeletal system; it may also prevent injuries and soreness and improve performance in all physical activities.

Joint Health

Good flexibility is essential to good joint health. When the muscles and other tissues that support a joint are tight, the joint is subject to abnormal stresses that can cause joint deterioration. For example, tight thigh muscles cause excessive pressure on the kneecap, leading to pain in the knee joint. Tight shoulder muscles can compress sensitive soft tissues in the shoulder, leading to pain and disability in the joint. Poor joint flexibility can also cause abnormalities in joint lubrication, leading to deterioration of the sensitive cartilage cells lining the joint; pain and further joint injury can result.

Improved flexibility can greatly improve your quality of life, particularly as you get older. People tend to exercise less as they age, leading to loss of joint mobility. Aging also decreases the natural elasticity of muscles, tendons, and joints, resulting in stiffness. The problem is often compounded by arthritis. Good joint flexibility may prevent arthritis, and stretching may lessen pain in people who have the disease. Flexibility exercises also improve the elasticity in your tissues, making it easier to move your body and reducing the risk of injury. When you're flexible, everything from tying your shoes to reaching for a jar on an upper shelf becomes easier and safer.

Prevention of Low-Back Pain and Injuries

Low-back pain can be related to poor spinal alignment, which puts pressure on the nerves leading out from the spinal column. Strength and flexibility in the back, pelvis, and thighs may help prevent this type of back pain. Unfortunately, research studies have not yet clearly defined the relationship between back pain and lack of flexibility. Few studies have found that trunk flexibility improves back health or reduces the risk of injury; in some people, greater spinal mobility may actually increase the risk of low-back problems. However, good hip and knee flexibility has been found to protect the spine from excessive motion during the tasks of daily living. Maintaining normal levels of flexibility helps maintain healthy joints and is probably necessary for good back health.

Some but not all studies show that poor flexibility does increase the risk for injury. A general stretching program has been shown to be effective in reducing the frequency of injuries as well as their severity. When injuries do occur, flexibility exercises can be used in treatment: They reduce symptoms and help restore normal range of motion in affected joints.

Overstretching—stretching muscles to extreme ranges of motion—may actually decrease the stability of a joint. Although some activities, such as gymnastics and ballet, require extreme joint movements, such flexibility is not recommended for the average person. In fact, extreme flexibility may increase the risk of injury in activities such as skiing, basketball, and volleyball. Again, as with other types of exercise, moderation is the key to safe training.

Additional Potential Benefits

- *Relief of aches and pains.* Stretching helps relieve pain that develops from stress or prolonged sitting. Studying or working in one place for a long time can make your muscles tense. Stretching helps relieve tension, so you can go back to work refreshed and effective.

- *Relief of muscle cramps.* Recent research suggests that exercise-related muscle cramps are caused by increased electrical activity within the affected muscle. The best treatment for muscle cramps is gentle stretching, which reduces the electrical activity and allows the muscle to relax.

- *Improved body position and strength for sports (and life).* Good flexibility lets a person assume more efficient body positions and exert force through a greater range of motion. For example, swimmers with more flexible shoulders have stronger strokes because they can pull their arms through the water in the optimal position. Flexible joints and muscles let you move more fluidly. Some studies also suggest that flexibility training enhances strength development.

- *Maintenance of good posture and balance.* Good flexibility also contributes to body symmetry and good posture. Bad posture can gradually change your body structures. Sitting in a slumped position, for example, can lead to tightness in the muscles in the front of your chest and overstretching and looseness in the upper spine, causing a rounding of the upper back. This condition, called kyphosis, is common in older people. It may be prevented by stretching regularly. Another benefit of good flexibility to older adults is that it increases balance and stability.

- *Relaxation.* Flexibility exercises are a great way to relax. Studies have shown that doing flexibility exercises reduces mental tension, slows your breathing rate, and reduces blood pressure.

Flexibility and Lifetime Wellness

Part of wellness is being able to move without pain or hindrance. Flexibility exercises are an important part of this process. Sedentary people often effectively lose their mobility at an early age. Even relatively young people are often handicapped by back, shoulder, knee, and ankle pain. As they age, the pain can become debilitating, leading to injuries and a lower quality of life. Good flexibility helps keep your joints and muscles moving without pain so that you can do all the things you enjoy.

MOTIVATION FOR CHANGE! Make a list of five benefits of flexibility and stretching exercises that are particularly meaningful to you—for example, preventing back pain and relieving neck pain from long hours of computer work. Put the list in a prominent location and use it as a motivational tool for beginning and maintaining your stretching program.

ASSESSING FLEXIBILITY

Because flexibility is specific to each joint, there are no tests of general flexibility. The most commonly used flexibility test is the sit-and-reach test, which rates the flexibility of the muscles in the lower back and hamstrings. To assess your flexibility and identify inflexible joints, complete Lab 5.1.

CREATING A SUCCESSFUL PROGRAM TO DEVELOP FLEXIBILITY

A successful program for developing flexibility contains safe exercises executed with the most effective techniques. Your goal should be to attain normal flexibility in the major joints. Extreme flexibility causes joint instability, which can lead to pain in the back, hips, shoulders, and knees. Balanced flexibility (not too much or too little) provides joint stability and facilitates smooth, economical movement patterns. You can achieve balanced flexibility by performing stretching exercises regularly and by using a variety of stretches and stretching techniques.

Applying the FITT Principle

As with the programs described for developing other health-related components of fitness, the acronym FITT can be used to remember key components of a stretching program: frequency, intensity, time, and type of exercise.

Frequency The ACSM recommends that stretching exercises be performed a minimum of 2–3 days a week, ideally 5–7 days a week. Doing these exercises often will provide the most benefits. It's best to stretch when your muscles are warm, so try incorporating stretching into

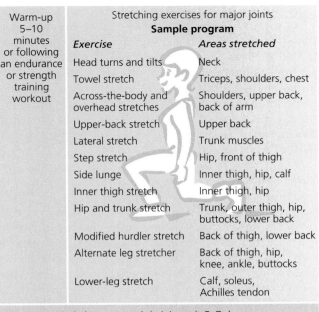

Warm-up 5–10 minutes or following an endurance or strength training workout	Stretching exercises for major joints Sample program	
	Exercise	*Areas stretched*
	Head turns and tilts	Neck
	Towel stretch	Triceps, shoulders, chest
	Across-the-body and overhead stretches	Shoulders, upper back, back of arm
	Upper-back stretch	Upper back
	Lateral stretch	Trunk muscles
	Step stretch	Hip, front of thigh
	Side lunge	Inner thigh, hip, calf
	Inner thigh stretch	Inner thigh, hip
	Hip and trunk stretch	Trunk, outer thigh, hip, buttocks, lower back
	Modified hurdler stretch	Back of thigh, lower back
	Alternate leg stretcher	Back of thigh, hip, knee, ankle, buttocks
	Lower-leg stretch	Calf, soleus, Achilles tendon

Frequency: 2–3 days per week (minimum); 5–7 days per week (ideal)

Intensity: Stretch to the point of mild discomfort, not pain

Time (duration): All stretches should be held for 15–30 seconds and performed 2–4 times

Type of activity: Stretching exercises that focus on major joints

Figure 5.2 A flexibility program.

your cool-down after cardiorespiratory endurance exercise or weight training.

Stretching can also be part of a warm-up, as long as the active part of the warm-up (for example, 5–10 minutes of walking) comes first. Never stretch when your muscles are cold; doing so can increase your risk of injury as well as limit the amount of flexibility you can develop. Although stretching before exercise is a time-honored ritual practiced by athletes in many sports, several studies have found that pre-exercise stretching decreases muscle strength and performance in explosive muscle activities, like jumping, for about 15–30 minutes after stretching. So, if your workout involves participation in a sport or high-performance activity, you may be better off stretching after your workout; for moderate-intensity activities like walking or cycling, stretching before your workout is unlikely to affect performance.

Intensity and Time (Duration) For each exercise, slowly stretch your muscles to the point of slight tension or mild discomfort. Hold the stretch for 15–30 seconds. As you hold the stretch, the feeling of slight tension should slowly subside; at that point, try to stretch a bit farther. Throughout the stretch, try to relax and breathe easily. Rest for about 30–60 seconds between each stretch, and do 2–4 repetitions of each stretch. A complete flexibility workout usually takes about 20–30 minutes (Figure 5.2).

Types of Stretching Techniques Stretching techniques vary from simply stretching the muscles during the course of normal activities to sophisticated methods based on patterns of muscle reflexes. Improper stretching can do more harm than good, so it's important to understand the different types of stretching exercises and how they affect the muscles. Four common techniques are static stretches, ballistic stretches, dynamic stretches, and PNF. These techniques can be performed passively or actively.

STATIC STRETCHING In **static stretching**, each muscle is gradually stretched, and the stretch is held for 15–30 seconds. A slow stretch prompts less reaction from stretch receptors, and the muscles can safely stretch farther than usual. Static stretching is the type most often recommended by fitness experts because it's safe and effective. The key to this technique is to stretch the muscles and joints to the point where a pull is felt, but not to the point of pain. (One note of caution: Excess static stretching can decrease joint stability and increase the risk of injury; this may be a particular concern for women, who naturally have joints that are less stable and more flexible than men.) Most experts consider static stretching the best and safest stretching technique, and the sample stretching program presented later in this chapter features static stretching exercises.

BALLISTIC STRETCHING In **ballistic stretching**, the muscles are stretched suddenly in a forceful bouncing movement. For example, touching the toes repeatedly in rapid succession is a ballistic stretch for the hamstrings. A problem with this technique is that the heightened activity of stretch receptors caused by the rapid stretches can continue for some time, possibly causing injuries during any physical activities that follow. Another concern is that triggering strong responses from the stretch receptors can cause a reflex muscle contraction that makes it harder to stretch. For these reasons, ballistic stretching is usually not recommended, especially for people of average fitness.

Ballistic stretching does train the elastic component of muscle, so it can be an appropriate stretching technique for some well-training athletes. For example, tennis players stretch their hamstrings and quadriceps ballistically when they lunge for a ball during a tennis match; because this movement is part of their sport, they might benefit from ballistic training of these muscle groups. For the average exerciser, however, the risks of ballistic stretching likely outweigh the benefits.

DYNAMIC (FUNCTIONAL) STRETCHING The emphasis in **dynamic stretching** is on functionally based movements. Dynamic stretching is similar to ballistic stretching in that it includes movement, but it differs in that it does not involve rapid bouncing. Instead, dynamic stretching involves moving the joints through the range of motion used in a specific exercise or sport in an exaggerated but controlled manner; movements are fluid rather than jerky. An example of a dynamic stretch is the lunge walk, in which a person takes slow steps with an exaggerated stride length; in each step, a lunge stretch position is reached. Slow dynamic stretches can lengthen the muscles in many directions without developing high tension in the tissues; these stretches elongate the tissues and train the neuromuscular system. Because dynamic stretches are based on sports movements or movements used in daily life, they develop functional flexibility that translates well into activities.

Dynamic stretches are more challenging than static stretches, however; they require balance and coordination and may carry a greater risk of muscle soreness and injury. People just beginning a flexibility program might want to start off with static stretches and try dynamic stretches only after they are comfortable with static stretching techniques and have improved their flexibility. Obtaining expert advice on dynamic stretching technique and program development is also recommended.

Serious athletes may use dynamic stretches as part of their warm-up before a competitive event or a high-intensity training session in order to move their joints through the range of motion required for the activity. Functional flexibility training can also be combined with functional strength training. For example, lunge curls, which combine dynamic lunges with free weights biceps curls, stretch the hip, thigh, and calf muscles; stabilize the core muscles in the trunk; and build strength in the arm muscles. Many activities build functional flexibility and strength at the same time, including yoga, Pilates, taijiquan, Olympic weight lifting, plyometrics, stability training (including Swiss and Bosu ball exercises), medicine ball exercises, and functional training machines (for example, Life Fitness and Cybex).

PROPRIOCEPTIVE NEUROMUSCULAR FACILITATION (PNF) PNF techniques use reflexes initiated by both muscle and joint receptors to cause greater training effects. The most popular PNF stretching technique is the contract-relax stretching method, in which a muscle is contracted before it is stretched. The contraction activates the Golgi tendon organs, causing relaxation in the muscle about to be stretched. For example, in a seated stretch of calf muscles, the first step in PNF is to contract the calf muscles. The individual or a partner can provide resistance for an isometric contraction. Following a brief period of relaxation, the next step is to stretch the calf muscles by pulling the tops of the feet toward the body. A duration of 6 seconds for the contraction and 15–30 seconds for the stretch is recommended. PNF appears to be most effective if the individual pushes hard during the isometric contraction.

Another example of a PNF stretch is the contract-relax-contract pattern. In this technique, begin by contracting the muscle to be stretched and then relaxing it.

Next, contract the opposing muscle (the antagonist). Finally, stretch the first muscle. For example, using this technique to stretch the hamstrings (the muscles in the back of the thigh) would require the following steps: contract the hamstrings, relax the hamstrings, contract the quadriceps (the muscles in the front of the thigh), stretch the hamstrings.

PNF appears to allow more effective stretching and greater increases in flexibility than static stretching, but it tends to cause more muscle stiffness and soreness. It also usually requires a partner and takes more time.

PASSIVE VERSUS ACTIVE STRETCHING   Stretches can be done either passively or actively. In **passive stretching,** an outside force or resistance provided by yourself, a partner, gravity, or a weight helps your joints move through their range of motion. For example, a seated stretch of the hamstring and back muscles can be done by reaching the hands toward the feet until a pull is felt in those muscles. You can achieve a greater range of motion (a more intense stretch) using passive stretching. However, because the stretch is not controlled by the muscles themselves, there is a greater risk of injury. Communication between partners in passive stretching is important to ensure joints aren't forced outside their normal functional range of motion.

In **active stretching,** a muscle is stretched by a contraction of the opposing muscle (the muscle on the opposite side of the limb). For example, an active seated stretch of the calf muscles occurs when a person actively contracts the muscles on the top of the shin. The contraction of this opposing muscle produces a reflex that relaxes the muscles to be stretched. The muscle can be stretched farther with a low risk of injury.

The only disadvantage of active stretching is that a person may not be able to produce enough stress (enough stretch) to increase flexibility using only the contraction of opposing muscle groups. The safest and most convenient technique is active static stretching, with an occasional passive assist. For example, you might stretch your calves both by contracting the muscles on the top of your shin and by pulling your feet toward you. This way you combine the advantages of active stretching—safety and the relaxation reflex—with those of passive stretching—greater range of motion. People who are just beginning flexibility training may be better off doing active rather than passive stretches. For PNF techniques, it is particularly important to have a knowledgeable partner.

Putting Exercises Together in a Complete Program
Your program should include stretches for all major joints; a complete sample program is found on pp. 148–153. Refer back to Figure 5.2 and the box "Safe Stretching" for a summary of guidelines for creating a safe and successful stretching program. Complete Lab 5.2 when you're ready to start your own program.

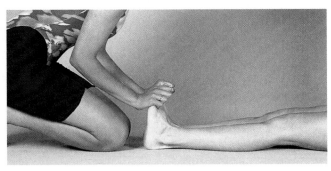

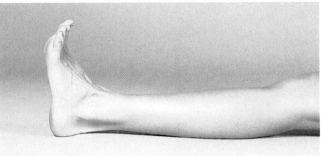

In passive stretching (top), an outside force—such as pressure exerted by another person—helps move the joint and stretch the muscles. In active stretching (bottom), the force to move the joint and stretch the muscles is provided by a contraction of the opposing muscles.

MOTIVATION FOR CHANGE!   Stretching exercises are sometimes given a low priority among fitness activities, especially among people with busy schedules. If you are having trouble motivating yourself to make time for flexibility training, try reminding yourself about the role of stretching in promoting relaxation. Make your stretching workout your "recess" or reward at the end of a busy day. Warm up your muscles for a few minutes first, and then stretch to reduce both mental and physical tension. The immediate benefits of your stretching routine will provide powerful positive reinforcement and help motivate you to stretch on a regular basis.

Terms

static stretching A technique in which a muscle is slowly and gently stretched and then held in the stretched position.

ballistic stretching A technique in which muscles are stretched by the force generated as a body part is repeatedly bounced, swung, or jerked.

dynamic stretching A technique in which muscles are stretched by moving joints slowly and fluidly through their range of motion in a controlled manner; also called *functional stretching*.

passive stretching A technique in which muscles are stretched by force applied by an outside source.

active stretching A technique in which muscles are stretched by the contraction of the opposing muscles.

Safe Stretching

- Do stretching exercises statically. Stretch to the point of mild discomfort, hold the position for 15–30 seconds, rest for 30–60 seconds, and repeat, trying to stretch a bit farther.

- Do not stretch to the point of pain. Any soreness after a stretching workout should be mild and last no more than 24 hours. If you are sore for a longer period, you stretched too intensely.

- Relax and breathe easily as you stretch. Inhale through the nose and exhale through pursed lips during the stretch. Try to relax the muscles being stretched.

- Perform all exercises on both sides of your body.

- Increase intensity and duration gradually over time. Improved flexibility takes many months to develop.

- Stretch when your muscles are warm. Do gentle warm-up exercises such as easy jogging or calisthenics before doing a pre-exercise stretching routine.

- There are large individual differences in joint flexibility. Don't feel you have to compete with others during stretching workouts.

- Engaging in a variety of physical activities will help you develop well-rounded functional physical fitness and allow you to perform all types of training more safely and effectively.

Making Progress

As with any type of training, you will make progress and improve your flexibility if you stick with your program. Follow the guidelines outlined in this chapter and train at least 2–3 days per week—ideally, 5–7 days per week. Judge your progress by noting your body position while stretching. For example, note how far you can lean forward during a modified hurdler stretch. If you wish, you can repeat the assessment tests that appear in Lab 5.1 periodically; be sure to take the test at the same time of day each time. You will likely notice some improvement after only 2–3 weeks of a stretching program; however, attaining significant improvements will take at least 2 months. By then, you can expect flexibility increases of about 10–20% in many joints.

Exercises to Improve Flexibility

There are hundreds of exercises that can improve flexibility. Your program should include exercises that work all the major joints of the body by stretching their associated muscle groups. The exercises illustrated here are simple to do and pose a minimum risk of injury. Use the exercises on pp. 148–153, or substitute your favorite stretches, to create a well-rounded program for developing flexibility. Be sure to perform each stretch using the proper technique. Hold each position for 15–30 seconds and perform 2–4 repetitions of each exercise. Avoid exercises that put excessive pressure on your joints (see the box "Stretches to Avoid" on p. 152).

FLEXIBILITY EXERCISES

EXERCISE 1   HEAD TURNS AND TILTS

Areas stretched: Neck

Instructions

Head turns: Turn your head to the right and hold the stretch. Repeat to the left.

Head tilts: Tilt your head to the right and hold the stretch. Repeat to the left.

Variation: Place your right palm on your right cheek; try to turn your head to the right as you resist with your hand. Repeat on the left side.

EXERCISE 2 TOWEL STRETCH

Areas stretched: Triceps, shoulders, chest

Instructions: Roll up a towel and grasp it with both hands, palms down. With your arms straight, slowly lift it back over your head as far as possible. The closer together your hands are, the greater the stretch.

Variation: Repeat the stretch with your arms down and the towel behind your back. Grasp the towel with your palms forward and thumbs pointing out. Gently raise your arms behind your back.

EXERCISE 3 ACROSS-THE-BODY AND OVERHEAD STRETCHES

Areas stretched: Shoulders, upper back, back of the arm (triceps)

Instructions: (a) Keeping your back straight, cross your right arm in front of your body and grasp it with your left hand. Stretch your arm, shoulders, and back by gently pulling your arm as close to your body as possible. Hold. **(b)** Bend your right arm over your head, placing your right elbow as close to your right ear as possible. Grasp your right elbow with your left hand over your head. Stretch the back of your arm by gently pulling your right elbow back and toward your head. Hold. Repeat both stretches on your left side.

(a)

(b)

EXERCISE 4 UPPER-BACK STRETCH

Areas stretched: Upper back

Instructions: Stand with your feet shoulder-width apart, knees slightly bent, and pelvis tucked under. Clasp your hands in front of your body and press your palms forward.

Variation: In the same position, wrap your arms around your body as if you were giving yourself a hug.

EXERCISE 5 LATERAL STRETCH

Areas stretched: Trunk muscles

Instructions: Stand with your feet shoulder-width apart, knees slightly bent, and pelvis tucked under. Raise one arm over your head and bend sideways from the waist. Support your trunk by placing the hand or forearm of your other arm on your thigh or hip for support. Be sure you bend directly sideways and don't move your body below the waist. Repeat on the other side.

Variation: Perform the same exercise in a seated position.

EXERCISE 6 STEP STRETCH

Areas stretched: Hip, front of thigh (quadriceps)

Instructions: Step forward and flex your forward knee, keeping your knee directly above your ankle. Stretch your other leg back so that it is parallel to the floor. Press your hips forward and down to stretch. Your arms can be at your sides, on top of your knee, or on the ground for balance. Repeat on the other side.

Variation: Increase the benefits of this exercise by placing your front and rear feet in different directions.

EXERCISE 7 SIDE LUNGE

Areas stretched: Inner thigh, hip, calf

Instructions: Stand in a wide straddle with your legs turned out from your hip joints and your hands on your thighs. Lunge to one side by bending one knee and keeping the other leg straight. Keep your knee directly over your ankle; do not bend it more than 90 degrees. Repeat on the other side.

Variation: In the same position, lift the heel of the bent knee to provide additional stretch. The exercise may also be performed with your hands on the floor for balance.

EXERCISE 8 INNER THIGH STRETCH

Areas stretched: Inner thigh, hip

Instructions: Sit with the soles of your feet together. Push your knees toward the floor using your hands or forearms.

Variation: When you first begin to push your knees toward the floor, use your legs to resist the movement. Then relax and press your knees down as far as they will go.

EXERCISE 9 HIP AND TRUNK STRETCH

Areas stretched: Trunk, outer thigh and hip, buttocks, lower back

Instructions: Sit with your left leg straight, right leg bent and crossed over the left knee, and right hand on the floor next to your right hip. Turn your trunk as far as possible to the right by pushing against your right leg with your left forearm or elbow. Keep your right foot on the floor. Repeat on the other side.

EXERCISE 10 | MODIFIED HURDLER STRETCH (SEATED SINGLE-TOE TOUCH)

Areas stretched: Back of the thigh (hamstring), lower back

Instructions: Sit with your left leg straight and your right leg tucked close to your body. Reach toward your left foot as far as possible. Repeat for the other leg.

Variation: As you stretch forward, alternately flex and point the foot of your extended leg.

EXERCISE 11 | ALTERNATE LEG STRETCHER

Areas stretched: Back of the thigh (hamstring), hip, knee, ankle, buttocks

Instructions: Lie flat on your back with both legs straight. **(a)** Grasp your left leg behind the thigh, and pull in to your chest. **(b)** Hold this position, and then extend your left leg toward the ceiling. **(c)** Hold this position, and then bring your left knee back to your chest and pull your toes toward your shin with your left hand. Stretch the back of the leg by attempting to straighten your knee. Repeat for the other leg.

Variation: Perform the stretch on both legs at the same time.

(a)

(b)

(c)

Areas stretched: Back of the lower leg (calf, soleus, Achilles tendon)

Instructions: Stand with one foot about 1–2 feet in front of the other, with both feet pointing forward. **(a)** Keeping your back leg straight, lunge forward by bending your front knee and pushing your rear heel backward. Hold. **(b)** Then pull your back foot in slightly, and bend your back knee. Shift your weight to your back leg. Hold. Repeat on the other side.

Variation: Place your hands on a wall and extend one foot back, pressing your heel down to stretch; or stand with the balls of your feet on a step or bench and allow your heels to drop below the level of your toes.

(a)

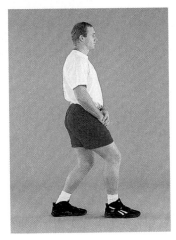

(b)

PREVENTING AND MANAGING LOW-BACK PAIN

More than 85% of Americans experience back pain at some time in their lives. Low-back pain is the second most common ailment in the United States—headache tops the list—and the second most common reason for absences from work and visits to a physician. Low-back pain is estimated to cost as much as $50 billion a year in lost productivity, medical and legal fees, and disability insurance and compensation.

Back pain can result from sudden traumatic injuries, but it is more often the long-term result of weak and inflexible muscles, poor posture, or poor body mechanics during activities like lifting and carrying. Any abnormal strain on the back can result in pain. Most cases of low-back pain clear up within a few weeks or months, but some people have recurrences or suffer from chronic pain.

Function and Structure of the Spine

The spinal column performs many important functions in the body.

- It provides structural support for the body, especially the thorax (upper-body cavity).
- It surrounds and protects the spinal cord.
- It supports much of the body's weight and transmits it to the lower body.
- It serves as an attachment site for a large number of muscles, tendons, and ligaments.
- It allows movement of the neck and back in all directions.

The spinal column is made up of bones called **vertebrae** (Figure 5.3, p. 155). The spine consists of 7 cervical vertebrae in the neck, 12 thoracic vertebrae in the upper back, and 5 lumbar vertebrae in the lower back. The 9 vertebrae at the base of the spine are fused into two sections and form the sacrum and the coccyx (tailbone). The spine has four curves: the cervical, thoracic, lumbar, and sacral curves. These curves help bring the body weight supported by the spine in line with the axis of the body.

Although the structure of vertebrae depends on their location on the spine, the different types of vertebrae do share common characteristics. Each consists of a body, an arch, and several bony processes (Figure 5.4, p. 155). The vertebral body is cylindrical, with flattened surfaces where **intervertebral disks** are attached. The vertebral body is designed to carry the stress of body weight and physical activity. The vertebral arch surrounds and protects the spinal cord. The bony processes serve as joints for adjacent vertebrae and attachment sites for muscles and ligaments. **Nerve roots** from the spinal cord pass through notches in the vertebral arch.

Intervertebral disks, which absorb and disperse the stresses placed on the spine, separate vertebrae from each

Terms

vertebrae Bony segments composing the spinal column that provide structural support for the body and protect the spinal cord.

intervertebral disk An elastic disk located between adjoining vertebrae consisting of a gel- and water-filled nucleus surrounded by fibrous rings; it serves as a shock absorber for the spinal column.

nerve root Base of each of the 31 pairs of spinal nerves that branch off the spinal cord through spaces between vertebrae.

The safe alternatives listed here are described and illustrated on pages 148–153 as part of the complete program of safe flexibility exercises presented in this chapter.

Standing Toe Touch

Problem: Puts excessive strain on the spine.

Alternatives: Modified hurdler stretch (Exercise 10), alternate leg stretcher (Exercise 11), and lower-leg stretch (Exercise 12).

Standing Hamstring Stretch

Problem: Puts excessive strain on the knee and lower back.

Alternatives: Modified hurdler stretch (Exercise 10) and alternate leg stretcher (Exercise 11).

Standing Ankle-to-Buttocks Quadriceps Stretch

Problem: Puts excessive strain on the ligaments of the knee.

Alternative: Step stretch (Exercise 6).

Yoga Plow

Problem: Puts excessive strain on the neck, shoulders, and back.

Alternatives: Head turns and tilts (Exercise 1), across-the-body and overhead stretches (Exercise 3), and upper-back stretch (Exercise 4).

Full Squat

Problem: Puts excessive strain on the ankles, knees, and spine.

Alternatives: Alternate leg stretcher (Exercise 11) and lower-leg stretch (Exercise 12).

Hurdler Stretch

Problem: Turning out the bent leg can put excessive strain on the ligaments of the knee.

Alternatives: Modified hurdler stretch (Exercise 10).

Prone Arch

Problem: Puts excessive strain on the spine, knees, and shoulders.

Alternatives: Towel stretch (Exercise 2) and step stretch (Exercise 6).

Neck Circles

Problem: Puts excessive strain on the neck and cervical disks.

Alternatives: Head turns and tilts (Exercise 1).

Note: Prone leg extensions, in which a person lifts both the chest and the legs while lying on the stomach but without grabbing the ankles, should also be avoided; spine extensions (p. 119) provide a safe alternative.

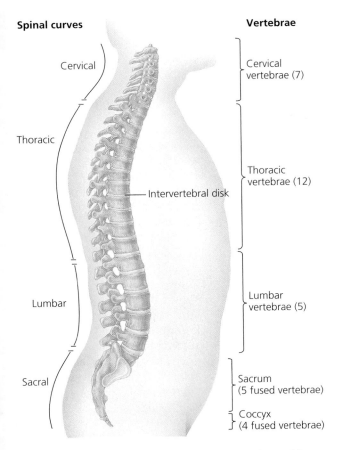

Spinal curves

Cervical

Thoracic

Lumbar

Sacral

Intervertebral disk

Vertebrae

Cervical vertebrae (7)

Thoracic vertebrae (12)

Lumbar vertebrae (5)

Sacrum (5 fused vertebrae)

Coccyx (4 fused vertebrae)

Figure 5.3 The spinal column. The spine is made up of five separate regions and has four distinct curves. An intervertebral disk is located between vertebrae.

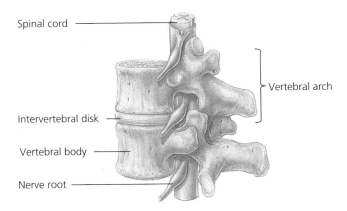

Spinal cord

Intervertebral disk

Vertebral body

Nerve root

Vertebral arch

Figure 5.4 Vertebrae and an intervertebral disk.

other. Disks are made up of a gel- and water-filled nucleus surrounded by a series of fibrous rings. The liquid nucleus can change shape when it is compressed, allowing the disk to absorb shock. The intervertebral disks also help maintain the spaces between vertebrae where the spinal nerve roots are located.

Core Muscle Fitness

The core muscles include those in the abdomen, pelvic floor, sides of the trunk, back, buttocks, hip, and pelvis. Twenty-nine muscles attach to the core, so a stable midsection is vital to all movements and body positions. As described in Chapter 4, the core muscles stabilize the spine and help transfer force between the upper body and lower body. They stabilize the midsection when you sit, stand, reach, walk, jump, twist, squat, throw, or bend. The muscles on the front, back, and sides of your trunk support your spine when you sit in a chair and fix your midsection as you use your legs to stand up. When hitting a forehand in tennis or batting a softball, most of the force is transferred from the legs, across the core, to the arms. Strong core muscles make movements more forceful and help prevent back pain.

The torso region needs stability to transmit forces between the upper and lower body. During any dynamic movement (hitting a tennis ball or picking up a bag of groceries), the core muscles work together: Some shorten to cause movement, while others contract and hold to provide stability, lengthen to brake the movement, or send signals to the brain about the movements and positions of the muscles and bones (proprioception). When specific core muscles are weak or tired, the nervous system steps in and uses other muscles. This substitution causes abnormal stresses on the joints, decreases power, and increases the risk of injury. For example, weakness in the transverse abdominis—a muscle deep in the abdomen—creates an unstable spine and can stress muscles and joints in both the upper and lower body.

The core maintains body control by keeping the body mass over its base of support during dynamic movements. Core support works much like a camping tent. The spine is like the pole holding up the tent, and the muscles are like the ropes that stabilize the pole. The tent is most stable when all the ropes are tight and adjusted at the same tension. The core muscles lie in layers—some are deep and some are superficial—which increases central body stabilization. The layer effect works much like the layers of plywood to increase strength and stability. The entire core is strongest and provides the most support when all of its elements are fit and toned.

How can a person strengthen the core muscles for low-back health? The best exercises are whole-body exercises that force the core muscles to stabilize the spine in many different directions. The low-back exercises presented later in this chapter include several exercises that focus on the core, including the step stretch (lunge), side bridges, and spine extensions. These exercises are generally safe for beginning exercisers and, with physician approval, people with some back pain. More challenging core exercises utilize stability balls or free weights. Stability ball exercises require the core muscles to stabilize the ball (and the body) while performing nearly any type of exercise. Many traditional free weights exercises can strengthen the core if you do them in a standing position. Weight machines train muscles in isolation, while standing free weights exercises help train the body for real-world movements. For example, no one carries a bag of groceries or a toddler while their body is supported by the frame of a weight machine. *An essential principle of core training is to train movements—not muscles.*

Causes of Back Pain

Back pain can occur at any point along your spine; the lumbar area, because it bears the majority of your weight, is the most common site. Any movement that causes excessive stress on the spinal column can cause injury and pain. The spine is well equipped to bear body weight and the force or stress of body movements along its long axis. However, it is less capable of bearing loads at an angle to its long axis. You do not have to carry a heavy load or participate in a vigorous contact sport to injure your back. Picking a pencil up from the floor using poor body mechanics—reaching too far out in front of you or bending over with your knees straight, for example—can also result in back pain.

Risk factors associated with low-back pain include age greater than 34 years, degenerative diseases such as arthritis or osteoporosis, a family or personal history of back pain or trauma, a sedentary lifestyle, low job satisfaction, and low socioeconomic status. Smoking increases risk because smoking appears to increase degenerative changes in the spine. Excess body weight also increases strain on the back, and psychological stress or depression can cause muscle tension and back pain. Occupations and activities associated with low-back pain are those involving physically hard work, such as frequent lifting, twisting, bending, standing up, or straining in forced positions; those requiring high concentration demands (such as computer programming); and those involving vibrations affecting the entire body (such as truck driving).

Underlying causes of back pain include poor muscle endurance and strength in the muscles of the core; excess body weight; poor posture or body position when standing, sitting, or sleeping; and poor body mechanics when performing actions like lifting and carrying, or sports movements. Abnormal spinal loading resulting from any of these causes can have short-term or long-term direct and indirect effects on the spine. Strained muscles, tendons, or ligaments can cause pain and can, over time, lead to injuries to vertebrae or the intervertebral disks.

Stress can cause disks to break down and lose some of their ability to absorb shock. A damaged disk may bulge out between vertebrae and put pressure on a nerve root, a condition commonly referred to as a slipped disk. Painful pressure on nerves can also occur if damage to a disk narrows the space between two vertebrae. With age, you lose fluid from the disks, making them more likely to bulge and put pressure on nerve roots. Depending on the amount of pressure on a nerve, symptoms may include numbness in the back, hip, leg, or foot; radiating pain; loss of muscle function; depressed reflexes; and muscle spasm. If the pressure is severe enough, loss of function can be permanent.

Preventing Low-Back Pain

Incorrect posture when standing, sitting, lying, and lifting is responsible for many back injuries. In general, think about moving your spine as a unit, with the force directed through its long axis. Strategies for maintaining good posture during daily activities are presented in the box "Good Posture and Low-Back Health." Follow the same guidelines for posture and movement when you engage in sports or recreational activities. Maintain control over your body movements and warm up thoroughly before you exercise. Take special care when lifting weights as part of a resistance training program (see Chapter 4).

The role of exercise in preventing and treating back pain is still being investigated. However, many experts do recommend exercise, especially for people who have already experienced an episode of low-back pain. Regular exercise aimed at increasing muscle endurance and strength in the back and abdomen is often recommended to prevent back pain, as is lifestyle physical activity such as walking. Movement helps lubricate your spinal disks and increases muscle fitness in your trunk and legs. Other lifestyle recommendations for preventing back pain include

- Lose weight, stop smoking, and reduce emotional stress.
- Avoid sitting, standing, or working in the same position for too long. Stand up every hour or half-hour and move around. The cat stretch (p. 159) is a good exercise to perform when you take a break during a long period of sitting.
- Use a supportive seat and a medium-firm mattress. Use lumbar support when driving, particularly for long distances, to prevent muscle fatigue and pain.
- Warm up thoroughly before engaging in vigorous exercise or sports.
- Progress gradually when attempting to improve strength or fitness.

Managing Acute Back Pain

Sudden back pain usually involves tissue injury. Symptoms may include pain, muscle spasms, stiffness, and inflammation. Many cases of acute back pain go away by themselves within a few days or weeks. You may be able to reduce pain and inflammation by applying cold and then heat (see Chapter 3). Begin with a cold treatment: Apply ice several times a day; once inflammation and spasms subside, you can apply heat using a heating pad or a warm bath. If the pain is bothersome, an over-the-counter, nonsteroidal anti-inflammatory medication such as ibuprofen or naproxen may be helpful; stronger pain medications and muscle relaxants are available by prescription.

Changes in everyday posture and behavior can help prevent and alleviate low-back pain.

- *Lying down.* When resting or sleeping, lie on your side with your knees and hips bent. If you lie on your back place a pillow under your knees. Don't lie on your stomach. Use a medium-firm mattress.

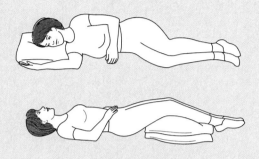

- *Sitting.* Sit with your lower back slightly rounded, knees bent, and feet flat on the floor. Alternate crossing your legs, or use a footrest to keep your knees higher than your hips. If this position is uncomfortable or if your back flattens when you sit, try using a lumbar roll pillow behind your lower back.

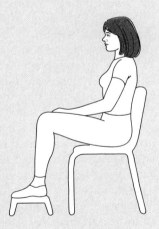

- *Lifting.* If you need to lower yourself to grasp an object, bend at the knees and hips rather than at the waist. Your feet should be about shoulder-width apart. Lift gradually, keeping your arms straight, by standing up or by pushing with your leg muscles. Keep the object close to your body. Don't twist, if you have to turn with the object, change the position of your feet.

- *Standing.* When you are standing, a straight line should run from the top of your ear through the center of your shoulder, the center of your hip, the back of your kneecap, and the front of your ankle bone. Support your weight mainly on your heels, with one or both knees slightly bent. Try to keep your lower back flat by placing one foot on a stool. Don't let your pelvis tip forward or your back arch. Shift your weight back and forth from foot to foot. Avoid prolonged standing. (To check your posture, stand in a normal way with your back to a wall. Your upper back and buttocks should touch the wall; your heels may be a few inches away. Slide one hand into the space between your lower back and the wall. It should slide in easily but should almost touch both your back and the wall. Adjust your posture as needed, and try to hold this position as you walk away from the wall.)

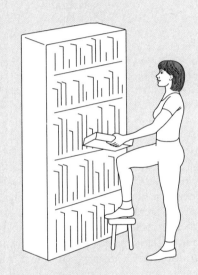

- *Walking.* Walk with your toes pointed straight ahead. Keep your back flat, head up and centered over your body, and chin in. Swing your arms freely. Don't wear tight or high-heeled shoes.

Expressive Writing and Chronic Conditions

The act of writing down feelings and thoughts about stressful life events has been shown to help people with chronic conditions improve their health. In one recent study, people with asthma or rheumatoid arthritis were asked to write down their feelings about the most stressful event in their lives; they wrote for 20 minutes a day over a three-day period. In follow-up exams four months later, nearly half of the patients who engaged in expressive writing experienced positive changes in their condition such as reduced joint pain. Only about a quarter of the control group, who wrote about their daily plans, experienced a positive change in health.

Investigators remain unsure why writing about one's feelings has beneficial effects. It is possible that expressing feelings about a traumatic event helps people work through the event and put it behind them. The resulting sense of release and control may reduce stress levels and have positive physical effects. Alternatively, expressive writing may change the way people think about previous stressful events in their lives and help them cope with new stressors. Whatever the cause, it's clear that expressive writing can be a safe, inexpensive, and effective supplement to standard treatment of certain chronic conditions.

What about the effects of expressive writing on otherwise healthy individuals? Other studies have, in fact, found such a benefit: People who wrote about traumatic experiences reported fewer symptoms, fewer days off work, fewer visits to the doctor, improved mood, and a more positive outlook.

If you'd like to try expressive writing to help you deal with a traumatic event, set aside a special time—15 minutes a day for four consecutive days, for example, or on one day a week for four weeks. Write in a place where you won't be interrupted or distracted. Explore your deepest thoughts and feelings and why you feel the way you do. Don't worry about grammar or coherence or about what someone else might think about what you're writing; you are writing just for yourself. You may find the writing exercise to be distressing in the short term—sadness and depression are common when dealing with feelings about a stressful event—but most people report relief and contentment soon after writing for several days.

SOURCES: Pennebaker, J. W. 2004. *Writing to Heal: A Guided Journal for Recovery from Trauma and Emotional Upheaval.* Oakland, Calif.: New Harbinger. Smyth, J. M., et al. 1999. Effects of writing about stressful experiences on symptom reduction in patients with asthma or rheumatoid arthritis: A randomized trial. *Journal of the American Medical Association* 281(14): 1304–1309. Spiegel, D. 1999. Healing words: Emotional expression and disease outcome. *Journal of the American Medical Association* 281(14): 1328–1329.

Bed rest immediately following the onset of back pain may make you feel better, but it should be of very short duration. Prolonged bed rest—5 days or more—was once thought to be an effective treatment for back pain, but most physicians now advise against it because it may weaken muscles and actually worsen pain. Limit bed rest to one day and begin moderate physical activity as soon as possible. Exercise can increase muscular endurance and flexibility and protect your disks from loss of fluid. Three of the back exercises discussed later in the chapter may be particularly helpful following an episode of acute back pain: curl-ups, side bridges, and spine extensions.

See your physician if acute back pain doesn't resolve within a short time. Other warning signals of a more severe problem that requires a professional evaluation include severe pain, numbness, pain that radiates down one or both legs, problems with bladder or bowel control, fever, or rapid weight loss.

Managing Chronic Back Pain

Low-back pain is considered chronic if it persists for more than 3 months. Symptoms vary—some people experience stabbing or shooting pain, others a steady ache accompanied by stiffness. Sometimes pain is localized; in other cases, it radiates to another part of the body. Psychological symptoms may also occur. Underlying causes of chronic back pain include injuries, infection, muscle or ligament strains, and disk herniations.

Because symptoms and causes are so varied, different people benefit from different treatment strategies, and researchers have found that many treatments have only limited benefits. Potential treatments may include over-the-counter or prescription medications; exercise; physical therapy, massage, or chiropractic care; acupuncture; percutaneous electrical nerve stimulation (PENS), in which acupuncture-like needles are used to deliver an electrical current; education and advice about posture, exercise, and body mechanics; and surgery.

Psychological therapy may also be beneficial in some cases. Reducing emotional stress that causes muscle tension can provide direct benefits, and other therapies can help people deal better with chronic pain and its effects on their daily lives. Support groups and expressive writing are strategies that have been found beneficial for people with chronic pain and other conditions (see the box "Expressive Writing and Chronic Conditions.").

Exercises for the Prevention and Management of Low-Back Pain

The tests in Labs 5.3 and 5.4 can help you assess low-back muscular endurance and posture. The exercises that follow are designed to help you maintain a healthy back by stretching and strengthening the major muscle groups that affect the back—the abdominal muscles, the muscles along your spine and sides, and the muscles of your hips and thighs. If you have back problems, check with your physician before beginning any exercise program. Perform the exercises slowly and progress very gradually. Stop and consult your physician if any exercise causes back pain. General guidelines for back exercise programs include the following:

- Do low-back exercises at least 3 days per week; many experts recommend that back exercises be done daily.

- Emphasize muscular endurance rather than muscular strength—endurance may be more protective. Many back injuries are caused by problems with motor control: If you attempt complex trunk movements (such as picking up a book from the floor) when your muscles are tired, you are more likely to strain muscles and/or put pressure on nerves, thereby causing pain.

- Don't do spine exercises involving a full range of motion early in the morning because your disks have

a high fluid content early in the day and injuries may occur as a result.

- Engage in regular endurance exercise such as cycling or walking in addition to performing exercises that specifically build muscular endurance and flexibility. Brisk walking with a vigorous arm swing may help relieve back pain. Start with fast walking if your core muscles are weak or you have back pain. After you get in shape, integrate other endurance activities that you enjoy—jogging, cycling, treadmill, elliptical trainer, or stair-climber.

- Be patient and stick with your program. Increased back fitness and pain relief may require as long as 3 months of regular exercise.

LOW-BACK EXERCISES

EXERCISE 1   CAT STRETCH

Target: Improved flexibility, relaxation, and reduced stiffness in the spine

Instructions: Begin on all fours with your knees below your hips and your hands below your shoulders. Slowly and deliberately move through a cycle of extension and flexion of your spine. **(a)** Begin by slowly pushing your back up and dropping your head slightly until your spine is extended (rounded). **(b)** Then, slowly lower your back and lift your chin slightly until your spine is flexed (relaxed and slightly arched). *Do not press at the ends of the range of motion.* Stop if you feel pain. Do 10 slow, continuous cycles of the movement.

(a)

(b)

EXERCISE 2   STEP STRETCH

(see Exercise 6 in the flexibility program, p. 150)

Target: Improved flexibility, strength, and endurance in the muscles of the hip and the front of the thigh

Instructions: Hold each stretch for 15–30 seconds and do 2–4 repetitions on each side.

EXERCISE 3 ALTERNATE LEG STRETCHER

(see Exercise 11 in the flexibility program, p. 152)

Target: Improved flexibility in the back of the thigh, hip, knee, and buttocks

Instructions: Hold each stretch for 15–30 seconds and do 2–4 repetitions on each side.

EXERCISE 4 TRUNK TWIST

Target: Improved flexibility in the lower back and sides

Instructions: Lie on your side with top knee bent, lower leg straight, lower arm extended out in front of you on the floor, and upper arm at your side. Push down with your upper knee while you twist your trunk backward. Try to get your shoulders and upper body flat on the floor, turning your head as well. Return to the starting position, and then repeat on the other side. Hold the stretch for 15–30 seconds and do 2–4 repetitions on each side.

EXERCISE 5 CURL-UP

Target: Improved strength and endurance in the abdomen

Instructions: Lie on your back with one or two knees bent and arms crossed on your chest or hands under your lower back. Tilt your pelvis under, flattening your back. Tuck your chin in and slowly curl up, one vertebra at a time, as you use your abdominal muscles to lift your head first and then your shoulders. Stop when you can see your knees and hold for 5–10 seconds before returning to the starting position. Do 10 or more repetitions.

Variation: Add a twist to develop other abdominal muscles. When you have curled up so that your shoulder blades are off the floor, twist your upper body so that one shoulder is higher than the other; reach past your knee with your upper arm. Hold and then return to the starting position. Repeat on the opposite side. Curl-ups can also be done using an exercise ball (see p. 102).

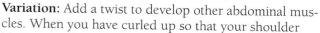

EXERCISE 6 ISOMETRIC SIDE BRIDGE

(see Exercise 11 in the free weights program in Chapter 4, p. 119)

Target: Increased strength and endurance in the muscles along the sides of the abdomen

Instructions: Hold the bridge position for 10 seconds, breathing normally. Work up to a 60-second hold. Perform one or more repetitions on each side.

Variation: You can make the exercise more difficult by keeping your legs straight and supporting yourself with your feet and forearm (see Lab 5.3) or with your feet and hand (with elbow straight).

EXERCISE 7   SPINE EXTENSIONS

(see Exercise 10 in the free weights program in Chapter 4, p. 119)

Target: Increased strength and endurance in the back, buttocks, and back of the thighs

Instructions: Hold each position for 10–30 seconds. Begin with one repetition on each side and work up to several repetitions.

Variation: If you have experienced back pain in the past or if this exercise is difficult for you, do the exercise with both hands on the ground rather than with one arm lifted. You can make this exercise more difficult by doing it balancing on an exercise ball. Find a balance point on your chest while lying face down on the ball with one arm and the opposite leg on the ground. Tense your abdominal muscles while reaching and extending with one arm and reaching and extending with the opposite leg. Repeat this exercise using the other arm and leg.

EXERCISE 8   WALL SQUAT (PHANTOM CHAIR)

Target: Increased strength and endurance in the lower back, thighs, and abdomen

Instructions: Lean against a wall and bend your knees as though you are sitting in a chair. Support your weight with your legs. Begin by holding the position for 5–10 seconds. Build up to 1 minute or more. Perform one or more repetitions.

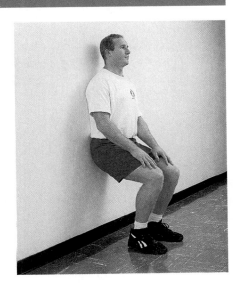

EXERCISE 9   PELVIC TILT

Target: Increased strength and endurance in the abdomen and buttocks

Instructions: Lie on your back with knees bent and arms extended to the side. Tilt your pelvis under and try to flatten your lower back against the floor. Tighten your buttock and abdominal muscles while you hold this position for 5–10 seconds. Don't hold your breath. Work up to 10 repetitions of the exercise. Pelvic tilts can also be done standing or leaning against a wall. (Note: Although this is a popular exercise with many therapists, some experts question the safety of pelvic tilts. Stop if you feel pain in your back at any time during the exercise.)

Target: Increased strength and endurance in the hips and buttocks

Instructions: Lie on your back with knees bent and arms extended to the side. Tuck your pelvis under, and then lift your tailbone, buttocks, and lower back from the floor. Hold this position for 5–10 seconds with your weight resting on your feet, arms, and shoulders, and then return to the starting position. Work up to 10 repetitions of the exercise. (Note: Although this is a popular exercise with many therapists, some experts question the safety of back bridges. Stop if you feel pain in your back at any time during the exercise.)

Good flexibility and proper posture improve the health of your joints and muscles and may prevent injuries and low-back pain, contributing to long-term quality of life. Stretching exercises are also a great way to relax and relieve aches and pains. To improve and maintain your flexibility, perform stretches that work the major joints at least twice a week.

Right now you can

- Stand up and stretch—do either the upper-back stretch or the across-the-body stretch shown in the chapter.

- Practice the recommended sitting and standing postures suggested in the chapter. If needed, adjust your chair or find something to use as a footrest.

- If you frequently work at a computer, check the position in which you typically sit and make any needed adjustments to improve your posture. Your back should be flat or slightly rounded, feet flat on the floor (or a footrest), and knees at or slightly above hip level. When your hands are on the keyboard, your shoulders should be relaxed, your forearms and hands should be in a straight line, and the top of the monitor screen should be at or slightly below eye level. Your eyes should be about 18–30 inches from the screen.

SUMMARY

- Flexibility, the ability of joints to move through their full range of motion, is highly adaptable and specific to each joint.

- Range of motion can be limited by joint structure, muscle inelasticity, and stretch receptor activity.

- Developing flexibility depends on stretching the elastic tissues within muscles regularly and gently until they lengthen. Overstretching can make connective tissue brittle and lead to rupture.

- Signals sent between muscle and tendon receptors and the spinal cord can enhance flexibility because contracting a muscle stimulates a relaxation response, thereby allowing a longer muscle stretch, and because stretch receptors become less sensitive after repeated stretches, initiating fewer contractions.

- The benefits of flexibility include preventing abnormal stresses that lead to joint deterioration and possibly reducing the risk of injuries and low-back pain.

- Stretches should be held for 15–30 seconds; perform 2–4 repetitions. Flexibility training should be done a minimum of 2–3 days per week (ideally, 5–7 days per week), preferably following activity, when muscles are warm.

- Static stretching is done slowly and held to the point of mild tension; ballistic stretching consists of bouncing stretches and can lead to injury. Dynamic stretching involves moving joints slowly and fluidly through their range of motion in a controlled manner. Proprioceptive neuromuscular facilitation uses muscle receptors in contracting and relaxing a muscle.

- Passive stretching, using an outside force in moving muscles and joints, achieves a greater range of motion (and has a higher injury risk) than active stretching, which uses opposing muscles to initiate a stretch.

- The spinal column consists of vertebrae separated by intervertebral disks. It provides structure and support for the body and protects the spinal cord. The muscles in the core work together to stabilize the spine and transfer force between the upper body and lower body.

- Acute back pain can be treated as a soft tissue injury, with cold treatment followed by application of heat (once swelling subsides); prolonged bed rest is not recommended. A variety of treatments have been suggested for chronic back pain, including regular exercise, physical therapy, acupuncture, education, and psychological therapy.

- In addition to good posture, proper body mechanics, and regular physical activity, a program for preventing low-back pain includes exercises that develop flexibility, strength, and endurance in the muscle groups that affect the lower back.

Is stretching the same as warming up?
No. People often confuse stretching with a pre-exercise warm-up. Although they are complementary, they are two distinct activities. A warm-up is light exercise that involves moving the joints through the same motions used during the activity; it increases body temperature so your metabolism works better when you're exercising at high intensity. Stretching increases the movement capability of your joints, so you can move more easily with less risk of injury. Stretching may also induce cellular changes that protect muscles from injury.

Whenever you stretch, first spend 5–10 minutes engaged in some form of low-intensity exercise, such as walking, jogging, or low-intensity calisthenics. When your muscles are warmed, begin your stretching routine. Warmed muscles stretch better than cold ones and are less prone to injury.

How much flexibility do I need? This question is not always easy to answer. If you're involved in a sport such as gymnastics, figure skating, or ballet, you are often required to reach extreme joint motions to achieve success. However, nonathletes do not need to reach these extreme joint positions. In fact, too much flexibility may, in some cases, increase your risk of injury. As with other types of fitness, moderation is the key. You should regularly stretch your major joints and muscle groups but not aspire to reach extreme flexibility.

Can I stretch too far? Yes. As muscle tissue is progressively stretched, it reaches a point where it becomes damaged and may rupture. The greatest danger occurs during passive stretching when a partner is doing the stretching for you. It is critical that your stretching partner not force your joint outside its normal functional range of motion.

Can physical training limit flexibility? Weight training, jogging, or any physical activity will decrease flexibility if the exercises are not performed through a full range of motion. When done properly, weight training increases flexibility. However, because of the limited range of motion used during the running stride, jogging tends to compromise flexibility. It is important for runners to practice flexibility exercises for the hamstrings and quadriceps regularly.

Does stretching affect muscular strength? Several recent studies have found that stretching decreases strength and power for about 5 minutes following the stretch. This is one reason some experts suggest that people not stretch as part of their exercise warm-up. However, the effects of stretching on muscle strength and athletic performance are still being investigated. Regardless of when you choose to stretch, it is still important to warm up before any workout by engaging in 5–10 minutes of light exercise such as walking or slow jogging.

Visit the Online Learning Center for more answers to common questions about flexibility and low-back health.

For Further Exploration

VW Fit and Well Online Learning Center (www.mhhe.com/fahey)

Use the learning objectives, study guide questions, and glossary flashcards to review key terms and concepts and prepare for exams. You can extend your knowledge of flexibility and low-back health and gain experience in using the Internet as a resource by completing the activities and checking out the Web links for the topics in Chapter 5 marked with the World Wide Web icon. For this chapter, Internet activities explore the types of stretching techniques, different exercises that build flexibility, and techniques for preventing and managing back pain; there is also a helpful set of Web links.

Daily Fitness and Nutrition Journal

Complete the flexibility portion of the program plan by setting goals and selecting exercises. Fill in the information for the specific exercises you will perform, including which joints they work.

Books

Alter, M. J. 2004. *Science of Flexibility,* 3rd ed. Champaign, Ill.: Human Kinetics. *An extremely well-researched book that discusses the scientific basis of stretching exercises and flexibility.*

Anderson, B., and J. Anderson. 2003. *Stretching,* 20th anniv. ed. Bolinas, Calif.: Shelter Publications. *A best-selling exercise book, updated with more than 200 stretches for 60 sports and activities.*

Blahnik, J. 2004. *Full-Body Flexibility.* Champaign, Ill.: Human Kinetics. *Presents a blend of stretching techniques derived from sports training, martial arts, yoga, and Pilates.*

Jemmet, M. 2001. *Spinal Stabilization: The New Science of Back Pain.* Halifax, Nova Scotia: RMJ Fitness and Rehabilitation Consultants. *Provides information on anatomy, biomechanics, common back problems, and helpful exercises.*

McGill, S. 2004. *Ultimate Back Fitness and Performance.* Waterloo, Canada: Wabuno. *Written by one of the premier researchers in the world on back biomechanics and back pain. It describes mechanisms of back pain and exercises and movement patterns for preventing it.*

VW Organizations and Web Sites

American Academy of Orthopaedic Surgeons: Public Information. Provides information about a variety of joint problems, including back, neck, and shoulder pain.
http://orthoinfo.aaos.org

CUErgo: Cornell University Ergonomics Web Site. Provides information about how to arrange a computer workstation to prevent back pain and repetitive strain injuries as well as other topics related to ergonomics.
http://ergo.human.cornell.edu

Exercise: A Guide from the National Institute on Aging. Practical advice on fitness for seniors; includes animated instructions for specific flexibility exercises.

http://weboflife.ksc.nasa.gov/exerciseandaging/toc.html

Georgia State University: Flexibility. Provides information about the benefits of stretching and how to develop a safe and effective program; includes illustrations of stretches.

http://www.gsu.edu/~wwwfit/flexibility.html

MedlinePlus Back Pain Tutorial. An interactive, illustrated tutorial of the causes and prevention of back pain.

http://www.nlm.nih.gov/medlineplus/tutorials/backpain.html

NIH Back Pain Fact Sheet. Basic information on the prevention and treatment of back pain.

http://www.ninds.nih.gov/disorders/backpain/backpain.htm

Southern California Orthopedic Institute. Provides information about a variety of orthopedic problems, including back injuries; also has illustrations of spinal anatomy.

http://www.scoi.com

Stretching and Flexibility. Provides information about the physiology of stretching and different types of stretching exercises.

http://www.ifafitness.com/stretch/index.html

See also the listings for Chapters 2 and 4.

Selected Bibliography

Amako, M., et al. 2003. Effect of static stretching on prevention of injuries for military recruits. *Military Medicine* 168:442–446.

American College of Sports Medicine. 2006. *ACSM's Guidelines for Exercise Testing and Prescription.* Philadelphia: Lippincott Williams & Wilkins.

American College of Sports Medicine. 2006. *ACSM's Resource Manual for Guidelines for Exercise Testing and Prescription,* 5th ed. Philadelphia: Lippincott Williams & Wilkins.

Barr, K. P., Griggs, M., and Cadby, T. 2005. Lumbar stabilization: Core concepts and current literature. Part 1. *American Journal of Physical Medicine and Rehabilitation* 84(6): 473–480.

Beach, T. A., et al. 2005. Effects of prolonged sitting on the passive flexion stiffness of the in vivo lumbar spine. *Spine Journal* 5(2): 145–154.

Buchbinder, R., and J. Hoving. 2002. Specific spinal exercise substantially reduces the risk of low back pain recurrence. *Australian Journal of Physiotherapy* 48:55.

Davis, D. S., et al. 2005. The effectiveness of three stretching techniques on hamstring flexibility using consistent stretching parameters. *Journal of Strength and Conditioning Research* 19(1): 27–32.

Friedrich, M., et al. 2005. Long-term effect of a combined exercise and motivational program on the level of disability of patients with chronic low back pain. *Spine* 30(9): 995–1000.

Funk, D. C., et al. 2003. Impact of prior exercise on hamstring flexibility: A comparison of proprioceptive neuromuscular facilitation and static stretching. *Journal of Strength and Conditioning Research* 17:489–492.

Gajdosik, R. L., et al. 2005. Effects of an eight-week stretching program on the passive-elastic properties and function of the calf muscles of older women. *Clinical Biomechanics* 20(9): 973–983.

Grenier, S. G., C. Russell, and S. M. McGill. 2003. Relationships between lumbar flexibility, sit-and-reach test, and a previous history of low back discomfort in industrial workers. *Canadian Journal of Applied Physiology* 28:165–177.

Hakkinen, A., et al. 2005. Effects of home strength training and stretching versus stretching alone after lumbar disk surgery: A randomized study with a 1-year follow-up. *Archives of Physical Medicine and Rehabilitation* 86(5): 865–870.

Hart, L. 2005. Effect of stretching on sport injury risk: A review. *Clinical Journal of Sports Medicine* 15(2): 113.

Hayden, J. A., van Tulder, M. W., and Tomlinson, G. (2005). Systematic review: Strategies for using exercise therapy to improve outcomes in chronic low back pain. *Annals of Internal Medicine* 142(9): 776–785.

Hodges, P. W. 2003. Core stability exercise in chronic low back pain. *Orthopedic Clinics of North America* 34:245–254.

Hurwitz, E. L., H. Morgenstern, and C. Chiao. 2005. Effects of recreational physical activity and back exercises on low back pain and psychological distress: findings from the UCLA Low Back Pain Study. *American Journal of Public Health* 95(10): 1817–1824.

Kovacs, F. M., et al. 2003. Effect of firmness of mattress on chronic nonspecific low-back pain: Randomised, double-blind, controlled, multicentre trial. *Lancet* 362(9396): 1594–1595.

Liu-Ambrose, T. Y., et al. 2005. Both resistance and agility training reduce back pain and improve health-related quality of life in older women with low bone mass. *Osteoporosis International,* 9 February [Epub ahead of print].

Manek, N. J., and MacGregor, A. J. 2005. Epidemiology of back disorders: Prevalence, risk factors, and prognosis. *Current Opinion in Rheumatology* 17(2): 134–140.

McGill, S. M. 1998. Low back exercises: Evidence for improving exercise regimens. *Physical Therapy* 78(7): 754–765.

National Institute of Arthritis and Musculoskeletal and Skin Diseases. 2005. *Back Pain.* NIH Publication No. 05-5285.

Nelson, A. G., et al. 2005. Acute effects of passive muscle stretching on sprint performance. *Journal of Sports Science* 23(5): 449–454.

Nieman, D. C. 2007. *Exercise Testing and Prescription: A Health-Related Approach,* 6th ed. New York: McGraw-Hill.

Nieman, D. C. 2004. You asked for it: Low back pain. *ACSM's Health and Fitness Journal,* January/February.

Palmer, K. T., et al. 2003. Smoking and musculoskeletal disorders: Findings from a British national survey. *Annals of Rheumatoid Diseases* 62:33–36.

Parks, K. A., et al. 2003. A comparison of lumbar range of motion and functional ability scores in patients with low back pain: Assessment for range of motion validity. *Spine* 28:380–384.

Power, C., et al. 2001. Predictors of low back pain onset in a prospective British study. *American Journal of Public Health* 91(10): 1671–1678.

Shrier, I. 2004. Does stretching improve performance? A systematic and critical review of the literature. *Clinical Journal of Sports Medicine* 14(5): 267–273.

Ten nice-to-know facts about flexibility and stretching. 2003. *ACSM's Health & Fitness Journal,* July/August.

Thacker, S. B., et al. 2004. The impact of stretching on sports injury risk: A systematic review of the literature. *Medicine and Science in Sports and Exercise* 36(3): 371–378.

LAB 5.1 *Assessing Your Current Level of Flexibility* ViW

Part I Sit-and-Reach Test

Equipment

Use a modified Wells and Dillon flexometer or construct your own measuring device using a firm box or two pieces of wood about 30 centimeters (12 inches) high attached at right angles to each other. Attach a metric ruler to measure the extent of reach. With the low numbers of the ruler toward the person being tested, set the 26-centimeter mark of the ruler at the footline of the box. (Individuals who cannot reach as far as the footline will have scores below 26 centimeters; those who can reach past their feet will have scores above 26 centimeters.)

Preparation

Warm up your muscles with a low-intensity activity such as walking or easy jogging. Then perform slow stretching movements.

Instructions

1. Remove your shoes and sit facing the flexibility measuring device with your knees fully extended and your feet flat against the device about 10 centimeters (4 inches) apart.
2. Reach as far forward as you can, with palms down, arms evenly stretched, and knees fully extended; hold the position of maximum reach for about 2 seconds.
3. Perform the stretch 2 times, recording the distance of maximum reach to the nearest 0.5 centimeters: _____ cm

Rating Your Flexibility

Find the score in the table below to determine your flexibility rating. Record it here and on the final page of this lab.

Rating: _____

Ratings for Sit-and-Reach Test

	Rating/Score (cm)*				
Men	Needs Improvement	Fair	Good	Very Good	Excellent
Age: 15–19	Below 24	24–28	29–33	34–38	Above 38
20–29	Below 25	25–29	30–33	34–39	Above 39
30–39	Below 23	23–27	28–32	33–37	Above 37
40–49	Below 18	18–23	24–28	29–34	Above 34
50–59	Below 16	16–23	24–27	28–34	Above 34
60–69	Below 15	15–19	20–24	25–32	Above 32
Women					
Age: 15–19	Below 29	29–33	34–37	38–42	Above 42
20–29	Below 28	28–32	33–36	37–40	Above 40
30–39	Below 27	27–31	32–35	36–40	Above 40
40–49	Below 25	25–29	30–33	34–37	Above 37
50–59	Below 25	25–29	30–32	33–38	Above 38
60–69	Below 23	23–26	27–30	31–34	Above 34

*Footline is set at 26 cm.

SOURCE: *The Canadian Physical Activity, Fitness & Lifestyle Approach: CSEP-Health & Fitness Program's Health-Related Appraisal and Counselling Strategy*, 3rd edition, 2003. Reprinted with permission from the Canadian Society for Exercise Physiology.

Part II Range-of-Motion Assessment

This portion of the lab can be completed by doing visual comparisons or by measuring joint range of motion with a goniometer or other instrument.

Equipment

1. A partner to do visual comparisons or to measure the range of motion of your joints. (You can also use a mirror to perform your own visual comparisons.)
2. For the measurement method, you need a goniometer, flexometer, or other instrument to measure range of motion.

Preparation

Warm up your muscles with some low-intensity activity such as walking or easy jogging.

Instructions

On the following pages, the average range of motion is illustrated and listed quantitatively for some of the major joints. Visually assess the range of motion in your joints and compare it to that shown in the illustrations. For each joint, note (with a check mark) whether your range of motion is above average, average, or below average and in need of improvement. Average values for range of motion are given in degrees for each joint in the assessment. You can also complete the assessment by measuring your range of motion with a goniometer, flexometer, or other instrument. If you are using this measurement method, identify your rating (above average, average, or below average) and record your range of motion in degrees next to the appropriate category. Although the measurement method is more time-consuming, it allows you to track the progress of your stretching program more precisely and to note changes within the broader ratings categories (below average, above average).

Record your ratings on the following pages and on the chart on the final page of this lab. (Ratings were derived from several published sources.)

Assessment of range of motion using a goniometer.

1. Shoulder Abduction and Adduction

For each position and arm, check one of the following; fill in degrees if using the measurement method.

***Shoulder abduction**—raise arm up to the side*

Right	Left	
_____	_____	Below average/needs improvement
_____	_____	Average (92–95°)
_____	_____	Above average

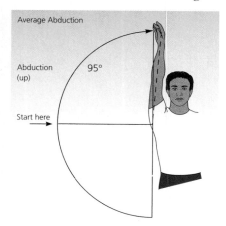

***Shoulder adduction**—move arm down and in front of body*

Right	Left	
_____	_____	Below average/needs improvement
_____	_____	Average (124–127°)
_____	_____	Above average

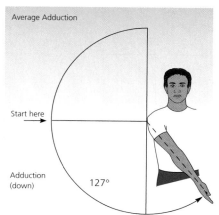

2. Shoulder Flexion and Extension

For each position and arm, check one of the following; fill in degrees if using the measurement method.

Shoulder flexion—raise arm up in front of the body

Right   Left

_____   _____   Below average/needs improvement

_____   _____   Average (92–95°)

_____   _____   Above average

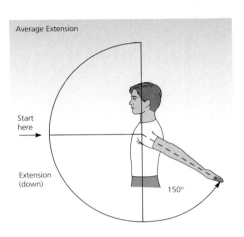

Shoulder extension—move arm down and behind the body

Right   Left

_____   _____   Below average/needs improvement

_____   _____   Average (145–150°)

_____   _____   Above average

3. Trunk/Low-Back Lateral Flexion

Bend directly sideways at your waist. To prevent injury, keep your knees slightly bent, and support your trunk by placing your hand or forearm on your thigh. Check one of the following for each side; fill in degrees if using the measurement method.

Right   Left

_____   _____   Below average/needs improvement

_____   _____   Average (36–40°)

_____   _____   Above average

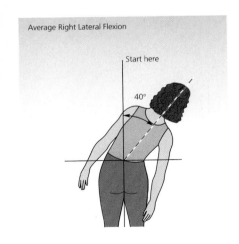

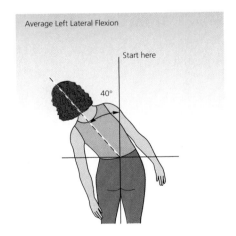

4. Hip Abduction

Raise your leg to the side at the hip. Check one of the following for each leg; fill in degrees if using the measurement method.

Right   Left

_____ _____ Below average/needs improvement
_____ _____ Average (40–45°)
_____ _____ Above average

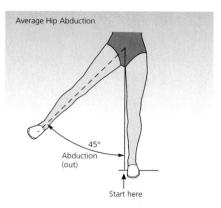

5. Hip Flexion (Bent Knee)

With one leg flat on the floor, bend the other knee and lift the leg up at the hip. Check one of the following for each leg; fill in degrees if using the measurement method.

Right   Left

_____ _____ Below average/needs improvement
_____ _____ Average (121–125°)
_____ _____ Above average

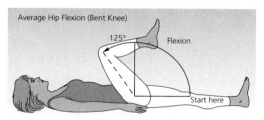

6. Hip Flexion (Straight Leg)

With one leg flat on the floor, raise the other leg at the hip, keeping both legs straight. Take care not to put excess strain on your back. Check one of the following for each leg; fill in degrees if using the measurement method.

Right   Left

_____ _____ Below average/needs improvement
_____ _____ Average (79–81°)
_____ _____ Above average

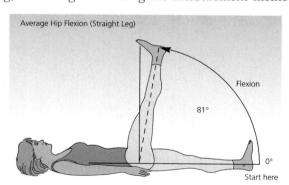

7. Ankle Dorsiflexion and Plantar Flexion

For each position and foot, check one of the following; fill in degrees if using the measurement method.

Ankle dorsiflexion—pull your toes toward your shin

Right   Left

_____ _____ Below average/needs improvement

_____ _____ Average (9–13°)

_____ _____ Above average

Plantar flexion—point your toes

Right   Left

_____ _____ Below average/needs improvement

_____ _____ Average (50–55°)

_____ _____ Above average

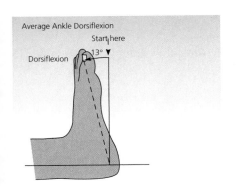

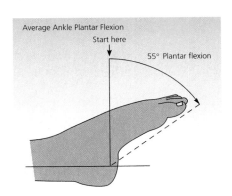

Rating Your Flexibility

Sit-and-Reach Test: Score: _____ cm   Rating: _____

Range-of-Motion Assessment

Identify your rating for each joint on each side of the body. If you used the comparison method, put check marks in the appropriate categories; if you measured range of motion, enter the degrees for each joint in the appropriate category.

Joint/Assessment		Right			Left		
		Below Average	Average	Above Average	Below Average	Average	Above Average
1. Shoulder abduction and adduction	Abduction						
	Adduction						
2. Shoulder flexion and extension	Flexion						
	Extension						
3. Trunk/low-back lateral flexion	Flexion						
4. Hip abduction	Abduction						
5. Hip flexion (bent knee)	Flexion						
6. Hip flexion (straight leg)	Flexion						
7. Ankle dorsiflexion and plantar flexion	Dorsiflexion						
	Plantar flexion						

Using Your Results

How did you score? Are you at all surprised by your ratings for flexibility? Are you satisfied with your current ratings?

If you're not satisfied, set a realistic goal for improvement: _____

Are you satisfied with your current level of flexibility as expressed in your daily life—for example, your ability to maintain good posture and move easily and without pain?

If you're not satisfied, set some realistic goals for improvement:

What should you do next? Enter the results of this lab in the Preprogram Assessment column in Appendix D. If you've set goals for improvement, begin planning your flexibility program by completing the plan in Lab 5.2. After several weeks of your program, complete this lab again and enter the results in the Postprogram Assessment column of Appendix D. How do the results compare?

LAB 5.2 *Creating a Personalized Program for Developing Flexibility* Ww

Goals: List goals for your flexibility program. On the left, include specific, measurable goals that you can use to track the progress of your fitness program. These goals might be things like raising your sit-and-reach score from fair to good or your bent-leg hip flexion rating from below average to average. On the right, include long-term and more qualitative goals, such as reducing your risk for back pain.

Specific Goals: Current Status   Final Goals

_____   _____
_____   _____
_____   _____

Other goals: _____
_____

Exercises: The exercises in the program plan below are from the general stretching program presented in Chapter 5. You can add or delete exercises depending on your needs, goals, and preferences. For any exercises you add, fill in the areas of the body affected.

Frequency: A minimum frequency of 2–3 days per week is recommended; 5–7 days per week is ideal. You may want to do your stretching exercises the same days you plan to do cardiorespiratory endurance exercise or weight training, because muscles stretch better following exercise, when they are warm.

Intensity: All stretches should be done to the point of mild discomfort, not pain.

Time/duration: All stretches should be held for 15–30 seconds. (PNF techniques should include a 6-second contraction followed by a 10–30-second assisted stretch.) All stretches should be performed 2–4 times.

Program Plan for Flexibility

Exercise	Areas Stretched	Frequency (check ✔)						
		M	T	W	Th	F	Sa	Su
Head turns and tilts	Neck							
Towel stretch	Triceps, shoulders, chest							
Across-the-body and overhead stretches	Shoulders, upper back, back of the arm							
Upper-back stretch	Upper back							
Lateral stretch	Trunk muscles							
Step stretch	Hip, front of thigh							
Side lunge	Inner thigh, hip, calf							
Inner thigh stretch	Inner thigh, hip							
Trunk rotation	Trunk, outer thigh and hip, lower back							
Modified hurdler stretch	Back of the thigh, lower back							
Alternate leg stretcher	Back of the thigh, hip, knee, ankle, buttocks							
Lower-leg stretch	Back of the lower leg							

You can monitor your program using a chart like the one on the next page.

Flexibility Program Chart

Fill in the dates you perform each stretch, the number of seconds you hold each stretch (should be 15–30), and the number of repetitions of each (should be 2–4). For an easy check on the duration of your stretches, count "one thousand one, one thousand two," and so on. You will probably find that over time you'll be able to hold each stretch longer (in addition to being able to stretch farther).

Exercise/Date																						
	Duration																						
	Reps																						
	Duration																						
	Reps																						
	Duration																						
	Reps																						
	Duration																						
	Reps																						
	Duration																						
	Reps																						
	Duration																						
	Reps																						
	Duration																						
	Reps																						
	Duration																						
	Reps																						
	Duration																						
	Reps																						
	Duration																						
	Reps																						
	Duration																						
	Reps																						
	Duration																						
	Reps																						
	Duration																						
	Reps																						
	Duration																						
	Reps																						
	Duration																						
	Reps																						
	Duration																						
	Reps																						

LAB 5.3 *Assessing Muscular Endurance for Low-Back Health*

The three tests in this lab evaluate the muscular endurance of major spine-stabilizing muscles.

Side Bridge Endurance Test

Equipment

1. Stopwatch or clock with a second hand
2. Exercise mat
3. Partner

Preparation

Warm up your muscles with some low-intensity activity such as walking or easy jogging. Practice assuming the side bridge position described below.

Instructions

1. Lie on the mat on your side with your legs extended. Place your top foot in front of your lower foot for support. Lift your hips off the mat so you are supporting yourself on one elbow and your feet (see photo). Your body should maintain a straight line. Breathe normally; don't hold your breath.
2. Hold the position as long as possible. Your partner should keep track of the time and make sure that you maintain the correct position. Your final score is the total time you are able to hold the side bridge with correct form—from the time you lift your hips until your hips return to the mat.
3. Rest for 5 minutes and then repeat the test on the other side. Record your times here and on the chart at the end of the lab. Right side bridge time: _____ sec   Left side bridge time: _____ sec

Trunk Flexors Endurance Test

Equipment

1. Stopwatch or clock with a second hand
2. Exercise mat or padded exercise table
3. Two helpers
4. Jig angled at 60° from the floor or padded bench (optional)

Preparation

Warm up with some low-intensity activity such as walking or easy jogging.

Instructions

1. To start, assume a sit-up posture with your back supported at an angle of 60° from the floor; support can be provided by a jig, a padded bench, or a spotter (see photos). Your knees and hips should both be flexed at 90°, and your arms should be folded across your chest with your hands placed on the opposite shoulders. Your toes should be secured under a toe strap or held by a partner.
2. Your goal is to hold the starting position (isometric contraction) as long as possible after the support is pulled away. To begin the test, a helper should pull the jig or other support back about 10 cm (4 inches). A helper should keep track of the time; if a spotter is acting as your support, she or he should be ready to support your weight as soon as your torso begins to move back. Your final score is the total time you are able to hold the contraction—from the time the support is removed until any part of your back touches the support. Remember to breathe normally throughout the test.
3. Record your time here and on the chart at the end of the lab. Trunk flexors endurance time: _____ sec

Back Extensors Endurance Test

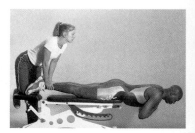

Equipment

1. Stopwatch or clock with a second hand
2. Extension bench with padded ankle support or any padded bench
3. Partner

Preparation

Warm up with some low-intensity activity such as walking or easy jogging.

Instructions

1. Lie face down on the test bench with the upper body extending out over the end of the bench and the pelvis, hips, and knees flat on the bench. Your arms should be folded across your chest with your hands placed on the opposite shoulders. Your feet should be secured under a padded strap or held by a partner.
2. Your goal is to hold your upper body in a straight horizontal line with your lower body as long as possible. Keep your neck straight and neutral; don't raise your head and don't arch your back. Breathe normally. Your partner should keep track of the time and watch your form. Your final score is the total time you are able to hold the horizontal position—from the time you assume the position until your upper body drops from the horizontal position.
3. Record your time here and on the chart below. Back extensors endurance time: _____ sec

Rating Your Test Results for Muscular Endurance for Low-Back Health

The table below shows mean endurance test times for healthy young college students with a mean age of 21 years. Compare your scores with the times shown in the table. (If you are older or have suffered from low-back pain in the past, these ratings are less accurate; however, your time scores can be used as a point of comparison.)

Mean Endurance Times (sec)

	Right side bridge	Left side bridge	Trunk flexors	Back extensors
Men	95	99	136	161
Women	75	78	134	185

SOURCE: From S. M. McGill, 2002, *Low Back Disorders: Evidence-Based Prevention and Rehabilitation*, page 227, table 12.1. © 2002 by Stuart McGill. Reprinted with permission from Human Kinetics (Champaign, IL).

Right side bridge: _____ sec   Rating (above mean, at mean, below mean): _____
Left side bridge: _____ sec   Rating (above mean, at mean, below mean): _____
Trunk flexors: _____ sec   Rating (above mean, at mean, below mean): _____
Back extensors: _____ sec   Rating (above mean, at mean, below mean): _____

Using Your Results

How did you score? Are you at all surprised by your scores for the low-back tests? Are you satisfied with your current ratings?

If you're not satisfied, set a realistic goal for improvement. The norms in this lab are based on healthy young adults, so a score above the mean may or may not be realistic for you. Instead, you may want to set a specific goal based on time rather than rating; for example, set a goal of improving your time by 10%. Imbalances in muscular endurance have been linked with back problems, so if your rating is significantly lower for one of the three tests, you should focus particular attention on that area of the body.

Goal: _____

What should you do next? Enter the results of this lab in the Preprogram Assessment column in Appendix D. If you've set a goal for improvement, begin a program of low-back exercises such as that suggested in this chapter. After several weeks of your program, complete this lab again and enter the results in the Postprogram Assessment column of Appendix D. How do the results compare?

Name _____ **Section** _____ **Date** _____

LAB 5.4 *Posture Evaluation*

For each row, have a partner record the point total that corresponds to the illustration that most closely matches your posture.

5 points	3 points	1 point	Your Score

  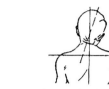

Head erect (gravity line passes directly through center)   Head twisted or turned to one side slightly   Head twisted or turned to one side markedly   _____

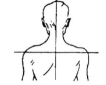

Shoulders level (horizontally)   One shoulder slightly higher than other   One shoulder markedly higher than other   _____

Spine straight   Spine slightly curved laterally   Spine markedly curved laterally   _____

Hips level (horizontally)   One hip slightly higher   One hip markedly higher   _____

Feet pointed straight ahead   Feet pointed out   Feet pointed out markedly; ankles sag in (pronation)   _____

Arches high   Arches lower; feet slightly flat   Arches low; feet markedly flat   _____

5 points	3 points	1 point	Your Score
Neck erect, chin in, head in balance directly above shoulders	Neck slightly forward, chin slightly out	Neck markedly forward, chin markedly out	_____
Chest elevated (breast-bone farthest forward part of body)	Chest slightly depressed	Chest markedly depressed (flat)	_____
Shoulders centered	Shoulders slightly forward	Shoulders markedly forward (shoulder blades protruding in rear)	_____
Upper back normally rounded	Upper back slightly more rounded	Upper back markedly rounded	_____
Trunk erect	Trunk inclined slightly to rear	Trunk inclined to rear markedly	_____
Abdomen flat	Abdomen protruding	Abdomen protruding and sagging	_____
Lower back normally curved	Lower back slightly hollow	Lower back markedly hollow	_____

TOTAL SCORE (from both pages) (Scores should be between 13 and 65.) _____

If your posture needs improvement, review the information in the box on good posture and low-back health on p. 157. If you scored "1 point" for any item in the evaluation, you may want to consider seeing a physician; professional advice, physical therapy, orthotic devices, or other therapies may help you improve your posture.

SOURCE: Reproduced with the permission of The University of the State of New York, author, and publisher.

Looking

AHEAD

After reading this chapter, you should be able to

- Define fat-free mass, essential fat, and nonessential fat and describe their functions in the body
- Explain how body composition affects overall health and wellness
- Describe how body mass index, body composition, and body fat distribution are measured and assessed
- Explain how to determine recommended body weight and body fat distribution

6

Body Composition

Test Your

Knowledge

1. **Exercise helps reduce the risks associated with overweight and obesity even if it doesn't result in improvements in body composition.**
   True or false?

2. **Which of the following is the most significant risk factor for the most common type of diabetes (type 2 diabetes)?**
   a. smoking
   b. low-fiber diet
   c. overweight or obesity
   d. inactivity

3. **In women, excessive exercise and low energy (calorie) intake can cause which of the following?**
   a. unhealthy reduction in body fat levels
   b. amenorrhea (absent menstruation)
   c. bone density loss and osteoporosis
   d. muscle wasting and fatigue

ANSWERS

1. TRUE. Regular physical activity provides protection against the health risks of overweight and obesity. It lowers the risk of death for people who are overweight or obese as well as for those at a normal weight.

2. C. All four are risk factors for diabetes, but overweight/obesity is the most significant. It's estimated that 90% of cases of type 2 diabetes could be prevented if people adopted healthy lifestyle behaviors. About 7% of Americans have type 2 diabetes, and more than 6 million of those with diabetes don't know it. The direct and indirect costs exceed $130 billion per year.

3. ALL FOUR. Very low levels of body fat, and the behaviors used to achieve them, have serious health consequences for both men and women.

W Fit and Well Online Learning Center   www.mhhe.com/fahey

Visit the *Fit and Well* Online Learning Center for study aids, online labs, additional information about body composition, links, Internet activities that explore how body composition can influence wellness, and much more.

Body composition, the body's relative amounts of fat and fat-free mass, is an important component of fitness for health and wellness. People whose body composition is optimal tend to be healthier, to move more efficiently, and to feel better about themselves. They also have a lower risk of many chronic diseases. To reach wellness, you must determine what body composition is right for you and then work to achieve and maintain it.

Although people pay lip service to the idea of exercising for health, a more immediate goal for many is to look fit and healthy. Unfortunately, many people don't succeed in their efforts to obtain a fit and healthy body because they set unrealistic goals and emphasize short-term weight loss rather than the permanent changes in lifestyle that lead to fat loss and a healthy body composition. Successful management of body composition requires the long-term, consistent coordination of many aspects of a wellness program. However, even in the absence of changes in body composition, an active lifestyle can improve wellness (see the box "Can You Be Fit and Fat?"). This chapter focuses on defining and measuring body composition. The aspects of lifestyle that affect body composition are discussed in detail in other chapters: physical activity and exercise in Chapters 2–5 and 7, sound nutritional habits in Chapter 8, strategies for weight management in Chapter 9, and techniques for managing stress in Chapter 10.

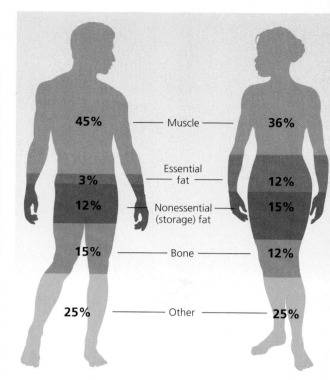

Figure 6.1 Body composition of a typical man and woman, 20–24 years old. SOURCE: Adapted from Brooks, G. A., et al. 2005. *Exercise Physiology: Human Bioenergetics and Its Applications,* 4th ed. New York: McGraw-Hill.

WHAT IS BODY COMPOSITION, AND WHY IS IT IMPORTANT?

The human body can be divided into fat-free mass and body fat. Fat-free mass is composed of all the body's nonfat tissues: bone, water, muscle, connective tissue, organ tissues, and teeth. Body fat includes both essential and nonessential (storage) body fats (Figure 6.1). **Essential fat** includes lipids incorporated into the nerves, brain, heart, lungs, liver, and mammary glands. These fat deposits, crucial for normal body functioning, make up 3–5% of total body weight in men and 8–12% in women. (The larger percentage in women is natural and healthy and is due to fat deposits in the breasts, uterus, and other gender-specific sites.) **Nonessential (storage) fat** exists primarily within fat cells, or **adipose tissue,** often located just below the skin and around major organs. In general, when the amount of fat in the body changes, fat cells increase or decrease in size (rather than in number). The amount of storage fat varies from individual to individual based on many factors, including gender, age, heredity, metabolism, diet, and activity level. Excess storage fat is usually the result of consuming more energy (as food) than is expended (in metabolism and physical activity).

Overweight and Obesity Defined

How much body fat is too much for health and wellness? In the past, many people relied on height-weight tables based on insurance company mortality statistics to answer this question. Unfortunately, these tables can be

Terms

essential fat The fat in the body necessary for normal body functioning.

nonessential (storage) fat Extra fat or fat reserves stored in the body.

adipose tissue Connective tissue in which fat is stored.

percent body fat The percentage of total body weight that is composed of fat.

overweight Characterized by a body weight above a recommended range for good health; ranges are set through large-scale population surveys.

obese Severely overweight, characterized by an excessive accumulation of body fat; overfat. Obesity may also be defined in terms of some measure of total body weight.

Can You Be Fit and Fat?

Obesity is linked to many serious diseases and physical problems, including cardiovascular disease, diabetes, certain cancers, gallbladder disease, arthritis, and premature death. Regular physical activity can help prevent obesity, but activity is also extremely important for health *even if it results in no changes in body composition.*

Exercise blocks many of the destructive health effects of obesity even in individuals who remain overweight. It improves blood pressure, blood fat and blood glucose levels, and body fat distribution; it lowers the risk of diabetes, heart disease, and early death. It is particularly important for the many Americans who have metabolic syndrome or prediabetes, both characterized by insulin resistance.

Physical activity as risk factor operates independently of body composition. That is, activity reduces the risk of health problems and mortality for people of all levels of body fat (see figure). So, while it is best to have both a healthy level of body fat *and* an active lifestyle, activity is important for people regardless of their body composition.

Is physical activity or physical fitness more important for fighting the adverse health effects of obesity? The results of a large number of published studies suggest that physical activity and fitness are both important—the more fit and active you are, the lower your risk of dying prematurely or having health problems. Of the two, however, daily physical activity appears to be more important for health than physical fitness.

SOURCES: Hu, F. B., et al. 2004. Adiposity compared with physical activity in predicting mortality among women. *New England Journal of Medicine* 351(26): 2694–2703. Blair, S. N., Y. Cheng, and J. S. Holder. 2001. Is physical activity or physical fitness more important in defining health benefits? *Medicine and Science in Sports and Exercise* 33(Suppl.): 379–399.

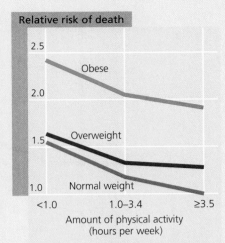

Relationship among amount of activity, body weight, and risk of death.

---

highly inaccurate for some people; at best, they provide only an indirect measure of fatness. Because, as explained in Chapter 4, muscle tissue is denser and heavier than fat, a fit person can easily weigh more and an unfit person weigh less than recommended weights on a height-weight table.

The most important consideration when a person is looking at body composition is the proportion of the body's total weight that is fat—the **percent body fat.** For example, two women may both be 5 feet, 5 inches tall and weigh 130 pounds. But one women, a runner, may have only 20% of her body weight as fat, whereas the other, sedentary, woman could have 40% body fat. Although neither woman is overweight by most standards, the second woman is overfat. Too much body fat (not total weight) has a negative effect on health and well-being.

Some of the most commonly used methods to assess and classify body composition are described later in the chapter. Although less accurate than standards based on body fat, some methods are based on total body weight because it is easier to measure. **Overweight** is usually defined as total body weight above the recommended range for good health (as determined by large-scale population surveys). **Obesity** is defined as a more serious degree of overweight; the cutoff point for obesity may be set in terms of percent body fat or in terms of some measure of total body weight.

Prevalence of Overweight and Obesity Among Americans

By any measure, Americans are getting fatter. Since 1960, the average weight among adult men increased from 166 to 191 pounds; among women, from 140 to 164 pounds. The prevalence of obesity has increased from about 13% in 1960 to about 31% today, and more than 60% of American adults are now overweight (Figure 6.2). Possible explanations for this increase include more time spent in sedentary work and leisure activities, fewer short trips on foot and more by automobile, fewer daily gym classes for students, more meals eaten outside the home, greater consumption of fast food, increased portion sizes, and increased consumption of soft drinks and convenience foods. Fewer than half of Americans meet the minimum recommendation of 30 minutes per day of moderate physical activity, and the Centers for Disease Control and Prevention has estimated that caloric intake has increased by 250–500 calories a day since 1970. (For more on the causes of obesity, see Chapter 9.)

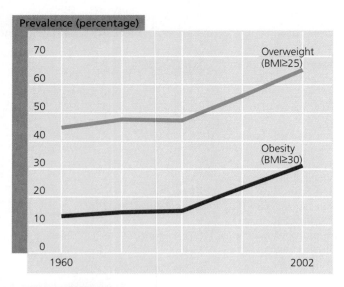

Figure 6.2 Prevalence of overweight and obesity among Americans. SOURCE: National Center for Health Statistics. 2005. *Health, United States, 2005.* Hyattsville, Md.: National Center for Health Statistics.

MOTIVATION FOR CHANGE! Do a check of your home living space to eliminate cues that trigger behaviors you are trying to reduce or eliminate and to add cues that trigger behaviors you want to develop or increase. For example, do you have unhealthy snacks stuffed into your desk drawers or in easy reach in the kitchen? If so, remove these and make healthier choices just as available. Where are your exercise clothes located? Placing them in an easily accessible and obvious location can help them serve as a reminder and motivate you to be active by making it more convenient. Place motivational notes and reminders in appropriate locations—on the bathroom mirror, on the refrigerator, by the front door. Once you've shaped your home environment to support your behavior change program, repeat the process in other locations—your office or study space, your car, and so on.

Excess Body Fat and Wellness

As rates of overweight and obesity increase, so do the problems associated with them. Obesity reduces life expectancy by 10–20 years, causes more than 100,000 premature deaths each year, and costs the United States more than $100 billion annually. Excess body fat can decrease overall wellness through its effects on chronic disease risk, ability to perform physical activities, and body image.

Risk of Chronic Disease and Premature Death Obese people have an overall mortality rate almost twice that of nonobese people, and even mild to moderate overweight is associated with a substantial increase in the risk of premature death. Obesity is associated with unhealthy blood fat levels, impaired heart function, and death from cardiovascular disease. It is estimated that if all Americans had a healthy body composition, the incidence of coronary heart disease would drop by more than 24%. Obesity is also associated with increased risk of death from many types of cancer. Other health problems associated with obesity include hypertension, impaired immune function, gallbladder and kidney diseases, skin problems, sleep and breathing disorders, impotence, pregnancy complications, back pain, arthritis, and other bone and joint disorders. Of particular note is the strong association between excess body fat and diabetes mellitus: Obese people are more than three times as likely as nonobese people to develop diabetes, and the incidence of diabetes among Americans has increased dramatically as the rate of obesity has climbed (see the box "Diabetes").

The distribution of fat is also an important indicator of future health. Studies suggest that people who tend to gain weight in the abdominal area (an apple shape) have a risk of coronary heart disease, high blood pressure, diabetes, and stroke twice as high as that of people who tend to gain weight in the hip area (a pear shape). The reason for this increased risk is not entirely clear, but it appears that fat in the abdomen is more easily mobilized and sent into the bloodstream, increasing disease-related blood fat levels. In general, men tend to gain weight in the abdominal area and premenopausal women in the hip area, but women who exhibit the male pattern of fat distribution face the increased health risks associated with it. Researchers have also found ethnic differences in the relative significance of increased abdominal fat, but more studies are needed to clarify the relationships among fat distribution, ethnicity, and disease.

Performance of Physical Activities Too much body fat makes all types of physical activity more difficult because just moving the body through everyday activities means working harder and using more energy. In general, overfat people are less fit than others and don't have the muscular strength, endurance, and flexibility that make normal activity easy. Because exercise is more difficult, they do less of it, depriving themselves of an effective way to improve body composition.

Emotional Wellness and Self-Image Obesity can affect psychological as well as physical wellness. Being perceived as fat can be a source of ridicule, ostracism, and sometimes discrimination from others; it can contribute to psychological problems such as depression, anxiety, and low self-esteem. Regardless of your body composition, strive to lead a healthier lifestyle and take pride in all your accomplishments. A person's worth is not dependent on their appearance. Everyone should

Diabetes mellitus is a disease that causes a disruption of normal metabolism. The pancreas, a long, thin organ located behind the stomach, normally secretes the hormone insulin, which stimulates cells to take up glucose to produce energy. In a person with diabetes, this process is disrupted, causing a buildup of glucose in the bloodstream. Over the long term, diabetes is associated with kidney failure; nerve damage; circulation problems; retinal damage and blindness; and increased rates of heart attack, stroke, and hypertension. The rate of diabetes has increased steadily over the past 40 years, jumping a dramatic 33% in the 1990s; it is currently the sixth leading cause of death in the United States.

Types of Diabetes

Approximately 20.8 million (1 in 14) Americans have one of two major forms of diabetes. About 5–10% of people with diabetes have the more serious form, known as type 1 diabetes. In this type of diabetes, the pancreas produces little or no insulin, so daily doses of insulin are required. (Without insulin, a person with type 1 can lapse into a coma.) Type 1 diabetes usually strikes before age 30.

About 90% of Americans with diabetes have type 2 diabetes. This condition can develop slowly, and about a third of affected individuals are unaware of their condition. In type 2 diabetes, the pancreas doesn't produce enough insulin, cells are resistant to insulin, or both. This condition is usually diagnosed in people over age 40, but the recent rise in rates of obesity has led to a significant increase in the number of children and young adults with type 2 diabetes. About one-third of people with type 2 diabetes must inject insulin; others may take medications that increase insulin production or stimulate cells to take up glucose.

A third type of diabetes occurs in about 2–5% of women during pregnancy. So-called gestational diabetes usually disappears after pregnancy but 20–50% of women who experience it develop type 2 diabetes within 5–10 years.

The U.S. Department of Health and Human Services and the American Diabetes Association adopted the term *pre-diabetes* to describe blood glucose levels that are higher than normal but not high enough for a diagnosis of full-blown diabetes. About 41 million Americans have pre-diabetes, and most people with the condition will develop type 2 diabetes within 10 years unless they adopt preventive lifestyle measures.

The major factors involved in the development of diabetes are age, obesity, physical inactivity, a family history of diabetes, and lifestyle. Excess body fat reduces cell sensitivity to insulin, and it is a major risk factor for type 2 diabetes; excess abdominal fat is particularly linked to diabetes risk. Ethnic background also plays a role. African Americans and people of Hispanic background are 55% more likely than non-Hispanic whites to develop type 2 diabetes; more than 20% of Hispanics over age 65 have diabetes. Native Americans also have a higher-than-average incidence of diabetes.

Treatment

There is no cure for diabetes, but it can be successfully managed by keeping blood sugar levels within safe limits through diet, exercise, and, if necessary, medication. Blood sugar levels can be monitored using a home test, and close control of glucose levels can significantly reduce the rate of serious complications. Nearly 90% of people with type 2 diabetes are overweight when diagnosed, and an important step in treatment is to lose weight. Even a small amount of exercise and weight loss can be beneficial. People with diabetes should obtain carbohydrate from whole grains, fruits, vegetables, and low-fat dairy products; carbohydrate and monounsaturated fat together should provide 60–70% of total daily calories. Regular exercise and a healthy diet are often sufficient to control type 2 diabetes.

Prevention

It is estimated that 90% of cases of type 2 diabetes could be prevented if people adopted healthy lifestyle behaviors, including regular physical activity, a moderate diet, and modest weight loss. For people with pre-diabetes, lifestyle measures are more effective than medication for delaying or preventing the development of diabetes. Exercise (endurance and/or strength training) makes cells more sensitive to insulin and helps stabilize blood glucose levels; it also helps keep body fat at healthy levels.

Eating a moderate diet to help control body fat is perhaps the most important dietary recommendation for the prevention of diabetes. However, there is some evidence that the composition of the diet may also be important. Studies have linked diets low in fiber and high in sugar, refined carbohydrates, saturated fat, red meat, and high-fat dairy products to increased risk of diabetes; diets rich in whole grains, fruits, vegetables, legumes, fish, and poultry may be protective. Specific foods linked to higher diabetes risk include regular (nondiet) cola beverages, white bread, white rice, french fries, processed meats (bacon, sausage, hot dogs), and sugary desserts. (See Chapter 8 for more information on different types of carbohydrates.)

Warning Signs and Testing

A wellness lifestyle that includes a healthy diet and regular exercise is the best strategy for preventing diabetes. If you do develop diabetes, the best way to avoid complications is to recognize the symptoms and get early diagnosis and treatment. Be alert for the following warning signs:

- Frequent urination
- Extreme hunger or thirst
- Unexplained weight loss
- Extreme fatigue
- Blurred vision
- Frequent infections
- Cuts and bruises that are slow to heal
- Tingling or numbness in the hands and feet
- Generalized itching, with no rash

Type 2 diabetes is often asymptomatic in the early stages, and major health organizations now recommend routine screening for people over age 45 and anyone younger who is at high risk, including anyone who is obese. (The Web site for the American Diabetes Association, listed in the For Further Exploration section at the end of the chapter, includes an interactive diabetes risk assessment). Screening involves a blood test to check glucose levels after either a period of fasting or the administration of a set dose of glucose. A fasting glucose level of 126 mg/dl or higher indicates diabetes; a level of 100–125 mg/dl indicates pre-diabetes. If you are concerned about your risk for diabetes, talk with your physician about being tested.

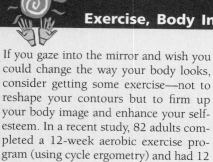

If you gaze into the mirror and wish you could change the way your body looks, consider getting some exercise—not to reshape your contours but to firm up your body image and enhance your self-esteem. In a recent study, 82 adults completed a 12-week aerobic exercise program (using cycle ergometry) and had 12 months of follow-up. Compared with the control group, the participants improved their fitness and also benefited psychologically in tests of mood, anxiety, and self-concept. These same physical and psychological benefits were still significant at the 1-year follow-up.

One reason for the findings may be that people who exercise regularly often gain a sense of mastery and competence that enhances their self-esteem and body image. In addition, exercise contributes to a more toned look, which many adults prefer. Research suggests that physically active people are more comfortable with their bodies and their image than sedentary people are. In one workplace study, 60 employees were asked to complete a 36-session stretching program whose main purpose was to prevent muscle strains at work. At the end of the program, besides the significant increase by all participants in measurements of flexibility, their perceptions of their bodies improved and so did their overall sense of self-worth.

Similar results were obtained in a Norwegian study, in which 219 middle-aged people at risk for heart disease were randomly assigned to one of four groups: diet, diet plus exercise, exercise, and no intervention. The greater the participation of individuals in the exercise component of the program, the higher were their scores in perceived competence/self-esteem and coping.

SOURCES: DiLorenzo, T. M., et al. 1999. Long-term effects of aerobic exercise on psychological outcomes. *Preventive Medicine* 28(1): 75–85. Sorensen, M., et al. 1999. The effect of exercise and diet on mental health and quality of life in middle-aged individuals with elevated risk factors for cardiovascular disease. *Journal of Sports Science* 17(5): 369–377. Moore, T. M. 1998. A workplace stretching program. *AAOHN Journal* 46(12): 563–568.

judge themselves and others by what they say and do, not by their body type.

The "fashionable" body image has changed dramatically during the past 50 years, varying from slightly plump to an almost unhealthy thinness. Today, a fit and healthy-looking body, developed through a healthy lifestyle, is the goal for most people (see the box "Exercise, Body Image, and Self-Esteem"). The key to this "look" is a balance of proper nutrition and exercise—in short, a lifestyle that emphasizes wellness.

Goals for body composition should be realistic, however; a person's ability to change body composition through diet and exercise depends not only on a wellness program, but also on heredity. The "ideal" body presented in the media—from dolls and action figures to fashion models—is an unrealistic goal for the vast majority of Americans. Unrealistic expectations about body composition can have a negative impact on self-image and can lead to the development of eating disorders. Remember, an active lifestyle improves wellness regardless of body weight and composition. (For more information on body image and eating disorders, see Chapter 9.)

For most people, body fat percentage falls somewhere between ideal and a level that is significantly unhealthy. If they consistently maintain a wellness lifestyle that includes a healthy diet and regular exercise, the right body composition will naturally develop.

Wellness for Life   A healthy body composition is vital for wellness throughout life. Strong scientific evidence suggests that controlling your weight will increase your life span; reduce the risk of heart disease, cancer, diabetes, insulin resistance, and back pain; increase your energy level; and improve your self-esteem.

Problems Associated with Very Low Levels of Body Fat

Though not as prevalent a problem as overweight or obesity, having too little body fat is also dangerous. Essential fat is necessary for the functioning of the body, and health experts generally view too little body fat—less than 8–12% for women and 3–5% for men—as a threat to health and well-being. Extreme leanness is linked with reproductive, circulatory, and immune system disorders and with premature death. Extremely lean people may experience muscle wasting and fatigue. They are also more likely to have dangerous eating disorders, which are described in more detail in Chapter 9. For women, an extremely low percentage of body fat is associated with **amenorrhea** and loss of bone mass (see the box "The Female Athlete Triad").

Terms

amenorrhea Absent or infrequent menstruation, sometimes related to low levels of body fat and excessive quantity or intensity of exercise.

female athlete triad A condition consisting of three interrelated disorders: abnormal eating patterns (and excessive exercising) followed by lack of menstrual periods (amenorrhea) and decreased bone density (premature osteoporosis).

body mass index (BMI) A measure of relative body weight correlating highly with more direct measures of body fat, calculated by dividing total body weight (in kilograms) by the square of body height (in meters).

While obesity is at epidemic levels in the United States, many girls and women strive for unrealistic thinness in response to pressure from peers and a society obsessed with appearance. This quest for thinness has led to an increasingly common, underreported condition called the **female athlete triad.**

The triad consists of three interrelated disorders: abnormal eating patterns (and excessive exercising), followed by lack of menstrual periods (amenorrhea), followed by decreased bone density (premature osteoporosis). Left untreated, the triad can lead to decreased physical performance, increased incidence of bone fractures, disturbances of heart rhythm and metabolism, and even death.

Abnormal eating is the event from which the other two components of the triad flow. Abnormal eating ranges from moderately restricting food intake, to binge eating and purging (bulimia), to severely restricting food intake (anorexia nervosa). Whether serious or relatively mild, eating disorders prevent women from consuming enough calories to meet their bodies' needs.

Disordered eating, combined with intense exercise and emotional stress, can suppress the hormones that control the menstrual cycle. If the menstrual cycle stops for three consecutive months, the condition is called amenorrhea. Prolonged amenorrhea can lead to osteoporosis; bone density may erode to the point that a woman in her 20s will have the bone density of a woman in her 60s. Women with osteoporosis have fragile, easily fractured, bones. Some researchers have found that even a few missed menstrual periods can decrease bone density.

All physically active women and girls have the potential to develop one or more components of the female athlete triad; for example, it is estimated that 5–20% of women who exercise regularly and vigorously may develop amenorrhea. But the triad is most prevalent among athletes who participate in certain sports: those in which appearance is highly important, those that emphasize a prepubertal body shape, those that require contour-revealing clothing for competition, those that require endurance, and those that use weight categories for participation. Such sports include gymnastics, figure skating, swimming, distance running, cycling, cross-country skiing, track, volleyball, rowing, horse racing, and cheerleading.

The female athlete triad can be life-threatening, and health professionals are taking it seriously. Typical signs of the eating disorders that trigger the condition are extreme weight loss, dry skin, loss of hair, brittle fingernails, cold hands and feet, low blood pressure and heart rate, swelling around the ankles and hands, and weakening of the bones. Female athletes who have repeated stress fractures may be suffering from the condition. Early intervention is the key to stopping this series of interrelated conditions. Unfortunately, once the condition has progressed, long-term consequences, especially bone loss, are unavoidable. Teenagers may need only to learn about good eating habits; college-age women with a long-standing problem may require intensive psychological counseling.

Abnormal eating patterns and excessive exercising

Premature osteoporosis

Amenorrhea

SOURCES: Brunet, M. 2005. Female athlete triad. *Clinics in Sports Medicine* 24(3): 623–636. Otis, C. 1998. Too slim, amenorrheic, fracture-prone: The female athlete triad. *ACSM's Health and Fitness Journal* 2(1): 20–25. Art: Adapted from Yeager, K. K., et al. 1993. The female athlete triad: Disordered eating, amenorrhea, osteoporosis. *Medicine and Science in Sports and Exercise* 25:775–777. Reprinted by permission of Lippincott Williams & Wilkins.

ASSESSING BODY MASS INDEX, BODY COMPOSITION, AND BODY FAT DISTRIBUTION

The morning weighing ritual on the bathroom scale can't reveal whether a fluctuation in weight is due to a change in muscle, body water, or fat and can't differentiate between overweight and overfat. A 260-pound football player may be overweight according to population height-weight standards yet may actually have much less body fat than average. Likewise, a 40-year-old woman may weigh the same as she did 20 years earlier yet have a considerably different body composition.

There are a number of simple, inexpensive ways to estimate healthy body weight and healthy body composition that are more accurate than the bathroom scale. These assessments can provide you with information about the health risks associated with your current body weight and body composition. They can also help you establish reasonable goals and set a starting point for current and future decisions about weight loss and weight gain.

Calculating Body Mass Index

Body mass index (BMI) is a measure of body weight that is useful for classifying the health risks of body weight if you don't have access to more sophisticated methods. Though more accurate than height-weight tables, body mass index is also based on the concept that a person's weight should be proportional to their height. BMI is a fairly accurate measure of the health risks of body weight

Table 6.1 Body Mass Index (BMI) Classification and Disease Risk

Classification	BMI (kg/m²)	Obesity Class	Disease Risk Relative to Normal Weight and Waist Circumference* Men ≤ 40 in. (102 cm) Women ≤ 35 in. (88 cm)	> 40 in. (102 cm) > 35 in. (88 cm)
Underweight**	<18.5		—	—
Normal†	18.5–24.9		—	—
Overweight	25.0–29.9		Increased	High
Obesity	30.0–34.9	I	High	Very high
	35.0–39.9	II	Very high	Very high
Extreme obesity	≥40.0	III	Extremely high	Extremely high

*Disease risk for type 2 diabetes, hypertension, and cardiovascular disease. The waist circumference cutoff points for increased risk are 40 inches (102 cm) for men and 35 inches (88 cm) for women.

**Research suggests that a low BMI can be healthy in some cases, as long as it is not the result of smoking, an eating disorder, or an underlying disease process. A BMI of 17.5 or less is sometimes used as a diagnostic criterion for the eating disorder anorexia nervosa.

†Increased waist circumference can also be a marker for increased risk, even in persons of normal weight.

SOURCE: Adapted from National Heart, Lung, and Blood Institute. 1998. *Clinical Guidelines on the Identification, Evaluation, and Treatment of Overweight and Obesity in Adults: The Evidence Report.* Bethesda, Md.: National Institutes of Health.

for average (nonathletic) people, and it is easy to calculate and rate. Researchers frequently use BMI in studies that examine the health risks associated with body weight. However, because BMI doesn't distinguish between fat weight and fat-free weight, it can be very inaccurate for some groups. For example, athletes who weight train have more muscle mass than average people and may be classified as overweight by the BMI scale; however, because their "excess" weight is in the form of muscle, it is healthy. If you are an athlete, a serious weight trainer, or a person of short stature, do not use BMI as your primary means of assessing whether your current weight is healthy; instead, try one of the methods described in the next section for estimating percent body fat.

BMI is calculated by dividing your body weight (expressed in kilograms) by the square of your height (expressed in meters). The formula appears below. Space for your own calculations can be found in Lab 6.1, and a complete BMI chart appears in Lab 6.2.

1. Divide body weight in pounds by 2.2 to convert weight to kilograms.

2. Multiply height in inches by 0.0254 to convert height to meters.

3. Multiply the result in step 2 by itself to obtain the square of the height measurement.

4. Divide the result of step 1 by the result of step 3 to obtain BMI.

For example, a person who weighs 130 pounds (130 ÷ 2.2 = 59.1 kg) and is 5 feet, 3 inches tall (63 inches × 0.0254 = 1.6 meters) has a BMI of 59.1 kg ÷ (1.6 m)², or 23 kg/m².

Under guidelines from the National Institutes of Health (NIH), a person is classified as overweight if he or she has a BMI of 25 or above and obese if he or she has a BMI of 30 or above (Table 6.1). More than 60% of American adults have a BMI of 25 or above. At high values of BMI (over 25), the risk of arthritis, diabetes, hypertension, endometrial cancer, and other disorders increases substantially. The increased risk of type 2 diabetes at even fairly low values of BMI, especially among women, is of particular concern (Figure 6.3).

In classifying the health risks associated with overweight and obesity, the NIH guidelines consider body fat distribution and other disease risk factors in addition to BMI. As described earlier, excess fat in the abdomen is of greater concern than excess fat in other areas. Methods of assessing body fat distribution are discussed later in the chapter; the NIH guidelines use measurement of waist circumference (see Table 6.1). At a given level of overweight, people with a large waist circumference and/or additional disease risk factors are at greater risk for health problems. For example, a man with a BMI of 27, a waist circumference of more than 40 inches, and high blood pressure is at greater risk for health problems than another man who has a BMI of 27 but has a smaller waist circumference and no other risk factors.

Thus, optimal BMI for good health depends on many factors; if your BMI is 25 or above, consult a physician for help in determining a healthy BMI for you. (Weight loss recommendations based on the NIH guidelines are discussed further in Chapter 9.) Despite its widespread use, BMI does have limitations. Although it is good for large

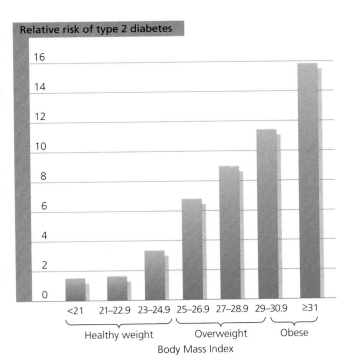

Relative risk of type 2 diabetes

Figure 6.3 Body mass index (BMI) and risk of type 2 diabetes in women. The risk of diabetes goes up even for women at the high end of the healthy BMI range, but it is extremely high in overweight and obese women. SOURCE: Hankinson, S. E., et al. 2001. *Healthy Women, Healthy Lives: A Guide to Preventing Disease from the Landmark Nurses' Health Study.* New York: Simon and Schuster.

population studies, it is less useful for measuring changes in body composition in individuals.

Estimating Percent Body Fat

Assessing body composition involves estimating percent body fat. The only method for directly measuring the percentage body weight that is fat is autopsy—the dissection and chemical analysis of the body. However, there are indirect techniques that can provide an estimate of percent body fat. One of the most accurate is underwater weighing. Other techniques include skinfold measurements, the Bod Pod, bioelectrical impedance analysis, and dual-energy X-ray absorptiometry. All of these methods have a margin of error, so it is important not to focus too much on precise values. For example, underwater weighing has an error of about ±3%, meaning that if a person's percent body fat is actually 17%, the test result may be between 14% and 20%. The results of different methods may also vary, so if you plan to track changes in body composition over time, be sure to use the same method each time to perform the assessment. Table 6.2 provides estimated ranges for healthy percent body fat.

Underwater Weighing Hydrostatic (underwater) weighing is the standard used for several other techniques, including skinfold measurements. For this method,

Table 6.2 — Percent Body Fat Classification

	Percent Body Fat (%)		
	20–39 years	40–59 years	60–79 years
Women			
Essential*	8–12	8–12	8–12
Low/athletic**	13–20	13–22	13–23
Recommended	21–32	23–33	24–35
Overfat†	33–38	34–39	36–41
Obese†	≥39	≥40	≥42
Men			
Essential*	3–5	3–5	3–5
Low/athletic**	6–7	6–10	6–12
Recommended	8–19	11–21	13–24
Overfat†	20–24	22–27	25–29
Obese†	≥25	≥28	≥30

The cutoffs for recommended, overfat, and obese ranges in this table are based on a study that linked body mass index classifications from the National Institutes of Health with predicted percent body fat (measured using dual energy X-ray absorptiometry).

*Essential body fat is necessary for the basic functioning of the body.

**Percent body fat in the low/athletic range may be appropriate for some people as long as it is not the result of illness or disordered eating habits; see pp. 182–183 for more on low levels of percent body fat.

†Health risks increase as percent body fat exceeds the recommended range.

SOURCES: Gallagher, D., et al. 2000. Healthy percentage body fat ranges: An approach for developing guidelines based on body mass index. *American Journal of Clinical Nutrition* 72: 694–701. American College of Sports Medicine. 2006. *ACSM's Resource Manual for Guidelines for Exercise Testing and Prescription.* 5th ed. Philadelphia: Lippincott Williams & Wilkins.

an individual is submerged and weighed under water. The percentages of fat and fat-free weight are calculated from body density. Muscle has a higher density and fat a lower density than water (1.1 grams per cubic centimeter for fat-free mass, 0.91 gram per cubic centimeter for fat, and 1 gram per cubic centimeter for water). Therefore, fat people tend to float and weigh less under water, and lean people tend to sink and weigh more under water. Most university exercise physiology departments or sports medicine laboratories have an underwater weighing facility. If you want an accurate assessment of your body composition, find a place that does underwater weighing.

Skinfold Measurements Skinfold measurement is a simple, inexpensive, and practical way to assess body composition. Skinfold measurements can be used to

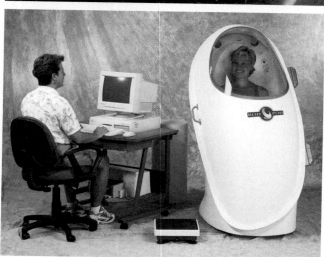

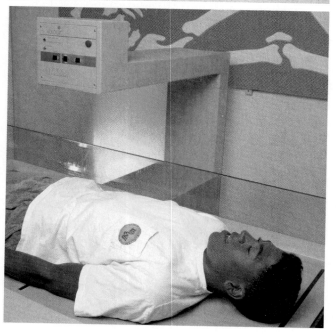

assess body composition because equations can link the thickness of skinfolds at various sites to percent body fat calculations from more precise laboratory techniques.

Skinfold assessment typically involves measuring the thickness of skinfolds at several different sites on the body. You can use these measurements in different ways. You can sum up the skinfold values as an indirect measure of body fatness. For example, if you plan to create a fitness (and dietary change) program to improve body composition, you can compare the sum of skinfold values over time as an indicator of your program's progress and of improvements in body composition. You can also plug your skinfold values into equations like those in Lab 6.1 that predict percent body fat. When using these equations, however, it is important to remember that they have a fairly substantial margin of error (±4% if performed by a skilled technician)—so, don't focus too much on specific values. The sum represents only a relative measure of body fatness.

Skinfolds are measured with a device called a **caliper,** which consists of a pair of spring-loaded, calibrated jaws. High-quality calipers are made of metal and have parallel jaw surfaces and constant spring tension. Inexpensive plastic calipers are also available; to ensure accuracy, plastic calipers should be spring-loaded and have metal jaws. Refer to Lab 6.1 for instructions on how to take skinfold measurements. Taking accurate measurements with calipers requires patience, experience, and considerable practice. It's best to take several measurements at each site (or have several different people take each measurement) to help ensure accuracy. Be sure to take the measurements in the exact location called for in the procedure. Because the amount of water in your body changes during the day, skinfold measurements taken in the morning and evening often differ. If you repeat the measurements in the future to track changes in your body composition, measure skinfolds at approximately the same time of day.

The Bod Pod The Bod Pod, a small chamber containing computerized sensors, measures body composition by air displacement rather than water displacement; the technical name of the technique is *plethysmography*. It determines the percentage of fat by calculating how much air is displaced by the person sitting inside the chamber. Many people prefer this short, 5-minute test over underwater weighing because it takes the place of the difficult "dunking" process and is about as accurate. It has an

In underwater weighing (top) percent body fat is calculated from body density; muscle has a higher density than water, so people with more muscle weigh relatively more under water. The Bod Pod (middle) measures air displacement, which can be used to calculate percent body fat. DEXA (bottom) uses high- and low-energy X-ray beams to measure fat and lean tissue.

error rate of about ±2–4% in determining percent body fat.

Bioelectrical Impedance Analysis (BIA)
The BIA technique works by sending a small electrical current through the body and measuring the body's resistance to it. Fat-free tissues, where most body water is located, are good conductors of electrical current, whereas fat is not. Thus, the amount of resistance to electrical current is related to the amount of fat-free tissue in the body (the lower the resistance, the greater the fat-free mass) and can be used to estimate percent body fat. Bioelectrical impedance analysis is fairly accurate for most people, with an error rate of about ±4–5%. To reduce error, it is important to follow the manufacturer's instructions carefully and to avoid overhydration or underhydration (more or less body water than normal). Because measurement varies with the type of BIA analyzer, use the same instrument to compare measurements over time.

Advanced Techniques: DEXA and TOBEC
Dual-energy X-ray absorptiometry (DEXA) was originally developed to measure bone mineral content but has been expanded to analyze fat and lean tissue. DEXA works by measuring the tissue absorption of high- and low-energy X-ray beams; studies thus far indicate that it has an error rate of about ±2%. Total body electrical conductivity (TOBEC) estimates lean body mass by passing a body through a magnetic field. Although the DEXA and TOBEC equipment is sophisticated and expensive, some fitness centers and sports medicine research facilities offer these body composition assessment techniques.

Assessing Body Fat Distribution

Researchers have studied many different methods for determining the risk associated with body fat distribution. Two of the simplest to perform are waist circumference measurement and waist-to-hip ratio calculation. In the first method, you measure your waist circumference; in the second, you divide your waist circumference by your hip circumference. Waist circumference has been found to be a better indicator of abdominal fat than waist-to-hip ratio. More research is needed to determine the precise degree of risk associated with specific values for these two assessments of body fat distribution. However, a total waist measurement of more than 40 inches (102 cm) for men and 35 inches (88 cm) for women and a waist-to-hip ratio above 0.94 for young men and 0.82 for young women are associated with a significantly increased risk of heart disease and diabetes. Follow the instructions in Lab 6.1 to measure and rate your body fat distribution.

SETTING BODY COMPOSITION GOALS

If assessment tests indicate that fat loss would be beneficial for your health, your first step is to establish a goal. You can use the ratings in Table 6.1 or Table 6.2 to choose a target value for BMI or percent body fat (depending on which assessment you completed).

Make sure your goal is realistic and will ensure good health. Genetics limits your capacity to change your body composition, and few people can expect to develop the body of a fashion model or competitive bodybuilder. However, you can improve your body composition through a program of regular exercise and a healthy diet. If your body composition is in or close to the recommended range, you may want to set a lifestyle goal rather than a specific percent body fat or BMI goal. For example, you might set a goal of increasing your daily physical activity from 20 to 60 minutes or beginning a program of weight training, and then let any improvements in body composition occur as a secondary result of your primary target (physical activity). Remember, a lifestyle that includes regular exercise may be more important for health than trying to reach any ideal weight.

If you are significantly overfat or if you have known risk factors for disease (such as high blood pressure or high cholesterol), consult your physician to determine a body composition goal for your individual risk profile. For people who are obese, small losses of body weight (5–15%) over a 6–12 month period can result in significant health improvements.

Once you've established a body composition goal, you can then set a target range for body weight. Although body weight is not an accurate method of assessing body composition, it's a useful method for tracking progress in a program to change body composition. If you're losing a small or moderate amount of weight and exercising, you're probably losing fat while building muscle mass. Lab 6.2 will help you determine a range for recommended body weight.

Using percent body fat or BMI will generate a fairly accurate target body weight for most people. However, it's best not to stick rigidly to a recommended body weight calculated from any formula; individual genetic, cultural, and lifestyle factors are also important. Decide whether the body weight that the formulas generate for you is realistic, meets all your goals, is healthy, *and* is reasonable for you to maintain.

Terms

caliper A pressure-sensitive measuring instrument with two jaws that can be adjusted to determine thickness.

MAKING CHANGES IN BODY COMPOSITION

Chapter 9 includes specific strategies for losing or gaining weight and improving body composition. In general, lifestyle should be your focus—regular physical activity, endurance exercise, strength training, and a moderate energy intake. Making significant cuts in food intake in order to lose weight and body fat is a difficult strategy to maintain; focusing on increased physical activity is a better approach for many people. In studies of people who have lost weight and maintained the loss, physical activity was the key to long-term success.

You can track your progress toward your target body composition by checking your body weight periodically. However, it is best not to focus too much on body weight, especially if your goal is modest. Look instead at other factors, such as how much energy you have and how your clothes fit.

To get a more accurate idea of your progress, you should directly reassess your body composition occasionally during your program: Body composition changes as weight changes. Losing a lot of weight usually includes losing some muscle mass no matter how hard a person exercises, partly because carrying less weight requires the muscular system to bear a smaller burden. (Conversely, a large gain in weight without exercise still causes some gain in muscle mass because muscles are working harder to carry the extra weight.)

Tips for Today

Your current body composition is the result of many factors, including gender, heredity, and your activity and eating habits. A healthy body composition reduces your risk of premature death and many diseases, and it improves the quality of your life. Adopting a wellness lifestyle can lead naturally to a body composition that is healthy and appropriate for you.

Right now you can

- Find out what types of body composition assessment techniques are available at facilities on your campus or in your community.

- Do 15 minutes of physical activity—walk, jog, bike, swim, or climb stairs.

- Drink a glass of water instead of a regular (nondiet) soda, and include a high-fiber food such as whole-grain bread or cereal, popcorn, apples, berries, or beans in your next snack or meal. (These types of dietary changes are associated with reduced risk for type 2 diabetes.)

- Think about your image of the ideal body type for your sex. Consider where your idea comes from, whether you use this image to judge your own body shape and body composition, and whether it is a realistic goal for you. Write down five positive things about your body.

MOTIVATION FOR CHANGE! If modifying your body composition is one of your fitness goals, choose a method of monitoring your progress that works for you. For some people, too close attention to body weight or percent body fat can lead to unhealthy behaviors and actually reduce motivation; for others, frequent weighing or body fat checks help keep a program on track. If you fall into the first group, consider scheduling regular but infrequent checks of your weight or body composition; in the interims, track such factors as your level of physical activity or your daily energy level. Changes in body composition require long-term effort, so working toward short-term goals that focus on factors other than specific amounts of fat-loss can provide more opportunities for rewards and positive feedback.

SUMMARY

- The human body is composed of fat-free mass (which includes bone, muscle, organ tissues, and connective tissues) and body fat (essential and nonessential).

- Having too much body fat has negative health consequences, especially in terms of cardiovascular disease and diabetes. Distribution of fat is also a significant factor in health.

- A fit and healthy-looking body, with the right body composition for a particular person, develops from habits of proper nutrition and exercise.

- Measuring body weight is not an accurate way to assess body composition because it does not differentiate between muscle weight and fat weight.

- Body mass index (calculated from weight and height measurements) can help classify the health risks associated with overweight.

- Techniques for estimating percent body fat include underwater weighing, skinfold measurements, the Bod Pod, bioelectrical impedance analysis, DEXA, and TOBEC.

- Body fat distribution can be assessed through the total waist measurement or the waist-to-hip ratio.

- Recommended body composition and weight can be determined by choosing a target BMI or target body fat percentage. Keep heredity in mind when setting a goal, and focus on positive changes in lifestyle.

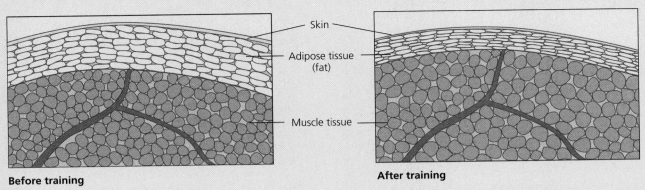

Before training

After training

Effects of exercise on body composition. Endurance exercise and strength training reduce body fat and increase muscle mass.

Is spot reducing effective? No. Spot reducing refers to attempts to lose body fat in specific parts of the body by doing exercises for those parts. For example, a person might try to spot reduce in the legs by doing leg lifts. Spot-reducing exercises contribute to fat loss only to the extent that they burn calories. The only way you can reduce fat in any specific area is to create an overall negative energy balance: Take in less energy (food) than you use up through exercise and metabolism.

How does exercise affect body composition? Cardiorespiratory endurance exercise burns calories, thereby helping create a negative energy balance. Weight training does not use many calories and therefore is of little use in creating a negative energy balance. However, weight training increases muscle mass, which maintains a high metabolic rate (the body's energy level) and helps improve body composition. To minimize body fat and increase muscle mass, thereby improving body composition, combine cardiorespiratory endurance exercise and weight training (see figure).

How do I develop a toned, healthy-looking body? The development of a healthy-looking body requires regular exercise, proper diet, and other good health habits. However, it helps to have heredity on your side. Some people put on or take off fat more easily than others just as some people are taller than others. Be realistic in your goals, and be satisfied with the improvements in body composition you can make by observing the principles of a wellness lifestyle.

Are people who have a desirable body composition physically fit? Having a healthy body composition is not necessarily associated with overall fitness. For example, many bodybuilders have very little body fat but have poor cardiorespiratory capacity and flexibility. To be fit, you must rate high on all the components of fitness.

What is liposuction, and will it help me lose body fat? Suction lipectomy, popularly known as liposuction, has become the most popular type of elective surgery in the United States. The procedure involves removing limited amounts of fat from specific areas. Typically, no more than 2.5 kg (5.5 lb) of adipose tissue is removed at a time. The procedure is usually successful if the amount of excess fat is limited and skin elasticity is good. The procedure is most effective if integrated into a program of dietary restriction and exercise. Side effects include infection, dimpling, and wavy skin contours. Liposuction has a death rate of 1 in 5000 patients, primarily from pulmonary thromboembolism (a blood clot in the lungs) or fat embolism (circulatory blockage caused by a dislodged piece of fat). Other serious complications include shock, bleeding, and impaired blood flow to vital organs.

What is cellulite, and how do I get rid of it? Cellulite is the name commonly given to ripply, wavy fat deposits that collect just under the skin. However, these rippling fat deposits are really the same as fat deposited anywhere else in the body. The only way to control them is to create a negative energy balance—burn up more calories than are taken in. There are no creams or lotions that will rub away surface (subcutaneous) fat deposits, and spot reducing is also ineffective. The solution is sensible eating habits and exercise.

Visit the Online Learning Center for more answers to common questions about body composition.

For Further Exploration

Ｖ|ｗ **Fit and Well Online Learning Center**
(www.mhhe.com/fahey)

Use the learning objectives, study guide questions, and glossary flashcards to review key terms and concepts and prepare for exams.

You can extend your knowledge of body composition and gain experience in using the Internet as a resource by completing the activities and checking out the Web links for the topics in Chapter 6 marked with the World Wide Web icon. For this chapter, Internet activities explore the health risks of too much or too little body fat, body mass index, and diabetes; there are also Web links for major chapter topics.

Daily Fitness and Nutrition Journal

Fill in the body composition portion of the fitness program plan. If you plan to make changes in your body composition, you may also want to begin reviewing the steps in the weight management section of the journal.

Books

Bray, G. A., and C. A. Bray. 2002. *An Atlas of Obesity and Weight Control.* London: CRC Press. *Provides detailed information about assessment, classification, and treatment of obesity.*

Gaesser, G. A. 2002. *Big Fat Lies: The Truth About Your Weight and Your Health.* Updated Edition. Carlsbad, Calif.: Gurze Books. *Emphasizes the importance of diet and exercise in maintaining metabolic health.*

Heyward, V. H., and D. R. Wagner. 2004. *Applied Body Composition Assessment.* 2nd ed. Champaign, Ill.: Human Kinetics. *Describes different methods of measuring and assessing body composition.*

Nathan, D. M., and L. Delahanty. 2005. *Beating Diabetes: A Harvard Medical School Book.* New York: McGraw-Hill. Provides information on identifying and changing lifestyle behaviors that contribute to the development and worsening of diabetes.

Otis, C. L., and R. Goldingay. 2000. *The Athletic Woman's Survival Guide.* Champaign, Ill.: Human Kinetics. *Information on the female athlete triad and suggestions for changing attitudes toward weight, self-esteem, and body image.*

WW Organizations and Web Sites

American Diabetes Association. Provides information, a free newsletter, and referrals to local support groups; the Web site includes an online diabetes risk assessment.

800-342-2383

http://www.diabetes.org

Methods of Body Composition Analysis Tutorials. Provides information about body composition assessment techniques, including underwater weighing, BIA, and DEXA.

http://nutrition.uvm.edu/bodycomp

National Heart, Lung, and Blood Institute. Provides information on the latest federal obesity standards and a BMI calculator.

http://www.nhlbi.nih.gov/guidelines/obesity/ob_home.htm

National Institute of Diabetes and Digestive and Kidney Diseases Health Information/Nutrition and Obesity. Provides information about adult obesity: how it is defined and assessed, the risk factors associated with it, and its causes.

877-946-4627

http://www.niddk.nih.gov/health/nutrit/nutrit.htm

USDA Food and Nutrition Information Center: Reports and Studies on Obesity. Provides links to recent reports and studies on the issue of obesity among Americans.

http://www.nal.usda.gov/fnic/reports/obesity.html

See also the listings for Chapters 2, 8, and 9.

Selected Bibliography

American College of Sports Medicine. 2006. *ACSM's Resource Manual for Guidelines for Exercise Testing and Prescription,* 5th ed. Philadelphia: Lippincott Williams & Wilkins.

American Diabetes Association. 2004. *How to Tell if You Have Pre-Diabetes* (http://www.diabetes.org/pre-diabetes/pre-diabetes-symptoms.jsp; retrieved March 27, 2005).

Bigaard, J., et al. 2005. Waist circumference and body composition in relation to all-cause mortality in middle-aged men and women. *International Journal of Obesity and Related Metabolic Disorders* 29:778–784.

Calle, E. E., et al. 2003. Overweight, obesity, and mortality from cancer in a prospectively studied cohort of U.S. adults. *New England Journal of Medicine* 348(17): 1625–1638.

Centers for Disease Control and Prevention. 2005. *Frequently Asked Questions About Calculating Obesity-Related Risk* (http://www.cdc.gov/od/oc/media/pressrel/r050614.htm; retrieved June 28, 2005).

Centers for Disease Control and Prevention. 2005. National Diabetes Fact Sheet (http://www.cdc.gov/diabetes/pubs/general.htm; retrieved November 10, 2005).

Deurenberg, P. 2003. Validation of body composition methods and assumptions. *British Journal of Nutrition* 90(3): 485–486.

Fang, J., et al. 2003. Exercise, body mass index, caloric intake, and cardiovascular mortality. *American Journal of Preventive Medicine* 25(4): 283–289.

Fenicchia, L. M., et al. 2004. Influence of resistance exercise training on glucose control in women with type 2 diabetes. *Metabolism* 53(3): 284–289.

Frisard, M. I., F. L. Greenway, and J. P. Delany. 2005. Comparison of methods to assess body composition changes during a period of weight loss. *Obesity Research* 13:845–854.

Green, J. S., et al. 2004. The effects of exercise training on abdominal visceral fat, body composition, and indicators of the metabolic syndrome in postmenopausal women with and without estrogen replacement therapy: The HERITAGE family study. *Metabolism* 53:1192–1196.

Holten, M. K., et al. 2004. Strength training increases insulin-mediated glucose uptake, GLUT4 content, and insulin signaling in skeletal muscle in patients with type 2 diabetes. *Diabetes* 53(2): 294–305.

Jiang, R., et al. 2004. Body iron stores in relation to risk of type 2 diabetes in apparently healthy women. *Journal of the American Medical Association* 291(6): 711–717.

Joyner, M. J. 2005. Muscle strength, body composition, hormones, and aging. *Exercise and Sport Sciences Reviews* 33:61–62.

Krakauer, J. C., et al. 2004. Body composition profiles derived from dual-energy X-ray absorptiometry, total body scan, and mortality. *Preventive Cardiology* 7:109–115.

Mokdad, A. H., et al. 2003. Prevalence of obesity, diabetes, and obesity-related health risk factors, 2001. *Journal of the American Medical Association* 289(1): 76–79.

Nielsen, S. J., and B. M. Popkin. 2003. Patterns and trends in food portion sizes, 1977–1996. *Journal of the American Medical Association* 289(4): 450–453.

Plank, L. D. 2005. Dual-energy X-ray absorptiometry and body composition. *Current Opinion in Clinical Nutrition and Metabolic Care* 8:305–309.

Soriano, J. M., et al. 2004. Pencil-beam vs fan-beam dual-energy X-ray absorptiometry comparisons across four systems: Body composition and bone mineral. *Journal of Clinical Densitometry* 7:281–289.

Stookey, J. D., L. S. Adair, and B. M. Popkin. 2005. Do protein and energy intakes explain long-term changes in body composition? *Journal of Nutrition, Health and Aging* 9:5–17.

Suk, S.-H., et al. 2003. Abdominal obesity and risk of ischemic stroke. *Stroke* 34:1586–1592.

Sullivan, P. W., et al. 2005. Abstract: Obesity, inactivity, and the prevalence of diabetes and diabetes-related cardiovascular comorbidities in the U.S., 2000–2002. *Diabetes Care* 28(7): 1599–1603.

U.S. Department of Health and Human Services. 2005. *Dietary Guidelines for Americans, 2005* (http://www.healthierus.gov/dietaryguidelines; retrieved January 15, 2005).

Wong, S. L., et al. 2004. Cardiorespiratory fitness is associated with lower abdominal fat independent of body mass index. *Medicine and Science in Sports and Exercise* 36(2): 286–291.

Zhu, S., et al. 2005. Lifestyle behaviors associated with lower risk of having the metabolic syndrome. *Metabolism* 53(11): 1503–1511.

LAB 6.1 *Assessing Body Mass Index and Body Composition*   VitaWrap

Body Mass Index

Equipment

1. Weight scale
2. Tape measure or other means of measuring height

Instructions

Measure your height and weight, and record the results. Be sure to record the unit of measurement.

Height: _____   Weight: _____

Calculating BMI (see also the shortcut chart of BMI values in Lab 6.2)

1. Convert your body weight to kilograms by dividing your weight in pounds by 2.2.

   Body weight _____ lb ÷ 2.2 lb/kg = body weight _____ kg

2. Convert your height measurement to meters by multiplying your height in inches by 0.0254.

   Height _____ in. × 0.0254 m/in. = height _____ m

3. Square your height measurement.

   Height _____ m × height _____ m = height _____ m^2

4. BMI equals body weight in kilograms divided by height in meters squared (kg/m^2).

   Body weight _____ kg ÷ height _____ m^2 = BMI _____ kg/m^2
   _(from step 1) _(from step 3)

Rating Your BMI

Refer to the table for a rating of your BMI. Record the results below and on the final page of this lab.

Classification	BMI (kg/m^2)
Underweight	<18.5
Normal	18.5–24.9
Overweight	25.0–29.9
Obesity (I)	30.0–34.9
Obesity (II)	35.0–39.9
Extreme obesity (III)	≥40.0

(See complete version of table on p. 184 for additional information.)

BMI _____ kg/m^2

Classification (from table) _____

 ## Skinfold Measurements

Equipment

1. Skinfold calipers
2. Partner to take measurements
3. Marking pen (optional)

Instructions

1. *Select and locate the correct sites for measurement.* All measurements should be taken on the right side of the body with the subject standing. Skinfolds are normally measured on the natural fold line of the skin, either vertically or at a slight angle. The skinfold measurement sites for males are chest, abdomen, and thigh; for females, triceps, suprailium, and thigh. If the person taking skinfold measurements is inexperienced, it may be helpful to mark the correct sites with a marking pen.

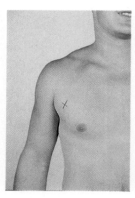 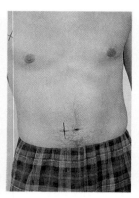 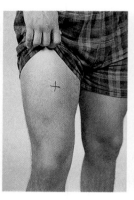  

(a) Chest   (b) Abdomen   (c) Thigh   (d) Triceps   (e) Suprailium

(a) Chest. Pinch a diagonal fold halfway between the nipple and the shoulder crease. *(b) Abdomen.* Pinch a vertical fold about 1 inch to the right of the umbilicus (navel). *(c) Thigh.* Pinch a vertical fold midway between the top of the hipbone and the kneecap. *(d) Triceps.* Pinch a vertical skinfold on the back of the right arm midway between the shoulder and elbow. The arm should be straight and should hang naturally. *(e) Suprailium.* Pinch a fold at the top front of the right hipbone. The skinfold here is taken slightly diagonally according to the natural fold tendency of the skin.

2. *Measure the appropriate skinfolds.* Pinch a fold of skin between your thumb and forefinger. Pull the fold up so that no muscular tissue is included; don't pinch the skinfold too hard. Hold the calipers perpendicular to the fold and measure the skinfold about 0.25 inch away from your fingers. Allow the tips of the calipers to close on the skinfold and let the reading settle before marking it down. Take readings to the nearest half-millimeter. Continue to repeat the measurements until two consecutive measurements match, releasing and repinching the skinfold between each measurement. Make a note of the final measurement for each site.

Time of day of measurements: _____

Men	*Women*
Chest: _____ mm	Triceps: _____ mm
Abdomen: _____ mm	Suprailium: _____ mm
Thigh: _____ mm	Thigh: _____ mm

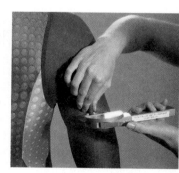

Determining Percent Body Fat

Add the measurements of your three skinfolds. Use this sum as a point of comparison for future assessments and/or find the percent body fat that corresponds to your total in the appropriate table. For example, a 19-year-old female with measurements of 16 mm, 19 mm, and 22 mm would have a skinfold sum of 57 mm; according to the table on page 193, her percent body fat is 22.7.

Sum of three skinfolds: _____ mm   Percent body fat: _____ %

Percent Body Fat Estimate for Women: Sum of Triceps, Suprailium, and Thigh Skinfolds

Sum of Skinfolds (mm)	Age								
	Under 22	23–27	28–32	33–37	38–42	43–47	48–52	53–57	Over 57
23–25	9.7	9.9	10.2	10.4	10.7	10.9	11.2	11.4	11.7
26–28	11.0	11.2	11.5	11.7	12.0	12.3	12.5	12.7	13.0
29–31	12.3	12.5	12.8	13.0	13.3	13.5	13.8	14.0	14.3
32–34	13.6	13.8	14.0	14.3	14.5	14.8	15.0	15.3	15.5
35–37	14.8	15.0	15.3	15.5	15.8	16.0	16.3	16.5	16.8
38–40	16.0	16.3	16.5	16.7	17.0	17.2	17.5	17.7	18.0
41–43	17.2	17.4	17.7	17.9	18.2	18.4	18.7	18.9	19.2
44–46	18.3	18.6	18.8	19.1	19.3	19.6	19.8	20.1	20.3
47–49	19.5	19.7	20.0	20.2	20.5	20.7	21.0	21.2	21.5
50–52	20.6	20.8	21.1	21.3	21.6	21.8	22.1	22.3	22.6
53–55	21.7	21.9	22.1	22.4	22.6	22.9	23.1	23.4	23.6
56–58	22.7	23.0	23.2	23.4	23.7	23.9	24.2	24.4	24.7
59–61	23.7	24.0	24.2	24.5	24.7	25.0	25.2	25.5	25.7
62–64	24.7	25.0	25.2	25.5	25.7	26.0	26.7	26.4	26.7
65–67	25.7	25.9	26.2	26.4	26.7	26.9	27.2	27.4	27.7
68–70	26.6	26.9	27.1	27.4	27.6	27.9	28.1	28.4	28.6
71–73	27.5	27.8	28.0	28.3	28.5	28.8	29.0	29.3	29.5
74–76	28.4	28.7	28.9	29.2	29.4	29.7	29.9	30.2	30.4
77–79	29.3	29.5	29.8	30.0	30.3	30.5	30.8	31.0	31.3
80–82	30.1	30.4	30.6	30.9	31.1	31.4	31.6	31.9	32.1
83–85	30.9	31.2	31.4	31.7	31.9	32.2	32.4	32.7	32.9
86–88	31.7	32.0	32.2	32.5	32.7	32.9	33.2	33.4	33.7
89–91	32.5	32.7	33.0	33.2	33.5	33.7	33.9	34.2	34.4
92–94	33.2	33.4	33.7	33.9	34.2	34.4	34.7	34.9	35.2
95–97	33.9	34.1	34.4	34.6	34.9	35.1	35.4	35.6	35.9
98–100	34.6	34.8	35.1	35.3	35.5	35.8	36.0	36.3	36.5
101–103	35.3	35.4	35.7	35.9	36.2	36.4	36.7	36.9	37.2
104–106	35.8	36.1	36.3	36.6	36.8	37.1	37.3	37.5	37.8
107–109	36.4	36.7	36.9	37.1	37.4	37.6	37.9	38.1	38.4
110–112	37.0	37.2	37.5	37.7	38.0	38.2	38.5	38.7	38.9
113–115	37.5	37.8	38.0	38.2	38.5	38.7	39.0	39.2	39.5
116–118	38.0	38.3	38.5	38.8	39.0	39.3	39.5	39.7	40.0
119–121	38.5	38.7	39.0	39.2	39.5	39.7	40.0	40.2	40.5
122–124	39.0	39.2	39.4	39.7	39.9	40.2	40.4	40.7	40.9
125–127	39.4	39.6	39.9	40.1	40.4	40.6	40.9	41.1	41.4
128–130	39.8	40.0	40.3	40.5	40.8	41.0	41.3	41.5	41.8

SOURCE: Jackson, A. S., and M. L. Pollock. 1985. Practical assessment of body composition. *The Physician and Sportsmedicine* 13(5): 76–90, Tables 6 & 7, pp. 86, 87. Copyright © 2005 The McGraw-Hill Companies. All rights reserved. Reprinted with permission from The McGraw-Hill Companies.

Percent Body Fat Estimate for Men: Sum of Chest, Abdomen, and Thigh Skinfolds

Sum of Skinfolds (mm)	Age								
	Under 22	23–27	28–32	33–37	38–42	43–47	48–52	53–57	Over 57
8–10	1.3	1.8	2.3	2.9	3.4	3.9	4.5	5.0	5.5
11–13	2.2	2.8	3.3	3.9	4.4	4.9	5.5	6.0	6.5
14–16	3.2	3.8	4.3	4.8	5.4	5.9	6.4	7.0	7.5
17–19	4.2	4.7	5.3	5.8	6.3	6.9	7.4	8.0	8.5
20–22	5.1	5.7	6.2	6.8	7.3	7.9	8.4	8.9	9.5
23–25	6.1	6.6	7.2	7.7	8.3	8.8	9.4	9.9	10.5
26–28	7.0	7.6	8.1	8.7	9.2	9.8	10.3	10.9	11.4
29–31	8.0	8.5	9.1	9.6	10.2	10.7	11.3	11.8	12.4
32–34	8.9	9.4	10.0	10.5	11.1	11.6	12.2	12.8	13.3
35–37	9.8	10.4	10.9	11.5	12.0	12.6	13.1	13.7	14.3
38–40	10.7	11.3	11.8	12.4	12.9	13.5	14.1	14.6	15.2
41–43	11.6	12.2	12.7	13.3	13.8	14.4	15.0	15.5	16.1
44–46	12.5	13.1	13.6	14.2	14.7	15.3	15.9	16.4	17.0
47–49	13.4	13.9	14.5	15.1	15.6	16.2	16.8	17.3	17.9
50–52	14.3	14.8	15.4	15.9	16.5	17.1	17.6	18.2	18.8
53–55	15.1	15.7	16.2	16.8	17.4	17.9	18.5	19.1	19.7
56–58	16.0	16.5	17.1	17.7	18.2	18.8	19.4	20.0	20.5
59–61	16.9	17.4	17.9	18.5	19.1	19.7	20.2	20.8	21.4
62–64	17.6	18.2	18.8	19.4	19.9	20.5	21.1	21.7	22.2
65–67	18.5	19.0	19.6	20.2	20.8	21.3	21.9	22.5	23.1
68–70	19.3	19.9	20.4	21.0	21.6	22.2	22.7	23.3	23.9
71–73	20.1	20.7	21.2	21.8	22.4	23.0	23.6	24.1	24.7
74–76	20.9	21.5	22.0	22.6	23.2	23.8	24.4	25.0	25.5
77–79	21.7	22.2	22.8	23.4	24.0	24.6	25.2	25.8	26.3
80–82	22.4	23.0	23.6	24.2	24.8	25.4	25.9	26.5	27.1
83–85	23.2	23.8	24.4	25.0	25.5	26.1	26.7	27.3	27.9
86–88	24.0	24.5	25.1	25.7	26.3	26.9	27.5	28.1	28.7
89–91	24.7	25.3	25.9	26.5	27.1	27.6	28.2	28.8	29.4
92–94	25.4	26.0	26.6	27.2	27.8	28.4	29.0	29.6	30.2
95–97	26.1	26.7	27.3	27.9	28.5	29.1	29.7	30.3	30.9
98–100	26.9	27.4	28.0	28.6	29.2	29.8	30.4	31.0	31.6
101–103	27.5	28.1	28.7	29.3	29.9	30.5	31.1	31.7	32.3
104–106	28.2	28.8	29.4	30.0	30.6	31.2	31.8	32.4	33.0
107–109	28.9	29.5	30.1	30.7	31.3	31.9	32.5	33.1	33.7
110–112	29.6	30.2	30.8	31.4	32.0	32.6	33.2	33.8	34.4
113–115	30.2	30.8	31.4	32.0	32.6	33.2	33.8	34.5	35.1
116–118	30.9	31.5	32.1	32.7	33.3	33.9	34.5	35.1	35.7
119–121	31.5	32.1	32.7	33.3	33.9	34.5	35.1	35.7	36.4
122–124	32.1	32.7	33.3	33.9	34.5	35.1	35.8	36.4	37.0
125–127	32.7	33.3	33.9	34.5	35.1	35.8	36.4	37.0	37.6

SOURCE: Jackson, A. S., and M. L. Pollock. 1985. Practical assessment of body composition. *The Physician and Sportsmedicine* 13(5): 76–90, Tables 6 & 7, pp. 86, 87. Copyright © 2005 The McGraw-Hill Companies. All rights reserved. Reprinted with permission from The McGraw-Hill Companies.

LABORATORY ACTIVITIES

Rating Your Body Composition

Refer to the figure to rate your percent body fat. Record it below and in the chart at the end of this lab.

Rating: _____

Percent Body Fat Classification

	Percent Body Fat (%)				Percent Body Fat (%)		
	20–39 years	*40–59 years*	*60–79 years*		*20–39 years*	*40–59 years*	*60–79 years*
Women				**Men**			
Essential*	8–12	8–12	8–12	Essential*	3–5	3–5	3–5
Low/athletic**	13–20	13–22	13–23	Low/athletic**	6–7	6–10	6–12
Recommended	21–32	23–33	24–35	Recommended	8–19	11–21	13–24
Overfat†	33–38	34–39	36–41	Overfat†	20–24	22–27	25–29
Obese†	≥39	≥40	≥42	Obese†	≥25	≥28	≥30

The cutoffs for recommended, overfat, and obese ranges in this table are based on a study that linked body mass index classifications from the National Institutes of Health with predicted percent body fat (measured using dual-energy X-ray absorptiometry).

*Essential body fat is necessary for the basic functioning of the body.

**Percent body fat in the low/athletic range may be appropriate for some people as long as it is not the result of illness or disordered eating habits; see pp. 182–183 for more on low levels of percent body fat.

†Health risks increase as percent body fat exceeds the recommended range.

SOURCES: Gallagher, D., et al. 2000. Healthy percentage body fat ranges: An approach for developing guidelines based on body mass index. *American Journal of Clinical Nutrition* 72:694–701. American College of Sports Medicine. 2006. *ACSM's Resource Manual for Guidelines for Exercise Testing and Prescription.* 5th ed. Philadelphia: Lippincott Williams & Wilkins.

Other Methods of Assessing Percent Body Fat

If you use a different method, record the name of the method and the result below and in the chart at the end of this lab. Find your body composition rating on the chart above.

Method used: _____   Percent body fat: _____ %   Rating (from chart above): _____

Waist Circumference and Waist-to-Hip Ratio

Equipment

1. Tape measure
2. Partner to take measurements

Preparation

Wear clothes that will not add significantly to your measurements.

Instructions

Stand with your feet together and your arms at your sides. Raise your arms only high enough to allow for taking the measurements. Your partner should make sure the tape is horizontal around the entire circumference and pulled snugly against your skin. The tape shouldn't be pulled so tight that it causes indentations in your skin. Record measurements to the nearest millimeter or one-sixteenth of an inch.

Waist. Measure at the smallest waist circumference. If you don't have a natural waist, measure at the level of your navel. Waist measurement: _____

Hip. Measure at the largest hip circumference. Hip measurement: _____

Waist-to-Hip Ratio: You can use any unit of measurement (for example, inches or centimeters) as long as you're consistent. Waist-to-hip ratio equals waist measurement divided by hip measurement.

Waist-to-hip ratio: _____ ÷ _____ = _____
                    (waist measurement)   (hip measurement)

Determining Your Risk

The table below indicates values for waist circumference and waist-to-hip ratio above which the risk of health problems increases significantly. If your measurement or ratio is above either cutoff point, put a check on the appropriate line below and in the chart at the end of this lab.

Waist circumference: _____ (✔ high risk)   Waist-to-hip ratio: _____ (✔ high risk)

Body Fat Distribution

Cutoff Points for High Risk

	Waist Circumference	Waist-to-Hip Ratio
Men	more than 40 in. (102 cm)	more than 0.94
Women	more than 35 in. (88 cm)	more than 0.82

SOURCES: National Heart, Lung, and Blood Institute. 1998. *Clinical Guidelines on the Identification, Evaluation, and Treatment of Overweight and Obesity in Adults: The Evidence Report.* Bethesda, Md.: National Institutes of Health. Heyward, V. H., and D. R. Wagner. 2004. *Applied Body Composition Assessment.* 2nd ed. Champaign, Ill.: Human Kinetics.

Rating Your Body Composition

Assessment	Value	Classification
BMI	_____ kg/m²	_____
Skinfold measurements or alternative method of determining percent body fat Specify method: _____	_____ % body fat	_____
Waist circumference Waist-to-hip ratio	_____ in. or cm _____ (ratio)	_____ (✔ high risk) _____ (✔ high risk)

Using Your Results

How did you score? Are you at all surprised by your ratings for body composition and body fat distribution? Are your current ratings in the range for good health? Are you satisfied with your current body composition? Why or why not?

If you're not satisfied, set a realistic goal for improvement: _____

What should you do next? Enter the results of this lab in the Preprogram Assessment column in Appendix D. If you've determined that you need to improve your body composition, set a specific goal by completing Lab 6.2, and then plan your program using the labs in Chapters 8 and 9 and the weight management section of the Daily Fitness and Nutrition Journal. After several weeks or months of an exercise and/or dietary change program, complete this lab again and enter the results in the Postprogram Assessment column of Appendix D. How do the results compare?

LAB 6.2 *Determining a Target Body Weight*

LABORATORY ACTIVITIES

Complete this lab if the results of Lab 6.1 indicate that a change in body composition would be beneficial for your health and well-being. This lab will help you set a target body weight based on a goal for BMI or percent body fat. Remember, though, that a wellness lifestyle that includes a sensible diet and regular exercise is more important for most people than achieving any specific target weight. In addition, you may have other health risk factors that could affect your body composition goals. You may decide to choose a lifestyle goal for your body composition target instead of a specific BMI, percent body fat, or target body weight. For example, you may set goals of increasing physical activity and improving your diet, and then let your body composition change as a result. Choose an approach that best fits your goals and preferences.

Equipment

Calculator (or pencil and paper for calculations)

Preparation

Determine percent body fat and/or calculate BMI as described in Lab 6.1. Keep track of height and weight as measured for these calculations.

Height: _____ Weight: _____

Instructions: Target Body Weight from Target BMI

Use the chart below to find the target body weight that corresponds to your target BMI. Find your height in the left column and then move across the appropriate row until you find the weight that corresponds to your target BMI. Remember, BMI is only an indirect measurement of body composition. It is possible to improve body composition without any significant change in weight. For example, a weight training program may result in increased muscle mass and decreased fat mass without any change in overall weight. For this reason, you may want to set alternative or additional goals, such as improving the fit of your clothes or decreasing your waist measurement.

	<18.5 Underweight		18.5–24.9 Normal						25–29.9 Overweight					30–34.9 Obesity (Class I)					35–39.9 Obesity (Class II)					≥40 Extreme Obesity
BMI	17	18	19	20	21	22	23	24	25	26	27	28	29	30	31	32	33	34	35	36	37	38	39	40
Height												Body Weight (pounds)												
4' 10"	81	86	91	96	101	105	110	115	120	124	129	134	139	144	148	153	158	163	168	172	177	182	187	192
4' 11"	84	89	94	99	104	109	114	119	124	129	134	139	144	149	154	159	163	168	173	178	183	188	193	198
5'	87	92	97	102	108	113	118	123	128	133	138	143	149	154	159	164	169	174	179	184	190	195	200	205
5' 1"	90	95	101	106	111	117	122	127	132	138	143	148	154	159	164	169	175	180	185	191	196	201	207	212
5' 2"	93	98	104	109	115	120	126	131	137	142	148	153	159	164	170	175	181	186	191	197	202	208	213	219
5' 3"	96	102	107	113	119	124	130	136	141	147	153	158	164	169	175	181	186	192	198	203	209	215	220	226
5' 4"	99	105	111	117	122	128	134	140	146	152	157	163	169	175	181	187	192	198	204	210	216	222	227	233
5' 5"	102	108	114	120	126	132	138	144	150	156	162	168	174	180	186	192	198	204	210	216	222	229	235	241
5' 6"	105	112	118	124	130	136	143	149	155	161	167	174	180	186	192	198	205	211	217	223	229	236	242	248
5' 7"	109	115	121	128	134	141	147	153	160	166	173	179	185	192	198	204	211	217	224	230	236	243	249	256
5' 8"	112	118	125	132	138	145	151	158	165	171	178	184	191	197	204	211	217	224	230	237	244	250	257	263
5' 9"	115	122	129	136	142	149	156	163	169	176	183	190	197	203	210	217	224	230	237	244	251	258	264	271
5' 10"	119	126	133	139	146	153	160	167	174	181	188	195	202	209	216	223	230	237	244	251	258	265	272	279
5' 11"	122	129	136	143	151	158	165	172	179	187	194	201	208	215	222	230	237	244	251	258	265	273	280	287
6'	125	133	140	148	155	162	170	177	184	192	199	207	214	221	229	236	243	251	258	266	273	280	288	295
6' 1"	129	137	144	152	159	167	174	182	190	197	205	212	220	228	235	243	250	258	265	273	281	288	296	303
6' 2"	132	140	148	156	164	171	179	187	195	203	210	218	226	234	242	249	257	265	273	281	288	296	304	312
6' 3"	136	144	152	160	168	176	184	192	200	208	216	224	232	240	248	256	264	272	280	288	296	304	312	320
6' 4"	140	148	156	164	173	181	189	197	206	214	222	230	238	247	255	263	271	280	288	296	304	312	321	329

SOURCE: Ratings from the National Heart, Lung, and Blood Institute. 1998. *Clinical Guidelines on the Identification, Evaluation, and Treatment of Overweight and Obesity in Adults.* Bethesda, Md.: National Institutes of Health.

Current BMI _____ Target BMI _____ Target body weight (from chart) _____

Alternative/additional goals _____

_____

Note: You can calculate target body weight from target BMI more precisely by using the following formula: (1) convert your height measurement to meters, (2) square your height measurement, (3) multiply this number by your target BMI to get your target weight in kilograms, and (4) convert your target weight from kilograms to pounds:

1. Height _____ in. $\times$ 0.0254 m/in. = height _____ m

2. Height _____ m $\times$ height _____ m = _____ m^2

3. Target BMI _____ $\times$ height _____ m^2 = target weight _____ kg

4. Target weight _____ kg $\times$ 2.2 lb/kg = target weight _____ lb

Instructions: Target Body Weight from Target Body Fat Percentages

Use the formula below to determine the target body weight that corresponds to your target percent body fat.

Current percent body fat _____ Target percent body fat _____

Formula

Example: 180-lb male, current percent body fat of 24%, goal of 21%

1. To determine the fat weight in your body, multiply your current weight by percent body fat (determined through skinfold measurements and expressed as a decimal).

180 lb $\times$ 0.24 = 43.2 lb

2. Subtract the fat weight from your current weight to get your current fat-free weight.

180 lb $-$ 43.2 lb = 136.8 lb

3. Subtract your target percent body fat from 1 to get target percent fat-free weight.

1 $-$ 0.21 = 0.79

4. To get your target body weight, divide your fat-free weight by your target percent fat-free weight.

136.8 lb $\div$ 0.79 = 173 lb

Note: Weight can be expressed in either pounds or kilograms, as long as the unit of measurement is used consistently.

1. Current body weight _____ $\times$ percent body fat _____ = fat weight _____

2. Current body weight _____ $-$ fat weight _____ = fat-free weight _____

3. 1 $-$ target percent body fat _____ = target percent fat-free weight _____

4. Fat-free weight _____ $\div$ target percent fat-free weight _____ = target body weight _____

Setting a Goal

Based on these calculations and other factors (including heredity, individual preference, and current health status), select a target weight or range of weights for yourself.

Target body weight: _____

Looking **AHEAD**

After reading this chapter, you should be able to

- Explain the steps for putting together a successful personal fitness program
- Describe strategies that can help you maintain a fitness program over the long term
- Tailor a fitness program to accommodate special health concerns and different life stages

7

Putting Together a Complete Fitness Program

Test Your Knowledge

1. **In surveys, how many Americans report that they've engaged in no physical activity in the past month?**
   a. 7%
   b. 17%
   c. 27%

2. **Falling asleep in a boring class means a person needs more sleep.**
   True or false?

3. **Exercise is not recommended for people with asthma or diabetes.**
   True or false?

ANSWERS

1. C. More than a quarter of Americans are completely sedentary, putting them at risk for early death and a wide variety of diseases and disabling conditions.

2. TRUE. A fully rested person may become bored during an uninteresting or monotonous event but will not fall asleep. Daytime sleepiness is a sign of inadequate sleep, which negatively affects health and athletic performance.

3. FALSE. Although special precautions may be needed, people with many types of chronic conditions can exercise safely and obtain significant health benefits. Regular exercise reduces the risks of acute asthma attacks and improves insulin sensitivity.

ViV *Fit and Well* **Online Learning Center**   www.mhhe.com/fahey

Visit the *Fit and Well* Online Learning Center for study aids, online labs, additional information about putting together a complete fitness program, links, Internet activities that explore fitness, consumer resources, and much more.

199

U nderstanding the physiological basis and wellness benefits of health-related physical fitness, as explained in Chapters 1–6, is the first step toward creating a well-rounded exercise program. The next challenge is to combine activities into a program that develops all the fitness components and maintains motivation. This chapter presents a step-by-step procedure for creating and maintaining a well-rounded program. Following the chapter, you'll find sample programs based on popular activities. The structure these programs provide can be helpful if you're beginning an exercise program for the first time.

DEVELOPING A PERSONAL FITNESS PLAN

If you're ready to create a complete fitness program based on the activities you enjoy most, begin by preparing the program plan and contract in Lab 7.1. By carefully developing your plan and signing a contract, you'll increase your chances of success. The step-by-step procedure outlined here will guide you through the steps of Lab 7.1 to create an exercise program that's right for you. Refer to Figure 7.1 for a sample personal fitness program plan and contract.

If you'd like additional help in setting up your program, choose one of the sample programs at the end of this chapter. Sample programs are provided for walking/jogging/running, cycling, swimming, and in-line skating; they include detailed instructions for starting a program and developing and maintaining fitness.

I. Set Goals

Setting goals to reach through exercise is a crucial first step. Ask yourself, "What do I want from my fitness program?" Develop different types of goals—general and specific, long term and short term. General or long-term goals might include things like lowering your risk for chronic disease, improving posture, having more energy, and improving the fit of your clothes. It's a good idea to also develop some specific, short-term goals based on measurable factors. Specific goals might be raising $\dot{V}O_{2max}$ by 10%, reducing the time it takes you to jog 2 miles from 22 minutes to 19 minutes, increasing the number of push-ups you can do from 15 to 25, and lowering BMI from 26 to 24.5. Having specific goals will allow you to track your progress and enjoy the measurable changes brought about by your fitness program. Finally, break your specific goals into several smaller steps (mini-goals), such as those shown in Figure 7.1.

Physical fitness assessment tests are essential to determining your goals. They help you decide which types of exercise you should emphasize, and they help you understand the relative difficulty of attaining specific goals. If you have health problems, such as high blood pressure,

An overall fitness program includes activities to develop all the components of physical fitness.

heart disease, obesity, or serious joint or muscle disabilities, see your physician before taking assessment tests. Measure your progress by taking these tests about every 3 months.

You'll find it easier to stick with your program if you choose goals that are both important to you and realistic. Remember that heredity, your current fitness level, and other individual factors influence the amount and rate of improvement and the ultimate level of fitness you can expect to obtain through physical training. Fitness improves most quickly during the first 6 months of an exercise program. After that, gains come more slowly and usually require a higher-intensity program. Don't expect to improve indefinitely: Improve your fitness to a reasonable target level, and then train consistently to maintain it. Some-times you may lose fitness—due to illness, injury, missed workouts, or a vacation—so you must begin again at a lower level. Developing fitness is a dynamic process that involves gains and losses. Even if you lose ground occasionally, stay with your program, and you'll be able to achieve your goals.

Think carefully about your reasons for exercising, and then fill in the goals portion of your plan in Lab 7.1.

2. Select Activities

If you have already chosen activities and created separate program plans for different fitness components in Chapters 3, 4, and 5, you can put those plans together into a single program. It's usually best to include exercises to develop each of the health-related components of fitness.

- Cardiorespiratory endurance is developed by activities such as walking, cycling, and aerobic dance that involve continuous rhythmic movements of large-muscle groups like those in the legs (see Chapter 3).

- Muscular strength and endurance are developed by training against resistance (see Chapter 4).

A. I [Tracie Kaufman] am contracting with myself to follow a physical
(name)
fitness program to work toward the following goals:

Specific or short-term goals

1. Improving cardiorespiratory fitness by raising my $\dot{V}O_{2max}$ from 34 to 37 ml/kg/min
2. Improving upper body muscular strength and endurance rating from fair to good
3. Improving body composition (from 28% to 25% body fat)
4. Improving my tennis game (hitting 20 playable shots in a row against the ball machine)

General or long-term goals

1. Developing a more positive attitude about myself
2. Improving the fit of my clothes
3. Building and maintaining bone mass to reduce my risk of osteoporosis
4. Increasing my life expectancy and reducing my risk for diabetes and heart disease

B. **My program plan is as follows:**

Activities	Components (Check X)					Time	Frequency (Check X)							Intensity*
	CRE	MS	ME	F	BC		M	Tu	W	Th	F	S	S	
Swimming	X	X	X	X	X	35min	X		X		X			140–170 bpm
Tennis	X	X	X	X	X	90min					X			RPE= 13–16
Weight training		X	X	X	X	30min		X		X	X			see Lab 4–3
Stretching				X		25min	X		X		X	X		—

*List your target heart rate range or an RPE value if appropriate.

C. My program will begin on [Sept. ▲] [21 ▲] My program includes the following schedule
of mini-goals. For each step in my program, I will give myself the reward listed.

Completing 2 full weeks of program (mini-goal 1)	Oct. ▲	5 ▲	movie with friends (reward)
$\dot{V}O_{2max}$ of 35 ml/kg/min (mini-goal 2)	Nov. ▲	2 ▲	new CD (reward)
Completing 10 full weeks of program (mini-goal 3)	Nov. ▲	30 ▲	new sweater (reward)
Percent body fat of 27% (mini-goal 4)	Dec. ▲	22 ▲	weekend away (reward)
$\dot{V}O_{2max}$ of 36 ml/kg/min (mini-goal)	Jan. ▲	18 ▲	new CD (reward)

D. My program will include the addition of physical activity to my daily routine (such
as climbing stairs or walking to class):

1. Walking to and from campus job
2. Taking the stairs to dorm room instead of elevator
3. Bicycling to the library instead of driving
4. Doing one active chore a day
5.

E. I will use the following tools to monitor my program and my progress toward
my goals:

I'll use a chart that lists the number of laps and minutes I swim and the
charts for strength and flexibility from Labs 4-3 & 5-2.

I sign this contract as an indication of my personal commitment to reach my goal.

Tracie Kaufman   Sep. ▲ 10 ▲
(your signature)

I have recruited a helper who will witness my contract and
swim with me three days per week
(list any way your helper will participate in your program)

Russell Walker   Sep. ▲ 10 ▲
(witness's signature)

Figure 7.1   A sample personal fitness program plan and contract.

Table 7.1 A Summary of Sports and Fitness Activities

This table classifies sports and activities as high (H), moderate (M), or low (L) in terms of their ability to develop each of the five components of physical fitness: cardiorespiratory endurance (CRE), muscular strength (MS), muscular endurance (ME), flexibility (F), and body composition (BC). The skill level needed to obtain fitness benefits is noted: Low (L) means little or no skill is required to obtain fitness benefits; moderate (M) means average skill is needed to obtain fitness benefits; and high (H) means much skill is required to obtain fitness benefits. The fitness prerequisite, or conditioning needs of a beginner, is also noted: Low (L) means no fitness prerequisite is required, moderate (M) means some preconditioning is required, and high (H) means substantial fitness is required. The last two columns list the calorie cost of each activity when performed moderately and vigorously. To determine how many calories you burn, multiply the value in the appropriate column by your body weight and then by the number of minutes you exercise. Work up to using 300 or more calories per workout.

Sports and Activities	Components					Skill Level	Fitness Prerequisite	Approximate Calorie Cost (cal/lb/min)	
	CRE	MS*	ME*	F*	BC			Moderate	Vigorous
Aerobic dance	H	M	H	H	H	L	L	.046	.062
Backpacking	H	M	H	M	H	L	M	.032	.078
Badminton, skilled, singles	H	M	M	M	H	M	M	—	.071
Ballet (floor combinations)	M	M	H	H	M	M	L	—	.058
Ballroom dancing	M	L	M	L	M	M	L	.034	.049
Baseball (pitcher and catcher)	M	M	H	M	M	H	M	.039	—
Basketball, half court	H	M	H	M	H	M	M	.045	.071
Bicycling	H	M	H	M	H	M	L	.049	.071
Bowling	L	L	L	L	L	L	L	—	—
Calisthenic circuit training	H	M	H	M	H	L	L	—	.060
Canoeing and kayaking (flat water)	M	M	H	M	M	M	M	.045	—
Cheerleading	M	M	M	M	M	M	L	.033	.049
Fencing	M	M	H	H	M	M	L	.032	.078
Field hockey	H	M	H	M	H	M	M	.052	.078
Folk and square dancing	M	L	M	L	M	L	L	.039	.049
Football, touch	M	M	M	M	M	M	M	.049	.078
Frisbee, ultimate	H	M	H	M	H	M	M	.049	.078
Golf (riding cart)	L	L	L	M	L	L	L	—	—
Handball, skilled, singles	H	M	H	M	H	M	M	—	.078
Hiking	H	M	H	L	H	L	M	.051	.073
Hockey, ice and roller	H	M	H	M	H	M	M	.052	.078
Horseback riding	M	M	M	L	M	M	M	.052	.065
Interval circuit training	H	H	H	M	H	L	L	—	.062
Jogging and running	H	M	H	L	H	L	L	.060	.104

*Ratings are for the muscle groups involved.

- Flexibility is developed by stretching the major muscle groups (see Chapter 5).
- Healthy body composition can be developed by combining a sensible diet and a program of regular exercise, including cardiorespiratory endurance exercise to burn calories and resistance training to build muscle mass (see Chapter 6).

Table 7.1 rates many popular activities for their ability to develop each of the health-related components of fitness. Check the ratings of the activities you're considering to make sure the program you put together will develop all fitness components and help you achieve your goals. One strategy is to select one activity for each component of fitness—bicycling, weight training, and stretching, for example. Another strategy applies the principle of cross-training, using several different activities to develop a particular fitness component—aerobics classes, swimming, and volleyball for cardiorespiratory endurance, for example. Cross-training is discussed in the next section.

If you select activities that support your commitment rather than activities that turn exercise into a chore, the right program will be its own incentive for continuing. Consider the following factors in making your choices.

- *Fun and interest.* Your fitness program is much more likely to be successful if you choose activities that

| Sports and Activities | Components | | | | | Skill Level | Fitness Prerequisite | Approximate Calorie Cost (cal/lb/min) | |
	CRE	MS*	ME*	F*	BC			Moderate	Vigorous
Judo	M	H	H	M	M	M	L	.049	.090
Karate	H	M	H	H	H	L	M	.049	.090
Lacrosse	H	M	H	M	H	H	M	.052	.078
Modern dance (moving combinations)	M	M	H	H	M	L	L	—	.058
Orienteering	H	M	H	L	H	L	M	.049	.078
Outdoor fitness trails	H	M	H	M	H	L	L	—	.060
Popular dancing	M	L	M	M	M	M	L	—	.049
Racquetball, skilled, singles	H	M	M	M	H	M	M	.049	.078
Rock climbing	M	H	H	H	M	H	M	.033	.033
Rope skipping	H	M	H	L	H	M	M	.071	.095
Rowing	H	H	H	H	H	L	L	.032	.097
Rugby	H	M	H	M	H	M	M	.052	.097
Sailing	L	L	M	L	L	M	L	—	—
Skating, ice, roller, and in-line	M	M	H	M	M	H	M	.049	.095
Skiing, alpine	M	H	H	M	M	H	M	.039	.078
Skiing, cross-country	H	M	H	M	H	M	M	.049	.104
Soccer	H	M	H	M	H	M	M	.052	.097
Squash, skilled, singles	H	M	M	M	H	M	M	.049	.078
Stretching	L	L	L	H	L	L	L	—	—
Surfing (including swimming)	M	M	M	M	M	H	M	—	.078
Swimming	H	M	H	M	H	M	L	.032	.088
Synchronized swimming	M	M	H	H	M	H	M	.032	.052
Table tennis	M	L	M	M	M	M	L	—	.045
Tennis, skilled, singles	H	M	M	M	H	M	M	—	.071
Volleyball	M	L	M	M	M	M	M	—	.065
Walking	H	L	M	L	H	L	L	.029	.048
Water polo	H	M	H	M	H	H	M	—	.078
Water skiing	M	M	H	M	M	H	M	.039	.055
Weight training	L	H	H	H	M	L	L	—	—
Wrestling	H	H	H	H	H	H	H	.065	.094
Yoga	L	L	M	H	L	H	L	—	—

*Ratings are for the muscle groups involved.

SOURCE: Kusinitz, I., and M. Fine, *Physical Fitness for Practically Everybody*, Consumer Reports® 1983. Consumers Union of the U.S., Inc., Yonkers, NY 10703-1057, a nonprofit organization. Reprinted with permission for educational purposes only. No commercial use or reproduction permitted. www.ConsumerReports.org®.

you enjoy doing. Start by considering any activities you currently engage in and enjoy. Often you can modify your current activities to fit your fitness program. As you consider new activities, ask yourself, "Is this activity fun?" "Will it hold my interest over time?" For new activities, it is a good idea to undertake a trial period before making a final choice.

- *Your current skill and fitness level.* Although many activities are appropriate for beginners, some sports and activities require participants to have a moderate level of skill to obtain fitness benefits. For example, a beginning tennis player will probably not be able to sustain rallies long enough to develop cardiorespiratory endurance. Re-

fer to the skill level column in Table 7.1 to determine the level of skill needed for full participation in the activities you're considering. If your current skill level doesn't meet the requirement, you may want to begin your program with a different activity. For example, a beginning tennis player may be better off with a walking program while improving his or her tennis game—or practicing with a ball machine to guarantee steady activity. To build skill for a particular activity, consider taking a class or getting some instruction from a coach or fellow participant.

Your current fitness level may also limit the activities that are appropriate for your program. For example, if you have been inactive, a walking program would

	Cardiorespiratory endurance training	Strength training	Flexibility training
Frequency	3–5 days per week	2–3 nonconsecutive days per week	2–3 days per week (minimum); 5–7 days per week (ideal)
Intensity	55/65–90% of maximum heart rate	Sufficient resistance to fatigue muscles	Stretch to the point of tension
Time	20–60 minutes in sessions lasting 10 minutes or more	8–12 repetitions of each exercise, 1 or more sets	2–4 repetitions of each exercise, held for 15–30 seconds
Type	Continuous rhythmic activities using large muscle groups	Resistance exercises for all major muscle groups	Stretching exercises for all major joints

Figure 7.2   A summary of the FITT principle for the health-related components of fitness

be more appropriate than a jogging program. Activities in which participants control the intensity of effort—walking, cycling, and swimming, for example—are more appropriate for a beginning fitness program than sports and activities that are primarily "other paced"—soccer, basketball, and tennis, for example. Refer to the fitness prerequisite column of Table 7.1 to determine the minimum level of fitness required for participation in the activities you're considering. However, staying active is the most important thing. If you like to play tennis but don't like to take walks or jog, then play tennis.

• *Time and convenience.* Unless exercise fits easily into your daily schedule, you are unlikely to maintain your program over the long term. As you consider activities, think about whether a special location or facility is required. Can you participate in the activity close to your residence, school, or job? Are the necessary facilities open and available at times convenient to you (see Lab 7.2)? Do you need a partner or a team to play? Can you participate in the activity year-round, or will you need to find an alternative during the summer or winter? Would a home treadmill make you more likely to exercise regularly?

• *Cost.* Some sports and activities require equipment, fees, or some type of membership investment. If you are on a tight budget, limit your choices to activities that are inexpensive or free. Investigate the facilities on your campus, which you may be able to use at little or no cost. Many activities require no equipment beyond an appropriate pair of shoes (see the box "Choosing Exercise Footwear" for more information). Refer back to Chapters 2 and 3 for consumer guidelines for evaluating exercise equipment and facilities.

• *Special health needs.* If you have special exercise needs due to a particular health problem, choose activities that will conform to your needs and enhance your ability to cope. If necessary, consult your physician about how best to tailor an exercise program to your particular needs and goals. Guidelines and safety tips for exercisers with common chronic conditions are provided later in the chapter.

MOTIVATION FOR CHANGE!   To add variety and enjoyment to your workouts and to boost your motivation, try exercising to music. Researchers have found that working out to music can boost mood and even keep people working out longer and harder without feeling like they are expending extra effort. Just make sure that music provides a safe distraction and doesn't increase your risk of injury; for example, don't wear headphones while walking, jogging, or cycling on the street.

3. Set a Target Frequency, Intensity, and Time (Duration) for Each Activity

The next step is to apply the FITT principle and set a starting frequency, intensity, and time (duration) for each type of activity you've chosen (see the summary in Figure 7.2 and the sample in Figure 7.1). Refer to the calculations and plans you completed in Chapters 3, 4, and 5.

Cardiorespiratory Endurance Exercise   An appropriate frequency for cardiorespiratory endurance exercise is 3–5 times per week. For intensity, note your target heart rate zone or RPE value. Your target total workout time (duration) should be about 20–60 minutes, depending on the intensity of the activity (shorter durations are appropriate for high-intensity activities, longer durations for activities of more moderate intensity). You can exercise in a single session or in multiple sessions of 10 or more minutes. One way to check whether the total duration you've set is appropriate is to use the **calorie costs** (calories per minute per pound of body weight)

Terms

Ww **calorie cost** The amount of energy used to perform a particular activity, usually expressed in calories per minute per pound of body weight.

Footwear is perhaps the most important item of equipment for almost any activity. Shoes protect and support your feet and improve your traction. When you jump or run, you place as much as six times more force on your feet than when you stand still. Shoes can help cushion against the stress that this additional force places on your lower legs, thereby preventing injuries. Some athletic shoes are also designed to help prevent ankle rollover, another common source of injury.

General Guidelines

When choosing athletic shoes, first consider the activity you've chosen for your exercise program. Shoes appropriate for different activities have very different characteristics. For example, running shoes typically have highly cushioned midsoles, rubber outsoles with elevated heels, and a great deal of flexibility in the forefoot. The heels of walking shoes tend to be lower, less padded, and more beveled than those designed for running. For aerobic dance, shoes must be flexible in the forefoot and have straight, nonflared heels to allow for safe and easy lateral movements. Court shoes also provide substantial support for lateral movements; they typically have outsoles made from white rubber that will not damage court surfaces.

Also consider the location and intensity of your workouts. If you plan to walk or run on trails, you should choose shoes with water-resistant, highly durable uppers and more outsole traction. If you work out intensely or have a relatively high body weight, you'll need thick, firm midsoles to avoid bottoming-out the cushioning system of your shoes.

Foot type is another important consideration. If your feet tend to roll inward excessively, you may need shoes with additional stability features on the inner side of the shoe to counteract this movement. If your feet tend to roll outward excessively, you may need highly flexible and cushioned shoes that promote foot motion. For aerobic dancers with feet that tend to roll inward or outward, mid-cut to high-cut shoes may be more appropriate than low-cut aerobic shoes or cross-trainers (shoes designed to be worn for several different activities). Compared to men, women have narrower feet overall and narrower heels relative to the forefoot. Most women will get a better fit if they choose shoes that are specifically designed for women's feet rather than shoes that are downsized versions of men's shoes.

Successful Shopping

For successful shoe shopping, keep the following strategies in mind:

- Shop at an athletic shoe or specialty store that has personnel trained to fit athletic shoes and a large selection of styles and sizes.

- Shop late in the day or, ideally, following a workout. Your foot size increases over the course of the day and as a result of exercise.

- Wear socks like those you plan to wear during exercise. If you have an old pair of athletic shoes, bring them with you.

The wear pattern on your old shoes can help you select a pair with extra support or cushioning in the places you need it the most.

- Ask for help. Trained salespeople know which shoes are designed for your foot type and your level of activity. They can also help fit your shoes properly.

- Don't insist on buying shoes in what you consider to be your typical shoe size. Sizes vary from shoe to shoe. In addition, foot sizes change over time, and many people have one foot that is larger or wider than the other. Try several sizes in several widths, if necessary. Don't buy shoes that are too small.

- Try on both shoes and wear them around for 10 or more minutes. Try walking on a noncarpeted surface. Approximate the movements of your activity: walk, jog, run, jump, and so on.

- Check the fit and style carefully:

  Is the toe box roomy enough? Your toes will spread out when your foot hits the ground or you push off. There should be at least one thumb's width of space from the longest toe to the end of the toe box.

  Do the shoes have enough cushioning? Do your feet feel supported when you bounce up and down? Try bouncing on your toes and on your heels.

  Do your heels fit snugly into the shoe? Do they stay put when you walk, or do they rise up?

  Are the arches of your feet right on top of the shoes' arch supports?

  Do the shoes feel stable when you twist and turn on the balls of your feet? Try twisting from side to side while standing on one foot.

  Do you feel any pressure points?

- If the shoes are not comfortable in the store, don't buy them. Don't expect athletic shoes to stretch over time in order to fit your feet properly.

- If you exercise at dawn or dusk, choose shoes with reflective sections for added visibility and safety.

- Replace athletic shoes about every 3 months or 300–500 miles of jogging or walking.

Name Tracie Kaufman

Enter time, distance, or another factor to track your progress.

Activity/Date	M	Tu	W	Th	F	S	S	Weekly Total	M	Tu	W	Th	F	S	S	Weekly Total
1 Swimming	800 yd		725 yd		800 yd			2325 yd	800 yd		800 yd		850 yd			2450 yd
2 Tennis				90 min				90 min						95 min		95 min
3 Weight Training		X		X		X				X		X		X	X	
4 Stretching	X		X		X	X			X		X	X	X	X		

Figure 7.3 A sample program log.

given in Table 7.1. Your goal should be to work up to burning about 300 calories per workout; beginners should start with a calorie cost of about 100–150 calories per workout. You can calculate the calorie cost of your activities by multiplying the appropriate factor from Table 7.1 by your body weight and the duration of your workout. For example, walking at a moderate pace burns about 0.029 calorie per minute per pound of body weight. A person weighing 150 pounds could begin her exercise program by walking for 30 minutes, burning about 130 calories. Once her fitness improves, she might choose to start cycling for her cardiorespiratory endurance workouts. Cycling at a moderate pace has a higher calorie cost than walking (0.049 calorie per minute per pound), and if she cycled for 40 minutes, she would burn the target 300 calories during her workout.

Muscular Strength and Endurance Training

A frequency of 2–3 days per week for strength training is recommended. As described in Chapter 4, a general fitness strength training program includes 1 or more sets of 8–12 repetitions of 8–10 exercises that work all major muscle groups. For intensity, choose a weight that is heavy enough to fatigue your muscles but not so heavy that you cannot complete the full number of repetitions with proper form.

Flexibility Training Stretches should be performed when muscles are warm at least 2–3 days per week (5–7 days per week is ideal). Stretches should be performed for all major muscle groups. For each exercise, stretch to the point of slight tension or mild discomfort and hold the stretch for 15–30 seconds; do 2–4 repetitions of each exercise.

4. Set Up a System of Mini-Goals and Rewards

To keep your program on track, it is important to set up a system of goals and rewards. Break your specific goals into several steps, and set a target date for each step. For example, if one of the goals of an 18-year-old male student's

program is to improve upper-body strength and endurance, he could use the push-up test in Lab 4.2 to set intermediate goals. If he can currently perform 15 push-ups (for a rating of "very poor"), he might set intermediate goals of 17, 20, 25, and 30 push-ups (for a final rating of "fair"). By allowing several weeks between mini-goals and specifying rewards, he'll be able to track his progress and reward himself as he moves toward his final goal. Reaching a series of small goals is more satisfying than working toward a single, more challenging, goal that may take months to achieve. Realistic goals, broken into achievable mini-goals, can boost your chances of success. For more on choosing appropriate rewards, refer to page 18 in Chapter 1 and Activity 4 in the Behavior Change Workbook at the end of the text.

5. Include Lifestyle Physical Activity in Your Program

As described in Chapter 2, daily physical activity is an important part of a fit and well lifestyle. As part of your fitness program plan, specify ways to be more active during your daily routine. You may find it helpful to first use your health journal to track your activities for several days. Review the records in your journal, identify routine opportunities to be more active, and add these to your program plan in Lab 7.1.

6. Develop Tools for Monitoring Your Progress

A record that tracks your daily progress will help remind you of your ongoing commitment to your program and give you a sense of accomplishment. Figure 7.3 shows you how to create a general program log and record the activity type, frequency, and times (durations). Or, if you wish, complete specific activity logs like those in Labs 3.2, 4.3, and 5.2 in addition to, or instead of, a general log. Post your log in a place where you'll see it often as a reminder and as an incentive for improvement. If you have specific, measurable, goals, you can also graph your weekly or monthly progress toward your goal (Figure 7.4). To monitor the overall progress of your fitness

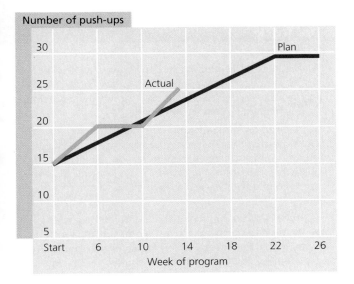

Figure 7.4 **A sample program progress chart.**

program, you may choose to reassess your cardiorespiratory endurance, muscular, strength and endurance, flexibility, and body composition every 3 months or so during the improvement phase of your program. Because the results of different fitness tests vary, be sure to compare results for the same assessments over time.

7. Make a Commitment

Your final step in planning your program is to make a commitment by signing a contract. Find a witness for your contract—preferably one who will be actively involved in your program. Keep your contract in a visible spot to remind you of your commitment.

PUTTING YOUR PLAN INTO ACTION

Once you've developed a detailed plan and signed your contract, you are ready to begin your fitness program. Refer to the specific training suggestions provided in Chapters 2–5 for advice on beginning and maintaining your program. Many people find it easier to plan a program than to put their plan into action and stick with it over time. For that reason, adherence to healthy lifestyle programs has become an important area of study for psychologists and health researchers. The guidelines below and in the next section reflect research into strategies that help people succeed in sticking with an exercise program:

- *Start slowly and increase fitness gradually.* Overzealous exercising can result in discouraging discomforts and injuries. Your program is meant to last a lifetime. The important first step is to break your established pattern of inactivity. Be patient and realistic. Once your body has adjusted to your starting level of exercise,

slowly increase the amount of overload. Small increases are the key—achieving a large number of small improvements will eventually result in substantial gains in fitness. It's usually best to increase duration and frequency before increasing intensity.

- *Find an exercise buddy.* The social side of exercise is an important factor for many regular exercisers. Working out with a friend will make exercise more enjoyable and increase your chances of sticking with your program. Find an exercise partner who shares your goals and general fitness level.

- *Ask for support from others.* You have a much greater chance of exercising consistently if you have the support of important people in your life, such as parents, spouse, partner, and friends. Talk with them about your program and let them know the importance of exercise and wellness in your life. Exercise is not a frivolous pursuit you follow after your work is finished. Rather, it is a critical component of your day (just like sleeping and eating). Good communication will help others become more supportive and enthusiastic about the time you spend on your wellness program.

- *Vary your activities.* You can make your program more fun over the long term if you participate in a variety of different activities that you enjoy. You can also add interest by strategies such as varying the routes you take when walking, running, biking, or in-line skating; finding a new tennis or racquetball partner; changing your music for aerobic dance; or switching to a new volleyball or basketball court.

Varying your activities, a strategy known as cross-training, has other benefits. It can help you develop balanced, total body, fitness. For example, by alternating running with swimming, you build both upper- and lower-body strength. Cross-training can thus prepare you for a wider range of activities and physical challenges. It can also reduce the risk of injury and overtraining because the same muscles, bones, and joints are not continuously subjected to the stresses of the same activity. Cross-training can be done either by choosing different activities on different days or by alternating activities within a single workout.

- *Cycle the volume and intensity of your workouts.* Olympic athletes use a technique called periodization of training, meaning that they vary the volume and intensity of their workouts. Sometimes they exercise very intensely; at other times they train lightly or rest. You can use the same technique to improve fitness faster and make your training program more varied and enjoyable. For example, if your program consists of walking, weight training, and stretching, pick one day a week for each activity to train a little harder or longer than you normally do. If you usually walk 2 miles in 16 minutes per mile, increase the pace to 15 minutes per mile once a week. If you lift weights twice a week,

Take Charge

Lapses are a normal part of any behavior change program. The important point is to move on and avoid becoming discouraged. Try again, and keep trying. Know that continued effort will lead to success.

• Don't judge yourself harshly. Some people make faster gains in fitness than others. Focus on the improvements you've already obtained from your program and how good you feel after exercise—both physically and mentally.

• Visualize what it will be like to reach your goals. Keep these pictures in your mind as an incentive to stick with your program.

• Use your exercise journal to identify thoughts and behaviors that are causing noncompliance. Devise strategies to combat these problematic patterns. If needed, make additional changes in your environment or obtain more social support. Call a friend to walk with you. Keep exercise clothes in your car or backpack.

• Make changes in your plan and reward system to help renew your enthusiasm and commitment to your program. Try changing fitness activities or your exercise schedule. Build in more opportunities to reward yourself.

• Plan ahead for difficult situations. Think about what circumstances might make it tough to keep up your fitness routine. Develop strategies to increase your chances of sticking with your program. For example, devise strategies for your program during vacation, travel, bad weather, and so on.

• If you're in a bad mood or just don't feel like exercising, remind yourself that physical activity is probably the one thing you can do that will make you feel better. Even if you can only do half your scheduled workout, you'll boost your energy, improve your mood, and help keep your program on track.

train more intensely during one of the workouts by using more resistance or performing multiple sets.

• *Adapt to changing environments and schedules.* Most people are creatures of habit and have trouble adjusting to change. Don't use wet weather or a new job as excuses to give up your exercise program. If you walk in the summer, put on a warm coat and walk in the winter. If you can't go out because of darkness, join a gym and walk on a treadmill. Changes in your job or family situation can also affect your exercise program. Taking a job with a longer commute or having a new baby can rob you of the time you used to spend exercising. Remember that physical activity is important for your energy level, self-esteem, and well-being. You owe it to yourself to include physical activity in your day. Try to exercise before going to work or do some physical activity during your lunch hour—even if it's only a short walk or a few trips up and down the stairs.

• *Expect fluctuations and lapses.* On some days, your progress will be excellent, but, on others, you'll barely be able to drag yourself through your scheduled activities. Don't let off-days or lapses discourage you or make you feel guilty. Instead, feel a renewed commitment for your fitness program (see the box "Getting Your Fitness Program Back on Track").

MOTIVATION FOR CHANGE! In addition to tracking the basic progress of your fitness program, you may find that directly monitoring some of your program's benefits can help keep you motivated and on track. For example, try tracking your energy level. Develop a point scale (1–10 or 1–20), record a value for your energy level each day, and graph the results. Most people find that increasing physical activity quickly boosts their energy level.

MAINTAINING YOUR PROGRAM: FIT FOR LIFE

Exercise should not be something you do just during January and February to satisfy a New Year's resolution—or during a class to satisfy a course requirement. You must make it a permanent part of your life. Choose activities you enjoy and make them part of your daily routine, just like sleeping, eating, brushing your teeth, and going to school and work. Scientists gather more evidence every year that regular exercise is the most important activity you can do to contribute to wellness. It is not a frill or a treat—it is a necessity. You will be a healthier, more vital, person if you make physical activity a habit. The following strategies can help keep you active for life:

• *Be safe.* Minimize the risk of injury or problems from activity by following safety guidelines, using proper technique and equipment, respecting signals from your body that something may be wrong, and treating any injuries that occur. Warm up, cool down, and drink plenty of fluids before and after exercise. (See Appendix A for more on personal safety.)

• *Have several exercise options.* Don't depend on a single location, activity, or person to be active. Cultivate many enjoyable activities that can be done in all seasons and circumstances. Take up a new sport or activity to keep your program fresh and enjoyable. And don't forget to include lifestyle physical activity in your daily routine.

• *Keep an exercise journal.* A journal can help keep your program on track, identify sources of problems, and give you a continuing sense of accomplishment.

• *Reward yourself.* Don't stop rewarding yourself once you reach your fitness goals. Continue to give yourself regular rewards for sticking with your program.

If you could do something simple, safe, and free to dramatically improve your mental, physical, and psychological health, would you do it? The opportunity is yours starting tonight—all you have to do is go to bed earlier! The majority of Americans suffer from chronic sleep deprivation. Most of us get between one-half and two fewer hours of sleep each night than we need in order to be fully alert during the day. One hundred years ago, Americans slept on average one and a half more hours each night than we do now. With the advent of electric lights, sleep times decreased dramatically.

Many people view sleep as a luxury or a waste of time, but sleep is absolutely essential for life and health. Humans and other animals who are deprived of sleep for many days will become ill and even die. Less extreme sleep deprivation over a long period of time makes us vulnerable to a wide variety of illnesses including CVD, diabetes, high blood pressure, and psychological disorders such as anxiety and depression. It has also been linked to weight gain. Inadequate sleep depresses the immune system, making people more vulnerable to infectious diseases. It affects learning, memory, and attention span, all critical to academic performance. Athletes who fail to get sufficient sleep cannot perform at their peak because fatigue slows reaction time and lessens endurance. Every aspect of life is easier and more pleasurable when you are well rested.

Sleep deprivation also takes a huge toll on society. The National Sleep Foundation estimates that sleepy employees cost U.S. businesses $18 billion every year in lost productivity alone. The costs are much higher if you factor in mistakes, accidents, and health problems caused by lack of sleep. Drowsiness is a factor in at least one-third of all auto crashes; it impairs driving ability as much as alcohol use. Many of us think that no matter how tired we may be, we can force ourselves to be alert. But we can't: People who are sleep deprived may think they are wide awake but often fall asleep at the wheel for brief periods without even realizing it.

College students are particularly vulnerable to sleep deprivation and poor quality of sleep. Most students lead hectic lives as they juggle studies, work, socializing, and family obligations. Students who live in dormitories are often awakened by nighttime noise. Partying, especially if alcohol and other drugs are used, further disrupts sleep. To make matters worse, teens and young adults actually need more sleep than older individuals—more than 9 hours of sleep a night—to be well rested.

Financial necessity dictates that many students work part-time or even full-time. There are only so many hours in the day, and many working students find it nearly impossible to get enough sleep to function well in school or at work. What can you do if you are faced with this dilemma? Cut back on work hours if at all possible. Obtaining financial aid or a loan or taking an extra year to get your degree may be worth it to preserve your health and happiness.

How do you know if you're getting enough sleep? If you need an alarm to get yourself up every morning, rather than awakening naturally at the appropriate time, chances are you are significantly sleep deprived. Another clue is if you fall asleep within just a few minutes of getting into bed, or if you fall asleep during the day when you don't intend to, such as during lectures or while reading or watching TV. Sleep you need but don't get is referred to as "sleep debt." Whenever you get less sleep than your body requires, you add to your sleep debt. Week after week, sleep debt can build, leaving you chronically groggy. If you have a large sleep debt, sleeping in a few extra hours on the weekends won't solve the problem, although it can help a bit. The real solution is to make sleep a priority in your daily life. Remember that the time you spend sleeping will pay for itself in increased productivity. For example, if you go to bed one hour earlier instead of trying to study when you're half awake, you are likely to get the work done in a fraction of the time when you're more alert the next day. Knowing that the quality of your life depends on getting adequate sleep, make sleep a priority part of your wellness lifestyle.

• *Choose other healthy lifestyle behaviors.* Exercise provides huge benefits for your health, but other behaviors are also important. Choose a nutritious diet and avoid harmful habits like smoking and overconsumption of alcohol. Don't skimp on sleep, which has a mutually beneficial relationship with exercise. Physical activity improves sleep, and adequate sleep can improve physical performance (see the box "Sleep").

EXERCISE GUIDELINES FOR PEOPLE WITH SPECIAL HEALTH CONCERNS

Regular, appropriate exercise is safe and beneficial for many people with chronic conditions or other special health concerns. For example, people with heart disease or hypertension who exercise may lower their blood pressure and improve their cholesterol levels. For people with diabetes, exercise can improve insulin sensitivity and body composition. For people with asthma, regular exercise may reduce the risk of acute attacks during exertion. For many people with special health concerns, the risks associated with *not* exercising are far greater than those associated with a moderate program of regular exercise.

The fitness recommendations for the general population presented in this text can serve as a general guideline for any exercise program. However, for people with special health concerns, certain precautions and monitoring may be required. Anyone with special health concerns should consult a physician before beginning an exercise program. Guidelines and cautions for some common conditions are described below.

Arthritis

• Begin an exercise program as early as possible in the course of the disease.

- Warm up thoroughly before each workout to loosen stiff muscles and lower the risk of injury.
- For cardiorespiratory endurance exercise, avoid high-impact activities that may damage arthritic joints; consider swimming, water walking, or another type of exercise in a warm pool.
- Strength train the whole body; pay special attention to muscles that support and protect affected joints (for example, build quadriceps, hamstring, and calf strength for the knee). Start with small loads and build intensity gradually.
- Perform flexibility exercises daily to maintain joint mobility.

Asthma

- Exercise regularly. Acute attacks are more likely if you exercise only occasionally.
- Carry medication during workouts and avoid exercising alone. Use your inhaler before exercise, if recommended by your physician.
- Warm up and cool down slowly to reduce the risk of acute attacks.
- When starting an exercise program, choose self-paced endurance activities, especially those involving **interval training** (short bouts of exercise followed by a rest period). Increase the intensity of cardiorespiratory endurance exercise gradually.
- Educate yourself about circumstances that may trigger an asthma attack, and act accordingly. For example, cold, dry air can trigger or worsen an attack. Pollen, dust, and polluted air can also trigger an attack. To avoid attacks in dry air, drink water before, during, and after a workout to moisten your airways. In cold weather, cover your mouth with a mask or scarf to warm and humidify the air you breathe. Also, avoid outdoor activities during pollen season or when the air is polluted or dusty.

Diabetes

- Don't begin an exercise program unless your diabetes is under control and you have checked about exercise safety with your physician. Because people with diabetes have an increased risk for heart disease, an exercise stress test may be recommended.
- Don't exercise alone. Wear a bracelet identifying yourself as having diabetes.

Terms

W̌w̌

interval training A training technique that alternates exercise intervals with rest intervals or intense exercise intervals with low-to-moderate intervals.

- If you are taking insulin or another medication, you may need to adjust the timing and amount of each dose. Work with your physician and check your blood sugar levels regularly so you can learn to balance your energy intake and output and your medication dosage.
- To prevent abnormally rapid absorption of injected insulin, inject it over a muscle that won't be exercised and wait at least an hour before exercising.
- Check blood sugar levels before, during, and after exercise and adjust your diet or insulin dosage if needed. Carry high-carbohydrate foods during a workout. Avoid exercises if your blood sugar level is above 250 mg/dl and ingest carbohydrates prior to exercise if your blood sugar level is below 100 mg/dl.
- Don't lift heavy weights. Straining can damage blood vessels. Perform a higher number of repetitions (15–20) using a lighter load.
- If you have poor circulation or numbness in your extremities, check your skin regularly for blisters and abrasions, especially on your feet. Avoid high-impact activities and wear comfortable shoes.
- For maximum benefit and minimum risk, choose low-to-moderate-intensity activities.

Heart Disease and Hypertension

- Check with your physician about exercise safety before increasing your activity level.
- Exercise at moderate rather than high intensity. Keep your heart rate below the level at which abnormalities appear on an exercise stress test.
- Warm-up and cool-down sessions should be gradual and last at least 10 minutes.
- Monitor your heart rate during exercise and stop if you experience dizziness or chest pain.
- If your physician has prescribed it, carry nitroglycerin with you during exercise. If you are taking beta-blockers for hypertension, use RPE rather than heart rate to monitor exercise intensity (beta-blockers reduce heart rate). Exercise at an RPE level of "fairly light" to "somewhat hard"; your breathing should be unlabored, and you should be able to talk.
- Don't hold your breath when exercising. Doing so can cause sudden, steep increases in blood pressure. Take special care during weight training; don't lift heavy loads. Exhale during the exertion phase of lifts.
- Increase exercise frequency, intensity, and time very gradually.

Obesity

- For maximum benefit and minimum risk, begin by choosing low-to-moderate-intensity activities. Increase intensity slowly as your fitness improves. Studies of overweight people show that exercising

Low-impact activities like walking are a good choice for people who are overweight because they can provide a good workout and are less likely than high-impact activities to cause joint problems or injuries. This man lost 100 pounds in the year after this photo was taken.

at moderate-to-high intensities causes more fat loss than training at low intensities.

- The 2005 Dietary Guidelines recommend that people who want to lose weight or maintain lost weight exercise moderately 60 minutes or more every day. To get the benefit of 60 minutes of exercise, you can exercise all at once or divide your total activity time into sessions of 10, 20, or 30 minutes.

- Choose non-or low-weight-bearing activities such as swimming, water exercises, cycling, or walking. Low-impact activities are less likely to lead to joint problems or injuries.

- Stay alert for symptoms of heat-related problems during exercise (see Chapter 3). People who are obese are particularly vulnerable to problems with heat intolerance.

- Ease into an exercise program and increase overload gradually. Increase time and frequency of exercise before increasing intensity.

- Include strength training in your fitness program to build or maintain muscle mass.

- Try to include as much lifestyle physical activity in your daily routine as possible.

Osteoporosis

- For cardiorespiratory endurance activities, exercise at the maximum intensity that causes no significant discomfort. If possible, choose low-impact weight-bearing activities to help safely maintain bone density (see Chapter 8 for more strategies for building and maintaining bone density).

- To prevent fractures, avoid any activity or movement that stresses the back or carries a risk of falling.

- Include weight training in your exercise program to improve strength and balance and reduce the risk of falls and fractures. Avoid lifting heavy loads.

Exercise guidelines for people with disabilities are discussed in Chapter 2 and for people with low-back pain, in Chapter 5.

MOTIVATION FOR CHANGE!   If you have a special health concern and have hesitated becoming more active, one helpful strategy is to take a class or join an exercise group specifically designed for your condition. Many health centers and support groups sponsor specially tailored activity programs. Such a class can provide you with both expert advice and exercise partners who share your concerns and goals.

EXERCISE GUIDELINES FOR LIFE STAGES

A fitness program may also need to be adjusted to accommodate the requirements of different life stages.

Children and Adolescents

Only 50% of all young people age 12–21 in the United States participate regularly in vigorous activity, and 25% report no vigorous activity at all. This lack of physical activity has led to alarming increases in overweight and obesity in children and adolescents. If you have children or are in a position to influence children, keep these guidelines in mind:

- Provide opportunities for children and adolescents to exercise every day. Minimize sedentary activities, such as watching television and playing video games. Children and adolescents should aim for at least 60 minutes of moderate activity most, but preferably all, days.

- During family outings, choose dynamic activities. For example, go for a walk, park away from a mall and then walk to the stores, and take the stairs instead of the escalator.

- For children younger than 12, emphasize skill development and fitness rather than excellence in competitive sports. For adolescents, combine participation and training in lifetime sports with traditional, competitive, sports.

- Make sure children are developmentally capable of participating in an activity. For example, catching skills are difficult for young children because their nervous system is not developed enough to fully master the skill. When teaching a child to catch a ball, start with a large ball and throw it from a short range. Gradually increase the complexity of the skill once the child has mastered the simpler skill.

- Make sure children get plenty of water when exercising in the heat. Make sure they are dressed properly when exercising in the cold.

Pregnant Women

Exercise is important during pregnancy, but women should be cautious because some types of exercise can pose increased risk to the mother and the unborn child. The following guidelines are consistent with the recommendations of the American College of Obstetrics and Gynecology:

- See your physician about possible modifications needed for your particular pregnancy.

- Continue mild-to-moderate exercise routines at least three times a week. Avoid exercising vigorously or to exhaustion, especially in the third trimester. Monitor exercise intensity by assessing how you feel rather than by monitoring your heart rate; RPE levels of 11–13 are appropriate.

- Favor non- or low-weight-bearing exercises such as swimming or cycling over weight-bearing exercises, which can carry increased risk of injury.

- Avoid exercise in a supine position—lying on your back—after the first trimester. This position restricts blood flow to the uterus. Also avoid prolonged periods of motionless standing.

- Avoid exercise that could cause loss of balance, especially in the third trimester, and exercise that might injure the abdomen, stress the joints, or carry a risk of falling (such as contact sports, vigorous racquet sports, skiing, and in-line skating).

- Avoid activities involving extremes in barometric pressure—for example, scuba diving and mountain climbing.

- Especially during the first trimester, drink plenty of fluids and exercise in well-ventilated areas to avoid heat stress.

- Do 3–5 sets of 10 Kegel exercises daily. These exercises involve tightening the muscles of the pelvic floor for 5–15 seconds. Kegel exercises are thought to help prevent incontinence (involuntary loss of urine) and speed recovery after giving birth.

- After giving birth, resume prepregnancy exercise routines gradually, based on how you feel.

Older Adults

Older people readily adapt to endurance exercise and strength training. Exercise principles are the same as for younger people, but some specific guidelines apply:

- Include the three basic types of exercise—resistance, endurance, and flexibility.

- For strength training, the ACSM recommends that older adults use a lighter weight and perform more (10–15) repetitions than those recommended for young adults.

- Drink plenty of water and avoid exercising in excessively hot or cold environments. (Older people sometimes have a decreased ability to regulate body temperature during exercise.) Wear clothes that speed heat loss in warm environments and that prevent heat loss in cold environments.

- Warm up slowly and carefully. Increase intensity and duration of exercise gradually.

- Cool down slowly, continuing very light exercise until the heart rate is below 100.

- To help prevent soft tissue pain, do static stretching after a normal workout.

Sample fitness programs begin on p. 214.

Sample fitness programs begin on p. 214.

Tips for Today

A complete fitness program includes activities to build and maintain cardiorespiratory endurance, muscular strength and endurance, and flexibility. It takes time, energy, and commitment to begin and maintain a fitness program, but the many benefits are well worth the effort. Begin today, and you'll be on your way to enjoying fitness and wellness for the rest of your life.

Right now you can

- Obtain a journal to track your daily physical activity and exercise routine.

- Put away your remote control devices—every bit of physical activity can benefit your health.

- Put the clothes and equipment for your next workout in a convenient and obvious location.

- Set a firm time for your next workout with your training partner (buddy).

- Plan to go to bed 15 minutes earlier than usual.

- Make a list of situations such as bad weather that may challenge your ability to stick with your fitness program, develop a strategy for dealing with each one.

SUMMARY

- Steps for putting together a complete fitness program include (1) setting realistic goals; (2) selecting activities to develop all the health-related components of fitness; (3) setting a target frequency, intensity, and time (duration) for each activity; (4) setting up a system of mini-goals and rewards; (5) making lifestyle physical activity a part of the daily routine; (6) developing tools for monitoring progress; and (7) making a commitment.

Common Questions Answered

Should I exercise every day? Some daily exercise is beneficial, and health experts recommend that you engage in at least 30 minutes of moderate physical activity over the course of every day. Back experts suggest that you also do back pain prevention exercises daily. However, if you train intensely every day without giving yourself a rest, you will likely get injured or become overtrained. When strength training, for example, rest at least 48 hours between workouts before exercising the same muscle group. For cardiorespiratory endurance exercise, rest or exercise lightly the day after an intense or lengthy workout. Balancing the proper amount of rest and exercise will help you feel better and improve your fitness faster.

I'm just starting an exercise program. How much activity should I do at first? Be conservative. Walking is a good way to begin almost any fitness program. At first, walk for approximately 10 minutes, and then increase the distance and pace. After several weeks, you can progress to something more vigorous. Let your body be your guide. If the intensity and duration of a workout seem easy, increase them a little the next time. The key is to be progressive; don't try to achieve physical fitness in one or two workouts. Build your fitness gradually.

Visit the Online Learning Center for more answers to common questions about developing and maintaining a fitness program.

- In selecting activities, consider fun and interest, your current skill and fitness levels, time and convenience, cost, and any special health concerns.
- Keys to beginning and maintaining a successful program include starting slowly, increasing intensity and duration gradually, finding a buddy, varying the activities and intensity of the program, and expecting fluctuations and lapses.
- Regular exercise is appropriate and highly beneficial for people with special health concerns or in particular stages of life; program modifications may be necessary to maximize safety.

For Further Exploration

Fit and Well Online Learning Center (www.mhhe.com/fahey)

Use the learning objectives, study guide questions, and glossary flashcards to review key terms and concepts and prepare for exams. You can extend your knowledge of personal fitness and gain experience in using the Internet as a resource by completing the activities and checking out the Web links for the topics in Chapter 7 marked with the World Wide Web icon. For this chapter, Internet activities explore fitness activities and strategies for creating a complete fitness program; there are also links for chapter topics.

Daily Fitness and Nutrition Journal

Complete the program plan and fitness contract, and begin your program. Use the journal to record your activities and track your progress.

Books, Organizations, and Web Sites

See the listings for Chapters 2–6.

Selected Bibliography

American College of Obstetrics and Gynecology Committee on Obstetric Practice. 2002. Exercise during pregnancy and the postpartum period. Committee Opinion No. 267. *International Journal of Gynaecology and Obstetrics* 77:79–81.

American College of Sports Medicine. 2006. *ACSM's Guidelines for Exercise Testing and Prescription,* 7th ed. Philadelphia: Lippincott Williams & Wilkins.

American College of Sports Medicine. 2006. *ACSM's Resource Manual for Guidelines for Exercise Testing and Prescription,* 5th ed. Philadelphia: Lippincott Williams & Wilkins.

American Diabetes Association. 2003. Physical activity/exercise and diabetes mellitus. *Diabetes Care* 26:S73–S77.

American Heart Association. 2003. Exercise and physical activity in the prevention and treatment of atherosclerotic cardiovascular disease. *Circulation* 107:3109–3116.

Bernstein, M. S., M. C. Costanza, and A. Morabia. 2004. Association of physical activity intensity levels with overweight and obesity in a population-based sample of adults. *Preventive Medicine* 38(1): 94–104.

Brunet, S., et al. 2005. For the patient. Exercise is important to preventing and controlling type 2 diabetes. *Ethnicity and Disease* 15:353–354.

Fenicchia, L. M., et al. 2004. Influence of resistance exercise training on glucose control in women with type 2 diabetes. *Metabolism* 53(3): 284–289.

Hogan, M. 2005. Physical and cognitive activity and exercise for older adults: A review. *International Journal of Aging and Human Development* 60:95–126.

Lee, S., et al. 2005. Exercise without weight loss is an effective strategy for obesity reduction in obese individuals with and without type 2 diabetes. *Journal of Applied Physiology* 99:1220–1225.

Morris, S. N., and N. R. Johnson. 2005. Exercise during pregnancy: A critical appraisal of the literature. *Journal of Reproductive Medicine* 50:181–188.

National Sleep Foundation. 2002. *2002 Sleep in America Poll* (http://www.sleepfoundation.org/2002poll.html; retrieved May 14, 2002).

Nieman, D. C. 2002. How do I adapt current ACSM exercise prescription guidelines for my obese clients? *ACSM Health and Fitness Journal,* January/February.

Pescatello, L. S., et al. 2004. American College of Sports Medicine Position Stand: Exercise and hypertension. *Medicine and Science in Sports and Exercise* 36(3): 533–553.

Riebe, D., et al. 2005. Long-term maintenance of exercise and healthy eating behaviors in overweight adults. *Preventive Medicine* 40:769–778.

Satta, A. 2000. Exercise training in asthma. *Journal of Sports Medicine and Physical Fitness* 40(4): 277–283.

Seguin, R., and M. E. Nelson. 2003. The benefits of strength training for older adults. *American Journal of Preventive Medicine* 25(3 Suppl. 2): 141–149.

Vorona, R. D., et al. 2005. Overweight and obese patients in a primary care population report less sleep than patients with a normal body mass index. *Archives of Internal Medicine* 165(1): 25–30.

Sample programs based on four different types of cardiorespiratory activities—walking/jogging/running, bicycling, swimming, and in-line skating—are presented below. Each sample program includes regular cardiorespiratory endurance exercise, resistance training, and stretching. To choose a sample program, first compare your fitness goals with the benefits of the different types of endurance exercise featured in the sample programs (see Table 7.1). Identify the programs that meet your fitness needs. Next, read through the descriptions of the programs you're considering, and decide which will work best for you based on your present routine, the potential for enjoyment, and adaptability to your lifestyle. If you choose one of these programs, complete the personal fitness program plan in Lab 7.1, just as if you had created a program from scratch.

No program will produce enormous changes in your fitness level in the first few weeks. Give your program a good chance. Follow the specifics of the program for 3–4 weeks. Then if the exercise program doesn't seem suitable, make adjustments to adapt it to your particular needs. But retain the basic elements of the program that make it effective for developing fitness.

GENERAL GUIDELINES

The following guidelines can help make the activity programs more effective for you.

- *Frequency and time.* To experience training effects, you should exercise for 20–60 minutes at least three times a week.

- *Intensity.* To work effectively for cardiorespiratory endurance training or to improve body composition, raise your heart rate into its target zone. Monitor your pulse or use rates of perceived exertion to monitor your intensity.

  If you've been sedentary, begin very slowly. Give your muscles a chance to adjust to their increased workload. It's probably best to keep your heart rate below target until your body has had time to adjust to new demands. At first you may not need to work very hard to keep your heart rate in its target zone, but as your cardiorespiratory endurance improves, you will probably need to increase intensity.

- *Interval training.* Some of the sample programs involve continuous activity. Others rely on interval training, which calls for alternating a relief interval with exercise (walking after jogging, for example, or coasting after biking uphill). Interval training is an effective way to achieve progressive overload: When your heart rate gets too high, slow down to lower your pulse rate until you're at the low end of your target zone. Interval training can also prolong the total time you spend in exercise and delay the onset of fatigue.

- *Warm-up and cool-down.* Begin each exercise session with a 10-minute warm-up. Begin your activity at a slow pace and work up gradually to your target heart rate. Always slow down gradually at the end of your exercise session to bring your system back to its normal state. It's a good idea to do stretching exercises to increase your flexibility after cardiorespiratory exercise or strength training because your muscles will be warm and ready to stretch.

- *Record keeping.* After each exercise session, record your daily distance or time on a progress chart.

WALKING/JOGGING/RUNNING SAMPLE PROGRAM

Walking, jogging, and running are the most popular forms of training for people who want to improve cardiorespiratory endurance; they also improve body composition and muscular endurance of the legs. It's not always easy to distinguish among these three endurance activities. For clarity and consistency, we'll consider walking to be any on-foot exercise of less than 5 miles per hour, jogging any pace between 5 and 7.5 miles per hour, and running any pace faster than that. Table 1 divides walking, jogging, and running into nine categories, with rates of speed (in both miles per hour and minutes per mile) and calorie costs for each. The faster your pace or the longer you exercise, the more calories you burn. The greater the number of calories burned, the higher the potential training effects of these activities. Tables 2 and 3 contain sample walking/jogging programs by time and distance.

Equipment and Technique

These activities require no special skills, expensive equipment, or unusual facilities. Comfortable clothing, well-fitted walking or running shoes, and a stopwatch or ordinary watch with a second hand are all you need.

Developing Cardiorespiratory Endurance

The four variations of the basic walking/jogging/running sample program that follow are designed to help you regulate the intensity, duration, and frequency of your program. Use the following guidelines to choose the variation that is right for you.

- *Variation 1: Walking (Starting).* Choose this program if you have medical restrictions, are recovering from illness or surgery, tire easily after short walks, are obese, or have a sedentary lifestyle, and if you want to prepare for the advanced walking program to improve cardiorespiratory endurance, body composition, and muscular endurance.

- *Variation 2: Advanced Walking.* Choose this program if you already can walk comfortably for 30 minutes and if you want to develop and maintain cardiorespiratory fitness, a lean body, and muscular endurance.

- *Variation 3: Preparing for a Jogging/Running Program.* Choose this program if you already can walk comfortably for 30 minutes and if you want to prepare for the jogging/running program to improve cardiorespiratory endurance, body composition, and muscular endurance.

SAMPLE PROGRAM TABLE 1 *Calorie Costs for Walking/Jogging/Running*

This table gives the calorie costs of walking, jogging, and running for slow, moderate, and fast paces. Calculations for calorie costs are approximate and assume a level terrain. A hilly terrain would result in higher calorie costs. To get an estimate of the number of calories you burn, multiply your weight by the calories per minute per pound for the speed at which you're doing the activity, and then multiply that by the number of minutes you exercise.

| | Speed | | Calories per Minute per Pound |
Activity	Miles per Hour	Minutes: Seconds per Mile	
Walking			
Slow	2.0	30:00	.020
	2.5	24:00	.023
Moderate	3.0	20:00	.026
	3.5	17:08	.029
Fast	4.0	15:00	.037
	4.5	13:20	.048
Jogging			
Slow	5.0	12:00	.060
	5.5	11:00	.074
Moderate	6.0	10:00	.081
	6.5	9:00	.088
Fast	7.0	8:35	.092
	7.5	8:00	.099
Running			
Slow	8.5	7:00	.111
Moderate	9.0	6:40	.116
Fast	10.0	6:00	.129
	11.0	5:30	.141

SOURCE: Kusinitz, I., and M. Fine, *Physical Fitness for Practically Everybody*, Consumer Reports®, 1983. Consumers Union of the U.S., Inc., Yonkers, NY 10703-1057, a nonprofit organization. Reprinted with permission for educational purposes only. No commercial use or reproduction permitted. www.ConsumerReports.org®.

- *Variation 4: Jogging/Running.* Choose this program if you already can jog comfortably without muscular discomfort, if you already can jog for 15 minutes without stopping or 30 minutes with brief walking intervals within your target heart rate range, and if you want to develop and maintain a high level of cardiorespiratory fitness, a lean body, and muscular endurance.

Variation 1: Walking (Starting)

FIT—frequency, intensity, and time: Walk at first for 15 minutes at a pace that keeps your heart rate below your target zone. Gradually increase to 30-minute sessions. The distance you travel will probably be 1–2 miles. At the beginning, walk every other day. You can gradually increase to daily walking if you want to burn more calories (helpful if you want to change body composition).

Calorie cost: Work up to using 90–135 calories in each session (see Table 1). To increase calorie costs to the target level, walk for a longer time or for a longer distance rather than sharply increasing speed.

At the beginning: Start at whatever level is most comfortable. Maintain a normal, easy pace, and stop to rest as often as you need to. Never prolong a walk past the point of comfort. When walking with a friend (a good motivation), let a comfortable conversation be your guide to pace.

As you progress: Once your muscles have become adjusted to the exercise program, increase the duration of your sessions—but by no more than 10% each week. Increase your intensity only enough to keep your heart rate just below your target. When you're able to walk 1.5 miles in 30 minutes, using 90–135 calories per session, you should consider moving on to variation 2 or 3. Don't be discouraged by lack of immediate progress and don't try to speed things up by overdoing. Remember that pace and heart rate can vary with the terrain, the weather, and other factors.

Variation 2: Advanced Walking

FIT—frequency, intensity, and time: Start at a pace at the lower end of your target heart rate zone and begin soon afterward to increase your pace. This might boost your heart rate into the upper levels of your target zone, which is fine for brief periods. But don't overdo the intervals of fast walking. Slow down after a short time to drop your pulse rate. Vary your pattern to allow for intervals of slow, medium, and fast walking. Walk at first for 30 minutes and gradually increase your walking time until eventually you reach 60 minutes, all the while maintaining your target heart rate. The distance you walk will probably be 2–4 miles. Walk at least every other day.

Calorie cost: Work up to using about 200–350 calories in each session (see Table 1).

At the beginning: Begin by walking somewhat faster than you did in Variation 1. Check your pulse to make sure you keep your heart rate within your target zone. Slow down when necessary to lower your heart rate when going up hills or when extending the duration of your walks.

As you progress: As your heart rate adjusts to the increased workload, gradually increase your pace and your total walking time. Gradually lengthen the intervals of fast walking and shorten the relief intervals of slow walking, always maintaining target heart rate. Eventually, you will reach the fitness level you would like to maintain. And to maintain that level of fitness, continue to burn the same amount of calories in each session.

Vary your program by changing the pace and distance walked, or by walking routes with different terrains and views. Gauge your progress toward whatever calorie goal you've set by using Table 1.

Variation 3: Preparing for a Jogging/Running Program

FIT—frequency, intensity, and time: Start by walking at a moderate pace (3–4 miles per hour or 15–20 minutes per mile).

SAMPLE PROGRAM TABLE 2 *Walking/Jogging Progression by Time*

This table is based on a walking interval of 3.75 miles per hour, measured in seconds, and a jogging interval of 5.5 miles per hour, measured in minutes:seconds. The combination of the two intervals equals a single set. In the Number of Sets column, the higher figure represents the maximum number of sets to be completed.

	Walk Interval (sec)	Jog Interval (min:sec)	Number of Sets	Total Distance (mi)	Total Time (min:sec)
Stage 1	:60	:30	10–15	1.0–1.7	15:00–22:30
Stage 2	:60	:60	8–13	1.2–2.0	16:00–26:00
Stage 3	:60	2:00	5–19	1.3–2.3	15:00–27:00
Stage 4	:60	3:00	5–7	1.6–2.4	16:00–28:00
Stage 5	:60	4:00	3–6	1.5–2.7	15:00–30:00

SOURCE: Kusinitz, I., and M. Fine, *Physical Fitness for Practically Everybody,* Consumer Reports®, 1983. Consumers Union of the U.S., Inc., Yonkers, NY 10703-1057, a nonprofit organization. Reprinted with permission for educational purposes only. No commercial use or reproduction permitted. www.ConsumerReports.org®.

SAMPLE PROGRAM TABLE 3 *Walking/Jogging Progression by Distance*

This table is based on a walking interval of 3.75 miles per hour, measured in yards, and a jogging interval of 5.5 miles per hour, also measured in yards. The combination of the two intervals equals a single set. (One lap around a typical track is 440 yards.)

	Walk Interval (yd)	Jog Interval (yd)	Number of Sets	Total Distance (mi)	Total Time (min:sec)
Stage 1	110	55	11–21	1.0–2.0	15:00–28:12
Stage 2	110	110	16	2.0	26:56
Stage 3	110	220	11	2.0	26:02
Stage 4	110	330	8	2.0	24:24
Stage 5	110	440	7	2.2	26:05
Stage 6	110	440	8	2.5	29:49

SOURCE: Kusinitz, I., and M. Fine, *Physical Fitness for Practically Everybody,* Consumer Reports®, 1983. Consumers Union of the U.S., Inc., Yonkers, NY 10703-1057, a nonprofit organization. Reprinted with permission for educational purposes only. No commercial use or reproduction permitted. www.ConsumerReports.org®.

Staying within your target heart rate zone, begin to add brief intervals of slow jogging (5–6 miles per hour or 10–12 minutes per mile). Keep the walking intervals constant at 60 seconds or at 110 yards, but gradually increase the jogging intervals until eventually you jog 4 minutes for each minute of walking. You'll probably cover between 1.5 and 2.5 miles. Each exercise session should last 15–30 minutes. Exercise every other day. If your goals include changing body composition and you want to exercise more frequently, walk on days you're not jogging.

Calorie cost: Work up to using 200–350 calories in each session (see Table 1).

At the beginning: Start slowly. Until your muscles adjust to jogging, you may need to exercise at less than your target heart rate. At the outset, expect to do two to four times as much walking as jogging, even more if you're relatively inexperienced. Be guided by how comfortable you feel—and by your heart rate—in setting the pace for your progress. Follow the guidelines presented in Chapter 3 for exercising in hot or cold weather. Drink enough liquids to stay adequately hydrated, particularly in hot weather. In addition, use the proper running technique, described below.

- Run with your back straight and your head up. Look straight ahead, not at your feet. Shift your pelvis forward and tuck your buttocks in.

- Hold your arms slightly away from your body. Your elbows should be bent so that your forearms are parallel to the ground. You may cup your hands, but do not clench your fists. Allow your arms to swing loosely and rhythmically with each stride.

- Your heel should hit the ground first in each stride. Then roll forward onto the ball of your foot and push off for the next stride. If you find this difficult, you can try a more flat-footed style, but don't land on the balls of your feet.

- Keep your steps short by allowing your foot to strike the ground in line with your knee. Keep your knees bent at all times.

- Breathe deeply through your mouth. Try to use your abdominal muscles rather than just your chest muscles to take deep breaths.

- Stay relaxed.

As you progress: Adjust your ratio of walking to jogging to keep within your target heart rate zone as much as possible. When you have progressed to the point where most of your 30-minute session is spent jogging, consider moving on to Variation 4. To find a walking/jogging progression that suits you, refer to Tables 2 and 3 (one uses time, the other distance). Which one you choose will depend, to some extent, on where you work out. If you have access to a track or can use a measured distance with easily visible landmarks to indicate yardage covered, you may find it convenient to use distance as your organizing principle. If you'll be using parks, streets, or woods, time intervals (measured with a watch) would probably work better. The progressions in Tables 2 and 3 are not meant to be rigid; they are guidelines to help you develop your own rate of progress. Let your progress be guided by your heart rate and increase your intensity and duration only to achieve your target zone.

Variation 4: Jogging/Running

FIT—frequency, intensity, and time: The key is to exercise within your target heart rate zone. Most people who sustain a continuous jog/run program will find that they can stay within their target heart rate zone with a speed of 5.5–7.5 miles per hour (8–11 minutes per mile). Start by jogging steadily for 15 minutes. Gradually increase your jog/run session to a regular 30–60 minutes (or about 2.5–7 miles). Exercise at least every other day. Increasing frequency by doing other activities on alternate days will place less stress on the weight-bearing parts of your lower body than will a daily program of jogging/running.

Calorie cost: Use about 300–750 calories in each session (see Table 1).

At the beginning: The greater number of calories you burn per minute makes this program less time-consuming for altering body composition than the three other variations in the walking/jogging/running program.

As you progress: If you choose this variation, you probably already have a moderate-to-high level of cardiorespiratory fitness. To stay within your target heart rate zone, increase your distance or both pace and distance as needed. Add variety to your workouts by varying your route, intensity, and duration. Alternate short runs with long runs. If you run for 60 minutes one day, try running for 30 minutes the next session. Or try doing sets that alternate hard and easy intervals—even walking, if you feel like it. You can also try a road race now and then, but be careful not to do too much too soon.

Developing Muscular Strength and Endurance

Walking, jogging, and running provide muscular endurance workouts for your lower body; they also develop muscular strength of the lower body to a lesser degree. To develop muscular strength and endurance of the upper body, and to make greater and more rapid gains in lower-body strength, you need to include resistance training in your fitness program. Use the general wellness weight training program in Chapter 4, or tailor one to fit your personal fitness goals. If you'd like to increase your running speed and performance, you might want to focus your program on lower-body exercises. (Don't neglect upper-body strength, however; it is important for overall wellness.) Regardless of the strength training exercises you choose, follow the guidelines for successful training:

- Train 2–3 nonconsecutive days per week.

- Perform 1 or more sets of 8–12 repetitions of 8–10 exercises.

- Include exercises that work all the major muscle groups: neck, shoulders, chest, arms, upper and lower back, abdomen, thighs, and calves.

Depending on the amount of time you are able to set aside for exercise, you may find it more convenient to alternate between your cardiorespiratory endurance workouts and your muscular strength and endurance workouts. In other words, walk or jog one day and strength train the next day.

Developing Flexibility

To round out your fitness program, you also need to include exercises that develop flexibility. The best time for a flexibility workout is when your muscles are warm, as they are immediately following cardiorespiratory endurance exercise or strength training. Perform the stretching routine presented in Chapter 5 or one that you have created to meet your own goals and preferences. Be sure to pay special attention to the hamstrings and quadriceps, which are not worked through their complete range of motion during walking or jogging. As you put your program together, remember the basic structure of a successful flexibility program:

- Stretch at least 2–3 days per week (ideally 5–7 days per week), preferably when muscles are warm.

- Stretch all the major muscle groups.

- Stretch to the point of mild discomfort and hold for 15–30 seconds.

- Repeat each stretch 2–4 times.

BICYCLING SAMPLE PROGRAM

Bicycling can also lead to large gains in physical fitness. For many people, cycling is a pleasant and economical alternative to driving and a convenient way to build fitness.

Equipment and Technique

Cycling has its own special array of equipment, including headgear, lighting, safety pennants, and special shoes. The bike is the most expensive item, ranging from about $100 to well over $1000. Avoid making a large investment until you're sure you'll use your bike regularly. While investigating what the marketplace has to offer, rent or borrow a bike. Consider your intended use of the bike. Most cyclists who are interested primarily in fitness are best served by a sturdy 10-speed rather than a mountain bike or sport bike. Stationary cycles are good for rainy days and areas that have harsh winters.

Clothing for bike riding shouldn't be restrictive or binding, nor should it be so loose-fitting or so long that it might get caught in the chain. Clothing worn on the upper body should be comfortable but not so loose that it catches the wind and slows you down. Always wear a helmet to help prevent injury in case of a fall or crash. Wearing glasses or goggles can protect the eyes from dirt, small objects, and irritation from wind.

To avoid saddle soreness and injury, choose a soft or padded saddle and adjust it to a height that allows your legs to almost reach full extension while pedaling. Make certain the saddle doesn't put too much pressure on sensitive areas. Wear a pair of well-padded gloves if your hands tend to become numb while riding or if you begin to develop blisters or calluses. To prevent backache and neck strain, warm up thoroughly and periodically shift the position of your hands on the handlebars and your body in the saddle. Keep your arms relaxed and don't lock your elbows. To protect your knees from strain, pedal with your feet pointed straight ahead or very slightly inward and don't pedal in high gear for long periods.

Bike riding requires a number of precise skills that practice makes automatic. If you've never ridden before, consider taking a course. In fact, many courses are not just for beginners. They'll help you develop skills in braking, shifting, and handling emergencies, as well as teach you ways of caring for and repairing your bike. For safe cycling, follow these rules:

- Always wear a helmet.

- Keep on the correct side of the road. Bicycling against traffic is usually illegal and always dangerous.

- Obey all traffic signs and signals.

- On public roads, ride in single file, except in low-traffic areas (if the law permits). Ride in a straight line; don't swerve or weave in traffic.

- Be alert; anticipate the movements of other traffic and pedestrians. Listen for approaching traffic that is out of your line of vision.

- Slow down at street crossings. Check both ways before crossing.

- Use hand signals—the same as for automobile drivers—if you intend to stop or turn. Use audible signals to warn those in your path.

- Maintain full control. Avoid anything that interferes with your vision. Don't jeopardize your ability to steer by carrying anything (including people) on the handlebars.

- Keep your bicycle in good shape. Brakes, gears, saddle, wheels, and tires should always be in good condition.

- See and be seen. Use a headlight at night and equip your bike with rear reflectors. Use side reflectors on pedals, front and rear. Wear light-colored clothing or use reflective tape at night; wear bright colors or use fluorescent tape by day.

- Be courteous to other road users. Anticipate the worst and practice preventive cycling.

- Use a rear-view mirror.

Developing Cardiorespiratory Endurance

Cycling is an excellent way to develop and maintain cardiorespiratory endurance and a healthy body composition.

FIT—frequency, intensity, and time: If you've been inactive for a long time, begin your cycling program at a heart rate that is 10–20% below your target zone. Beginning cyclists should

pedal at about 80–100 revolutions per minute; adjust the gear so that you can pedal at that rate easily. Your bicycle may display different types of useful information, including speed, distance traveled, heart rate, altitude, and revolutions per minute, and it may provide a cadence signal to help you maintain your pace. Once you feel at home on your bike, try 1 mile at a comfortable speed, and then stop and check your heart rate. Increase your speed gradually until you can cycle at 12–15 miles per hour (4–5 minutes per mile), a speed fast enough to bring most new cyclists' heart rate into their target zone. Allow your pulse rate to be your guide: More highly fit individuals may need to ride faster to achieve their target heart rate. Cycling for at least 20 minutes three times a week will improve your fitness.

Calorie cost: Use Table 4 to determine the number of calories you burn during each outing. You can increase the number of calories burned by cycling faster or for a longer time (it's usually better to increase distance than to add speed).

At the beginning: It may require several outings to get the muscles and joints of your legs and hips adjusted to this new activity. Begin each outing with a 10-minute warm-up that includes stretches for your hamstrings and your back and neck muscles. Until you become a skilled cyclist, select routes with the fewest hazards and avoid heavy automobile traffic.

As you progress: Interval training is also effective with bicycling. Simply increase your speed for periods of 4–8 minutes or for specific distances, such as 1–2 miles. Then coast for 2–3 minutes. Alternate the speed intervals and slow intervals for a total of 20–60 minutes, depending on your level of fitness. Hilly terrain is also a form of interval training.

Developing Muscular Strength and Endurance

Bicycling develops a high level of endurance and a moderate level of strength in the muscles of the lower body. To develop muscular strength and endurance of the upper body—and to make greater and more rapid gains in lower-body strength—you need to include resistance training as part of your fitness program. Use the general wellness weight training program from Chapter 4, or tailor one to fit your personal fitness goals. If one of your goals is to increase your cycling speed and performance, be sure to include exercises for the quadriceps, hamstrings, and buttocks muscles in your strength training program. No matter which exercises you include in your program, follow the general guidelines for successful and safe training:

- Train 2–3 nonconsecutive days per week.

- Perform 1 or more sets of 8–12 repetitions of 8–10 exercises.

- Include exercises that work all the major muscle groups: neck, shoulders, chest, arms, upper and lower back, abdomen, thighs, and calves.

Depending on your schedule, you may find it more convenient to alternate between your cardiorespiratory endurance workouts and your muscular strength and endurance workouts. In other words, cycle one day and strength train the next day.

Developing Flexibility

A complete fitness program also includes exercises that develop flexibility. The best time for a flexibility workout is when your muscles are warm, as they are immediately following a session of cardiorespiratory endurance exercise or strength training. Perform

SAMPLE PROGRAM TABLE 4 *Calorie Costs for Bicycling*

This table gives the approximate calorie costs per pound of body weight for cycling from 5 to 60 minutes for distances of .50 mile up to 15 miles on a level terrain. To use the table, find on the horizontal line the time most closely approximating the number of minutes you cycle. Next, locate on the vertical column the approximate distance in miles you cover. The figure at the intersection represents an estimate of the calories used per minute per pound of body weight. Multiply this figure by your body weight. Then multiply the product of these two figures by the number of minutes you cycle to get the total number of calories burned. For example, assuming you weigh 154 pounds and cycle 6 miles in 40 minutes, you would burn 260 calories: 154 × .042 (calories per pound, from table) = 6.5 × 40 (minutes) = 260 calories burned.

Distance (mi)	Time (min)											
	5	10	15	20	25	30	35	40	45	50	55	60
.50	.032											
1.00	.062	.032										
1.50		.042	.032									
2.00		.062	.039	.032								
3.00			.062	.042	.036	.032						
4.00				.062	.044	.039	.035	.032				
5.00				.097	.062	.045	.041	.037	.035	.032		
6.00					.088	.062	.047	.042	.039	.036	.034	.032
7.00						.081	.062	.049	.043	.040	.038	.036
8.00							.078	.062	.050	.044	.041	.039
9.00								.076	.062	.051	.045	.042
10.00								.097	.074	.062	.051	.045
11.00									.093	.073	.062	.052
12.00										.088	.072	.062
13.00											.084	.071
14.00												.081
15.00												.097

SOURCE: Kusinitz, I., and M. Fine, *Physical Fitness for Practically Everybody,* Consumer Reports®, 1983. Consumers Union of the U.S., Inc., Yonkers, NY 10703-1057, a nonprofit organization. Reprinted with permission for educational purposes only. No commercial use or reproduction permitted. www.ConsumerReports.org®.

the stretching routine presented in Chapter 5, or develop one that meets your own goals and preferences. Pay special attention to the hamstrings and quadriceps, which are not worked through their complete range of motion during bike riding, and to the muscles in your lower back, shoulders, and neck. As you put your stretching program together, remember these basic guidelines:

- Stretch at least 2–3 days per week (ideally 5–7 days per week), preferably when muscles are warm.

- Stretch all the major muscle groups.
- Stretch to the point of mild discomfort and hold for 15–30 seconds.
- Repeat each stretch 2–4 times.

SWIMMING SAMPLE PROGRAM

Swimming is excellent for developing all-around fitness. Because water supports the body weight of the swimmer, swimming places less stress than weight-bearing activities on joints, ligaments, and tendons and tends to cause fewer injuries.

Equipment and Safety Guidelines

Aside from having access to a swimming pool, the only equipment required for a swimming program is a swimsuit and a pair of swimming goggles (that fit and do not leak) to protect the eyes from irritation in chlorinated pools. Following these few

simple rules can help keep you safe and healthy during your swimming sessions:

- Swim only in a pool with a qualified lifeguard on duty.
- Always walk carefully on wet surfaces.
- Dry your ears well after swimming. If you experience the symptoms of swimmer's ear (itching, discharge, or even a partial hearing loss), consult your physician. If you swim while recovering from swimmer's ear, protect your ears with a few drops of lanolin on a wad of lamb's wool.

- To avoid back pain, try not to arch your back excessively when you swim.
- Be courteous to others in the pool.

If you swim in a setting other than a pool with a lifeguard, remember the following important rules:

- Don't swim beyond your skill and endurance limits.
- Avoid being chilled: don't swim in water colder than 70°F.
- Never drink alcohol before going swimming.
- Never swim alone.

Developing Cardiorespiratory Endurance

Any one or any combination of common swimming strokes—front crawl stroke, breaststroke, backstroke, butterfly stroke, sidestroke, or elementary backstroke—can help develop and maintain cardiorespiratory fitness. (Swimming may not be as helpful as walking, jogging, or cycling for body fat loss.)

FIT—frequency, intensity, and time: Because swimming is not a weight-bearing activity and is not done in an upright position, it elicits a lower heart rate per minute. Therefore, you'll need to adjust your target heart rate zone. To calculate your target heart rate for swimming, use this formula:

Maximum swimming heart rate (MSHR) = 205 − age

Target heart rate zone = 65–90% of MSHR

For example, a 19-year-old would calculate her target heart rate zone for swimming as follows:

MSHR = 205 − 19 = 186 bpm

65% intensity: 0.65 × 186 = 121 bpm

90% intensity: 0.90 × 186 = 167 bpm

Base your duration of swimming on your intensity and target calorie costs. Swim at least three times a week.

Calorie cost: Calories burned while swimming are the result of the pace: how far you swim and how fast (Table 5). Work up to using at least 300 calories per session.

At the beginning: If you are an inexperienced swimmer, invest in the time and money for instruction. You'll make more rapid gains in fitness if you learn correct swimming technique. If you've been sedentary and haven't done any swimming for a long time, begin your program with 2–3 weeks, three times a week, of leisurely swimming at a pace that keeps your heart rate 10–20% below your target zone. Start swimming laps of the width of the pool if you can't swim the length. To keep your heart rate below target, take rest intervals as needed. Swim one lap, then rest 15–90 seconds as needed. Start with 10 minutes of swim/rest intervals and work up to 20 minutes. How long it takes will depend on your swimming skills and muscular fitness.

As you progress: Gradually increase the duration, or the intensity, or both duration and intensity of your swimming to raise your heart rate to a comfortable level within your target zone. Gradually increase your swimming intervals and decrease your rest intervals as you progress. Once you can swim the length of the pool at a pace that keeps your heart rate on target, continue swim/rest intervals for 20 minutes. Your rest intervals should be 30–45 seconds. You may find it helpful to get out of the pool during your rest intervals and walk until you've lowered your heart rate. Next, swim two laps of the pool length per swim interval and

SAMPLE PROGRAM TABLE 5 *Calorie Costs for Swimming*

To use this table, find on the top horizontal row the distance in yards that most closely approximates the distance you swim. Next, locate on the appropriate vertical column (below the distance in yards) the time it takes you to swim the distance. Then locate in the first column on the left the approximate number of calories burned per minute per pound for the time and distance. To find the total number of calories burned, multiply your weight by the calories per minute per pound. Then multiply the product of these two numbers by the time it takes you to swim the distance (minutes:seconds). For example, assuming you weigh 130 pounds and swim 500 yards in 20 minutes, you would burn 106 calories: 130 × .041 (calories per pound, from table) = 5.33 × 20 (minutes) = 106 calories burned.

Calories per Minute per Pound	Distance (yd)					
	25	100	150	250	500	750
.033	1:15	5:00	7:30	12:30	25:00	30:30
.041	1:00	4:00	6:00	10:00	20:00	30:00
.049	0:50	3:20	5:00	8:20	18:40	25:00
.057	0:43	2:52	4:18	7:10	17:20	21:30
.065	0:37.5	2:30	3:45	6:15	10:00	
.073	0:33	2:13	3:20	5:30	8:50	
.081	0:30	2:00	3:00	5:00	8:00	
.090	0:27	1:48	2:42	4:30	7:12	
.097	0:25	1:40	2:30	4:10	6:30	

SOURCE: Kusinitz, I., and M. Fine, *Physical Fitness for Practically Everybody*, Consumer Reports®, 1983. Consumers Union of the U.S., Inc., Yonkers, NY 10703-1057, a nonprofit organization. Reprinted with permission for educational purposes only. No commercial use or reproduction permitted. www.ConsumerReports.org®.

continue swim/rest intervals for 30 minutes. For the 30-second rest interval, walk (or rest) until you've lowered your heart rate. Gradually increase the number of laps you swim consecutively and the total duration of your session until you reach your target calorie expenditure and fitness level. But take care not to swim at too fast a pace: It can raise your heart rate too high and limit your ability to sustain your swimming. Alternating strokes can rest your muscles and help prolong your swimming time. A variety of strokes will also let you work more muscle groups. You can also vary your program by incorporating kick boards, pull-buoys, hand paddles, or fins into some of your workouts.

Developing Muscular Strength and Endurance

The swimming program outlined in this section will result in moderate gains in strength and large gains in endurance in the muscles used during the strokes you've chosen. To develop strength and endurance in all the muscles of the body, you need to include resistance training as part of your fitness program. Use the general wellness weight training program from Chapter 4, or tailor one to fit your personal fitness goals. To improve your swimming performance, include exercises that work key muscles. For example, if you swim primarily front crawl, include exercises to increase strength in your shoulders, arms, and upper back. (Training the muscles you use during swimming can also help prevent injuries.) Regardless of which strength training exercise you include in your program, follow the general guidelines for successful training:

- Train 2–3 nonconsecutive days per week.
- Perform 1 or more sets of 8–12 repetitions of 8–10 exercises.
- Include exercises that work all the major muscle groups: neck, shoulders, chest, arms, upper and lower back, abdomen, thighs, and calves.

Depending on the amount of time you have for exercise, you might want to schedule your cardiorespiratory endurance workouts and your muscular strength and endurance workouts on alternate days. In other words, swim one day and strength train the next day.

Developing Flexibility

For a complete fitness program, you also need to include exercises that develop flexibility. The best time for a flexibility workout is when your muscles are warm, as they are immediately following cardiorespiratory endurance exercise or strength training. Perform the stretching routine presented in Chapter 5 or one you have created to meet your own goals and preferences. Be sure to pay special attention to the muscles you use during swimming, particularly the shoulders and back. As you put your program together, remember the basic structure of a successful flexibility program:

- Stretch at least 2–3 days per week (ideally 5–7 days per week), preferably when muscles are warm.
- Stretch all the major muscle groups.
- Stretch to the point of mild discomfort and hold for 15–30 seconds.
- Repeat each stretch 2–4 times.

IN-LINE SKATING SAMPLE PROGRAM

In-line skating is convenient and inexpensive (after the initial outlay for equipment); it can be done on city streets, on paved bike paths and trails, and in parks. If done intensively enough, skating can provide a cardiorespiratory endurance workout comparable to the workouts provided by jogging and cycling. Studies indicate that skating consumes about as many calories as jogging. An advantage of skating over jogging is that skating is low impact, so it is less harmful to the knees and ankles. An advantage of skating over bicycling is that it works the hamstring muscle in the back of the thigh. Skating develops lower-body strength and endurance, working all the muscles of the leg and hip and strengthening the muscles and connective tissues surrounding the ankles, knees, and hips.

Equipment

To skate safely and enjoyably, you will need a pair of comfortable, sturdy, quality skates and adequate safety equipment. The skate consists of a hard polyurethane shell or outer boot; a padded foam liner; and a frame or chassis that holds the wheels, bearings, spacers, and brake. If you want to try out the sport before making a commitment, rent your skates and equipment from a skate shop. If you are buying, plan to spend about $110–$200 for skates that meet the basic needs of most recreational skaters. Shop for the best combination of price, quality, comfort, and service.

Essential safety equipment includes a helmet, elbow pads, knee pads, and wrist guards. (Wrist injuries are the most common in-line skating injury.) You may want to put reflective tape on your skates for those occasions when you don't get home before dark. Carry moleskin or adhesive bandages with you in case you start to develop a blister while skating. (For more on safety, see Appendix A.)

Technique

In-line skating uses many of the skills and techniques of ice skating, roller skating, and skiing, so if you have ever participated in any of those activities, you will probably take to in-line skating fairly readily. Many people begin without instruction, but instruction will allow you to progress more quickly.

To begin, center your weight equally over both skates, bend your knees slightly so your nose, knees, and toes are all in the same line, and look straight ahead. Keep your weight forward over the balls of your feet; don't lean back.

To skate, use a stroke, glide, stroke, glide rhythm (rather than a series of quick, short strokes). Push with one leg while gliding with the other. Shift your body weight back and forth so it is always centered over the gliding skate.

To stop, use your brake, located on the back of the right skate in most skates. With knees bent and arms extended in front of your body, move the right foot forward, shift your weight to your left leg, and lift your right toe until the brake pad touches the ground and stops you. An alternative stop is the T-stop, in which you drag one skate behind the other at a 90-degree angle to the direction of your forward motion.

If you lose your balance and are about to fall, lower your center of gravity by bending at the waist and putting your hands on your knees. If you can't regain your balance, try to fall forward, directing the impact to your wrist guards and knee pads. Try not to fall backward.

Again, instruction can help you learn many moves and techniques that will make the sport safer and more enjoyable.

Developing Cardiorespiratory Endurance

Studies have shown that in-line skaters raise their heart rates and oxygen consumption comparably to joggers, bicyclers, and walkers. Skaters reached 60–75% of $\dot{V}O_{2max}$ by skating continuously (not pushing off and gliding for several seconds) at 10.6–12.5 mph for 20–30 minutes. It may be difficult for recreational skaters to safely skate this fast for this long, however, given the typical constraints of city and suburban streets. Experts suggest skating uphill as much as possible to reach the

SAMPLE PROGRAM TABLE 6 *Calorie Costs for In-Line Skating*

To estimate the number of calories you burn, first determine your approximate speed (use the Minutes: Seconds per Mile column if necessary), multiply the calories per minute per pound by your weight, and then multiply that figure by the number of minutes you skate. For example, assuming you weigh 145 pounds and skate at 10 mph for 30 minutes, you would burn 273 calories: 145 × .063 (calories per pound, from table) = 9.1 × 30 (minutes) = 273 calories burned. Calculations are approximate.

Speed		
Miles per Hour	Minutes:Seconds per Mile	Calories per Minute per Pound
8	7:30	.041
9	6:40	.053
10	6:00	.063
11	5:25	.072
12	5:00	.084
13	4:35	.095
14	4:20	.105
15	4:00	.115

SOURCES: Adapted from International Inline Skating Association. 1999. *Health Benefits of Inline Skating* (http://www.iisa.org/numbers/health.htm, retrieved April 7, 2000); Wallick, M. E., et al. 1995. Physiological responses to in-line skating compared to treadmill running. *Medicine and Science in Sports and Exercise* 27(2): 242–248.

level of intensity that builds cardiorespiratory endurance. If you can reach and maintain higher speeds in parks or on paved paths, do so, but always skate safely.

FIT—frequency, intensity, and time: Start your early skating sessions at a pace that keeps your heart rate about 10–20% below your target zone. Skate for 5–10 minutes, and then check your heart rate. Increase your speed gradually until you can skate at about 10 miles per hour (6 minutes per mile). Use your pulse as a guide to speed, aiming for 65% of your target heart rate zone. To achieve cardiorespiratory benefits, you will have to skate at a continuous and relatively intense pace for at least 20 minutes three times a week. The more fit you are, the more intensively you will need to skate to reach your target heart rate.

Calorie cost: Use Table 6 to determine the approximate number of calories you burn during each outing. You can increase the number of calories burned by skating faster, for a longer time, or uphill.

At the beginning: If you are a beginner, practice skating in an empty schoolyard or parking lot. As you become confident with the basic techniques, move on to streets, parks, and paved bike trails. Maintain an easy pace, alternating stroking and gliding.

Begin each outing with a 5- to 10-minute warm-up of walking, jogging, or even slow skating. Once your muscles are warm, you can do some stretches to help loosen and warm up the primary muscles used during skating. These muscles include the quadriceps, hamstrings, buttocks, hips, groin, ankles, calves, and lower back. You can also save the stretches for the end of the workout.

To launch an in-line skating fitness program, aim for slow, long-distance workouts at first. Start by skating for 15 minutes and gradually increase your sessions to 20–30 minutes of continuous skating (about 3.5–5 miles). Try to skate about 20 miles a week, or 5 miles a day (about 30 minutes) 4 days a week.

As you progress: After the first week or two, add about a mile a day, up to 40 miles per week (60 minutes a day). To increase intensity, add some hills, sprints (bursts of short, rapid striding), and interval training (periods of intensive exercise at your target heart rate alternating with timed rest periods when your heart rate drops below your target zone). Try to skate 30–60 minutes a day four or more times a week.

The harder and faster you skate, the more intensive your workout will be and the more your cardiorespiratory endurance and muscular strength will improve. The longer and more often you skate, the more your endurance will increase.

Developing Muscular Strength and Endurance

In-line skating develops the muscles in the entire upper leg, buttocks, and hip; lower back; and upper arms and shoulders when arms are swung vigorously. To make greater gains in lower-body strength and to develop the entire upper body, include resistance training in your overall fitness program. Use the general wellness weight training program from Chapter 4, or tailor one to fit your personal fitness goals. No matter which exercises you include in your program, follow the general guidelines for successful and safe training:

- Train 2–3 nonconsecutive days per week.

- Perform 1 or more sets of 8–12 repetitions of 8–10 exercises.

- Include exercises that work all the major muscle groups: neck, shoulders, chest, arms, upper and lower back, thighs, and calves.

Depending on your schedule, you may find it more convenient to skate and strength train on alternate days.

Developing Flexibility

The best times for a flexibility workout are when your muscles are warm, so stretch after a short warm-up at the beginning of your skating session, or after your skating session, or after a weight training session. Use the stretching routine presented in Chapter 5, or develop one that meets your own goals and preferences. Pay particular attention to your quadriceps, hamstrings, buttocks, hips, groin, ankles, calves, and lower back. Remember these basic guidelines:

- Stretch at least 2–3 days per week (ideally 5–7 days per week), preferably when muscles are warm.

- Stretch all the major muscle groups.

- Stretch to the point of mild discomfort and hold for 15–30 seconds.

- Repeat each stretch 2–4 times.

Name _____   Section _____   Date _____

LAB 7.1   *A Personal Fitness Program Plan and Contract*

A. I, _____, am contracting with myself to follow a physical fitness pro-
        (name)

gram to work toward the following goals:

Specific or short-term goals (include current status for each)

1. _____

2. _____

3. _____

4. _____

General or long-term goals

1. _____

2. _____

3. _____

4. _____

B. My program plan is as follows:

Activities	Components (Check ✓)					Frequency (Check ✓)							Intensity*	Time (duration)
	CRE	MS	ME	F	BC	M	Tu	W	Th	F	Sa	Su		

*Conduct activities for achieving CRE goals in your target range for heart rate or RPE.

C. My program will begin on _____. My program includes the following schedule of mini-goals. For each step
                              (date)

in my program, I will give myself the reward listed.

_____	_____	_____
(mini-goal 1)	(date)	(reward)
_____	_____	_____
(mini-goal 2)	(date)	(reward)
_____	_____	_____
(mini-goal 3)	(date)	(reward)
_____	_____	_____
(mini-goal 4)	(date)	(reward)
_____	_____	_____
(mini-goal 5)	(date)	(reward)

D. My program will include the addition of physical activity to my daily routine (such as climbing stairs or walking to class):

1. _____

2. _____

3. _____

4. _____

5. _____

E. I will use the following tools to monitor my program and my progress toward my goals:

_____

(list any charts, graphs, or journals you plan to use)

_____

_____

I sign this contract as an indication of my personal commitment to reach my goal.

_____   _____
(your signature)   (date)

I have recruited a helper who will witness my contract and _____

_____

(list any way your helper will participate in your program)

_____

_____   _____
(witness's signature)   (date)

LAB 7.2 *Getting to Know Your Fitness Facility*

To help create a successful training program, take time out to learn more about the fitness facility you plan to use.

Basic Information

Name and location of facility: _____

Hours of operation: _____

Times available for general use: _____

Times most convenient for your schedule: _____

Can you obtain an initial session or consultation with a trainer to help you create a program? _____ yes _____ no

If so, what does the initial planning session involve? _____

_____

Are any of the staff certified? Do any have special training? If yes, list/describe: _____

_____

What types of equipment are available for the development of cardiorespiratory endurance? Briefly list/describe:

_____

_____

_____

Are any group activities or classes available? If so, briefly describe: _____

_____

_____

What types of weight training equipment are available for use? _____

_____

Yes	No	
____	____	Is there a fee for using the facility? If so, how much? $ _____
____	____	Is a student ID required for access to the facility?
____	____	Do you need to sign up in advance to use the facility or any of the equipment?
____	____	Is there typically a line or wait to use the equipment during the times you use the facility?
____	____	Is there a separate area with mats for stretching and/or cool-down?
____	____	Do you need to bring your own towel?
____	____	Are lockers available? If so, do you need to bring your own lock? _____ yes _____ no
____	____	Are showers available? If so, do you need to bring your own soap and shampoo? _____ yes _____ no
____	____	Is drinking water available? (If not, be sure to bring your own bottle of water.)

Describe any other amenities, such as vending machines or saunas, that are available at the facility.

_____

_____

Information About Equipment

Fill in the specific equipment and exercise(s) that you can use to develop cardiorespiratory endurance and each of the major muscle groups. For cardiorespiratory endurance, list the type(s) of equipment and a sample starting workout: frequency, intensity, time, and other pertinent information (such as a setting for resistance or speed). For muscular strength and endurance, list the equipment and exercises, and indicate the order in which you'll complete them during a workout session (see p. 104 for suggestions on order of weight training exercises).

Cardiorespiratory Endurance Equipment

Equipment	Sample Starting Workout

Muscular Strength and Endurance Equipment

Order	Muscle Groups	Equipment	Exercises(s)
	Neck		
	Chest		
	Shoulders		
	Upper back		
	Front of arms		
	Back of arms		
	Buttocks		
	Abdomen		
	Lower back		
	Front of thighs		
	Back of thighs		
	Calves		
	Other:		
	Other:		

LABORATORY ACTIVITIES

Looking AHEAD

After reading this chapter, you should be able to

- List the essential nutrients and describe the functions they perform in the body
- Describe the guidelines that have been developed to help people choose a healthy diet, avoid nutritional deficiencies, and protect themselves from diet-related chronic diseases
- Discuss nutritional guidelines for vegetarians and for special population groups
- Explain how to use food labels and other consumer tools to make informed choices about foods
- Put together a personal nutrition plan based on affordable foods that you enjoy and that will promote wellness, today and in the future

8

Nutrition

Test Your Knowledge

1. **It is recommended that all adults consume one to two servings each of fruits and vegetables every day.**
   True or false?

2. **Candy is the leading source of added sugars in the American diet.**
   True or false?

3. **Which of the following is NOT a whole grain?**
   a. brown rice
   b. wheat flour
   c. popcorn

ANSWERS

1. FALSE. For someone consuming 2000 calories, a minimum of nine servings per day—four of fruits and five of vegetables—is recommended, the equivalent of 4½ cups per day. Most Americans fail to meet this goal; half of all the vegetables we do eat are potatoes—and half of those are french fried.

2. FALSE. Regular (nondiet) sodas are the leading source, with an average of 55 gallons consumed per person per year. Each 12-ounce soda supplies about 10 teaspoons of sugar, or nearly 10% of the calories in a 2000-calorie diet. On average, Americans consume more than 140 pounds of sugar and sweeteners per year.

3. B. Unless labeled "whole wheat," wheat flour is processed to remove the bran and germ and is not a whole grain.

VW *Fit and Well* **Online Learning Center**   www.mhhe.com/fahey

Visit the *Fit and Well* Online Learning Center for study aids, online labs, additional information about nutrition, links, Internet activities that explore the role of nutrition in wellness, and much more.

In your lifetime, you'll spend about 6 years eating—about 70,000 meals and 60 tons of food. What you eat affects your energy level, well-being, and overall health (see the box "Eating Habits and Total Wellness"). Of particular concern is the connection between lifetime nutritional habits and risk of the major chronic diseases, including heart disease, cancer, stroke, and diabetes. Choosing foods that provide adequate amounts of the nutrients you need while limiting the substances linked to disease should be an important part of your daily life. The food choices you make will significantly influence your health—both now and in the future.

Choosing a healthy diet that supports maximum fitness and protects against disease is a two-part project. First, you have to know which nutrients are necessary and in what amounts. Second, you have to translate those requirements into a diet consisting of foods you like to eat that are both available and affordable. Once you have an idea of what constitutes a healthy diet for you, you may also have to make adjustments in your current diet to bring it into line with your goals.

This chapter provides the basic principles of **nutrition.** It introduces the six classes of essential nutrients, explaining their role in the functioning of the body. It also provides different sets of guidelines that you can use to design a healthy diet plan. Finally, it offers practical tools and advice to help you apply the guidelines to your life. Diet is an area of your life in which you have almost total control. Using your knowledge and understanding of nutrition to create a healthy diet plan is a significant step toward wellness.

NUTRITIONAL REQUIREMENTS: COMPONENTS OF A HEALTHY DIET

When you think about your diet, you probably do so in terms of the foods you like to eat—a turkey sandwich and a glass of milk, or black beans and rice. What's important

for your health, though, are the nutrients contained in those foods. Your body requires proteins, fats, carbohydrates, vitamins, minerals, and water—about 45 **essential nutrients.** The word *essential* in this context means that you must get these substances from food because your body is unable to manufacture them at all, or at least not fast enough to meet your physiological needs. The six classes of nutrients, along with their functions and major sources, are listed in Table 8.1.

Nutrients are released into the body by the process of **digestion,** which breaks them down into compounds that the gastrointestinal tract can absorb and the body can use (Figure 8.1, p. 230). A diet containing adequate amounts of all essential nutrients is vital because various nutrients provide energy, build and maintain body tissues, and regulate body functions. Some essential nutrients are needed by the body in relatively large amounts. These **macronutrients** include protein, fat, and carbohydrate. **Micronutrients,** such as vitamins and minerals, are required in much smaller amounts.

The energy in foods is expressed as **kilocalories.** One kilocalorie represents the amount of heat it takes to raise the temperature of 1 liter of water 1°C. A person needs about 2000 kilocalories a day to meet energy needs. In common usage, people usually refer to kilocalories as *calories,* which is a much smaller energy unit: 1 kilocalorie contains 1000 calories. We'll use the familiar word *calorie* in this chapter to stand for the larger energy unit; you'll also find *calorie* used on food labels.

Of the six classes of essential nutrients, three supply energy:

- Fat = 9 calories per gram
- Protein = 4 calories per gram
- Carbohydrate = 4 calories per gram

(Alcohol, although it is not an essential nutrient, also supplies energy, providing 7 calories per gram.) The high caloric content of fat is one reason experts often advise against high fat consumption; most of us do not need the extra calories to meet energy needs. Regardless of their source, calories consumed in excess of energy needs are converted to fat and stored in the body.

Terms

Vⁱⁱw

nutrition The science of food and how the body uses it in health and disease.

essential nutrients Substances the body must get from food because it cannot manufacture them at all or fast enough to meet its needs. These nutrients include proteins, fats, carbohydrates, vitamins, minerals, and water.

digestion The process of breaking down foods in the gastrointestinal tract into compounds the body can absorb.

macronutrients Essential nutrients required by the body in relatively large amounts.

micronutrients Essential nutrients required by the body in minute amounts.

kilocalorie A measure of energy content in food; 1 kilocalorie represents the amount of heat needed to raise the temperature of 1 liter of water 1°C; commonly referred to as *calorie.*

Healthy eating does more than nourish your body—it enhances your ability to enjoy life to the fullest by improving overall wellness, both physical and mental. One study examined a group of adults who followed a healthy eating plan for four years. At the end of this period, the study subjects were more confident with their food choices and more satisfied with their lives in general than their peers who did not make any dietary changes. The reverse is also true—when people overeat they often have feelings of guilt, anger, discouragement, and even self-loathing. Out-of-control eating can erode self-confidence and lead to depression. How we eat is a reflection of how we feel about ourselves. Enjoying food and eating well is a major part of a healthy and happy life.

Can individual foods affect the way we feel? Limited scientific evidence points to some correlation between certain foods and one's mood. Many people, especially women, seem to crave chocolate when they are "blue." Studies show that chocolate, in small quantities, may indeed give you a lift. Sugary foods tend to temporarily raise serotonin levels in the brain, which can improve mood (serotonin is a neurotransmitter associ-

ated with a calm, relaxed state). The fat found in chocolate acts to increase endorphins, brain chemicals that reduce pain and increase feelings of well-being. Chocolate also contains caffeine, theobromine, phenylethylamine, and a variety of other less studied chemicals that may have a positive impact on mood.

A commonly held belief about the connection between food and the mind is that eating sugary foods makes people (especially children) hyperactive. Parents often comment on the wild behavior observed at parties and festive events where lots of sweets are consumed. However, several carefully controlled studies showed no correlation between behavior and the consumption of sugary foods. Researchers speculate that high-sugar foods tend to be eaten at birthday parties and other exciting occasions when children tend to be highly stimulated regardless of what they eat.

Some recent research shows that eating certain carbohydrate-rich foods, such as a plain baked potato or a bagel with jelly, can have a temporary calming effect. Scientists postulate that this occurs because carbohydrates stimulate insulin release, which improves the transport of the amino acid tryptophan (the major building block for serotonin) into the

brain. This effect is most pronounced when rapidly digestible carbohydrates are consumed alone, with no fats or proteins in the meal. The practical implications of this research are uncertain.

If you are looking for a mental boost, some scientists think that eating a meal consisting primarily of protein-rich foods may be helpful. The theory is that proteins contain the amino acid tyrosine, which is used by the body to manufacture the neurotransmitters dopamine and norepinephrine. Some researchers postulate that eating protein-rich foods could increase the synthesis of these neurotransmitters, which can speed reaction time and increase alertness. Whether this really works, especially in well-nourished individuals who have not been lacking these nutrients to begin with, remains to be seen. In the meantime, it wouldn't hurt, and might even help, to include some protein in the meal you eat prior to your next big exam.

What we know about how food affects mood remains limited. But evidence points to the commonsense conclusion that enjoying reasonable portions of a variety of healthy and tasty foods is a great way to optimize your physical and mental health.

Table 8.1	The Six Classes of Essential Nutrients	
Nutrient	**Function**	**Major Sources**
Proteins (4 calories/gram)	Form important parts of muscles, bone, blood, enzymes, some hormones, and cell membranes; repair tissue; regulate water and acid-base balance; help in growth; supply energy	Meat, fish, poultry, eggs, milk products, legumes, nuts
Carbohydrates (4 calories/gram)	Supply energy to cells in brain, nervous system, and blood; supply energy to muscles during exercise	Grains (breads and cereals), fruits, vegetables, milk
Fats (9 calories/gram)	Supply energy; insulate, support, and cushion organs; provide medium for absorption of fat-soluble vitamins	Animal foods, grains, nuts, seeds, fish, vegetables
Vitamins	Promote (initiate or speed up) specific chemical reactions within cells	Abundant in fruits, vegetables, and grains; also found in meat and dairy products
Minerals	Help regulate body functions; aid in the growth and maintenance of body tissues; act as catalysts for the release of energy	Found in most food groups
Water	Makes up 50–70% of body weight; provides a medium for chemical reactions; transports chemicals; regulates temperature; removes waste products	Fruits, vegetables, and liquids

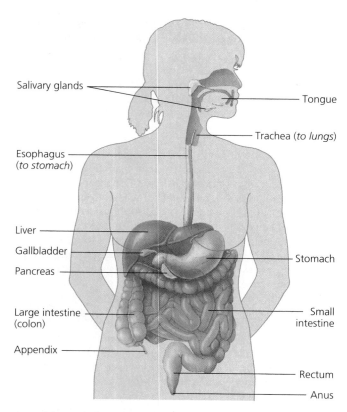

Salivary glands

Tongue

Trachea (*to lungs*)

Esophagus
(*to stomach*)

Liver

Gallbladder

Pancreas

Stomach

Large intestine
(colon)

Small
intestine

Appendix

Rectum

Anus

Figure 8.1 The digestive system. Food is partially broken down by being chewed and mixed with saliva in the mouth. As food moves through the digestive tract, it is mixed by muscular contractions and broken down by chemicals. After traveling to the stomach via the esophagus, food is broken down further by stomach acids. Most absorption of nutrients occurs in the small intestine, aided by secretions from the pancreas, gallbladder, and intestinal lining. The large intestine reabsorbs excess water; the remaining solid wastes are collected in the rectum and excreted through the anus.

But just meeting energy needs is not enough; our bodies need adequate amounts of all the essential nutrients to grow and function properly. Practically all foods contain mixtures of nutrients, although foods are commonly classified according to their predominant nutrients. For example, spaghetti is considered a carbohydrate food although it contains small amounts of other nutrients. Let's take a closer look at the functions and sources of the six classes of nutrients.

Proteins—The Basis of Body Structure

Proteins form important parts of the body's main structural components: muscles and bones. Proteins also form important parts of blood, enzymes, cell membranes, and some hormones. As mentioned above, protein can also provide energy at 4 calories per gram of protein weight.

Amino Acids The building blocks of proteins are called **amino acids.** Twenty common amino acids are found in food; nine of these are essential: histidine, iso-

leucine, leucine, lysine, methionine, phenylalanine, threonine, tryptophan, and valine. The other eleven amino acids can be produced by the body as long as the necessary components are supplied by foods.

Complete and Incomplete Proteins Individual protein sources are considered "complete" if they supply all the essential amino acids in adequate amounts and "incomplete" if they do not. Meat, fish, poultry, eggs, milk, cheese, and soy provide complete proteins. Incomplete proteins, which come from plant sources such as **legumes** and nuts, are good sources of most essential amino acids, but are usually low in one or two.

Combining two vegetable proteins, such as wheat and peanuts in a peanut butter sandwich, allows each vegetable protein to make up for the amino acids missing in the other protein. The combination yields a complete protein. Your concern with amino acids and complete protein in your diet should focus on what you consume throughout the day, rather than at each meal. It was once believed that vegetarians had to "complement" their proteins at each meal in order to receive the benefit of a complete protein. It is now known, however, that proteins consumed throughout the course of the day can complement each other to form a pool of amino acids from which the body can draw to produce the necessary proteins. Vegetarians should include a variety of vegetable protein sources in their diets to make sure they get all the essential amino acids in adequate amounts. (Healthy vegetarian diets are discussed later in the chapter.)

Recommended Protein Intake Adequate daily intake of protein for adults is 0.8 gram per kilogram (0.36 gram per pound) of body weight, corresponding to 50 grams of protein per day for someone who weighs 140 pounds and 65 grams of protein for someone who weighs 180 pounds. This amount of protein is easily obtained from popular foods: 3 ounces of lean meat, poultry, or fish or ½ cup of tofu contains about 20–25 grams of protein; 1 cup of legumes such as pinto and kidney beans, 15–20 grams; 1 cup of milk or yogurt or 1½ ounces of cheese, 8–12 grams; and cereals, grains, nuts, and vegetables, about 2–4 grams of protein per serving.

Most Americans meet or exceed the protein intake needed for adequate nutrition. Protein consumed beyond what the body needs is synthesized into fat for energy storage or burned for energy requirements. Consuming somewhat above our needs is not harmful, but it does contribute fat to the diet because protein-rich foods are often fat-rich as well. A very high protein intake can strain the kidneys and lead to dehydration. A fairly broad range of protein intake is associated with good health, and the Food and Nutrition Board of the National Academies recommends that the amount adults eat should fall within the range of 10–35% of the total daily calorie intake. The average American diet includes about 15–16% of total daily

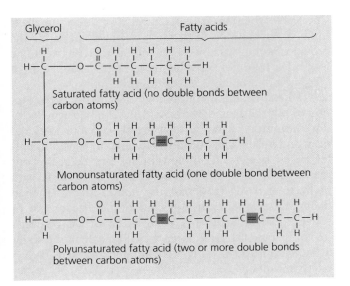

Figure 8.2 Chemical structures of saturated and unsaturated fatty acids. This example of a triglyceride consists of a molecule of glycerol with three fatty acids attached. Fatty acids can differ in the length of their carbon chains and their degree of saturation.

calories as protein. (See Chapter 9 for more information about high-protein diets advocated for weight loss.)

Fats—Essential in Small Amounts

Fats, also known as lipids, are the most concentrated source of energy, at 9 calories per gram. The fats stored in your body represent usable energy, help insulate your body, and support and cushion your organs. Fats in the diet help your body absorb fat-soluble vitamins and add important flavor and texture to foods. Fats are the major fuel for the body during periods of rest and light activity. Two fats—linoleic acid and alpha-linolenic acid—are essential to the diet; they are key regulators of such body functions as the maintenance of blood pressure and the progress of a healthy pregnancy.

Types and Sources of Fats Most of the fats in food are in the form of triglycerides, which are composed of a glycerine molecule (an alcohol) plus three fatty acids. A fatty acid is made up of a chain of carbon atoms with oxygen attached at the end and hydrogen atoms attached along the length of the chain. Fatty acids differ in the length of their carbon atom chains and in their degree of saturation (the number of hydrogens attached to the chain). If every available bond from each carbon atom in a fatty acid chain is attached to a hydrogen atom, the fatty acid is said to be **saturated** (Figure 8.2). If not all the available bonds are taken up by hydrogens, the carbon atoms in the chain will form double bonds with each other. Such fatty acids are called unsaturated fats. If there is only one double bond, the fatty acid is called **monounsaturated.** If there are two or more double bonds, the

fatty acid is called **polyunsaturated.** The essential fatty acids, linoleic and alpha-linolenic acids, are both polyunsaturated. The different types of fatty acids have different characteristics and different effects on your health.

Food fats are often composed of both saturated and unsaturated fatty acids; the dominant type of fatty acid determines the fat's characteristics. Food fats containing large amounts of saturated fatty acids are usually solid at room temperature; they are generally found naturally in animal products. The leading sources of saturated fat in the American diet are red meats (hamburger, steak, roasts), whole milk, cheese, and hot dogs and lunch meats. Food fats containing large amounts of monounsaturated and polyunsaturated fatty acids are usually from plant sources and are liquid at room temperature. Olive, canola, safflower, and peanut oils contain mostly monounsaturated fatty acids. Corn, soybean, and cottonseed oils contain mostly polyunsaturated fatty acids.

There are notable exceptions to these generalizations. When unsaturated vegetable oils undergo the process of **hydrogenation,** a mixture of saturated and unsaturated fatty acids is produced. Hydrogenation turns many of the double bonds in unsaturated fatty acids into single bonds, increasing the degree of saturation and producing a more solid fat from a liquid oil. Hydrogenation also changes some unsaturated fatty acids into **trans fatty acids,** unsaturated fatty acids with an atypical shape that affects their behavior in the body. Food manufacturers use hydrogenation to increase the stability of an oil so it can be reused for deep frying; to improve the texture of certain foods (to make pastries and pie crusts flakier, for example); and to extend the shelf life of foods made with oil. Hydrogenation is also used to transform liquid vegetable oils into margarine or shortening.

Terms

protein An essential nutrient; a compound made of amino acids that contains carbon, hydrogen, oxygen, and nitrogen.

amino acids The building blocks of proteins.

legumes Vegetables such as peas and beans that are high in fiber and are also important sources of protein.

saturated fat A fat with no carbon-carbon double bonds; usually solid at room temperature.

monounsaturated fat A fat with one carbon-carbon double bond; liquid at room temperature.

polyunsaturated fat A fat containing two or more carbon-carbon double bonds; liquid at room temperature.

hydrogenation A process by which hydrogens are added to unsaturated fats, increasing the degree of saturation and turning liquid oils into solid fats. Hydrogenation produces a mixture of saturated fatty acids and standard and trans forms of unsaturated fatty acids.

trans fatty acid A type of unsaturated fatty acid produced during the process of hydrogenation; trans fats have an atypical shape that affects their chemical activity.

Many baked and fried foods are prepared with hydrogenated vegetable oils, so they can be relatively high in saturated and trans fatty acids. Leading sources of trans fats in the American diet are deep-fried fast foods such as french fries and fried chicken (typically fried in vegetable shortening rather than oil); baked and snack foods such as pot pies, cakes, cookies, pastries, doughnuts, and chips; and stick margarine. In general, the more solid a hydrogenated oil is, the more saturated and trans fats it contains; for example, stick margarines typically contain more saturated and trans fats than do tub or squeeze margarines. Small amounts of trans fatty acids are also found naturally in meat and milk.

Hydrogenated vegetable oils are not the only plant fats that contain saturated fats. Palm and coconut oils, although derived from plants, are also highly saturated. Yet fish oils, derived from an animal source, are rich in polyunsaturated fats.

Fats and Health   Different types of fats have very different effects on health. Many studies have examined the effects of dietary fat intake on blood **cholesterol** levels and the risk of heart disease. Saturated and trans fatty acids raise blood levels of **low-density lipoprotein (LDL)**, or "bad" cholesterol, thereby increasing a person's risk of heart disease. Unsaturated fatty acids, on the other hand, lower LDL. Monounsaturated fatty acids, such as those found in olive and canola oils, may also increase levels of **high-density lipoproteins (HDL)**, or "good" cholesterol, providing even greater benefits for heart health. In large amounts, trans fatty acids may lower HDL. Thus, to reduce the risk of heart disease, it is important to choose unsaturated fats instead of saturated and trans fats. (See Chapter 11 for more on cholesterol and a heart-healthy diet.)

Most Americans consume more saturated fat than trans fat (12% versus 2–4% of total daily calories). However, health experts are particularly concerned about trans fats because of their double negative effect on heart health—they both raise LDL and lower HDL—and because there is less public awareness of trans fats. The saturated fat content of prepared foods has been listed on nutrition labels since 1994; the trans fat content wasn't required on labels until January 2006. Consumers can also check for the presence of trans fats by examining the ingredient list of a food: If a food contains "partially hydrogenated oil" or "vegetable shortening," it contains trans fat.

For heart health, it's important to limit your consumption of both saturated and trans fats. The best way to reduce saturated fat in your diet is to lower your intake of meat and full-fat dairy products (whole milk, cream, butter, cheese, ice cream). To lower trans fats, decrease your intake of deep-fried foods and baked goods made with hydrogenated vegetable oils; use liquid oils rather than margarine or shortening for cooking; and favor tub or squeeze margarines or those labeled low-trans or trans-free over standard stick margarines. Remember, the softer or more liquid a fat is, the less saturated and trans fat it is likely to contain.

Although saturated and trans fats pose health hazards, other fats are beneficial. Monounsaturated fatty acids, as found in avocados, most nuts, and olive, canola, peanut, and safflower oils, improve cholesterol levels and may help protect against some cancers. **Omega-3 fatty acids,** a form of polyunsaturated fat found primarily in fish, may be even more healthful. An omega-3 fatty acid has its endmost double bond three carbons from the end of the fatty acid chain. (The polyunsaturated fatty acid shown in Figure 8.2 is an omega-3 form.) Omega-3s and the compounds the body makes from them have a number of heart-healthy effects: They reduce the tendency of blood to clot, inhibit inflammation and abnormal heart rhythms, and reduce blood pressure and risk of heart attack and stroke in some people. Because of these benefits, nutritionists recommend that Americans increase the proportion of omega-3s in their diet by eating fish two or more times a week. Salmon, tuna, trout, mackerel, herring, sardines, and anchovies are all good sources of omega-3s; lesser amounts are found in plant sources, including dark green leafy vegetables; walnuts; flaxseeds; and canola, walnut, and flaxseed oils.

Another form of polyunsaturated fat, omega-6 fatty acid, has its endmost double bond at the sixth carbon atom. Most of the polyunsaturated fats currently consumed by Americans are omega-6s, primarily from corn oil and soybean oil. Foods rich in omega-6s are important because they contain the essential nutrient linoleic acid. However, some nutritionists recommend that people reduce the proportion of omega-6s they consume in favor of omega-3s. To make this adjustment, use canola oil rather than corn oil in cooking, and check for corn, soybean, or cottonseed oil in products such as mayonnaise, margarine, and salad dressing.

In addition to its effects on heart disease risk, dietary fat can affect health in other ways. Diets high in fatty red meat are associated with an increased risk of certain forms of cancer, especially colon cancer. A high-fat diet can also make weight management more difficult. Because fat is a

Terms

cholesterol A waxy substance found in the blood and cells and needed for cell membranes, vitamin D, and hormone synthesis.

low-density lipoprotein (LDL) Blood fat that transports cholesterol to organs and tissues; excess amounts result in the accumulation of fatty deposits on artery walls.

high-density lipoprotein (HDL) Blood fat that helps transport cholesterol out of the arteries, thereby protecting against heart disease.

omega-3 fatty acids Polyunsaturated fatty acids commonly found in fish oils that are beneficial to cardiovascular health; the endmost double bond occurs three carbons from the end of the fatty acid chain.

	Type of Fatty Acid	Found In[a]	Possible Effects o...
Keep Intake Low	SATURATED	Animal fats (especially fatty meats and poultry fat and skin) Butter, cheese, and other high-fat dairy products Palm and coconut oils	Raises total cholesterol and L... levels Increases risk of heart disease... May increase risk of colon an...
	TRANS	French fries and other deep-fried fast foods Stick margarines, shortening Packaged cookies and crackers Processed snacks and sweets	Raises total cholesterol and LD... levels Lowers HDL cholesterol levels May increase risk of heart dise... cancer
Choose Moderate Amounts	MONOUNSATURATED	Olive, canola, and safflower oils Avocados, olives Peanut butter (without added fat) Many nuts, including almonds, cashews, pecans, and pistachios	Lowers total cholesterol and LDL cholesterol levels May reduce blood pressure and lower triglyceride levels (a risk factor for CVD) May reduce risk of heart disease, stroke, and some cancers
	POLYUNSATURATED (two groups)[b]		
	Omega-3 fatty acids	Fatty fish, including salmon, white albacore tuna, mackerel, anchovies, and sardines Lesser amounts in walnut, flaxseed, canola, and soybean oils; tofu; walnuts; flaxseeds; and dark green leafy vegetables	Reduces blood clotting and inflammation and inhibits abnormal heart rhythms Lowers triglyceride levels (a risk factor for CVD) May lower blood pressure in some people May reduce risk of fatal heart attack, stroke, and some cancers
	Omega-6 fatty acids	Corn, soybean, and cottonseed oils (often used in margarine, mayonnaise, and salad dressing)	Lowers total cholesterol and LDL cholesterol levels May lower HDL cholesterol levels May reduce risk of heart disease May slightly increase risk of cancer if omega-6 intake is high and omega-3 intake is low

[a] Food fats contain a combination of types of fatty acids in various proportions; for example, canola oil is composed mainly of monounsaturated fatty acids (62%) but also contains polyunsaturated (32%) and saturated (6%) fatty acids. Food fats are categorized here according to their predominant fatty acid.

[b] The essential fatty acids are polyunsaturated: Linoleic acid is an omega-6 fatty acid and alpha-linolenic acid is an omega-3 fatty acid.

Figure 8.3 Types of fatty acids and their possible effects on health. The health effects of dietary fats are still being investigated. In general, nutritionists recommend that we consume a diet moderate in fat overall and that we substitute unsaturated fats for saturated and trans fats. Monounsaturated fats and omega-3 polyunsaturated fats may be particularly good choices for promoting health. Eating lots of fat of any type can provide excess calories because all types of fats are rich sources of energy (9 calories per gram).

concentrated source of calories (9 calories per gram versus 4 calories per gram for protein and carbohydrate), a high-fat diet is often a high-calorie diet that can lead to weight gain. In addition, there is some evidence that calories from fat are more easily converted to body fat than calories from protein or carbohydrate.

Although more research is needed on the precise effects of different types and amounts of fat on overall health, a great deal of evidence points to the fact that most people benefit from lowering their overall fat intake to recommended levels and choosing unsaturated fats instead of saturated and trans fats. The types of fatty acids and their effects on health are summarized in Figure 8.3.

Recommended Fat Intake   To meet the body's need for essential fats, adult men need about 17 grams per day of linoleic acid and 1.6 grams per day of alpha-linolenic acid; for women, the daily need is 12 grams of linoleic acid and

1.1 grams of alpha-linolenic acid. About 3–4 teaspoons (15–20 grams) of vegetable oil per day incorporated into your diet will supply the essential fats. Most Americans consume sufficient amounts of the essential fats, and limiting unhealthy fats is a much greater health concern.

Limits for total, saturated, and trans fat intake have been set by a number of government and research organizations. In 2002, the Food and Nutrition Board released recommendations for the balance of energy sources in a healthful diet. These recommendations, called Acceptable Macronutrient Distribution Ranges (AMDRs), are based on ensuring adequate intake of essential nutrients while also reducing the risk of chronic diseases like heart disease and cancer. As with protein, a range of levels of fat intake is associated with good health; the AMDR for total fat is 20–35% of total calories. Although more difficult for consumers to monitor, AMDRs have also been set for omega-6 fatty acids (5–10%) and omega-3 fatty acids (0.6–1.2%) as part of

Nutritional Requirements: Components of a Healthy Diet

Goals have been established by the Food and Nutrition Board to help ensure adequate intake of the essential amino acids, fatty acids, and carbohydrate. The daily goals for adequate intake for adults are as follows:

	Men	Women
Protein	56 grams	46 grams
Fat: Linoleic acid	17 grams	12 grams
Alpha-linolenic acid	1.6 grams	1.1 grams
Carbohydrate	130 grams	130 grams

Protein intake goals can be calculated more specifically by multiplying your body weight in kilograms by 0.8 or your body weight in pounds by 0.36. (Refer to the Nutrition Resources section at the end of the chapter for information for specific age groups and life stages.)

To meet your daily energy needs, you need to consume more than the minimally adequate amounts of the energy-providing nutrients listed above, which alone supply only about 800–900 calories. The Food and Nutrition Board provides additional guidance in the form of AMDRs. These ranges can help you balance your intake of energy-providing nutrients in ways that ensure adequate intake and reduce the risk of chronic disease. The AMDRs for protein, total fat, and carbohydrate are as follows:

Protein	10–35% of total daily calories
Total fat	20–35% of total daily calories
Carbohydrate	45–65% of total daily calories

To set individual goals, begin by estimating your total daily energy (calorie) needs; if your weight is stable, your current energy intake is the number of calories you need to maintain your weight at your current activity level. Next, select percentage goals for protein, fat, and carbohydrate. You can allocate your total daily calories among the three classes of macronutrients to suit your preferences; just make sure that the three percentages you select total 100% and that you meet the minimum intake goals listed. Two samples reflecting different total energy intake and nutrient intake goals are shown in the table below.

To translate your percentage goals into daily intake goals expressed in calories and grams, multiply the appropriate percentages by total calorie intake and then divide the results by the corresponding calories per gram. For example, a fat limit of 35% applied to a 2200-calorie diet would be calculated as follows: $0.35 \times 2200 = 770$ calories of total fat; $770 \div 9$ calories per gram $= 86$ grams of total fat. (Remember that fat has 9 calories per gram and that protein and carbohydrate have 4 calories per gram.)

Two Sample Macronutrient Distributions

		Sample 1		Sample 2	
Nutrient	**AMDR**	**Individual Goals**	**Amounts for a 1600-Calorie Diet**	**Individual Goals**	**Amounts for a 2800-Calorie Diet**
Protein	10–35%	15%	240 calories = 60 grams	20%	560 calories = 140 grams
Fat	20–35%	30%	480 calories = 53 grams	20%	560 calories = 62 grams
Carbohydrate	45–65%	55%	880 calories = 220 grams	60%	1680 calories = 420 grams

SOURCE: Food and Nutrition Board, Institute of Medicine, National Academies, 2002. *Dietary Reference Intakes: Energy, Carbohydrates, Fiber, Fat, Fatty Acids, Cholesterol, Protein, and Amino Acids,* Washington, D.C., National Academies Press. Reprinted with permission from *Dietary Reference Intakes for Energy, Carbohydrate, Fiber, Fat, Fatty Acids, Cholesterol, Protein, and Amino Acids (Macronutrients).* Copyright © 2003 by the National Academy of Sciences. Courtesy of the National Academies Press, Washington, D.C.

total fat intake. Because any amount of saturated and trans fat increases the risk of heart disease, the Food and Nutrition Board recommends that saturated and trans fat intake be kept as low as possible and that most fat in a healthy diet should be unsaturated. American adults currently consume about 33% of total calories as fat, including 11–12% of calories as saturated fat and 2–4% as trans fat.

For advice on setting individual intake goals, see the box, "Setting Intake Goals for Protein, Fat, and Carbohydrate." To determine how close you are to meeting these intake goals for fat, keep a running total over the course of the day. For prepared foods, food labels list the number of grams of fat, protein, and carbohydrate; the breakdown

for many foods and popular fast-food items can be found in Appendixes B and C. Nutrition information is also available in many grocery stores, in published nutrition guides, and online (see For Further Exploration at the end of the chapter). By checking these resources, you can keep track of the total grams of fat, protein, and carbohydrate you eat and assess how close your current diet is to the recommended intake goals.

In reducing fat intake to recommended levels, the emphasis should be on lowering saturated and trans fats (see Figure 8.3). You can still eat high-fat foods, but it makes good sense to limit the size of your portions and to balance your intake with low-fat foods. For example, peanut butter is high in fat, with 8 grams (72 calories) of fat in each 90-calorie tablespoon. Two tablespoons of peanut butter eaten on whole-wheat bread and served with a banana, carrot sticks, and a glass of nonfat milk makes a nutritious lunch—high in protein and carbohydrate, relatively low in total and saturated fat (500 calories, 18 grams of total fat, 4 grams of saturated fat). Four tablespoons of peanut butter on high-fat crackers with potato chips, cookies, and whole milk is a less healthy combination (1000 calories, 62 grams of total fat, 15 grams of saturated fat). So although it's important to evaluate individual food items for their fat content, it is more important to look at them in the context of your overall diet.

Carbohydrates—An Ideal Source of Energy

Carbohydrates are needed in the diet primarily to supply energy to body cells. Some cells, such as those in the brain and other parts of the nervous system and in the blood, use only carbohydrates for fuel. During high-intensity exercise, muscles also get most of their energy from carbohydrates.

Simple and Complex Carbohydrates
Carbohydrates are classified into two groups: simple and complex. Simple carbohydrates contain only one or two sugar units in each molecule; they include sucrose (table sugar), fructose (fruit sugar, honey), maltose (malt sugar), and lactose (milk sugar). Providing much of the sweetness in foods, they are found naturally in fruits and milk and are added to soft drinks, fruit drinks, candy, and sweet desserts. There is no evidence that any type of simple sugar is more nutritious than any other.

Complex carbohydrates consist of chains of many sugar molecules; they include starches and most types of dietary fiber. Starches are found in a variety of plants, especially grains (wheat, rye, rice, oats, barley, millet), legumes, and tubers (potatoes and yams). Most other vegetables contain a mix of starches and simple carbohydrates. Fiber, discussed in the next section, is found in fruits, vegetables, and grains.

During digestion in the mouth and small intestine, your body breaks down starches and double sugars into single sugar molecules, such as **glucose,** for absorption. Once the glucose is in the bloodstream, the pancreas releases insulin, which allows cells to take up glucose and use it for energy. The liver and muscles also take up glucose and store it in the form of a starch called **glycogen.** The muscles use glucose from glycogen as fuel during endurance events or long workouts. Carbohydrates consumed in excess of the body's energy needs are changed into fat and stored. Whenever calorie intake exceeds calorie expenditure, fat storage can lead to weight gain. This is true whether the excess calories come from carbohydrates, proteins, fat, or alcohol.

Refined Carbohydrates Versus Whole Grains
Complex carbohydrates can be further divided between

Our bodies require adequate amounts of all essential nutrients—water, proteins, carbohydrates, fats, vitamins, and minerals—to grow and function properly. Choosing foods to satisfy these nutritional requirements is an important part of a healthy lifestyle.

refined, or processed, carbohydrates and unrefined carbohydrates, or whole grains. Before they are processed, all grains are **whole grains,** consisting of an inner layer of germ, a middle layer called the endosperm, and an outer layer of bran. During processing, the germ and bran are often removed, leaving just the starchy endosperm. The refinement of whole grains transforms whole-wheat flour into white flour, brown rice into white rice, and so on.

Refined carbohydrates usually retain all the calories of their unrefined counterparts, but they tend to be much lower in fiber, vitamins, minerals, and other beneficial compounds. Unrefined carbohydrates tend to take longer to chew and digest than refined ones; they also enter the bloodstream more slowly. This slower digestive pace tends to make people feel full sooner and for a longer period, lessening the chance that they will overeat. Also, a slower rise in blood glucose levels following consumption of

Terms

carbohydrate An essential nutrient; sugars, starches, and dietary fiber are all carbohydrates.

glucose A simple sugar that is the body's basic fuel.

glycogen An animal starch stored in the liver and muscles.

whole grain The entire edible portion of a grain such as wheat, rice, or oats, including the germ, endosperm, and bran. During milling or processing, parts of the grain are removed, often leaving just the endosperm.

What Are Whole Grains?

The first step in increasing your intake of whole grains is to correctly identify them. The following are whole grains:

whole wheat	whole-grain corn
whole rye	popcorn
whole oats	brown rice
oatmeal	barley

Other choices include bulgur (cracked wheat), millet, kasha (roasted buckwheat kernels), quinoa, teff, wheat and rye berries, amaranth, graham flour, whole-grain kamut, whole-grain spelt, and whole-grain triticale.

Wheat flour, unbleached flour, enriched flour, and degerminated corn meal are not whole grains. Wheat germ and wheat bran are also not whole grains, but they are the constituents of wheat typically left out when wheat is processed and so are healthier choices than regular wheat flour, which typically contains just the endosperm.

Reading Food Packages to Find Whole Grains

To find packaged foods rich in whole grains, read the list of ingredients and check for special health claims related to whole grains. *The first item on the list of ingredients should be one of the whole grains listed above.* In addition, the FDA allows manufacturers to include special health claims for foods that contain 51% or more whole-grain ingredients. Such products may contain a statement such as the following on their packaging: "Rich in whole grain," "Made with 100% whole grain," or "Diets rich in whole-grain foods may help reduce the risk of heart disease and certain cancers." However, many whole-grain products will not carry such claims.

Incorporating Whole Grains into Your Daily Diet

- *Bread:* Look for sandwich breads, bagels, English muffins, buns, and pita breads with a whole grain listed as the first ingredient. Color and name can be misleading; always check the list of ingredients.

- *Breakfast cereals:* Whole-grain choices include oatmeal, muesli, shredded wheat, and some types of raisin bran, bran flakes, wheat flakes, toasted oats, and granola. Check the ingredient list for whole grains.

- *Rice:* Choose brown rice or rice blends that include brown rice.

- *Pasta:* Look for whole-wheat, whole-grain kamut, or whole-grain spelt pasta.

- *Tortillas:* Choose whole-wheat or whole-corn tortillas.

- *Crackers and snacks:* Some varieties of crackers are made from whole grains, including some flatbreads or crispbreads, woven wheat crackers, and rye crackers. Other whole-grain snack possibilities include popcorn, popcorn cakes, brown rice cakes, whole-corn tortilla chips, and whole-wheat fig cookies. Be sure to check food labels for fat content, as many popular snacks are also high in fat.

- *Mixed-grain dishes:* Combine whole grains with other foods to create healthy mixed dishes such as tabouli; soups made with hulled barley or wheat berries; and pilafs, casseroles, and salads made with brown rice, whole-wheat couscous, kasha, millet, wheat bulgur, and quinoa.

If your grocery store doesn't carry these items, try your local health food store.

---

complex carbohydrates may help in the prevention and management of diabetes. Whole grains are also high in dietary fiber and so have all the benefits of fiber. Consumption of whole grains has been linked to reduced risk for heart disease, diabetes, high blood pressure, stroke, and certain forms of cancer. For all these reasons, whole grains are recommended over those that have been refined. This does not mean that you should never eat refined carbohydrates such as white bread or white rice, simply that whole-wheat bread, brown rice, and other whole grains are healthier choices. Federal dietary guidelines recommend a minimum of three servings of whole grains per day; however, Americans currently average less than one serving of whole grains per day. See the box "Choosing More Whole-Grain Foods" for tips on increasing your intake of whole grains.

Glycemic Index   Insulin and glucose levels rise and fall following a meal or snack containing any type of carbohydrate. Some foods cause a quick and dramatic rise in glucose and insulin levels; others have a slower, more moderate effect. A food that has a strong effect on blood glucose levels is said to have a high **glycemic index.**

Research findings have been mixed, but some studies have found that a meal containing high glycemic index foods may increase appetite in some people; over the long term, diets rich in high glycemic index foods are linked to increased risk of diabetes and heart disease. High glycemic index foods do not, as some popular diets claim, directly cause weight gain beyond the calories they contain.

Attempting to base food choices on glycemic index is a difficult task, however. Although one can say generally that unrefined complex carbohydrates and high-fiber foods tend to have a low glycemic index, patterns are less clear for other types of foods and do not follow a simple distinction such as that of simple versus complex carbohydrates. For example, some fruits with fairly high levels of simple carbohydrates have only a moderate effect on blood glucose levels, while white rice, potatoes, and white bread, which are rich in complex carbohydrates, have a high glycemic index. Watermelon has a glycemic index more than twice that of strawberries, and the glycemic index of a banana changes dramatically as it ripens. The acid and fat content of a food also affect glycemic index—the more acidic and higher in fat a food is, the lower its effect on glucose levels. Other factors that affect the body's response to carbohydrates include how foods are combined and prepared and the fitness status of the individual.

This complexity is one reason why major health organizations have not issued specific guidelines for glycemic index. For people with particular health concerns, glycemic index may be an important consideration; however, it should not be the sole criterion for food choices. For example, ice cream has a much lower glycemic index than brown rice or carrots—but that doesn't make it a healthier choice overall. Glycemic index and its effects on appetite and heart health are discussed further in Chapters 9 and 11. For now, remember that most unrefined grains, fruits, vegetables, and legumes are rich in nutrients and have a low-to-moderate glycemic index. Choose a variety of vegetables daily, and avoid heavy consumption of white potatoes. Limit foods that are high in added sugars but provide few other nutrients. Some studies have singled out regular soda, with its large dose of rapidly absorbable sugar, as specifically linked to increased diabetes risk.

Recommended Carbohydrate Intake   On average, Americans consume 200–300 grams of carbohydrate per day, well above the 130 grams needed to meet the body's requirement for essential carbohydrate. A range of intakes is associated with good health, and experts recommend that adults consume 45–65% of total daily calories as carbohydrate, about 225–325 grams of carbohydrate for someone consuming 2000 calories per day. The focus should be on consuming a variety of foods rich in complex carbohydrates, especially whole grains.

Health experts offer separate guidelines for intake of added sugars as part of total carbohydrate consumption. The Food and Nutrition Board set an AMDR for added sugars of 25% or less of total daily calories, but many health experts recommend a substantially lower intake. Guidelines released by the World Health Organization in 2003 suggested a limit of 10% of total daily calories from added sugars. Limits set by the USDA in 2005 are even lower, with a maximum of about 8 teaspoons (32 grams) suggested for someone consuming 2000 calories per day. Foods high in added sugar are generally high in calories and low in nutrients and fiber, thus providing "empty" calories. To reduce your intake of added sugars, limit soft drinks, candy, sweet desserts, and sweetened fruit drinks. The simple carbohydrates in your diet should come from food sources in which they are found naturally—including fruits, which are excellent sources of vitamins and minerals, and from milk, which is high in protein and calcium.

Athletes in training can especially benefit from high-carbohydrate diets (60–70% of total daily calories), which enhance the amount of carbohydrates stored in their muscles (as glycogen) and therefore provide more carbohydrate fuel for use during endurance events or long workouts. In addition, carbohydrates consumed during prolonged athletic events can help fuel muscles and extend the availability of the glycogen stored in muscles. Caution is in order, however, because overconsumption of carbohydrates can lead to feelings of fatigue and underconsumption of other nutrients. (For more on the special nutritional needs of athletes, see p. 256.)

Fiber—A Closer Look

Fiber is the term given to nondigestible carbohydrates provided mainly by plants. Instead of being digested, like starch, fiber passes through the intestinal tract and provides bulk for feces in the large intestine, which in turn facilitates elimination. In the large intestine, some types of fiber are broken down by bacteria into acids and gases, which explains why consuming too much fiber can lead to intestinal gas. Because humans cannot digest fiber, it is not a source of carbohydrate in the diet; however, the consumption of fiber is necessary for good health.

Types of Dietary Fiber   The Food and Nutrition Board has defined two types of fiber: dietary fiber and functional fiber. **Dietary fiber** refers to nondigestible carbohydrates and lignin that are present naturally in plants such as grains, legumes, and vegetables. **Functional fiber** refers to nondigestible carbohydrates that have been either isolated from natural sources or synthesized in a lab and then added to a food product or supplement. **Total fiber** is the sum of dietary and functional fiber.

Fibers have different properties that lead to different physiological effects in the body. **Soluble (viscous) fiber** slows the body's absorption of glucose and binds cholesterol-containing compounds in the intestine, lowering blood cholesterol levels and reducing the risk of cardiovascular disease. **Insoluble fiber** binds water, making the feces bulkier and softer so they pass more quickly and easily through the intestines.

Both kinds of fiber contribute to disease prevention. A diet high in soluble fiber can help people manage diabetes

Terms

glycemic index A measure of how the ingestion of a particular food affects blood glucose levels.

dietary fiber Nondigestible carbohydrates and lignin that are intact in plants.

functional fiber Nondigestible carbohydrates either isolated from natural sources or synthesized; these may be added to foods and dietary supplements.

total fiber The total amount of dietary fiber and functional fiber in the diet.

soluble (viscous) fiber Fiber that dissolves in water or is broken down by bacteria in the large intestine.

insoluble fiber Fiber that does not dissolve in water and is not broken down by bacteria in the large intestine.

and high blood cholesterol levels. A diet high in insoluble fiber can help prevent a variety of health problems, including constipation, hemorrhoids, and **diverticulitis.** Some studies have linked diets high in fiber-rich fruits, vegetables, and grains with a lower risk of some kinds of cancer; however, it is unclear whether fiber or other food components are responsible for this reduction in risk.

Sources of Dietary Fiber   All plant foods contain some dietary fiber, but fruits, legumes, oats (especially oat bran), and barley are particularly rich in it. Wheat (especially wheat bran), cereals, grains, and vegetables are all good sources of insoluble fiber. Psyllium, which is often added to cereals or used in fiber supplements and laxatives, improves intestinal health and also helps control glucose and cholesterol levels. The processing of packaged foods can remove fiber, so it's important to depend on fresh fruits and vegetables and foods made from whole grains as sources of dietary fiber.

Recommended Intake of Dietary Fiber   To reduce the risk of chronic disease and maintain intestinal health, the Food and Nutrition Board recommends a daily fiber intake of 38 grams for adult men and 25 grams for adult women. Americans currently consume about half this amount. Fiber should come from foods, not supplements, which should be used only under medical supervision.

To increase the amount of fiber in your diet, try the following:

- Choose breads, crackers, and cereals that list whole grain first in the ingredient list: Whole-wheat flour, whole-grain oats, and whole-grain rice are whole grains; wheat flour is not. Choose a breakfast cereal with 5 or more grams of fiber per serving.
- Eat whole, unpeeled fruits rather than drinking fruit juice. Top cereals, yogurt, and desserts with berries, apple slices, or other fruit.
- Include beans in soups and salads. Combine raw vegetables with pasta, rice, or beans in salads.
- Substitute bean dip for cheese-based or sour cream–based dips or spreads. Use raw vegetables rather than chips for dipping.

Terms

Ⓦ

diverticulitis A digestive disorder in which abnormal pouches form in the walls of the intestine and become inflamed.

vitamins Organic substances needed in small amounts to help promote and regulate chemical reactions and processes in the body.

antioxidant A substance that protects against the breakdown of body constituents by free radicals; actions include binding oxygen, donating electrons to free radicals, and repairing damage to molecules.

Vitamins—Organic Micronutrients

Vitamins are organic (carbon-containing) substances required in very small amounts to regulate various processes within living cells (Table 8.2). Humans need 13 vitamins. Four are fat-soluble (A, D, E, and K), and nine are water-soluble (C and the eight B-complex vitamins: thiamin, riboflavin, niacin, vitamin B-6, folate, vitamin B-12, biotin, and pantothenic acid). Solubility affects how a vitamin is absorbed, transported, and stored in the body. The water-soluble vitamins are absorbed directly into the bloodstream, where they travel freely; excess water-soluble vitamins are detected and removed by the kidneys and excreted in urine. Fat-soluble vitamins require a more complex absorptive process; they are usually carried in the blood by special proteins and are stored in the body in the liver and in fat tissues rather than excreted.

Functions of Vitamins   Many vitamins help chemical reactions take place. They provide no energy to the body directly but help unleash the energy stored in carbohydrates, proteins, and fats. Vitamins are critical in the production of red blood cells and the maintenance of the nervous, skeletal, and immune systems. Some vitamins also form substances that act as **antioxidants,** which help preserve healthy cells in the body. Key vitamin antioxidants include vitamin E, vitamin C, and the vitamin A precursor beta-carotene. (The actions of antioxidants are described later in the chapter.)

Sources of Vitamins   The human body does not manufacture most of the vitamins it requires and must obtain them from foods. Vitamins are abundant in fruits, vegetables, and grains. In addition, many processed foods, such as flour and breakfast cereals, contain added vitamins. A few vitamins are made in certain parts of the body: The skin makes vitamin D when it is exposed to sunlight, and intestinal bacteria make vitamin K. Nonetheless, you still need to obtain vitamin D and vitamin K from foods.

Vitamin Deficiencies and Excesses   If your diet lacks sufficient amounts of a particular vitamin, characteristic symptoms of deficiency develop (see Table 8.2). For example, vitamin A deficiency can cause blindness, and vitamin B-6 deficiency can cause seizures. Vitamin deficiency diseases are most often seen in developing countries; they are relatively rare in the United States because vitamins are readily available from our food supply. However, intakes below recommended levels can have adverse effects on health even if they are not low enough to cause a deficiency disease. For example, low intake of folate increases a woman's chance of giving birth to a baby with a neural tube defect (a congenital malformation of the central nervous system). Low intake of folate and vitamins B-6 and B-12 has been linked to increased heart disease risk. Many Americans consume less-than-recommended amounts of vitamins A, C, D, and E.

| | | **Table 8.2** | **Facts About Vitamins** | | |

Vitamin	Important Dietary Sources	Major Functions	Signs of Prolonged Deficiency	Toxic Effects of Megadoses
Fat-Soluble				
Vitamin A	Liver, milk, butter, cheese, and fortified margarine; carrots, spinach, and other orange and deep green vegetables and fruits	Maintenance of vision, skin, linings of the nose, mouth, digestive and urinary tracts, immune function	Night blindness; dry, scaling skin; increased susceptibility to infection; loss of appetite; anemia; kidney stones	Liver damage, miscarriage and birth defects, headache, vomiting and diarrhea, vertigo, double vision, bone abnormalities
Vitamin D	Fortified milk and margarine, fish oils, butter, egg yolks (sunlight on skin also produces vitamin D)	Development and maintenance of bones and teeth, promotion of calcium absorption	Rickets (bone deformities) in children; bone softening, loss, and fractures in adults	Kidney damage, calcium deposits in soft tissues, depression, death
Vitamin E	Vegetable oils, whole grains, nuts and seeds, green leafy vegetables, asparagus, peaches	Protection and maintenance of cellular membranes	Red blood cell breakage and anemia, weakness, neurological problems, muscle cramps	Relatively nontoxic, but may cause excess bleeding or formation of blood clots
Vitamin K	Green leafy vegetables; smaller amounts widespread in other foods	Production of proteins essential for blood clotting and bone metabolism	Hemorrhaging	None reported
Water-Soluble				
Biotin	Cereals, yeast, egg yolks, soy flour, liver; widespread in foods	Synthesis of fat, glycogen, and amino acids	Rash, nausea, vomiting, weight loss, depression, fatigue, hair loss	None reported
Folate	Green leafy vegetables, yeast, oranges, whole grains, legumes, liver	Amino acid metabolism, synthesis of RNA and DNA, new cell synthesis	Anemia, weakness, fatigue, irritability, shortness of breath, swollen tongue	Masking of vitamin B-12 deficiency
Niacin	Eggs, poultry, fish, milk, whole grains, nuts, enriched breads and cereals, meats, legumes	Conversion of carbohydrates, fats, and proteins into usable forms of energy	Pellagra (symptoms include diarrhea, dermatitis, inflammation of mucous membranes, dementia)	Flushing of the skin, nausea, vomiting, diarrhea, liver dysfunction, glucose intolerance
Pantothenic acid	Animal foods, whole grains, broccoli, potatoes; widespread in foods	Metabolism of fats, carbohydrates, and proteins	Fatigue, numbness and tingling of hands and feet, gastrointestinal disturbances	None reported
Riboflavin	Dairy products, enriched breads and cereals, lean meats, poultry, fish, green vegetables	Energy metabolism; maintenance of skin, mucous membranes, and nervous system structures	Cracks at corners of mouth, sore throat, skin rash, hypersensitivity to light, purple tongue	None reported
Thiamin	Whole-grain and enriched breads and cereals, organ meats, lean pork, nuts, legumes	Conversion of carbohydrates into usable forms of energy, maintenance of appetite and nervous system function	Beriberi (symptoms include muscle wasting, mental confusion, anorexia, enlarged heart, nerve changes)	None reported
Vitamin B-6	Eggs, poultry, fish, whole grains, nuts, soybeans, liver, kidney, pork	Metabolism of amino acids and glycogen	Anemia, convulsions, cracks at corners of mouth, dermatitis, nausea, confusion	Neurological abnormalities and damage
Vitamin B-12	Meat, fish, poultry, fortified cereals	Synthesis of blood cells; other metabolic reactions	Anemia, fatigue, nervous system damage, sore tongue	None reported
Vitamin C	Peppers, cruciferous vegetables, spinach, citrus fruits, strawberries, tomatoes, potatoes, other fruits and vegetables	Maintenance and repair of connective tissue, bones, teeth, and cartilage; promotion of healing; aid in iron absorption	Scurvy, anemia, reduced resistance to infection, loosened teeth, joint pain, poor wound healing, hair loss, poor iron absorption	Urinary stones in some people, acid stomach from ingesting supplements in pill form, nausea, diarrhea, headache, fatigue

SOURCES: Food and Nutrition Board, Institute of Medicine, National Academies. 2001. *Dietary Reference Intakes Tables* (http://www.iom.edu/file.asp?id=21372; retrieved December 21, 2004). The complete Dietary Reference Intake reports are available from the National Academy Press (http://www.nap.edu). Shils, M. E., et al., eds. 1998. *Modern Nutrition in Health and Disease*, 9th ed. Baltimore: Williams & Wilkins.

Extra vitamins in the diet can be harmful, especially when taken as supplements. High doses of vitamin A are toxic and increase the risk of birth defects, for example. Vitamin B-6 can cause irreversible nerve damage when taken in large doses. Megadoses of fat-soluble vitamins are particularly dangerous because the excess will be stored in the body rather than excreted, increasing the risk of toxicity. Even when supplements are not taken in excess, relying on them for an adequate intake of vitamins can be a problem: There are many substances in foods other than vitamins and minerals, and some of these compounds may have important health effects. Later in the chapter we discuss specific recommendations for vitamin intake and when a supplement is advisable. For now, keep in mind that it's best to obtain most of your vitamins from foods rather than supplements.

When preparing foods, remember that vitamins and minerals in vegetables can be easily lost or destroyed during storage or cooking. To retain their value, eat or process vegetables immediately after buying them. If you can't do this, then store them in a cool place, covered to retain moisture—either in the refrigerator (for a few days) or in the freezer (for a longer term). To reduce nutrient losses during food preparation, minimize the amount of water used and the total cooking time. Develop a taste for a crunchier texture in cooked vegetables. Baking, steaming, broiling, and microwaving are all good methods of preparing vegetables.

Minerals—Inorganic Micronutrients

Minerals are inorganic (non-carbon-containing) elements you need in small amounts to help regulate body functions, aid in the growth and maintenance of body tissues, and help release energy (Table 8.3). There are about 17 essential minerals. The major minerals, those that the body needs in amounts exceeding 100 milligrams, include calcium, phosphorus, magnesium, sodium, potassium, and chloride. The essential trace minerals, those that you need in minute amounts, include copper, fluoride, iodine, iron, selenium, and zinc.

Terms

Ww

minerals Inorganic compounds needed in small amounts for regulation, growth, and maintenance of body tissues and functions.

anemia A deficiency in the oxygen-carrying material in the red blood cells.

osteoporosis A condition in which the bones become thin and brittle and break easily.

free radical An electron-seeking compound that can react with fats, proteins, and DNA, damaging cell membranes and mutating genes in its search for electrons; produced through chemical reactions in the body and by exposure to environmental factors such as sunlight and tobacco smoke.

Characteristic symptoms develop if an essential mineral is consumed in a quantity too small or too large for good health. The minerals most commonly lacking in the American diet are iron, calcium, magnesium, and potassium. Focus on good food choices for these nutrients (see Table 8.3). Lean meats are rich in iron; low-fat or fat-free dairy products are excellent choices for calcium. Plant foods such as whole grains and leafy vegetables are good sources of magnesium. Potassium-rich foods include spinach and other leafy greens, cantaloupe, bananas, mushrooms, and white and sweet potatoes. Iron-deficiency **anemia** is a problem in some age groups, and researchers fear poor calcium intakes are sowing the seeds for future **osteoporosis,** especially in women. See the box "Eating for Healthy Bones" on p. 242 to learn more.

Water—A Vital Component

Water is the major component in both foods and the human body: You are composed of about 60% water. Your need for other nutrients, in terms of weight, is much less than your need for water. You can live up to 50 days without food but only a few days without water.

Water is distributed all over the body, among lean and other tissues and in urine and other body fluids. Water is used in the digestion and absorption of food and is the medium in which most of the chemical reactions take place within the body. Some water-based fluids like blood transport substances around the body; other fluids serve as lubricants or cushions. Water also helps regulate body temperature.

Water is contained in almost all foods, particularly in liquids, fruits, and vegetables. The foods and fluids you consume provide 80–90% of your daily water intake; the remainder is generated through metabolism. You lose water each day in urine, feces, and sweat and through evaporation in your lungs.

As described in Chapter 3, severe dehydration causes weakness and can lead to death. However, most people maintain a healthy water balance by consuming beverages at meals and drinking fluids in response to thirst. In 2004, the Food and Nutrition Board set levels of adequate water intake to maintain hydration; all fluids, including those containing caffeine, can count toward your total daily fluid intake. Water and other beverages typically make up about 80% of your fluid intake; the remainder comes from foods, especially fruits and vegetables. Men need to consume about 3.7 total liters of water, with 3.0 liters (about 13 cups) coming from beverages; women need 2.7 total liters, with 2.2 liters (about 9 cups) coming from beverages. (See Table 1 in the Nutrition Resources section at the end of the chapter for recommendations for specific age groups.) If you exercise vigorously or live in a hot climate, you need to consume additional fluids to maintain a balance between water consumed and water lost. See p. 256 for more on the fluid needs of athletes and active people.

| Table 8.3 | Facts About Selected Minerals |

Mineral	Important Dietary Sources	Major Functions	Signs of Prolonged Deficiency	Toxic Effects of Megadoses
Calcium	Milk and milk products, tofu, fortified orange juice and bread, green leafy vegetables, bones in fish	Formation of bones and teeth; control of nerve impulses, muscle contraction, blood clotting	Stunted growth in children, bone mineral loss in adults; urinary stones	Kidney stones, calcium deposits in soft tissues, inhibition of mineral absorption, constipation
Fluoride	Fluoridated water, tea, marine fish eaten with bones	Maintenance of tooth and bone structure	Higher frequency of tooth decay	Increased bone density, mottling of teeth, impaired kidney function
Iodine	Iodized salt, seafood, processed foods	Essential part of thyroid hormones, regulation of body metabolism	Goiter (enlarged thyroid), cretinism (birth defect)	Depression of thyroid activity, hyperthyroidism in susceptible people
Iron	Meat and poultry, fortified grain products, dark green vegetables, dried fruit	Component of hemoglobin, myoglobin, and enzymes	Iron-deficiency anemia, weakness, impaired immune function, gastrointestinal distress	Nausea, diarrhea, liver and kidney damage, joint pains, sterility, disruption of cardiac function, death
Magnesium	Widespread in foods and water (except soft water); especially found in grains, legumes, nuts, seeds, green vegetables, milk	Transmission of nerve impulses, energy transfer, activation of many enzymes	Neurological disturbances, cardiovascular problems, kidney disorders, nausea, growth failure in children	Nausea, vomiting, diarrhea, central nervous system depression, coma; death in people with impaired kidney function
Phosphorus	Present in nearly all foods, especially milk, cereal, peas, eggs, meat	Bone growth and maintenance, energy transfer in cells	Impaired growth, weakness, kidney disorders, cardiorespiratory and nervous system dysfunction	Drop in blood calcium levels, calcium deposits in soft tissues, bone loss
Potassium	Fruits and vegetables, especially leafy greens, cantaloupe, bananas, mushrooms, potatoes	Basic functioning of cells, water balance, acid-base balance	Elevated blood pressure, bone mineral loss, kidney stones, increased salt sensitivity, cardiac arrhythmia, muscle weakness	Cardiac arrhythmia and arrest, gastrointestinal discomfort
Selenium	Seafood, meat, eggs, whole grains	Defense against oxidative stress and regulation of thyroid hormone action	Muscle pain and weakness, heart disorders	Hair and nail brittleness and loss, nausea and vomiting, weakness, irritability
Sodium	Salt, soy sauce, fast food, and processed foods, especially lunch meats, canned soups and vegetables, salty snacks, and processed cheese	Body water balance, acid-base balance, nerve function	Muscle weakness, loss of appetite, nausea, vomiting; deficiency is rarely seen	Increased blood pressure (even at fairly low levels of intake), renal stones, edema
Zinc	Whole grains, meat, eggs, liver, seafood (especially oysters)	Synthesis of proteins, RNA, and DNA; wound healing; immune response; ability to taste	Growth failure, loss of appetite, impaired taste acuity, skin rash, impaired immune function, poor wound healing	Vomiting, impaired immune function, decline in blood HDL levels, impaired copper absorption

SOURCES: Food and Nutrition Board, Institute of Medicine, National Academies. 2001. *Dietary Reference Intakes Tables* (http://www.iom.edu/file.asp?id=21372; retrieved December 21, 2004). The complete Dietary Reference Intake reports are available from the National Academy Press (http://www.nap.edu). Shils, M. E., et al., eds. 1998. *Modern Nutrition in Health and Disease,* 9th ed. Baltimore: Williams & Wilkins.

Other Substances in Food

There are many substances in food that are not essential nutrients but that may influence health.

Antioxidants When the body uses oxygen or breaks down certain fats or proteins as a normal part of metabo-lism, it gives rise to substances called **free radicals.** Environmental factors such as cigarette smoke, exhaust fumes, radiation, excessive sunlight, certain drugs, and stress can increase free radical production. A free radical is a chemically unstable molecule that is missing an electron; it will react with any molecule it encounters from which it can take an electron. In their search for electrons, free radicals

Osteoporosis is a condition in which the bones become danger- ously thin and fragile over time. An estimated 10 million Ameri- cans over age 50 have osteoporosis, and another 34 million are at risk. Women account for about 80% of osteoporosis cases. Most bone mass is built by age 18. After bone density peaks between ages 25 and 35, bone mass is slowly lost over time. To prevent os- teoporosis, the best strategy is to build as much bone as possible during your young years and then do everything you can to maintain it as you age. Up to 50% of bone loss is determined by controllable lifestyle factors. Key nutrients include the following:

Calcium   Consuming an adequate amount of calcium is im- portant throughout life to build and maintain bone mass. Milk, yogurt, and calcium-fortified orange juice, bread, and cereals are all good sources.

Vitamin D   Vitamin D is necessary for bones to absorb cal- cium; a daily intake of 5 μg is recommended for adults age 19–50. Vitamin D can be obtained from foods and is manu- factured by the skin when exposed to sunlight. Candidates for vitamin D supplements include people who don't eat many foods rich in vitamin D; those who don't expose their face, arms, and hands to the sun (without sunscreen) for 5–15 minutes a few times each week; and people who live north of an imaginary line roughly between Boston and the Oregon– California border (the sun is weaker in northern latitudes).

Vitamin K   Vitamin K promotes the synthesis of proteins that help keep bones strong. Broccoli and leafy-green vegetables are rich in vitamin K.

Other Nutrients   Other nutrients that may play an important role in bone health include vitamin C, magnesium, potassium, manganese, zinc, copper, and boron. On the flip side, there are several dietary substances that may have a *negative* effect on bone health, especially if consumed in excess: alcohol, sodium, caffeine, and retinol (a form of vitamin A). Drinking lots of soda, which often replaces milk in the diet and which is high in phosphorus (a mineral that may interfere with calcium absorp- tion), has been shown to increase the risk of bone fracture in teenage girls. For healthy bones, it is important to be moderate in your consumption of alcohol, sodium, caffeine, retinol, and sodas.

The effect of protein intake on bone mass depends on other nutrients: Protein helps build bone as long as calcium and vita- min D intake are adequate; but if intake of calcium and vitamin D is low, high protein intake can lead to bone loss.

Finally, it is important to combine a healthy diet with other wellness behaviors. Weight-bearing aerobic activities, if per- formed regularly, help build and maintain bone mass through- out life. Strength training improves bone density, muscle mass, strength, and balance, protecting against both bone loss and falls, a major cause of fractures. Drinking alcohol only in mod- eration, refraining from smoking, and managing depression and stress are also important for maintaining strong bones. For peo- ple who do develop osteoporosis, a variety of medications is available to treat the condition.

---

react with fats, proteins, and DNA, damaging cell mem- branes and mutating genes. Because of this, free radicals have been implicated in aging, cancer, cardiovascular dis- ease, and other degenerative diseases like arthritis.

Antioxidants found in foods can help protect the body by blocking the formation and action of free radicals and repairing the damage they cause. Some antioxidants, such as vitamin C, vitamin E, and selenium, are also essential nutrients; others, such as carotenoids, found in yellow, orange, and dark green leafy vegetables, are not. Many fruits and vegetables are rich in antioxidants.

Phytochemicals   Antioxidants fall into the broader category of **phytochemicals,** substances found in plant foods that may help prevent chronic disease. Researchers have just begun to identify and study all the different compounds found in foods, and many preliminary find- ings are promising. For example, certain proteins found in soy foods may help lower cholesterol levels. Sul- foraphane, a compound isolated from broccoli and other **cruciferous vegetables,** may render some carcinogenic compounds harmless. Allyl sulfides, a group of chemicals found in garlic and onions, appear to boost the activity of cancer-fighting immune cells. Further research on

phytochemicals may extend the role of nutrition to the prevention and treatment of many chronic diseases.

To increase your intake of phytochemicals, it is best to obtain them by eating a variety of fruits and vegetables rather than relying on supplements. Like many vitamins and minerals, isolated phytochemicals may be harmful if taken in high doses. In addition, it is likely that their health benefits are the result of chemical substances work- ing in combination. The role of phytochemicals in disease prevention is discussed further in Chapters 11 and 12.

NUTRITIONAL GUIDELINES: PLANNING YOUR DIET

The second part of putting together a healthy food plan— after you've learned about necessary nutrients—is choos- ing foods that satisfy nutritional requirements and meet your personal criteria. Various tools have been created by scientific and government groups to help people design healthy diets. The **Dietary Reference Intakes (DRIs)** are standards for nutrient intake designed to prevent nutritional deficiencies and reduce the risk of chronic disease. **Dietary Guidelines for Americans** have been established to promote health and reduce the risk for major chronic diseases through diet and physical activity. Further guidance symbolized by **MyPyramid** provides daily food intake patterns that meet the DRIs and are consistent with the Dietary Guidelines for Americans.

Dietary Reference Intakes (DRIs)

How much vitamin C, iron, calcium, and other nutrients do you need to stay healthy? The Food and Nutrition Board establishes dietary standards, or recommended intake levels, for Americans of all ages. The current set of standards, called Dietary Reference Intakes (DRIs), is relatively new, having been introduced in 1997. An earlier set of standards, called the **Recommended Dietary Allowances (RDAs)**, focused on preventing nutritional deficiency diseases such as anemia. The newer DRIs have a broader focus because recent research has looked not just at the prevention of nutrient deficiencies but also at the role of nutrients in promoting optimal health and preventing chronic diseases such as cancer, osteoporosis, and heart disease.

The DRIs include standards for both recommended intakes and maximum safe intakes. The recommended intake of each nutrient is expressed as either a *Recommended Dietary Allowance (RDA)* or *Adequate Intake (AI)*. An AI is set when there is not enough information available to set an RDA value; regardless of the type of standard used, however, the DRI represents the best available estimate of intake for optimal health. The *Tolerable Upper Intake Level (UL)* sets the maximum daily intake by a healthy person that is unlikely to cause health problems. For example, the RDA for calcium for an 18-year-old female is 1300 milligrams per day; the UL is 2500 milligrams per day. Because of lack of data, ULs have not been set for all nutrients. This does not mean that people can tolerate chronic intakes of these vitamins and minerals above recommended levels. Like all chemical agents, nutrients can produce adverse effects if intakes are excessive. There is no established benefit from consuming nutrients at levels above the RDA or AI. The DRIs can be found in the Nutrition Resources section at the end of the chapter. For more information, visit the Web site of the National Academies' Food and Nutrition Board (see For Further Exploration at the end of the chapter).

Should You Take Supplements?

The aim of the DRIs is to guide you in meeting your nutritional needs primarily with food, rather than with vitamin and mineral supplements. This goal is important because recommendations have not yet been set for some essential nutrients. Many supplements contain only nutrients with established recommendations, so using them to meet nutrient needs can leave you deficient in other nutrients. Supplements also lack potentially beneficial phytochemicals that are found only in whole foods. Most Americans can obtain most of the vitamins and minerals they need by consuming a varied, nutritionally balanced, diet.

The question of whether to take supplements is a serious one. Some vitamins and minerals are dangerous when ingested in excess, as described in Tables 8.2 and 8.3. Large doses of particular nutrients can also cause health problems by affecting the absorption of other vitamins and minerals. For all these reasons, you should think carefully about whether to take supplements; consider consulting a physician or registered dietitian.

In setting the DRIs, the Food and Nutrition Board recommended supplements of particular nutrients for the following groups:

- Women who are capable of becoming pregnant should take 400 micrograms (μg) per day of folic acid (the synthetic form of the vitamin folate) from fortified foods and/or supplements in addition to folate from a varied diet. Research indicates that this level of folate intake will reduce the risk of neural tube defects. (This defect occurs early in pregnancy, before most women know they are pregnant; therefore, the recommendation for folate applies to all women of reproductive age rather than only to pregnant women.) Since 1998, enriched breads, flours, corn meals, rice, noodles, and other grain products have been fortified with small amounts of folic acid. Folate is found naturally in green leafy vegetables, legumes, oranges and orange juice, and strawberries.

- People over age 50 should consume foods fortified with vitamin B-12, B-12 supplements, or a combination of the two in order to meet the majority of the DRI of

Terms

phytochemical A naturally occurring substance found in plant foods that may help prevent and treat chronic diseases such as heart disease and cancer; *phyto* means plant.

cruciferous vegetables Vegetables of the cabbage family, including cabbage, broccoli, brussels sprouts, kale, and cauliflower; the flower petals of these plants form the shape of a cross, hence the name.

Dietary Reference Intakes (DRIs) An umbrella term for four types of nutrient standards: Adequate Intake (AI), Estimated Average Requirement (EAR), and Recommended Dietary Allowance (RDA) set levels of intake considered adequate to prevent nutrient deficiencies and reduce the risk of chronic disease; Tolerable Upper Intake Level (UL) sets the maximum daily intake that is unlikely to cause health problems.

Dietary Guidelines for Americans General principles of good nutrition intended to help prevent certain diet-related diseases.

MyPyramid A food-group plan that provides practical advice to ensure a balanced intake of the essential nutrients.

Recommended Dietary Allowances (RDAs) Amounts of certain nutrients considered adequate to prevent deficiencies in most healthy people; will eventually be replaced by the Dietary Reference Intakes (DRIs).

2.4 milligrams of B-12 daily. Up to 30% of people over 50 may have problems absorbing protein-bound B-12 in foods. Vitamin B-12 in supplements and fortified foods is more readily absorbed and can help prevent a deficiency.

Because of the oxidative stress caused by smoking, the Food and Nutrition Board also recommends that smokers consume 35 milligrams *more* vitamin C per day than the DRI intake level set for their age and sex (for adults, recommended daily vitamin C intakes for nonsmokers are 90 mg for men and 75 mg for women). However, supplements are not usually needed because this extra vitamin C can easily be obtained from foods. For example, one cup of orange juice has about 100 milligrams of vitamin C.

Supplements may also be recommended in other cases. Women with heavy menstrual flows may need extra iron to compensate for the monthly loss. Older people, people with dark skin, and people exposed to little sunlight may need extra vitamin D from vitamin D–fortified foods and/or supplements. Some vegetarians may need supplemental calcium, iron, zinc, and vitamin B-12, depending on their food choices. Newborns need a single dose of vitamin K, which must be administered under the direction of a physician. People who consume few calories, who have certain diseases, or who take certain medications may need specific vitamin and mineral supplements; such supplement decisions must be made by a physician because some vitamins and minerals counteract the actions of certain medications.

In deciding whether to take a vitamin and mineral supplement, consider whether you already regularly consume a fortified breakfast cereal. Many breakfast cereals contain almost as many nutrients as a vitamin pill. If you do decide to take a supplement, choose a balanced formulation that contains 50–100% of the Daily Value for vitamins and minerals. Avoid supplements containing large doses of particular nutrients. See pp. 257–260 for more on choosing and using supplements.

Daily Values Because the DRIs are far too cumbersome to use as a basis for food labels, the U.S. Food and Drug Administration developed another set of dietary standards, the **Daily Values.** The Daily Values are based on several different sets of guidelines and include standards for fat, cholesterol, carbohydrate, dietary fiber, and selected vitamins and minerals. The Daily Values represent appropriate intake levels for a 2000-calorie diet. The percent Daily Value shown on a food label shows how well that food contributes to your recommended daily intake. Food labels are described in detail later in the chapter.

Terms

VW **Daily Values** A simplified version of the RDAs used on food labels; also included are values for nutrients with no established RDA.

Dietary Guidelines for Americans

To provide general guidance for choosing a healthy diet, the U.S. Department of Agriculture (USDA) and the U.S. Department of Health and Human Services (DHHS) have jointly issued Dietary Guidelines for Americans, most recently in 2005. These guidelines are intended for healthy children age 2 and older and adults of all ages. Key recommendations include the following:

- Consume a variety of nutrient-dense foods within and among the basic food groups, while staying within energy needs.
- Control calorie intake to manage body weight.
- Be physically active every day.
- Increase daily intake of foods from certain groups: fruits and vegetables, whole grains, and fat-free or low-fat milk and milk products.
- Choose fats wisely for good health, limiting intake of saturated and trans fats.
- Choose carbohydrates wisely for good health, limiting intake of added sugars.
- Choose and prepare foods with little salt, and consume potassium-rich foods.
- If you drink alcoholic beverages, do so in moderation.
- Keep foods safe to eat.

Following these guidelines promotes health and reduces risk for chronic diseases, including heart disease, cancer, diabetes, stroke, osteoporosis, and obesity. Each of the recommendations in the 2005 Dietary Guidelines for Americans is supported by an extensive review of scientific and medical evidence. What follows is a brief summary of the guidelines.

Adequate Nutrients Within Calorie Needs

Many people consume more calories than they need while failing to meet recommended intakes for all nutrients. Meeting the DRIs provides a foundation not only for current health but also for reducing chronic disease risk. Many adults don't get enough calcium, potassium, fiber, magnesium, and vitamins A, C, and E; many children don't get enough calcium, potassium, fiber, magnesium, and vitamin E. Most people need to choose meals and snacks that are high in nutrients but low to moderate in calories.

Two eating plans that translate nutrient recommendations into food choices are the USDA's MyPyramid and the DASH eating plan. MyPyramid is described in detail in the next section (pp. 249–253); the DASH plan appears in the Nutrition Resources section at the end of the chapter. You can obtain all the nutrients and other substances you need by choosing the recommended number of daily servings from basic food groups and following the advice about selecting nutrient-dense foods within the groups.

For many Americans, general dietary changes needed to meet dietary guidelines include consuming more fruits, whole grains, and dark green vegetables. Most fats in the diet should be unsaturated, like those found in fish and nuts.

Following these plans would mean that many Americans would have to make some general dietary changes:

- Eat more dark green vegetables, orange vegetables, legumes, fruits, whole grains, and low-fat and fat-free milk and milk products.
- Eat less refined grains, saturated fat, trans fat, cholesterol, added sugars, and calories.

Your nutrients should come primarily from foods that contain not only the vitamins and minerals often found in supplements but also hundreds of naturally occurring substances that may benefit health, such as antioxidants. Situations in which a supplement might be recommended were described earlier in the chapter.

For maximum nutrition, it is important to consume foods from all the food groups daily and to consume a variety of nutrient-dense foods within the groups. Nutrient-dense foods are those that provide substantial amounts of vitamins and minerals and relatively few calories. Americans currently consume many foods and beverages that are low in nutrient density, making it difficult or impossible to meet nutrient needs without overconsuming calories. Selecting nutrient-dense foods—low-fat forms of foods in each group and those free of added sugars—allows you to meet your nutrient needs without overconsuming calories and unhealthy food components such as saturated and trans fats.

People's food choices can be affected by individual and cultural preferences, moral beliefs, the cost and availability of food, and food intolerances and allergies. But healthy eating is possible no matter how foods are prepared or combined. If you avoid most or all foods from any of the major food groups, be sure to get enough nutrients from the other groups. MyPyramid can be applied to vegetarian diets.

Weight Management   Overweight and obesity are a major public health problem in the United States.

Calorie intake and physical activity work together to influence body weight. Most Americans need to reduce the amount of calories they consume, increase their level of physical activity, and make wiser food choices. Many adults gain weight slowly over time, but even small changes in behavior can help avoid weight gain.

Evaluate your body weight in terms of body mass index (BMI), a measure of relative body weight that also takes height into account (see Chapter 6 for instructions on how to determine your BMI). If your current weight is healthy, aim to avoid weight gain. Do so by increasing physical activity and making small cuts in calorie intake. Choose nutrient-dense foods and sensible portion sizes. Avoiding weight gain is easier than losing weight: For example, for most adults, a reduction of 50 to 100 calories per day may prevent gradual weight gain, whereas a reduction of 500 calories or more per day may be needed initially for weight loss.

Monitoring weight regularly helps people know if they need to adjust their food intake or physical activity to maintain a healthy weight. Those who need to lose weight should aim for slow, steady weight loss by decreasing calorie intake, maintaining adequate nutrient intake, and increasing physical activity. In terms of macronutrient intake, use the AMDR ranges described earlier in the chapter for dietary planning; within these healthy ranges, total calorie intake is what counts for weight management rather than specific percentages of particular macronutrients.

Physical Activity   As described earlier, regular physical activity improves fitness, helps manage weight, promotes psychological well-being, and reduces risk of heart disease, high blood pressure, cancer, and diabetes. Become active if you are inactive, and maintain or increase physical activity if you are already active. The amount of daily physical activity recommended for you depends on your current health status and goals.

- To reduce the risk of chronic disease, aim to accumulate at least 30 minutes (adults) or 60 minutes (children) of moderate physical activity—the equivalent of brisk walking at a pace of 3–4 miles per hour—beyond your usual activity at work, home, and school. Greater health benefits can be obtained by engaging in more vigorous activity or activity of longer duration.
- To help manage body weight and prevent gradual, unhealthy weight gain, engage in 60 minutes of moderate-to-high-intensity activity on most days of the week.
- To sustain weight loss in adulthood, engage daily in at least 60–90 minutes of moderate physical activity.

You can do the activity all at once or spread it out over several 10-minute or longer bouts during the day; choose activities you enjoy and can do regularly. You can boost fitness by engaging in exercises specifically designed for the health-related fitness components: cardiorespiratory endurance exercises, stretching exercises for flexibility, and resistance training for muscular strength and endurance. See Chapters 2–7 for advice on increasing daily physical activity and creating a complete fitness program.

Food Groups to Encourage Many Americans do not consume the recommended amounts of fruits, vegetables, whole grains, and low-fat or fat-free milk products—all of which have health benefits.

FRUITS AND VEGETABLES Fruits and vegetables are important sources of dietary fiber, vitamins, and minerals. For a 2000-calorie diet, about 4½ cups or the equivalent (9 servings) of fruits and vegetables each day is recommended. Eat a variety of fruits—fresh, frozen, canned, or dried—rather than fruit juice for most of your fruit choices. For vegetables, choose a variety of colors and kinds. Eat more of the following types of vegetables:

- Dark green vegetables, such as broccoli, kale, and other dark leafy greens
- Orange vegetables, such as carrots, sweet potatoes, pumpkin, and winter squash
- Legumes, such as pinto beans, kidney beans, black beans, garbanzo beans, split peas, and lentils

Other fruits and vegetables that are important sources of nutrients of concern include tomatoes and tomato products, red sweet peppers, cabbage and other cruciferous vegetables, bananas, citrus fruits, berries, and melons. See the discussion of MyPyramid for more advice on choosing fruits and vegetables.

WHOLE GRAINS Whole grains provide more fiber and nutrients than refined grains, and intake of whole grains reduces the risk of chronic disease and helps with weight maintenance. For a 2000-calorie diet, 6 ounce-equivalents (6 servings) of grains each day are recommended; at least half of these servings should be whole grains. (One ounce is about 1 slice of bread, 1 cup of breakfast cereal flakes, or ½ cup of cooked pasta or rice.) The remaining grain servings should be from enriched or whole-grain products. Refer back to p. 235 for information on identifying whole-grain products.

LOW-FAT AND FAT-FREE MILK AND MILK PRODUCTS Milk and other dairy products are important sources of calcium and other nutrients. Regular consumption of milk and milk products can reduce the risk of low bone mass throughout life. Choosing low-fat and fat-free dairy products helps to control calorie intake and reduce intake of saturated fat and cholesterol. For adults, the equivalent of 3 cups daily of fat-free or low-fat milk or milk products is recommended; 1½ ounces of cheese is the equivalent of 1 cup of milk. Yogurt and lactose-free milk are options for

Whole grains provide more nutrients and fiber than refined grains, and they may help reduce the risk of chronic disease. Half of your daily grain servings should come from whole grains. To check if a food contains whole grains, read the ingredient list on the food label.

people who are lactose intolerant, as is use of the enzyme lactase prior to the consumption of milk products. For individuals who avoid all milk products, nondairy calcium sources include fortified cereals and beverages, tofu prepared with calcium sulfate, green leafy vegetables, soybeans, and certain fish and seafood.

Fats Fats and oils provide the essential fatty acids needed for a healthy diet, but, as described earlier in the chapter, the type and amount of fats consumed can make a difference for health. A diet low in saturated fat, trans fat, and cholesterol helps keep blood cholesterol low and reduces the risk for heart disease; a diet containing omega-3 fats from fish also reduces the risk for heart disease. Goals for fat intake for most adults are as follows:

Total fat: 20–35% of total daily calories

Saturated fat: Less than 10% of total daily calories

Trans fat: As little as possible

Cholesterol: Less than 300 mg per day

Most fats in the diet should come from sources of unsaturated fats, such as fish, nuts, and vegetable oils. When

Your overall goal is to limit total fat intake to no more than 35% of total calories. Within that limit, favor unsaturated fats from vegetable oils, nuts, and fish over saturated and trans fats from animal products and foods made with hydrogenated vegetable oils or shortening. Saturated and trans fat intake should be kept as low as possible within a nutritionally adequate diet.

- Be moderate in your consumption of foods high in fat, including fast foods, commercially prepared baked goods and desserts, deep-fried food, meat, poultry, nuts and seeds, and regular dairy products.
- When you do eat high-fat foods, limit your portion sizes, and balance your intake with foods low in fat.
- Choose lean cuts of meat, and trim any visible fat from meat before and after cooking. Remove skin from poultry before or after cooking.
- Drink fat-free or low-fat milk instead of whole milk, and use lower-fat milk in puddings, soups, and baked products. Substitute plain low-fat yogurt, blender-whipped low-fat cottage cheese, or buttermilk for sour cream.
- Use vegetable oil instead of butter or margarine. Use tub or squeeze margarine instead of stick margarine. Look for margarines that are free of trans fats. Minimize intake of coconut or palm oil.
- Season vegetables, seafood, and meats with herbs and spices rather than with creamy sauces, butter, or margarine.
- Try lemon juice on salad, or use a yogurt-based salad dressing instead of mayonnaise or sour cream dressings.
- Steam, boil, bake, or microwave vegetables, or stir-fry them in a small amount of vegetable oil.
- Roast, bake, or broil meat, poultry, or fish so that fat drains away as the food cooks.
- Use a nonstick pan for cooking so that added fat will be unnecessary; use a vegetable spray for frying. Kitchen stores sell non-aerosol spray bottles to use with regular cooking oils.
- Chill broths from meat or poultry until the fat becomes solid. Spoon off the fat before using the broth.
- Substitute egg whites for whole eggs when baking; limit the number of egg yolks when scrambling eggs.
- Choose fruits as desserts most often.
- Eat a low-fat vegetarian main dish at least once a week.

selecting and preparing meat, poultry, dry beans, and milk or milk products, make choices that are lean, low-fat, or fat-free. To reduce trans fat intake, limit intake of foods made with hydrogenated vegetable oils. Refer to the box "Reducing the Saturated and Trans Fats in Your Diet" for additional specific suggestions.

Cholesterol is found only in animal foods. If you need to reduce your cholesterol intake, limit your intake of foods that are particularly high in cholesterol, including egg yolks, dairy fats, certain shellfish, and liver and other organ meats; watch your serving sizes of animal foods. Food labels list the fat and cholesterol content of foods.

Two servings per week of fish rich in heart-healthy omega-3 fatty acids are also recommended for people at high risk for heart disease. However, for certain groups, intake limits are set for varieties of fish that may contain mercury; see p. 262 for more information. Fish rich in omega-3 fatty acids include salmon, mackerel, and trout.

Carbohydrates Carbohydrates are an important energy source in a healthy diet. Foods rich in carbohydrates may also be rich in dietary fiber, which promotes healthy digestion and helps reduce the risk of type 2 diabetes and heart disease. Fruits, vegetables, whole grains, and fat-free or low-fat milk can provide the recommended amount of carbohydrate. Choose foods rich in fiber often—for example, choose whole fruits instead of juices and whole grains instead of refined grains. Legumes are another good source of fiber.

People who consume foods and beverages high in added sugars tend to consume more calories but smaller amounts of vitamins and minerals than those who limit their intake of added sugars. A food is high in sugar if one of the following appears first or second in the list of ingredients or if several are listed: sugar (any type, including beet, brown, invert, raw, and cane), corn syrup or sweetener, fruit juice concentrate, honey, malt syrup, molasses, syrup, cane juice or dextrose, fructose, glucose, lactose, maltose, or sucrose.

To reduce added sugar consumption, cut back on soft drinks, candies, sweet desserts (cakes, cookies, pies), fruit drinks, and other foods high in added sugars. Drink water rather than sweetened drinks, and don't let sodas and other sweets crowd out more nutritious foods, such as low-fat milk. Regular soda is the leading source of both added sugars and calories in the American diet; it provides little in the way of nutrients except sugar (Figure 8.4, p. 248). The 10 teaspoons of sugar in a 12-ounce soda can exceed the recommended daily limit for added sugars for someone consuming 2000 calories per day; for more on added sugar limits, see the discussion of MyPyramid.

Keep your teeth and gums healthy by limiting consumption of sweet or starchy foods between meals and brushing and flossing regularly; drinking fluoridated water also reduces the risk of dental caries.

Sodium and Potassium Many people can reduce their chance of developing high blood pressure or lower already elevated blood pressure by consuming less salt;

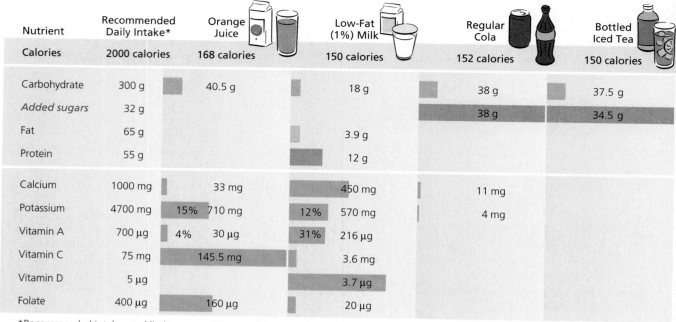

Nutrient	Recommended Daily Intake*	Orange Juice		Low-Fat (1%) Milk		Regular Cola		Bottled Iced Tea	
Calories	2000 calories	168 calories		150 calories		152 calories		150 calories	
Carbohydrate	300 g		40.5 g		18 g		38 g		37.5 g
Added sugars	32 g						38 g		34.5 g
Fat	65 g				3.9 g				
Protein	55 g				12 g				
Calcium	1000 mg		33 mg		450 mg		11 mg		
Potassium	4700 mg	15%	710 mg	12%	570 mg		4 mg		
Vitamin A	700 µg	4%	30 µg	31%	216 µg				
Vitamin C	75 mg		145.5 mg		3.6 mg				
Vitamin D	5 µg				3.7 µg				
Folate	400 µg		160 µg		20 µg				

*Recommended intakes and limits appropriate for a 20-year-old woman consuming 2000 calories per day.

Figure 8.4 Nutrient density of 12-ounce portions of selected beverages.   The four beverages shown have approximately the same number of calories in a 12-ounce serving. However, regular cola and iced tea provide few nutrients besides added sugars; both contain more than the total daily recommended limit of added sugars (about 8 teaspoons). Orange juice is rich in potassium, vitamin C, and folate; low-fat milk is an excellent source of protein, calcium, potassium, vitamin A, and vitamin D. (Color bars represent percentage of recommended daily intake or limit for each nutrient.)

reducing blood pressure lowers the risk for stroke, heart disease, and kidney disease. Salt is made up of the minerals sodium and chloride; and, although both of these minerals are essential for normal body function, we need only small amounts (1500 mg per day for adults). Most Americans consume much more salt than they need. The goal is to reduce sodium intake to less than 2300 milligrams per day, the equivalent of about 1 teaspoon of salt. Certain groups, including people with hypertension, African Americans, and older adults, benefit from an even lower sodium intake of no more than 1500 mg per day.

Salt is found mainly in processed and prepared foods; smaller amounts may also be added during cooking or at the table. To lower your intake of salt, choose fresh or plain frozen meat, poultry, seafood, and vegetables most often; these are lower in salt than processed forms are. Check and compare the sodium content in processed foods, including frozen dinners, cheeses, soups, salad dressings, sauces, and canned mixed dishes. Add less salt during cooking and at the table, and limit your use of high-sodium condiments like soy sauce, ketchup, mustard, pickles, and olives. Use lemon juice, herbs, and spices instead of salt to enhance the flavor of foods.

Along with lowering salt intake, increasing potassium intake helps lower blood pressure. Fruits, vegetables, and most milk products are available in forms that contain no salt, and many of these are sources of potassium. Potassium-rich foods include leafy green vegetables, sweet and white potatoes, winter squash, soybeans, tomato sauce, bananas, peaches, apricots, cantaloupes, and orange juice.

Alcoholic Beverages   Alcoholic beverages supply calories but few nutrients. Drinking in moderation—that is, no more than one drink per day for women and no more than two drinks per day for men—is associated with mortality reduction among some groups, primarily males age 45 and older and women age 55 and older. Among younger people, alcohol use provides little if any health benefit, and heavy drinking is associated with motor vehicle injuries and deaths, liver disease, stroke, violence, and other health problems.

People who should not drink at all include individuals who cannot restrict their drinking to moderate levels; women who are pregnant or breastfeeding or who may become pregnant; children and adolescents; people with specific health conditions; individuals who plan to drive or operate machinery or engage in any activity that requires attention, skill, or coordination; and individuals taking prescription or over-the-counter medications that can interact with alcohol. If you choose to drink alcoholic beverages, do so sensibly, moderately, and with meals. Never drink in situations where it may put you or others at risk.

Figure 8.5   USDA's MyPyramid.
The USDA food guidance system, called MyPyramid, can be personalized based on an individual's sex, age, and activity level; visit MyPyramid.gov to obtain a food plan appropriate for you. MyPyramid contains five main food groups plus oils (yellow band). Key consumer messages include the following:

- Grains: Make half your grains whole
- Vegetables: Vary your veggies
- Fruits: Focus on fruits
- Milk: Get your calcium-rich foods
- Meat and Beans: Go lean with protein

SOURCE: U.S. Department of Agriculture. 2005. *MyPyramid* (http://mypyramid.gov; retrieved April 20, 2005).

Grains Vegetables Fruits Milk Meat and Beans

Food Safety   Safe foods are those that pose little risk from harmful bacteria, viruses, parasites, toxins, or chemical or physical contaminants. Foodborne diseases affect about 76 million Americans each year. Actions by consumers can reduce the occurrence of foodborne illness significantly. It is especially important to be careful with perishable foods such as poultry, meats, eggs, shellfish, milk products, and fresh fruits and vegetables. Refer to the section on foodborne illness (pp. 259–261) for specific food safety tips.

USDA's MyPyramid

The first USDA daily food guide, published in 1916, emphasized the importance of fats and sugars in obtaining adequate calories to support daily activity. But nutrition needs have changed over time: Now the guidelines stress the importance of limiting additional fats and added sugars to keep calorie intake under control. Many Americans are familiar with the USDA Food Guide Pyramid, the food guidance system that was first released in 1992. Since the initial release of the Pyramid, scientists have updated both nutrient recommendations (the DRIs) and the Dietary Guidelines for Americans. So, as the 2005 Dietary Guidelines were prepared, the USDA reassessed its overall food guidance system and released MyPyramid in April 2005 (Figure 8.5).

A variety of experts have proposed other food-group plans. Some of these address perceived shortcomings in the USDA plans, and some adapt the basic 1992 Pyramid to special populations. Two alternative food plans appear in the Nutrition Resources section at the end of the chapter: the DASH eating plan and the Harvard Healthy Eating Pyramid. The USDA Center for Nutrition Policy and Promotion (www.usda.gov/cnpp) has more on alternative food plans for special populations such as young children, older adults, and people choosing particular ethnic diets.

Key Messages of MyPyramid   The new MyPyramid symbol (see Figure 8.5) has been developed to remind consumers to make healthy food choices and to be active every day. Consuming a balance of servings from each food group will not only meet nutrient needs but also help to reduce chronic disease risk. Key messages include the following:

- *Personalization* is represented by the person on the steps and the MyPyramid.gov site, which includes individualized recommendations, interactive assessments of food intake and physical activity, and tips for success.
- *Daily physical activity,* represented by the person climbing the steps, is important for maintaining a healthy weight and reducing the risk of chronic disease.
- *Moderation* of food intake is represented by the narrowing of each food group from bottom to top. The wider base stands for foods with little or no solid fats or added sugars, which should be selected more often; the narrower top represents food containing more solid fats and added sugars, which should be limited.
- *Proportionality* is represented by the different widths of the food group bands. The widths provide a general guide for how much food a person should choose from each group.
- *Variety* is represented by the six color bands representing the five food groups of MyPyramid and oils. Foods from all groups are needed daily for good health.

Daily Amount of Food from Each Group

Food group amounts shown in cups (c) or ounce-equivalents (oz-eq), with number of daily servings (srv) shown in parentheses; vegetable subgroup amounts are per week

Calorie level	1600	1800	2000	2200	2400	2600	2800	3000
Grains	5 oz-eq	6 oz-eq	6 oz-eq	7 oz-eq	8 oz-eq	9 oz-eq	10 oz-eq	10 oz-eq
Whole grains	3 oz-eq	3 oz-eq	3 oz-eq	3.5 oz-eq	4 oz-eq	4.5 oz-eq	5 oz-eq	5 oz-eq
Other grains	2 oz-eq	3 oz-eq	3 oz-eq	3.5 oz-eq	4 oz-eq	4.5 oz-eq	5 oz-eq	5 oz-eq
Vegetables	2 c (4 srv)	2.5 c (5 srv)	2.5 c (5 srv)	3 c (6 srv)	3 c (6 srv)	3.5 c (7 srv)	3.5 c (7 srv)	4 c (8 srv)
Dark green	2 c/wk	3 c/wk	3 c/wk	3 c/wk	3 c/wk	3 c/wk	3 c/wk	3 c/wk
Orange	1.5 c/wk	2 c/wk	2 c/wk	2 c/wk	2 c/wk	2.5 c/wk	2.5 c/wk	2.5 c/wk
Legumes	2.5 c/wk	3 c/wk	3 c/wk	3 c/wk	3 c/wk	3.5 c/wk	3.5 c/wk	3.5 c/wk
Starchy	2.5 c/wk	3 c/wk	3 c/wk	6 c/wk	6 c/wk	7 c/wk	7 c/wk	9 c/wk
Other	5.5 c/wk	6.5 c/wk	6.5 c/wk	7 c/wk	7 c/wk	8.5 c/wk	8.5 c/wk	10 c/wk
Fruits	1.5 c (3 srv)	1.5 c (3 srv)	2 c (4 srv)	2 c (4 srv)	2 c (4 srv)	2 c (4 srv)	2.5 c (5 srv)	2.5 c (5 srv)
Milk	3 c	3 c	3 c	3 c	3 c	3 c	3 c	3 c
Lean meat and beans	5 oz-eq	5 oz-eq	5.5 oz-eq	6 oz-eq	6.5 oz-eq	6.5 oz-eq	7 oz-eq	7 oz-eq
Oils	5 tsp	5 tsp	6 tsp	6 tsp	7 tsp	8 tsp	8 tsp	10 tsp

The discretionary calorie allowances shown below are the calories remaining at each level after nutrient-dense foods in each food group are selected. Those trying to lose weight may choose not to use discretionary calories. For those wanting to maintain weight, discretionary calories may be used to increase the amount of food from each food group; to consume foods that are not in the lowest fat form or that contain added sugars; to add oil, fat, or sugars to foods; or to consume alcohol. The amounts below show how discretionary calories may be divided between solid fats and added sugars.

Discretionary calories	132	195	267	290	362	410	426	512
Solid fats	11 g	15 g	18 g	19 g	22 g	24 g	24 g	29 g
Added sugars	12 g (3 tsp)	20 g (5 tsp)	32 g (8 tsp)	38 g (9 tsp)	48 g (12 tsp)	56 g (14 tsp)	60 g (15 tsp)	72 g (18 tsp)

Figure 8.6   MyPyramid food intake patterns.   To determine an appropriate amount of food from each group, find the column with your approximate daily energy intake. That column lists the daily recommended intake from each food group. Visit MyPyramid.gov for a personalized intake plan and for intakes for other calorie levels.   SOURCE: U.S. Department of Health and Human Services and U.S. Department of Agriculture. 2005. *Dietary Guidelines for Americans, 2005* (http://www.health. gov/dietaryguidelines; retrieved January 20, 2005).

• *Gradual improvement* is a good strategy; people can benefit from taking small steps to improve their diet and activity habits each day.

The MyPyramid chart in Figure 8.6 shows the food intake patterns recommended for different levels of calorie intake; Table 8.4 provides guidance for determining an appropriate calorie intake for weight maintenance. Use the table to identify an energy intake that is about right for you; then refer to the appropriate column in Figure 8.6. A personalized version of MyPyramid recommendations can also be obtained by visiting MyPyramid.gov. Each food group is described briefly below. Past experiences have shown that many Americans have trouble identifying serving sizes, so recommended daily intakes from each group are now given in terms of cups and ounces; see the box "Judging Portion Sizes" for additional advice.

Studies have shown that most people underestimate the size of their food portions, in many cases by as much as 50%. If you need to retrain your eye, try using measuring cups and spoons and an inexpensive kitchen scale when you eat at home. With a little practice, you'll learn the difference between 3 and 8 ounces of chicken or meat, and what a half-cup of rice really looks like. For quick estimates, use the following equivalents:

- 1 teaspoon of margarine = the tip of your thumb
- 1 ounce of cheese = your thumb, four dice stacked together, or an ice cube
- 3 ounces of chicken or meat = a deck of cards or an audio-cassette tape.

- 1 cup of pasta = a small fist or a tennis ball
- ½ cup of rice or cooked vegetables = an ice cream scoop or one-third of a can of soda
- 2 tablespoons of peanut butter = a ping-pong ball or large marshmallow
- 1 medium potato = a computer mouse
- 1–2-ounce muffin or roll = plum or large egg
- 2-ounce bagel = hockey puck or yo-yo
- 1 medium fruit (apple or orange) = baseball
- ¼ cup nuts = golf ball
- Small cookie or cracker = poker chip

Grains Foods from this group are usually low in fat and rich in complex carbohydrates, dietary fiber (if grains are unrefined), and many vitamins and minerals, including thiamin, riboflavin, iron, niacin, folic acid (if enriched or fortified), and zinc. Someone eating 2000 calories a day should include 6 ounce-equivalents each day, with half of those servings from whole grains such as whole-grain bread, whole-wheat pasta, high-fiber cereal, and brown rice. The following count as 1 ounce-equivalent:

[handwritten: Grains]
[handwritten: 6 oz each day]
[handwritten: 3 should be whole grains]

- 1 slice of bread
- 1 small (2½-inch diameter) muffin
- 1 cup ready-to-eat cereal flakes
- ½ cup cooked cereal, rice, grains, or pasta
- 1 6-inch tortilla

Choose foods that are typically made with little fat or sugar (bread, rice, pasta) over those that are high in fat and sugar (croissants, chips, cookies, doughnuts).

Vegetables Vegetables contain carbohydrates, dietary fiber, vitamin A, vitamin C, folate, potassium, and other nutrients. They are also naturally low in fat. In a 2000-calorie diet, 2½ cups (5 servings) of vegetables should be included daily. Each of the following counts as ½ cup or equivalent (1 serving) of vegetables:

[handwritten: 5 servings or 2½ cups]

- ½ cup raw or cooked vegetables
- 1 cup raw leafy salad greens
- ½ cup vegetable juice

Because vegetables vary in the nutrients they provide, it is important to consume a variety of types of vegetables to obtain maximum nutrition. Many Americans consume only a few types of vegetables, with white potatoes (baked or served as french fries) being the most popular. To help boost variety, MyPyramid recommends servings from five different subgroups within the Vegetables group; choose vegetables from several subgroups each day. (For clarity,

Table 8.4	MyPyramid Daily Calorie Intake Levels		
Age (years)	Sedentary*	Moderately Active**	Active†
Child			
2–3	1000	1000–1400	1000–1400
Female			
4–8	1200–1400	1400–1600	1400–1800
9–13	1400–1600	1600–2000	1800–2200
14–18	1800	2000	2400
19–30	1800–2000	2000–2200	2400
31–50	1800	2000	2200
51+	1600	1800	2000–2200
Male			
4–8	1200–1400	1400–1600	1600–2000
9–13	1600–2000	1800–2200	2000–2600
14–18	2000–2400	2400–2800	2800–3200
19–30	2400–2600	2600–2800	3000
31–50	2200–2400	2400–2600	2800–3000
51+	2000–2200	2200–2400	2400–2800

*A lifestyle that includes only the light physical activity associated with typical day-to-day life.
**A lifestyle that includes physical activity equivalent to walking about 1.5 to 3 miles per day at 3 to 4 miles per hour (30–60 minutes a day of moderate physical activity), in addition to the light physical activity associated with typical day-to-day life.
†A lifestyle that includes physical activity equivalent to walking more than 3 miles per day at 3 to 4 miles per hour (60 or more minutes a day of moderate physical activity), in addition to the light physical activity associated with typical day-to-day life.

SOURCE: U.S. Department of Agriculture, 2005. *MyPyramid Food Intake Pattern Calorie Levels* (http://mypyramid.gov/professionals; retrieved April 20, 2005).

...ngs from the subgroups in terms of

...es like spinach, chard, collards, ...ale, romaine, and turnip and

...w vegetables like carrots, win-...es, and pumpkin

...s, kidney beans, black ...peas, soybeans, split peas, and ...mes can be counted as servings of vegeta-...bles or as alternatives to meat

- Starchy vegetables like corn, green peas, and white potatoes
- Other vegetables; tomatoes, bell peppers (red, orange, yellow, or green), green beans, and cruciferous vegetables like cauliflower are good choices

Fruits   Fruits are rich in carbohydrates, dietary fiber, and many vitamins, especially vitamin C. For someone eating a 2000-calorie diet, 2 cups (4 servings) of fruits are recommended daily. The following each count as ½ cup or equivalent (1 serving) of fruit:

- ½ cup fresh, canned, or frozen fruit
- ½ cup fruit juice (100% juice)
- 1 small whole fruit
- ¼ cup dried fruit

2 cups or 4 servings

Good choices from this group are citrus fruits and juices, melons, pears, apples, bananas, and berries. Choose whole fruits often—they are higher in fiber and often lower in calories than fruit juices. Fruit *juices* typically contain more nutrients and less added sugar than fruit *drinks*. Choose canned fruits packed in 100% fruit juice or water rather than in syrup.

Milk   This group includes all milk and milk products, such as yogurt, cheeses (except cream cheese), and dairy desserts, as well as lactose-free and lactose-reduced products. Foods from this group are high in protein, carbohydrate, calcium, riboflavin, and vitamin D (if fortified). Those consuming 2000 calories per day should include 3 cups of milk or the equivalent daily. Each of the following counts as the equivalent of 1 cup:

- 1 cup milk or yogurt
- ½ cup ricotta cheese
- 1½ ounces natural cheese
- 2 ounces processed cheese

3 cups

Cottage cheese is lower in calcium than most other cheeses; ½ cup is equivalent to ¼ cup milk. Ice cream is also lower in calcium and higher in sugar and fat than many other dairy products; one scoop counts as ⅓ cup milk. To limit calories and saturated fat in your diet, it is best to choose servings of low-fat and fat-free items from this group.

Meat and Beans   This group includes meat, poultry, fish, dry beans and peas, eggs, nuts, and seeds. These foods provide protein, niacin, iron, vitamin B-6, zinc, and thiamin; the animal foods in the group also provide vitamin B-12. For someone consuming a 2000-calorie diet, 5½ ounce-equivalents is recommended. The following each count as equivalent to 1 ounce:

- 1 ounce cooked lean meat, poultry, or fish
- ¼ cup cooked dry beans (legumes) or tofu
- 1 egg
- 1 tablespoon peanut butter
- ½ ounce nuts or seeds

5½ oz

One egg at breakfast, ½ cup of pinto beans at lunch, and a 3-ounce (cooked weight) hamburger at dinner would add up to the equivalent of 6 ounces of lean meat for the day. To limit your intake of fat and saturated fat, choose lean cuts of meat and skinless poultry, and watch your serving sizes carefully. Choose at least one serving of plant proteins, such as black beans, lentils, or tofu, every day.

Oils   The Oils group represents the oils that are added to foods during processing, cooking, or at the table; oils and soft margarines include vegetable oils and soft vegetable oil table spreads that have no trans fats. These are major sources of vitamin E and unsaturated fatty acids, including the essential fatty acids. For a 2000-calorie diet, 6 teaspoons of oils per day are recommended. One teaspoon is the equivalent of the following:

- 1 teaspoon vegetable oil or soft margarine
- 1 tablespoon salad dressing or light mayonnaise

Foods that are mostly oils include nuts, olives, avocados, and some fish. The following portions include about 1 teaspoon of oil: 8 large olives, ⅙ medium avocado, ½ tablespoon peanut butter, and ⅓ ounce roasted nuts. Food labels can help consumers identify the type and amount of fat in various foods.

Discretionary Calories, Solid Fats, and Added Sugars   The suggested intakes from the basic food groups in MyPyramid assume that nutrient-dense foods are selected from each group; nutrient-dense foods are those that are fat-free or low-fat and that contain no added sugars. If this pattern is followed, then a small amount of additional calories can be consumed—the *discretionary calorie allowance*. Figure 8.6 shows the discretionary calorie allowance at each calorie level in MyPyramid.

People who are trying to lose weight may choose not to use discretionary calories. For those wanting to maintain weight, discretionary calories may be used to increase the amount of food from a food group; to consume foods that

Table 8-5	**Top Ten Sources of Calories in the American Diet**
Food	**Percent of Total Calories**
Regular soft drinks	7.1
Cake, sweet rolls, doughnuts, pastries	3.6
Hamburgers, cheeseburgers, meatloaf	3.1
Pizza	3.1
Potato chips, corn chips, popcorn	2.9
Rice	2.7
Rolls, buns, English muffins, bagels	2.7
Cheese or cheese spread	2.6
Beer	2.6
French fries, fried potatoes	2.2

SOURCE: Block, G. 2004. Foods contributing to energy intake in the US: Data from NHANES III and NHANES 1999–2000. *Journal of Food Composition and Analysis* 17(2004): 439–447.

are not in the lowest fat form or that contain added sugars; to add oil, fat, or sugars to foods; or to consume alcohol. The amounts shown in Figure 8.6 show how discretionary calories may be divided between solid fats and added sugars. The values for additional fat target no more than 30% of total calories from fat and less than 10% of calories from saturated fat. Examples of discretionary solid fat calories include choosing higher-fat meats such as sausages or chicken with skin; whole milk instead of fat-free milk; and topping foods with butter. For example, 1 cup of whole milk has 60 calories more than 1 cup of fat-free milk; these 60 calories would be counted as discretionary calories.

As described earlier in the chapter, added sugars are the sugars added to foods and beverages in processing or preparation, not the naturally occurring sugars in fruits or milk. The suggested amounts of added sugars may be helpful limits for including some sweetened foods or beverages in the daily diet without exceeding energy needs or underconsuming other nutrients. For example, in a 2000-calorie diet, MyPyramid lists 32 grams (8 teaspoons) for discretionary intake of added sugars. In the American diet, added sugars are often found in sweetened beverages (regular soda, sweetened teas, fruit drinks), dairy products (ice cream, some yogurts), and grain products (bakery goods). For example, a 20-ounce regular soda has 260 calories from added sugars that would be counted as discretionary calories. The current American diet includes higher-than-recommended levels of sugar intake.

Remember, the amounts listed in Figure 8.6 for solid fats and added sugars assume that you selected nutrient-dense foods from the major food groups; don't just add fats and sugars to your diet. The average American diet is overrich in foods that contain relatively large amounts of added sugars and fats and that are low in essential nutrients (Table 8.5). To control weight and obtain adequate amounts of essential nutrients, it is important to choose nutrient-dense foods for most of your daily servings.

MOTIVATION FOR CHANGE! Maintaining a healthy diet can be a challenge in an environment filled with convenient but less-than-ideal food choices. To help increase your commitment and motivation, complete an analysis of the short-term and long-term advantages and disadvantages of your current diet and your goal diet (see Chapter 1 for tips on completing this type of analysis). Keep your list of the advantages of change handy to help overcome challenging situations.

The Vegetarian Alternative

Some people choose a diet with one essential difference from the diets we've already described: Foods of animal origin (meat, poultry, fish, eggs, milk) are eliminated or restricted. Many do so for health reasons; vegetarian diets tend to be lower in saturated fat, cholesterol, and animal protein and higher in complex carbohydrates, dietary fiber, folate, vitamins C and E, carotenoids, and phytochemicals. Some people adopt a vegetarian diet out of concern for the environment, for financial considerations, or for reasons related to ethics or religion.

Types of Vegetarian Diets There are various vegetarian styles; the wider the variety of the diet eaten, the easier it is to meet nutritional needs. **Vegans** eat only plant foods. **Lacto-vegetarians** eat plant foods and dairy products. **Lacto-ovo-vegetarians** eat plant foods, dairy products, and eggs. According to some polls, about 5 million American adults never eat meat, poultry, or fish and fall into one of these three groups. Others can be categorized as **partial vegetarians, semivegetarians,** or **pescovegetarians;** these individuals eat plant foods, dairy products, eggs, and usually a small selection of poultry, fish, and other seafood. Many other people choose vegetarian meals frequently but are not strictly vegetarian. Including some animal protein (such as dairy products) in a mostly vegetarian diet makes planning easier, but it is not necessary.

Terms

vegan A vegetarian who eats no animal products at all.

lacto-vegetarian A vegetarian who includes milk and cheese products in the diet.

lacto-ovo-vegetarian A vegetarian who eats no meat, poultry, or fish, but does eat eggs and milk products.

partial vegetarian, semivegetarian, or **pescovegetarian** A vegetarian who includes eggs, dairy products, and small amounts of poultry and seafood in the diet.

A Food Plan for Vegetarians MyPyramid can be adapted for use by vegetarians with only a few key modifications. For the meat and beans group, vegetarians can focus on the nonmeat choices of dry beans (legumes), nuts, seeds, eggs, and soy foods like tofu (soybean curd) and tempeh (a cultured soy product). Vegans and other vegetarians who do not consume any dairy products must find other rich sources of calcium (see below). Fruits, vegetables, and whole grains are healthy choices for people following all types of vegetarian diets.

A healthy vegetarian diet emphasizes a wide variety of plant foods. Although plant proteins are generally incomplete, choosing a variety of plant foods will supply all of the essential amino acids. Choosing minimally processed and unrefined foods will maximize nutrient value and provide ample dietary fiber. Daily consumption of a variety of plant foods in amounts that meet total energy needs can provide all needed nutrients, except vitamin B-12 and possibly vitamin D. Strategies for obtaining these and other nutrients of concern include the following:

- *Vitamin B-12* is found naturally only in animal foods; if dairy products and eggs are limited or avoided, B-12 can be obtained from fortified foods such as ready-to-eat cereals, soy beverages, meat substitutes, and special yeast products or from supplements.

- *Vitamin D* can be obtained by spending 5–15 minutes a day out in the sun, by consuming vitamin D-fortified products like ready-to-eat cereals and soy or rice milk, or by taking a supplement.

- *Calcium* is found in legumes, tofu processed with calcium, dark-green leafy vegetables, nuts, tortillas made from lime-processed corn, and fortified orange juice, soy milk, bread, and other foods.

- *Iron* is found in whole grains, fortified bread and breakfast cereals, dried fruits, green leafy vegetables, nuts and seeds, legumes, and soy foods. The iron in plant foods is more difficult for the body to absorb than the iron from animal sources; consuming a good source of vitamin C with most meals is helpful because vitamin C improves iron absorption.

- *Zinc* is found in whole grains, nuts, legumes, and soy foods.

It takes a little planning and common sense to put together a good vegetarian diet. If you are a vegetarian or are considering becoming one, devote some extra time and thought to your diet. It's especially important that you eat as wide a variety of foods as possible to ensure that all your nutritional needs are satisfied. Consulting with a registered dietitian will make your planning even easier. Vegetarian diets for children, teens, and pregnant and lactating women warrant professional guidance.

Dietary Challenges for Special Population Groups

MyPyramid and the Dietary Guidelines for Americans provide a basis that everyone can use to create a healthy diet. However, some population groups face special dietary challenges.

Women Women tend to be smaller and to weigh less than men, meaning they have lower energy needs and therefore need fewer calories. Because of this, women may have more difficulty getting adequate amounts of all the essential nutrients and need to focus on nutrient-dense foods. Two nutrients of special concern are calcium and iron, minerals for which many women fail to meet the RDAs. Low calcium intake may be linked to the development of osteoporosis in later life. The *Healthy People 2010* report sets a goal of increasing from 40% to 75% the proportion of women ages 20–49 who meet the dietary recommendation for calcium. Nonfat and low-fat dairy products and fortified cereal, bread, and orange juice are good choices. Iron is also a concern: Menstruating women have higher iron requirements than other groups, and a lack of iron in the diet can lead to iron-deficiency anemia. Lean red meat, green leafy vegetables, and fortified breakfast cereals are good sources of iron. As discussed earlier, all women capable of becoming pregnant should consume adequate folate or folic acid from fortified foods and/or supplements.

Men Men are seldom thought of as having nutritional deficiencies because they generally have high-calorie diets. However, many men have a diet that does not follow recommended food intake patterns but that includes more red meat and fewer fruits, vegetables, and grains than recommended. This dietary pattern is linked to heart disease and some types of cancer. A high intake of calories can lead to weight gain in the long term if a man's activity level decreases as he ages. Men should use MyPyramid as a basis for their overall diet and focus on increasing their consumption of fruits, vegetables, and grains to obtain vitamins, minerals, dietary fiber, and phytochemicals. The "5 a Day for Better Health" program created by the National Cancer Institute and Department of Health and Human Services to promote increased intake of fruits and vegetables has been adapted to create the "Shoot for 9 for Better Health" message for men; for strategies and guidelines for consuming more fruits and vegetables, visit http://5aday.gov.

College Students Foods that are convenient for college students are not always the healthiest choices. However, it is possible to make healthy eating both convenient and affordable (see the tips in the box "Eating Strategies for College Students"). Two settings of concern often found on college campuses are buffet-style dining

General Guidelines

• Eat slowly and enjoy your food. Set aside a separate time to eat. Don't eat while you study.

• Eat a colorful, varied diet. The more colorful your diet is, the more varied and rich in fruits and vegetables it will be. Many Americans eat few fruits and vegetables, despite the fact that these foods are typically inexpensive, delicious, rich in nutrients, and low in fat and calories. Don't limit your vegetable choices to french fries, which are typically high in saturated and trans fats.

• Consider nutrient density in your food choices, and avoid large servings of foods that provide calories but few essential nutrients. Spend your daily calorie budget wisely on healthy, nutrient-rich, foods.

• Check out the labels and ingredient lists of foods you commonly eat so that you are aware of their general nutrient profile.

• Eat breakfast. You'll have more energy in the morning and be less likely to grab an unhealthy snack later on. Whole-grain cereals or whole-grain toast are excellent breakfast choices.

• Choose healthy snacks—fruits, vegetables, grains, and cereals—as often as you can.

• Drink water more often than soft drinks or other sweetened beverages. Rent a mini-refrigerator for your dorm room and stock up on healthy beverages.

• Pay attention to portion sizes. Read food labels carefully, and take special note of serving sizes and the total number of servings in the package. You may find that your favorite bottled drinks and packaged snack foods—which you treat as a single serving—actually provide multiple servings and that you are consuming more calories, fat, and added sugars than you realize.

• Combine physical activity with healthy eating. You'll look and feel better and have a much lower risk of many chronic diseases. Even a little exercise is better than none.

Eating in the Dining Hall

• Choose a meal plan that includes breakfast—and don't skip it.

• Accept that dining hall food is not going to be as good as home cooking. Find dishes that you like that are nutritious.

• If menus are posted or distributed, decide what you want to eat before getting in line and stick to your choices. Consider what you plan to do and eat for the rest of the day before making your choices.

• Ask for large servings of vegetables and small servings of meat and other high-fat main dishes. Build your meals around grains and vegetables.

• Try whole grains like brown rice, whole-wheat bread, and whole-grain cereals.

• Choose leaner poultry, fish, or bean dishes rather than high-fat meats and fried entrees.

• Ask that gravies and sauces be served on the side; limit your intake.

• Choose broth-based or vegetable soups rather than cream soups.

• At the salad bar, load up on leafy greens, beans, and fresh vegetables. Avoid mayonnaise-coated salads, bacon, croutons, and high-fat dressings. Put dressing on the side; dip your fork into it rather than pouring it over the salad.

• Drink nonfat milk, water, mineral water, or 100% fruit juice rather than heavily sweetened fruit drinks, whole milk, soft drinks, or beer.

• Choose fruit for dessert rather than pastries, cookies, or cakes.

• Do some research about the foods and preparation methods used in your dining hall or cafeteria. Discuss any suggestions you have with your food service manager.

Eating in Fast-Food Restaurants

• Most fast-food chains can provide a brochure with a nutritional breakdown of the foods on the menu. Ask for it and identify the healthiest options. (See also the information in Appendix C.)

• Order small single burgers with no cheese instead of double burgers with many toppings. If possible, ask for them broiled instead of fried.

• Ask for items to be prepared without mayonnaise, tartar sauce, sour cream, or other high-fat sauces. Ketchup, mustard, and fat-free mayonnaise or sour cream are better choices and are available at many fast-food restaurants.

• Choose whole-grain buns or bread for burgers, hot dogs, and sandwiches.

• Choose chicken items made from chicken breast, not processed chicken.

• Order vegetable pizzas without extra cheese.

• If you order french fries or onion rings, get the smallest size and/or share them with a friend.

Fast-food meals are a health concern not just because of what they typically provide—significant amounts of calories, fat, added sugars, and sodium—but also because of what they often lack—fiber and many vitamins and minerals. A large cheeseburger, large order of fries, and large (32 oz) nondiet soda may provide about 1600 calories, 75 grams of fat, and 30 teaspoons of added sugars. It is important to balance any fast-food meals you consume by choosing healthy, nutrient-rich foods during the rest of the day.

Eating on the Run

Are you chronically short of time? The following healthy and filling items can be packed for a quick snack or meal: fresh or dried fruit, fruit juices, raw fresh vegetables, plain bagels, bread sticks, whole-wheat fig bars, low-fat cheese sticks or cubes, low-fat crackers or granola bars, nonfat or low-fat yogurt, snack-size cereal boxes, pretzels, rice or corn cakes, plain popcorn, soup (if you have access to a microwave), or water.

halls and fast-food restaurants. Both may offer foods that are low in nutrient density—and in very large portions. While no foods are entirely "bad," consuming moderate portions of a wide variety of foods is critical for a healthy diet.

Older Adults As people age, they tend to become less active, so they require fewer calories to maintain their weight. At the same time, the absorption of nutrients tends to be lower in older adults because of age-related changes in the digestive tract. Thus, they must consume nutrient-dense foods to meet their nutritional requirements. As discussed earlier, foods fortified with vitamin B-12 and/or B-12 supplements are recommended for people over age 50. Because constipation is a common problem, consuming foods high in dietary fiber and obtaining adequate fluids are important goals.

Athletes Key dietary concerns for athletes are meeting increased energy and fluid requirements for training and making healthy food choices throughout the day.

ENERGY INTAKE Individuals engaged in vigorous training programs expend more energy (calories) than sedentary and moderately active individuals and may have energy needs ranging from 2000 to more than 6000 calories per day. For athletes, the American Dietetic Association recommends a diet with 60–65% of calories coming from carbohydrate, 10–15% from protein, and no more than 30% from fat. Athletes for whom maintaining low body weight and body fat is important—such as gymnasts, skaters, and wrestlers—should consume adequate calories and nutrients and avoid falling into unhealthy patterns of eating. The combination of low levels of body fat, high physical activity, disordered eating habits, and, in women, amenorrhea, is associated with stress fractures and other injuries and with osteoporosis. (The female athlete triad was discussed in Chapter 6; see Chapter 9 for more on eating disorders.)

CARBOHYDRATE Endurance athletes involved in competitive events lasting longer than 90 minutes may benefit from increasing carbohydrate intake to 65–70% of total calories; this increase should come in the form of complex, rather than simple, carbohydrates. High carbohydrate intake builds and maintains muscle glycogen stores, resulting in greater endurance and delayed fatigue during competitive events. Some endurance athletes engage in "carbohydrate loading"—a practice that involves increasing carbohydrate intake in the days before a competition. Before exercise, the ACSM recommends that an active adult or athlete consume a meal or snack that is relatively high in carbohydrate, moderate in protein, and low in fat. Soon after exercise, particularly following a strenuous competition or training session, a mixed meal containing carbohydrates, protein, and fat should be consumed to replace muscle glycogen and provide amino acids for building and repairing muscle tissue. Consuming some simple carbohydrate immediately after exercise can help replenish glycogen stores in the liver and muscles.

PROTEIN For endurance athletes, the ACSM recommends a protein intake of 1.2–1.4 grams of protein per kilogram (0.55–0.64 gram per pound) of body weight per day, up from the standard DRI of 0.8 gram per kilogram (0.36 gram per pound); for athletes engaged in heavy strength training, protein needs may be as high as 1.6–1.7 grams per kilogram (0.73–0.77 gram per pound) of body weight. This level of protein intake is easily obtainable from foods, however. A 160-pound athlete consuming 3500 calories per day needs to obtain only 12% of total calories as protein to achieve the upper end of the range for endurance athletes. The average American diet includes about 16% of total calories as protein, and a balanced high-carbohydrate, moderate protein, moderate-fat diet can provide the nutrients athletes need.

There is no evidence that consuming supplements containing vitamins, minerals, protein, or specific amino acids will build muscle or improve sports performance. Strength and muscle are built with exercise, not extra protein, and carbohydrates provide the fuel needed for muscle-building exercise. Strenuous physical activity does increase the need for protein and some vitamins and minerals; however, the increased energy intake of athletes more than compensates for this increased need.

FLUIDS Moderately active people should consume adequate fluids as described earlier in the chapter. People who exercise heavily and/or live in a hot climate need to consume additional fluids to maximize performance and prevent heat illness. For a strenuous endurance event, prepare yourself the day before by drinking plenty of fluid. On the day of the event, the ACSM recommends that you consume 14–22 ounces (400–600 ml) of fluid about 2 hours before exercise, and then 6–12 ounces (150–350 ml) of fluid every 15–20 minutes during exercise—or as much of this amount as you can tolerate. Afterward, drink enough to replace lost fluids—16–24 ounces for every pound of weight lost. (Weight loss during a workout or athletic event comes primarily from fluid loss through sweat; as described in Chapter 3, checking your weight can help you monitor your fluid balance.)

Water is a good choice for fluid replacement for workouts and events lasting less than 60–90 minutes, especially if you are trying to avoid the additional calories in many other beverages. However, for workouts or events lasting longer, a sports drink can be a good choice. These contain water, electrolytes, and carbohydrates. The advantage of sports drinks is that they can provide you with some extra energy (in the form of rapidly digestible carbohydrates that help maintain blood glucose levels) and replace electrolytes like sodium that are lost in sweat.

People with Special Health Concerns Many Americans have special health concerns that affect their dietary needs. For example, women who are pregnant or breastfeeding require extra calories, vitamins, and minerals. People with diabetes benefit from a well-balanced diet that is low in simple sugars, high in complex carbohydrates, and relatively rich in monounsaturated fats. And people with high blood pressure need to limit their sodium consumption and control their weight. If you have a health problem or concern that may require a special diet, discuss your situation with a physician or registered dietitian.

NUTRITIONAL PLANNING: MAKING INFORMED CHOICES ABOUT FOOD

Now that you know the nutrients you need and the amounts required for maximum wellness, you are almost ready to create a diet that works for you. Depending on your needs and dietary habits, you may have some specific areas of concern you want to address first, such as interpreting food labels, understanding food additives, or avoiding foodborne illnesses. We turn to these and other topics next.

Reading Food Labels

Consumers can get help in applying the principles of MyPyramid and the Dietary Guidelines for Americans from food labels. Since 1994, all processed foods regulated by either the FDA or the USDA have included standardized nutrition information on their labels. Every food label shows serving sizes and the amount of fat, saturated fat, cholesterol, protein, dietary fiber, and sodium in each serving. To make intelligent choices about food, learn to read and understand food labels (see the box "Using Food Labels" on p. 258). Research has shown that people who read food labels eat less fat.

Because most meat, poultry, fish, fruits, and vegetables are not processed, they were not covered by the 1994 law. You can obtain information on the nutrient content of these items from basic nutrition books, registered dietitians, nutrient analysis computer software, the World Wide Web, and the companies that produce or distribute these foods. Also, supermarkets often have posters or pamphlets listing the nutrient contents of these foods. Lab 8.3 gives you the opportunity to compare foods using the information provided on their labels.

Reading Dietary Supplement Labels

Dietary supplements include vitamins, minerals, amino acids, herbs, enzymes, and other compounds. Although dietary supplements are often thought of as safe and natural, they do contain powerful, bioactive chemicals that have the potential for harm. About one-quarter of all pharmaceutical drugs are derived from botanical sources,

and even essential vitamins and minerals can have toxic effects if consumed in excess.

In the United States, supplements are not legally considered drugs and are not regulated the way drugs are. Before they are approved by the FDA and put on the market, drugs undergo clinical studies to determine safety, effectiveness, side effects and risks; possible interactions with other substances; and appropriate dosages. The FDA does not authorize or test dietary supplements, and supplements are not required to demonstrate either safety or effectiveness before they are marketed. Although dosage guidelines exist for some of the compounds in dietary supplements, dosages for many are not well established.

Many ingredients in dietary supplements are classified by the FDA as "generally recognized as safe," but some have been found to be dangerous on their own or to interact with prescription or over-the-counter drugs in dangerous ways. Garlic supplements, for example, can cause bleeding if taken with anticoagulant ("blood-thinning") medications. Even products that are generally considered safe can have side effects—St. John's wort, for example, increases the skin's sensitivity to sunlight and may decrease the effectiveness of oral contraceptives, drugs used to treat HIV infection, and many other medications.

There are also key differences between drugs and supplements in their manufacture. FDA-approved medications are standardized for potency, and quality control and proof of purity are required. Dietary supplement manufacture is not as closely regulated, and there is no guarantee that a product even contains a given ingredient, let alone in the appropriate amount. The potency of herbal supplements can vary widely due to differences in growing and harvesting conditions, preparation methods, and storage. Contamination and misidentification of plant compounds are also potential problems.

In an effort to provide consumers with more reliable and consistent information about supplements, the FDA has developed labeling regulations. Since March 1999, labels similar to those found on foods have been required for dietary supplements; for more information, see the box "Using Dietary Supplement Labels" on p. 260.

Remember that dietary supplements are no substitute for a healthy diet. Supplements do not provide all the known—or yet-to-be-discovered—benefits of whole foods. Supplements should also not be used as a replacement for medical treatment for serious illnesses.

Food Additives

Today, some 2800 substances are intentionally added to foods for one or more of the following reasons: (1) to maintain or improve nutritional quality, (2) to maintain freshness, (3) to help in processing or preparation, or (4) to alter taste or appearance. Additives make up less than 1% of our food. The most widely used are sugar, salt, and corn syrup; these three, plus citric acid, baking soda,

Using Food Labels

Vw

Food labels are designed to help consumers make food choices based on the nutrients that are most important to good health. In addition to listing nutrient content by weight, the label puts the information in the context of a daily diet of 2000 calories that includes no more than 65 grams of fat (approximately 30% of total calories). For example, if a serving of a particular product has 13 grams of fat, the label will show that the serving represents 20% of the daily fat allowance. If your daily diet contains fewer or more than 2000 calories, you need to adjust these calculations accordingly.

Food labels contain uniform serving sizes. This means that if you look at different brands of salad dressing, for example, you can compare calories and fat content based on the serving amount. (Food label serving sizes may be larger or smaller than MyPyramid serving size equivalents, however.) Regulations also require that foods meet strict definitions if their packaging includes the terms *light, low-fat,* or *high-fiber* (see below). Health claims such as "good source of dietary fiber" or "low in saturated fat" on packages are signals that those products can wisely be included in your diet. Overall, the food label is an important tool to help you choose a diet that conforms to MyPyramid and the Dietary Guidelines.

Selected Nutrient Claims and What They Mean

Healthy   A food that is low in fat, is low in saturated fat, has no more than 360–480 mg of sodium and 60 mg of cholesterol, *and* provides 10% or more of the Daily Value for vitamin A, vitamin C, protein, calcium, iron, or dietary fiber.

Light or lite   One-third fewer calories or 50% less fat than a similar product.

Reduced or fewer   At least 25% less of a nutrient than a similar product; can be applied to fat ("reduced fat"), saturated fat, cholesterol, sodium, and calories.

Extra or added   10% or more of the Daily Value per serving when compared to what a similar product has.

Good source   10–19% of the Daily Value for a particular nutrient per serving.

High, rich in, or excellent source of   20% or more of the Daily Value for a particular nutrient per serving.

Low calorie   40 calories or less per serving.

High fiber   5 g or more of fiber per serving.

Good source of fiber   2.5–4.9 g of fiber per serving.

Fat-free   Less than 0.5 g of fat per serving.

Low-fat   3 g of fat or less per serving.

Saturated fat-free   Less than 0.5 g of saturated fat and 0.5 g of trans fatty acids per serving.

Low saturated fat   1 g or less of saturated fat per serving and no more than 15% of total calories.

Cholesterol-free   Less than 2 mg of cholesterol and 2 g or less of saturated fat per serving.

Low cholesterol   20 mg or less of cholesterol and 2 g or less of saturated fat per serving.

Low sodium   140 mg or less of sodium per serving.

Very low sodium   35 mg or less of sodium per serving.

Lean   Cooked seafood, meat, or poultry with less than 10 g of fat, 4.5 g or less of saturated fat, and less than 95 mg of cholesterol per serving.

Extra lean   Cooked seafood, meat, or poultry with less than 5 g of fat, 2 g of saturated fat, and 95 mg of cholesterol per serving.

Note: As of June 2005, the FDA had not yet defined nutrient claims relating to carbohydrate, so foods labeled low- or reduced-carbohydrate do not conform to any approved standard.

1. Serving size: Determine how many servings there are in the food package and compare it to how much you actually eat. You may need to adjust the rest of the nutrient values based on your typical serving size.

2. Calories and calories from fat: Note whether a serving is high in calories and fat. The sample food shown here is low in fat, with only 30 of its 235 calories from fat.

3. Daily Values: Based on a 2000-calorie diet, Daily Value percentages tell you whether the nutrients in a serving of food contribute a lot or a little to your total daily diet.
  5% or less is low
  20% or more is high

4. Limit these nutrients: Look for foods low in fat, saturated fat, trans fat, cholesterol, and sodium.

5. Get enough of these nutrients: Look for foods high in dietary fiber, vitamin A, vitamin C, calcium, and iron.

Nutrition Facts

Serving Size 1 cup (265g)
Servings per Container 2

Amount per Serving

Calories 235   Calories from Fat 30

	% Daily Value*
Total Fat 3g	**5%**
Saturated Fat 1g	**5%**
Trans Fat 0.5g	
Cholesterol 30mg	**10%**
Sodium 775mg	**32%**
Total Carbohydrate 34g	**11%**
Dietary Fiber 9g	**36%**
Sugars 5g	
Protein 18g	

Vitamin A 25%	•	Vitamin C 0%	
Calcium 12%	•	Iron 20%	

*Percent Daily Values are based on a 2,000 calorie diet. Your daily values may be higher or lower depending on your calorie needs:

		Calories	2,000	2,500
Total Fat	Less than		65g	80g
Sat Fat	Less than		20g	25g
Cholesterol	Less than		300mg	300mg
Sodium	Less than		2,400mg	2,400mg
Total Carbohydrate			300g	375g
Dietary Fiber			25g	30g

Calories per gram:
Fat 9 • Carbohydrate 4 • Protein 4

Footnote: This section shows recommended daily intake for two levels of calorie consumption and values for dietary calculations; it's the same on all labels.

vegetable colors, mustard, and pepper, account for 98% by weight of all food additives used in the United States.

Food additives pose no significant health hazard to most people because the levels used are well below any that could produce toxic effects. Two additives of potential concern for some people are sulfites, used to keep vegetables from turning brown, and monosodium glutamate (MSG), used as a flavor enhancer. Sulfites can cause severe reactions in some people, and the FDA strictly limits their use and requires clear labeling on any food containing sulfites. MSG may cause some people to experience episodes of sweating and increased blood pressure. To protect yourself, eat a variety of foods in moderation. If you have any sensitivity to an additive, check food labels when you shop and ask questions when you eat out.

Foodborne Illness

Many people worry about additives or pesticide residues in their food. However, a greater threat to the safety of the food supply comes from microorganisms that cause foodborne illnesses. Raw or undercooked animal products, such as chicken, hamburger, and oysters, pose the greatest risk for contamination. The CDC estimates that 76 million Americans become sick each year as a result of foodborne illness, 325,000 are hospitalized, and 5000 die. In most cases, foodborne illness produces acute gastroenteritis, characterized by diarrhea, vomiting, fever, and weakness. People often mistake foodborne illness for a bout of the flu. Although the effects of foodborne illness are usually not serious, some groups, such as children and older people, are at risk for severe complications, including rheumatic diseases, kidney failure, seizures, blood poisoning, and death.

Causes of Foodborne Illnesses Most cases of foodborne illness are caused by **pathogens**, disease-causing microorganisms that contaminate food, usually from improper handling. The threats are numerous and varied; among them are the sometimes deadly *Escherichia coli* (*E. coli*) O157:H7 in meat and water; *Salmonella* in eggs, on vegetables, and on poultry; *Vibrio* in shellfish; *Cyclospora* and hepatitis A virus on fruit; *Cryptosporidium* in drinking water; *Campylobacter jejuni* in meat and poultry; and *Listeria monocytogenes* in lunch meats, sausages, and hot dogs.

You can't tell by taste, smell, or sight whether a food is contaminated. Some studies have revealed high levels of contamination. In 2003, *Consumer Reports* tested 484 chickens purchased in grocery stores and found that half were contaminated with *Campylobacter* and/or *Salmonella*. Although pathogens are usually destroyed during cooking, the U.S. government is taking steps to bring down levels of contamination by improving national testing and surveillance. Raw meat and poultry products are now sold with safe handling and cooking instructions, and all packaged, unpasteurized fresh fruit and vegetable juices carry warnings about potential contamination. It is important to note that while foodborne illness outbreaks associated with food-processing plants make headlines, most cases of illness trace back to poor food handling in the home or in food-service establishments.

A potential threat from food is bovine spongiform encephalopathy (BSE), or "mad cow disease," a fatal degenerative neurological disease caused by an abnormal protein that forms deposits in the brain. A variant form of this disease, known as Creutzfeldt-Jakob disease (CJD), is believed to be caused by eating beef contaminated with central nervous system tissue from BSE-infected cows. To date, there have been about 150 confirmed cases worldwide of CJD among the hundreds of thousands of people who may have consumed BSE-contaminated products. In December 2003, the first BSE-infected cow was identified in the United States. Although the USDA states that the risk to human health from BSE is extremely low, additional steps are being taken to prevent the BSE protein from entering the food supply; visit the USDA Web site for more information (www.aphis.usda.gov).

Preventing and Treating Foodborne Illness

The key to protecting yourself from foodborne illness is to handle, cook, and store foods in ways that prevent bacteria from spreading and multiplying:

- Don't buy food in containers that leak, bulge, or are severely dented. Refrigerated foods should be cold, and frozen foods should be solid.
- Refrigerate perishable items as soon as possible after purchase. Use or freeze fresh meats within 3–5 days and fresh poultry, fish, and ground meat within 1–2 days.
- Thaw frozen food in the refrigerator or in the microwave oven, not on the kitchen counter.
- Thoroughly wash your hands with warm soapy water for 20 seconds before and after handling food, especially raw meat, fish, poultry, or eggs.
- Make sure counters, cutting boards, dishes, and other equipment are thoroughly cleaned before and after use. If possible, use separate cutting boards for meat and for foods that will be eaten raw, such as fruits and vegetables. Wash dishcloths and kitchen towels frequently.
- Thoroughly rinse and scrub fruits and vegetables with a brush, if possible, or peel off the skin.
- Cook foods thoroughly, especially beef, poultry, fish, pork, and eggs. Cooking kills most microorganisms, as long as an appropriately high temperature is reached. The USDA now recommends that consumers, especially high-risk individuals, use a food thermometer to

Terms

pathogen A microorganism that causes disease.

Nutritional Planning: Making Informed Choices About Food **259**

Since 1999, specific types of information have been required on the labels of dietary supplements. In addition to basic information about the product, labels include a "Supplement Facts" panel, modeled after the "Nutrition Facts" panel used on food labels (see the figure). Under the Dietary Supplement Health and Education Act (DSHEA) and food labeling laws, supplement labels can make three types of health-related claims.

- *Nutrient-content claims,* such as "high in calcium," "excellent source of vitamin C," or "high potency." The claims "high in" and "excellent source of" mean the same as they do on food labels. A "high potency" single-ingredient supplement must contain 100% of its Daily Value; a "high potency" multi-ingredient product must contain 100% or more of the Daily Value of at least two-thirds of the nutrients present for which Daily Values have been established.

- *Health claims,* if they have been authorized by the FDA or another authoritative scientific body. The association between adequate calcium intake and lower risk of osteoporosis is an example of an approved health claim. Since 2003, the FDA has also allowed so-called *qualified* health claims for situations in which there is emerging but as yet inconclusive evidence for a particular claim. Such claims must include qualifying language such as "scientific evidence suggests but does not prove" the claim.

- *Structure-function claims,* such as "antioxidants maintain cellular integrity" or "this product enhances energy levels." Because these claims are not reviewed by the FDA, they must carry a disclaimer (see the sample label).

Tips for Choosing and Using Dietary Supplements

- Check with your physician before taking a supplement. Many are not meant for children, older people, women who are pregnant or breastfeeding, people with chronic illnesses or upcoming surgery, or people taking prescription or OTC medications.

- Follow the cautions, instructions for use, and dosage given on the label.

- Look for the USP-DSVP mark on the label, indicating that the product meets minimum safety and purity standards developed under the Dietary Supplement Verification Program (DSVP) by the United States Pharmacopeia (USP). The USP-DSVP mark means that the product (1) contains the ingredients stated on the label, (2) has the declared amount and strength of ingredients, (3) will dissolve effectively, (4) has been screened for harmful contaminants, and (5) has been manufactured using safe, sanitary, and well-controlled procedures. The National Nutritional Foods Association (www.nnfa.org) has a self-regulatory testing program for its members; other, smaller associations and labs, including ConsumerLab.Com, also test and rate dietary supplements.

- Choose brands made by nationally known food and drug manufacturers or "house brands" from large retail chains. Due to their size and visibility, such sources are likely to have higher manufacturing standards.

- If you experience side effects, discontinue use of the product and contact your physician. Report any serious reactions to the FDA's MedWatch monitoring program (1-888-INFO-FDA; http://www.fda.gov/medwatch).

For More Information About Dietary Supplements

ConsumerLab.Com: http://www.consumerlab.com

Food and Drug Administration: http://vm.cfsan.fda.gov/~dms/supplmnt.html

National Center for Complementary and Alternative Medicine: nccam.nih.gov/health/supplements.htm

National Institutes of Health, Office of Dietary Supplements: http://dietary-supplements.info.nih.gov

U.S. Department of Agriculture: http://www.nal.usda.gov/fnic/etext/000015.html

U.S. Pharmacopeia: http://www.usp.org/uspverified

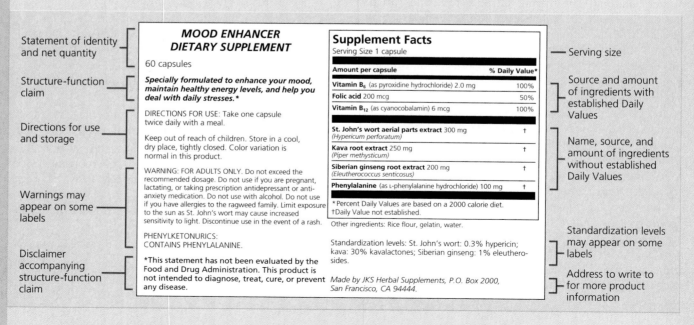

Statement of identity and net quantity

MOOD ENHANCER DIETARY SUPPLEMENT

60 capsules

Structure-function claim

Specially formulated to enhance your mood, maintain healthy energy levels, and help you deal with daily stresses.*

Directions for use and storage

DIRECTIONS FOR USE: Take one capsule twice daily with a meal.

Keep out of reach of children. Store in a cool, dry place, tightly closed. Color variation is normal in this product.

Warnings may appear on some labels

WARNING: FOR ADULTS ONLY. Do not exceed the recommended dosage. Do not use if you are pregnant, lactating, or taking prescription antidepressant or anti-anxiety medication. Do not use with alcohol. Do not use if you have allergies to the ragweed family. Limit exposure to the sun as St. John's wort may cause increased sensitivity to light. Discontinue use in the event of a rash.

PHENYLKETONURICS: CONTAINS PHENYLALANINE.

Disclaimer accompanying structure-function claim

*This statement has not been evaluated by the Food and Drug Administration. This product is not intended to diagnose, treat, cure, or prevent any disease.

Supplement Facts
Serving Size 1 capsule — Serving size

Amount per capsule	% Daily Value*
Vitamin B$_6$ (as pyroxidine hydrochloride) 2.0 mg	100%
Folic acid 200 mcg	50%
Vitamin B$_{12}$ (as cyanocobalamin) 6 mcg	100%
St. John's wort aerial parts extract 300 mg (Hypericum perforatum)	†
Kava root extract 250 mg (Piper methysticum)	†
Siberian ginseng root extract 200 mg (Eleutherococcus senticosus)	†
Phenylalanine (as L-phenylalanine hydrochloride) 100 mg	†

* Percent Daily Values are based on a 2000 calorie diet.
†Daily Value not established.

Other ingredients: Rice flour, gelatin, water.

Standardization levels: St. John's wort: 0.3% hypericin; kava: 30% kavalactones; Siberian ginseng: 1% eleuthero-sides.

Made by JKS Herbal Supplements, P.O. Box 2000, San Francisco, CA 94444.

Source and amount of ingredients with established Daily Values

Name, source, and amount of ingredients without established Daily Values

Standardization levels may appear on some labels

Address to write to for more product information

Careful food handling greatly reduces the risk of foodborne illness. Helpful strategies include washing hands and all fruits and vegetables, using separate cutting boards for meat and for foods that will be eaten raw, cooking meat thoroughly, and refrigerating leftovers promptly.

verify that hamburgers are cooked to 160°F. When eating out, order red meat cooked "well done."

- Cook stuffing separately from poultry; or wash poultry thoroughly, stuff immediately before cooking, and transfer the stuffing to a clean bowl immediately after cooking.

- Refrigerate foods at or below 40°F and freeze at or below 0°F. Do not leave cooked or refrigerated foods, such as meats or salads, at room temperature for more than 2 hours. Use refrigerated leftovers within 3–4 days.

- Don't eat raw animal products, including raw eggs in Caesar salad, hollandaise sauce, or eggnog. Use only pasteurized milk and juice, and look for pasteurized eggs, which are now available in some states.

- Cook eggs until they're firm and fully cook foods containing eggs. Store eggs in the coldest part of the refrigerator, not on the door, and use them within 3–5 weeks.

- Because of possible contamination with *E. coli* O157:H7 and *Salmonella,* avoid raw sprouts, or eat sprouts only after submerging them in boiling water for 10 seconds.

- According to the USDA, "When in doubt, throw it out."

Additional precautions are recommended for people at particularly high risk for foodborne illness—pregnant women, young children, older persons, and people with weakened immune systems or certain chronic illnesses. If you are a member of one of these groups, don't eat or drink any of the following products: unpasteurized juices; raw sprouts; raw (unpasteurized) milk and products made from unpasteurized milk; raw or undercooked meat, poultry, eggs, fish, and shellfish; and soft cheeses such as feta, Brie, Camembert, or blue-veined varieties. It's also important to avoid ready-to-eat foods such as hot dogs, luncheon meats, and cold cuts unless they are reheated until they are steaming hot.

If you think you may be having a bout of foodborne illness, drink plenty of clear fluids to prevent dehydration and rest to speed recovery. To prevent further contamination, wash your hands often and always before handling food until you recover. A fever higher than 102°F, blood in the stool, or dehydration deserves a physician's evaluation, especially if the symptoms persist for more than 2–3 days. In cases of suspected botulism—characterized by symptoms such as double vision, paralysis, dizziness, and vomiting—consult a physician immediately.

Irradiated Foods

Food irradiation is the treatment of foods with gamma rays, X-rays, or high-voltage electrons to kill potentially harmful pathogens, including bacteria, parasites, insects, and fungi that cause foodborne illness. It also reduces spoilage and extends shelf life. Even though irradiation has been generally endorsed by agencies such as the World Health Organization, the Centers for Disease Control and Prevention, and the American Medical Association, few irradiated foods are currently on the market due to consumer resistance and skepticism. Studies haven't conclusively identified any harmful effects of food irradiation, and newer methods of irradiation involving electricity and X-rays do not require the use of any radioactive materials. Studies indicate that when consumers are given information about the process of irradiation and the benefits of irradiated foods, most want to purchase them.

All primary irradiated foods (meat, vegetables, and so on) are labeled with the flowerlike radura symbol and a brief information label; spices and foods that are merely ingredients do not have to be labeled. It is important to remember that although irradiation kills most pathogens, it does not completely sterilize foods. Proper handling of irradiated foods is still critical for preventing foodborne illness.

Terms

food irradiation The treatment of foods with gamma rays, X-rays, or high-voltage electrons to kill potentially harmful pathogens and increase shelf life.

Environmental Contaminants and Organic Foods

Contaminants are present in the food-growing environment, but few of them ever enter the food and water supply in amounts sufficient to cause health problems. Environmental contaminants include various minerals, antibiotics, hormones, pesticides, and industrial chemicals. Safety regulations attempt to keep our exposure to contaminants at safe levels, but monitoring is difficult and many substances (such as pesticides) persist in the environment long after being banned from use.

Organic Foods Some people who are concerned about pesticides and other environmental contaminants choose to buy foods that are **organic.** In December 2000, the USDA enacted a new national standard for organic foods to replace the older system of local, state, and private standards. To be certified as organic, foods must meet strict production, processing, handling, and labeling criteria. Organic crops must meet limits on pesticide residues; for meat, milk, eggs, and other animal products to be certified organic, animals must be given organic feed and access to the outdoors and may not be given antibiotics or growth hormones. The use of genetic engineering, ionizing radiation, and sewage sludge are prohibited. Products can be labeled "100% organic" if they contain all organic ingredients and "organic" if they contain at least 95% organic ingredients; all such products may carry the new USDA organic seal. A product with at least 70% organic ingredients can be labeled "made with organic ingredients" but cannot use the USDA seal.

Foods that are organic may not be chemical-free, however. They may be contaminated with pesticides used on neighboring lands or on foods transported in the same train or truck. However, they do tend to have lower levels of pesticide residues than conventionally grown crops. There are strict pesticide limits for all foods—organic and conventional—and the debate about the potential health effects of long-term exposure to small amounts of pesticide residues is ongoing. Supporters of organic foods also note that practices associated with organic farming help maintain biodiversity of crops and are less likely to degrade soil, contaminate water, or expose farmworkers to dangerous chemicals.

Guidelines for Fish Consumption A specific area of concern has been possible mercury contamination in fish. Overall, fish and shellfish are healthy sources of pro-tein, omega-3 fats, and other nutrients; and prudent choices can minimize the risk of any possible negative health effects. High mercury concentrations are most likely to be found in predator fish—large fish that eat smaller fish. Mercury can cause brain damage to fetuses and young children. In 2004, the FDA and Environmental Protection Agency (EPA) released an advisory with specific guidelines for certain groups. To reduce exposure to the harmful effects of mercury, women who are or who may become pregnant and nursing mothers should follow these guidelines:

- Do not eat shark, swordfish, king mackerel, or tilefish.
- Eat up to 12 ounces a week of a variety of fish and shellfish that is lower in mercury, such as shrimp, canned light tuna, salmon, pollock, and catfish. Limit consumption of albacore tuna to 6 ounces per week.
- Check advisories about the safety of recreationally caught fish from local lakes, rivers, and coastal areas; if no information is available, limit consumption to 6 ounces per week.

The same FDA/EPA guidelines apply to children, although they should consume smaller servings.

Some experts have also expressed concern about the presence of toxins such as PCBs in farmed fish, especially farmed salmon. Although no federal guidelines have been set, some researchers suggest that consumers limit themselves to 8 ounces of farmed salmon per month. Fish should be labeled with its country of origin and whether it is wild or farmed; most canned salmon is wild.

A PERSONAL PLAN: APPLYING NUTRITIONAL PRINCIPLES

You've learned the basics of good nutrition, know how to interpret food and supplement labels, and have some guidelines for protecting yourself from foodborne illness. With this foundation, you can now put together a diet that works for you. Based on your particular nutrition and health status, there probably is an ideal diet for you, but there is no single type of diet that provides optimal health for everyone. Many cultural dietary patterns can meet people's nutritional requirements (see the box "Ethnic Foods"). Customize your food plan based on your age, gender, weight, activity level, medical risk factors—and, of course, personal tastes.

Assessing and Changing Your Diet

The first step in planning a healthy diet is to examine what you currently eat. Labs 8.1 and 8.2 are designed to help you analyze your current diet and compare it with optimal dietary goals. (This analysis can be completed using Appendix B, a nutritional analysis software program, or one of several Web sites.)

Terms

organic A designation applied to foods grown and produced according to strict guidelines limiting the use of pesticides, nonorganic ingredients, hormones, antibiotics, genetic engineering, irradiation, and other practices.

There is no one ethnic diet that clearly surpasses all others in providing people with healthful foods. However, every diet has its advantages and disadvantages and, within each cuisine, some foods are better choices. The dietary guidelines described in this chapter can be applied to any ethnic cuisine. For additional guidance, refer to the table below.

	Choose More Often	Choose Less Often
Chinese	Dishes that are steamed, poached (jum), boiled (chu), roasted (kow), barbecued (shu), or lightly stir-fried Hoisin sauce, oyster sauce, wine sauce, plum sauce, velvet sauce, or hot mustard Fresh fish and seafood, skinless chicken, tofu Mixed vegetables, Chinese greens Steamed rice, steamed spring rolls, soft noodles	Fried wontons or egg rolls Crab rangoon Crispy (Peking) duck or chicken Sweet-and-sour dishes made with breaded and deep-fried meat, poultry, or fish Fried rice Fried or crispy noodles
French	Dishes prepared au vapeur (steamed), en brochette (skewered and broiled), or grillé (grilled) Fresh fish, shrimp, scallops, or mussels or skinless chicken, without sauces Clear soups	Dishes prepared à la crème (in cream sauce), au gratin or gratinée (baked with cream and cheese), or en croûte (in pastry crust) Drawn butter, hollandaise sauce, and remoulade (mayonnaise-based sauce)
Greek	Dishes that are stewed, broiled, or grilled, including shish kabobs (souvlaki) Dolmas (grape leaves) stuffed with rice Tzatziki (yogurt, cucumbers, and garlic) Tabouli (bulgur-based salad) Pita bread, especially whole wheat	Moussaka, saganaki (fried cheese) Vegetable pies such as spanakopita and tyropita Baba ghanoush (eggplant and olive oil) Deep-fried falafel (chickpea patties) Gyros stuffed with ground meat Baklava
Indian	Dishes prepared masala (curry), tandoori (roasted in a clay oven), or tikke (pan roasted); kabobs Raita (yogurt and cucumber salad) and other yogurt-based dishes and sauces Dal (lentils), pullao or pilau (basmati rice) Chapati (baked bread)	Ghee (clarified butter) Korma (meat in cream sauce) Samosas, pakoras (fried dishes) Molee and other coconut milk–based dishes Poori, bhatura, or paratha (fried breads)
Italian	Pasta primavera or pasta, polenta, risotto, or gnocchi with marinara, red or white wine, white or red clam, or light mushroom sauce Dishes that are grilled or prepared cacciatore (tomato-based sauce), marsala (broth and wine sauce), or piccata (lemon sauce) Cioppino (seafood stew) Vegetable soup, minestrone or fagioli (beans)	Antipasto (cheese, smoked meats) Dishes that are prepared alfredo, frito (fried), crema (creamed), alla panna (with cream), or carbonara Veal scaloppini Chicken, veal, or eggplant parmigiana Italian sausage, salami, and prosciutto Buttered garlic bread Cannoli
Japanese	Dishes prepared nabemono (boiled), shabu-shabu (in boiling broth), mushimono (steamed), nimono (simmered), yaki (broiled), or yakimono (grilled) Sushi or domburi (mixed rice dish) Steamed rice or soba (buckwheat), udon (wheat), or rice noodles	Tempura (battered and fried) Agemono (deep fried) Katsu (fried pork cutlet) Sukiyaki Fried tofu
Mexican	Soft corn or wheat tortillas Burritos, fajitas, enchiladas, soft tacos, and tamales filled with beans, vegetables, or lean meats Refried beans, nonfat or low-fat; rice and beans Ceviche (fish marinated in lime juice) Salsa, enchilada sauce, and picante sauce Gazpacho, menudo, or black bean soup Fruit or flan for dessert	Crispy, fried tortillas Dishes that are fried, such as chile rellenos, chimichangas, flautas, and tostadas Nachos and cheese, chili con queso, and other dishes made with cheese or cheese sauce Guacamole, sour cream, and extra cheese Refried beans made with lard Fried ice cream
Thai	Dishes that are barbecued, sautéed, broiled, boiled, steamed, braised, or marinated Sàté (skewered and grilled meats) Fish sauce, basil sauce, chili or hot sauces Bean thread noodles, Thai salad	Coconut milk soup Peanut sauce or dishes topped with nuts Mee-krob (crispy noodles) Red, green, and yellow curries, which typically contain coconut milk

SOURCES: National Heart, Lung, and Blood Institute. 1998. Tips for Healthy Multicultural Dining Out. In *Clinical Guidelines on the Identification, Evaluation, and Treatment of Overweight and Obesity in Adults*. Bethesda, Md.: National Institutes of Health. Duyff, R. L. 1998. *The American Dietetic Association's Complete Food and Nutrition Guide*. Minneapolis, Minn.: Chronimed. Kirby, J. 1998. *Dieting for Dummies*. Foster City, Calif.: IDG Books.

Next, experiment with additions and substitutions to your current diet to bring it closer to your goals. If you are consuming too much fat, for example, try substituting fruit for a calorie-rich dessert. If you aren't getting enough iron, try adding some raisins to your cereal or garbanzo beans to your salad. If you need to plan your diet from the ground up, use the Dietary Guidelines and the MyPyramid food guidance system.

To put your plan into action, use the behavioral self-management techniques and tips described in Chapter 1. If you identify several changes you want to make, focus on one at a time. You might start, for example, by substituting nonfat or low-fat milk for whole milk. When you become used to that, you can try substituting whole-wheat bread for white bread. The information on eating behavior in Lab 8.1 will help you identify and change unhealthy patterns of eating.

MOTIVATION FOR CHANGE! Are you one of the many people who choose fast food or packaged snack foods often because they are quick and convenient? You can't eliminate these choices from your environment, but you can make healthier choices by finding other options that are just as convenient. Review the menus of the restaurants you visit most often and identify choices that meet your dietary goals and that you enjoy. Next, locate other inexpensive restaurants or food sources that are near your campus or home. Finally, identify ready-to-eat foods like prewashed vegetables and fruit salad that you could stock at home and pack for an inexpensive bag lunch. Make a list of restaurants, stores, and specific food items that are convenient and that are a match for your dietary goals. When you are tempted by less healthy choices, refer to your list for both practical information and a motivation boost.

Staying Committed to a Healthy Diet

Beyond knowledge and information, you also need support in difficult situations. Keeping to your plan is easiest when you choose and prepare your own food at home. Advance planning is the key: mapping out meals and shopping appropriately, cooking in advance when possible, and preparing enough food for leftovers later in the week. A tight budget does not necessarily make it more difficult to eat healthy meals. It makes good health sense and good budget sense to use only small amounts of meat and to have a few meatless meals each week.

In restaurants, keeping to food plan goals becomes somewhat more difficult. Portion sizes in restaurants tend to be larger than MyPyramid serving size equivalents, but by remaining focused on your goals, you can eat only part of your meal and take the rest home for a meal later in the week. Don't hesitate to ask questions when you're eating in a restaurant. Most restaurant personnel are glad to

explain how menu selections are prepared and to make small adjustments, such as serving salad dressings and sauces on the side so they can be avoided or used sparingly. To limit your fat intake, order meat or fish broiled or grilled rather than fried or sauteed, choose rice or a plain baked potato over french fries, and select a clear soup rather than a creamy one. Desserts that are irresistible can, at least, be shared.

Strategies like these are helpful, but small changes cannot change a fundamentally high-fat, high-calorie meal into a moderate, healthful one. Often, the best advice is to bypass a large steak with potatoes au gratin for a flavorful but low-fat entree. Many of the selections offered in ethnic restaurants are healthy choices (refer to the box on ethnic foods for suggestions).

Fast-food restaurants offer the biggest challenge to a healthy diet. Surveys show that about 70% of 18- to 24-year-olds and 64% of 25- to 34-year-olds visit a fast-food restaurant at least once a week. Fast-food meals are often high in calories, total fat, saturated fat, trans fat, sodium, and sugar; they may be low in fiber and in some vitamins and minerals (see Appendix C). If you do eat at a fast-food restaurant, make sure the rest of your meals that day are low-fat meals rich in fruits and vegetables.

Knowledge of food and nutrition is essential to the success of your program. The information provided in this chapter should give you the tools you need to design and implement a diet that promotes long-term health and well-being. If you need additional information or have questions about nutrition, be sure the source you consult is reliable.

Tips for Today

Eating is one of life's great pleasures. There are many ways to satisfy your nutrient needs so you can create a healthy diet that takes into account your personal preferences and favorite foods. If your current eating habits are not as healthy as they could be, you can choose equally delicious foods that offer both short-term and long-term health benefits. Opportunities to improve your diet present themselves every day, and small changes add up.

Right now you can

- Substitute a healthy snack—an apple, a banana, or plain popcorn—for a bag of chips or cookies.

- Drink a glass of water and put a bottle of water in your backpack for tomorrow.

- Plan to make healthy selections when you go to dinner, such as grilled or steamed vegetables instead of french fries or salmon instead of steak.

- Study the box on ethnic foods in this chapter and plan to order a healthy selection the next time you eat at your favorite ethnic restaurant. Do the same with the fast-food restaurants listed in Appendix C.

SUMMARY

- The six classes of nutrients are carbohydrates, proteins, fats, vitamins, minerals, and water.

- The nutrients essential to humans are released into the body through digestion. Nutrients in foods provide energy, measured in kilocalories (commonly called calories); build and maintain body tissues; and regulate body functions.

- Protein, an important component of body tissue, is composed of amino acids; nine are essential to good health. Foods from animal sources provide complete proteins; plants provide incomplete proteins.

- Fats, a major source of energy, also insulate the body and cushion the organs; 3–4 teaspoons of vegetable oil per day supplies the essential fats. For most people, dietary fat intake should be 20–35% of total calories, and unsaturated fats should be favored over saturated and trans fats.

- Carbohydrates provide energy to the brain, nervous system, and blood and to muscles during high-intensity exercise. Naturally occurring simple carbohydrates and unrefined complex carbohydrates should be favored over added sugars and refined carbohydrates.

- Fiber includes plant substances that are impossible for the human body to digest. It helps reduce cholesterol levels and promotes the passage of wastes through the intestines.

- The 13 essential vitamins are organic substances that promote specific chemical and cell processes and act as antioxidants. The 17 known essential minerals are inorganic substances that regulate body functions, aid in growth and tissue maintenance, and help in the release of energy from food. Deficiencies in vitamins and minerals can cause severe symptoms over time, but excess doses are also dangerous.

- Water aids in digestion and food absorption, allows chemical reactions to take place, serves as a lubricant or cushion, and helps regulate body temperature.

- Foods contain other substances, such as phytochemicals, that may not be essential nutrients but that may protect against chronic diseases.

- The Dietary Reference Intakes, Dietary Guidelines for Americans, and MyPyramid food guidance system provide standards and recommendations for getting all essential nutrients from a varied, balanced diet and for eating in ways that protect against chronic disease.

- The Dietary Guidelines for Americans advise us to consume a variety of foods while staying within calorie needs; manage body weight through calorie control and regular physical activity; eat more fruits, vegetables, whole grains, and reduced-fat dairy products; choose fats and carbohydrates wisely; eat less salt and more potassium; be moderate with alcohol intake; and handle foods safely.

- Choosing foods from each group in MyPyramid every day helps ensure the appropriate amounts of necessary nutrients.

- A vegetarian diet requires special planning but can meet all human nutritional needs.

- Different population groups, such as college students and athletes, face special dietary challenges and should plan their diets to meet their particular needs.

- Consumers can get help applying nutritional principles by reading the standardized labels that appear on all packaged foods and on dietary supplements.

- Although nutritional basics are well established, no single diet provides wellness for everyone. Individuals should focus on their particular needs and adapt general dietary principles to meet them.

For Further Exploration

For reliable nutrition advice, talk to a faculty member in the nutrition department on your campus, a registered dietitian (RD), or your physician. Many large communities have a telephone service called Dial a Dietitian. By calling this number, you can receive free nutrition information from an RD.

Experts on quackery suggest that you steer clear of anyone who puts forth any of the following false statements: Most diseases are caused primarily by faulty nutrition, large doses of vitamins are effective against many diseases, hair analysis can be used to determine a person's nutritional state, or a computer-scored nutritional deficiency test is a basis for prescribing vitamins. Any practitioner—licensed or not—who sells supplements in his or her office should be thoroughly scrutinized.

W W *Fit and Well* Online Learning Center (www.mhhe.com/fahey)

Use the learning objectives, study guide questions, and glossary flashcards to review key terms and concepts and prepare for exams. You can extend your knowledge of nutrition and gain experience in using the Internet as a resource by completing the activities and checking out the Web links for the topics in Chapter 8 marked with the World Wide Web icon. For this chapter, Internet activities explore specialized food pyramids, food composition analysis, osteoporosis prevention, and dietary supplements; there are Web links for the Vital Statistics table, the Critical Consumer boxes on food labels and dietary supplements, and the chapter as a whole. The Online Learning Center also includes handouts on such topics as judging portion sizes, finding food sources of key nutrients, and learning to cook.

Daily Fitness and Nutrition Journal

Review the resources and complete the activities available in the nutrition portion of the journal. Take the portion sizes quiz, complete the preprogram nutrition log, and analyze the results. Based on what you find, set healthy goals for change and complete the contract. Once you put your plan into action, complete the postprogram nutrition log to determine how successful you've been at improving your diet and moving toward the goals you've set.

Books

Duyff, R. L. 2002. *ADA Complete Food and Nutrition Guide,* 2nd ed. Chicago, Ill.: American Dietetic Association. *An excellent review of current nutrition information.*

Insel, P., R. E. Turner, and D. Ross. 2006. *Discovering Nutrition,* 2nd ed. Sudbury, Mass.: Jones and Bartlett. *A comprehensive review of major concepts in nutrition.*

Which should I eat—butter or margarine? Both butter and margarine are concentrated sources of fat, containing about 11 grams of fat and 100 calories per tablespoon. Butter is higher in saturated fat, which raises levels of artery-clogging LDL ("bad" cholesterol). Each tablespoon of butter has about 8 grams of saturated fat; margarine has about 2. Butter also contains cholesterol, which margarine does not.

Margarine, on the other hand, contains trans fat, which not only raises LDL but lowers HDL ("good" cholesterol). A tablespoon of stick margarine contains about 2 grams of trans fat. Butter contains a small amount of trans fat as well. Although butter has a combined total of saturated and trans fats that is twice that of stick margarine, the trans fat in stick margarine may be worse for you. Clearly, you should avoid both butter and stick margarine. To solve this dilemma, remember that softer is better. The softer or more liquid a margarine or spread is, the less hydrogenated it is and the less trans fat it contains. Tub and squeeze margarines contain less trans fat than stick margarines; some margarines are modified to be low-trans or trans-free and are labeled as such. Vegetable oils are an even better choice for cooking and for table use (such as olive oil for dipping bread) because most are low in saturated fat and completely free of trans fats.

MyPyramid recommends such large amounts of vegetables and fruit. How can I possibly eat that many servings without gaining weight? First, consider your typical portion sizes—you may be closer to meeting the recommendations than you think. Many people consume large servings of foods and underestimate the size of their portions. For example, a large banana may contain the equivalent of a cup of fruit, or half the recommended daily total for someone consuming 2000–2600 calories per day. Likewise, a medium baked potato (3-inch diameter) or an ear of corn (8-inch length) counts as a cup of vegetables. Use a measuring cup or a food scale for a few days to train your eye to accurately estimate food portion sizes. The MyPyramid.gov Web site includes charts of portion-size equivalents for each food group.

If an analysis of your diet indicates that you do need to increase your overall intake of fruits and vegetables, look for healthy substitutions. If you are like most Americans, you are consuming more than the recommended number of calories from added sugars and solid fats; trim some of these calories to make room for additional servings of fruits and vegetables. Your beverage choices may be a good place to start. Do you routinely consume regular sodas, sweetened bottled teas or fruit drinks, or whole milk? One regular 12-ounce soda contains the equivalent of about 150 calories of added sugars; one 8-ounce glass of whole milk provides about 75 calories as discretionary fats. Substituting water, diet soda, or low-fat milk would free up calories for additional servings of fruits and vegetables. A half-cup of carrots, tomatoes, apples, or melon has only about 25 calories; you could consume 6 cups of these foods for the calories in one can of regular soda. Substituting lower-fat condiments for such full-fat items as butter, mayonnaise, and salad dressing is another good way to trim calories to make room for additional servings of nutrient-rich fruits and vegetables.

Also consider your portion sizes and/or the frequency with which you consume foods high in discretionary calories: You may not need to eliminate a favorite food—instead, just cut back. For example, cut your consumption of fast-food fries from four times a week to once a week, or reduce the size of your ice cream dessert from a cup to half a cup. Treats should be consumed appropriately—infrequently, and in small amounts.

For additional help on improving food choices to meet dietary recommendations, visit the MyPyramid.gov Web site and the family-friendly chart of "Go, Slow, and Whoa" foods at the site for the National Heart, Lung, and Blood Institute (www.nhlbi.nih.gov/health/public/heart/obesity/wecan/downloads/gswtips.pdf).

What exactly are genetically modified foods? Are they safe? How can I recognize them on the shelf, and how can I know when I'm eating them? Genetic engineering involves altering the characteristics of a plant, animal, or microorganism by adding, rearranging, or replacing genes in its DNA; the result is a genetically modified (GM)

Jacobson, M. F., and J. Hurley. 2002. *Restaurant Confidential*. New York: Workman. *Provides information about restaurant foods, including tips for making healthier choices.*

Selkowitz, A. 2000. *The College Student's Guide to Eating Well on Campus*. Bethesda, Md.: Tulip Hill Press. *Provides practical advice for students, including how to make healthy choices when eating in a dorm or restaurant and how to stock a first pantry.*

Wardlaw, G. M., and A. M. Smith. 2006. *Perspectives in Nutrition*, 7th ed. New York: McGraw-Hill. *An easy-to-understand review of major concepts in nutrition.*

Williams, M. H. 2005. *Nutrition for Health, Fitness, and Sport*, 7th ed. New York: McGraw-Hill. *An overview of the role of nutrition in enhancing health, fitness, and sport performance.*

Newsletters

Environmental Nutrition (800-829-5384; http://www.environmentalnutrition.com)

Nutrition Action Health Letter (202-332-9110; http://www.cspinet.org)

Tufts University Health and Nutrition Letter (800-274-7581; http://www.healthletter.tufts.edu)

VW Organizations, Hotlines, and Web Sites

American Dietetic Association. Provides a wide variety of educational materials on nutrition.
800-877-1600
http://www.eatright.org

organism. New DNA may come from related species or organisms or from entirely different types of organisms. Many GM crops are already grown in the United States: About 75% of the current U.S. soybean crop has been genetically modified to be resistant to an herbicide used to kill weeds, and about a third of the U.S. corn crop carries genes for herbicide resistance or to produce a protein lethal to a destructive type of caterpillar. Products made with GM organisms include juice, soda, nuts, tuna, frozen pizza, spaghetti sauce, canola oil, chips, salad dressing, and soup.

The potential benefits of GM foods cited by supporters include improved yields overall and in difficult growing conditions, increased disease resistance, improved nutritional content, lower prices, and less use of pesticides. Critics of biotechnology argue that unexpected effects may occur: Gene manipulation could elevate levels of naturally occurring toxins or allergens, permanently change the gene pool and reduce biodiversity, and produce pesticide-resistant insects through the transfer of genes. In 2000, a form of GM corn approved for use only in animal feed was found to have commingled with other varieties of corn and to have been used in human foods; this mistake sparked fears of allergic reactions and led to recalls. Opposition to GM foods is particularly strong in Europe; in many developing nations that face food shortages,

responses to GM crops have tended to be more positive.

In April 2000, the National Academy of Sciences released a report stating that there is no proof that GM food on the market is unsafe but that changes are needed to better coordinate regulation of GM foods and to assess potential problems.

Labeling has been another major concern. Surveys indicate that the majority of Americans want to know if their foods contain GMO. However, under current rules, the FDA requires special labeling only when a food's composition is changed significantly or when a known allergen is introduced. For example, soybeans that contain a gene from a peanut would have to be labeled because peanuts are a common allergen. The only foods guaranteed not to contain GM ingredients are those certified as organic.

How can I tell if I'm allergic to a food?
A true food allergy is a reaction of the body's immune system to a food or food ingredient, usually a protein. This immune reaction can occur within minutes of ingesting the food, resulting in symptoms such as hives, diarrhea, difficulty breathing, or swelling of the lips or tongue. The most severe response is a systemic reaction called anaphylaxis, which involves a potentially life-threatening drop in blood pressure. Food allergies affect only about 2% of the adult population and about 4–6% of infants. Just a few foods

account for more than 90% of the food allergies in the United States: cow's milk, eggs, peanuts, tree nuts (walnuts, cashews, and so on), soy, wheat, fish, and shellfish.

Many people who believe they have food allergies may actually suffer from a food intolerance, a much more common source of adverse food reactions that typically involves problems with metabolism rather than with the immune system. The body may not be able to adequately digest a food or the body may react to a particular food compound. Food intolerances have been attributed to lactose (milk sugar), gluten (a protein in some grains), tartrazine (yellow food coloring), sulfite (a food additive), MSG, and the sweetener aspartame. Although symptoms of a food intolerance may be similar to those of a food allergy, they are typically more localized and not life-threatening. Many people with food intolerance can safely and comfortably consume small amounts of the food that affects them.

If you suspect you have a food allergy or intolerance, a good first step is to keep a food diary. Note everything you eat or drink, any symptoms you develop, and how long after eating the symptoms appear. Then make an appointment with your physician to go over your diary and determine if any additional tests are needed. People at risk for severe allergic reactions must diligently avoid trigger foods and carry medications to treat anaphylaxis.

Visit the Online Learning Center for more answers to common questions about nutrition.

American Heart Association: Delicious Decisions. Provides basic information about nutrition, tips for shopping and eating out, and heart-healthy recipes.

http://www.deliciousdecisions.org

FDA Center for Food Safety and Applied Nutrition. Offers information about topics such as food labeling, food additives, and foodborne illness.

http://vm.cfsan.fda.gov

Food Safety Hotlines. Provide information on the safe purchase, handling, cooking, and storage of food.

888-SAFEFOOD (FDA)

800-535-4555 (USDA)

Gateways to Government Nutrition Information. Provides access to government resources relating to food safety, including consumer advice and information on specific pathogens.

http://www.nutrition.gov

http://www.foodsafety.gov

Harvard School of Public Health: Nutrition Source. Provides advice on interpreting news on nutrition; an overview of the Healthy Eating Pyramid, an alternative to the basic USDA pyramid; and suggestions for building a healthy diet.

http://www.hsph.harvard.edu/nutritionsource

Health Canada: Food and Nutrition. Provides information about Canada's Food Guide to Healthy Eating as well as advice for people with special dietary needs.

http://www.hc-sc.gc.ca/fn-an/index_e.html

MedlinePlus: Nutrition. Provides links to information from government agencies and major medical associations on a wide variety of nutrition topics.

http://www.nlm.nih.gov/medlineplus/nutrition.html

MyPyramid. Provides personalized dietary plans and interactive food and activity tracking tools.

 http://mypyramid.gov

National Academies' Food and Nutrition Board. Provides information about the Dietary Reference Intakes and related guidelines.

 http://www.iom.edu/board.asp?id=3788

National Cancer Institute: Eat 5 to 9 a Day for Better Health. Promotes the consumption of fruits and vegetables every day.

 http://5aday.gov

National Institutes of Health: Osteoporosis and Related Bone Diseases— National Resource Center. Provides information about osteoporosis prevention and treatment; includes a special section on men and osteoporosis.

 http://www.osteo.org

National Osteoporosis Foundation. Provides information on the causes, prevention, detection, and treatment of osteoporosis.

 http://www.nof.org

USDA Center for Nutrition Policy and Promotion. Click on the Healthy Eating Index for an assessment of Americans' diets and a comparison with the Dietary Guidelines and the Food Guide Pyramid.

 http://www.usda.gov/cnpp

USDA Food and Nutrition Information Center. Provides a variety of materials relating to the Dietary Guidelines, food labels, Food Guide Pyramid, MyPyramid, and many other topics.

 http://www.nal.usda.gov/fnic

Vegetarian Resource Group. Information and links for vegetarians and people interested in learning more about vegetarian diets.

 http://www.vrg.org

You can obtain nutrient breakdowns of individual food items from the following sites:

Nutrition Analysis Tools and System (NATS)
 http://nat.crgq.com
USDA Food and Nutrition Information Center
 http://www.nal.usda.gov/fnic/foodcomp

See also the resources listed in Chapters 9, 11, and 12.

Selected Bibliography

Aldana, S. G., et al. 2005. Effects of an intensive diet and physical activity modification program on the health risks of adults. *Journal of the American Dietetic Association* 105(3): 371–381.

American College of Sports Medicine, American Dietetic Association, and Dietitians of Canada. 2000. Joint Position Statement: Nutrition and athletic performance. *Medicine and Science in Sports and Exercise* 32(12): 2130–2145.

American Diabetes Association. 2002. Evidence-based nutrition principles and recommendations for the treatment and prevention of diabetes and related complications. *Diabetes Care* 25:148–198.

American Heart Association Nutrition Committee. 2000. AHA Dietary Guidelines: Revision 2000. *Circulation* 102:2296–2311.

Block, G. 2004. Foods contributing to energy intake in the US: Data from NHANES III and NHANES 1999–2000. *Journal of Food Composition and Analysis* 17(2004): 439–447.

Clifton, P. M., J. B. Keogh, and M. Noakes. 2004. Trans fatty acids in adipose tissue and the food supply are associated with myocardial infarction. *Journal of Nutrition* 134:874–879.

Corle, D. K., et al. 2001. Self-rated quality of life measures: Effect of change to a low-fat, high-fiber, fruit and vegetable enriched diet. *Annals of Behavioral Medicine* 23(3): 198–207.

Ervin, R. B., et al. 2004. Dietary intake of selected minerals for the United States Population: 1999–2000. *Advance Data from Vital and Health Statistics,* 341.

Food and Drug Administration. 2004. *Backgrounder for the 2004 FDA/EPA Consumer Advisory: What You Need to Know About Mercury in Fish and Shellfish* (http://www.fda.gov/oc/opacom/hottopics/mercury/backgrounder.html; retrieved April 27, 2004).

Food and Drug Administration. 2004. *Commonly Asked Questions About BSE in Products Regulated by FDA's Center for Food Safety and Applied Nutrition.* (http://www.cfsan.fda.gov/~comm/bsefaq.html; retrieved April 28, 2004).

Food and Drug Administration. 2004. *Fact Sheet: Carbohydrates* (http://www.fda.gov/oc/initiatives/obesity/factsheet.html; retrieved April 28, 2004).

Food and Nutrition Board, Institute of Medicine. 2004. *Dietary Reference Intakes for Water, Potassium, Sodium, Chloride, and Sulfate.* Washington, D.C.: National Academies Press.

Food and Nutrition Board, Institute of Medicine. 2002. *Dietary Reference Intakes for Energy, Carbohydrate, Fiber, Fat, Fatty Acids, Cholesterol, Protein, and Amino Acids.* Washington, D.C.: National Academies Press.

Hanley, D. A., and K. S. Davison. 2005. Vitamin D insufficiency in North America. *Journal of Nutrition* 135(2): 332–337.

Hites, R. A., et al. 2004. Global assessment of organic contaminants in farmed salmon. *Science* 303(5655): 226–229.

Houston, D. K., et al. 2005. Dairy, fruit, and vegetable intakes and functional limitations and disability in a biracial cohort. *American Journal of Clinical Nutrition* 81(2): 515–522.

Joint WHO/FAO Expert Consultation. 2003. *Diet, Nutrition, and the Prevention of Chronic Diseases.* Geneva: World Health Organization.

Kranz, S., et al. 2005. Adverse effect of high added sugar consumption on dietary intake in American preschoolers. *Journal of Pediatrics* 46(1): 105–111.

Ma, Y., et al. 2005. Association between dietary carbohydrates and body weight. *American Journal of Epidemiology* 161(4): 359–367.

Nanney, M. S., et al. 2004. Rationale for a consistent "powerhouse" approach to vegetable and fruit messages. *Journal of the American Dietetic Association* 104(3): 352–356.

National Center for Health Statistics. 2003. Dietary intake of ten key nutrients for public health, United States: 1999–2000. *Advance Data from Vital and Health Statistics* No. 334.

Of birds and bacteria. 2003. *Consumer Reports,* January.

Opotowsky, A. R., et al. 2004. Serum vitamin A concentration and the risk of hip fracture among women 50 to 74 years old in the United States. *American Journal of Medicine* 117(3): 169–174.

U.S. Department of Agriculture, Center for Food Safety and Applied Nutrition. 2003. *Examples of Revised Nutrition Facts Panel Listing Trans Fat* (http://www.cfsan.fda.gov/~dms/labtr.html; retrieved January 5, 2004).

U.S. Department of Agriculture, Center for Nutrition Policy and Promotion. 2005. *MyPyramid* (http://mypyramid.gov; retrieved April 20, 2005).

U.S. Department of Agriculture, Center for Nutrition Policy and Promotion. 2004. *2005 Dietary Guidelines Advisory Committee report* (http://www.health.gov/dietaryguidelines/dga2005/report; retrieved January 5, 2005).

U.S. Department of Agriculture, Economic Research Service. 2005. *U.S. Food Consumption Up 16 Percent Since 1970* (http://www.ers.usda.gov/AmberWaves/November05/Findings/USFoodConsumption.htm).

U.S. Department of Health and Human Services and U.S. Department of Agriculture. 2005. *Dietary Guidelines for Americans, 2005* (http://www.health.gov/dietaryguidelines; retrieved January 20, 2005).

U.S. Department of Health and Human Services and U.S. Department of Agriculture. 2005. Finding your way to a healthier you: Based on the Dietary Guidelines for Americans. *Home and Garden Bulletin* No. 232-CP.

Wong, S. H. S., and S. Chung. 2003. Glycemic index: An educational tool for health and fitness professionals? *ACSM's Health and Fitness Journal,* November/December.

Wyshak, G. 2000. Teenaged girls, carbonated beverage consumption, and bone fracture. *Archives of Pediatric and Adolescent Medicine* 154:610–613.

Table 1 — Dietary Reference Intakes (DRIs): Recommended Levels for Individual Intake

Life Stage	Group	Biotin (μg/day)	Choline (mg/day)[a]	Folate (μg/day)[b]	Niacin (mg/day)[c]	Pantothenic Acid (mg/day)	Riboflavin (mg/day)	Thiamin (mg/day)	Vitamin A (μg/day)[d]	Vitamin B-6 (mg/day)	Vitamin B-12 (μg/day)	Vitamin C (mg/day)[e]	Vitamin D (μg/day)[f]	Vitamin E (mg/day)[g]
Infants	0–6 months	5	125	65	2	1.7	0.3	0.2	400	0.1	0.4	40	5	4
	7–12 months	6	150	80	4	1.8	0.4	0.3	500	0.3	0.5	50	5	5
Children	1–3 years	8	200	150	6	2	0.5	0.5	300	0.5	0.9	15	5	6
	4–8 years	12	250	200	8	3	0.6	0.6	400	0.6	1.2	25	5	7
Males	9–13 years	20	375	300	12	4	0.9	0.9	600	1.0	1.8	45	5	11
	14–18 years	25	550	400	16	5	1.3	1.2	900	1.3	2.4	75	5	15
	19–30 years	30	550	400	16	5	1.3	1.2	900	1.3	2.4	90	5	15
	31–50 years	30	550	400	16	5	1.3	1.2	900	1.3	2.4	90	5	15
	51–70 years	30	550	400	16	5	1.3	1.2	900	1.7	2.4[h]	90	10	15
	>70 years	30	550	400	16	5	1.3	1.2	900	1.7	2.4[h]	90	15	15
Females	9–13 years	20	375	300	12	4	0.9	0.9	600	1.0	1.8	45	5	11
	14–18 years	25	400	400[i]	14	5	1.0	1.0	700	1.2	2.4	65	5	15
	19–30 years	30	425	400[i]	14	5	1.1	1.1	700	1.3	2.4	75	5	15
	31–50 years	30	425	400[i]	14	5	1.1	1.1	700	1.3	2.4	75	5	15
	51–70 years	30	425	400	14	5	1.1	1.1	700	1.5	2.4[h]	75	10	15
	>70 years	30	425	400	14	5	1.1	1.1	700	1.5	2.4[h]	75	15	15
Pregnancy	≤18 years	30	450	600[j]	18	6	1.4	1.4	750	1.9	2.6	80	5	15
	19–30 years	30	450	600[j]	18	6	1.4	1.4	770	1.9	2.6	85	5	15
	31–50 years	30	450	600[j]	18	6	1.4	1.4	770	1.9	2.6	85	5	15
Lactation	≤18 years	35	550	500	17	7	1.6	1.4	1200	2.0	2.8	115	5	19
	19–30 years	35	550	500	17	7	1.6	1.4	1300	2.0	2.8	120	5	19
	31–50 years	35	550	500	17	7	1.6	1.4	1300	2.0	2.8	120	5	19
Tolerable Upper Intake Levels for Adults (19–70)			3500	1000[k]	35[k]				3000	100		2000	50	1000[k]

NOTE: The table includes values for the type of DRI standard—Adequate Intake (AI) or Recommended Dietary Allowance (RDA)—that has been established for that particular nutrient and life stage; RDAs are shown in **bold type**. The final row of the table shows the Tolerable Upper Intake Levels (ULs) for adults; refer to the full DRI report for information on other ages and life stages. A UL is the maximum level of daily nutrient intake that is likely to pose no risk of adverse effects. There is insufficient data to set ULs for all nutrients, but this does not mean that there is no potential for adverse effects; source of intake should be from food only to prevent high levels of intake of nutrients without established ULs. In healthy individuals, there is no established benefit from nutrient intakes above the RDA or AI.

[a] Although AIs have been set for choline, there are few data to assess whether a dietary supply of choline is needed at all stages of the life cycle, and it may be that the choline requirement can be met by endogenous synthesis at some of these stages.
[b] As dietary folate equivalents (DFE): 1 DFE = 1 μg food folate = 0.6 μg folate from fortified food or as a supplement consumed with food = 0.5 μg of a supplement taken on an empty stomach.
[c] As niacin equivalents (NE): 1 mg niacin = 60 mg tryptophan.

Table 1 — Dietary Reference Intakes (DRIs): Recommended Levels for Individual Intake (*continued*)

Life Stage	Group	Vitamin K (µg/day)	Calcium (mg/day)	Chromium (µg/day)	Copper (µg/day)	Fluoride (mg/day)	Iodine (µg/day)	Iron (mg/day)[l]	Magnesium (mg/day)	Manganese (mg/day)	Molybdenum (µg/day)	Phosphorus (mg/day)	Selenium (µg/day)	Zinc (mg/day)[m]
Infants	0–6 months	2.0	210	0.2	200	0.01	110	0.27	30	0.003	2	100	15	2
	7–12 months	2.5	270	5.5	220	0.5	130	11	75	0.6	3	275	20	3
Children	1–3 years	30	500	11	340	0.7	90	7	80	1.2	17	460	20	3
	4–8 years	55	800	15	440	1	90	10	130	1.5	22	500	30	5
Males	9–13 years	60	1300	25	700	2	120	8	240	1.9	34	1250	40	8
	14–18 years	75	1300	35	890	3	150	11	410	2.2	43	1250	55	11
	19–30 years	120	1000	35	900	4	150	8	400	2.3	45	700	55	11
	31–50 years	120	1000	35	900	4	150	8	420	2.3	45	700	55	11
	51–70 years	120	1200	30	900	4	150	8	420	2.3	45	700	55	11
	>70 years	120	1200	30	900	4	150	8	420	2.3	45	700	55	11
Females	9–13 years	60	1300	21	700	2	120	8	240	1.6	34	1250	40	8
	14–18 years	75	1300	24	890	3	150	15	360	1.6	43	1250	55	9
	19–30 years	90	1000	25	900	3	150	18	310	1.8	45	700	55	8
	31–50 years	90	1000	25	900	3	150	18	320	1.8	45	700	55	8
	51–70 years	90	1200	20	900	3	150	8	320	1.8	45	700	55	8
	>70 years	90	1200	20	900	3	150	8	320	1.8	45	700	55	8
Pregnancy	≤18 years	75	1300	29	1000	3	220	27	400	2.0	50	1250	60	13
	19–30 years	90	1000	30	1000	3	220	27	350	2.0	50	700	60	11
	31–50 years	90	1000	30	1000	3	220	27	360	2.0	50	700	60	11
Lactation	≤18 years	75	1300	44	1300	3	290	10	360	2.6	50	1250	70	14
	19–30 years	90	1000	45	1300	3	290	9	310	2.6	50	700	70	12
	31–50 years	90	1000	45	1300	3	290	9	320	2.6	50	700	70	12
Tolerable Upper Intake Levels for Adults (19–70)			2500		10,000	10	1100	45	350[k]	11	2000	4000	400	40

d As retinol activity equivalents (RAEs). 1 RAE = 1 µg retinol, 12 µg β-carotene, or 24 µg α-carotene or β-cryptoxanthin. Preformed vitamin A (retinol) is abundant in animal-derived foods; provitamin A carotenoids are abundant in some dark yellow, orange, red, and deep-green fruits and vegetables. For preformed vitamin A and for provitamin A carotenoids in supplements, 1RE = 1 RAE; for provitamin A carotenoids in foods, divide the REs by 2 to obtain RAEs. The UL applies only to preformed vitamin A.

e Individuals who smoke require an additional 35 mg/day of vitamin C over that needed by nonsmokers; nonsmokers regularly exposed to tobacco smoke should ensure they meet the RDA for vitamin C.

f As cholecalciferol. 1 µg cholecalciferol = 40 IU vitamin D. DRI values are based on the absence of adequate exposure to sunlight.

g As α-tocopherol. Includes naturally occurring RRR-α-tocopherol and the 2R-stereoisomeric forms from supplements; does not include the 2S-stereoisomeric forms from supplements.

h Because 10–30% of older people may malabsorb food-bound B-12, those over age 50 should meet their RDA mainly with supplements or foods fortified with B-12.

i In view of evidence linking folate intake with neural tube defects in the fetus. It is recommended that all women capable of becoming pregnant consume 400 µg from supplements or fortified foods in addition to consuming folate from a varied diet.

j It is assumed that women will continue consuming 400 µg from supplements or fortified food until their pregnancy is confirmed and they enter prenatal care, which ordinarily occurs after the end of the periconceptional period—the critical time for formation of the neural tube.

k The UL applies only to intake from supplements, fortified foods, and/or pharmacological agents and not to intake from foods.

l Because the absorption of iron from plant foods is low compared to that from animal foods, the RDA for strict vegetarians is approximately 1.8 times higher than the values established for omnivores (14 mg/day for adult male vegetarians; 33 mg/day for premenopausal female vegetarians). Oral contraceptives (OCs) reduce menstrual blood losses, so women taking them need less daily iron; the RDA for premenopausal women taking OCs is 10.9 mg/day. For more on iron requirements for other special situations, refer to Dietary Reference Intakes for Vitamin A, Vitamin K, Arsenic, Boron, Chromium, Copper, Iodine, Iron, Manganese, Molybdenum, Nickel, Silicon, Vanadium, and Zinc (visit http://www.nap.edu for the complete report).

m Zinc absorption is lower for those consuming vegetarian diets so the zinc requirement for vegetarians is approximately twofold greater than for those consuming a nonvegetarian diet.

Table 1   Dietary Reference Intakes (DRIs): Recommended Levels for Individual Intake (*continued*)

Life Stage	Group	Potassium (g/day)	Sodium (g/day)	Chloride (g/day)	Carbohydrate RDA/AI (g/day)	Carbohydrate AMDRᵒ (%)	Total Fiber RDA/AI (g/day)	Total Fat AMDRᵒ (%)	Linoleic Acid RDA/AI (g/day)	Linoleic Acid AMDRᵒ (%)	Alpha-linolenic Acid RDA/AI (g/day)	Alpha-linolenic Acid AMDRᵒ (%)	Protein RDA/AI (g/day)	Protein AMDRⁿ (%)	Waterᵖ (L/day)
Infants	0–6 months	0.4	0.12	0.18	60	NDq	ND	r	4.4	NDq	0.5	NDq	9.1	NDq	0.7
	7–12 months	0.7	0.37	0.57	95	NDq	ND	r	4.6	NDq	0.5	NDq	13.5	NDq	0.8
Children	1–3 years	3.0	1.0	1.5	130	45–65	19	30–40	7	5–10	0.7	0.6–1.2	13	5–20	1.3
	4–8 years	3.8	1.2	1.9	130	45–65	25	25–35	10	5–10	0.9	0.6–1.2	19	10–30	1.7
Males	9–13 years	4.5	1.5	2.3	130	45–65	31	25–35	12	5–10	1.2	0.6–1.2	34	10–30	2.4
	14–18 years	4.7	1.5	2.3	130	45–65	38	25–35	16	5–10	1.6	0.6–1.2	52	10–30	3.3
	19–30 years	4.7	1.5	2.3	130	45–65	38	20–35	17	5–10	1.6	0.6–1.2	56	10–35	3.7
	31–50 years	4.7	1.5	2.3	130	45–65	38	20–35	17	5–10	1.6	0.6–1.2	56	10–35	3.7
	51–70 years	4.7	1.3	2.0	130	45–65	30	20–35	14	5–10	1.6	0.6–1.2	56	10–35	3.7
	>70 years	4.7	1.2	1.8	130	45–65	30	20–35	14	5–10	1.6	0.6–1.2	56	10–30	2.1
Females	9–13 years	4.5	1.5	2.3	130	45–65	26	25–35	10	5–10	1.0	0.6–1.2	34	10–30	2.3
	14–18 years	4.7	1.5	2.3	130	45–65	26	25–35	11	5–10	1.1	0.6–1.2	46	10–30	2.7
	19–30 years	4.7	1.5	2.3	130	45–65	25	20–35	12	5–10	1.1	0.6–1.2	46	10–35	2.7
	31–50 years	4.7	1.5	2.3	130	45–65	25	20–35	12	5–10	1.1	0.6–1.2	46	10–35	2.7
	51–70 years	4.7	1.3	2.0	130	45–65	21	20–35	11	5–10	1.1	0.6–1.2	46	10–35	2.7
	>70 years	4.7	1.2	1.8	130	45–65	21	20–35	11	5–10	1.1	0.6–1.2	46	10–35	3.0
Pregnancy	≦18 years	4.7	1.5	2.3	175	45–65	28	20–35	13	5–10	1.4	0.6–1.2	71	10–35	3.0
	19–30 years	4.7	1.5	2.3	175	45–65	28	20–35	13	5–10	1.4	0.6–1.2	71	10–35	3.0
	31–50 years	4.7	1.5	2.3	175	45–65	28	20–35	13	5–10	1.4	0.6–1.2	71	10–35	3.8
Lactation	≦18 years	5.1	1.5	2.3	210	45–65	29	20–35	13	5–10	1.3	0.6–1.2	71	10–35	3.8
	19–30 years	5.1	1.5	2.3	210	45–65	29	20–35	13	5–10	1.3	0.6–1.2	71	10–35	3.8
	31–50 years	5.1	1.5	2.3	210	45–65	29	20–35	13	5–10	1.3	0.6–1.2	71	10–35	

Tolerable Upper Intake
Level for Adults (19–70)   Sodium 2.3   Chloride 3.6

ⁿDaily protein recommendations are based on body weight for reference body weights. To calculate for a specific body weight, use the following values: 1.5 g/kg for infants, 1.1 g/kg for 1–3 years, 0.95 g/kg for 4–13 years, 0.85 g/kg for 14–18 years, 0.8 g/kg for adults, and 1.1 g/kg for pregnant (using prepregnancy weight) and lactating women.

ᵒAcceptable Macronutrient Distribution Range (AMDR), expressed as a percent of total daily calories, is the range of intake for a particular energy source that is associated with reduced risk of chronic disease while providing intakes of essential nutrients. If an individual consumes in excess of the AMDR, there is a potential for increasing the risk of chronic diseases and/or insufficient intakes of essential nutrients.

ᵖTotal water intake from fluids and food.

qNot determinable due to lack of data of adverse effects in this age group and concern with regard to lack of ability to handle excess amounts. Source of intake should be from food only to prevent high levels of intake.

rFor infants, Adequate Intake of total fat is 31 grams/day (0–6 months) and 30 grams per day (7–12 months) from breast milk and, for infants 7–12 months, complementary food and beverages.

SOURCE: Food and Nutrition Board, Institute of Medicine, National Academies. 2004. *Dietary Reference Intakes Tables* (http://www.iom.edu/file.asp?id = 21372; retrieved December 21, 2004). The complete Dietary Reference Intake reports are available from the National Academy Press (http://www.nap.edu).

Reprinted with permission from *Dietary Reference Intakes Applications in Dietary Planning.* Copyright © 2003 by the National Academy of Sciences. Reprinted with permission from the National Academies Press, Washington, D.C.

Nutrition Resources

Number of servings per day (or per week, as noted)

Food groups	1600 calories	2000 calories	2600 calories	3100 calories	Serving sizes and notes
Grains	6	7–8	10–11	12–13	1 slice bread, 1 oz dry cereal, 1/2 cup cooked rice, pasta, or cereal; choose whole grains
Vegetables	3–4	4–5	5–6	6	1 cup raw leafy vegetables, 1/2 cup cooked vegetables, 6 oz vegetable juice
Fruits	4	4–5	5–6	6	6 oz fruit juice, 1 medium fruit, 1/4 cup dried fruit, 1/2 cup fresh, frozen, or canned fruit
Low-fat or fat-free dairy foods	2–3	2–3	3	3–4	8 oz milk; 1 cup yogurt, 1-1/2 oz cheese; choose fat-free or lowfat types
Meat, poultry, fish	1–2	2 or less	2	2–3	3 oz cooked meats, poultry, or fish: select only lean; trim away visible fats; broil, roast, or boil instead of frying; remove skin from poultry
Nuts, seeds, legumes	3–4	4–5	1	1	1/3 cup or 1-1/2 oz nuts, 2 Tbsp or 1/2 oz seeds, 1/2 cup cooked dry beans/peas
Fats and oils	2 servings/ week	2–3	3	4	1 tsp soft margarine; 1 Tbsp low-fat mayonnaise, 2 Tbsp light salad dressing, 1 tsp vegetable oil; DASH has 27% of calories as fat (low in saturated fat)
Sweets	0	5 servings/ week	2	2	1 Tbsp sugar, 1 Tbsp jelly or jam, 1/2 oz jelly beans, 8 oz lemonade; sweets should be low in fat

Figure 1   The DASH Eating Plan.   SOURCE: U.S. Department of Health and Human Services and U.S. Department of Agriculture. 2005. *Dietary Guidelines for Americans, 2005* (http://www.health.gov/dietaryguidelines; retrieved January 20, 2005).

Figure 2   Healthy Eating Pyramid. The Healthy Eating Pyramid is an alternative food-group plan developed by researchers at the Harvard School of Public Health; this pyramid reflects many major research studies that have looked at the relationship between diet and long-term health. The Healthy Eating Pyramid differentiates between the various dietary sources of fat, protein, and carbohydrates, and it emphasizes whole grains, vegetable oils, fruits and vegetables, nuts, and dried peas and beans.   SOURCE: Reprinted by permission of Simon & Schuster Adult Publishing Group from *Eat, Drink, and Be Healthy: The Harvard Medical School Guide to Healthy Eating* by Walter C. Willett, M.D. Copyright © 2001 by the President and Fellows of Harvard College.

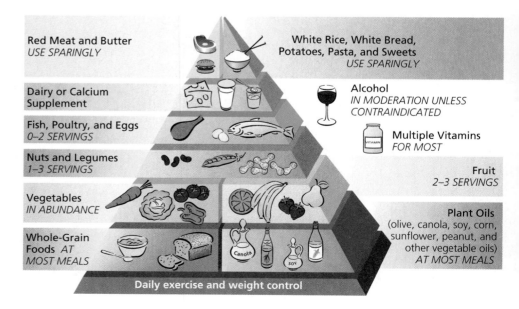

LAB 8.1 *Your Daily Diet Versus MyPyramid*

Use the worksheets in this lab to keep track of everything you eat for 3 consecutive days. Break down each food item into its component parts and list them separately in the column labeled "Food." Then enter the portion size you consumed in the correct food group column. For example, a turkey sandwich might be listed as follows: whole-wheat bread, 2 oz-equiv of whole grains; turkey, 2 oz-equiv of meat/beans; tomato, 1/3 cup other vegetables; romaine lettuce, 1/4 cup dark green vegetables; 1 tablespoon mayonnaise dressing, 1 teaspoon oils. It can be challenging to track values for added sugars and, especially, oils and fats, but use food labels and the information in Appendix B to be as accurate as you can. MyPyramid.gov has additional guidelines for counting discretionary calories.

For vegetables, enter your portion sizes in both the Total column and the column corresponding to the correct subgroup; for example, the spinach in a spinach salad would be entered under Dark Green and carrots would be entered under Orange. For the purpose of this 3-day activity, you will compare only your total vegetable consumption against MyPyramid guidelines; as described in the chapter, vegetable subgroup recommendations are based on weekly consumption. However, it is important to note which vegetable subgroups are represented in your diet; over a 3-day period, you should consume several servings from each of the subgroups.

This activity can also be completed online using the Pyramid Tracker program at the MyPyramid.gov Web site.

DAY 1

Food	Grains (oz-eq)		Vegetables (cups)						Fruits (cups)	Milk (cups)	Meat/ Beans (oz-eq)	Oils (tsp)	Discretionary Calories	
	Whole	Other	Total	Dark Green	Orange	Legume	Starchy	Other					Solid Fats (g)	Added Sugars (g/tsp)
Daily TOTAL														

DAY 2

Food	Grains (oz-eq)		Vegetables (cups)						Fruits (cups)	Milk (cups)	Meat/ Beans (oz-eq)	Oils (tsp)	Discretionary Calories	
	Whole	Other	Total	Dark Green	Orange	Legume	Starchy	Other					Solid Fats (g)	Added Sugars (g/tsp)
Daily TOTAL														

DAY 3

Food	Grains (oz-eq)		Vegetables (cups)						Fruits (cups)	Milk (cups)	Meat/ Beans (oz-eq)	Oils (tsp)	Discretionary Calories	
	Whole	Other	Total	Dark Green	Orange	Legume	Starchy	Other	Fruits (cups)	Milk (cups)	Meat/ Beans (oz-eq)	Oils (tsp)	Solid Fats (g)	Added Sugars (g/tsp)
Daily TOTAL														

Next, average your daily intake totals for the 3 days and enter them in the chart below. For example, if your three daily totals for the fruit group were 1 cup, 1½ cups, and 2 cups, your average daily intake would be 1½ cups. Fill in the recommended intake totals that apply to you from Figure 8.6 and Table 8.4.

MyPyramid Food Group	Recommended Daily Amounts or Limits	Your Actual Average Daily Intake
Grains (total)	oz-eq	oz-eq
Whole grains	oz-eq	oz-eq
Other grains	oz-eq	oz-eq
Vegetables (total)	cups	cups
Fruits	cups	cups
Milk	cups	cups
Meat and beans	oz-eq	oz-eq
Oils	tsp	tsp
Solid fats	g	g
Added sugars	g/tsp	g/tsp

Using Your Results

How did you score? How close is your diet to that recommended by MyPyramid? Are you at all surprised by the actual amount of food you're consuming from each food group or from added sugars and solid fats?

What should you do next? If the results of the assessment indicate that you could boost your level of wellness by improving your diet, set realistic goals for change. Do you need to increase or decrease your consumption of any food groups? List any areas of concern below, along with a goal for change and strategies for achieving the goal you've set. If you see that you are falling short in one food group, such as fruits or vegetables, but have many foods that are rich in discretionary calories from solid fats and added sugars, you might try decreasing those items in favor of an apple, a bunch of grapes, or some baby carrots. Think carefully about the reasons behind your food choices. For example, if you eat doughnuts for breakfast every morning because you feel rushed, make a list of ways to save time to allow for a healthier breakfast.

Problem: _____
Goal: _____
Strategies for change: _____
_____
_____

Problem: _____
Goal: _____
Strategies for change: _____
_____
_____

Problem: _____
Goal: _____
Strategies for change: _____
_____
_____

Enter the results of this lab in the Preprogram Assessment column in Appendix D. If you've set goals and identified strategies for change, begin putting your plan into action. Additional dietary tracking grids are available on the Online Learning Center and in the *Daily Fitness and Nutrition Journal*. After several weeks of your program, complete this lab again and enter the results in the Postprogram Assessment column of Appendix D. How do the results compare?

LAB 8.2 *Dietary Analysis*

WW

You can complete this activity using either a nutrition analysis software program or the food composition data in Appendix B and the charts printed below. Information about the nutrient content of foods is also available online; see the For Further Exploration section for recommended Web sites. (This lab asks you to analyze one day's diet. For a more complete and accurate assessment of your diet, analyze the results from several different days, including a weekday and a weekend day.)

DATE _____   DAY: M Tu W Th F Sa Su

Food	Amount	Calories	Protein (g)	Carbohydrate (g)	Dietary fiber (g)	Fat, total (g)	Saturated fat (g)	Cholesterol (mg)	Sodium (mg)	Vitamin A (RE)	Vitamin C (mg)	Calcium (mg)	Iron (mg)
Recommended totals*			10–35%	45–65%	25–38 g	20–35%	<10%	≤300 mg	≤2300 mg	RE	mg	mg	mg
Actual totals**		cal	g / %	g / %	g	g / %	g / %	mg	mg	RE	mg	mg	mg

*Fill in the appropriate DRI values for vitamin A, vitamin C, calcium, and iron from Table 1 in the Nutrition Resources section.
**Total the values in each column. To calculate the percentage of total calories from protein, carbohydrate, fat, and saturated fat, use the formula on p. 280. Protein and carbohydrate provide 4 calories per gram; fat provides 9 calories per gram. For example, if you consume a total of 270 grams of carbohydrate and 2000 calories, your percentage of total calories from carbohydrate would be (270 g × 4 cal/g) ÷ 2000 cal = 54%. Do not include data for alcoholic beverages in your calculations. Percentages may not total 100% due to rounding.

Using Your Results

How did you score? How close is your diet to that recommended by the Dietary Guidelines, Dietary Reference Intakes, and other guidelines? Are you surprised by any of the results of this assessment?

What should you do next? Enter the results of this lab in the Preprogram Assessment column in Appendix D. If your daily diet meets all the recommended intakes, congratulations—and keep up the good work. If the results of the assessment pinpoint areas of concern, then work with your food record on the previous page to determine what changes you could make to meet all the guidelines. Make changes, additions, and deletions until it conforms to all or most of the guidelines. Or, if you prefer, start from scratch to create a day's diet that meets the guidelines. Use the chart below to experiment and record your final, healthy sample diet for one day. Then put what you learned from this exercise into practice in your daily life. After several weeks of your program, complete this lab again and enter the results in the Postprogram Assessment column of Appendix D. How do the results compare?

DATE _____ DAY: M Tu W Th F Sa Su

Food	Amount	Calories	Protein (g)	Carbohydrate (g)	Dietary fiber (g)	Fat, total (g)	Saturated fat (g)	Cholesterol (mg)	Sodium (mg)	Vitamin A (RE)	Vitamin C (mg)	Calcium (mg)	Iron (mg)
Recommended totals			10–35%	45–65%	25–38 g	20–38%	<10%	≤300 mg	≤2300 mg	RE	mg	mg	mg
Actual totals		cal	g / %	g / %	g	g / %	g / %	mg	mg	RE	mg	mg	mg

LAB 8.3 *Informed Food Choices*

Part I   Using Food Labels

Choose three food items to evaluate. You might want to select three similar items, such as regular, low-fat, and non-fat salad dressing, or three very different items. Record the information from their food labels in the table below.

Food Items			
Serving size			
Total calories	cal	cal	cal
Total fat—grams	g	g	g
—% Daily Value	%	%	%
Saturated fat—grams	g	g	g
—% Daily Value	%	%	%
Trans fat—grams	g	g	g
Cholesterol—milligrams	mg	mg	mg
—% Daily Value	%	%	%
Sodium—milligrams	mg	mg	mg
—% Daily Value	%	%	%
Carbohydrates (total)—grams	g	g	g
—% Daily Value	%	%	%
Dietary fiber—grams	g	g	g
—% Daily Value	%	%	%
Sugars—grams	g	g	g
Protein—grams	g	g	g
Vitamin A—% Daily Value	%	%	%
Vitamin C—% Daily Value	%	%	%
Calcium—% Daily Value	%	%	%
Iron—% Daily Value	%	%	%

How do the items you chose compare? You can do a quick nutrient check by totaling the Daily Value percentages for nutrients you should limit (total fat, cholesterol, sodium) and the nutrients you should favor (dietary fiber, vitamin A, vitamin C, calcium, iron) for each food. Which food has the largest percent Daily Value sum for nutrients to limit? For nutrients to favor?

Food Items			
Calories	cal	cal	cal
% Daily Value total for nutrients to limit (total fat, cholesterol, sodium)	%	%	%
% Daily Value total for nutrients to favor (fiber, vitamin A, vitamin C, calcium, iron)	%	%	%

Part II Evaluating Fast Food

Use the information from Appendix C, Nutritional Content of Popular Items from Fast-Food Restaurants, to complete the chart on this page for the last fast-food meal you ate. Add up your totals for the meal. Compare the values for fat, protein, carbohydrate, cholesterol, and sodium content for each food item and for the meal as a whole with the levels suggested by the Dietary Guidelines for Americans. Calculate the percent of total calories derived from fat, saturated fat, protein, and carbohydrate using the formulas given.

If you haven't recently been to one of the restaurants included in the appendix, fill in the chart for any sample meal you might eat. If some of the food items you selected don't appear in Appendix C, ask for a nutrition information brochure when you visit the restaurant, or check out online fast-food information: Arby's (http://www.arbysrestaurant.com), Burger King (http://www.burgerking.com), Domino's Pizza (http://www.dominos.com), Jack in the Box (http://www.jackinthebox.com), KFC (http://www.kfc.com), McDonald's (http://www.mcdonalds.com), Subway (http://www.subway.com), Taco Bell (http://www.tacobell.com), Wendy's (http://www.wendys.com).

FOOD ITEMS

	Dietary Guidelines							Total**
Serving size (g)		g	g	g	g	g	g	g
Calories		cal	cal	cal	cal	cal	cal	cal
Total fat—grams		g	g	g	g	g	g	g
—% calories*	20–35%	%	%	%	%	%	%	%
Saturated fat—grams		g	g	g	g	g	g	g
—% calories*	<10%	%	%	%	%	%	%	%
Protein—grams		g	g	g	g	g	g	g
—% calories*	10–35%	%	%	%	%	%	%	%
Carbohydrate—grams		g	g	g	g	g	g	g
—% calories*	45–65%	%	%	%	%	%	%	%
Cholesterol†	100 mg	mg	mg	mg	mg	mg	mg	mg
Sodium†	800 mg	mg	mg	mg	mg	mg	mg	mg

*To calculate the percent of total calories from each food energy source (fat, carbohydrate, protein), use the following formula:

$$\frac{(\text{number of grams of energy source}) \times (\text{number of calories per gram of energy source})}{(\text{total calories in serving of food item})}$$

(*Note:* Fat and saturated fat provide 9 calories per gram; protein and carbohydrate provide 4 calories per gram.) For example, the percent of total calories from protein in a 150-calorie dish containing 10 grams of protein is

$$\frac{(10 \text{ grams of protein}) \times (4 \text{ calories per gram})}{(150 \text{ calories})} = \frac{40}{150} = 0.27, \text{ or } 27\% \text{ of total calories from protein}$$

**For the Total column, add up the total grams of fat, carbohydrate, and protein contained in your sample meal and calculate the percentages based on the total calories in the meal. (Percentages may not total 100% due to rounding.) For cholesterol and sodium values, add up the total number of milligrams.

†Recommended daily limits of cholesterol and sodium are divided by 3 here to give an approximate recommended limit for a single meal.

SOURCE: Insel, P. M., and W. T. Roth. 2006. Wellness Worksheet 66. *Core Concepts in Health,* 10th ed. Copyright © 2006 The McGraw-Hill Companies, Inc. Reprinted with permission.

Looking **AHEAD**

After reading this chapter, you should be able to

- Explain the health risks associated with overweight and obesity
- Explain the factors that may contribute to a weight problem, including genetic, physiological, lifestyle, and psychosocial factors
- Describe lifestyle factors that contribute to weight gain and loss, including the role of food choices, exercise, and emotional factors
- Identify and describe the symptoms of eating disorders and the health risks associated with them
- Design a personal plan for successfully managing body weight

9

Weight Management

Test Your Knowledge

1. **People who are overweight get less sleep than people who are at a healthy body weight.**
   True or false?

2. **Approximately how many female high school and college students have either anorexia or bulimia?**
   a. 1 in 250
   b. 1 in 100
   c. 1 in 30

3. **Which of the following snacks contains the fewest calories—about 100 for the serving size listed?**
   a. 8 ounces (⅔ can) of soda
   b. 2 fat-free sandwich cookies
   c. 4 pretzel twists
   d. 2 cups strawberries
   e. 20 baby carrots

ANSWERS

1. TRUE. It is unclear whether there is a cause-and-effect relationship between lack of sleep and increased body weight, but insufficient sleep may affect hormones, metabolism, and appetite. Adequate sleep may also help prevent eating in response to feelings of stress and low energy.

2. C. About 2–4% of female students suffer from bulimia or anorexia, and many more occasionally engage in behaviors associated with these disorders.

3. ALL FIVE ARE EQUAL. Each of these snacks provides about 100 calories; however, the servings of strawberries and carrots are much larger because they are lower in energy (calorie) density.

ViW *Fit and Well* **Online Learning Center**   www.mhhe.com/fahey

Visit the *Fit and Well* Online Learning Center for study aids, online labs, additional information about weight management, links, Internet activities that explore the role of weight management in wellness, and much more.

Achieving and maintaining a healthy body weight is a serious public health challenge in the United States and a source of distress for many Americans. Under standards developed by the National Institutes of Health, only 34% of American adults are at a healthy weight: More than 60% of American adults are overweight, including more than 30% who are obese (Table 9.1). The rate of obesity has more than doubled since 1960, and it continues to rise. If current rates of weight gain continue, *all* American adults will be overweight by 2030. Rates of obesity among children are also increasing, with 15% of 6- to 19-year-olds now classified as obese.

Controlling body weight is really a matter of controlling body fat. As explained in Chapter 6, the most important consideration for health is not total weight but body composition—the proportion of fat to fat-free mass. Many people who are "overweight" are also "overfat," and the health risks they face are due to the latter condition. Although this chapter uses the common terms *weight management* and *weight loss,* the goal for wellness is to adopt healthy behaviors and achieve an appropriate body composition, not to conform to rigid standards of total body weight. Chapter 6 includes a variety of methods for assessing body composition.

Although not completely understood, managing body weight is not a mysterious process. The "secret" is balancing calories consumed with calories expended in daily activities—in other words, eating a moderate diet and getting regular physical activity. Unfortunately, this formula is not as exciting as the latest fad diet or "scientific breakthrough" that promises slimness without effort. Many people fail in their efforts to manage their weight because they emphasize short-term weight loss rather than permanent changes in lifestyle. Dieting is not part of a wellness lifestyle. Successful weight management requires the long-term coordination of many aspects of a wellness lifestyle, including proper nutrition, adequate physical activity, and stress management. The goal is the adoption of healthy and sustainable habits that maximize energy and well-being and reduce the risk of chronic diseases.

Body image is a related area of concern. More and more people are becoming unhappy with their bodies and obsessed with their weight. In recent surveys, more than half of Americans have stated that they are dissatisfied with their weight; only about 10% report being completely satisfied with their bodies. Dissatisfaction with body weight and shape is associated with dangerous eating patterns such as binge eating or self-starvation and with eating disorders.

This chapter explores the factors that contribute to the development of overweight and obesity as well as to eating disorders. It also takes a closer look at weight management through lifestyle and suggests specific strategies for reaching and maintaining a healthy weight. This information is designed to provide the tools necessary for integrating effective weight management into a wellness lifestyle.

VITAL STATISTICS

Table 9.1 — Prevalence of Healthy Weight Among Adults

Group	Estimated Prevalence of Healthy Weight*
Gender	
Women	35%
Men	32%
Ethnicity	
White	35%
Latino	26%
African American	29%
Age	
20–39 years	40%
40–59 years	31%
60+ years	28%
Health status	
People with disabilities	29%
People with diabetes	12%
All adults	34%

*A healthy weight is defined as BMI 18.5–25.0. The *Healthy People 2010* target is for 60% of adults to be at a healthy weight.

SOURCE: National Center for Health Statistics. 2004. *DATA2010: The Healthy People 2010 Database: November 2004 Edition* (http://wonder.cdc.gov/data2010/obj.htm; retrieved August 15, 2005).

HEALTH IMPLICATIONS OF OVERWEIGHT AND OBESITY

As rates of **overweight** and **obesity** have risen in the United States, so has the prevalence of the health conditions associated with overweight—including a more than 33% rise in the rate of type 2 diabetes in just the past decade. It's estimated that inactivity and overweight account for more than 100,000 premature deaths annually in the United States, second only to tobacco-related deaths. More than $75 billion per year is spent treating obesity-related health problems. Overweight and obesity

Terms

overweight Characterized by a body weight that falls above the range associated with minimum mortality: weighing 10% or more over recommended weight or having a BMI over 25.

obesity Severely overweight, with an excess of body fat: weighing 20% or more over recommended weight or having a BMI over 30.

resting metabolic rate (RMR) The energy required (in calories) to maintain vital body functions, including respiration, heart rate, body temperature, and blood pressure, while the body is at rest.

are two of the most serious and widespread challenges to wellness.

As described in Chapter 6, excess body fat increases a person's risk of developing numerous diseases and unhealthy conditions. Obesity is one of six major controllable risk factors for heart disease; it also increases risk for other forms of cardiovascular disease (CVD), hypertension, certain forms of cancer, diabetes, gallbladder disease, respiratory problems, joint diseases, skin problems, impaired immune function, and sleep disorders. Obese people have an overall mortality rate almost twice that of nonobese people. Gaining weight over the years has also been found dangerous; in one study, women who gained more than 22 pounds since they were 18 years old had a sevenfold increase in the risk of heart disease. Many studies have confirmed that overweight and obesity shorten lives.

At the same time, research has shown that even modest weight loss can have a significant positive impact on health. A weight loss of just 5–10% in obese individuals can reduce the risk of coronary heart disease, hypertension, stroke, diabetes, and other weight-related conditions and increase life expectancy.

FACTORS CONTRIBUTING TO EXCESS BODY FAT

Much research has been done in an effort to pinpoint the cause of overweight and obesity. It appears, however, that body weight and body composition are determined by multiple factors that may vary with each individual. These factors can be grouped into genetic, physiological, lifestyle, and psychosocial factors.

Genetic Factors

Estimates of the genetic contribution to obesity vary widely, from about 25% to 40% of an individual's body fat. More than 300 genes have been linked to obesity, but their actions are still under study. Genes influence body size and shape, body fat distribution, and metabolic rate. Genetic factors also affect the ease with which weight is gained as a result of overeating and where on the body extra weight is added. If both parents are overweight, their children are twice as likely to be overweight as children who have only one overweight parent. In studies that compared adoptees and their biological parents, the weights of the adoptees were found to be more like those of the biological parents than the adoptive parents, again indicating a strong genetic link.

Research thus suggests a genetic component in the determination of body weight. However, hereditary influences must be balanced against the contribution of environmental factors. Not all children of obese parents become obese, and normal-weight parents also have overweight children. In a study comparing men born and raised in Ireland with their biological brothers who lived in the United States, the American men were found to weigh, on average, 6% more than their Irish brothers. Environmental factors like diet and exercise are probably responsible for this difference in weight. Thus, the *tendency* to develop obesity may be inherited, but the expression of this tendency is affected by environmental influences.

The message you should take from this research is that genes are not destiny. It is true that some people have a harder time losing weight and maintaining weight loss than others. However, with increased exercise and attention to diet, even those with a genetic tendency toward obesity can maintain a healthy body weight. And regardless of genetic factors, lifestyle choices remain the cornerstone of successful weight management.

Physiological Factors

Metabolism is a key physiological factor in the regulation of body fat and body weight; hormones also play a role. Another physiological factor that has been proposed as contributing to obesity is weight cycling.

Metabolism and Energy Balance Metabolism is the sum of all the vital processes by which food energy and nutrients are made available to and used by the body. The largest component of metabolism, **resting metabolic rate (RMR)**, is the energy required to maintain vital body functions, including respiration, heart rate, body temperature, and blood pressure, while the body is at rest. As shown in Figure 9.1, RMR accounts for about 55–75% of daily energy expenditure. The energy required to digest food accounts for an additional 5–15% of daily energy expenditure. The remaining 20–40% is expended during physical activity.

Both heredity and behavior affect metabolic rate. Men, who have a higher proportion of muscle mass than do women, have a higher RMR (muscle tissue is more metabolically active than fat). Also, some individuals inherit a higher or lower RMR than others. A higher RMR means that a person burns more calories while at rest and can therefore take in more calories without gaining weight.

Exercise has a positive effect on metabolism. When people exercise, they slightly increase their RMR—the number of calories their bodies burn at rest. They also increase their muscle mass, which is associated with a higher metabolic rate. The exercise itself also burns calories, raising total energy expenditure. The higher the energy expenditure, the more the person can eat without gaining weight. Weight loss or gain also affects metabolic rate. When a person loses weight, both RMR and the energy required to perform physical tasks decrease. The reverse occurs when weight is gained. (One of the reasons exercise is so important during a weight-loss program is that exercise, especially resistance training, helps maintain muscle mass and metabolic rate.)

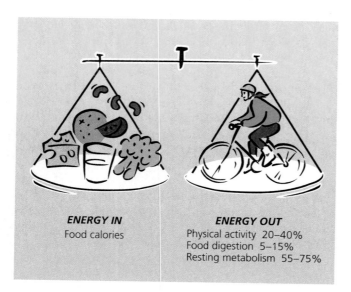

Figure 9.1 The energy-balance equation. To maintain your current weight, you must burn up as many calories as you take in as food each day.

ENERGY IN	**ENERGY OUT**
Food calories	Physical activity 20–40%
	Food digestion 5–15%
	Resting metabolism 55–75%

If the energy-balance equation is even, an individual is burning the same amount of energy as he or she is taking in, and weight remains constant. If more calories are consumed than expended—a positive energy balance—weight will increase; the reverse is true if more calories are expended than consumed—a negative energy balance. The two parts of the energy-balance equation over which you have the most control are the energy you take in as food and the energy you burn during physical activity. To create a negative energy balance and lose weight and body fat, you can increase the amount of energy you burn by increasing your level of physical activity and/or decrease the amount of energy you take in by consuming fewer calories. Specific strategies for altering energy balance are discussed later in the chapter.

Hormones Hormones clearly play a role in the accumulation of body fat, especially for women. Hormonal changes at puberty, during pregnancy, and at menopause contribute to the amount and location of body fat. For example, during puberty, hormones cause the development of secondary sex characteristics, including larger breasts, wider hips, and a fat layer under the skin. This addition of body fat at puberty is normal and healthy.

One hormone thought to be linked to obesity is leptin. Secreted by the body's fat cells, leptin is carried to the brain, where it appears to let the brain know how big or small the body's fat stores are. With this information, the brain can regulate appetite and metabolic rate accordingly. Other hormones that may be involved in the regulation of appetite are cholecystokinin (CCK), peptide YY, and glucagon-like peptide-1 (GLP-1). Researchers hope to use these hormones to develop treatments for obesity based on appetite control; however, as most of us will admit, hunger is often *not* the primary reason we overeat. Cases of obesity based solely or primarily on hormone abnormalities do exist, but they are rare. Lifestyle choices still account for the largest proportion of the differences in body composition among individuals.

Weight Cycling It has been hypothesized that repeatedly losing and regaining weight, known as weight cycling or yo-yo dieting, might be harmful to both overall health and to efforts at weight loss. Weight cycling, it was thought, might make the body more efficient at extracting and storing calories from food; thus, with each successive diet, it would become more difficult to lose weight. Most studies, however, have not supported this idea or found weight cycling to be harmful to the health of an obese person. Most researchers believe that obese individuals should continue to try to control their weight. Losing even a few pounds brings substantial health benefits that appear to exceed any potential risks that might be incurred from weight loss or weight cycling.

Lifestyle Factors

Genetic and physiological factors may increase risk for excess body fat, but they are not sufficient to explain the increasingly high rate of obesity seen in the United States. The gene pool has not changed dramatically in the past 40 years, during which time the rate of obesity among Americans has doubled. Clearly, other factors are at work—particularly lifestyle factors such as increased energy intake and decreased physical activity.

Eating Americans have access to an abundance of highly palatable and calorie-dense foods, and many have eating habits that contribute to weight gain. Most overweight adults will admit to eating more than they should of high-fat, high-sugar, high-calorie foods. Americans eat out more frequently now than in the past, and we rely more heavily on fast food and packaged convenience foods. Restaurant and convenience food portion sizes tend to be very large, and the foods themselves are more likely to be high in fat, sugar, and calories and low in nutrients. A 2004 study found that one-third of American children eat fast food on any given day, and children who eat fast food consume almost 200 more calories per day than those who don't. Studies of adults have also found that the more people eat out, the more calories they consume, especially when they choose a fast-food restaurant.

Studies have consistently found that people underestimate portion sizes by as much as 25%. When participants in one study were asked to report their food intake over the previous 24 hours, the majority underestimated their actual intake by about 600 calories. Many Americans may be unaware of how many calories they actually consume each day.

According to the CDC, the average calorie intake by Americans has increased by about 250–500 calories per day since 1970, and levels of physical activity have declined. The net result has been a substantial increase in the number of Americans who are overweight. Even small increases in energy intake make a difference. For example, 150 additional calories per day, the amount of calories in one can of soda or beer, can translate into a 15-pound weight gain in one year (3500 calories corresponds to one pound of body fat). Compared to 1970, Americans today consume significantly more carbohydrate (about 65 more grams per day), slightly more fat, and about the same amount of protein. These additional carbohydrate calories do not come from the fruits, vegetables, and whole grains recommended by health experts but rather from salty snacks, soft drinks, pizza, and sweet desserts. Other factors contributing to increased calorie intake include increased portion sizes and consumption of more high-calorie meals away from home.

Physical Activity Activity levels among Americans are declining, beginning in childhood and continuing throughout the life cycle. Most adults drive to work, sit all day, and then relax in front of the TV at night. During leisure time, both children and adults surf the Internet, play video games, or watch TV rather than bicycle, participate in sports, or just do yard work or chores around the house. One study found that 60% of the incidence of overweight can be linked to excessive television viewing. On average, Americans exercise 15 minutes per day and watch 170 minutes of TV and movies. Modern conveniences such as remote controls, elevators, and power mowers have also reduced daily physical activity.

Psychosocial Factors Many people have learned to use food as a means of coping with stress and negative emotions. Eating can provide a powerful distraction from difficult feelings—loneliness, anger, boredom, anxiety, shame, sadness, inadequacy. It can be used to combat low moods, low energy levels, and low self-esteem. When food and eating become the primary means of regulating emotions, **binge eating** or other unhealthy eating patterns can develop.

Obesity is strongly associated with socioeconomic status. The prevalence of obesity goes down as income level goes up. More women are obese at lower income levels than men, but men are somewhat more obese at higher levels. These differences may reflect the greater sensitivity and concern for a slim physical appearance among upper-income women, as well as greater access to information about nutrition and to low-fat and low-calorie foods. It may also reflect the greater acceptance of obesity among certain ethnic groups, as well as different cultural values related to food choices.

In some families and cultures, food is used as a symbol of love and caring. It is an integral part of social gatherings and celebrations. In such cases, it may be difficult to change established eating patterns because they are linked to cultural and family values.

College living often makes it difficult to maintain a healthy weight. Poor food choices, excessive snacking, and sedentary habits can lead to weight problems in both the short and the long term.

MOTIVATION FOR CHANGE! Successful weight management is a lifelong project, not a temporary change of habit. To help keep your attitude positive and your commitment and motivation strong, state your weight management goals and strategies positively. Don't make a weight-management program based on denying yourself foods or activities. Focus on what you *are* eating and on what physical activities you enjoy. View any temporary feelings of hunger as a positive sign that your body is using the fuel you're providing. Practice positive self-talk and give yourself lots of rewards and encouragement.

ADOPTING A HEALTHY LIFESTYLE FOR SUCCESSFUL WEIGHT MANAGEMENT

When all the research has been assessed, it is clear that most weight problems are lifestyle problems. Looking at these problems in a historical context reveals why fad diets and other quick-fix approaches are not effective in reversing overweight. About 100 years ago, Americans consumed a diet very different from today's diet and got much more exercise as well. Americans now eat more calories, fat, and refined sugars and fewer complex carbohydrates. Americans today also get far less exercise than their great-grandparents did. Walking, bicycling, and farm and manual labor have all declined, resulting in a decrease in daily energy expenditure of about 200 calories.

Terms

binge eating A pattern of eating in which normal food consumption is interrupted by episodes of high consumption.

Permanent weight loss is not something you start and stop. You need to adopt healthy behaviors that you can maintain throughout your life. Lifestyle factors that are critical for successful long-term weight management include diet and eating habits, physical activity and exercise, an ability to think positively and manage your emotions effectively, and the coping strategies you use to deal with the stresses and challenges in your life.

Diet and Eating Habits

In contrast to "dieting," which involves some form of food restriction, "diet" refers to your daily food choices. Everyone has a diet, but not everyone is dieting. It's important to develop a diet that you enjoy and that enables you to maintain a healthy body composition.

Use MyPyramid or DASH as the basis for planning a healthy diet (see Chapter 8); choose the healthiest options within each food group. For weight management, you may need to pay special attention to total calories, portion sizes, energy density, fat and carbohydrate intake, and eating habits.

Total Calories MyPyramid suggests approximate daily energy intakes based on gender, age, and activity level (see Table 8.4). However, the precise number of calories needed to maintain weight will vary from individual to individual based on heredity, fitness status, level of physical activity, and other factors. It may be more important to focus on individual energy balance than on a general recommendation for daily calorie intake. To maintain your current weight, the total number of calories you eat must equal the number you burn (refer to the energy-balance equation in Figure 9.1). To lose weight, you must decrease your calorie intake and/or increase the number of calories you burn; to gain weight, the reverse is true. (One pound of body fat represents 3500 calories.) To calculate your approximate daily caloric needs, complete the calculations in Lab 9.1.

The best approach for weight loss is probably combining an increase in physical activity with moderate calorie restriction. Don't go on a crash diet. You need to consume enough food to meet your need for essential nutrients. Also, to maintain weight loss, you will probably have to maintain some degree of the calorie restriction you used to lose the weight. Therefore, it is important that you adopt a level of food intake that you can live with over the long term. For most people, maintaining weight loss is more difficult than losing the weight in the first place. To identify weight-loss goals and ways to meet them, complete Lab 9.2.

Portion Sizes Overconsumption of total calories is closely tied to portion sizes. Many Americans are unaware that the portion sizes of packaged foods and of foods served at restaurants have increased in size, and most of us significantly underestimate the amount of food we eat. Limiting portion sizes is critical for weight management. For many people, concentrating on portion sizes is also a

Large portions make it difficult to consume a moderate diet and manage weight. Most people significantly underestimate the amount of food they eat.

much easier method of monitoring and managing total food intake than counting calories.

To counteract portion distortion, weigh and measure your food at home for a few days every now and then. In addition, check the serving sizes listed on packaged foods. With practice, you'll learn to judge portion sizes more accurately. When eating out, try to order the smallest-sized items on the menu. When a small isn't small enough, take some home or share it with a friend. It is especially important to limit serving sizes of foods that are high in calories and low in nutrients. Don't supersize your meals and snacks; although huge servings may seem like the best deal, it is more important to order just what you need. Refer to Chapter 8 and the Online Learning Center for more information and hints on choosing appropriate portion sizes.

Energy (Calorie) Density Experts also recommend that you pay attention to energy density—the number of calories per ounce or gram of weight in a food. Studies suggest that it isn't consumption of a certain amount of fat or calories in food that reduces hunger and leads to feelings of fullness and satisfaction; rather, it is consumption of a certain weight of food. Foods that are low in energy density have more volume and bulk—that is, they are relatively heavy but have few calories. For example, for the same 100 calories, you could consume 20 baby carrots or 4 pretzel twists; you are more likely to feel full after eating the serving of carrots because it weighs 10 times that of the serving of pretzels (10 ounces versus 1 ounce).

To cut back on calories and still feel full, then, you should favor foods with a low energy density. Fresh fruits and vegetables, with their high water and fiber content, are low in energy density, as are whole-grain foods. Fresh fruits contain fewer calories and more fiber than fruit juices or drinks. Meat, ice cream, potato chips, croissants, crackers, and low-fat cakes and cookies are examples of foods high in energy density. Strategies for lowering the energy density of your diet include the following:

- Eat fruit with breakfast and for dessert.
- Add extra vegetables to sandwiches, casseroles, stirfry dishes, pizza, pasta dishes, and fajitas.
- Start meals with a bowl of broth-based soup; include a green salad or fruit salad.
- Snack on fresh fruits and vegetables rather than crackers, chips, or other energy-dense snack foods.
- Limit serving sizes of energy-dense foods such as butter, mayonnaise, cheese, chocolate, fatty meats, croissants, and snack foods that are fried or high in added sugars (including reduced-fat products).

Fat Calories   Although some fat is needed in the diet to provide essential nutrients, you should avoid overeating fatty foods, especially those high in saturated and trans fats. There is some evidence that fat calories are more easily converted to body fat than calories from protein or carbohydrate. Limiting fat in the diet can also help you limit your total calories. As described in Chapter 8, most people should consume no more than 35% of their average total daily calories from fat, which translates into no more than 78 grams of fat in a 2000-calorie diet each day. Most of the fat in your diet should be in the form of unsaturated fats from plant and fish sources. Saturated and trans fats should be limited for weight control and disease prevention; foods high in unhealthy fats include full-fat dairy products, fatty meats, stick margarine, deep-fried foods, and other processed and fast foods.

Some people are higher fat burners than others; that is, they burn more of the fat they take in as calories and therefore have less fat to store. Low fat burners convert more dietary fat to stored body fat. This tendency to hoard fat calories may be an important part of the genetic tendency toward obesity. For low fat burners, restricting fat calories to a level even below 35% may be helpful in weight management.

As Chapter 8 made clear, then, moving toward a diet strong in whole grains and fresh fruits and vegetables, and away from a reliance on meat, processed foods, and fast foods is an effective approach to reducing saturated and trans fat consumption. Watch out for processed foods labeled "fat-free" or "reduced-fat" because they may be high in calories (see the box "Evaluating Fat and Sugar Substitutes" on p. 288). In addition, researchers have found that many Americans compensate for a lower-fat diet by consuming more calories overall. A low-fat diet that is high in calories will not lead to weight loss.

Carbohydrate   Most experts agree that people should consume about 45–65% of total daily calories as carbohydrate, with special emphasis on whole grains, vegetables, fruits, and other foods high in fiber. Americans currently consume most of their carbohydrate calories in the form of foods high in refined carbohydrates, added sugars, and easily digestible starch—soft drinks and heavily sweetened fruit drinks, white rice, white potatoes, and breads, cereals, and snack foods made with refined grains. Such foods are typically high in calories and low in fiber and essential nutrients. They also often cause dramatic swings in blood glucose and insulin levels that may affect hunger levels and that have been implicated in the development of heart disease and type 2 diabetes. (See Chapters 8 and 11 for more on the concept of glycemic index.)

Food rich in whole grains and fiber are typically lower in calorie density, saturated fat, and added sugars and may promote feelings of satiety (fullness)—all characteristic features of a successful dietary pattern for weight management. They also help maintain normal blood glucose and insulin levels and reduce the risk of heart disease and diabetes. For weight management and overall health, choose a diet rich in complex carbohydrates from whole grains, vegetables, and fruits, and be moderate in your consumption of starchy vegetables like white potatoes and corn. Avoid high-calorie preparation methods such as deep-frying, and limit consumption of high-fat toppings, added sugars (especially sugary soft drinks, fruit drinks, and desserts), and refined carbohydrates.

Protein   The typical American consumes an adequate amount of protein to meet nutritional needs. Dietary supplements with extra protein are unnecessary for most people, and protein not needed by the body for growth and tissue repair will be stored as fat. Some studies have found that increasing protein intake somewhat—while cutting calories from fat—helps people feel less hungry. If you do decide to increase your protein intake, stay within the recommended intake range of 10–35% of total daily calories, and favor plant sources of protein rather than high-fat animal products.

Eating Habits   Equally important to weight management is eating small, frequent meals—three or more a day plus snacks—on a dependable, regular schedule. Skipping meals leads to excessive hunger; feelings of deprivation; and increased vulnerability to binge eating or snacking on high-calorie, high-fat, or sugary foods. A regular pattern of eating, along with some personal decision rules governing food choices, is a way of thinking about and then internalizing the many details that go into a healthy, low-fat diet. Decision rules governing breakfast might be these, for example: Choose a sugar-free, high-fiber cereal with nonfat milk and fruit most of the time; have a hard-boiled egg no more than once a week; save pancakes and waffles for special occasions.

Evaluating Fat and Sugar Substitutes

Critical Consumer

For successful weight management, some people find it helpful to limit their intake of foods high in fat and simple sugars. Foods made with fat and sugar substitutes are often promoted for weight loss. But just what are fat and sugar substitutes? And can they really contribute to weight management?

Fat Substitutes

A variety of substances are used to replace fats in processed foods and other products. Some contribute calories, protein, fiber, and/or other nutrients; others do not. Fat replacers can be classified into three general categories:

- *Carbohydrate-based fat replacers* include starch, fibers, gums, cellulose, polydextrose, and fruit purees. They are the oldest and most widely used form of fat replacer and are found in dairy and meat products, baked goods, salad dressing, and many other prepared foods. Newer types such as Oatrim, Z-trim, and Nu-trim are made from types of dietary fiber that may actually lower cholesterol levels. Carbohydrate-based fat replacers contribute 0–4 calories per gram.

- *Protein-based fat replacers* are typically made from milk, egg whites, soy, or whey; trade names include Simplesse, Dairy-lo, and Supro. They are used in cheese, sour cream, mayonnaise, margarine spreads, frozen desserts, salad dressings, and baked goods. Protein-based fat replacers typically contribute 1–4 calories per gram.

- *Fat-based fat replacers* include glycerides, olestra, and other types of fatty acids. Some of these compounds are not absorbed well by the body and so provide fewer calories per gram (5 calories compared with the standard 9 for fats); others are impossible for the body to digest and so contribute no calories at all. Olestra, marketed under the trade name Olean and used in fried snack foods, is an example of the latter type of compound. Concerns have been raised about the safety of olestra because it reduces the absorption of fat-soluble nutrients and certain antioxidants and because it causes gastrointestinal distress in some people.

Nonnutritive Sweeteners and Sugar Alcohols

Sugar substitutes are often referred to as nonnutritive sweeteners because they provide no calories or essential nutrients. By 2005, five types of nonnutritive sweeteners had been approved for use in the United States: acesulfame-K (Sunett, Sweet One), aspartame (NutraSweet, Equal, NatraTaste), saccharin (Sweet 'N Low), sucralose (Splenda), and neotame. They are used in beverages, desserts, baked goods, yogurt, chewing gum, and products such as toothpaste, mouthwash, and cough syrup. Another sweetener, stevia, is an extract of a South American shrub; it is classified as a dietary supplement and so is not regulated by the FDA.

Sugar alcohols are made by altering the chemical form of sugars extracted from fruits and other plant sources; they include erythritol, isomalt, lactitol, maltitol, mannitol, sorbitol, and xylitol. Sugar alcohols provide 0.2 to 2.5 calories per gram, compared to 4 calories per gram in standard sugar. They have typically been used to sweeten sugar-free candies but are now being added to many sweet foods (candy, cookies, and so on) promoted as low-carbohydrate products, often combined with other sweeteners. Sugar alcohols are digested in a way that can create gas, cramps, and diarrhea if they are consumed in large amounts—more than about 10 grams in one meal. To avoid problems, check ingredient lists and food labels to determine if a food contains sugar alcohols and in what amount.

Fat and Sugar Substitutes in Weight Management

Whether fat and sugar substitutes help you achieve and maintain a healthy weight depends on your lifestyle—your overall eating and activity habits. The increase in the availability of fat-free and sugar-free foods in the United States has *not* been associated with a drop in calorie consumption. When evaluating foods containing fat and sugar substitutes, consider these issues:

- *Is the food lower in calories or just lower in fat?* Reduced-fat foods often contain extra sugar to improve the taste and texture lost when fat is removed, so such foods may be as high or even higher in total calories than their fattier counterparts. Limiting fat intake is an important goal for weight management, but so is controlling total calories.

- *Are you choosing foods with fat and/or sugar substitutes* instead of *foods you typically eat or* in addition to *foods you typically eat?* If you consume low-fat, no-sugar-added ice cream instead of regular ice cream, you may save calories. But if you add such ice cream to your daily diet simply because it is lower in fat and sugar, your overall calorie consumption—and your weight —may increase.

- *How many foods containing fat and sugar substitutes do you consume each day?* Although the FDA has given at least provisional approval to all the fat and sugar substitutes currently available, health concerns about some of these products linger. One way to limit any potential adverse effects is to read labels and monitor how much of each product you consume.

- *Is an even healthier choice available?* Many of the foods containing fat and sugar substitutes are low-nutrient snack foods. Although substituting a lower-fat or lower-sugar version of the same food may be beneficial, fruits, vegetables, and whole grains are healthier snack choices.

Decreeing some foods off-limits generally sets up a rule to be broken. The better rule is "everything in moderation." No foods need to be entirely off-limits, though some should be eaten judiciously. Making the healthier choice more often than not is the essence of moderation.

Physical Activity and Exercise

Regular physical activity is another important lifestyle factor in weight management. Physical activity and exercise burn calories and keep the metabolism geared to using food for energy instead of storing it as fat. Making significant cuts in

Table 9.2	Calorie Costs of Selected Physical Activities*

To determine how many calories you burn when you engage in a particular activity, multiply the calorie multiplier given below by your body weight (in pounds) and then by the number of minutes you exercise.

Activity	Cal/lb/ min ×	Body weight ×	min =	Total Calories
Cycling (13 mph)	.071	____	____	____
Dancing (popular)	.049	____	____	____
Digging	.062	____	____	____
Driving a car	.020	____	____	____
Housework	.029	____	____	____
Painting a house	.034	____	____	____
Shoveling snow	.052	____	____	____
Sitting quietly	.009	____	____	____
Sleeping and resting	.008	____	____	____
Standing quietly	.012	____	____	____
Typing or writing	.013	____	____	____
Walking briskly (4.5 mph)	.048	____	____	____

*See Chapter 7 for the energy costs of fitness activities.

SOURCE: Adapted from Kusinitz, I., and M. Fine. 1995. *Your Guide to Getting Fit*, 3rd ed. Mountain View, Calif.: Mayfield.

food intake in order to lose weight is a difficult strategy to maintain; increasing your physical activity is a much better strategy. Regular physical activity also protects against weight gain and is essential for maintaining weight loss.

Physical Activity The first step in becoming more active is to incorporate more physical activity into your daily life. If you are currently sedentary, start by accumulating 30 minutes or more of moderate-intensity physical activity—walking, gardening, housework, and so on—on most, or preferably all, days of the week, for a total of 150 minutes or more per week. Take advantage of routine opportunities to be more active. Take the stairs instead of the elevator, walk or bike instead of driving. In the long term, even a small increase in activity level can help maintain your current weight or help you lose a moderate amount of weight (Table 9.2). In fact, research suggests that fidgeting—stretching, squirming, standing up, and so on—may help prevent weight gain in some people. If you simply walked around during TV commercials while watching 2 hours of prime-time programming, you'd accumulate more than 30 minutes of physical activity. Short bouts of activity spread throughout the day can produce many of the same health benefits as continuous physical activity.

If you are overweight and want to lose weight, or if you are trying to maintain a lower weight following weight loss, a greater amount of physical activity can help. Researchers have found that people who lose weight and don't regain it typically burn about 2800 calories per week in physical activity—the equivalent of about 1 hour of brisk walking per day. The 2005 Dietary Guidelines for Americans recommend at least 60 minutes of daily physical activity to avoid slow weight gain in adulthood, and at least 60–90 minutes of activity to lose weight or maintain weight loss.

Exercise Once you become more active every day, begin a formal exercise program that includes cardiorespiratory endurance exercise, resistance training, and stretching exercises. (See Chapter 7 for advice on creating a complete, personalized exercise program.) Moderate-intensity endurance exercise, if performed frequently for a relatively long duration, can burn a significant number of calories. Endurance training also increases the rate at which your body uses calories after your exercise session is over—burning an additional 5–180 extra calories, depending on the intensity of exercise. Resistance training builds muscle mass, and more muscle translates into a higher metabolic rate. Resistance training can also help you maintain your muscle mass during a period of weight loss, helping you avoid the significant drop in RMR associated with weight loss.

The body's fuel-use patterns vary with exercise intensity and change during recovery. During low-intensity exercise, a higher proportion of energy comes from fat (50%) than does during high-intensity exercise (40%). However, high-intensity exercise burns more calories overall, so even though a lower proportion of those calories comes from fat, high-intensity exercise tends to burn more fat than low-intensity exercise. Intense exercise also causes the body to use more fat as fuel during the recovery period. However, high-intensity exercise is not necessarily the best strategy for controlling weight. All physical activity will help you manage your weight, and most people find that a program of moderate-intensity exercise is easier to maintain over the long term.

Regular physical activity, maintained throughout life, makes weight management easier. The sooner you establish good habits, the better. The key to success is making exercise an integral part of a lifestyle you can enjoy now and will enjoy in the future.

Thoughts and Emotions

The way you think about yourself and your world influences, and is influenced by, how you feel and how you act. In fact, research on people who have a weight problem indicates that low self-esteem and the negative emotions that accompany it are significant problems. People with low self-esteem mentally compare the actual self to an internally held picture of the "ideal self," an image based on perfectionistic goals and beliefs about how they and others should be. The more these two pictures differ, the larger the impact on self-esteem and the more likely the presence of negative emotions.

Besides the internal picture we carry of ourselves, all of us carry on a internal dialogue about events happening to us and around us. This **self-talk** can be either self-deprecating or positively motivating, depending on our beliefs and attitudes. Having realistic beliefs and goals and engaging in positive self-talk and problem solving support a healthy lifestyle. (Chapter 10 and Activity 11 in the Behavior Change Workbook at the end of the text include strategies for developing realistic self-talk.)

Coping Strategies

Adequate and appropriate coping strategies for dealing with the stresses and challenges of life are another lifestyle factor in weight management. One strategy that many people adopt for coping is eating. (Others may cope by turning to drugs, alcohol, smoking, or gambling.) Those who overeat might use food to alleviate loneliness, as a pickup for fatigue, as an antidote to boredom, or as a distraction from problems. Some people even overeat to punish themselves for real or imagined transgressions.

Those who recognize that they are using food in these ways can analyze their eating habits with fresh eyes. They can consciously attempt to find new coping strategies and begin to use food appropriately—to fuel life's activities, to foster growth, and to bring pleasure, *not* to manage stress. For a summary of the components of weight management through healthy lifestyle choices, see the box "Lifestyle Strategies for Successful Weight Management."

MOTIVATION FOR CHANGE!   Your environment may not always support your efforts at weight management, but you are in charge of your own behavior. Weight management is about choice. You have many opportunities to make positive choices about food and physical activity every day. For long-term success, you need to make the best choices whenever possible. Keep a journal to help raise your awareness of the choices you are making. Watch out for automatic eating or eating in response to emotions rather than hunger—think before you eat, and ask yourself why you are eating now and why you are choosing certain foods. View daily energy intake as a personal budget that you get to spend however you choose each day. Strategies like these can help build your sense of confidence and control over your daily eating and activity habits and improve your chance of long-term success.

Terms

self-talk A person's internal comments and discussion; instrumental in shaping self-image.

APPROACHES TO OVERCOMING A WEIGHT PROBLEM

Now you know the factors that contribute to a weight problem, and you understand the importance of diet and physical activity in successful weight management. If you are overweight, you may already be planning how to go about losing weight and keeping it off. There are many options available to you.

Doing It Yourself

If you need to lose weight, focus on adopting the healthy lifestyle described throughout this book. The "right" weight for you will naturally evolve, and you won't have to diet. Combine modest cuts in energy intake with exercise, and avoid very-low-calorie diets. By producing a negative energy balance of 250–1000 calories per day, you'll produce the recommended weight loss of ½–2 pounds per week. Realize that most low-calorie diets cause a rapid loss of body water at first. When this phase passes, weight loss declines. As a result, dieters are often misled into believing that their efforts are not working. They give up, not realizing that smaller losses later in the diet are actually better than the initial big losses, because later loss is mostly fat loss, whereas initial loss was primarily fluid. For someone who is overweight, reasonable weight loss is 8–10% of body weight over 6 months.

For many Americans, maintaining weight loss is a bigger challenge than losing weight. Most weight lost during a period of dieting is regained. When planning a weight-management program, it is extremely important to include strategies that you can maintain over the long term, both for food choices and for physical activity. Weight management is a lifelong project. A registered dietitian or nutritionist can recommend an appropriate plan for you when you want to lose weight on your own. For more tips on losing weight on your own, refer to the section later in the chapter on creating an individual weight-management plan.

Diet Books

Many people who try to lose weight by themselves fall prey to one or more of the dozens of diet books on the market. Although a very few of these do contain useful advice and tips for motivation, most make empty promises. Here are some guidelines for evaluating and choosing a diet book:

1. Reject books that advocate an unbalanced way of eating, such as a high-carbohydrate-only diet or low-carbohydrate, high-protein diets. Also reject books promoting a single food, such as cabbage or grapefruit.

Food Choices

• Follow the recommendations in MyPyramid for eating a moderate, varied diet. Focus on making good choices from within each food group.

• Pay attention to the energy density and nutrient density of your food choices. Favor foods with a low energy density and a high nutrient density.

• Check food labels for serving sizes, calories, and nutrient levels.

• Watch for hidden calories. Reduced-fat foods often have as many calories as their full-fat versions. Fat-based condiments like butter, margarine, mayonnaise, and salad dressings provide about 100 calories per tablespoon; added sugars such as jams, jellies, and syrup are also packed with calories.

• Drink fewer calories. Many Americans consume high-calorie beverages such as soda, fruit drinks, sports drinks, alcohol, and specialty coffees and teas. (People who get extra calories from solid food tend to compensate by eating less later; people whose extra calories come in liquid form don't compensate and consume more calories overall.)

• For problem foods, try eating small amounts under controlled conditions. Go out for a scoop of ice cream, for example, rather than buying half a gallon for your freezer.

Planning and Serving

• Keep a log of what you eat. Before you begin your program, your log will provide a realistic picture of your current diet and what changes you can make. Once you start your program, a log will keep you focused on your food choices and portion sizes. Consider tracking the following:

food eaten
hunger level
circumstances (location, other activities)
outside influences (environment, other people)
thoughts and emotions

• Eat three meals a day, *including breakfast;* in studies, people who eat breakfast consume fewer calories overall over the course of the day. Fix more meals yourself and eat out less often. Replace impulse snacking with planned, healthy snacks. Keep low-calorie snacks on hand to combat the "munchies": baby carrots, popcorn, and fresh fruits and vegetables are good choices.

• When shopping for food, make a list and stick to it. Don't shop when you're hungry. Avoid aisles that contain problem foods.

• In a cafeteria, examine all the possible food choices before you begin making selections. This will help you avoid overloading your plate. Don't take dessert during your first trip through the line: What seems like an appropriate choice and portion size for dessert may look very different *after* you've eaten a meal.

• Pay special attention to portion sizes. Use measuring cups and spoons and a food scale to become more familiar with appropriate portion sizes.

• Serve meals on small plates and in small bowls to help you eat smaller portions without feeling deprived.

• Eat only in specifically designated spots. Remove food from other areas of your house or apartment.

• When you eat, just eat—don't do anything else, such as read or watch TV.

• Avoid late night eating, a behavior specifically associated with weight gain among college students.

• Eat more slowly. It takes time for your brain to get the message that your stomach is full. Take small bites and chew food thoroughly. Pay attention to every bite, and enjoy your food. Between bites, try putting your fork or spoon down and taking sips of water or another beverage.

• When you're done eating, remove your plate. Cue yourself that the meal is over—drink a glass of water, suck on a mint, chew gum, or brush your teeth.

Special Occasions

• When you eat out, choose a restaurant where you can make healthy food choices. Ask the server not to put bread and butter on the table before the meal and request that sauces and salad dressings be served on the side. If portion sizes are large, take half your food home for a meal later in the week. Don't choose supersized meals.

• If you cook a large meal for friends, send leftovers home with your guests.

• If you're eating at a friend's, eat a little and leave the rest. Don't eat to be polite; if someone offers you food you don't want, thank the person and decline firmly: "No thank you, I've had enough" or "It's delicious, but I'm full."

• Take care during the winter holidays. Research indicates that people gain less than they think during the winter holidays (about a pound) but that the weight isn't lost during the rest of the year, leading to slow, steady weight gain.

Physical Activity and Stress Management

• Increase your level of daily physical activity. If you have been sedentary for a long time or are seriously overweight, increase your level of activity slowly. Start by walking 10 minutes at a time, and work toward 30–60 minutes or more of moderate physical activity per day.

• Begin a formal exercise program that includes cardiorespiratory endurance exercise, strength training, and stretching.

• Develop techniques for handling stress—go for a walk or use a relaxation technique. Practice positive self-talk. Get adequate sleep. See Chapter 10 for more on stress management.

• Develop strategies for coping with nonhunger cues to eat, such as boredom, sleepiness, or anxiety. Try calling a friend, taking a shower, or reading a magazine.

• Tell family members and friends that you're making some changes in your eating and exercise habits. Ask them to be supportive.

Visit the Small Steps site for more tips (www.smallstep.gov).

2. Reject books that claim to be based on a "scientific breakthrough" or to have the "secret" to success.

3. Reject books that use gimmicks, like matching eating to blood type, hyping insulin resistance as the single cause of obesity, combining foods in special ways to achieve weight loss, rotating levels of calories, or purporting that a weight problem is due to food allergies, food sensitivities, yeast infections, or hormone imbalances.

4. Reject books that promise quick weight loss or that limit the selection of foods.

5. Accept books that advocate a balanced approach to diet plus exercise and offer sound nutrition advice.

Many diets cause weight loss if maintained; the real difficulty is finding a safe and healthy pattern of food choices and physical activity that results in long-term maintenance of a healthy body weight and reduced risk of chronic disease (see the box "Is Any Diet Best for Weight Loss?"). In addition to the health concerns associated with some diets recommended by popular books, researchers have found low long-term success rates for many diets—again reinforcing the idea that weight management is a lifelong project that requires commitment to reasonable eating and exercise habits. Research into diet and exercise strategies for weight loss is ongoing, so you can expect to hear about further findings that may help you make informed decisions about your own weight-management program. Worksheets for evaluating diet books and commercial weight-loss plans can be found on the Online Learning Center.

Dietary Supplements and Diet Aids

The number of dietary supplements and other weight-loss aids on the market has also increased in recent years. Promoted in advertisements, magazines, direct mail campaigns, infomercials, and Web sites, these products typically promise a quick and easy path to weight loss. Most of these products are marketed as dietary supplements and so are subject to fewer regulations than over-the-counter medications. A 2002 report from the Federal Trade Commission stated that more than half of advertisements for weight-loss products made representations that are likely to be false. In addition, use of OTC products doesn't help in the adoption of lifestyle behaviors that can help people achieve and maintain a healthy weight over the long term.

The bottom line on nonprescription diet aids is caveat emptor—let the buyer beware. There is no quick and easy way to lose weight. The most effective approach is to develop healthy diet and exercise habits and make them a permanent part of your lifestyle. Some commonly marketed OTC products for weight loss are described below.

There are many plans and supplements promoted for weight loss, but few have any research supporting their effectiveness for long-term weight management. Developing lifelong healthy eating and exercise habits is the best approach for achieving and maintaining a healthy body composition.

Formula Drinks and Food Bars Canned diet drinks, powders used to make shakes, and diet food bars and snacks are designed to achieve weight loss by substituting for some or all of a person's daily food intake. However, most people find it difficult to use these products for long periods, and muscle loss and other serious health problems may result if they are used as the sole source of nutrition for an extended period. Use of such products sometimes results in rapid short-term weight loss, but the weight is typically regained because users haven't changed the eating and lifestyle behaviors that caused the weight problem in the first place.

Herbs and Herbal Products As described in Chapter 8, herbs are marketed as dietary supplements, so there is little information about effectiveness, proper dosage, drug interactions, and side effects. In addition, labels may not accurately reflect the ingredients and dosages present, and safe manufacturing practices are not guaranteed. For example, the substitution of a toxic herb for another compound during the manufacture of a Chinese herbal weight-loss preparation caused more than 100 cases of kidney damage and cancer among users in Europe.

In 2004, the FDA banned the sale of ephedra (*ma huang*), stating that it presented a significant and unreasonable risk to human health. (Lawsuits to overturn the ban were subsequently filed in several states.) Ephedrine, the active ingredient in ephedra, is structurally similar to amphetamine and was widely used in weight-loss supplements.

Experts agree that reducing energy (calorie) intake promotes weight loss. However, many popular commercial and published weight-loss plans include a special hook and promote specific food choices and macronutrient (protein, fat, carbohydrate) combinations as best for weight loss. Research findings have been mixed, but two points are clear. Total calorie intake matters, and the best diet is probably the one that an individual can stick with.

Low-Carbohydrate Diets

Recent popular diet books have advocated a diet very low in carbohydrate—with fewer than 10% of total calories from carbohydrate, compared to the 45–65% recommended by the Food and Nutrition Board. Some suggest daily carbohydrate intake below the 130 grams needed to provide essential carbohydrate in the diet. Small studies have found that low-carbohydrate diets can help with weight loss and be safe for relatively short periods of time—although unpleasant effects such as bad breath, constipation, and headache are fairly common.

There are concerns about the long-term effects of very low-carb diets, because they tend to be very high in saturated fat and protein and low in fiber, whole grains, vegetables, fruits, and some vitamins, minerals, and phytochemicals. Over the long term, this dietary pattern has been linked to increased risk of heart disease, high blood pressure, and cancer. Diets very high in protein can also stress the kidneys.

Low-Fat Diets

Many experts advocate diets that are relatively low in fat, high in carbohydrate, and moderate in protein. Critics of these diets blame them for rising rates of obesity and note that very-low-fat, very-high-carbohydrate diets can increase triglyceride levels and lower levels of good (HDL) cholesterol in some people. However, these negative effects can be counteracted with moderate-intensity exercise, and low-fat diets combined with physical activity can be safe and effective for many people.

Few experts take the position that low-fat, high-carbohydrate diets, apart from overall diet and activity patterns, are responsible for the increase in obesity among Americans. However, the debate has highlighted the importance of total calorie intake and the quality of carbohydrate choices. Most Americans consume large amounts of refined carbohydrates and added sugars from energy-dense, nutrient-poor foods; they do not consume the recommended whole grains, vegetables, and fruits. A low-fat diet is not a license to consume excess calories, even in the form of low-fat foods.

How Do Popular Diets Measure Up?

In one recent study, obese people on a very-low-carbohydrate, high-fat diet lost more weight over a 6-month period than people following a moderate-fat diet. However, after a year, the difference in weight loss between the two groups was no longer significant, and the dropout rate from both groups was high.

A 2005 study followed participants in four popular diets that emphasize different strategies—Weight Watchers (restricted portion sizes and calories), Atkins (low-carbohydrate, high-fat), Zone (relatively high protein, moderate fat and carbohydrate), and Ornish (very low fat). Each of these diets modestly reduced body weight and heart disease risk factors. There was no significant difference in weight loss at 1 year among the diets, and the more closely people adhered to each diet, the more weight they lost. The dropout rates were high—about 50% for Atkins and Ornish and about 35% for Weight Watchers and Zone. The message from this study? Finding a dietary approach that you can stick to is key to long-term success.

Energy Balance Counts: The National Weight Control Registry

Future research may determine that certain macronutrient patterns may be somewhat more helpful for disease reduction in people with particular risk profiles. However, in terms of weight loss, such differences among diets are likely overshadowed by the importance of total calorie intake and physical activity. Important lessons about energy balance can be drawn from the National Weight Control Registry, an ongoing study of people who have lost significant amounts of weight and kept it off. The average participant in the registry has lost 71 pounds and kept the weight off for more than 5 years. Nearly all participants use a combination of diet and exercise to manage their weight. Most consume diets moderate in calories and relatively low in fat and fried foods; they monitor their body weight and their food intake frequently. Participants engage in an average of 60 minutes of moderate physical activity daily. The National Weight Control Registry study illustrates that to lose weight and keep it off, you must decrease daily calorie intake and/or increase daily physical activity—and continue to do so over your lifetime.

A Balanced Approach

For short-term weight loss, many types of diets can be safe and successful. However, long-term maintenance of healthy body weight and reduction of chronic disease risk requires permanent changes in lifestyle. Diets advocating strict limits on any nutrient or food groups may be impractical and difficult to maintain over the long term. The latest USDA guidelines provide a good model for healthy food and activity choices. Basic guidelines for weight loss and risk reduction advocated by many experts include the following:

- Set reasonable goals; even small amounts of weight loss benefit health.

- Reduce your intake of saturated and trans fats, refined carbohydrates, and added sugars. Favor unsaturated fats, lean protein sources, whole grains, vegetables, and fruits. Select nutrient-dense choices within each food group.

- Incorporate 60 or more minutes of physical activity into your daily routine; begin a formal exercise program for even greater health and fitness benefits.

- Choose a healthy dietary pattern that works for you over the long term.

SOURCES: Dansinger, M. L., et al. 2005. Comparison of the Atkins, Ornish, Weight Watchers, and Zone diets for weight loss and heart disease risk reduction. *Journal of the American Medical Association* 293(1): 43–53. Hays, N. P., et al. 2004. Effects of an ad libitum low-fat, high-carbohydrate diet on body weight, body composition, and fat distribution in older men and women. *Archives of Internal Medicine* 164(2): 210–217. Hill, J., and R. Wing. 2003. The National Weight Control Registry. *Permanente Journal* 7(3): 34–37. Bravata, D. M., et al. 2003. Efficacy and safety of low-carbohydrate diets. *Journal of the American Medical Association* 289:1837–1850. Foster, G. D., et al. 2003. A randomized trial of low-carbohydrate diet for obesity. *New England Journal of Medicine* 348:2082–2090. Samaha, F. F., et al. 2003. A low-carbohydrate as compared with a low-fat diet in severe obesity. *New England Journal of Medicine* 348:2074–2081.

Table 9.3 Ingredients in Over-the-Counter Weight-Loss Aids

Common Name	Use/Claim	Safety Issues
Bitter orange extract	Stimulant chemically related to ephedrine; appetite suppressant	Concentrated extracts may increase blood pressure; contraindicated for people with cardiac problems
Chitosan (fiber derived from shellfish)	Interference with fat absorption	Can cause constipation or gas; contraindicated for people with shellfish allergies
Chromium picolinate	Increased muscle mass, decreased body fat	Short-term use of moderate doses generally considered safe; studies on effectiveness mixed
Conjugated linoleic acid (CLA)	Increased muscle mass, decreased body fat	Short-term use generally considered safe; no long-term studies support efficacy
Dieter's tea (made from aloe, buckthorn, senna, and other herbs)	Stimulant, diuretic, laxative	Acts as a stimulant laxative; in excess amounts can cause diarrhea, vomiting, nausea, fainting, laxative dependence, and electrolyte imbalances that can lead to heart rhythm problems
Garcinia cambogia	Interference with fat metabolism or appetite suppression	Generally considered safe, but common side effects include upper respiratory and gastrointestinal symptoms
Psyllium (fiber derived from seeds)	Appetite suppressant	Short-term use generally considered safe; hasn't been shown to be effective for weight loss
Pyruvate	Increased metabolism, decreased body fat	Generally considered safe
Yerba mate (tea); guarana; damiana	Stimulant, appetite suppression (active ingredient is caffeine)	Restlessness, anxiety, insomnia; symptoms of caffeine overdose in sensitive people

SOURCES: Evaluating 10 ingredients in weight-loss pills. No clear winners. 2004. *Environmental Nutrition*, June. Sarubin, A. 2000. *The Health Professional's Guide to Popular Dietary Supplements*. Chicago: American Dietetic Association. Food and Drug Administration. 1998. *Supplements Associated with Illnesses and Injuries* (http://www.fda.gov/fdac/features/1998/dietchrt.html; retrieved January 15, 2004).

It may suppress appetite, but adverse effects have included elevated blood pressure, panic attacks, seizures, insomnia, and increased risk of heart attack or stroke, particularly when combined with another stimulant, such as caffeine. The synthetic stimulant phenylpropanolamine was banned in 2000 for similar reasons. Other herbal stimulants are still on the market (Table 9.3).

Other Supplements and Diet Aids Fiber is another common ingredient in OTC diet aids, promoted for appetite control. However, dietary fiber acts as a bulking agent in the large intestine, not the stomach, so it doesn't have a pronounced effect on appetite. In addition, many diet aids contain only 3 or fewer grams of fiber, which does not contribute much toward the recommended daily intake of 25–38 grams. Other compounds marketed as diet aids include conjugated linoleic acid, carnitine, chromium, pyruvate, and a number of products labeled "fat absorbers," "fat blockers," and "starch blockers." Research has not found these products to be effective, and many have potentially adverse side effects.

Weight-Loss Programs

Weight-loss programs come in a variety of types, including noncommercial support organizations, commercial programs, Web sites, and medically supervised clinical programs.

Noncommercial Weight-Loss Programs Noncommercial programs such as TOPS (Take Off Pounds Sensibly) and Overeaters Anonymous (OA) mainly provide group support. They do not advocate any particular diet, but they do recommend seeking professional advice for creating an individualized diet and exercise plan. Like Alcoholics Anonymous, OA is a 12-step program with a spiritual orientation that promotes abstinence from compulsive overeating. These types of programs are generally free. Your physician or a registered dietitian can also provide information and support for weight loss.

Commercial Weight-Loss Programs Commercial programs such as Weight Watchers, Jenny Craig, Diet Workshop, and Richard Simmons Slimmons typically provide group support, nutrition education, physical activity recommendations, and behavior modification advice. Some also make available packaged foods to assist in following dietary advice. Many commercial programs voluntarily belong to the Partnership for Healthy Weight Management established by the Federal Trade Commission in 1999. By doing so, they agree to provide clients with information on staff training and education, the risks associated with overweight and obesity, the risks associated with each program or product, the costs of the program, and the expected outcomes of the program, including rates of success. A responsible and safe weight-loss program should have the following features:

1. The recommended diet should be safe and balanced, include all the food groups, and meet the DRIs for all nutrients. Physical activity and exercise should be strongly encouraged.

2. The program should promote slow, steady weight loss averaging ½–2 pounds per week. (There may be rapid weight loss initially due to fluid loss.)

3. If a participant plans to lose more than 20 pounds, has any health problems, or is taking medication on a regular basis, physician evaluation and monitoring should be recommended. The staff of the program should include qualified counselors and health professionals.

4. The program should include plans for weight maintenance after the weight-loss phase is over.

5. The program should provide information on all fees and costs, including those of supplements and prepackaged foods, as well as data on risks and expected outcomes of participating in the program.

You should also consider whether a program fits your lifestyle and whether you are truly ready to make a commitment to it. A strong commitment and a plan for maintenance are especially important because studies indicate that only 10–15% of program participants maintain their weight loss—the rest gain back all or more than they had lost. One study of participants found that regular exercise was the best predictor of maintaining weight loss, whereas frequent television viewing was the best predictor of weight gain. This reinforces the idea that successful weight management requires long-term lifestyle changes.

Online Weight-Loss Programs   A recent addition to the weight-loss program scene is the Internet-based program. Most such Web sites include a cross between self-help and group support through chat rooms, bulletin boards, and e-newsletters. Many sites offer online self-assessment for diet and physical activity habits as well as a meal plan; some provide access to a staff professional for individualized help. Many are free but some charge a small weekly or monthly fee. Preliminary research suggests that this type of program provides an alternative to in-person diet counseling and can lead to weight loss for some people. Studies found that people who logged on more frequently tended to lose more weight; weekly online contact in terms of behavior therapy proved most successful for weight loss. The criteria used to evaluate commercial programs can also be applied to Internet-based programs. In addition, check whether a program offers member-to-member support and access to staff professionals.

Clinical Weight-Loss Programs   Medically supervised clinical programs are usually located in a hospital or other medical setting. Designed to help those who are severely obese, these programs typically involve a closely monitored very-low-calorie diet. The cost of a clinical program is usually high, but insurance often covers part of the fee.

Prescription Drugs

For a medicine to cause weight loss, it must reduce energy consumption, increase energy expenditure, and/or interfere with energy absorption. The medications most often prescribed for weight loss are appetite suppressants that reduce feelings of hunger or increase feelings of fullness. Appetite suppressants usually work by increasing levels of catecholamine or serotonin, two brain chemicals that affect mood and appetite. All prescription weight-loss drugs have potential side effects. Those that affect catecholamine levels, including phentermine (Ionamin, Obenix, Fastin, and Adipex-P), diethylpropion (Tenuate), and mazindol (Sanorex), may cause sleeplessness, nervousness, and euphoria. Sibutramine (Meridia) acts on both the serotonin and catecholamine systems; it may trigger increases in blood pressure and heart rate. Headaches, constipation or diarrhea, dry mouth, and insomnia are other side effects.

Most appetite suppressants are approved by the FDA only for short-term use. Two drugs, however, are approved for longer-term use: sibutramine and orlistat (Xenical). Sibutramine's safety and efficacy record is good, but regular monitoring of blood pressure is required during therapy. Orlistat lowers calorie consumption by blocking fat absorption in the intestines; it prevents about 30% of the fat in food from being digested. Similar to the fat substitute olestra, orlistat also reduces the absorption of fat-soluble vitamins and antioxidants. Therefore, taking a vitamin supplement is highly recommended if taking orlistat. Side effects include diarrhea, cramping, and other gastrointestinal problems if users do not follow a low-fat diet.

It is important to remember that these medications work best in conjunction with behavior modification. Studies have generally found that appetite suppressants produce modest weight loss—about 5–22 pounds above the loss expected with nondrug obesity treatments. Individuals respond very differently, however, and some experience more weight loss than others. Unfortunately, weight loss tends to level off or reverse after 4–6 months on a medication, and many people regain the weight they've lost when they stop taking the drug.

Side effects and risks are other concerns. In 1997, the FDA removed from the market two prescription weight-loss drugs, fenfluramine (Pondimin) and dexfenfluramine (Redux), after their use was linked to potentially life-threatening heart valve problems. (Fenfluramine was used most often in combination with phentermine, an off-label combination referred to as "fen/phen.") It appears that people who took these drugs over a long period or at high dosages are at greatest risk for problems, but the FDA recommends that anyone who has taken either of these drugs be examined by a physician.

Prescription weight-loss drugs are not for people who want to lose a few pounds to wear a smaller size of jeans. The latest federal guidelines advise people to try lifestyle modification for at least 6 months before trying drug therapy. Prescription drugs are recommended—in conjunction with lifestyle changes—only in certain cases: for people who have been unable to lose weight with nondrug options and who have a BMI over 30 (or over 27 if two or more additional risk factors such as diabetes and high blood pressure are present).

Surgery

About 3–5% of Americans are severely obese, meaning they have a BMI of 40 or higher or are 100 pounds or more over recommended weight. For such people, obesity is a serious medical condition that is often complicated by other health problems such as diabetes, sleep disorders, heart disease, and arthritis. Surgical intervention may be necessary as a treatment of last resort for those who have not been successful in permanently reducing weight through other methods. According to a National Institutes of Health Consensus Conference, gastric bypass surgery may be recommended for patients with a BMI greater than 40, or greater than 35 with obesity-related illnesses. Due to the increasing prevalence of severe obesity, surgical treatment of obesity is growing worldwide. Obesity-related health conditions, as well as risk of premature death, generally improve after surgical weight loss. However, surgery is not without risks and is generally only appropriate for people experiencing severe obesity-related health problems.

Gastric bypass surgery modifies the gastrointestinal tract by changing either the size of the stomach or how the intestine drains, thereby reducing food intake. The two most common surgeries are the Roux-en-Y gastric bypass and the vertical banded gastroplasty. Complications of surgery include nutritional deficiencies, fat intolerance, nausea, vomiting, and reflux; as many as 10–20% of patients may require follow-up surgery to address complications. Weight loss from surgery generally ranges between 40% and 70% of total body weight over the course of a year. The key to success is to have adequate follow-up and to stay motivated so that life behaviors and eating patterns are changed permanently.

The surgical technique of liposuction, in which small amounts of fat are removed from specific locations, was described in Chapter 6. Liposuction is not a technique designed to treat obesity.

Psychological Help

Many people can lose weight just by increasing their physical activity level and moderately restricting total calories, especially fat calories. When concern about body weight and shape have developed into an eating disorder, the help of a professional is recommended. A therapist should have experience working with weight management, body image issues, eating disorders, addictions, and abuse issues. Your physician may be able to provide a referral.

BODY IMAGE

The collective picture of the body as seen through the mind's eye, **body image** consists of perceptions, images, thoughts, attitudes, and emotions. A negative body image is characterized by dissatisfaction with the body in general or some part of the body in particular. Recent surveys indicate that the majority of Americans, many of whom are not actually overweight, are unhappy with their body weight or with some aspect of their appearance. Developing a positive body image is an important aspect of psychological wellness.

Severe Body Image Problems

Poor body image can cause significant psychological distress. A person can become preoccupied by a perceived defect in appearance, thereby damaging self-esteem and interfering with relationships. Adolescents and adults who have a negative body image are more likely to diet restrictively, eat compulsively, or develop some other form of disordered eating.

When dissatisfaction becomes extreme, the condition is called body dysmorphic disorder (BDD). BDD affects about 2% of Americans, males and females in equal numbers; BDD usually begins before age 18 but can begin in adulthood. People with BDD are overly concerned with physical appearance, often focusing on what they perceive to be slight "flaws" of the face or head. Individuals with BDD may spend hours every day thinking about their flaws and looking at themselves in mirrors; they may desire and seek repeated cosmetic surgeries. BDD is related to obsessive-compulsive disorder and can lead to depression, social phobia, and suicide if left untreated. Medication and psychotherapy can help people with BDD.

In some cases, body image may bear little resemblance to fact. A person with the eating disorder anorexia nervosa typically has a severely distorted body image—she believes herself to be fat even when she has become emaciated (see the next section for more on anorexia). Distorted body image is also a hallmark of **muscle dysmorphia**, a disorder experienced by some bodybuilders in which they see themselves as small and out of shape despite being very muscular. People with muscle dysmorphia may let obsessive bodybuilding interfere with their work and relationships. They may also use steroids and other potentially dangerous muscle-building drugs.

To assess your body image, complete the body image self-test in Lab 9.3.

Acceptance and Change

Most Americans, young and old, are unhappy with some aspect of their appearance, often their weight. The "can-do" attitude of Americans, together with the belief that there is a solution to this dissatisfaction, leads to even more problems with body image, as well as to dieting, disordered eating, and the desire for cosmetic surgery to fix perceived defects.

In fact, there are limits to the changes that can be made to body weight and body shape, both of which are influenced by heredity. The changes that can and should be made are lifestyle changes—engaging in regular physical activity, obtaining adequate nutrition, and maintaining healthy eating habits. With these changes, the body weight and shape that develop will be natural and appropriate for an individual's particular genetic makeup.

Knowing when the limits to healthy change have been reached—and learning to accept those limits—is crucial for overall wellness. Women in particular tend to measure self-worth in terms of their appearance; when they don't measure up to an unrealistic cultural ideal, they see themselves as defective and their self-esteem falls. The result can be negative body image, disordered eating, or even a full-blown eating disorder (see the box "Gender, Ethnicity, and Body Image" on p. 298).

Obesity is a serious health risk, but weight management needs to take place in a positive and realistic atmosphere. For an obese person, losing as few as 10 pounds can reduce blood pressure and improve mood. The hazards of excessive dieting and overconcern about body weight need to be countered by a change in attitude about what constitutes the perfect body and a reasonable body weight. A reasonable weight must take into account a person's weight history, social circumstances, metabolic profile, and psychological well-being.

EATING DISORDERS

Problems with body weight and weight control are not limited to excessive body fat. A growing number of people, especially adolescent girls and young women, experience **eating disorders**, characterized by severe disturbances in eating patterns and eating-related behavior. The major eating disorders are anorexia nervosa, bulimia nervosa, and binge-eating disorder. More than 8 million Americans, most of them women, have eating disorders. Many more people have abnormal eating habits and attitudes about food that, although not meeting the criteria for a full-blown eating disorder, do disrupt their lives (see the box "Borderline Disordered Eating" on p. 299). To assess your eating habits, complete Lab 9.3.

Although many different explanations for the development of eating disorders have been proposed, they share one central feature: a dissatisfaction with body image and body weight. Such dissatisfaction is created by distorted thinking, including perfectionistic beliefs, unreasonable demands for self-control, and excessive self-criticism. Dissatisfaction with body weight leads to dysfunctional attitudes about eating, such as fear of fat, preoccupation with food, and problematic eating behaviors.

Anorexia Nervosa

A person with **anorexia nervosa** does not eat enough food to maintain a reasonable body weight. A BMI of 17.5 or less is sometimes used as a diagnostic criterion for anorexia. Anorexia affects 1–3 million Americans, 95% of them female. Although it can occur later, anorexia typically develops between ages 12 and 18. People with anorexia have an intense fear of gaining weight or becoming fat. Their body image is distorted so that even when emaciated, they think they are fat. People with anorexia may engage in compulsive behaviors or rituals that help them keep from eating; they also commonly use vigorous and prolonged physical activity to reduce body weight. Although they may express a great interest in food, their diet becomes more and more extreme. Anorexics are typically introverted, emotionally reserved, and socially insecure. Their entire sense of self-esteem may be tied up in their evaluation of their body shape and weight.

Anorexia nervosa has been linked to a variety of medical complications, including disorders of the cardiovascular, gastrointestinal, and endocrine systems. Because of

Terms

body image The mental representation a person holds about her or his body at any given moment in time, consisting of perceptions, images, thoughts, attitudes, and emotions about the body.

muscle dysmorphia A disorder characterized by distorted body image; affected people inaccurately perceive themselves as small, with underdeveloped muscles.

eating disorder A serious disturbance in eating patterns or eating-related behavior, characterized by a negative body image and concerns about body weight or body fat.

anorexia nervosa An eating disorder characterized by a refusal to maintain body weight at a minimally healthy level and an intense fear of gaining weight or becoming fat; self-starvation.

Body Image and Gender

Women are much more likely than men to be dissatisfied with their bodies, often wanting to be thinner than they are. In one study, only 30% of eighth-grade girls reported being content with their bodies, while 70% of their male classmates expressed satisfaction with their looks. Girls and women are much more likely than boys and men to diet, develop eating disorders, and be obese.

One reason that girls and women are dissatisfied with their bodies is that they are influenced by the media—particularly advertisements and women's fashion magazines. Most teen girls report that the media influence their idea of the perfect body and their decision to diet. In a study of adult women, viewing pictures of thin models in magazines had an immediate negative effect on their mood. In another study, 68% of female college students felt worse about their own appearance after looking through women's magazines. Some 75% of normal-weight women think they are overweight. Clearly, media images affect women's self-image and self-esteem. For American women of all ages, success is still too often equated with how they look rather than who they are.

It is important to note that the image of the "perfect" woman presented in the media is often unrealistic and even unhealthy. In a review of BMI data for Miss America pageant winners since 1922, researchers noted a significant decline in BMI over time, with an increasing number of recent winners having BMIs in the "underweight" category. The average fashion model is 4–7 inches taller and more than 25 pounds lighter than the average American woman. Most fashion models are thinner than 98% of American women.

Our culture may be promoting an unattainable masculine ideal as well. Researchers studying male action figures such as GI Joe from the past 40 years noted that they have become increasingly muscular. A recent Batman action figure, if projected onto a man of average height, would result in someone with a 30-inch waist, 57-inch chest, and 27-inch biceps. Such media messages can be demoralizing; and although not as commonly, boys and men also suffer from body image problems.

Body Image and Ethnicity

The thin, toned look as a feminine ideal is just a fashion, one that is not shared by all cultures. Although some groups espouse thinness as an ideal body type, others do not. In many traditional African societies, for example, full-figured women's bodies are seen as symbols of health, prosperity, and fertility. African American teenage girls have a much more positive body image than white girls; in one survey, two-thirds of them defined beauty as "the right attitude," whereas white girls were more preoccupied with weight and body shape. Nevertheless, recent evidence indicates that African American women are as likely to engage in disordered eating behavior, especially binge eating and vomiting, as their Latina, Native American, and white counterparts. This finding underscores the complex nature of eating disorders and body image.

Avoiding Body Image Problems

To minimize your risk of developing a body image problem, keep the following strategies in mind:

- Focus on healthy habits and good physical health. Eat a moderate, balanced diet and choose physical activities you enjoy. Avoid chronic or repetitive dieting.

- Focus on good psychological health and put concerns about physical appearance in perspective. Your worth as a human being does not depend on how you look.

- Practice body acceptance. You can influence your body size and type through lifestyle to some degree, but the basic fact is that some people are genetically designed to be bigger or heavier than others. Focus on healthy behaviors and accept your body as it is.

- Find things to appreciate in yourself besides an idealized body image. Men and women whose self-esteem is based primarily on standards of physical attractiveness can find it difficult to age gracefully. Those who can learn to value other aspects of themselves are more accepting of the physical changes that occur naturally with age.

- View eating as a morally neutral activity—eating dessert isn't "bad" and doesn't make you a bad person. Healthy eating habits are an important part of a wellness lifestyle, but the things you really care about and do are more important in defining who you are.

- Don't judge yourself or others based on appearance. Watch your attitudes toward people of differing body sizes and shapes, and don't joke about someone's body type. Take people seriously for what they say and do, not for their appearance. Body size is just one external characteristic; there are millions of happy and successful people who just also happen to have a weight problem.

- See the beauty and fitness industries for what they are. Realize that one of their goals is to prompt dissatisfaction with yourself so that you will buy their products.

---

extreme weight loss, females with anorexia often stop menstruating. When body fat is virtually gone and muscles are severely wasted, the body turns to its organs in a desperate search for protein. Death can occur from heart failure caused by electrolyte imbalances. About one in 10 women with anorexia dies of starvation, cardiac arrest, or other medical complications—one of the highest death rates for any psychiatric disorder. Depression is also a serious risk, and about half the fatalities relating to anorexia are suicides.

Bulimia Nervosa

A person with **bulimia nervosa** engages in recurrent episodes of binge eating followed by **purging**. Although bulimia usually begins in adolescence or young adulthood, it has recently begun to emerge at increasingly younger (11–12 years) and older (40–60 years) ages. During a binge, a bulimic person may consume anywhere from 1000 to 60,000 calories within a few hours. This is followed by an attempt to get rid of the food by purging,

For every person diagnosed with a full-blown eating disorder, there are many more who don't meet all the criteria but who have eating problems that significantly disrupt their lives. People with borderline disordered eating have some symptoms of eating disorders—for example, excessive dieting or occasional binging or purging—but do not meet the full diagnostic criteria for anorexia, bulimia, or binge-eating disorder.

Eating habits and body image run a continuum from healthy to seriously disordered. Where we fall along that continuum can change depending on life stresses, illnesses, and many other factors. Meaningful statistics about borderline disordered eating are hard to come by, in part because it is difficult to define exactly when eating habits cross the line between normal and disordered. However, many experts feel that the majority of Americans, particularly women, have at least some unhealthy attitudes and behaviors in relation to food and self-image. Concerns about weight and dieting are so common as to be considered culturally normal for many Americans.

Ideally, our relationship to food should be a happy one. The biological urge to satisfy hunger is one of our most basic drives, and eating is associated with many pleasurable sensations. For some of us, food triggers pleasant memories of good times, family, holidays, and fun. But for too many people, food is a source of anguish rather than pleasure. Eating results in feelings of guilt and self-loathing rather than satisfaction, causing tremendous disruption in the lives of the affected individuals. And experts estimate that as many as one-quarter of people with borderline disordered eating will eventually develop a full eating disorder.

How do you know if you have disordered eating habits? When thoughts about weight and food dominate your life, you have a problem. If you're convinced that your worth as a person hinges on how you look and how much you weigh, it's time to get help. We've all overeaten at a delicious holiday meal, but if you habitually eat until your stomach hurts, and if you feel guilty after a meal or a snack, you may have borderline disordered eating. Self-induced vomiting or laxative use after meals, even if only once in a while, is reason for concern. Do you feel compelled to overexercise to compensate for what you've eaten? Do you routinely restrict your food intake and sometimes eat nothing in an effort to feel more in control? These are all danger signs and could mean that you are developing a serious problem.

What can you do if you suspect you have an eating problem? Don't try to go it alone. Eating problems tend to become worse when you cloak them in secrecy. Nearly all colleges have counselors and medical personnel who can help you or refer you to a specialist if needed. If you are initially intimidated about asking for help, an easy first step is to learn more about eating problems online by visiting a reliable Web site; several good resources are listed in For Further Exploration. Don't hesitate to get help, even if you think your problem is "not that bad." Problem eating can be a serious threat to your health and happiness—and even your life.

usually by vomiting or using laxatives or diuretics. During a binge, people with bulimia feel as though they have lost control and cannot stop or limit how much they eat. Some binge and purge only occasionally; others do so many times every day. Binges may be triggered by a major life change or other stressful event. Binge eating and purging may become a way of dealing with difficult feelings such as anger and disappointment.

The binge-purge cycle of bulimia places a tremendous strain on the body and can have serious health effects, including tooth decay, esophageal damage and chronic hoarseness, menstrual irregularities, depression, liver and kidney damage, and cardiac arrhythmia. Bulimia is often difficult to recognize because bulimics conceal their eating habits and usually maintain a normal weight, although they may experience fluctuations of 10–15 pounds. About 1–3% of Americans have bulimia.

Binge-Eating Disorder

Binge-eating disorder is characterized by uncontrollable eating without any compensatory purging behaviors. Common eating patterns are eating more rapidly than normal, eating until uncomfortably full, eating when not hungry, and preferring to eat alone. Uncontrolled eating is usually followed by weight gain and feelings of guilt, shame, and depression. Many people with binge-eating disorder mistakenly see rigid dieting as the only solution to their problem. However, rigid dieting usually causes feelings of deprivation and a return to overeating. Compulsive overeaters rarely eat because of hunger. Instead, they use food to cope with stress, conflict, and other difficult emotions or to provide solace or entertainment. Binge eaters are almost always obese, so they face all the health risks associated with obesity. In addition, binge eaters may have higher-than-average rates of depression and anxiety. Binge-eating disorder may affect 2–5% of all adults and 8% of obese adults.

Terms

bulimia nervosa An eating disorder characterized by recurrent episodes of binge eating and then purging to prevent weight gain.

purging The use of vomiting, laxatives, excessive exercise, restrictive dieting, enemas, diuretics, or diet pills to compensate for food that has been eaten and that the person fears will produce weight gain.

binge-eating disorder An eating disorder characterized by binge eating and a lack of control over eating behavior in general.

Secrecy and denial are two hallmarks of eating disorders, making these conditions potentially difficult to identify and treat. Signs that a friend may suffer from an eating disorder include sudden weight loss, extreme weight fluctuations, excessive dieting or exercise, excessive eating without weight gain, claiming to feel fat while at a normal weight, guilt or preoccupation with food and eating, frequent weighing, wearing of baggy and/or layered clothing, avoidance of food-related social events, evidence of binge eating (hoarding food, food wrappers) or self-induced vomiting (bathroom visits following a meal, sores or calluses on the back of the hand), and use of laxatives, diuretics, or diet pills to control weight. Approaching a friend with your concerns can be difficult, but the following strategies may help.

• Educate yourself about eating disorders and their risks and about treatment resources in your community. (See For Further Exploration at the end of this chapter for suggestions.) Consider consulting a professional about the best way to approach the situation. Obtain information about how and where your friend can get help.

• Realize that your friend may not admit to having a problem or needing help. You may see your friend's disordered eating as unhealthy, but for your friend, disordered eating habits may be an important coping mechanism for problems in her or his life.

• Arrange to speak privately with the person. Plan ahead so that you have enough time to talk in a place where you won't be interrupted.

• Express your caring for your friend. Offer specific incidents or observations about your friend's psychological state and behavior. For example, "I'm worried about you because you seem anxious and unhappy. I've noticed that you've been skipping meals and that you often talk about feeling fat."

• Even if your friend becomes angry or denies there is a problem, remain calm and nonjudgmental and continue to express your concern. Give your friend information about where she or he can get help; offer to go along. Tell your friend that you believe she or he needs and deserves help.

• After you raise your concerns, give your friend time to think and respond. Listen to your friend and express your support and understanding. Emphasize your friend's good characteristics, successes, and strengths. Help maintain the person's sense of personal responsibility and decision making.

• Avoid giving simplistic advice about eating habits and making comments about how someone looks. Many people with eating disorders are very sensitive to comments about appearance and do not want to discuss the details of their disorder.

• If an emergency situation arises—if the person has fainted or attempted suicide, for example—take immediate action. Call 911 for help.

If a friend is in treatment for an eating disorder, be patient and realistic. Recovery is a long process. If you feel very upset about the situation, seek professional help for yourself. Remember that you are not to blame for another person's eating disorder.

Treating Eating Disorders

The treatment of eating disorders must address both problematic eating behaviors and the misuse of food to manage stress and emotions. Treatment for anorexia nervosa first involves averting a medical crisis by restoring adequate body weight; then the psychological aspects of the disorder can be addressed. The treatment of bulimia nervosa or binge-eating disorder involves first stabilizing the eating patterns, then identifying and changing the patterns of thinking that lead to disordered eating. Treatment usually involves a combination of psychotherapy, medication, and medical management. Antidepressants such as Prozac are effective for some people with bulimia nervosa or body dysmorphic disorder. Friends and family members often want to know what they can do to help; for suggestions, see the box "If Someone You Know Has an Eating Disorder . . .".

People with milder patterns of disordered eating may benefit from getting a nutrition checkup with a registered dietitian. A professional can help determine appropriate body weight and calorie intake and offer advice on how to budget calories into a balanced, healthy diet.

Eating disorders can be seen as the logical extension of the concern with weight that pervades American society.

The challenge is to achieve a healthy body weight through sensible eating habits and an active lifestyle.

CREATING AN INDIVIDUAL WEIGHT-MANAGEMENT PLAN

Would you like to lose weight on your own? Here are some strategies for creating a program of weight management that will last a lifetime.

Assess Your Motivation and Commitment

Before starting your weight-management program, it's important that you take a fresh look within and assess your motivation and commitment. The point is not only to achieve success but also to guard against frustration, negative changes in self-esteem, and the sense of failure that attends broken resolutions or yo-yo dieting. Think about the reasons you want to lose weight. Self-focused reasons, such as to feel good about yourself or to have a greater sense of well-being, can often lead to success. Trying to lose weight for others or out of concern for how others view you is a poor foundation for a weight-management program. Make a list of your reasons for wanting to manage your weight and post it in a prominent place.

Set Reasonable Goals

Choose a goal weight or body fat percentage that is both healthy and reasonable. Refer to the calculations you completed in Lab 6.2 to arrive at a goal. Subdivide your long-term goal into a series of short-term goals. Be willing to renegotiate your final goal as your program moves along.

Assess Your Current Energy Balance

Your energy balance is the balance between calories consumed and calories used in physical activity. When your weight is constant, you are burning approximately the same number of calories you are taking in. To tip your energy balance toward weight loss, you must either consume fewer calories or burn more through physical activity. To lose the recommended ½–2 pounds a week, you'll need to create a negative energy balance of between 1750 and 7000 calories a week, or 250–1000 calories a day. (No diet should reduce calorie intake below 1500 a day for men or 1200 a day for women.) Complete Labs 9.1 and 9.2 to assess your current daily energy needs and to develop strategies for achieving a negative energy balance that will lead to gradual, moderate weight loss. (See p. 303 for guidelines for altering your energy balance to *gain* weight.)

Increase Your Level of Physical Activity

To generate a negative energy balance, it's usually best to exercise more rather than eat less. One reason is that dieting reduces RMR, whereas exercise raises it. Furthermore, studies have shown that being physically fit is even more important than weight loss in reducing your mortality risk (see Chapter 6). The key is keeping fit with moderate exercise.

(Table 9.2 lists the calorie costs of selected physical activities; refer to Table 7.1 for the calorie costs of different types of sports and fitness activities.)

Make Changes in Your Diet and Eating Habits

If you can't generate a large enough negative calorie balance solely by increasing physical activity, you may want to supplement exercise with some dietary strategies. Don't think of this as "going on a diet"; your goal is to make small changes in your diet that you can maintain for a lifetime. Don't try skipping meals, fasting, or a very-low-calorie diet. These strategies seldom work, and they can have negative effects on your ability to manage your weight and on your overall health. Instead, try monitoring calories or simply cutting portion sizes. Refer back to the box "Lifestyle Strategies for Successful Weight Management" for suggestions.

Another strategy is to limit your intake of certain foods, such as those high in saturated and trans fat, sugar, or refined carbohydrates. The strategy of simply eating more vegetables, fruits, and dietary fiber has helped many achieve and maintain a healthy weight. Visit MyPyramid .gov for more tips on making healthy food choices.

MOTIVATION FOR CHANGE!   Successful weight management is like many other behavior change projects in that it may require you to develop new skills to achieve your goals, such as developing new shopping habits, reading food labels, learning to cook or to cook in a more healthful style, keeping a food journal, making special requests in restaurants, and being aware of the influence of advertising and other cues in the environment supporting unhealthy dietary and activity habits. Identify the key skills you'll need for successful weight management, and include plans to master them as part of your behavior change program. Developing new skills will boost your motivation and self-efficacy and help keep your program on track.

Put Your Plan into Action

Be systematic in your efforts to change your behavior, both what you eat and how you exercise. Many of those who are successful at controlling their weight track their progress, enlist the support of others, and think positively. Here are tips gleaned from studies of people who have succeeded in long-term weight management.

Write Daily   Write down everything you eat, including how many calories it contains. (See Figure 1.6 for one example of a food journal.) Researchers have found that writing down the food choices you make every day increases your commitment and helps you stick to your diet, especially during high-risk times such as holidays, parties, and family gatherings. Writing every day also serves as a reminder to you that losing weight is important.

Besides tracking what you eat, keep track of your formal exercise program and other daily physical activities so you can begin increasing either their intensity or duration. People who succeed in their health program expend lots of energy in physical activity—according to one study, an average of 2700 calories a week. Popular activities are walking, cycling, aerobic dance, and stair climbing.

Get Others to Help   Enlist friends and family members to help and give them specific suggestions about what you would find helpful. You might, for instance, ask someone to leave you an encouraging voice mail once a day or twice a week, or ask someone to send you reminders by e-mail. Besides asking for regular moral support, find a buddy to work out with you regularly and to be there as an emergency support.

Keeping a journal is an excellent way to keep track of your calorie intake—the foods you eat each day—and expenditure—your daily physical activities. You can also write down your thoughts and feelings to make sure you're maintaining a positive self-image and a realistic attitude about weight management.

Think Positively   Give yourself lots of praise and rewards. Think about your accomplishments each day, and congratulate yourself. You can write these positive thoughts in your food journal. If you do slip, stay objective and don't waste time on self-criticism. If you are keeping a journal, you can see the slip for what it is—an easily contained lapse rather than a catastrophic relapse that ends in your losing confidence and control. Remember that as weight loss slows, the weight loss at this slower rate is more permanent than earlier, more dramatic, losses.

Tips for Today

Maintaining a healthy weight means balancing calories in with calories out. Many forces and factors in contemporary society work against a healthy balance, so it's imperative that individuals take active control of managing their weight. Many approaches work, but the simplest formula is moderate food intake coupled with regular exercise.

Right now you can

- Drink a glass of water instead of a soda.

- Throw away any high-calorie, low-nutrient snack foods in your kitchen or room and start a list of fruits and vegetables you can buy as snacks instead.

- Put a sign on your refrigerator reminding you of your weight-management goals.

- Go outside and walk, jog, or cycle for 15 minutes. Walk your dog, if you have one.

- Review the information on portion sizes in Chapter 8 and consider whether the portions you usually take at meals are larger than they need to be.

SUMMARY

- Excess body weight increases the risk of numerous diseases, particularly cardiovascular disease, cancer, and diabetes.

- Although genetic factors help determine a person's weight, the influence of heredity can be overcome.

- Physiological factors involved in the regulation of body weight and body fat include metabolic rate and hormones.

- Energy-balance components that an individual can control are calories taken in and calories expended in physical activity.

- Nutritional guidelines for weight management and wellness include controlling consumption of total calories, unhealthy fats and carbohydrates, and protein; monitoring portion sizes and calorie density; increasing consumption of whole grains, fruits, and vegetables; and developing an eating schedule based on decision rules.

- Activity guidelines for weight control emphasize engaging in moderate-intensity physical activity for 150 minutes or more per week; regular, prolonged endurance exercise and weight training can burn a significant number of calories while maintaining muscle mass.

- The sense of well-being that results from a well-balanced diet can reinforce commitment to weight control; improve self-esteem; and lead to realistic, as opposed to negative, self-talk. Successful weight management results in not using food as a way to cope with stress.

- In cases of extreme obesity, weight loss requires medical supervision; in less extreme cases, people can set up individual programs, perhaps getting guidance from reliable books, or they can get help by joining a formal weight-loss program.

- Dissatisfaction with body image and body weight can lead to physical problems and serious eating disorders, including anorexia nervosa, bulimia nervosa, and binge-eating disorder.

- A successful personal plan assesses motivation, sets reasonable and healthy goals, and emphasizes increased activity rather than decreased calories.

For Further Exploration

WW   *Fit and Well* **Online Learning Center**
(www.mhhe.com/fahey)

Use the learning objectives, study guide questions, and glossary flashcards to review key terms and concepts and prepare for exams. You can extend your knowledge of weight management and gain experience in using the Internet as a resource by completing the activities and checking out the Web links for the topics in Chapter 9 marked with the World Wide Web icon. For this chapter, Internet activities explore eating habits, online weight-loss programs, and body image; there are Web links for the Vital Statistics table, the box on popular diets, and the chapter as a whole.

How can I safely gain weight?

Just as for losing weight, a program for weight gain should be gradual and should include both exercise and dietary changes. The foundation of a successful and healthy program for weight gain is a combination of strength training and a high-carbohydrate, high-calorie diet. Strength training will help you add weight as muscle rather than fat.

Energy balance is also important in a program for gaining weight. You need to consume more calories than your body needs in order to gain weight, but you need to choose those extra calories wisely. Fatty, high-calorie foods may seem like an obvious choice, but consuming additional calories as fat can jeopardize your health and your weight-management program. A diet high in fat carries health risks, and your body is more likely to convert dietary fat into fat tissue than into muscle mass. A better strategy is to consume additional calories as complex carbohydrates from whole grains, fruits, and vegetables. A diet for weight gain should contain about 60–65% of total daily calories from carbohydrates. You probably do not need to be concerned with protein: Although protein requirements increase when you exercise, the protein consumption of most Americans is already well above the DRI.

In order to gain primarily muscle weight instead of fat, a gradual program of weight gain is your best bet. Try these strategies for consuming extra calories:

- Don't skip any meals.

- Add two or three snacks to your daily eating routine.

- Try a sports drink or supplement that has at least 60% of calories from carbohydrates, as well as significant amounts of protein, vitamins, and minerals. (But don't use supplements to replace meals, because they don't contain all food components.)

How can I achieve a "perfect" body?

The current cultural ideal of an ultra-thin, ultrafit body is impossible for most people to achieve. A reasonable goal for body weight and body shape must take into account an individual's heredity, weight history, social circumstances, metabolic rate, and psychological well-being. Don't set goals based on movie stars or fashion models. Modern photographic techniques can make people look much different on film or in magazines than they look in person. Many of these people are also genetically endowed with body shapes that are impossible for most of us to emulate. The best approach is to work with what you've got. Adopting a wellness lifestyle that includes regular exercise and a healthy diet will naturally result in the best possible body shape for you. Obsessively trying to achieve unreasonable goals can lead to problems such as eating disorders, overtraining, and injuries.

Visit the Online Learning Center for more answers to common questions about weight management.

Daily Fitness and Nutrition Journal

Review the resources and complete the activities in the weight management portion of the journal. Complete the program plan by setting goals and examining your activities and eating habits for ways to tip the energy balance equation in the appropriate direction. Once you put your plan into action, continue to monitor your behavior using a daily log.

Books

Beck, C. 2003. *Anorexia and Bulimia for Dummies*. Hoboken, N.J.: John Wiley and Sons. *An easy-to-understand guide to eating disorders.*

Critser, G. 2004. *Fat Land: How Americans Became the Fattest People in the World*. Boston: Mariner Books. *A look at the many factors in American life that have contributed to the increase in obesity rates.*

Ferguson, J. M., and C. Ferguson. 2003. *Habits Not Diets*. 4th ed. Boulder, Colo.: Bull Publishing. *A behavior-change approach to changing diet and activity habits that includes many practical tips, assessment worksheets, and tracking forms.*

Hensrud, D. D. 2005. *Mayo Clinic Healthy Weight for Everyone*. Rochester, Minn.: Mayo Clinic. *Provides guidelines for successful weight management.*

Nash, J. D. 2003. *Maximize Your Body Potential: Lifetime Skills for Successful Weight Management*. Boulder, Colo.: Bull Publishing. *A do-it-yourself guide that provides self-assessment tools and guidelines for setting realistic goals and creating a personal plan.*

Pope, H. G., K. A. Phillips, and R. Olivardia. 2000. *Adonis Complex: The Secret Crisis of Male Body Obsession*. New York: Free Press.
Provides a historical review of the changing fashions in male body type and information about male problems with body image.

VW Organizations and Web Sites

FDA Information About Losing Weight and Maintaining a Healthy Weight. Includes guidelines for a variety of weight-loss strategies and special tips for using food labels to aid in weight management.
http://www.cfsan.fda.gov/~dms/wh-wght.html

Federal Trade Commission (FTC): Consumer Information. Provides advice for evaluating advertising about weight-loss products.
http://www.ftc.gov/bcp/conline/edcams/fitness/coninfo.html

Frontline: Fat. Information from a PBS Frontline special that looked at how society, genetics, and biology have influenced our relationship with food and at current problems with obesity and eating disorders.
http://www.pbs.org/wgbh/pages/frontline/shows/fat

MedlinePlus: Obesity and Weight Loss. Provides reliable information from government agencies and key professional associations.
http://www.nlm.nih.gov/medlineplus/obesity.html
http://www.nlm.nih.gov/medlineplus/weightlossdieting.html

National Heart, Lung, and Blood Institute (NHLBI): Aim for a Healthy Weight. Provides information and tips on diet and physical activity, as well as a BMI calculator.
http://www.nhlbi.nih.gov/health/public/heart/obesity/lose_wt

National Institute of Diabetes and Digestive and Kidney Diseases (NIDDK). Health Information: Nutrition and Obesity. Provides information and referrals for problems related to obesity, weight control, and nutritional disorders.
877-946-4627
http://www.niddk.nih.gov/health/nutrit/nutrit.htm

Partnership for Healthy Weight Management. Provides information on evaluating weight-loss programs and advertising claims.

> http://www.consumer.gov/weightloss

SmallStep.gov. Provides resources for increasing activity and improving diet through small changes in daily habits.

> http://www.smallstep.gov

U.S. Consumer Gateway: Health—Dieting and Weight Control. Provides links to government sites with advice on evaluating claims about weight-loss products and programs.

> http://www.consumer.gov/health.htm

WHO: Obesity and Overweight. Provides information on WHO's global strategy on diet and physical activity.

> http://www.who.int/dietphysicalactivity

There are also many resources for people concerned about body image and eating disorders:

Something Fishy Website on Eating Disorders
> http://www.something-fishy.org

MedlinePlus: Eating Disorders
> http://www.nlm.nih.gov/medlineplus/eatingdisorders.html

National Association of Anorexia Nervosa and Associated Disorders
> 847-831-3438
> http://www.anad.org

National Eating Disorders Association
> 800-931-2237
> http://www.nationaleatingdisorders.org

Women's Body Image and Health
> http://www.4woman.gov/bodyimage

See also the listings in Chapters 1, 6, and 8.

Selected Bibliography

Bhuiyan, A. R., et al. 2003. Differences in body shape representations among young adults from a biracial (Black-White), semirural community. *American Journal of Epidemiology* 158(8): 792–797.

Bowman, S. A, et al. 2004. Effects of fast-food consumption on energy intake and diet quality among children in a national household survey. *Pediatrics* 113(1 Pt. 1): 112–118.

Calle, E. E., et al. 2003. Overweight, obesity, and mortality from cancer in a prospectively studied cohort of U.S. adults. *New England Journal of Medicine* 348(17): 1625–1638.

Centers for Disease Control and Prevention. 2004. *Overweight and Obesity: Economic Consequences* (http://www.cdc.gov/nccdphp/dnpa/obesity/economic_consequences.htm; retrieved January 3, 2005).

Centers for Disease Control and Prevention. 2004. Trends in intake of energy and macronutrients—United States, 1971–2000. *Morbidity and Mortality Weekly Report* 53(4): 80–82.

Dong, L., G. Block, and S. Mandel. 2004. Activities contributing to total energy expenditure in the United States: Results from the NHAPS Study. *International Journal of Behavioral Nutrition and Physical Activity* 1(4).

Farshchi, H. R., M. A. Taylor, and I. A. Macdonald. 2005. Deleterious effects of omitting breakfast on insulin sensitivity and fasting lipid profiles in healthy lean women. *American Journal of Clinical Nutrition* 81(2): 388–396.

Federal Trade Commission. 2002. *Weight Loss Advertising: An Analysis of Current Trends.* Washington, D.C.: Federal Trade Commission.

Fontaine, K. R., et al. 2003. Years of life lost due to obesity. *Journal of the American Medical Association* 289(2): 187–193.

Food and Drug Administration. 2003. *Questions and Answers about FDA's Actions on Ephedra Dietary Supplements* (http://www.fda.gov/oc/initiatives/ephedra/december2003/qu.html; retrieved January 5, 2004).

Food and Nutrition Board, Institute of Medicine, National Academies. 2002. *Dietary Reference Intakes: Energy, Carbohydrate, Fiber, Fat, Fatty Acids, Cholesterol, Protein, and Amino Acids.* Washington, D.C.: National Academy Press.

Graves, B. S., and R. L. Welsh. 2004. Recognizing the signs of body dysmorphic disorder and muscle dysmorphia. *ACSM's Health & Fitness Journal,* January/February.

Graves, M. M. 2005. Weighing in on losing weight. *ACSM Fit Society Page,* Spring.

Haller, C. A., N. L. Benowitz, and P. Jacob. 2005. Hemodynamic effects of ephedra-free weight-loss supplements in humans. *American Journal of Medicine* 118(9): 998–1003.

Hu, F. B., et al. 2003. Television watching and other sedentary behaviors in relation to risk of obesity and type 2 diabetes mellitus in women. *Journal of the American Medical Association* 289(14): 1785–1791.

Hu, F. B., et al. 2004. Adiposity as compared with physical activity in predicting mortality among women. *New England Journal of Medicine* 351(26): 2694–2703.

Kruskall, L. J., L. J. Johnson, and S. L. Meacham. 2002. Eating disorders and disordered eating—Are they the same? *ACSM's Health & Fitness Journal,* May/June.

Leit, R. A., J. J. Gray, and H. G. Pope Jr. 2002. The media's representation of the ideal male body: A cause for muscle dysmorphia? *International Journal of Eating Disorders* 31(3): 334–338.

Ma, Y., et al. 2005. Association between dietary carbohydrates and body weight. *American Journal of Epidemiology* 161(4): 359–367.

Nicklas, B. J., et al. 2004. Association of visceral adipose tissue with incident myocardial infarction in older men and women. *American Journal of Epidemiology* 160(8): 741–749.

Nielsen, S. J., and B. M. Popkin. 2003. Patterns and trends in food portion sizes, 1977–1996. *Journal of the American Medical Association* 289(4): 450–453.

Pereira, M. A., et al. 2005. Fast-food habits, weight gain, and insulin resistance (the CARDIA study): 15-year prospective analysis. *Lancet* 365(9453): 36–42.

Pope, H. G., Jr., et al. 1999. Evolving ideals of male body image as seen through action toys. *International Journal of Disorders* 26(1): 65–72.

Rubinstein, S., and B. Caballero. 2000. Is Miss America an undernourished role model? *Journal of the American Medical Association* 283(12): 1569.

Santry, H. P., D. L. Gillen, and D. S. Lauderdale. Trends in bariatric surgical procedures. *Journal of the American Medical Association* 294(15): 1909–1917.

Schulze, M. B., et al. 2004. Sugar-sweetened beverages, weight gain, and incidence of type 2 diabetes in young and middle-aged women. *Journal of the American Medical Association* 292(8): 927–934.

Sweeteners can sour your health. 2005. *Consumer Reports on Health,* January.

Tsai, A. G., and T. A. Wadden. 2005. Systematic review: An evaluation of major commercial weight loss programs in the United States. *Annals of Internal Medicine* 142(1): 56–66.

U.S. Department of Health and Human Services. 2005. *Dietary Guidelines for Americans* (http://www.healthierus/dietaryguidelines; retrieved January 15, 2005).

Vorona, R. D., et al. 2005. Overweight and obese patients in a primary care population report less sleep than patients with a normal body mass index. *Archives of Internal Medicine* 165:25–30.

Weigle, D. S., et al. 2005. A high-protein diet induces sustained reductions in appetite, ad libitum caloric intake, and body weight despite compensatory changes in diurnal plasma leptin and ghrelin concentrations. *American Journal of Clinical Nutrition* 82(1): 42–48.

Wong, S. L., et al. 2004. Cardiorespiratory fitness is associated with lower abdominal fat independent of body mass index. *Medicine and Science in Sports and Exercise* 36(2): 286–291.

LAB 9.1 *Calculating Daily Energy Needs*

WW

Part I   Estimating Current Energy Intake from a Food Record

If your weight is stable, your current daily energy intake is the number of calories you need to consume to maintain your weight at your current activity level. If you completed Lab 8.2, you should have a record of your current energy intake; if you didn't complete the lab, keep a careful and complete record of everything you eat for one day and then total the calories in all the foods and beverages you consumed. (This calculation can be done by hand or by using a nutrition analysis software program or Web site; for example, visit MyPyramid.gov and click on MyPyramid Tracker.) Record your total energy intake below:

Current energy intake (from food record): _____ **Calories per day**

Part II   Estimating Daily Energy Requirements Using Food and Nutrition Board Formulas

Many people underestimate the size of their food portions, and so energy goals based on estimates of current calorie intake from food records can be inaccurate. You can also estimate your daily energy needs using the formulas listed below. To use the appropriate formula for your sex, you'll need to plug in the following:

- Age (in years)   • Weight (in pounds)   • Height (in inches)
- Physical activity coefficient (PA) from the table below.

   To help estimate your physical activity level, consider the following guidelines: Someone who typically engages in 30 minutes of moderate-intensity activity, equivalent to walking 2 miles in 30 minutes, in addition to the activities in maintaining a sedentary lifestyle is considered "low active"; someone who typically engages in the equivalent of 90 minutes of moderate-intensity activity is rated as "active." You might find it helpful to refer back to Lab 2.2 to estimate your physical activity level.

	Physical Activity Coefficient (PA)	
Physical Activity Level	Men	Women
Sedentary	1.00	1.00
Low active	1.12	1.14
Active	1.27	1.27
Very active	1.54	1.45

Estimated Daily Energy Requirement for Weight Maintenance in Men

$$864 - (9.72 \times \text{Age}) + (PA \times [(6.39 \times \text{Weight}) + (12.78 \times \text{Height})])$$

1. $9.72 \times$ _____ Age (years) = _____

2. $864 -$ _____ Result from step 1 = _____ [*result may be a negative number*]

3. $6.39 \times$ _____ Weight (pounds) = _____

4. $12.78 \times$ _____ Height (inches) = _____

5. _____ Result from step 3 + _____ Result from step 4 = _____

6. _____ PA (from table) $\times$ _____ Result from step 5 = _____

7. _____ Result from step 2 + _____ Result from step 6 = _____ Calories per day

Estimated Daily Energy Requirement for Weight Maintenance in Women

$$387 - (7.31 \times \text{Age}) + (\text{PA} \times [(4.91 \times \text{Weight}) + (16.78 \times \text{Height})])$$

1. $7.31 \times$ _____ Age (years) = _____

2. $387 -$ _____ Result from step 1 = _____ [*result may be a negative number*]

3. $4.91 \times$ _____ Weight (pounds) = _____

4. $16.78 \times$ _____ Height (inches) = _____

5. _____ Result from step 3 + _____ Result from step 4 = _____

6. _____ PA (from table) $\times$ _____ Result from step 5 = _____

7. _____ Result from step 2 + _____ Result from step 6 = _____ Calories per day

Daily energy needs for weight maintenance (from formula): _____ **Calories/day**

Part III   Determining an Individual Daily Energy Goal for Weight Maintenance

If you calculated values for daily energy needs based on both methods, examine the two values. Some difference is likely—people tend to underestimate their food intake and overestimate their level of physical activity—but if the two values are very far off, check your food record and your physical activity estimate for accuracy and make any necessary adjustments. For an individualized estimate of daily calorie needs, average the two values:

Daily energy needs = (Food record result _____ **Calories/day + Formula result** _____ **Calories/day)**

$\div$ **2 =** _____ **Calories/day**

Using Your Results

How did you score? Are you surprised by the value you calculated for your approximate daily energy needs? If so, is the value higher or lower than you expected?

What should you do next? Enter the results of this lab in the Preprogram Assessment column in Appendix D. If you wish to change your energy balance to lose weight, complete Lab 9.2 to set goals and develop specific strategies for change. (If your goal is weight gain, see p. 303 for basic guidelines.) One of the best ways to tip your energy balance toward weight loss is to increase your daily physical activity. If you include increases in activity as part of your program, then you can use the results of this lab to chart changes in your daily energy expenditure (and needs). Look for ways to increase the amount of time you spend in physical activity, thus increasing your physical activity coefficient. After several weeks of your program, complete this lab again, and enter the results in the Postprogram Assessment column of Appendix D. How do the results compare? Did your program for boosting physical activity show up as an increase in your daily energy expenditure and need?

SOURCE: Estimating Daily Energy Requirements Using Food and Nutrition Board Formulas Part II: Reprinted with permission from *Dietary Reference Intakes for Energy, Carbohydrate, Fiber, Fat, Fatty Acids, Cholesterol, Protein, and Amino Acids (Macronutrients).* Copyright © 2002 by the National Academy of Sciences. Courtesy of the National Academies Press, Washington, D.C.

Name _____   **Section** _____   **Date** _____

LAB 9.2 *Identifying Weight-Loss Goals and Ways to Meet Them* WW

LABORATORY ACTIVITIES

Negative Calorie Balance

Complete the following calculations to determine your weekly and daily negative calorie balance goals and the number of weeks to achieve your target weight.

Current weight _____ lb − target weight (from Lab 6.2) _____ lb

   = total weight to lose _____ lb

Total weight to lose _____ lb ÷ weight to lose each week _____ lb

   = time to achieve target weight _____ weeks

Weight to lose each week _____ lb × 3500 cal/lb = weekly negative calorie balance _____ cal/week

Weekly negative calorie balance _____ cal/week ÷ 7 days/week

   = daily negative calorie balance _____ cal/day

To keep your weight-loss program on schedule, you must achieve the daily negative calorie balance by either decreasing your calorie consumption (eating less) or increasing your calorie expenditure (being more active). A combination of the two strategies will probably be most successful.

Changes in Activity Level

Adding a few minutes of exercise every day is a good way of expending calories. Use the calorie costs for different activities listed in Table 7.1 and Table 9.2 to plan ways for raising your calorie expenditure level.

Activity	Duration	Calories Used
_____	_____	_____
_____	_____	_____
_____	_____	_____
_____	_____	_____
	Total calories expended:	_____

Changes in Diet

Look closely at your diet from one day, as recorded in Lab 8.2. Identify ways to cut calorie consumption by eliminating certain items or substituting lower-calorie choices. Be realistic in your cuts and substitutions; you need to develop a plan you can live with.

Food Item	Substitute Food Item	Calorie Savings
_____	_____	_____
_____	_____	_____
_____	_____	_____
_____	_____	_____
	Total calories cut:	_____

Total calories expended ＿＿＿＿ + total calories cut ＿＿＿＿ = Total negative calorie balance ＿＿＿＿

Have you met your required negative energy balance? If not, revise your dietary and activity changes to meet your goal.

Common Problem Eating Behaviors

For each of the groups of statements that appear below, check those that are true for you. If you check several statements for a given pattern or problem, it will probably be a significant factor in your weight-management program. One possible strategy for dealing with each type of problem is given. For those eating problems you identify as important, add your own ideas to the strategies listed.

1. ＿＿＿ I often skip meals.

   ＿＿＿ I often eat a number of snacks in place of a meal.

   ＿＿＿ I don't have a regular schedule of meal and snack times.

   ＿＿＿ I make up for missed meals and snacks by eating more at the next meal.

   Problem: Irregular eating habits

   Possible solutions:

   • Write out a plan for each day's meals in advance. Carry it with you and stick to it.

   • ＿＿＿＿＿＿＿＿＿＿＿＿＿＿＿＿＿＿＿＿＿＿＿＿＿＿＿＿＿＿＿＿＿＿＿＿＿＿＿

   • ＿＿＿＿＿＿＿＿＿＿＿＿＿＿＿＿＿＿＿＿＿＿＿＿＿＿＿＿＿＿＿＿＿＿＿＿＿＿＿

2. ＿＿＿ I eat more than one sweet dessert or snack each day.

   ＿＿＿ I usually snack on foods high in calories and fat (chips, cookies, ice cream).

   ＿＿＿ I drink regular (not sugar-free) soft drinks.

   ＿＿＿ I choose types of meat that are high in fat.

   ＿＿＿ I consume more than one alcoholic beverage a day.

   Problem: Poor food choices

   Possible solutions:

   • Keep a supply of raw fruits and vegetables handy for snacks.

   • ＿＿＿＿＿＿＿＿＿＿＿＿＿＿＿＿＿＿＿＿＿＿＿＿＿＿＿＿＿＿＿＿＿＿＿＿＿＿＿

   • ＿＿＿＿＿＿＿＿＿＿＿＿＿＿＿＿＿＿＿＿＿＿＿＿＿＿＿＿＿＿＿＿＿＿＿＿＿＿＿

3. ＿＿＿ I always eat everything on my plate.

   ＿＿＿ I often go back for seconds and thirds.

   ＿＿＿ I take larger helpings than most people.

   ＿＿＿ I eat up leftovers instead of putting them away.

   Problem: Portion sizes too large

   Possible solutions:

   • Measure all portions with a scale or measuring cup.

   • ＿＿＿＿＿＿＿＿＿＿＿＿＿＿＿＿＿＿＿＿＿＿＿＿＿＿＿＿＿＿＿＿＿＿＿＿＿＿＿

   • ＿＿＿＿＿＿＿＿＿＿＿＿＿＿＿＿＿＿＿＿＿＿＿＿＿＿＿＿＿＿＿＿＿＿＿＿＿＿＿

LAB 9.3 *Checking for Body Image Problems and Eating Disorders*

Assessing Your Body Image

		Never	Sometimes	Often	Always
1.	I dislike seeing myself in mirrors.	0	1	2	3
2.	When I shop for clothing, I am more aware of my weight problem, and consequently I find shopping for clothes somewhat unpleasant.	0	1	2	3
3.	I'm ashamed to be seen in public.	0	1	2	3
4.	I prefer to avoid engaging in sports or public exercise because of my appearance.	0	1	2	3
5.	I feel somewhat embarrassed about my body in the presence of someone of the other sex.	0	1	2	3
6.	I think my body is ugly.	0	1	2	3
7.	I feel that other people must think my body is unattractive.	0	1	2	3
8.	I feel that my family or friends may be embarrassed to be seen with me.	0	1	2	3
9.	I find myself comparing myself with other people to see if they are heavier than I am.	0	1	2	3
10.	I find it difficult to enjoy activities because I am self-conscious about my physical appearance.	0	1	2	3
11.	Feeling guilty about my weight problem preoccupies most of my thinking.	0	1	2	3
12.	My thoughts about my body and physical appearance are negative and self-critical.	0	1	2	3

Now add up the number of points you have circled in each column: _____ 0 + _____ + _____ + _____

Score Interpretation

The lowest possible score is 0, and this indicates a positive body image. The highest possible score is 36, and this indicates an unhealthy body image. A score higher than 14 suggests a need to develop a healthier body image.

SOURCE: Nash, J. D. 1997. *The New Maximize Your Body Potential.* Palo Alto, Calif.: Bull Publishing. Reprinted with permission from Bull Publishing. All rights reserved.

Eating Disorder Checklist

		Always	Very Often	Often	Sometimes	Rarely	Never
1.	I like eating with other people.	0	0	0	1	2	3
2.	I like my clothes to fit tightly.	0	0	0	1	2	3
3.	I enjoy eating meat.	0	0	0	1	2	3
4.	I have regular menstrual periods.	0	0	0	1	2	3
5.	I enjoy eating at restaurants.	0	0	0	1	2	3
6.	I enjoy trying new rich foods.	0	0	0	1	2	3
7.	I prepare foods for others, but do not eat what I cook.	3	2	1	0	0	0
8.	I become anxious prior to eating.	3	2	1	0	0	0
9.	I am terrified about being overweight.	3	2	1	0	0	0
10.	I avoid eating when I am hungry.	3	2	1	0	0	0
11.	I find myself preoccupied with food.	3	2	1	0	0	0
12.	I have gone on eating binges where I feel that I may not be able to stop.	3	2	1	0	0	0
13.	I cut my food into small pieces.	3	2	1	0	0	0

	Always	Very Often	Often	Sometimes	Rarely	Never
14. I am aware of the calorie content of foods that I eat.	3	2	1	0	0	0
15. I particularly avoid foods with a high carbohydrate content (bread, potatoes, rice, etc.).	3	2	1	0	0	0
16. I feel bloated after meals.	3	2	1	0	0	0
17. I feel others would prefer me to eat more.	3	2	1	0	0	0
18. I vomit after I have eaten.	3	2	1	0	0	0
19. I feel extremely guilty after eating.	3	2	1	0	0	0
20. I am preoccupied with a desire to be thinner.	3	2	1	0	0	0
21. I exercise strenuously to burn off calories.	3	2	1	0	0	0
22. I weigh myself several times a day.	3	2	1	0	0	0
23. I wake up early in the morning.	3	2	1	0	0	0
24. I eat the same foods day after day.	3	2	1	0	0	0
25. I think about burning up calories when I exercise.	3	2	1	0	0	0
26. Other people think I am too thin.						
27. I am preoccupied with the thought of having fat on my body.	3	2	1	0	0	0
28. I take longer than others to eat my meals.	3	2	1	0	0	0
29. I take laxatives.	3	2	1	0	0	0
30. I avoid foods with sugar in them.						
31. I eat diet foods.	3	2	1	0	0	0
32. I feel that food controls my life.	3	2	1	0	0	0
33. I display self-control around foods.	3	2	1	0	0	0
34. I feel that others pressure me to eat.	3	2	1	0	0	0
35. I give too much time and thought to food.	3	2	1	0	0	0
36. I suffer from constipation.	3	2	1	0	0	0
37. I feel uncomfortable after eating sweets.	3	2	1	0	0	0
38. I engage in dieting behavior.	3	2	1	0	0	0
39. I like my stomach to be empty.						
40. I have the impulse to vomit after meals.	3	2	1	0	0	0

Now add up the number of points in each column for statements 1 through 40:_____

____ + ____ + ____ + ____ + ____ + ____

Score Interpretation

The possible range is 0–120. A score higher than 50 suggests an eating disorder. A score between 30 and 50 suggests a borderline eating disorder. A score less than 30 is within the normal range. Among those with normal eating habits, the average score is 15.4.

SOURCE: Garner, D. M., Omstead, M., Polivy, J., Development and Validation of a Multidimensional Eating Disorder Inventory for Anorexia Nervosa and Bulimia. *International Journal of Eating Disorders* 2:15–33, 1983. Copyright © 1983 John Wiley & Sons. Reprinted by permission of John Wiley & Sons, Inc.

Using Your Results

How did you score? Are you surprised by your scores? Do the results of either assessment indicate that you may have a problem with body image or disordered eating?

What should you do next? If your results are borderline, consider trying some of the self-help strategies suggested in the chapter. If body image or disordered eating is a significant problem for you, get professional advice; a physician, therapist, and/or registered dietitian can help. Make an appointment today.

After reading this chapter, you should be able to

- Explain what stress is and how people react to it—physically, emotionally, and behaviorally
- Describe the relationship between stress and disease
- List common sources of stress
- Describe techniques for preventing and managing stress
- Put together a plan for successfully managing the stress in your life

10

Stress

Test Your Knowledge

1. **Which of the following events can cause stress?**
   a. taking out a loan
   b. failing a test
   c. graduating from college
   d. watching a hockey game

2. **Moderate exercise can stimulate which of the following?**
   a. analgesia (pain relief)
   b. birth of new brain cells
   c. relaxation

3. **High levels of stress can impair memory and cause physical changes in the brain.**
   True or false?

ANSWERS

1. ALL FOUR. Stress-producing factors can be pleasant or unpleasant and can include physical challenges and goal achievement as well as what are perceived as negative events.

2. ALL THREE. Regular exercise is linked to improvement in many dimensions of wellness.

3. TRUE. Low levels of stress may improve memory, but high stress levels impair learning and memory and, over the long term, may shrink an area of the brain called the hippocampus.

WW *Fit and Well* **Online Learning Center** www.mhhe.com/fahey

Visit the *Fit and Well* Online Learning Center for study aids, online labs, additional information about stress, links, Internet activities that explore the role of stress management in wellness, and much more.   311

Like the term *fitness, stress* is a word many people use without really understanding its precise meaning. Stress is popularly viewed as an uncomfortable response to a negative event, which probably describes *nervous tension* more than the cluster of physical and psychological responses that actually constitute stress. In fact, stress is not limited to negative situations; it is also a response to pleasurable physical challenges and the achievement of personal goals. Whether stress is experienced as pleasant or unpleasant depends largely on the situation and the individual. Because learning effective responses to whatever induces stress can enhance psychological health and help prevent a number of serious diseases, stress management is an important component in any wellness program.

This chapter explains the physiological and psychological reactions that make up the stress response and describes how these reactions can be risks to good health. The chapter also presents ways of managing stress with a personal program or with the help of others.

Terms

stressor Any physical or psychological event or condition that produces stress.

stress response The physiological changes associated with stress.

stress The collective physiological and emotional responses to any stimulus that disturbs an individual's homeostasis.

autonomic nervous system The branch of the peripheral nervous system that, largely without conscious thought, controls basic body processes; consists of the sympathetic and parasympathetic divisions.

parasympathetic division A division of the autonomic nervous system that moderates the excitatory effect of the sympathetic division, slowing metabolism and restoring energy supplies.

sympathetic division A division of the autonomic nervous system that reacts to danger or other challenges by almost instantly accelerating body processes.

norepinephrine A neurotransmitter released by the sympathetic nervous system onto target tissues to increase their function in the face of increased activity; when released by the brain, it causes arousal (increased attention, awareness, and alertness); also called *noradrenaline*.

endocrine system The system of glands, tissues, and cells that secrete hormones into the bloodstream to influence metabolism and other body processes.

hormone A chemical messenger produced in the body and transported in the bloodstream to target cells or organs for specific regulation of their activities.

cortisol A steroid hormone secreted by the cortex (outer layer) of the adrenal gland; also called *hydrocortisone*.

epinephrine A hormone secreted by the medulla (inner core) of the adrenal gland that affects the functioning of organs involved in responding to a stressor; also called *adrenaline*.

endorphins Brain secretions that have pain-inhibiting effects.

fight-or-flight reaction A defense reaction that prepares an individual for conflict or escape by triggering hormonal, cardiovascular, metabolic, and other changes.

WHAT IS STRESS?

In common usage, *stress* refers to two different things: situations that trigger physical and emotional reactions *and* the reactions themselves. In this text, we'll use the more precise term **stressor** for a situation that triggers physical and emotional reactions and the term **stress response** for those reactions. A first date and a final exam, then, are *stressors;* sweaty palms and a pounding heart are symptoms of the stress response. We'll use the term **stress** to describe the general physical and emotional state that accompanies the stress response. So, a person taking a final exam experiences *stress*.

Physical Responses to Stressors

Imagine a near miss: As you step off the curb, a car careens toward you. With just a fraction of a second to spare, you leap safely out of harm's way. In that split second of danger and in the moments following it, you experience a predictable series of physical reactions. Your body goes from a relaxed state to one prepared for physical action to cope with a threat to your life. Two major control systems in your body are responsible for your physical response to stressors: the nervous system and the endocrine system. Through a variety of rapid chemical reactions affecting almost every part of your body, you are primed to act quickly and appropriately in time of danger.

Actions of the Nervous System The nervous system consists of the brain, spinal cord, and nerves. Part of the nervous system is under voluntary control, as when you tell your arm to reach for a chocolate. The part that is not under conscious supervision, such as what controls the digestion of the chocolate, is known as the **autonomic nervous system.** In addition to digestion, it controls your heart rate, breathing, blood pressure, and hundreds of other functions you normally take for granted.

The autonomic nervous system consists of two divisions. The **parasympathetic division** is in control when you are relaxed; it aids in digesting food, storing energy, and promoting growth. In contrast, the **sympathetic division** is activated during times of arousal, including exercise, and when there is an emergency, such as severe pain, anger, or fear. Sympathetic nerves use the neurotransmitter **norepinephrine** to exert their actions on nearly every organ, sweat gland, blood vessel, and muscle to enable your body to handle an emergency. In general, the sympathetic division commands your body to stop storing energy and instead to mobilize all energy resources to respond to the crisis.

Actions of the Endocrine System One important target of the sympathetic nervous system is the activation of the **endocrine system.** This system of

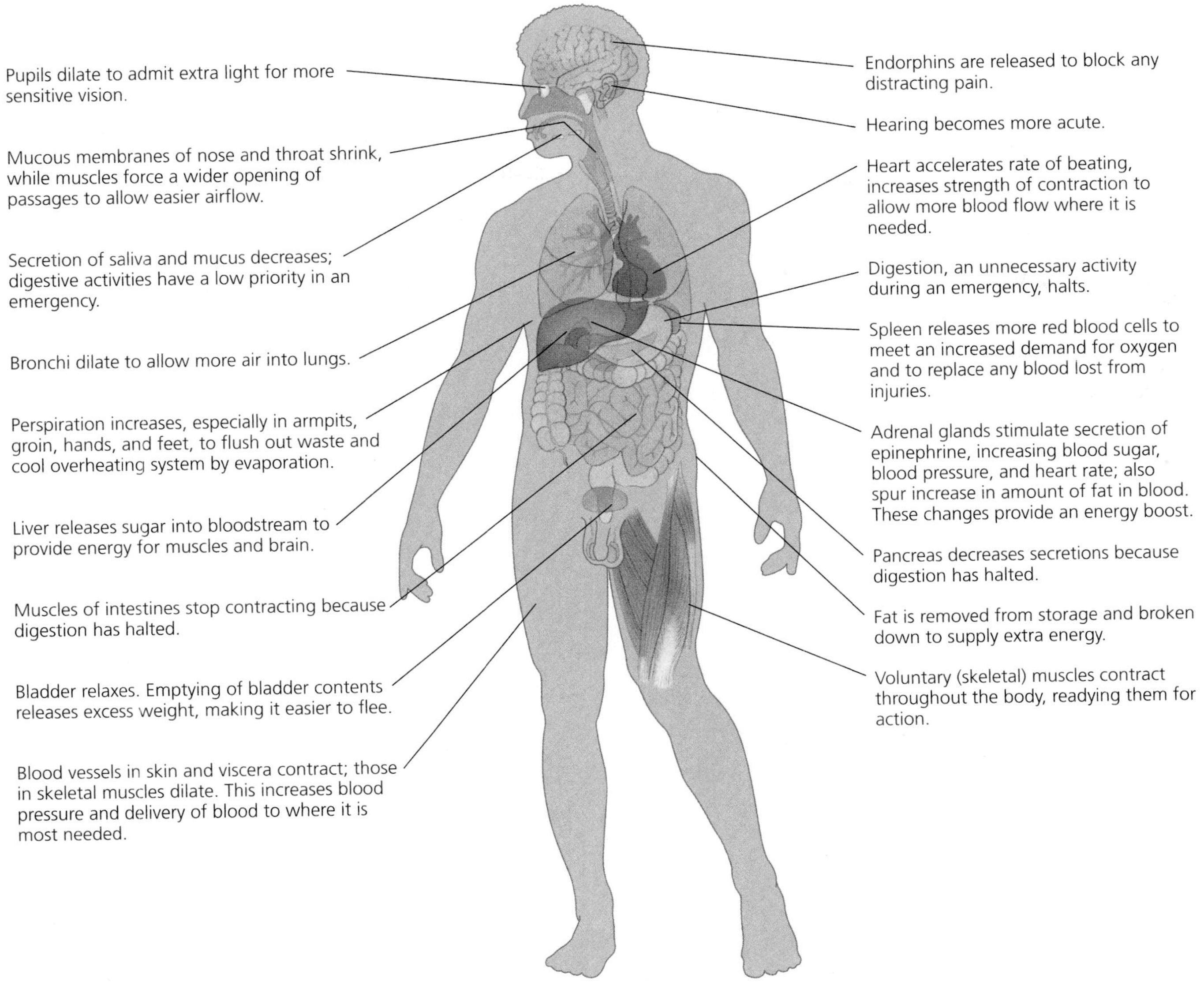

Pupils dilate to admit extra light for more sensitive vision.

Mucous membranes of nose and throat shrink, while muscles force a wider opening of passages to allow easier airflow.

Secretion of saliva and mucus decreases; digestive activities have a low priority in an emergency.

Bronchi dilate to allow more air into lungs.

Perspiration increases, especially in armpits, groin, hands, and feet, to flush out waste and cool overheating system by evaporation.

Liver releases sugar into bloodstream to provide energy for muscles and brain.

Muscles of intestines stop contracting because digestion has halted.

Bladder relaxes. Emptying of bladder contents releases excess weight, making it easier to flee.

Blood vessels in skin and viscera contract; those in skeletal muscles dilate. This increases blood pressure and delivery of blood to where it is most needed.

Endorphins are released to block any distracting pain.

Hearing becomes more acute.

Heart accelerates rate of beating, increases strength of contraction to allow more blood flow where it is needed.

Digestion, an unnecessary activity during an emergency, halts.

Spleen releases more red blood cells to meet an increased demand for oxygen and to replace any blood lost from injuries.

Adrenal glands stimulate secretion of epinephrine, increasing blood sugar, blood pressure, and heart rate; also spur increase in amount of fat in blood. These changes provide an energy boost.

Pancreas decreases secretions because digestion has halted.

Fat is removed from storage and broken down to supply extra energy.

Voluntary (skeletal) muscles contract throughout the body, readying them for action.

Figure 10.1   The fight-or-flight reaction.   In response to a stressor, the autonomic nervous system and the endocrine system cause physical changes that prepare the body to deal with an emergency.

glands, tissues, and cells helps control body functions by releasing **hormones** and other chemical messengers into the bloodstream. These chemicals act on a variety of targets throughout the body. Along with the nervous system with which it closely interacts, the endocrine system helps prepare the body to respond to a stressor.

The Two Systems Together   How do both systems work together in an emergency? Let's go back to your near collision with a car. Both reflexes and higher cognitive areas in your brain quickly make the decision that you are facing a threat—and your body prepares to meet the danger. Chemical messages and actions of sympathetic nerves cause the release of key hormones, including **cortisol** and **epinephrine.** These hormones trigger a series of profound physiological changes (Figure 10.1):

- Hearing and vision become more acute.
- The heart rate accelerates to pump more oxygen through the body.
- The liver releases extra sugar into the bloodstream to provide an energy boost.
- Perspiration increases to cool the skin.
- **Endorphins** are released to relieve pain in case of injury.

Taken together, these almost-instantaneous physical changes are called the **fight-or-flight reaction.** They give you the heightened reflexes and strength you need to dodge the car or deal with other stressors. Although these physical changes may vary in intensity, the same basic set of physical reactions occurs in response to any type of stressor, positive or negative, physical or psychological.

The Return to Homeostasis Once a stressful situation ends, the parasympathetic division of your autonomic nervous system takes command and halts the reaction. It initiates the adjustments necessary to restore **homeostasis,** a state in which blood pressure, heart rate, hormone levels, and other vital functions are maintained within a narrow range of normal. Your parasympathetic nervous system calms your body down, slowing a rapid heartbeat, drying sweaty palms, and returning breathing to normal. Gradually, your body resumes its normal "housekeeping" functions, such as digestion and temperature regulation. Damage that may have been sustained during the fight-or-flight reaction is repaired. The day after you narrowly dodge the car, you wake up feeling fine. In this way, your body can grow, repair itself, and acquire reserves of energy. When the next crisis comes, you'll be ready to respond—instantly—again.

The Fight-or-Flight Reaction in Modern Life The fight-or-flight reaction is a part of our biological heritage, and it's a survival mechanism that has served humans well. In modern life, however, it is often absurdly inappropriate. Many of the stressors we face in everyday life do not require a physical response—for example, an exam, a mess left by a roommate, or a red traffic light. The fight-or-flight reaction prepares the body for physical action regardless of whether such action is a necessary or appropriate response to a particular stressor.

Emotional and Behavioral Responses to Stressors

The physical response to a stressor may vary in intensity from person to person and situation to situation, but we all experience a similar set of physical changes—the fight-or-flight reaction. However, there is a great deal of variation in how people view potential stressors and in how they respond to them. For example, you may feel confident about taking exams but may be nervous about talking to people you don't know, while your roommate may love challenging social situations but may be very nervous about taking tests. Many factors, some external and some internal, help explain these differences. Your cognitive (mental) appraisal of a potential stressor will influence how it is viewed. Two factors that can reduce the magnitude of the stress response are successful prediction and the perception of having some control over the stressor. For instance, obtaining course syllabi at the beginning of the term allows you to predict the timing of major deadlines and exams. Having this predictive knowledge also allows you to exert some control over

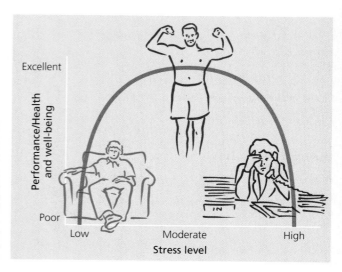

Figure. 10.2 Stress level, performance, and well-being. A moderate level of stress challenges individuals in a way that promotes optimal performance and well-being. Too little stress, and people are not challenged enough to improve; too much stress, and the challenges become stressors that can impair physical and emotional health.

your study plans and can thus help reduce the stress caused by exams.

Cognitive appraisal is highly individual and strongly related to emotions. The facts of a situation—Who? What? Where? When?—typically are evaluated fairly consistently from person to person. Evaluation with respect to personal outcome, however, varies: What does this mean for me? Can I do anything about it? Will it improve or worsen? If an individual perceives a situation as exceeding her or his ability to cope, the result can be negative emotions and an inappropriate stress response. If, on the other hand, a person perceives a situation as a challenge that is within her or his ability to manage, more positive and appropriate responses are likely. A certain amount of stress, if coped with appropriately, can help promote optimal performance (Figure 10.2).

Effective and Ineffective Responses Common emotional responses to stressors include anxiety, depression, and fear. Although emotional responses are determined in part by inborn personality or temperament, we often can moderate or learn to control them. Coping techniques are discussed later in the chapter.

Behavioral responses to stressors—controlled by the **somatic nervous system,** which manages our conscious actions—are entirely under our control. Effective behavioral responses such as talking, laughing, exercising, meditating, learning time-management skills, and finding a more compatible roommate can promote wellness and enable us to function at our best. Ineffective behavioral responses to stressors include overeating, expressing hostility, and using tobacco, alcohol, or other drugs.

Let's consider the individual variations demonstrated by two students, David and Amelia, responding to the same stressor—the first exam of the semester. David enters the exam with a feeling of dread and, as he reads the exam questions, responds to his initial anxiety with more anxiety. The more emotionally upset he gets, the less he can remember and the more anxious he becomes. Soon he's staring into space, imagining what will happen if he fails the course. Amelia, on the other hand, takes a deep breath to relax before she reads the questions, wills herself to focus on the answers she knows, and then goes back over the exam to deal with those questions she's not sure of. She leaves the room feeling calm, relaxed, and confident that she has done well.

It's not difficult to see that avoiding destructive responses to stress and adopting effective and appropriate ones can have a direct effect on well-being.

Personality and Stress   Some people seem to be nervous, irritable, and easily upset by minor annoyances; others are calm and composed even in difficult situations. Scientists remain unsure just why this is or how the brain's complex emotional mechanisms work. But personality, the sum of behavioral and emotional tendencies, clearly affects how people perceive and react to stressors. To investigate the links among personality, stress, and overall wellness, researchers have looked at different constellations of characteristics, or "personality types."

People with a Type A personality are described as ultracompetitive, controlling, impatient, aggressive, and hostile. Type A people tend to react more explosively to stressors, and they are upset by events that others would consider only mild annoyances. Type B individuals, on the other hand, are relaxed and contemplative. They tend to be less frustrated by daily events and more tolerant of the behavior of others. Studies indicate that certain characteristics of the Type A pattern—anger, cynicism, and hostility—increase the risk of heart disease. Type A people may have a higher perceived stress level and more problems coping with stress.

The Type C personality is characterized by difficulty expressing emotions, anger suppression, feelings of hopelessness and despair, and an exaggerated stress response to minor cognitive stressors. This heightened response may impair immune functions. People who consistently show Type C traits have lower levels of immune cells important in fighting and surviving cancer. Studies of Type A and C personalities suggest that expressing your emotions is beneficial but that habitually expressing exaggerated stress responses or hostility is unhealthy.

Researchers have also looked for personality traits that enable people to deal more successfully with stress, and they examined "hardiness," a particular form of optimism. People with a hardy personality view potential stressors as challenges and opportunities for growth and learning, rather than as burdens. Hardy people perceive fewer situations as stressful, and their reaction to stressors tends to be less intense. They are committed to their activities, have a sense of inner purpose and an

A person's emotional and behavioral responses to stressors depend on many different factors, including personality, gender, and cultural background. Research suggests that women are more likely than men to respond to stressors by seeking social support, a pattern referred to as tend-and-befriend.

inner locus of control, and feel at least partly in control of their lives.

Is there anything you can do to develop a more stress-resistant personality? It is unlikely that you can change your basic personality, but you can change your typical behaviors and patterns of thinking and develop positive coping strategies. Stress-management techniques are described later in the chapter.

Gender and Stress   Our gender role—the activities, abilities, and behaviors our culture expects of us based on whether we're male or female—can affect our experience of stress. Some behavioral responses to stressors, such as crying or openly expressing anger, may be deemed more appropriate for one gender than the other. Strict adherence to gender roles can thus place limits on how a person responds to stress and can itself become a source of stress. Adherence to traditional gender roles can also affect the perception of a potential stressor. For example, if a man derives most of his sense of self-worth from his work, retirement may be a more stressful life change for him than for a woman whose self-image is based on several different roles.

Terms

homeostasis A state of stability and consistency in an individual's physiological functioning.

somatic nervous system The branch of the peripheral nervous system that governs motor functions and sensory information, largely under conscious control.

Table 10.1 | Symptoms of Excess Stress

Physical Symptoms	Emotional Symptoms	Behavioral Symptoms
Dry mouth	Anxiety or edginess	Crying
Excessive perspiration	Depression	Disrupted eating habits
Frequent illnesses	Fatigue	Disrupted sleeping habits
Gastrointestinal problems	Hypervigilance	Harsh treatment of others
Grinding of teeth	Impulsiveness	Problems communicating
Headaches	Inability to concentrate	Sexual problems
High blood pressure	Irritability	Social isolation
Pounding heart	Trouble remembering things	Increased use of tobacco,
Stiff neck or aching lower back		alcohol, or other drugs

Although both men and women experience the fight-or-flight physiological response to stress, women are more likely to respond behaviorally with a pattern of "tend-and-befriend"—nurturing friends and family and seeking social support and social contacts. Rather than becoming aggressive or withdrawing from difficult situations, women are more likely to act to create and enhance their social networks in ways that reduce stress. Some evidence suggests that these gender differences may be partly tied to the hormone oxytocin, which is involved in social interaction and mood regulation and which is more plentiful and active in women.

Past Experiences   Past experiences can profoundly influence the evaluation of a potential stressor. Consider an individual who has had a bad experience giving a speech in the past. He or she is much more likely to perceive an upcoming speech assignment as stressful than someone who has had positive public speaking experiences. Effective behavioral responses, such as careful preparation and visualizing oneself giving a successful speech, can help overcome the effects of negative past experiences.

The Stress Experience as a Whole

Physical, emotional, and behavioral responses to stressors are intimately interrelated. The more intense the emotional response, the stronger the physical response. Effective behavioral responses can lessen stress; ineffective ones only worsen it. Sometimes people have such intense responses to stressors or such ineffective coping techniques that they need professional help. (Table 10.1 lists some symptoms of excess stress.) More often, however, people can learn to handle stressors on their own.

STRESS AND WELLNESS

The role of stress in health and disease is complex, and much remains to be learned. However, mounting evidence suggests that stress—interacting with a person's genetic predisposition, personality, social environment, and health-related behaviors—can increase vulnerability to numerous ailments. Several related theories have been proposed to explain the relationship between stress and disease.

The General Adaptation Syndrome

Biologist Hans Selye was one of the first scientists to develop a comprehensive theory of stress and disease. Based on his work in the 1930s and 1940s, Selye coined the term **general adaptation syndrome (GAS)** to describe what he believed is a universal and predictable response pattern to all stressors. He recognized that stressors could be pleasant, such as attending a party, or unpleasant, such as a bad grade. He called stress triggered by a pleasant stressor **eustress** and stress triggered by an unpleasant stressor **distress**. The sequence of physical responses associated with GAS is the same for both eustress and distress and occurs in three stages: alarm, resistance, and exhaustion (Figure 10.3).

Alarm   The alarm stage includes the complex sequence of events brought on by the activation of the sympathetic nervous system and the endocrine system—the fight-or-flight reaction. During this stage, the body is more susceptible to disease or injury because it is geared up to deal with a crisis. A person in this phase may experience headaches, indigestion, anxiety, and disrupted sleeping and eating patterns.

Resistance   Selye theorized that with continued stress, the body develops a new level of homeostasis in which it is more resistant to disease and injury than normal. During the resistance stage, a person can cope with normal life and added stress.

Exhaustion   Both the mobilization of forces during the alarm reaction and the maintenance of homeostasis during the resistance stage require a considerable amount of energy. If a stressor persists, or if several stressors occur in succession, general exhaustion results. This is not the sort of exhaustion people complain of after a long, busy

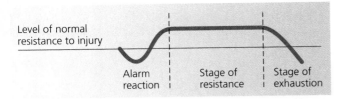

Figure 10.3 **The general adaptation syndrome.** Selye observed a predictable sequence of responses to stress. During the alarm phase, a lower resistance to injury is evident. With continued stress, resistance to injury is actually enhanced. With prolonged exposure to repeated stressors, exhaustion sets in, with a return of low resistance levels seen during acute stress. SOURCE: Insel, P. M., and W. T. Roth, 2004. *Core Concepts in Health*, 10th ed. Copyright © 2006 The McGraw-Hill Companies, Inc. Reprinted with permission of The McGraw-Hill Companies, Inc.

day. It's a life-threatening type of physiological exhaustion characterized by such symptoms as distorted perceptions and disorganized thinking.

Allostatic Load

While Selye's model of GAS is still viewed as a key contribution to modern stress theory, some aspects are now discounted. For example, increased susceptibility to disease after repeated or prolonged stress is now thought to be due to the effects of the stress response itself rather than to a depletion of resources (Selye's exhaustion stage). In particular, long-term overexposure to such stress hormones as cortisol has been linked with a variety of health problems. High cortisol levels are associated with metabolic syndrome, for example, a condition linked to increased risk of heart disease, type 2 diabetes, depression, and osteoporosis (see Chapter 11).

The long-term wear and tear of the stress response is called the *allostatic load*. An individual's allostatic load depends on many factors, including genetics, life experiences, and emotional and behavioral responses to stressors. A high allostatic load may be due to frequent stressors, poor adaptation to common stressors, an inability to shut down the stress response, or imbalances in the stress response of different body systems. High allostatic load has been linked with heart disease, high blood pressure, obesity, and reduced brain and immune system functioning. In other words, when your allostatic load exceeds your ability to cope, you are more likely to get sick.

Psychoneuroimmunology

One of the most fruitful areas of current research into the relationship between stress and disease is **psychoneuroimmunology (PNI)**. PNI is the study of the interactions among the nervous system, the endocrine system, and the immune system. The underlying premise of PNI is that stress, through the actions of the nervous and endocrine systems, impairs the immune system and thereby affects health.

Researchers have discovered a complex network of nerve and chemical connections between the nervous and endocrine systems and the immune system. We have already seen the profound physical effects of the hormones and other chemical messengers released during the stress response. These compounds also influence the immune system by affecting the number and efficiency of immune system cells, or lymphocytes.

The nervous, endocrine, and immune systems share other connections. Scientists have identified hormone-like substances called neuropeptides that appear to translate emotions into physiological events. Neuropeptides are produced and received by both brain and immune cells, so that the brain and the immune system share a biochemical "language," which also happens to be the language of emotions. The biochemical changes accompanying particular emotions can strongly influence the functioning of the immune system.

Links Between Stress and Specific Conditions

Although much remains to be learned, it is clear that people who have unresolved chronic stress in their lives or who handle stressors poorly are at risk for a wide range of health problems. In the short term, the problem might just be a cold, a stiff neck, or a stomachache. Over the long term, the problems can be more severe—cardiovascular disease or impairment of the immune system.

Cardiovascular Disease The stress response profoundly affects the cardiovascular system, and these changes have important implications for cardiovascular health, especially over the long term. During the stress response, heart rate increases and blood vessels constrict, causing blood pressure to rise. Chronic high blood pressure is a major cause of atherosclerosis, a disease in which the lining of the blood vessels becomes damaged and caked with fatty deposits. These deposits can block arteries, causing heart attacks and strokes (see Chapter 11).

Recent research suggests that certain types of emotional responses increase a person's risk of cardiovascular disease. "Hot reactors," people who exhibit extreme increases in heart rate and blood pressure in response to emotional stressors, may face an increased risk of cardiovascular problems.

Terms

general adaptation syndrome (GAS) A pattern of stress responses consisting of three stages: alarm, resistance, and exhaustion.

eustress Stress resulting from a pleasant stressor.

distress Stress resulting from an unpleasant stressor.

psychoneuroimmunology (PNI) The study of the interactions among the nervous system, the endocrine system, and the immune system.

Overcoming Insomnia

At some time in their lives, most people have trouble falling asleep or staying asleep. This condition is known as insomnia. Most people can overcome insomnia by discovering the cause of poor sleep and taking steps to remedy it. Insomnia that lasts for more than 6 months and interferes with daytime functioning requires consultation with a physician. Sleeping pills are not recommended for chronic insomnia because they can be habit-forming; they also lose their effectiveness over time.

If you're bothered by insomnia, here are some tips for getting a better night's sleep:

• Determine how much sleep you need to feel refreshed the next day, and don't sleep longer than that (but do make sure you get enough).

• Go to bed at the same time every night and, more important, get up at the same time every morning, 7 days a week, regardless of how much sleep you got. Don't nap during the day.

• Exercise every day, but not too close to bedtime. Your metabolism takes up to 6 hours to slow down after exercise.

• Avoid tobacco (nicotine is a stimulant), caffeine in the later part of the day, and alcohol before bedtime (it causes disturbed, fragmented sleep).

• Have a light snack before bedtime; you'll sleep better if you're not hungry.

• Deal with worries before bedtime. Try writing them down, along with some possible solutions, and then allow yourself to forget about them until the next day.

• Use your bed only for sleep. Don't eat, read, study, or watch television in bed.

• Relax before bedtime with a warm bath (again, not too close to bedtime—allow about 2 hours for your metabolism to slow down afterward), a book, music, or some relaxation exercises. Don't lie down in bed until you're sleepy.

• If you don't fall asleep in 15–20 minutes, or if you wake up and can't fall asleep again, get out of bed, leave the room if possible, and do something monotonous until you feel sleepy. Try distracting yourself with imagery instead of counting sheep; imagine yourself on a pleasant vacation or enjoying some beautiful scenery.

• Keep a perspective on your plight. Losing a night's sleep isn't the end of the world. Getting upset only makes it harder to fall asleep. Relax, and trust in your body's natural ability to drift off to sleep.

Altered Functioning of the Immune System

Sometimes you seem to get sick when you can least afford it—during exam week, when you're going on vacation, or when you have a job interview. As described earlier regarding PNI, research suggests that this is more than mere coincidence. Some of the health problems linked to stress-related changes in immune function include vulnerability to colds and other infections, asthma and allergy attacks, susceptibility to cancer, and flare-ups of chronic diseases such as genital herpes and HIV infection.

Other Health Problems   Many other health problems may be caused or worsened by uncontrolled stress, including the following:

• Digestive problems such as stomachaches, diarrhea, constipation, irritable bowel syndrome, and ulcers

• Tension headaches and migraines

• Insomnia and fatigue (see the box "Overcoming Insomnia")

• Injuries, including on-the-job injuries caused by repetitive strain

• Menstrual irregularities, impotence, and pregnancy complications

• Psychological problems, including depression, anxiety, panic attacks, eating disorders, and post-traumatic stress disorder (PTSD), which afflicts people who have suffered or witnessed severe trauma

COMMON SOURCES OF STRESS

We are surrounded by stressors—at home, at school, on the job, and within ourselves. Being able to recognize potential sources of stress is an important step in successfully managing the stress in our lives.

Major Life Changes

Any major change in your life that requires adjustment and accommodation can be a source of stress. Early adulthood and the college years are typically associated with many significant changes, such as moving out of the family home, establishing new relationships, setting educational and career goals, and developing a sense of identity and purpose. Even changes typically thought of as positive—graduation, job promotion, marriage—can be stressful.

Clusters of life changes, particularly those that are perceived negatively, may be linked to health problems in some people. Personality and coping skills are important moderating influences, however. People with a strong support network and a stress-resistant personality are less likely to become ill in response to major life changes than people with fewer internal and external resources.

Daily Hassles

Although major life changes are undoubtedly stressful, they seldom occur regularly. Researchers have proposed that minor problems—life's daily hassles—can be an even greater source of stress because they occur much more often. Daily hassles might include the following:

- Misplacing your keys, wallet, or an assignment
- Having an argument with a troublesome neighbor, coworker, or customer
- Waiting in a long line
- Being stuck in traffic or having another problem with transportation
- Worrying about money
- Being upset about the weather

People who perceive hassles negatively are likely to experience a moderate stress response every time they are faced with one. Over time, this can take a significant toll on health. Studies indicate that for some people, daily hassles contribute to a general decrease in overall wellness.

College Stressors

College is a time of major life changes and abundant minor hassles. You are learning new information and skills and making major decisions about your future. You may be away from home for the first time, or you may be adding extra responsibilities to a life already filled with job and family.

Academic Stressors   Exams, grades, and choosing a major are among the many academic stressors faced by college students. In addition to an increased workload compared to that in high school, high-quality efforts are expected of college students, so earning good grades takes more effort and dedication. Careful planning and preparation can help make academic stressors more predictable and manageable.

Students close to graduation may find themselves faced with the need to plan for life after college—a potentially daunting task. Remember that you'll have many opportunities to change career paths in the future and that the training and life experience gained from one path can often be transferred to other endeavors.

Interpersonal Stressors   The college years often involve such potential stressors as establishing new relationships and balancing multiple roles—student, employee, friend, spouse, parent, and so on. You'll have the opportunity to meet new people and make new friends at the start of every term and in every new class and activity. Viewed as an exciting challenge or a painful necessity, interacting with others involves attention, on-the-spot decision making, and energy expenditure. Be yourself and try not to be overly concerned with being liked by everyone you meet.

Time-Related Pressures   Time pressures are a problem for most students, but they may be particularly acute for those who also have job and family responsibilities. Most people do have enough time to fulfill all of their key responsibilities, but they don't manage their time or their priorities effectively. For these people, it's important to make a plan and stick to it. Effective time-management strategies are described later in the chapter.

Financial Concerns   As young adults leave home and become independent, such financial responsibilities as paying tuition, taking out loans, and managing living expenses are likely to arise, and such responsibilities are potential stressors. To complicate matters for students, tuition rates and competition for scholarships are at an all-time high. As college has become less affordable, more students have had to borrow—and borrow increasingly larger amounts—to pay for college. Most students work full-time during the summer and part-time during the school year to meet their financial needs. Some work full-time and support a family during the school year, which creates additional time pressures and stress. To help put your mind more at ease so that you can concentrate on your studies, develop a financial plan for each upcoming month or term. (A student budgeting Web site is listed in For Further Exploration at the end of the chapter.)

Job-Related Stressors

In recent surveys, Americans rate their jobs as one of the key sources of stress in their lives. Tight schedules and overtime leave less time to exercise, socialize, and engage in other stress-proofing activities. More than one-third of Americans report that they always feel rushed, and nearly half say they would give up a day's pay for a day off. Worries about job performance, salary, and job security and interactions with bosses, coworkers, and customers can contribute to stress. High levels of job stress are also common for people who are left out of important decisions relating to their jobs. When workers are given the opportunity to shape how their jobs are performed, job satisfaction goes up and stress levels go down.

If job-related (or college-related) stress is severe or chronic, the result can be **burnout**, a state of physical, mental, and emotional exhaustion. Burnout occurs most often in highly motivated and driven individuals who come to feel that their work is not recognized or that they are not accomplishing their goals. People in the helping professions—teachers, social workers, caregivers, police officers, and so on—are also prone to burnout. For some people who suffer from burnout, a vacation or leave of absence may be appropriate. For others, a reduced work schedule, better communication with superiors, or a change in job goals may be necessary. Improving time-management skills can also help.

Interpersonal and Social Stressors

Although social support is a key buffer against stress, your interactions with others can themselves be a source of stress. Your relationships with family members and old friends may change during your college years as you develop new interests and a new course for your life. You will be meeting new people and establishing new relationships.

The community and society in which you live can also be major sources of stress. Social stressors include prejudice and discrimination. You may feel stress as you try to relate to people of other ethnic or socioeconomic groups. As a member of a particular ethnic group, you may feel pressure to assimilate into mainstream society. If English is not your first language, you face the added burden of conducting many daily activities in a language with which you may not be completely comfortable.

Other Stressors

Other stressors are found in the environment and in ourselves. Environmental stressors—external conditions or events that cause stress—include loud noises, unpleasant smells, industrial accidents, violence, and natural disasters. (See Appendix A for preparation and coping strategies for large-scale disasters.) Internal stressors are found not in our interactions with our environment but within ourselves. We put pressure on ourselves to reach personal goals and then evaluate our progress and performance. Physical and emotional states such as illness and exhaustion are also internal stressors.

> MOTIVATION FOR CHANGE!   Set aside a few minutes at the end of each day to review the progress of your behavior change program. Think back over the course of the day and take note of your accomplishments—the positive choices you made and the challenges you overcame. Then, set a plan for the next day. This end-of-day review gives you the opportunity to engage in positive self-talk, and it can help you keep your behavior change program on track.

MANAGING STRESS

What can you do about all this stress? A great deal. By developing and maintaining healthy exercise, eating, and sleeping habits; shoring up your social support systems; improving your communication skills; developing spiritual wellness; and mastering simple techniques to identify and moderate individual stressors, you can learn to control the stress in your life—instead of allowing it to control you. The effort is well worth the time: People who manage stress effectively not only are healthier, they also have more time to enjoy life and accomplish their goals.

Counterproductive Strategies for Coping with Stress

Before we turn to helpful stress management techniques, let's take a closer look at some unhealthy strategies that you may be tempted to try to cope with stress. College is a time when many people develop habits in response to stress that are counterproductive and unhealthy and that may also last well beyond graduation. The following are a few unhealthy coping techniques to avoid:

- *Using tobacco:* The nicotine in cigarettes and other tobacco products can make you feel relaxed and even increase your ability to concentrate, but it is highly addictive. Smoking causes cancer, heart disease, impotence, and many other health problems and is the leading preventable cause of death in the United States.

- *Using alcohol:* Having a few drinks might make you feel temporarily at ease, and drinking until you're intoxicated may help you forget your current stressors. However, using alcohol to deal with stress places you at risk for all the short-term and long-term problems associated with alcohol abuse. It also does nothing to address the actual causes of stress in your life.

- *Using other drugs:* Altering your body chemistry in order to cope with stress is a strategy that has many pitfalls and does not directly address your stressors. For example, caffeine raises cortisol levels and blood pressure and disrupts sleep. Marijuana can elicit panic attacks with repeated use, and some research suggests that it enhances the stress response.

- *Binge eating:* The feelings of satiation and sedation that follow eating produce a relaxed state that reduces stress. However, regular use of eating as a means of coping with stress may lead to weight gain and to binge eating, a risky behavior associated with eating disorders. Maintain a regular schedule of meals and snacks, including breakfast, to keep your energy up and avoid hunger-driven binges late in the day.

For more on these unhealthy coping techniques, refer to Chapters 9 and 13.

Exercise

One study found that taking a long walk can be effective at reducing anxiety and blood pressure. Another study showed that a brisk walk of as little as 10 minutes' duration can leave people feeling more relaxed and energetic for up to 2 hours. Regular exercise has even more benefits. Researchers have found that people who exercise regularly react with milder physical stress responses before, during, and after exposure to stressors, and that their overall sense of well-being increases as well. Although even light exercise—a brisk walk, an easy bike outing—can have a beneficial effect, an integrated fitness program like the one recommended in this book can have a significant impact on stress. People who took three brisk 45-minute walks a week for

3 months reported that they perceived fewer daily hassles. Their sense of wellness also increased.

These findings are not surprising because, as described earlier, the stress response mobilizes energy resources and readies the body for physical emergencies. If you experience stress and do not physically exert yourself, you are not completing the energy cycle. You may not be able to exercise while your daily stressors occur—during class, for example, or while sitting in a traffic jam—but you can be active later in the day. Physical activity allows you to expend the nervous energy you have built up and trains your body to more readily return to homeostasis after stressful situations.

One warning: For some people, exercise can become just one more stressor in a highly stressed life. People who exercise compulsively risk overtraining, a condition characterized by fatigue, irritability, depression, and diminished athletic performance. An overly strenuous exercise program can even make a person sick by compromising immune function. For the details of a safe and effective exercise program, refer to Chapter 7.

Nutrition

A healthy, balanced diet will supply the energy needed to cope with stress. In addition, eating wisely will enhance your feelings of self-control and self-esteem. Avoiding or limiting caffeine is also important in stress management. Although one or two cups of coffee a day probably won't hurt you, caffeine is a mildly addictive stimulant that leaves some people jittery, irritable, and unable to sleep; consuming caffeine during stressful situations can raise blood pressure and increase levels of cortisol. For more on sound nutrition and for advice on evaluating dietary supplements, many of which are marketed for stress, see Chapter 8.

Sleep

Lack of sleep can be both a cause and an effect of excess stress. As described in Chapter 7, without sufficient sleep, our mental and physical processes steadily deteriorate. We get headaches, feel irritable, are unable to concentrate, forget things, and may be more susceptible to illness. Lack of sleep can also raise levels of stress hormones throughout the day. Fatigue and sleep deprivation are major factors in many fatal car, truck, and train crashes. Adequate sleep, on the other hand, improves mood, fosters feelings of competence and self-worth, and supports optimal mental and emotional functioning. Make time in your busy schedule to obtain adequate sleep; if insomnia is a problem for you, refer back to the tips in the box "Overcoming Insomnia."

Social Support

People need people. Sharing fears, frustrations, and joys not only makes life richer but also seems to contribute—indirectly but significantly—to the well-being of body and mind. Research supports this conclusion: One study of college students living in overcrowded apartments, for example, found that those with a strong social support system were less distressed by their cramped quarters than were the loners who navigated life's challenges on their own. Other studies have shown that married people live longer than single people and have lower death rates from a wide range of conditions. And people infected with HIV remain symptom-free longer if they have a strong social support network. The crucial common denominator in all these findings is the meaningful connection with others. For more on developing and maintaining your social network, see the box "Building Social Support" on p. 322.

Communication

Do you often find yourself angry at others? Some people express their anger directly by yelling or being aggressive; others express anger indirectly by excessively criticizing others or making cynical comments. A person who is angry with others often has difficulty forming and maintaining successful social relationships. Better communication skills can help. To learn strategies for managing anger, see the box "Dealing with Anger" on p. 323.

At the other extreme, you may suppress your feelings and needs entirely. You may have trouble saying no and allow people to take advantage of you. Many businesses encourage employees to take assertiveness training workshops to help them overcome shyness and resistance to communicating their needs. Such communication skills are also valuable in social relationships.

Strive for Spiritual Wellness

Spiritual wellness is associated with greater coping skills and higher levels of overall wellness. It is a very personal wellness component, and there are many ways to develop it (see the box "Paths to Spiritual Wellness"). Researchers have linked spiritual wellness to longer life expectancy, reduced risk of disease and faster recovery, and improved emotional health. Although spirituality is difficult to study, and researchers aren't sure how or why spirituality seems to improve health, several explanations have been offered:

- *Social support:* Attending religious services or participating in volunteer organizations helps people feel that they are part of a community with similar values, and it promotes social connectedness and caring.

- *Healthy habits:* Some of the paths to spiritual wellness may encourage healthy behaviors like eating a vegetarian diet or consuming less meat and alcohol, and may discourage harmful habits like smoking.

- *Positive attitude:* Spirituality can give a person a sense of meaning and purpose in life, and these qualities create a more positive attitude in a person, which in turn helps one cope with life's challenges.

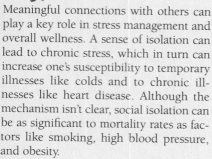

Meaningful connections with others can play a key role in stress management and overall wellness. A sense of isolation can lead to chronic stress, which in turn can increase one's susceptibility to temporary illnesses like colds and to chronic illnesses like heart disease. Although the mechanism isn't clear, social isolation can be as significant to mortality rates as factors like smoking, high blood pressure, and obesity.

There is no single best pattern of social support that works for everyone. However, research suggests that having a variety of types of relationships may be important for wellness. To help determine whether your social network measures up, answer true or false for each of the following statements:

1. If I needed an emergency loan of $100, there is someone I could get it from.

2. There is someone who takes pride in my accomplishments.

3. I often meet or talk with family or friends.

4. Most people I know think highly of me.

5. If I needed an early morning ride to the airport, there's no one I would feel comfortable asking to take me.

6. I feel there is no one with whom I can share my most private worries and fears.

7. Most of my friends are more successful making changes in their lives than I am.

8. I would have a hard time finding someone to go with me on a day trip to the beach or country.

To calculate your score, add the number of true answers to questions 1–4 and the number of false answers to questions 5–8. If your score is 4 or more, you should have enough support to protect your health. If your score is 3 or less, you may need to reach out. There are a variety of things you can do to strengthen your social ties:

• *Foster friendships.* Keep in regular contact with your friends. Offer respect, trust, and acceptance, and provide help and support in times of need. Express appreciation for your friends.

• *Keep your family ties strong.* Stay in touch with the family members you feel close to. Participate in family activities and celebrations. If your family doesn't function well as a support system for its members, create a second "family" of people with whom you have built meaningful ties.

• *Get involved with a group.* Do volunteer work, take a class, attend a lecture series, join a religious group. These types of activities can give you a sense of security, a place to talk about your feelings or concerns, and a way to build new friendships. Choose activities that are meaningful to you and that include direct involvement with other people.

• *Build your communication skills.* The more you share your feelings with others, the closer the bonds between you will become. When others are speaking, be a considerate and attentive listener.

Individual relationships change over the course of your life, but it's never too late to build friendships or become more involved in your community. Your investment of time and energy in your social network will pay off—in a brighter outlook now, and in better health and well-being for the future.

SOURCES: Friends Can Be Good Medicine. 1998. As found in the *Mind/Body Newsletter* 7(1): 3–6. Center for the Advancement of Health; quiz from Japenga, A. 1995. A Family of Friends. *Health*, November/December, 1994. Adapted with permission. Copyright © 2001 Health® magazine. For subscriptions please call 800-274-2522.

• *Moments of relaxation:* Spiritual practices like prayer, meditation, and immersion in artistic activities can reduce stress by eliciting the relaxation response (described later in the chapter).

Spirituality provides an ethical path to personal fulfillment that includes connectedness with self, others, and a higher power or larger reality. Spiritual wellness can make you more aware of your personal values and can help clarify them. Without an awareness of personal values, people's lives may be hurriedly driven forward by immediate desires and the passing demands of others. Living according to values means considering your options carefully before making a choice, choosing between options without succumbing to outside pressures that oppose your values, and making a choice and acting on it rather than doing nothing.

Lab 10.3 includes exercises designed to help you build spiritual wellness. For both stress management and overall wellness, take time out today to develop your spiritual side.

Confide in Yourself Through Writing

Keeping a diary is analogous to confiding in others, except that you are confiding in yourself. This form of coping with severe stress may be especially helpful for those who are shy or introverted and find it difficult to open up to others. Although writing about traumatic and stressful events may have a short-term negative effect on mood, over the long term, stress is reduced and positive changes in health occur. A key to promoting beneficial results with respect to health and well-being through journaling is to write about one's emotional responses to a stressful event. Set aside a special time each day or week to journal your feelings about stressful events in your life.

Time Management

Learning to manage your time successfully can be crucial to coping with everyday stressors. Overcommitment, procrastination, and even boredom are significant stressors

Anger is a natural response to something we perceive as a betrayal, injustice, threat, or other wrong—whether real or imagined. Angry responses include both emotions and physiological changes. Angry emotions can range from mild irritation to boiling mad, out-of-control rage. The body responds with faster heart and breathing rates, muscle tension, a knot in the stomach, trembling, or a red face. We can be angry with a person, a situation or condition, or ourselves. Anger is a useful emotion when it alerts us that something is wrong, and we respond with constructive action. But when anger gets out of control, it causes problems for ourselves and for others.

Managing Your Own Anger

How should you deal with anger? Popular wisdom has said that you should express rather than suppress anger to maintain psychological and physical wellness. However, recent studies have questioned this idea by showing that people who are overtly hostile seem to be at higher risk for heart attacks. Furthermore, angry words or actions won't contribute to wellness if they damage important personal or professional relationships or produce feelings of guilt or loss of control.

At one extreme are people who never express anger or any opinion that might offend others, even when their own rights and needs are being jeopardized. They may be chronically deprived of satisfaction at work and at home and may find themselves stuck in unhealthy relationships. At the other extreme are people whose anger is explosive or misdirected. Explosive anger, or rage, renders people temporarily unable to think straight or act in their own best interest; in the long run, frequent expressions of rage increase the risk for heart disease.

What is the best approach to anger, then? Try looking at each situation and distinguishing between a gratuitous expression of anger and a reasonable level of self-assertiveness. If you feel your anger building, ask yourself whether the situation is really important enough to get angry about, whether you are truly justified in getting angry, and whether expressing your anger is going to make a positive difference. If you can answer "yes" to all three questions, then calm but assertive communication may be an appropriate response.

If your anger isn't reasonable, try distracting or calming yourself rather than expressing anger. First, try to reframe what you're thinking at that moment. You'll be less angry at another person if there is a possibility that his or her behavior was not intentionally directed against you. Did the driver who cut into your lane on the freeway do it deliberately to spite you, or did he simply fail to see you? Look for possible mitigating factors that would make you less likely to blame him: Maybe he's late for a job interview and preoccupied with worries. If you're angry because you've just been criticized, avoid mentally replaying scenes from the past when you received similar unjust criticisms. Think about what is happening now and act analytically rather than defensively. Why are you taking it personally? Why are you acting like a jerk just because she did?

Second, try to distract yourself to calm down. Use the old trick of counting to 10 before you respond, or start concentrating on your breathing. Imagine yourself in a peaceful place. If needed, take a longer cooling-off period by leaving the situation until your anger has subsided.

These techniques do not mean that you should permanently avoid issues and people who make you angry. If you've decided that an expression of anger is the best response, return to the issue when you've had a chance to think about it more clearly and are ready to express yourself calmly and clearly. Use "I" statements ("I would like . . ." "I feel . . .") when expressing your feelings, and listen carefully to the other person's point of view. Negotiate a constructive solution; don't attack verbally and make demands. If you decide it's not appropriate to express your anger, don't stay stuck in the feeling by fuming, dwelling on the injustice of the situation, or thinking how to get back at the person indirectly later. Express your feelings in a constructive manner or move on.

If you have trouble expressing anger, you might explore training in assertiveness to help you learn to express your needs, desires, and opinions constructively. If, on the other hand, your anger is out of control, consider counseling. With counseling, a highly angry person can move closer to a middle range of anger in about two to three months.

Dealing with Anger in Other People

If someone you're with becomes very angry, respond asymmetrically by reacting not with anger but with calm. Try to validate the other person by acknowledging that he or she had some reason to be angry. This does not mean apologizing, if you don't think you're to blame, or accepting verbal abuse, which is always inappropriate. Try to focus on solving the problem by allowing the individual to explain why he or she is so angry and what can be done to alleviate the situation. For instance, instead of "Quit yelling at me!" you might say, "I realize you're upset because I erased your messages. Is there anything I can do to help you find out who called?" Finally, if the person cannot be calmed, it may be best to disengage, at least temporarily. After a time-out, a rational problem-solving approach may be more successful.

Warning Signs of Violence

It's normal to feel angry or frustrated when you've been let down or betrayed. But anger and frustration don't justify violent action. If you notice the following signs over a period of time, the potential for violence exists: a history of making threats and engaging in aggressive behavior; serious drug or alcohol use; gang membership; access to or fascination with weapons; feeling rejected or alone; withdrawal from friends and usual activities; poor school performance; having been a victim of bullying; feeling constantly disrespected; and failing to acknowledge the rights of others. If you see these immediate warning signs, violence is a serious possibility:

- Daily loss of temper or frequent physical fighting
- Significant vandalism or property damage
- Increased risk-taking behavior or use of drugs or alcohol
- Threats or detailed plans to commit acts of violence
- Pleasure in hurting animals
- Carrying a weapon

If you or someone you know shows warning signs of violence, get help. Don't spend time alone with people who show warning signs. If you are worried about being a victim of violence, get someone in authority to help you. Do not resort to violence or use a weapon to protect yourself. Instead, ask an experienced professional for help.

Spiritual wellness means different things to different people. For many, it involves developing a set of guiding beliefs, principles, or values that give purpose and meaning to life. It helps people achieve a sense of wholeness within themselves and in their relationships with others. Spiritual wellness influences people on an individual level, as well as on a community level, where it can bond people together through compassion, love, forgiveness, and self-sacrifice.

Regardless of how spiritual wellness is defined, its development is critical for overall well-being. Spiritual wellness is closely tied to the other components of wellness, particularly psychological wellness. And although difficult to study, spiritual wellness, researchers have found, is associated with greater self-esteem, social support, coping skills, positive health outcomes, and overall feelings of well-being. In general, people seem to feel better if they have beliefs about the ultimate purpose of life and their own place in the universe.

There are many paths to spiritual wellness. One of the most common in our society is organized religion. The major religions provide paths for transforming the self in ways that can lead to greater happiness and serenity and reduce feelings of anxiety and hopelessness. For example, in Christianity salvation follows turning away from the selfish ego to God's sovereignty and grace, where a joy is found that frees the believer from anxious self-concern and despair. *Islam* is the word for a kind of self-surrender leading to peace with God. Buddhism teaches how to detach oneself from selfish desire, leading to compassion for the suffering of others and freedom from fear-engendering illusions. Judaism emphasizes the social and ethical redemption the Jewish community can experience if it follows the laws of God. Religions teach specific techniques for achieving these transformations of the self: prayer, both in groups and in private; meditation; the performance of rituals and ceremonies symbolizing religious truths; and good works

and service to others. Religious organizations also usually offer social and material support to members who might otherwise be isolated.

Spiritual wellness does not require participation in organized religion. Many people find meaning and purpose in other ways. By spending time in nature or working on environmental issues, people can experience continuity with the natural world. Spiritual wellness can come through helping others in one's community or by promoting human rights, peace and harmony among people, and opportunities for human development on a global level. Other people develop spiritual wellness through art or through their personal relationships.

How would you define spiritual wellness and its role in your life? What beliefs and practices do you associate with your sense of spiritual wellness? To achieve overall well-being, it is important to take time out to consider what you can do to help your spiritual side grow and flourish.

for many people. Along with gaining control of nutrition and exercise to maintain a healthy energy balance, time management is an important element in a wellness program. Try these strategies for improving your time-management skills:

• *Set priorities.* Divide your tasks into three groups: essential, important, and trivial. Focus on the first two. Ignore the third.

• *Schedule tasks for peak efficiency.* You've undoubtedly noticed you're most productive at certain times of the day (or night). Schedule as many of your tasks for those hours as you can and stick to your schedule.

• *Set realistic goals and write them down.* Attainable goals spur you on. Impossible goals, by definition, cause frustration and failure. Fully commit yourself to achieving your goals by putting them in writing.

• *Budget enough time.* For each project you undertake, calculate how long it will take to complete. Then tack on another 10–15%, or even 25%, as a buffer.

• *Break up long-term goals into short-term ones.* Instead of waiting for or relying on large blocks of time, use short amounts of time to start a project or keep it moving.

• *Visualize the achievement of your goals.* By mentally rehearsing your performance of a task, you will be able to reach your goal more smoothly.

• *Keep track of the tasks you put off.* Analyze the reasons why you procrastinate. If the task is difficult or unpleasant, look for ways to make it easier or more fun. For example, if you find the readings for one of your classes particularly difficult, choose an especially nice setting for your reading and then reward yourself each time you complete a section or chapter.

• *Consider doing your least-favorite tasks first.* Once you have the most unpleasant ones out of the way, you can work on the tasks you enjoy more.

• *Consolidate tasks when possible.* For example, try walking to the store so that you run your errands and exercise in the same block of time.

• *Identify quick transitional tasks.* Keep a list of 5- to 10-minute tasks you can do while waiting or between other tasks, such as watering your plants, doing the dishes, or checking a homework assignment.

• *Delegate responsibility.* Asking for help when you have too much to do is no cop-out; it's good time management. Just don't delegate to others the jobs you know you should do yourself.

• *Say no when necessary.* If the demands made on you don't seem reasonable, say no—tactfully, but without guilt or apology.

• *Give yourself a break.* Allow time for play—free, unstructured time when you ignore the clock. Don't

Managing the many commitments of adult life—including work, school, and relationships—can sometimes feel overwhelming and produce a great deal of stress. Time-management skills, including careful scheduling with a date book or handheld computer, can help people cope with busy days.

consider this a waste of time. Play renews you and enables you to work more efficiently.

- *Avoid your personal time sinks.* You can probably identify your own time sinks, activities like watching television, surfing the Internet, or talking on the phone that consistently use up more time than you anticipate and put you behind schedule. Some days, it may be best to avoid problematic activities altogether; for example, if you have a big paper due, don't sit down for a 5-minute TV break if it is likely to turn into a 2-hour break. Try a 5-minute walk if you need to clear your head.

- *Stop thinking or talking about what you're going to do, and just do it!* Sometimes the best solution for procrastination is to stop waiting for the right moment and just get started. You will probably find that things are not as bad as you feared, and your momentum will keep you going.

For more help with time management, complete Activity 10 in the Behavior Change Workbook.

Cognitive Techniques

Certain thought patterns and ways of thinking, including ideas, beliefs, and perceptions, can contribute to stress and have a negative impact on health. But other habits of mind, if practiced with patience and consistency, can help

break unhealthy thought patterns. Below are some suggestions for changing destructive thinking.

- Modify expectations; they often restrict experience and lead to disappointment. Try to accept life as it comes.

- Monitor your self-talk and attempt to minimize hostile, critical, suspicious, and self-deprecating thoughts (see the box "Realistic Self-Talk").

- Live in the present; clear your mind of old debris and fears for the future so you can enjoy life as it is now.

- "Go with the flow." Accept what you can't change; forgive faults; be flexible.

MOTIVATION FOR CHANGE! Feeling confident about your ability to tackle new challenges to your behavior change program can help keep you motivated and on track. Building the skill of problem solving is important for nearly every type of behavior change program, and it also helps in stress management. When faced with a new challenge or problem, don't stew over it; try the following systematic approach to solving your problem:

1. Define the problem in one or two sentences.
2. Identify the causes of the problem.
3. List a number of possible solutions; don't stop with just the most obvious one.
4. Weigh the positive and negative consequences of each possible solution.
5. Make a decision—choose a solution.
6. Make a list of what you will need to do to act on your decision.
7. Begin to carry out your list; if you're unable to act immediately, temporarily turn to other things.
8. Evaluate the outcome and revise your approach if necessary.

Cultivating your sense of humor is another key cognitive stress-management technique. Even a fleeting smile produces changes in your autonomic nervous system that can lift your spirits. Hearty laughter triggers the release of endorphins, and after a good laugh, your muscles go slack and your pulse and blood pressure dip below normal—you are relaxed. Try keeping a humor journal filled with funny things you and others say, including slips of the tongue. Collect funny and clever sayings and cartoons that make you smile; add them to your journal. Watch funny films and television programs. In a study of college students, those who watched an episode of *Seinfeld* prior to giving an impromptu speech were less anxious and had a lower heart rate than those who didn't watch the program. You can also collect funny props to put on the next time you feel stressed or anxious, or simply try making funny faces in front of a mirror.

Realistic Self-Talk

Do your patterns of thinking make events seem worse than they truly are? Do negative beliefs about yourself become self-fulfilling prophecies? Substituting realistic self-talk for negative self-talk can help you build and maintain self-esteem and cope better with the challenges in your life. Here are some examples of common types of distorted, negative self-talk, along with suggestions for more accurate and rational responses.

Cognitive Distortion	Negative Self-Talk	Realistic Self-Talk
Focusing on negatives	School is so discouraging—nothing but one hassle after another.	School is pretty challenging and has its difficulties, but there certainly are rewards. It's really a mixture of good and bad.
Expecting the worst	Why would my boss want to meet with me this afternoon if not to fire me?	I wonder why my boss wants to meet with me. I guess I'll just have to wait and see.
Overgeneralizing	(After getting a poor grade on a paper) Just as I thought—I'm incompetent at everything.	I'll start working on the next paper earlier. That way, if I run into problems, I'll have time to consult with the TA.
Minimizing	I won the speech contest, but none of the other speakers was very good. I wouldn't have done as well against stiffer competition.	It may not have been the best speech I'll ever give, but it was good enough to win the contest. I'm really improving as a speaker.
Blaming others	I wouldn't have eaten so much last night if my friends hadn't insisted on going to that restaurant.	I overdid it last night. Next time I'll make different choices.
Expecting perfection	I should have scored 100% on this test. I can't believe I missed that one problem through a careless mistake.	Too bad I missed one problem through carelessness, but overall I did very well on this test. Next time I'll be more careful.

SOURCE: Excerpt from *Stress Management for Wellness*, 3rd ed., by Walt Schafer. Copyright © 1996. Reprinted with permission of Wadsworth, a division of Thomson Learning: www.thomsonrights.com. Fax 800-730-2215.

Relaxation Techniques

First identified and described by Herbert Benson of Harvard Medical School, the **relaxation response** is a physiological state characterized by a feeling of warmth and quiet mental alertness. This response is the opposite of the fight-or-flight reaction. When the relaxation response is triggered by a relaxation technique, heart rate, breathing, and metabolism slow down; blood flow to the brain and skin increases; and brain waves shift from an alert beta rhythm to a relaxed alpha rhythm.

The techniques described in this section and in the box "Stress-Management Techniques from Around the World" are among the most popular techniques and the easiest to learn. All these techniques take practice, so it may be several weeks before the benefits become noticeable in everyday life.

Progressive Relaxation   In this simple relaxation technique, you tense, then relax the muscles of the body one by one. Also known as deep muscle relaxation, this technique addresses the muscle tension that occurs when the body is experiencing stress. Consciously relaxing tensed muscles sends a message to other body systems to reduce the stress response.

To practice progressive relaxation, begin by inhaling as you contract your right fist. Then exhale as you release your fist. Repeat. Contract and relax your right bicep. Repeat. Do the same using your left arm. Then, working from forehead to feet, contract and relax other muscles. (A complete script for progressive relaxation is included on the Online Learning Center.) Repeat each contraction at least once, inhaling as you tense and exhaling as you relax. To speed up the process, tense and relax more muscles at one time—for example, both arms simultaneously. With practice you'll be able to relax quickly by simply clenching and releasing only your fists.

Visualization   Visualization, also known as using imagery, is so effective in enhancing sports performance that it has become part of the curriculum at training camps for U.S. Olympic athletes. This same technique can be used to induce relaxation, to help change habits, or to improve performance on an exam, on stage, or on a playing field.

Terms

relaxation response A physiological state characterized by a feeling of warmth and quiet mental alertness.

The origins of techniques for relaxation span many continents and many centuries. Three techniques that are growing in popularity in the United States are meditation, hatha yoga, and taijiquan. Although you may not choose to adopt the philosophical bases of these techniques, all of them can help you manage stress by promoting the relaxation response.

Meditation

At its most basic level, meditation, or self-reflective thought, involves quieting or emptying the mind to achieve deep relaxation. Some practitioners of meditation view it on a deeper level as a means of focusing concentration, increasing self-awareness, and bringing enlightenment to their lives. The origins of meditation can be traced back to the sixth century B.C. in Asia. Meditation has been integrated into the practices of several religions—Buddhism, Hinduism, Confucianism, Taoism—but it is not a religion itself, nor does its practice require any special knowledge, belief, or background.

There are two general styles of meditation, centered on different ways of quieting the mind. In exclusive meditation, one focuses on a single word or thought, eliminating all others. In inclusive meditation, the mind is allowed to wander uncontrolled from thought to thought, but one observes the thoughts in a detached way, without judgment or emotion. Exclusive meditation tends to be easier to learn. Herbert Benson has developed a simple, practical technique for eliciting the relaxation response using exclusive meditation:

1. Pick a word, phrase, or object to focus on. You can choose a word or phrase that has a deep meaning for you, but any word or phrase will work. In Zen meditation, the word *mu* (literally, "absolutely nothing") is often used. Some meditators prefer to focus on their breathing.

2. Sit comfortably in a quiet place. Close your eyes if you're not focusing on an object.

3. Relax your muscles.

4. Breathe slowly and naturally. If you're using a focus word or phrase, silently repeat it each time you exhale. If you're using an object, focus on it as you breathe.

5. Keep your attitude passive. Disregard thoughts that drift in.

6. Continue for 10–20 minutes once or twice a day.

7. After you've finished, sit quietly for a few minutes with your eyes closed, then open. Then stand up.

Allow relaxation to occur at its own pace; don't try to force it. Don't be surprised if you can't tune your mind out for more than a few seconds at a time. It's nothing to get angry about. The more you ignore the intrusions, the easier it will become. If you want to time your session, peek at a watch or clock occasionally, but don't set a jarring alarm.

The technique works best on an empty stomach, before a meal or about 2 hours after eating. Avoid times of day when you're tired, unless you want to fall asleep.

Although you'll feel refreshed even after the first session, it may take a month or more to get noticeable results. Be patient. Eventually the relaxation response will become so natural that it will occur spontaneously or on demand when you sit quietly for a few moments.

Hatha Yoga

Yoga is an ancient Sanskrit word meaning "union"; it refers specifically to the union of mind, body, and soul and for some serves as a preliminary to meditation. The development and practice of yoga are rooted in the Hindu philosophy of spiritual enlightenment. The founders of yoga developed a system of physical postures, called *asanas,* designed to cleanse the body, unlock energy paths, and raise the level of consciousness.

Although there are many kinds of yoga, the one most commonly practiced in the Western world is hatha yoga. It emphasizes physical balance and breathing control. It also integrates components of flexibility, muscular strength and endurance, and muscle relaxation.

A session of hatha yoga typically involves a series of *asanas* held for a few seconds to several minutes. The combination of stretching and *asanas* can be very relaxing, as long as one stretches to the point of relaxation and not to the point of pain or injury. There are hundreds of different *asanas,* and they must be performed correctly to be beneficial. For this reason, qualified instruction is recommended, particularly for beginners. Yoga classes are offered through many community recreation centers, YMCAs and YWCAs, and private clubs. Regardless of whether you accept the philosophy and symbolism of different *asanas,* the practice of yoga can induce the relaxation response as well as develop flexibility, muscular strength and endurance, and body awareness.

Taijiquan

A martial art that developed in China, taijiquan (pronounced "tie jee choo-en" and often called simply "tai chi") has become a popular form of exercise in the United States. Its movements, called forms, resemble a slow, graceful dance that mimics animals such as the snake and the crane. At its core is the Taoist belief that good health results from balanced *chi,* an energy force that surrounds and permeates all things. The forms, which can be practiced almost anywhere, are performed to help balance the body's chi to promote health and spiritual growth. The goal is to become calm and centered and to conserve and concentrate energy. Taijiquan's slow, graceful movements reinforce the idea of moving *with* rather than *against* the stressors of everyday life. Researchers have found that taijiquan is an appropriate activity for people of all ages and that it helps older adults safely boost their level of physical functioning.

The practice of taijiquan promotes relaxation and concentration as well as the development of body awareness, balance, muscular strength and endurance, and flexibility. It usually takes some time and practice to reap the stress-management benefits of taijiquan, and, as with yoga, it's best to begin with some qualified instruction.

SOURCES: Adapted from Li, F., et al. 2001. An evaluation of the effects of tai chi exercise on physical function among older persons: A randomized controlled trial. *Annals of Behavioral Medicine* 23:139–146. Seaward, B. L. 1999. *Managing Stress: Principles and Strategies for Health and Well Being,* Web-enhanced 2nd ed. Boston: Jones and Bartlett. Can yoga make you fit? 1997. *University of California, Berkeley Wellness Letter,* May. Benson, H., with W. Proctor. 1984. *Beyond the Relaxation Response.* New York: Times Books.

Breathing for Relaxation

Diaphragmatic Breathing

1. Lie on your back with your body relaxed.
2. Place one hand on your chest and one on your abdomen. (You will use your hands to monitor the depth and location of your breathing.)
3. Inhale slowly and deeply through your nose into your abdomen. Your abdomen should push up as far as is comfortable. Your chest should expand only a little and only in conjunction with the movement of your abdomen.
4. Exhale gently through your mouth.
5. Continue for about 5–10 minutes per session. Focus on the sound and feel of your breathing.

Breathing In Relaxation, Breathing Out Tension

1. Assume a comfortable position, lying on your back or sitting in a chair.
2. Inhale slowly and deeply into your abdomen. Imagine the inhaled, warm air flowing to all parts of your body. Say to yourself, "Breathe in relaxation."
3. Exhale from your abdomen. Imagine tension flowing out of your body. Say to yourself. "Breathe out tension."
4. Pause before you inhale.
5. Continue for 5–10 minutes or until no tension remains.

Chest Expansion

1. Sit in a comfortable chair or stand.
2. Inhale slowly and deeply into your abdomen as you raise your arms out to the sides. Pull your shoulders and arms back and lift your chin slightly so that your chest opens up.
3. Exhale gradually as you lower your arms and chin and return to the starting position.
4. Repeat five to ten times or until your breathing is deep and regular and your body feels relaxed and energized.

Quick Tension Release

1. Inhale into your abdomen slowly and deeply as you count slowly to 4.
2. Exhale as you again count slowly to 4. As you exhale, concentrate on relaxing your face, neck, shoulders, and chest.
3. Repeat several times. With each exhalation, feel more tension leaving your body.

SOURCES: Stop stress with a deep breath. 1996. *Health,* October, 53. Breathing for health and relaxation. 1995. *Mental Medicine Update* 4(2): 3–6. When you're stressed, catch your breath. 1995. *Mayo Clinic Health Letter,* December, 5.

To practice visualization, imagine yourself floating on a cloud, sitting on a mountaintop, or lying in a meadow. Try to identify all the perceptible qualities of the environment—sight, sound, temperature, smell, and so on. Your body will respond as if your imagery were real. (A complete sample script for imagery is included on the Online Learning Center.)

An alternative is to close your eyes and imagine a deep purple light filling your body. Then change the color into a soothing gold. As the color lightens, so should your distress. Imagery can also enhance performance: Visualize yourself succeeding at a task that worries you.

Deep Breathing　Your breathing pattern is closely tied to your stress level. Deep, slow breathing is associated with relaxation. Rapid, shallow, often irregular breathing occurs during the stress response. With practice, you can learn to slow and quiet your breathing pattern, thereby also quieting your mind and relaxing your body. Try one of the breathing techniques described in the box "Breathing for Relaxation" for on-the-spot tension relief, as well as for long-term stress reduction.

Listening to Music　Music can relax us. It influences pulse, blood pressure, and the electrical activity of muscles. Listening to soothing, lyrical music can lessen depression, anxiety, and stress levels. To experience the stress-management benefits of music yourself, set aside a time to listen. Choose music you enjoy and selections that make you feel relaxed.

Other Techniques

Other stress-management techniques, such as biofeedback, hypnosis and self-hypnosis, and massage, require a partner or professional training or assistance. As with the relaxation techniques presented, all take practice, and it may be several weeks before the benefits are noticeable.

Biofeedback　Biofeedback helps people reduce their response to stress by enabling them to become more aware of their level of physiological arousal. In biofeedback, some measure of stress—perspiration, heart rate, skin temperature, or muscle tension—is mechanically monitored, and feedback is given using sound (a tone or music), light, or a meter or dial. With practice, people begin to exercise conscious control over their physiological stress responses. The point of biofeedback training is to develop the ability to transfer the skill to daily life without the use of electronic equipment. Biofeedback initially requires the help of a therapist, stress counselor, or technician.

Hypnosis and Self-Hypnosis　Hypnosis, a mental focusing technique that can profoundly affect the body, has been a part of healing since ancient times. Today, hypnosis is being used to help correct eating disorders, help people stop smoking, alleviate cancer pain, and hasten recovery from surgery. Many people have misconceptions about hypnosis and may associate it with sleep. But in sleep one's focus of attention dissolves, whereas in hypnosis it intensifies. A pioneer of medical hypnosis describes hypnosis as an "attentive perception and concentration, which leads to controlled imagination." Using that controlled imagination lets participants choose to feel something other than anxiety or stress or pain. Hypnosis works well for the subset of people who respond easily to being hypnotized. That same subset can be trained in self-hypnosis. In a sense, all hypnosis can be seen as self-hypnosis.

Massage   Massage, the manipulation of the body's tissues, is a time-honored part of health and medicine. Massage is known to subdue the stress response, diminish depression, and even increase alertness, though no one knows exactly how. Nowadays many workers are taking a few minutes at their office for a weekly back rub as a way of reducing stress. In a study of English medical workers, those who got 10 weekly rubdowns outscored their colleagues on timed math tests.

Although there are many ways in which massage helps our minds and bodies, the effects can be most dramatic with diseases that have stress as a small or even major component. Massage has been used successfully with premature infants to help them gain weight and with asthmatics to improve lung functioning and lessen their anxiety. It has also been used successfully with men who have HIV to strengthen their immune systems and significantly reduce their anxiety.

GETTING HELP

You can use the principles of behavioral self-management described in Chapter 1 to create a stress-management program tailored specifically to your needs. The starting point of a successful program is to listen to your body. When you learn to recognize the stress response and the emotions and thoughts that accompany it, you'll be in a position to take charge of how you handle stress. Labs 10.1 and 10.2 can guide you in identifying and finding ways to cope with stress-inducing situations. (Appendix A has some specific guidelines for coping after terrorism or mass violence.)

If you feel you need guidance beyond the information in this text, excellent self-help guides can be found in bookstores or the library; helpful Web sites are listed in For Further Exploration at the end of the chapter. Some people also find it helpful to express their feelings in a journal. Grappling with a painful experience in this way provides an emotional release and can help you develop more constructive ways of dealing with similar situations in the future.

Peer Counseling and Support Groups

If you have attempted to fashion a stress-management program to cope with the stressors in your life but still feel overwhelmed, you may want to seek outside help. Peer counseling, often available through the student health center or student affairs office, is usually staffed by volunteer students with special training that emphasizes maintaining confidentiality. Peer counselors can steer those seeking help to appropriate campus and community resources or just offer sympathetic listening.

Support groups are typically organized around a particular issue or problem: All group members might be entering a new school, reentering school after an interruption, struggling with single parenting, experiencing eating disorders, or coping with particular kinds of trauma. Simply voicing concerns that others share can relieve stress.

Professional Help

Psychotherapy, especially a short-term course of sessions, can also be tremendously helpful in dealing with stress-related problems. Not all therapists are right for all people, so it's a good idea to shop around for a compatible psychotherapist with reasonable fees. (See the box "Choosing and Evaluating Mental Health Professionals" on p. 330.)

Is It Stress or Something More Serious?

Most of us have had periods of feeling down when we become pessimistic, anxious, less energetic, and less able to enjoy life. Such feelings and thoughts can be normal responses to the ordinary challenges of life. Symptoms that may indicate a more serious problem that requires professional help include the following:

- Depression, anxiety, or other emotional problems begin to interfere seriously with school or work performance or in getting along with others.
- Suicide is attempted or is seriously considered (see below).
- Symptoms such as hallucinations, delusions, incoherent speech, or loss of memory occur.
- Alcohol or drugs are used to the extent that they impair normal functioning; finding or taking drugs occupies much of the week; or reducing the dosage leads to psychological or physical withdrawal symptoms.

Depression is of particular concern because severe depression is linked to suicide, one of the leading causes of death among college students. In some cases, depression, like severe stress, is a clear-cut reaction to a specific event,

Terms

depression A mood disorder characterized by loss of interest, sadness, hopelessness, loss of appetite, disturbed sleep, and other physical symptoms.

Choosing and Evaluating Mental Health Professionals

College students are usually in a good position to find convenient, affordable mental health care. Larger schools typically have both health services that employ psychiatrists and psychologists and counseling centers staffed by professionals and peer counselors. Resources in the community may include a school of medicine, a hospital, and a variety of professionals who work independently. It's a good idea to get recommendations from physicians, clergy, friends who have been in therapy, or community agencies rather than to pick a name at random.

Financial considerations are also important. Find out how much different services will cost and what your health insurance will cover. If you're not adequately covered by a health plan, don't let that stop you from getting help; investigate low-cost alternatives on campus and in your community. The cost of treatment is linked to how many therapy sessions will be needed, which in turn depends on the type of therapy and the nature of the problem. Psychological therapies focusing on specific problems may require eight or ten sessions at weekly intervals. Therapies aiming for psychological awareness and personality change can last months or years.

Deciding whether a therapist is right for you will require meeting the therapist in person. Before or during your first meeting, find out about the therapist's background and training:

- Does she or he have a degree from an appropriate professional school and a state license to practice?
- Has she or he had experience treating people with problems similar to yours?

- How much will therapy cost?

You have a right to know the answers to these questions and should not hesitate to ask them. After your initial meeting, evaluate your impressions:

- Does the therapist seem like a warm, intelligent person who would be able to help you and is interested in doing so?
- Are you comfortable with the personality, values, and beliefs of the therapist?
- Is he or she willing to talk about the techniques in use? Do these techniques make sense to you?

If you answer yes to these questions, this therapist may be satisfactory for you. If you feel uncomfortable—and you're not in need of emergency care—it's worthwhile to set up one-time consultations with one or two others before you make up your mind. Take the time to find someone who feels right for you.

Later in your treatment, evaluate your progress:

- Are you being helped by the treatment?
- If you are displeased, is it because you aren't making progress or because therapy is raising difficult, painful issues you don't want to deal with?
- Can you express dissatisfaction to your therapist? Such feedback can improve your treatment.

If you're convinced your therapy isn't working or is harmful, thank your therapist for her or his efforts and find another.

---

such as the loss of a loved one or failing in school or work. In other cases, no trigger event is obvious. Symptoms of depression include the following:

- Negative self-concept
- Pervasive feelings of sadness and hopelessness
- Loss of pleasure in usual activities
- Poor appetite and weight loss
- Insomnia or disturbed sleep
- Restlessness or fatigue
- Thoughts of worthlessness and guilt
- Trouble concentrating or making decisions
- Thoughts of death or suicide

Not all of these symptoms are present in everyone who is depressed, but most do experience a loss of interest or pleasure in their usual activities. Warning signs of suicide include expressing the wish to be dead; revealing contemplated suicide methods; increasing social withdrawal and isolation; and a sudden, inexplicable lightening of mood (which can indicate the person has finally decided to commit suicide). If you are severely depressed or know someone who is, expert help from a mental health professional is essential. Most communities and many colleges have hotlines and/or health services and counseling centers that can

provide help. The National Suicide Prevention Lifeline can be reached at 1-800-273-TALK. Treatments for depression and many other psychological disorders are highly effective.

Some stress is unavoidable in life. How you respond to it is what determines whether you become "stressed out" or maintain your serenity. For the stress you can't avoid, develop a range of stress-management techniques and strategies.

Right now you can

- Sit in a comfortable chair and practice deep breathing for 5 to 10 minutes.

- Visualize a relaxing, peaceful place and imagine yourself experiencing it as vividly as possible; you might "feel" a gentle breeze on your skin or "hear" the soothing sound of a waterfall. Stay there as long as you can.

- Stand up and do some stretching exercises, such as gently rolling your head from side to side, stretching your arms out in front of your body and over your head, and slowly bending over and letting your arms hang toward the floor.

- Get out your datebook and schedule what you'll be doing the rest of today and tomorrow. Pencil in a short walk and a conversation with a friend. Plan to go to bed 15 minutes earlier than usual.

Are there any relaxation techniques I can use in response to an immediate stressor? Yes. Try the deep breathing techniques described in the chapter, and try some of the following to see which work best for you:

- Do a full-body stretch while standing or sitting. Stretch your arms out to the sides and then reach them as far as possible over your head. Rotate your body from the waist. Bend over as far as is comfortable for you.

- Do a partial session of progressive muscle relaxation. Tense and then relax some of the muscles in your body. Focus on the muscles that are stiff or tense. Shake out your arms and legs.

- Take a short, brisk walk (3–5 minutes). Breathe deeply.

- Engage in realistic self-talk about the stressor. Mentally rehearse dealing successfully with the stressor. As an alternative, focus your mind on some other activity.

- Briefly reflect on something personally meaningful. In a 2005 study of college students, researchers found that self-reflection on important personal values prior to a stressful task reduced the hormonal response to the stressor.

Can stress cause headaches? Stress is one possible cause of the most common type of headache, the tension headache. About 90% of headaches are tension headaches, characterized by a dull, steady pain, usually on both sides of the head. It may feel as though a band of pressure is tightening around the head, and the pain may extend to the neck and shoulders. Acute tension headaches may last from hours to days, while chronic tension headaches may occur almost every day for months or even years. Stress, poor posture, and immobility are leading causes of tension headaches. There is no cure, but the pain can be relieved with over-the-counter painkillers; many people also try such therapies as massage, relaxation, hot or cold showers, and rest. Stress is also one possible trigger of migraine headaches, which are typically characterized by throbbing pain (often on one side of the head), heightened sensitivity to light and noise, visual disturbances such as flashing lights, nausea, and fatigue.

If your headaches are frequent, keep a journal with details about the events surrounding each one. Are your tension headaches associated with late nights, academic deadlines, or long periods spent sitting at a computer? Are migraines associated with certain foods, stress, fatigue, specific sounds or odors, or (in women) menstruation? If you can identify the stressors or other factors that are consistently associated with your headaches, you can begin to gain more control over the situation. If you suffer persistent tension or migraine headaches, consult your physician.

Visit the Online Learning Center for more answers to common questions about stress.

SUMMARY

- Stress is the collective physiological and emotional response to any stressor. Physiological responses to stressors are the same for everyone.

- The autonomic nervous system and the endocrine system are responsible for the body's physical response to stressors. The sympathetic nervous system mobilizes the body and activates key hormones of the endocrine system, causing the fight-or-flight reaction. The parasympathetic system returns the body to homeostasis.

- Behavioral responses to stress are controlled by the somatic nervous system and fall under a person's conscious control.

- The general adaptation syndrome model and research in psychoneuroimmunology contribute to our understanding of the links between stress and disease. People who have many stressors in their lives or handle stress poorly are at risk for cardiovascular disease, impairment of the immune system, and many other problems.

- Potential sources of stress include major life changes, daily hassles, college- and job-related stressors, and interpersonal and social stressors.

- Positive ways of managing stress include regular exercise, good nutrition, support from other people, clear communication, spiritual wellness, effective time management, cognitive techniques, and other relaxation techniques.

- If a personal program for stress management doesn't work, peer counseling, support groups, and psychotherapy are available.

For Further Exploration

Ⓦ **Fit and Well Online Learning Center**
(www.mhhe.com/fahey)

Use the learning objectives, study guide questions, and glossary flash cards to review key terms and concepts and prepare for exams. You can extend your knowledge of stress and gain experience in using the Internet as a resource by completing the activities and checking out the Web links for the topics in Chapter 10 marked with the World Wide Web icon. For this chapter, Internet activities explore college stressors, social support, and sleep; there are Web links for the Critical Consumer box on mental health professionals and the chapter as a whole.

Daily Fitness and Nutrition Journal

Engaging in regular physical activity and eating a healthy diet are two important strategies for successful stress management. Continue to use your journal to monitor your exercise program and, if needed, to keep records of your diet. You can also use your fitness and nutrition journal as a model for creating a stress-management journal. The Online Learning Center has samples of other types of journals you might use during a behavior change program.

Books

Blonna, R. 2005. *Coping with Stress in a Changing World*. 3rd ed. New York: McGraw-Hill. *A comprehensive guide to stress management that includes separate chapters on college stressors and spirituality.*

Kabat-Zinn, J. 2005. *Coming to Our Senses: Healing Ourselves and the World Through Mindfulness*. New York: Hyperion. *Explores the connections among mindfulness, health, and our physical and spiritual well-being.*

Pennebaker, J. W. 2004. *Writing to Heal: A Guided Journal for Recovering from Trauma and Emotional Upheaval*. Oakland, Calif.: New Harbinger Press. *Provides information about using journaling to cope with stress.*

Sapolsky, R. M. 2004. *Why Zebras Don't Get Ulcers*. 3rd ed. New York: Owl Books. *Describes the links between stress and disease in addition to strategies for stress management.*

Organizations and Web Sites

American Psychiatric Association: Healthy Minds, Healthy Lives. Provides information on mental wellness developed especially for college students.
> http://www.healthyminds.org/collegementalhealth.cfm

American Psychological Association. Provides information on stress management and psychological disorders.
> 800-374-2721; 800-964-2000 (referrals)
> http://www.apa.org; http://helping.apa.org

Harvard Mind-Body Medical Institute. Provides information about stress management and relaxation techniques.
> http://www.mbmi.org

Interactive Budgeting Worksheet. An interactive calculator designed to help students balance income and expenses.
> http://www.ed.gov/offices/OSFAP/DirectLoan/BudgetCalc/budget.html

National Institute of Mental Health (NIMH). Offers information about stress and stress management as well as other aspects of psychological health, including anxiety, depression, and eating disorders.
> 866-615-6464
> http://www.nimh.nih.gov

National Institute for Occupational Safety and Health (NIOSH). Provides information and links on job stress.
> http://www.cdc.gov/niosh/topics/stress

National Sleep Foundation. Provides information about sleep and how to overcome sleep problems such as insomnia and jet lag; brochures are available from the Web site or via fax.
> http://www.sleepfoundation.org

Student Counseling Virtual Pamphlet Collection. Links to online pamphlets from student counseling centers at colleges and universities across the country; topics include stress, sleep, and time management.
> http://www.dr-bob.org/vpc

Selected Bibliography

American Psychological Association. 2005. *Learning to Deal with Stress* (http://helping.apa.org/articles/article.php?id=71; retrieved February 17, 2005).

American Psychological Association. 1999. *Warning Signs: A Violence Prevention Guide for Youth from MTV and APA* (http://helping.apa.org/warningsigns; retrieved October 10, 1999).

Barnes, V. A., et al. 2004. Impact of meditation on resting and ambulatory blood pressure and heart rate in youth. *Psychosomatic Medicine* 66(6): 909–914.

Bernardi, L., C. Porta, and P. Sleight. 2005. Cardiovascular, cerebrovascular and respiratory changes induced by different types of music in musicians and non-musicians: The importance of silence. *Heart*, epub Sept 30.

Bovier, P. A., E. Chamot, and T. V. Perneger. 2004. Perceived stress, internal resources, and social support as determinants of mental health among young adults. *Quality of Life Research* 13(1): 161–170.

Creswell, J. D., et al. 2005. Affirmation of personal values buffers neuroendocrine and psychological stress responses. *Psychological Science* 16(11): 846–851.

Dew, M. S., et al. 2003. Healthy older adults' sleep predicts all-cause mortality at 4 to 19 years of follow-up. *Psychosomatic Medicine* 65(1): 63–73.

Gaab, J., et al. 2003. Randomized controlled evaluation of the effects of cognitive-behavioral stress management on cortisol responses to acute stress in healthy subjects. *Psychoneuroendocrinology* 28(6): 767–779.

Grewen, K. M., et al. 2005. Effects of partner support on resting oxytocin, cortisol, norepinephrine, and blood pressure before and after warm partner contact. *Psychosomatic Medicine* 67(4): 531–538.

Kivlighan, K. T., D. A. Granger, and A. Booth. 2005. Gender differences in testosterone and cortisol response to competition. *Psychoneuroendocrinology* 30(1): 58–71.

Koenig, H. G., L. K. George, and P. Titus. 2004. Religion, spirituality, and health in medically ill hospitalized older patients. *Journal of the American Geriatrics Society* 52(4): 554–562.

Laitinen, J., E. Ek, and U. Sovio. 2002. Stress-related eating and drinking behavior and body mass index and predictors of this behavior. *Preventive Medicine* 34(1): 29–39.

Lane, J. D., et al. 2002. Caffeine affects cardiovascular and neuroendocrine activation at work and home. *Psychosomatic Medicine* 64(4): 595–603.

Meier-Ewert, H. K., et al. 2004. Effect of sleep loss on C-reactive protein, an inflammatory marker of cardiovascular risk. *Journal of the American College of Cardiology* 43:678–683.

Miller, G. E., et al. 2004. Psychological stress and antibody response to influenza vaccination. *Psychosomatic Medicine* 66(2): 215–223.

Pennebaker, J. W. 2004. *Writing to Heal: A Guided Journal for Recovering from Trauma and Emotional Upheaval*. Oakland, Calif.: New Harbinger Press.

Pickering, T. G. 2003. Effects of stress and behavioral interventions in hypertension—Men are from Mars, women are from Venus: Stress, pets, and oxytocin. *Journal of Clinical Hypertension* 5(1): 86–88.

Rosenzweig, S., et al. 2003. Mindfulness-based stress reduction lowers psychological distress in medical students. *Teaching and Learning in Medicine* 15(2): 88–92.

Rothwell, J. D. 2004. *In the Company of Others: An Introduction to Communication*. 2nd ed. New York: McGraw-Hill.

Schwartz, A. R., et al. 2003. Toward a causal model of cardiovascular responses to stress and the development of cardiovascular disease. *Psychosomatic Medicine* 65(1): 22–35.

Segerstrom, S. C., and G. E. Miller. 2004. Psychological stress and the human immune system: A meta-analytic study of 30 years of inquiry. *Psychological Bulletin* 130:601–630.

Steptoe, A., et al. 2004. Loneliness and neuroendocrine, cardiovascular, and inflammatory stress responses in middle-aged men and women. *Psychoneuroendocrinology* 29(5): 593–611.

Steptoe, A., et al. 2003. Influence of socioeconomic status and job control on plasma fibrinogen responses to acute mental stress. *Psychosomatic Medicine* 65(1): 137–144.

Taylor, S. E., et al. 2000. Biobehavioral responses to stress in females. Tend-and-befriend, not fight-or-flight. *Psychological Review* 107(3): 411–429.

LAB 10.1 *Identifying Your Stress Level and Key Stressors*

WW

How Stressed Are You?

To help determine how much stress you experience on a daily basis, answer the following questions.

How many of the symptoms of excess stress in the list below do you experience frequently? _____

Symptoms of Excess Stress

Physical Symptoms
Dry mouth
Excessive perspiration
Frequent illnesses
Gastrointestinal problems
Grinding of teeth
Headaches
High blood pressure
Pounding heart
Stiff neck or aching lower back

Emotional Symptoms
Anxiety or edginess
Depression
Fatigue
Hypervigilance
Impulsiveness
Inability to concentrate
Irritability
Trouble remembering things

Behavioral Symptoms
Crying
Disrupted eating habits
Disrupted sleeping habits
Harsh treatment of others
Problems communicating
Sexual problems
Social isolation
Increased use of tobacco,
    alcohol, or other drugs

Yes	No	
____	____	1. Are you easily startled or irritated?
____	____	2. Are you increasingly forgetful?
____	____	3. Do you have trouble falling or staying asleep?
____	____	4. Do you continually worry about events in your future?
____	____	5. Do you feel as if you are constantly under pressure to produce?
____	____	6. Do you frequently use tobacco, alcohol, or other drugs to help you relax?
____	____	7. Do you often feel as if you have less energy than you need to finish the day?
____	____	8. Do you have recurrent stomachaches or headaches?
____	____	9. Is it difficult for you to find satisfaction in simple life pleasures?
____	____	10. Are you often disappointed in yourself and others?
____	____	11. Are you overly concerned with being liked or accepted by others?
____	____	12. Have you lost interest in intimacy or sex?
____	____	13. Are you concerned that you do not have enough money?

Experiencing some stress-related symptoms or answering "yes" to a few questions is normal. However, if you experience a large number of stress symptoms or you answered "yes" to a majority of the questions, you may be experiencing a high level of stress. Take time out to develop effective stress-management techniques. Many coping strategies that can aid you in dealing with college stressors are described in this chapter. Additionally, your school's counseling center can provide valuable support.

Weekly Stress Log

Now that you are familiar with the signals of stress, complete the weekly stress log to map patterns in your stress levels and identify sources of stress. Enter a score for each hour of each day according to the ratings listed below.

	A.M.							P.M.												*Average*
	6	7	8	9	10	11	12	1	2	3	4	5	6	7	8	9	10	11	12	
Monday																				
Tuesday																				
Wednesday																				
Thursday																				
Friday																				
Saturday																				
Sunday																				
Average																				

Ratings: 1 = No anxiety; general feeling of well-being
2 = Mild anxiety; no interference with activity
3 = Moderate anxiety; specific signal(s) of stress present
4 = High anxiety; interference with activity
5 = Very high anxiety and panic reactions; general inability to engage in activity

To identify daily or weekly patterns in your stress level, average your stress rating for each hour and each day. For example, if your scores for 6:00 A.M. are 3, 3, 4, 3, and 4, with blanks for Saturday and Sunday, your 6:00 A.M. rating would be 17 ÷ 5, or 3.4 (moderate to high anxiety). Then, calculate an average weekly stress score by averaging your daily average stress scores. Your weekly average will give you a sense of your overall level of stress.

Using Your Results

How did you score? How high are your daily and weekly stress scores? Are you at all surprised by your score for average stress level?

Are you satisfied with your stress rating? If not, set a specific goal: _____

What should you do next? Enter the results of this lab in the Preprogram Assessment column in Appendix D. If you've set a goal for improvement, begin by using your log to look for patterns and significant time periods in order to identify key stressors in your life. Below, list any stressors that caused you a significant amount of discomfort this week; these can be people, places, events, or recurring thoughts or worries. For each, enter one strategy that would help you deal more successfully with the stressor; examples of strategies might include practicing an oral presentation in front of a friend or engaging in positive self-talk.

Next, begin to put your strategies into action. In addition, complete Lab 10.2 to help you incorporate lifestyle stress-management techniques into your daily routine.

LAB 10.2 *Stress-Management Techniques*

Part I   Lifestyle Stress Management

For each of the areas listed in the table below, describe your current lifestyle as it relates to stress management. For example, do you have enough social support? How are your exercise and nutrition habits? Is time management a problem for you? For each area, list two ways that you could change your current habits to help you manage your stress. Sample strategies might include calling a friend before a challenging class, taking a short walk before lunch, and buying and using a datebook to track your time.

	Current lifestyle	Lifestyle change #1	Lifestyle change #2
Social support system			
Exercise habits			
Nutrition habits			
Time-management techniques			
Self-talk patterns			
Sleep habits			

Part II   Relaxation Techniques

Choose two relaxation techniques described in this chapter (progressive relaxation, visualization, deep breathing, meditation, yoga, taijiquan, massage, listening to music). If a taped recording is available for progressive relaxation or visualization, these techniques can be performed by your entire class as a group. Sample scripts for progressive relaxation and imagery can be found on the Online Learning Center.

List the techniques you tried.

1. _____

2. _____

How did you feel before you tried these techniques?

_____

_____

_____

What did you think or how did you feel during each of the techniques you tried?

1. _____

_____

_____

2. _____

_____

_____

How did you feel after you tried these techniques?

_____

_____

_____

LAB 10.3 *Developing Spiritual Wellness*

W|W

To develop spiritual wellness, it is important to take time out to think about what gives meaning and purpose to your life and what actions you can take to support the spiritual dimension of your life.

Look Inward

This week, spend some quiet time alone with your thoughts and feelings. Slow the pace of your day, remove your watch, turn your phone or pager off, and focus on your immediate experience. Try one of the following activities or develop another that is meaningful to you and that contributes to your sense of spiritual well-being.

- *Spend time in nature:* Experience continuity with the natural world by spending solitary time in a natural setting. Watch the sky (day or night), a sunrise, or a sunset; listen to waves on a shore or wind in the trees; feel the breeze on your face or raindrops on your skin; smell the grass, brush, trees, or flowers. Open all your senses to the beauty of nature.
- *Experience art, architecture, or music:* Spend time with a work of art or architecture or a piece of music. Choose one that will awaken your senses, engage your emotions, and challenge your understanding. Take a break and then repeat the experience to see how your responses change the second time.
- *Express your creativity:* Set aside time for a favorite activity, one that allows you to express your creative side. Sing, draw, paint, play a musical instrument, sculpt, build, dance, cook, garden—choose an activity in which you will be so engaged that you will lose track of time. Strive for feelings of joy and exhilaration.
- *Engage in a personal spiritual practice:* Pray, meditate, do yoga, chant. Choose a spiritual practice that is familiar to you or try one that is new. Tune out the outside world and turn your attention inward, focusing on the experience.

In the space below, describe the personal spiritual activity you tried and how it made you feel—both during the activity and after.

Reach Out

Spiritual wellness can be a bond among people and can promote values such as altruism, forgiveness, and compassion. Try one of the following spiritual activities that involve reaching out to others.

- *Share writings that inspire you:* Find two writings that inspire, guide, and comfort you—passages from sacred works, poems, quotations from literature, songs. Share them with someone else by reading them aloud and explaining what they mean to you.

- *Practice kindness:* Spend a day practicing small acts of personal kindness for people you know as well as for strangers. Compliment a friend, send a card, let someone go ahead of you in line, pick up litter, do someone else's chores, help someone with packages, say please and thank you, smile.

- *Perform community service:* Foster a sense of community by becoming a volunteer. Find a local nonprofit group and offer your time and talent. Mentor a youth, work at a food bank, support a literacy project, help build low-cost housing, visit seniors in a nursing home. You can also work on national or international issues by writing letters to your elected representatives and other officials.

In the space below, describe the spiritual activity you performed and how it made you feel—during the activity and after. Include details about the writings you chose or the acts of kindness or community service you performed.

Keep a Journal

One strategy for continuing on the path toward spiritual wellness is to keep a journal. Use a journal to record your thoughts, feelings, and experiences; to jot down quotes that engage you; to sketch pictures and write poetry about what is meaningful to you. Begin your spirituality journal today.

Source: Insel, P. M., and W. T. Roth. 2006. Wellness Worksheet 22. Copyright © 2006 The McGraw-Hill Companies, Inc. Reprinted with permission of The McGraw-Hill Companies, Inc.

After reading this chapter, you should be able to

- Describe the controllable and uncontrollable risk factors associated with cardiovascular disease
- Discuss the major forms of cardiovascular disease and how they develop
- List the steps you can take now to lower your personal risk of developing cardiovascular disease

11

Cardiovascular Health

Test Your Knowledge

1. **Women are about as likely to die of cardiovascular disease as they are to die of breast cancer.**
   True or false?

2. **How much earlier, on average, do sedentary people develop heart disease compared with people who exercise?**
   a. 6 months
   b. 2 years
   c. 6 years

3. **Which of the following foods would be a good choice for promoting heart health?**
   a. tofu
   b. salmon
   c. bananas

ANSWERS

1. FALSE. Cardiovascular disease kills far more. Among American women, about 1 in 2 deaths is due to CVD and about 1 in 30 is due to breast cancer. In addition, more women than men die each year from cardiovascular disease.

2. C. Both endurance exercise and strength training significantly improve cardiovascular health.

3. ALL THREE. Soy protein (tofu), foods with omega-3 fatty acids (salmon), and foods high in potassium and low in sodium (bananas) all improve cardiovascular health.

ViW *Fit and Well* **Online Learning Center**   www.mhhe.com/fahey

Visit the *Fit and Well* Online Learning Center for study aids, online labs, additional information about cardiovascular health, links, Internet activities that explore the prevention of cardiovascular disease, and much more.

Cardiovascular disease (CVD) is the leading cause of death in the United States; nearly half of all Americans alive today will die from CVD. If all major forms of CVD were eliminated, U.S. life expectancy would rise by almost 7 years. As previously discussed, much of the incidence of CVD is attributable to the American way of life. Too many Americans are overweight and sedentary, smoke cigarettes, manage stress ineffectively, have uncontrolled high blood pressure or high cholesterol levels, and don't know the signs of CVD. Not all risk factors for CVD are controllable—some people have an inherited tendency toward high cholesterol levels, for example—but many are within the control of the individual.

This chapter explains the major forms of CVD, including hypertension, atherosclerosis, and stroke. It also considers the factors that put people at risk for CVD. Most important, it explains the steps individuals can take to protect their hearts and promote cardiovascular health throughout their lives.

RISK FACTORS FOR CARDIOVASCULAR DISEASE

Researchers have identified a variety of factors associated with an increased risk of developing CVD. They are grouped into two categories: major risk factors and contributing risk factors. Some major risk factors, such as diet, exercise habits, and use of tobacco, are linked to controllable aspects of lifestyle and can therefore be changed. Others, such as age, sex, and heredity, are beyond an individual's control. (You can evaluate your personal CVD risk factors in Part I of Lab 11.1.)

Major Risk Factors That Can Be Changed

The American Heart Association (AHA) has identified six major risk factors for CVD that can be changed. These are tobacco use, high blood pressure, unhealthy blood cholesterol levels, physical inactivity, obesity, and diabetes. Most Americans, including young adults, have major risk factors for CVD. For example, among people age 18–34, about 1 in 10 have high cholesterol levels, 1 in 10 have hypertension, 1 in 4 smoke, 1 in 4 are completely sedentary, and half are overweight.

Tobacco Use   About one in five deaths from CVD can be attributed to smoking. People who smoke a pack of cigarettes a day have twice the risk of heart attack that nonsmokers have; smoking two or more packs a day triples the risk. And when smokers do have heart attacks, they are two to four times more likely than nonsmokers to die from them. Women who smoke and use oral contraceptives are up to 32 times more likely to have a heart attack and up to 20 times more likely to have a stroke than women who don't smoke and take the pill.

Smoking harms the cardiovascular system in several ways. It damages the linings of arteries and contributes to unhealthy blood fat levels by reducing levels of **high-density lipoproteins (HDL)**, "good" cholesterol, and by raising levels of triglycerides and **low-density lipoproteins (LDL)**, "bad" cholesterol. The psychoactive drug in tobacco, nicotine, is a central nervous system stimulant, causing increased blood pressure and heart rate. The carbon monoxide in cigarette smoke displaces oxygen in the blood, reducing the amount of oxygen available to the heart and other parts of the body. Smoking causes the **platelets** in blood to become sticky and cluster, promoting clotting. Smoking also permanently accelerates the rate at which fatty deposits are laid down in arteries. All these effects increase a person's risk of heart attack and other forms of CVD.

You don't have to smoke to be affected. **Environmental tobacco smoke (ETS)** in high concentrations has been linked to the development of cardiovascular disease. ETS and high cholesterol levels act together to damage the cells that line artery walls. Researchers estimate that as many as 62,000 nonsmokers die from heart attacks each year as a result of exposure to ETS.

High Blood Pressure   High blood pressure, or **hypertension**, is a risk factor for many forms of cardiovascular disease, including heart attacks and strokes, and is itself considered a form of CVD. Blood pressure, the force exerted by the blood on the vessel walls, is created by the pumping action of the heart. When the heart contracts (systole), blood pressure increases. When the heart relaxes (diastole), pressure decreases. Short periods of high blood pressure—such as in response to excitement or exertion—are normal, but blood pressure that is continually at an abnormally high level constitutes hypertension.

Blood pressure is measured with a stethoscope and an instrument called a sphygmomanometer. It is expressed as two numbers—for example, 120 over 80—and measured in millimeters of mercury. The first and larger number is the systolic blood pressure; the second is the diastolic blood pressure. A normal blood pressure reading for a healthy adult is 115 systolic over 75 diastolic; CVD risk increases when blood pressure rises above this level. High blood pressure in adults is defined as equal to or greater than 140 over 90 (Table 11.1).

High blood pressure results from either an increased output of blood by the heart or, most often, increased resistance to blood flow in the arteries. The latter condition can be caused by **atherosclerosis**, discussed later in the chapter, or by constriction of smooth muscle surrounding the arteries. When a person has high blood pressure, the heart must work harder than normal to force blood through the narrowed arteries, thereby straining both the heart and arteries. High blood pressure is often called a

Table 11.1 — Blood Pressure Classification for Healthy Adults

Category*	Systolic (mm Hg)		Diastolic (mm Hg)
Normal**	below 120	and	below 80
Prehypertension	120–139	or	80–89
Hypertension†			
Stage 1	140–159	or	90–99
Stage 2	160 and above	or	100 and above

*When systolic and diastolic pressure fall into different categories, the higher category should be used to classify blood pressure status.

**The risk of death from heart attack and stroke begins to rise when blood pressure is above 115/75.

†Based on the average of two or more readings taken at different physician visits. In persons over 50, systolic blood pressure greater than 140 is a much more significant CVD risk factor than diastolic blood pressure.

SOURCE: *The Seventh Report of the Joint National Committee on Prevention, Detection, Evaluation, and Treatment of High Blood Pressure.* 2003. Bethesda, Md.: National Heart, Lung, and Blood Institute. National Institutes of Health (NIH Publication No. 03-5233).

silent killer, because it usually has no symptoms. A person may have high blood pressure for years without realizing it. But, during that time, it damages vital organs and increases the risk of heart attack, congestive heart failure, stroke, kidney failure, and blindness.

Hypertension is common, occurring in nearly one in three adults. Its incidence rises dramatically with increasing age; however, it can occur among children and young adults. Overall, about 30% of adults have hypertension, 30% have prehypertension, and 40% have normal blood pressure. In most cases, hypertension cannot be cured, but it can be controlled. The key to avoiding complications is to have your blood pressure tested at least once every 2 years (more often if you have other CVD risk factors) and to follow your physician's advice about lifestyle changes and medication.

Lifestyle changes are recommended for everyone with prehypertension and hypertension (see Table 11.1). These lifestyle changes include weight reduction, regular physical activity, a healthy diet, and moderation of alcohol consumption. The DASH diet, described in Chapter 8, is recommended; it emphasizes fruits, vegetables, and whole grains—foods that are rich in potassium and fiber, both of which may reduce blood pressure. Sodium restriction is also helpful. Many people are salt-sensitive, meaning that their blood pressure will decrease significantly when salt intake is restricted. The 2005 Dietary Guidelines for Americans recommend restricting consumption to less than 2300 mg of sodium (about 1 teaspoon of salt) per day. People with hypertension, African Americans, and middle-aged and older adults should aim to consume no more than 1500 mg of sodium per day.

Adequate potassium intake is also important. For people whose blood pressure isn't adequately controlled with lifestyle changes, medication is prescribed.

Recent research has shed new light on the importance of lowering blood pressure to improve cardiovascular health. Death rates from CVD begin to rise when blood pressure is above 115 over 75, well below the traditional 140 over 90 cutoff for hypertension. People with blood pressures in the prehypertension range are at increased risk of heart attack and stroke as well as at significant risk of developing full-blown hypertension; preventive lifestyle measures are strongly recommended for people with prehypertension. The bottom line is that lowering your blood pressure through healthy lifestyle changes is beneficial, even if your current blood pressure is already below 140 over 90.

Unhealthy Cholesterol Levels Cholesterol is a fatty, waxlike substance that circulates through the bloodstream and is an important component of cell membranes, sex hormones, vitamin D, the fluid that coats the lungs, and the protective sheaths around nerves. Adequate cholesterol is essential for the proper functioning of the body. However, excess cholesterol can clog arteries and increase the risk of CVD (Figure 11.1, p. 342). Our bodies obtain cholesterol in two ways: from the liver, which manufactures it, and from the foods we eat. Cholesterol levels vary depending on diet, age, sex, heredity, and other factors.

GOOD VERSUS BAD CHOLESTEROL Cholesterol is carried in protein-lipid packages called **lipoproteins.** Lipoproteins can be thought of as shuttles that transport cholesterol to

Terms

cardiovascular disease (CVD) Disease of the heart and blood vessels.

high-density lipoproteins (HDL) Blood fats that help transport cholesterol out of the arteries, thereby protecting against heart disease; "good" cholesterol.

low-density lipoproteins (LDL) Blood fats that transport cholesterol to organs and tissues; excess amounts result in the accumulation of deposits on artery walls; "bad" cholesterol.

platelets Microscopic disk-shaped cell fragments in the blood that disintegrate on contact with foreign objects and release chemicals necessary for the formation of blood clots.

environmental tobacco smoke (ETS) Smoke that enters the atmosphere from the burning end of a cigarette, cigar, or pipe, as well as smoke that is exhaled by smokers; also called *second-hand smoke.*

hypertension Sustained abnormally high blood pressure.

atherosclerosis Cardiovascular disease in which the inner layers of artery walls are made thick and irregular by deposits of a fatty substance; the internal channels of the arteries thus become narrowed, and blood supply is reduced.

lipoproteins Blood fats formed in the liver that carry cholesterol throughout the body.

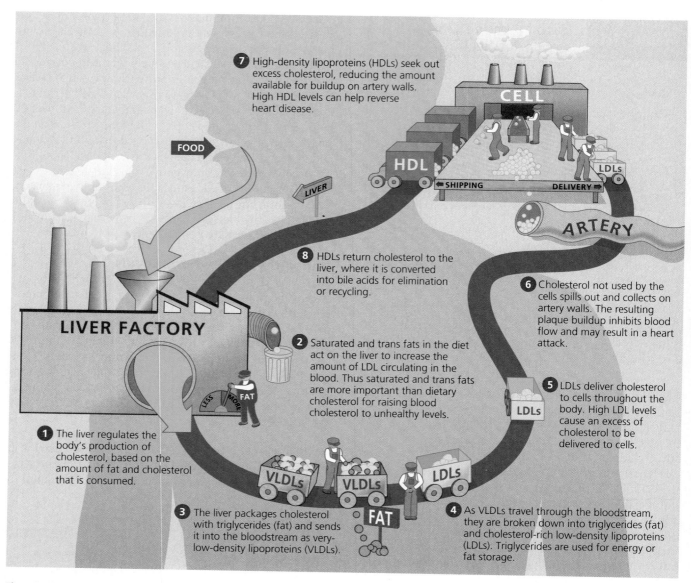

Figure 11.1 Travels with cholesterol.

The following labels appear within the figure:

7. High-density lipoproteins (HDLs) seek out excess cholesterol, reducing the amount available for buildup on artery walls. High HDL levels can help reverse heart disease.

8. HDLs return cholesterol to the liver, where it is converted into bile acids for elimination or recycling.

6. Cholesterol not used by the cells spills out and collects on artery walls. The resulting plaque buildup inhibits blood flow and may result in a heart attack.

2. Saturated and trans fats in the diet act on the liver to increase the amount of LDL circulating in the blood. Thus saturated and trans fats are more important than dietary cholesterol for raising blood cholesterol to unhealthy levels.

5. LDLs deliver cholesterol to cells throughout the body. High LDL levels cause an excess of cholesterol to be delivered to cells.

1. The liver regulates the body's production of cholesterol, based on the amount of fat and cholesterol that is consumed.

3. The liver packages cholesterol with triglycerides (fat) and sends it into the bloodstream as very-low-density lipoproteins (VLDLs).

4. As VLDLs travel through the bloodstream, they are broken down into triglycerides (fat) and cholesterol-rich low-density lipoproteins (LDLs). Triglycerides are used for energy or fat storage.

and from the liver through the circulatory system. Low-density lipoproteins (LDLs) shuttle cholesterol from the liver to the organs and tissues that require it. LDL is known as "bad" cholesterol because if there is more than the body can use, the excess is deposited in the blood vessels. LDL that accumulates and becomes trapped in artery walls may be oxidized by free radicals, speeding inflammation and damage to artery walls and increasing the likelihood that an artery will become blocked, causing a heart attack or stroke. High-density lipoproteins (HDLs), or "good" cholesterol, shuttle unused cholesterol back to the liver for recycling.

RECOMMENDED BLOOD CHOLESTEROL LEVELS The risk for CVD increases with increasing blood cholesterol levels, especially LDL. The National Cholesterol Education Program (NCEP) recommends testing at least once every 5 years for all adults, beginning at age 20. The recommended test is a lipoprotein profile that measures total cholesterol, LDL cholesterol, HDL cholesterol, and triglycerides (another blood fat). General cholesterol and triglyceride guidelines are given in Table 11.2. In general, high LDL levels and low HDL levels are associated with a high risk for CVD; low levels of LDL and high levels of HDL are associated with lower risk. HDL is important because a high HDL level seems to offer protection from CVD even in cases where total cholesterol is high, especially for women.

As shown in Table 11.2, LDL levels below 100 mg/dl (milligrams per deciliter) and total cholesterol levels below 200 mg/dl are desirable. An estimated 100 million American adults—over half the population—have total cholesterol levels of 200 mg/dl or higher. The CVD risk associated with elevated cholesterol levels also depends on other factors. For example, an above optimal level of

Table 11.2 Cholesterol Guidelines

LDL cholesterol (mg/dl)

Less than 100	Optimal
100–129	Near optimal/above optimal
130–159	Borderline high
160–189	High
190 or more	Very high

Total cholesterol (mg/dl)

Less than 200	Desirable
200–239	Borderline high
240 or more	High

HDL cholesterol (mg/dl)

Less than 40	Low (undesirable)
60 or more	High (desirable)

Triglycerides (mg/dl)

Less than 150	Normal
150–199	Borderline high
200–499	High
500 or more	Very high

SOURCE: Expert Panel on Detection, Evaluation, and Treatment of High Blood Cholesterol in Adults. 2001. Executive Summary of the Third Report of the National Cholesterol Education Program (NCEP) Expert Panel on Detection, Evaluation, and Treatment of High Blood Cholesterol in Adults (Adult Treatment Panel III). *Journal of the American Medical Association* 285(19).

Stress and social isolation can increase risk of cardiovascular disease. A strong social support network improves both heart health and overall wellness.

LDL would be of more concern for an individual who also smoked and had high blood pressure than for an individual without these additional CVD risk factors.

IMPROVING CHOLESTEROL LEVELS Your primary goal should be to reduce LDL to healthy levels. Important dietary changes for reducing LDL levels include choosing unsaturated fats instead of saturated and trans fats and increasing fiber intake. Decreasing your intake of saturated and trans fats is particularly important because they promote the production and excretion of cholesterol by the liver. Exercising regularly and eating more fruits, vegetables, and whole grains also help. You can raise your HDL levels by exercising regularly, losing weight if you are overweight, quitting smoking, and altering the amount and type of fat you consume. These and other lifestyle changes promoting heart health are discussed in greater detail later in this chapter.

Physical Inactivity An estimated 40–60 million Americans are so sedentary that they are at high risk for developing CVD. Exercise is thought to be the closest thing we have to a magic bullet against heart disease. It lowers CVD risk by helping decrease blood pressure and resting heart rate, increase HDL levels, maintain desirable weight,

improve the condition of the blood vessels, and prevent or control diabetes. One recent study found that women who accumulated at least 3 hours of brisk walking each week cut their risk of heart attack and stroke by more than half. (See Chapter 3 for more information on the physical and psychological effects of exercise.)

Obesity The risk of death from CVD is two to three times higher in obese people (BMI ≥ 30) than it is in lean people (BMI 18.5–24.9), and for every 5-unit increment of BMI, a person's risk of death from coronary heart disease increases by 30%. Excess weight increases the strain on the heart by contributing to high blood pressure and high cholesterol. It can also lead to diabetes, another CVD risk factor (see below). As discussed in Chapter 6, distribution of body fat is also significant: Fat that collects in the torso is more dangerous than fat that collects around the hips. Obesity in general, and abdominal obesity in particular, is significantly associated with narrowing of the coronary arteries, even in young adults in their twenties. A sensible diet and regular exercise are the best ways to achieve and maintain a healthy body weight. For someone who is overweight, even modest weight reduction can reduce CVD risk by lowering blood pressure, improving cholesterol levels, and reducing diabetes risk.

Diabetes As described in Chapter 6, diabetes is a disorder in which the metabolism of glucose is disrupted, causing a buildup of glucose in the bloodstream. People with diabetes are at increased risk for CVD, partly because elevated blood glucose levels can damage the lining of arteries, making them more vulnerable to atherosclerosis;

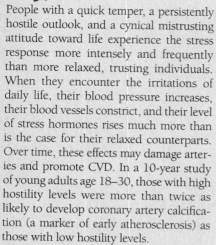
People with a quick temper, a persistently hostile outlook, and a cynical mistrusting attitude toward life experience the stress response more intensely and frequently than more relaxed, trusting individuals. When they encounter the irritations of daily life, their blood pressure increases, their blood vessels constrict, and their level of stress hormones rises much more than is the case for their relaxed counterparts. Over time, these effects may damage arteries and promote CVD. In a 10-year study of young adults age 18–30, those with high hostility levels were more than twice as likely to develop coronary artery calcification (a marker of early atherosclerosis) as those with low hostility levels.

Part II of Lab 11.1 includes a hostility self-assessment. If your results indicate a high level of hostility, begin by keeping a hostility journal to monitor your angry responses and identify your triggers. Familiarize yourself with the patterns of thinking that lead to angry or hostile feelings, and then try to head them off before they develop into full-blown anger. Ask yourself the following:

1. Is this really important enough to get angry about?

2. Am I really justified in getting angry?

3. Is getting angry going to make a real and positive difference in the situation?

If you answer yes to all three questions, then calm but assertive communication may be an appropriate response. If your anger isn't reasonable, try distracting yourself or removing yourself from the situation. Exercise, humor, social support, and other stress-management techniques can also help (see Chapter 10). Your heart—and the people around you—will benefit from your calmer, more positive outlook.

SOURCES: Olson, M. B., et al. 2005. Hostility scores are associated with increased risk of cardiovascular events in women undergoing coronary angiography. *Psychosomatic Medicine* 67(4): 546–552. Ibarren, C., et al. 2000. Association of hostility with coronary artery calcification in young adults. *Journal of the American Medical Association* 283(19): 2546–2551. Take it to heart: "Chill out." 2000, *Mind/Body Health Newsletter* 9(2): 1–2. Anger and heart disease risk. 2002. *Harvard Heart Letter*, July.

---

diabetics also often have other risk factors, including hypertension, obesity, unhealthy cholesterol and triglyceride levels, and platelet and blood coagulation abnormalities. Even people whose diabetes is under control face an increased risk of CVD; therefore, careful control of other risk factors is critical for people with diabetes. People with pre-diabetes also face a significantly increased risk of CVD.

Contributing Risk Factors That Can Be Changed

Various other factors that can be changed have been identified as contributing to CVD risk, including triglyceride levels, psychological and social factors, and alcohol and drug use.

High Triglyceride Levels   Like cholesterol, triglycerides are blood fats that are obtained from food and manufactured by the body. High triglyceride levels are a reliable predictor of heart disease, especially if associated with other risk factors, such as low HDL levels, obesity, and diabetes. Factors contributing to elevated triglyceride levels include excess body fat, physical inactivity, cigarette smoking, type 2 diabetes, excess alcohol intake, very high carbohydrate diets, and certain diseases and medications. A full lipid profile should include testing and evaluation of triglyceride levels (see Table 11.2). For people with borderline high triglyceride levels, increased physical activity, reduced intake of added sugars and starches, and weight reduction can help bring levels down into the healthy range; for people with high triglycerides, drug therapy may be needed. Being moderate in the use of alcohol and quitting smoking are also helpful.

Psychological and Social Factors   Many of the psychological and social factors that influence other areas of wellness are also important risk factors for CVD.

- *Stress.* Excessive stress can strain the heart and blood vessels over time and contribute to CVD. A full-blown stress response causes blood vessels to constrict and blood pressure to rise. Blood platelets become more likely to cluster, possibly enhancing the formation of artery-clogging clots. Stress can trigger abnormal heart rhythms, with potentially fatal consequences. People sometimes also adopt unhealthy habits such as smoking or overeating as a means of dealing with severe stress.

- *Chronic hostility and anger.* Certain traits in the hard-driving Type A personality—hostility, cynicism, and anger—are associated with increased risk of heart disease (see the box "Anger, Hostility, and Heart Disease").

- *Suppressing psychological distress.* Consistently suppressing anger and other negative emotions may also be hazardous to a healthy heart. People who hide psychological distress tend to have a higher rate of heart disease than people who experience similar distress but share it with others. People with so-called Type D personalities tend to be pessimistic, negative, and unhappy and to suppress these feelings.

- *Depression and anxiety.* Both mild and severe depression are linked to an increased risk of CVD. Researchers have also found a strong association between anxiety disorders and an increased risk of death from heart disease, particularly sudden death from heart attack.

- *Social isolation.* People with little social support are at higher risk of dying from CVD than people with close ties to others. Studies suggest that religious commitment has a positive effect on heart health, perhaps because of the strong community provided by church membership. A strong social support network is a major antidote to stress. Friends and family members can also promote and support a healthy lifestyle.

- *Low socioeconomic status.* Low socioeconomic status and low educational attainment also increase risk for CVD, probably because of a variety of factors, including lifestyle, response to stress, and access to health care.

Alcohol and Drugs Drinking too much alcohol raises blood pressure and can increase the risk of stroke and heart failure. Stimulant drugs, particularly cocaine, can also cause serious cardiac problems, including heart attack, stroke, and sudden cardiac death. Injection drug use can cause infection of the heart and stroke.

MOTIVATION FOR CHANGE! Psychological distress impacts quality of life, raises the risk of some chronic diseases, and is a key factor in lapses during a behavior change program. When people are stressed and upset, they are more likely to eat unhealthy foods, restart a smoking habit, drink too much alcohol, or engage in other unhealthy coping strategies. No matter what your target behavior, plan ahead for how you'll handle difficult times while sticking with your behavior change program. Make a list of positive strategies you can use to reduce stress and cope with difficult emotions—for example, a short walk, a phone call to a friend, a massage, or a time-out with a favorite piece of music. Keep your list handy as a "prescription" for help when you feel stressed or overwhelmed.

Major Risk Factors That Can't Be Changed

A number of major risk factors for CVD cannot be changed: heredity, aging, being male, and ethnicity.

Family History (Heredity) CVD is a genetically complex disease because there is no one gene that causes it. Instead, multiple genes contribute to the development of CVD and its risk factors. Having an unfavorable set of genes increases your risk, but risk is modifiable by lifestyle factors such as whether you smoke, exercise, or eat a healthy diet. People who inherit a tendency for CVD are not destined to develop it, but they may have to work harder than other people to prevent it.

Aging The risk of heart attack increases dramatically after age 65. About 70% of all heart attack victims are age 65 or over, and more than 4 out of 5 who suffer fatal heart attacks are over 65. For people over 55, the incidence of stroke more than doubles in each successive decade. However, many people in their thirties and forties, especially men, have heart attacks.

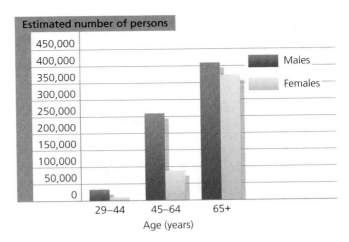

VITAL STATISTICS

Figure 11.2   Annual incidence of heart attack. Among heart attack victims under age 65, men significantly outnumber women; after age 65, women start to catch up.   SOURCE: American Heart Association. 2005. *2005 Heart and Stroke Facts Statistical Update.* Dallas, Tex.: American Heart Association.

Being Male Although CVD is the leading killer of both men and women in the United States, men face a greater risk of heart attack than women, especially earlier in life (Figure 11.2). Until age 55, men also have a greater risk of hypertension than women. The incidence of stroke is higher for males than females until age 65. Estrogen production, highest during the childbearing years, may offer premenopausal women some protection against CVD (see the box "Gender, Ethnicity, and CVD" on p. 346).

Ethnicity Death rates from heart disease vary among ethnic groups in the United States, with African Americans having much higher rates of hypertension, heart disease, and stroke than other groups. Puerto Rican Americans, Cuban Americans, and Mexican Americans are also more likely to suffer from high blood pressure and angina (a warning sign of heart disease) than non-Hispanic white Americans. Asian Americans historically have had far lower rates of CVD than white Americans. However, cholesterol levels among Asian Americans appear to be rising, presumably because of the adoption of a high-fat American diet.

Possible Risk Factors Currently Being Studied

In recent years, a number of other possible risk factors for cardiovascular disease have been identified.

High levels of a substance called C-reactive protein (CRP), which is released into the bloodstream during the inflammatory response, may indicate a substantially elevated risk of heart attack and stroke. CRP may be released into the bloodstream when an artery is injured by smoking, cholesterol, infectious agents, or other factors. In 2003, the CDC and the American Heart Association

CVD is the leading cause of death for all Americans, but significant differences exist between men and women and between white Americans and African Americans in the incidence, diagnosis, and treatment of this deadly disease.

CVD has been thought of as a "man's disease," but it actually kills more women than men. Polls indicate that women vastly underestimate their risk of dying of a heart attack and overestimate their risk of dying of breast cancer. In reality, nearly 1 in 2 women dies of CVD, while 1 in 30 dies of breast cancer. For women, CVD typically does not develop until after age 50.

The hormone estrogen, produced naturally by a woman's ovaries until menopause, improves blood lipid concentrations and other CVD risk factors. For the past several decades, many U.S. physicians encouraged menopausal women to take hormone replacement therapy (HRT) to relieve menopause symptoms and presumably to reduce their risk of CVD. However, some large studies have found that HRT may actually *increase* a woman's risk for heart disease and other health problems, and the U.S. Preventive Services Task Force currently recommends against the use of HRT for the prevention of chronic diseases such as CVD.

When women do have heart attacks, they are more likely than men to die within a year. One reason is that since they develop heart disease at older ages, they are more likely to have other health problems that complicate treatment. Women also have smaller hearts and arteries than men, possibly making diagnosis and surgery more difficult. Another reason is that medical personnel appear to evaluate and treat women less aggressively than men. Women are more likely than men to have a heart attack *without* chest pain; in one study of female heart attack victims, many women reported severe fatigue and disturbed sleep in the month leading up to the attack and fatigue, weakness, and shortness of breath during the attack. A woman who experiences these symptoms should be persistent in seeking accurate diagnosis and appropriate treatment.

Careful diagnosis of cardiac symptoms is also key in avoiding unnecessary invasive procedures in cases of stress cardiomyopathy ("broken heart syndrome"), which occurs much more commonly in women than in men. In this condition, exposure to hormones and neurotransmitters associated with a severe stress response stuns the heart and produces heart-attack-like symptoms without any corresponding damage to the heart muscle. Typically, the condition can be reversed quickly.

In addition to such positive lifestyle changes as quitting smoking and engaging in physical activity, women should be aware of their CVD risk factors—including blood pressure and cholesterol levels—and consult with a physician to assess their risk and determine the best way to meet personal prevention goals. Visit the "Go Red for Women" campaign on the American Heart Association's Web site (http://www.americanheart.org) for further information.

African Americans also have a different experience of CVD than do white men. Blacks are at substantially higher risk for death from CVD. The rate of hypertension among African Americans is among the highest of any group in the world. Blacks tend to develop hypertension at an earlier age than whites, and their average blood pressures are much higher. They also have a higher risk of stroke, have strokes at younger ages, and have more significant stroke-related disabilities. Some experts recommend that blacks be treated with antihypertensive drugs at an earlier stage—when blood pressure reaches 130/80 rather than the typical 140/90 cutoff for hypertension.

Possible genetic and biological factors in this CVD profile include heightened sensitivities to salt and a physiologically different response to stress, which can lead to high blood pressure and a greater tendency to develop diabetes, another CVD risk factor. Sickle-cell disease, a genetic disorder that occurs mainly in blacks, can contribute to CVD. Low income is another factor and is associated with reduced access to adequate health care, insurance, and information about prevention. Discrimination may also play a role, both by increasing stress and by affecting treatment by physicians and hospitals.

Although these factors are important, some evidence favors lifestyle explanations for the higher CVD rate among African Americans. For example, black New Yorkers born in the South have a much higher CVD risk than those born in the Northeast. (Researchers speculate that some lifestyle risk factors for CVD, including smoking and a high-fat diet, may be more common in the South.) People with low incomes, who are disproportionately black, tend to smoke more, use more salt, and exercise less than those with higher incomes. In addition, more than half of black women and one-third of black men are overweight.

The general preventive strategies recommended for all Americans may be particularly critical for African Americans. In addition, researchers have identified several dietary factors that may be of special importance for blacks. Studies have found that diets high in potassium and calcium improve blood pressure in African Americans. Fruits, vegetables, grains, and nuts are rich in potassium; dairy products are high in calcium.

jointly recommended testing of CRP levels for people at intermediate risk for CVD because people in this risk category who are found to also have high CRP levels may benefit from additional CVD testing or treatment. (This guideline assumes that people at high risk for CVD are already receiving treatment.) Lifestyle changes and certain drugs can reduce CRP levels. Statin drugs, widely prescribed to lower cholesterol, also decrease inflammation; this may be one reason why statin drugs seem to lower CVD risk even in people with normal blood lipid levels.

Elevated blood levels of homocysteine, an amino acid that may damage the lining of blood vessels, are associated with an increased risk of CVD. Men generally have higher homocysteine levels than women, as do individuals with diets low in folic acid, vitamin B-12, and vitamin B-6. Most people can lower homocysteine levels easily by adopting a healthy diet rich in fruits,

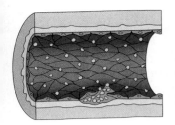
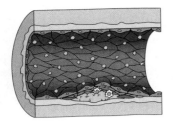
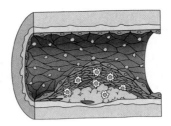

Plaque buildup begins when endothelial cells lining the arteries are damaged by smoking, high blood pressure, oxidized LDL, and other causes; excess cholesterol particles collect beneath these cells.

In response to the damage, platelets and other types of cells collect at the site; a fibrous cap forms, isolating the plaque within the artery wall. An early-stage plaque is called a fatty streak.

Chemicals released by cells in and around the plaque cause further inflammation and buildup; an advanced plaque contains LDL, white blood cells, connective tissue, smooth muscle cells, platelets, and other compounds.

The narrowed artery is vulnerable to blockage by clots. The risk of blockage and heart attack rises if the fibrous cap cracks (probably due to destructive enzymes released by white blood cells within the plaque).

Figure 11.3   Stages of plaque development.

vegetables, and grains and by taking supplements if needed.

High levels of a specific type of LDL called lipoprotein(a), or Lp(a), have been identified as a possible risk factor for coronary heart disease (CHD), especially when associated with high LDL or low HDL levels. Lp(a) levels have a strong genetic component and are difficult to treat. LDL particles differ in size and density, and people with a high proportion of small, dense LDL particles—a condition called LDL pattern B—also appear to be at greater risk for CVD. Exercise, a low-fat diet, and certain lipid-lowering drugs may help lower CVD risk in people with LDL pattern B.

Several infectious agents, including *Chlamydia pneumoniae, cytomegalovirus,* and *Helicobacter pylori,* have also been identified as possible risk factors. Infections may damage arteries and lead to chronic inflammation. Another marker for higher risk is fibrinogen, a protein involved in blood clotting.

Certain CVD risk factors are often found in a cluster. This special constellation of health problems is called metabolic syndrome, syndrome X, or insulin resistance syndrome. A person is diagnosed with metabolic syndrome if he or she has three or more of the risk factors associated with the condition: abdominal obesity (waist circumference greater than 40 inches in men and 35 inches in women); high blood pressure (130/85 or higher); high triglycerides (150 mg/dl or higher); low HDL cholesterol (below 40 mg/dl in men and 50 mg/dl in women); and insulin resistance (glucose of 100 mg/dl or higher). Nearly 25% of U.S. adults have metabolic syndrome, with the highest rates seen among Mexican American women. Weight control, physical activity, and a diet rich in unsaturated fats and fiber is recommended for people with metabolic syndrome (see the box "Glycemic Index and Glycemic Load" on p. 348). Exercise is especially important because it increases insulin sensitivity even if it doesn't produce weight loss.

MAJOR FORMS OF CARDIOVASCULAR DISEASE

Collectively, the various forms of CVD kill more Americans than the next four leading causes of death combined. The financial burden of CVD, including the costs of medical treatments and lost productivity, exceeds $360 billion annually. Although the main forms of CVD are interrelated and have elements in common, we treat them separately here for the sake of clarity. Hypertension, which is both a major risk factor and a form of CVD, was described earlier in the chapter.

Atherosclerosis

Atherosclerosis is a form of arteriosclerosis, or thickening and hardening of the arteries. In atherosclerosis, arteries become narrowed by deposits of fat, cholesterol, and other substances. The process begins when the cells lining the arteries (endothelial cells) become damaged, often through a combination of factors such as smoking, high blood pressure, and deposits of oxidized LDL particles. The body's response to this damage results in inflammation and changes in the artery lining. Deposits, called **plaques,** accumulate on artery walls; the arteries lose their elasticity and their ability to expand and contract, restricting blood flow. Once narrowed by a plaque, an artery is vulnerable to blockage by blood clots (Figure 11.3). Atherosclerosis often begins in childhood and has no early symptoms.

If the heart, brain, and/or other organs are deprived of blood, and thus the vital oxygen it carries, the effects of

Terms

plaque A deposit of fatty (and other) substances on the inner wall of the arteries.

As described in Chapter 8, all carbohydrate foods are broken down in the body into simple sugars that are absorbed into the bloodstream, causing blood glucose and insulin levels to rise. Some carbohydrates are broken down very quickly, resulting in a large and rapid increase in blood sugar; others are digested more slowly, causing a more gradual change in blood sugar level. **Glycemic index (GI)** is a measure of how fast and how high blood sugar rises after eating a particular food. When you eat high-GI foods, your blood sugar spikes rapidly, followed by a steep fall a little while later. Rapidly falling blood sugar levels may increase appetite. Foods with low GIs take longer to digest and cause a lower, longer-lasting rise in blood sugar; hunger tends to return much more slowly after eating low-GI foods. High-GI foods may also contribute to insulin resistance and oxidative stress, risk factors associated with type 2 diabetes and CVD.

The GI of a food is not always easy to predict. In general, rapidly digestible starchy or sugary foods such as white bread, white potatoes, and sweets tend to have relatively high GIs, while foods higher in fiber and fat are digested more slowly and have lower GIs. The GI values for some foods are surprising—white bread has a higher GI than table sugar, for example, and raisins have a higher GI than grapes.

Some experts have recommended using a slightly different measure, called **glycemic load,** to get a better picture of how the body responds to particular foods. Glycemic load is calculated by measuring the carbohydrate content of a specific amount of food and multiplying it by the GI. For example, carrots have a relatively high GI, yet the glycemic load of a serving consisting of one raw carrot is quite low. Why? The type of carbohydrate in carrots is rapidly digestible, resulting in a high glycemic *index,* but the total amount of carbohydrate in one serving of raw carrots is very small, resulting in a low glycemic *load.* In other words, eating a single serving of raw carrots is not going to raise your blood sugar very much, despite the high-GI value of carrots. (The GI and glycemic load values for some common foods are listed on a handout on the Online Learning Center.)

Why does any of this matter? Evidence is mounting that eating a diet rich in low-GI foods reduces the risk of developing type 2 diabetes and coronary heart disease, particularly among people who are overweight or who have the cluster of risk factors known as metabolic syndrome. However, glycemic index should not be the sole criterion for selecting foods: Low-GI hard cheese, high in calories and saturated fat, isn't a healthier choice than high-GI carrots; and diets high in carbohydrate-rich fruits, vegetables, and whole grains are linked to reduced risk of many diseases.

Some experts feel we don't yet understand enough about glycemic load to make specific diet recommendations. Limitations of the glycemic load concept include the fact that GI measurements vary from one study to another. How a food is prepared also changes the GI; for example, instant white rice and instant oatmeal have much higher GI values than regular white rice and old-fashioned oatmeal. Even factors such as ripeness can make a difference: The GI of a relatively ripe banana can be twice that of a less ripe one. Also, GI gives us information about what can happen to blood sugar when a given food is eaten by itself; estimating the glycemic load of a typical mixed meal is more complicated. Given the confusion and complexities, some experts are skeptical about whether glycemic index will ever be really useful in daily practice.

Despite all the uncertainty, the basic idea of glycemic index can be helpful if it is kept simple. Eating more low-GI foods can be one way to improve your health, especially if you have a family history of diabetes or heart disease, are overweight, or suspect you have metabolic syndrome. Rather than worrying about the exact GI of foods, keep in mind that certain classes of foods such as whole grains, nonstarchy vegetables, and fruits tend to have lower GIs than starchy or highly refined foods. Most of the carbohydrates in the current American diet come from refined or starchy foods, including soft drinks, sweets, white potatoes (including those served as french fries), white bread, and refined ready-to-eat cereals. Focus on choosing healthier sources of carbohydrate. In general, this translates to eating more of the fruits, vegetables, and whole-grain foods that nutrition experts have been recommending for a long time.

---

atherosclerosis can be deadly. Coronary arteries, which supply the heart with blood, are particularly susceptible to plaque buildup, a condition called **coronary heart disease (CHD),** or *coronary artery disease.* The blockage of a coronary artery causes a heart attack. If a cerebral artery (leading to the brain) is blocked, the result is a stroke. The main risk factors for atherosclerosis are cigarette smoking, physical inactivity, high levels of blood cholesterol, high blood pressure, and diabetes.

Heart Disease and Heart Attacks

Although a **heart attack,** or *myocardial infarction (MI),* may come without warning, it is usually the end result of a long-term disease process. The heart requires a steady supply of oxygen-rich blood to function properly (Figure 11.4). If one of the coronary arteries that supplies blood to the heart becomes blocked by a blood clot, a heart attack results. A heart attack caused by a clot is called a coronary thrombosis. During a heart attack, part of the heart muscle (myocardium) may die from lack of oxygen. If an MI is not fatal, the heart muscle may partially repair itself.

Chest pain called **angina pectoris** is a signal that the heart isn't getting enough oxygen to supply its needs. Although not actually a heart attack, angina—felt as an extreme tightness in the chest and heavy pressure behind the breastbone or in the shoulder, neck, arm, hand, or back—is a warning that the heart is overloaded.

If the electrical impulses that control heartbeat are disrupted, the heart may beat too quickly, too slowly, or in an irregular fashion, a condition known as **arrhythmia.** The symptoms of arrhythmia range from imperceptible to severe

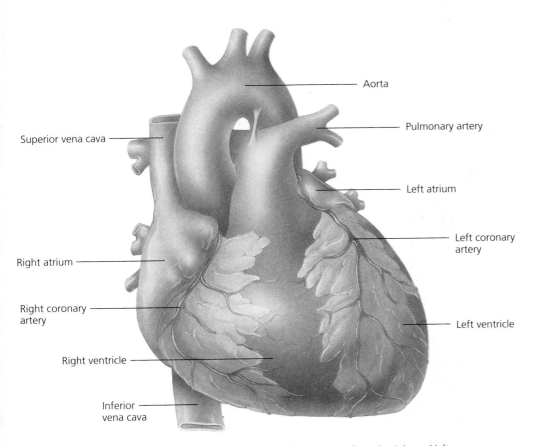

Aorta

Pulmonary artery

Superior vena cava

Left atrium

Left coronary
artery

Right atrium

Right coronary
artery

Left ventricle

Right ventricle

Inferior
vena cava

Figure 11.4 Blood supply to the heart. Blood is supplied to the heart from the right and left coronary arteries, which branch off the aorta. If a coronary artery becomes blocked by plaque buildup or a blood clot, a heart attack occurs; part of the heart muscle may die due to lack of oxygen.

and even fatal. **Sudden cardiac death,** also called *cardiac arrest,* is most often caused by an arrythmia called ventricular fibrillation, a kind of "quivering" of the ventricle that makes it ineffective in pumping blood. If ventricular fibrillation continues for more than a few minutes, it is fatal. Cardiac defibrillation, in which an electrical shock is delivered to the heart, can jolt the heart into a more efficient rhythm.

Remember that not all heart attacks involve sharp chest pain; women, in particular, are more likely to have different symptoms—shortness of breath, weakness, unusual fatigue, cold sweat, dizziness, and nausea. If symptoms of heart trouble do occur, it is critical to contact the emergency medical service or go immediately to the nearest hospital or clinic with a 24-hour emergency cardiac facility (see the box "What to Do in Case of a Heart Attack, Cardiac Arrest, or Stroke" on p. 350). An additional step recommended by many experts is to chew and swallow one adult aspirin tablet (325 mg); aspirin has an immediate anticlotting effect. If someone having a heart attack gets to the emergency room quickly enough, a clot-dissolving agent can be injected to dissolve a clot in the coronary artery, reducing the amount of damage to the heart muscle.

Physicians have a variety of diagnostic tools and treatments for heart disease. A patient may undergo a stress or

exercise test, in which he or she runs on a treadmill or pedals a stationary cycle while being monitored with an electrocardiogram (ECG or EKG). Certain characteristic changes in

Terms

glycemic index (GI) A measure of how high and how fast a particular food raises blood glucose levels.

glycemic load A measure of how a particular food affects blood glucose levels, calculated by multiplying the glycemic index of a food by its carbohydrate content.

coronary heart disease (CHD) Heart disease caused by hardening of the arteries that supply oxygen to the heart muscle; also called *coronary artery disease.*

heart attack Damage to, or death of, heart muscle, sometimes resulting in a failure of the heart to deliver enough blood to the body; also known as *myocardial infarction (MI).*

angina pectoris A condition in which the heart muscle does not receive enough blood, causing severe pain in the chest and often in the left arm and shoulder.

arrhythmia An irregularity in the force or rhythm of the heartbeat.

sudden cardiac death A nontraumatic, unexpected death from *sudden cardiac arrest,* most often due to arrhythmia; in most instances, victims had underlying heart disease.

Heart Attack Warning Signs

Some heart attacks are sudden and intense—the "movie heart attack," where no one doubts what's happening. But most heart attacks start slowly, with mild pain or discomfort. Often people affected aren't sure what's wrong and wait too long before getting help. Here are signs that can mean a heart attack is happening:

- **Chest discomfort.** Most heart attacks involve discomfort in the center of the chest that lasts more than a few minutes, or that goes away and comes back. It can feel like uncomfortable pressure, squeezing, fullness, or pain.
- **Discomfort in other areas of the upper body.** Symptoms can include pain or discomfort in one or both arms, the back, neck, jaw, or stomach.
- **Shortness of breath.** May occur with or without chest discomfort.
- **Other signs:** May include breaking out in a cold sweat, nausea, or lightheadedness.

If you or someone you're with has chest discomfort, especially with one or more of the other signs, don't wait more than 5 minutes before calling for help. Call 9-1-1 or get to a hospital right away.

Calling 9-1-1 is almost always the fastest way to get lifesaving treatment. Emergency medical services (EMS) staff can begin treatment when they arrive—up to an hour sooner than if someone gets to the hospital by car. The staff are also trained to revive someone whose heart has stopped. Patients with chest pain who arrive by ambulance usually receive faster treatment at the hospital, too.

If you can't access EMS, have someone drive you to the hospital right away. If you're the one having symptoms, don't drive yourself, unless you have absolutely no other option.

Stroke Warning Signs

The American Stroke Association says these are the warning signs of stroke:

- Sudden numbness or weakness of the face, arm, or leg, especially on one side of the body
- Sudden confusion, trouble speaking or understanding
- Sudden trouble seeing in one or both eyes
- Sudden trouble walking, dizziness, or loss of balance or coordination
- Sudden, severe headache with no known cause

If you or someone with you has one or more of these signs, don't delay! Immediately call 9-1-1 or EMS so an ambulance (ideally with advanced life support) can be sent for you. Also, check the time so you'll know when the first symptoms appeared. It's very important to take immediate action. If given within three hours of the start of symptoms, a clot-busting drug can reduce long-term disability for the most common type of stroke.

Cardiac Arrest Strikes Immediately and Without Warning.

Here are the signs:

- Sudden loss of responsiveness. No response to gentle shaking.
- No normal breathing. The victim does not take a normal breath when you check for several seconds.
- No signs of circulation. No movement or coughing.

If cardiac arrest occurs, call 9-1-1 and begin CPR immediately. If an automated external defibrillator (AED) is available and someone trained to use it is nearby, involve her or him.

SOURCE: American Heart Association, 2005. Heart Attack, Stroke, and Cardiac Arrest Warning Signs. Reproduced with permission. www.americanheart.org. Copyright © 2005 American Heart Association.

---

the heart's electrical activity while it is under stress can reveal particular heart problems, such as restricted blood flow to the heart muscle. Tools that allow the physician to visualize a patient's heart and arteries include magnetic resonance imaging (MRI), electron-beam computed tomography (EBC), echocardiograms, and angiograms.

If tests indicate a problem or if a person has already had a heart attack, several treatments are possible. Along with a low-fat diet, regular exercise, and smoking cessation, many patients are also advised to take aspirin daily to reduce clotting and inflammation. (Low-dose aspirin therapy appears to help prevent first and second heart attacks in men over age 45, second heart attacks in women over age 45, and first heart attacks and strokes in women over age 55.) Prescription drugs can also help reduce the strain on the heart. *Balloon angioplasty,* a common surgical treatment, involves threading a catheter with an inflatable balloon tip through a coronary artery until it reaches the area of blockage; the balloon is then inflated, flattening the plaque and widening the arterial opening. Many surgeons permanently implant coronary stents—flexible stainless steel tubes—to prop the artery open and prevent reclogging after angioplasty. In *coronary bypass surgery,* healthy blood vessels are grafted to coronary arteries to bypass blockages.

Stroke

For brain cells to function as they should, they must have a continuous and ample supply of oxygen-rich blood. If brain cells are deprived of blood for more than a few minutes, they die. A **stroke,** also called a *cerebrovascular accident (CVA),* occurs when the blood supply to the brain is cut off. Prompt treatment of stroke can greatly decrease the risk of permanent disability.

A stroke may be caused by a blood clot that blocks an artery (ischemic stroke) or by a ruptured blood vessel (hemorrhagic stroke). Ischemic strokes are often caused by atherosclerosis or certain types of arrhythmia; hemorrhagic strokes may occur if there is a weak spot in an artery wall or following a head injury. The interruption of the blood supply to any area of the brain prevents the nerve cells there from functioning—in some cases, causing death. Nerve cells control sensation and most body movements; depending on the area of the brain that is affected, a stroke may cause paralysis, walking disability, speech impairment, or memory loss. Of the 700,000 or more Americans who have strokes each year, nearly one-third die within a year; those who survive usually have some lasting disability.

Effective treatment requires the prompt recognition of symptoms and correct diagnosis of the type of stroke that has occurred. Treatment may involve the use of clot-dissolving and antihypertensive drugs. Even if brain tissue has been damaged or destroyed, nerve cells in the brain can make new pathways, and some functions can be taken over by other parts of the brain.

Congestive Heart Failure

A number of conditions—high blood pressure, heart attack, atherosclerosis, viral infections, **rheumatic fever,** birth defects—can damage the heart's pumping mechanism. When the heart cannot maintain its regular pumping rate and force, fluids begin to back up. When extra fluid seeps through capillary walls, edema (swelling) results, usually in the legs and ankles, but sometimes in other parts of the body as well. Fluid can collect in the lungs and interfere with breathing, particularly when a person is lying down. This condition is called *pulmonary edema,* and the entire process is known as **congestive heart failure.** Treatment includes reducing the workload on the heart, modifying salt intake, and using drugs that help the body eliminate excess fluid. Obesity is a significant independent risk factor for heart failure, and experts fear the incidence of heart failure will increase dramatically due to the rapid rise of obesity.

MOTIVATION FOR CHANGE! Many people, especially young adults, have trouble motivating themselves to improve their health habits to avoid a chronic disease that won't cause symptoms for another 20–30 years. Luckily in the case of CVD, many key prevention strategies—exercise, smoking cessation, improved diet—have immediate rewards. But if chronic disease prevention is one of your goals, one strategy for making your goal more powerful and real is to use imagery to engage your emotions. Imagine in detail what you'd like your life to be when you are 65; then imagine how your quality of life will be diminished if you have heart disease. Do research or talk to someone affected by CVD if you need more information; watch a relevant television program or film or read a book. Finding out more about your own personal risk factors can also help; if you haven't had your blood pressure or cholesterol levels checked recently, make an appointment today.

PROTECTING YOURSELF AGAINST CARDIOVASCULAR DISEASE

You can take several important steps right now to lower your risk of developing CVD in the future (Figure 11.5, p. 352). Reducing CVD risk factors when you are young can pay off with many extra years of life and health.

Eat Heart-Healthy

For most Americans, changing to a heart-healthy diet involves cutting total fat intake, substituting unsaturated fats for saturated and trans fats, and increasing intake of whole grains and fiber.

Decreased Fat and Cholesterol Intake   The National Cholesterol Education Program (NCEP) recommends that all Americans over age 2 adopt a diet in which total fat consumption is no more than 30% of total daily calories, with no more than one-third of those fat calories (10% of total daily calories) coming from saturated fat. For people with heart disease or high LDL levels, the NCEP recommends a total fat intake of 25–35% of total daily calories and a saturated fat intake of less than 7% of total calories. This higher total fat allowance is helpful for people who also have high triglyceride and low HDL levels. (Diets rich in high-glycemic-index carbohydrates may lower HDL levels and raise levels of triglycerides and glucose in some people, including those with metabolic syndrome. For this group, then, a diet slightly higher in unsaturated fats is allowed, while saturated fats are further restricted.)

Saturated fat is found in animal products, palm and coconut oil, and hydrogenated vegetable oils, which are also high in trans fats. Saturated and trans fats influence the production and excretion of cholesterol by the liver, so decreasing intake of these fats is the most important dietary change you can make to improve cholesterol levels. Animal products contain cholesterol as well as saturated fat, and the NCEP recommends that most Americans limit dietary cholesterol intake to no more than 300 mg per day; for people with heart disease or high LDL levels, the suggested daily limit is 200 mg.

Terms

stroke An impeded blood supply to some part of the brain resulting in the destruction of brain cells; also called *cerebrovascular accident (CVA).*

rheumatic fever A disease, mainly of children, characterized by fever, inflammation, and pain in the joints; often damages the heart muscle, a condition called *rheumatic heart disease.*

congestive heart failure A condition resulting from the heart's inability to pump out all the blood that returns to it. Blood backs up in the veins leading to the heart, causing an accumulation of fluid in various parts of the body.

- Eat a diet rich in fruits, vegetable, whole grains, and low-fat or fat-free dairy products. Eat 7–13 servings of fruits and vegetables each day.

- Eat several servings of high-fiber foods each day.

- Eat 2 or more servings of fish per week; try a few servings of nuts and soy foods each week.

- Choose unsaturated fats rather than saturated and trans fats.

- Be physically active; do both aerobic exercise and strength training on a regular basis.

- Achieve and maintain a healthy weight.

- Develop effective strategies for handling stress and anger. Nurture old friendships and family ties, and make new friends; pay attention to your spiritual side.

- Obtain recommended screening tests and follow your physician's recommendations.

- Don't use tobacco in any form: cigarettes, spit tobacco, cigars and pipes, bidis and clove cigarettes.

- Avoid exposure to environmental tobacco smoke.

- Limit consumption of fats, especially trans fats and saturated fats.

- Limit consumption of cholesterol, added sugars, and refined carbohydrates.

- Avoid excessive alcohol consumption—no more than one drink per day for women and two drinks per day for men.

- Limit consumption of salt to no more than 2300 mg of sodium per day (1500 mg if you have or are at high risk for hypertension).

- Avoid excess stress, anger, and hostility.

Figure 11.5   Strategies for reducing your risk of cardiovascular disease.

Increased Fiber Intake   Soluble (viscous) fiber traps the bile acids the liver needs to manufacture cholesterol and carries them to the large intestine, where they are excreted. It also slows the production of proteins that promote blood clotting. Insoluble fiber may interfere with the absorption of dietary fat and may also help you cut total food intake because foods rich in insoluble fiber tend to be filling. To obtain the recommended 25–38 grams of dietary fiber a day, choose a diet rich in whole grains, fruits, and vegetables. Good sources of fiber include oatmeal, some breakfast cereals, barley, legumes, and most fruits and vegetables.

Decreased Sodium Intake and Increased Potassium Intake   The recommended limit for sodium intake is 2300 milligrams per day; for population groups at special risk, including those with hypertension, middle-aged and older adults, and African Americans, the recommended limit is 1500 milligrams per day. To limit sodium intake, read food labels carefully, and avoid foods particularly high in sodium; foods that are fresh, less processed, and less sodium-dense are good choices. Adequate potassium intake is also important in control of blood pressure. Good food sources include leafy green vegetables like spinach and beet greens, root vegetables like white and sweet potatoes, vine fruits like cantaloupe and honeydew melon, winter squash, bananas, many dried fruits, and tomato sauce.

Alcohol   Moderate alcohol consumption may lower the risk of CHD among men over 45 and women over 55. (Moderate means no more than one drink per day for women and two drinks per day for men.) For most people under age 45, however, the risks of alcohol use probably outweigh any health benefit. If you do drink, do so moderately, with food and at times when drinking will not put you or others at risk.

DASH   A dietary plan that reflects many of the suggestions described here was released as part of a study called Dietary Approaches to Stop Hypertension, or DASH. This is the DASH diet plan:

- 7–8 servings a day of grains and grain products
- 4–5 servings a day of vegetables
- 4–5 servings a day of fruits
- 2–3 servings a day of low-fat or nonfat dairy products
- 2 or fewer servings a day of meats, poultry, and fish
- 4–5 servings a *week* of nuts, seeds, and legumes
- 2–3 servings a day of added fats, oils, and salad dressings
- 5 servings a *week* of snacks and sweets

The DASH diet also follows the dietary recommendations for lowering one's risk of cancer, osteoporosis, and heart disease. See Chapter 8 and the Online Learning Center for more information on DASH.

Exercise Regularly

You can significantly reduce your risk of CVD with a moderate amount of physical activity. Accumulate at least 30–60 minutes of moderate-intensity physical activity each day through such activities as brisk walking and stair climbing. A formal exercise program can provide even greater benefits. The American Heart Association recommends strength training in addition to aerobic exercise for building and maintaining cardiovascular health.

A diet high in fiber and low in saturated and trans fats can help lower levels of total cholesterol and LDL. This young woman is enjoying a vegetable sandwich on whole-grain bread with fresh fruit for lunch.

a family history of heart disease, and age above 45 years for men and 55 years for women. (An HDL level of 60 mg/dl or higher is protective and removes one risk factor from your total count of risk factors.)

If you have two or fewer risk factors, the NCEP sets an LDL goal of less than 160 mg/dl. If your LDL is above that level, begin the "Therapeutic Lifestyle Changes," or TLC, recommended by the NCEP, including weight management, increased physical activity, and the TLC diet, which suggests total fat intake of 25–35% of total daily calories, saturated fat intake less than 7% of daily calories, and, for some people, 10–25 grams per day of soluble fiber and 2 grams per day of plant stanols and sterols. If your LDL level is 190 mg/dl or higher, medication may also be recommended.

If you have two or more risk factors for heart disease, the NCEP sets an LDL goal of less than 130 mg/dl. If your LDL level is 130 or above, you should begin TLC. Depending on other factors, your physician may also suggest drug therapy.

If you have CVD or diabetes, your goal for LDL is less than 100 mg/dl or, for very-high-risk patients, 70 mg/dl. TLC is recommended for all people in this risk category, and a variety of medications is available to lower LDL and improve other blood fat levels.

Avoid Tobacco

Remember: The number one risk factor for CVD that you can control is smoking. If you smoke, quit. If you don't, don't start. The majority of people who start don't believe they will become hooked, but most do. If you live or work with people who smoke, encourage them to quit—for their sake and yours. If you find yourself breathing in smoke, take steps to prevent or stop this exposure. Quitting smoking will significantly reduce your CVD risk, but studies show that smoking and exposure to ETS may permanently increase the rate of plaque formation in arteries. Quitting smoking is highly beneficial, but abstaining from smoking and avoiding ETS throughout your life is even better.

Know and Manage Your Blood Pressure

Currently, only about 34% of Americans with hypertension have their blood pressure under control. If you have no CVD risk factors, have your blood pressure measured at least once every 2 years; yearly tests are recommended if you have other risk factors. If your blood pressure is high, follow your physician's advice on how to lower it.

Know and Manage Your Cholesterol Levels

Everyone age 20 and over should have a lipoprotein profile—which measures total cholesterol, HDL, LDL, and triglyceride levels—at least once every 5 years. Your goal for LDL depends in part on how many of the following major risk factors you have: cigarette smoking, high blood pressure, low HDL cholesterol (less than 40 mg/dl),

Develop Ways to Handle Stress and Anger

To reduce the psychological and social risk factors for CVD, develop effective strategies for handling the stress in your life. Shore up your social support network, and, if anger and hostility are problems for you, try some of the techniques described in Chapter 10 for managing stress and anger.

Know Your Risk Factors

Know your CVD risk factors and follow your physician's advice for testing, lifestyle changes, and any drug treatments. If you are at moderate to high risk for CVD, consult a physician about taking small doses of aspirin (50–325 mg per day).

Tips for Today

Risk factors for cardiovascular disease fall into two categories—those you can do something about, such as physical activity and levels of stress, and those you can't, such as age and ethnicity. Because cardiovascular disease is a long-term process that can begin when you're young, it's important to develop heart-healthy habits early in life.

Right now you can

- Plan to have fish for dinner two times this week.

- Go to the gym or fitness facility on your campus and get started on an aerobic exercise program.

- Practice time management by prioritizing your day's activities; work on accomplishing the most important tasks first.

- Resolve to address any nagging interpersonal issue that's been causing you stress.

I know what foods to avoid to prevent CVD, but are there any foods I should eat to protect myself from CVD? The most important dietary change for CVD prevention is a negative one: cutting back on foods high in saturated and trans fat. However, certain foods can be helpful. The positive effects of unsaturated fats, soluble fiber, and alcohol on heart health were discussed earlier in the chapter. Other potentially beneficial foods include those rich in the following:

- *Omega-3 fatty acids.* Found in fish, shellfish, and some nuts and seeds, omega-3 fatty acids reduce clotting and inflammation and may lower the risk of fatal arrhythmia.

- *Folic acid, vitamin B-6, and vitamin B-12.* These vitamins may affect CVD risk by lowering homocysteine levels; see Table 8.2 for a list of food sources.

- *Plant stanols and sterols.* Plant stanols and sterols, found in some types of trans-free margarines and other products, reduce the absorption of cholesterol in the body and help lower LDL levels.

- *Soy protein.* Replacing some animal protein with soy protein can lower LDL cholesterol. Soy-based foods include tofu, tempeh, and soy-based beverages.

- *Calcium.* Diets rich in calcium may help prevent hypertension and possibly stroke by reducing insulin resistance and platelet aggregation. Low-fat and fat-free dairy products are rich in calcium; refer to Chapter 8 for other sources.

The advice I hear from the news about protecting myself from CVD seems to be changing all the time. What am I supposed to believe? Health-related research is now described in popular newspapers and magazines rather than just medical journals, meaning that more and more people have access to the information. Researchers do not deliberately set out to mislead or confuse people. However, news reports may oversimplify the results of research studies, leaving out some of the qualifications and questions the researchers present with their findings. In addition, news reports may not differentiate between a preliminary finding and a result that has been verified by a large number of long-term studies. And researchers themselves must strike a balance between reporting promising preliminary findings to the public, thereby allowing people to act on them, and waiting 10–20 years until long-term studies confirm (or disprove) a particular theory.

Although you cannot become an expert on all subjects, there are some general strategies you can use to better assess the health advice that appears in the media; see the box "Evaluating Health News."

What's a heart murmur, and is it dangerous? A heart murmur is an extra or altered heart sound heard during a routine medical exam. The source is often a problem with one of the heart valves that separate the chambers of the heart. Congenital defects and certain infections can cause abnormalities in the valves. The most common heart valve disorder is mitral valve prolapse (MVP), which occurs in about 4% of the population. MVP is characterized by a "billowing" of the mitral valve, which separates the left ventricle and left atrium, during ventricular contraction; in some cases, blood leaks from the ventricle into the atrium. Most people with MVP have no symptoms; they have the same ability to exercise and live as long as people without MVP.

MVP can be confirmed with echocardiography. Treatment is usually unnecessary, although surgery may be needed in the rare cases where leakage through the faulty valve is severe. Experts disagree over whether patients with MVP should take antibiotics prior to dental procedures, a precautionary step used to prevent bacteria, which may be dislodged into the bloodstream during some types of dental and surgical procedures, from infecting the defective valve. Most often, only those patients with significant blood leakage are advised to take antibiotics.

Although MVP usually requires no treatment, more severe heart valve disorders can impair blood flow through the heart. Treatment depends on the location and severity of the problem. More serious defects may be treated with surgery to repair or replace a valve.

Visit the Online Learning Center for answers to common questions about heart health.

SUMMARY

- The major controllable risk factors for CVD are smoking, hypertension, unhealthy cholesterol levels, a sedentary lifestyle, obesity, and diabetes.

- Contributing factors for CVD that can be changed include high triglyceride levels, inadequate stress management, a hostile personality, depression, anxiety, lack of social support, poverty, and alcohol and drug use.

- Major risk factors that can't be changed are heredity, aging, being male, and ethnicity.

- Hypertension weakens the heart and scars and hardens arteries, causing resistance to blood flow. It is defined as blood pressure equal to or higher than 140 over 90.

- Atherosclerosis is a progressive hardening and narrowing of arteries that can lead to restricted blood flow and even complete blockage.

- Heart attacks, strokes, and congestive heart failure are the results of a long-term disease process; hypertension and atherosclerosis are usually involved.

- Reducing heart disease risk involves eating a heart-healthy diet, exercising regularly, avoiding tobacco, managing blood pressure and cholesterol levels, handling stress and anger, and knowing your risk factors.

Evaluating Health News

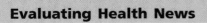

Americans face an avalanche of health information from newspapers, magazines, books, and television programs. It's not always easy to decide what to believe. The following questions can help you evaluate health news:

1. *Is the report based on research or on an anecdote?* Information or recommendations based on one or more carefully designed research studies has more validity than one person's experiences.

2. *What is the source of the information?* A study in a respected publication has been reviewed by editors and other researchers in the field—people who are in a position to evaluate the merits of a study and its results. Information put forth by government agencies and national research organizations is also usually considered fairly reliable.

3. *How big was the study?* A study that involves many subjects is more likely to yield reliable results than a study involving only a few people. Another indication that a finding is meaningful is if several different studies yield the same results.

4. *Who were the people involved in the study?* Research findings are more likely to apply to you if you share important characteristics with the subjects of the study. For example, the results of a study on men over age 50 who smoke may not be particularly meaningful for a 30-year-old nonsmoking woman. Even less applicable are studies done in test tubes or on animals.

5. *What kind of study was it?* Epidemiological studies involve observation or interviews in order to trace the relationships among lifestyle, physical characteristics, and diseases. Although epidemiological studies can suggest links, they cannot establish cause-and-effect relationships. Clinical or interventional studies involve testing the effects of different treatments on groups of people who have similar lifestyles and characteristics. They are more likely to provide conclusive evidence of a cause-and-effect relationship. The best interventional studies share the following characteristics:
   - *Controlled.* A group of people who receive the treatment is compared with a matched group who do not receive the treatment.

   - *Randomized.* The treatment and control groups are selected randomly.
   - *Double-blind.* Researchers and participants are unaware of who is receiving the treatment.
   - *Multicenter.* The experiment is performed at more than one institution.

6. *What do the statistics really say?* First, are the results described as "statistically significant"? If a study is large and well designed, its results can be deemed statistically significant, meaning there is less than a 5% chance that the findings resulted from chance. Second, are the results stated in terms of relative or absolute risk? Many findings are reported in terms of *relative risk,* how a particular treatment or condition affects a person's disease risk. Consider the following examples of relative risk:
   - According to some estimates, taking estrogen without progesterone can increase a postmenopausal woman's risk of dying from endometrial cancer by 233%.
   - Giving antiviral medication to HIV-infected pregnant women reduces prenatal transmission of HIV by 90%.

   The first of these two findings seems far more dramatic than the second—until one also considers *absolute risk,* the actual risk of the illness in the population being considered. The absolute risk of endometrial cancer is 0.3%; a 233% increase based on the effects of estrogen raises it to 1%, a change of 0.7%. Without treatment, about 25% of infants born to HIV-infected women will be infected with HIV; with treatment, the absolute risk drops to about 2%, a change of 23%. Because the absolute risk of an HIV-infected mother passing the virus to her infant is so much greater than a woman's risk of developing endometrial cancer (25% compared with 0.3%), a smaller change in relative risk translates into a much greater change in absolute risk.

7. *Is new health advice being offered?* If the media report new guidelines for health behavior or medical treatment, examine the source. Government agencies and national research foundations usually consider a great deal of evidence before offering health advice. Above all, use common sense, and check with your physician before making a major change in your health habits based on news reports.

For Further Exploration

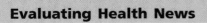 *Fit and Well* **Online Learning Center**
(www.mhhe.com/fahey)

Use the learning objectives, study guide questions, and glossary flashcards to review key terms and concepts and prepare for exams. You can extend your knowledge of cardiovascular health and gain experience in using the Internet as a resource by completing the activities and checking out the Web links for the topics in Chapter 11 marked with the World Wide Web icon. For this chapter, Internet activities explore CVD risk factors, major forms of CVD, and

prevention; there are Web links for the Vital Statistics figure, the Critical Consumer box on evaluating health news, and the chapter as a whole.

Daily Fitness and Nutrition Journal

Engaging in regular physical activity and eating a healthy diet are two important strategies for preventing CVD. Continue to use your journal to monitor your exercise program and, if needed, to keep records of your diet. You may want to use the nutrition journal to focus on a specific dietary factor related to CVD, such as saturated fat.

Books

Moore, T., et al. 2003. *The DASH Diet for Hypertension*. New York: Pocket Books. *Provides background information and guidelines for adopting the DASH diet; also includes recipes.*

Nelson, M. E., and A. Lichtenstein. 2005. *Strong Women, Strong Hearts*. New York: Putnam Adult. *Lifestyle advice for women to prevent heart disease.*

Reaven, G. M. 2001. *Syndrome X: Overcoming the Silent Killer That Can Give You a Heart Attack*. St. Louis, Mo.: Fireside. *Provides information about syndrome X and insulin resistance, including lifestyle strategies for affected individuals.*

Romaine, D. S., and O. S. Randall. 2005. *The Encyclopedia of Heart and Heart Disease*. New York: Facts on File. *Includes entries on the functioning of the cardiovascular system, types and causes of heart disease, and prevention and treatment.*

Ⓦ Organizations and Web Sites

American Heart Association. Provides information on hundreds of topics relating to the prevention and control of CVD. Special guidelines for women can be found in the section on the "Go Red for Women" campaign.

    800-AHA-USA1

    http://www.americanheart.org (general information)

    http://www.deliciousdecisions.org (dietary advice)

    http://www.justmove.org (fitness advice)

Franklin Institute Science Museum/The Heart: An On-Line Exploration. An online museum exhibit containing information on the structure and function of the heart, how to monitor your heart's health, and how to maintain a healthy heart.

    http://www.fi.edu/biosci/heart.html

HeartInfo—Heart Information Network. Provides information for heart patients and others interested in identifying and reducing their risk factors for heart disease; includes links to many related sites.

    http://www.heartinfo.org

MedlinePlus: Heart and Circulation Topics. Provides links to reliable sources of information on cardiovascular health.

    http://www.nlm.nih.gov/medlineplus/heartandcirculation.html

National Heart, Lung, and Blood Institute. Provides information on a variety of topics relating to cardiovascular health and disease, including cholesterol, smoking, obesity, and hypertension.

    800-575-WELL

    http://www.nhlbi.nih.gov; http://rover.nhlbi.nih.gov/chd

National Stroke Association. Provides information and referrals for stroke victims and their families; the Web site has a stroke risk assessment.

    800-STROKES

    http://www.stroke.org

See also the listings for Chapters 9 and 10.

Selected Bibliography

Ajani, U. A., et al. 2004. Body mass index and mortality among U.S. male physicians. *Annals of Epidemiology* 14(10): 731–739.

American Heart Association. 2005. *Heart and Stroke Statistical Update, 2005*. Dallas, Tex.: American Heart Association.

Centers for Disease Control and Prevention. 2005. Differences in disability among black and white stroke survivors. *Morbidity and Mortality Weekly Report* 54(1): 3–9.

Cooper, R. S., et al. 2005. An international comparative study of blood pressure in populations of European vs. African descent. *BMC Medicine* 3(1): 2.

Daviglus, M. L., et al. 2004. Favorable cardiovascular risk profile in young women and long-term risk of cardiovascular and all-cause mortality. *Journal of the American Medical Association* 292(113): 1588–1592.

Erkkila, A. T., et al. 2005. Cereal fiber and whole-grain intake are associated with reduced progression of coronary-artery atherosclerosis in postmenopausal women with coronary artery disease. *American Heart Journal* 150(1): 94–101.

Forman, J. P., et al. 2005. Folate intake and risk of incident hypertension among U.S. women. *Journal of the American Medical Association* 292(3): 320–329.

Greenland, P., et al. 2003. Major risk factors as antecedents of fatal and nonfatal coronary heart disease events. *Journal of the American Medical Association* 290(7): 891–897.

Grundy, S. M., et al. 2005. Diagnosis and management of the metabolic syndrome: An American Heart Association/National Heart, Lung, and Blood Institute Scientific Statement. *Circulation* 112(17): 2735–2752.

Hu, G., et al. 2005. Leisure time, occupational, and commuting physical activity and the risk of stroke. *Stroke* 36(9): 1994–1999.

Ludwig, D. S. 2002. The glycemic index: Physiological mechanisms relating to obesity, diabetes, and cardiovascular disease. *Journal of the American Medical Association* 287(18): 2414–2423.

McSweeney, J. C., et al. 2003. Women's early warning symptoms of acute myocardial infarction. *Circulation* 108:2619–2623.

Meadows, M. 2005. Brain attack: A look at stroke prevention and treatment. *FDA Consumer*, March/April.

Mosca, L., et al. 2004. Evidence-based guidelines for cardiovascular disease prevention in women. *Circulation* 109:672–693.

Mukamal, K. J., et al. 2005. Alcohol and risk of ischemic stroke in men: The role of drinking patterns and usual beverage. *Annals of Internal Medicine* 142(1): 11–19.

Nissen, S. E., et al. 2005. Statin therapy, LDL cholesterol, C-reactive protein, and coronary artery disease. *New England Journal of Medicine* 352(1): 29–38.

Olson, M. B., et al. 2005. Hostility scores are associated with increased risk of cardiovascular events in women undergoing coronary angiography. *Psychosomatic Medicine* 67(4): 546–552.

Qureshi, A. I., et al. 2005. Cigarette smoking among spouses: Another risk factor for stroke in women. *Stroke* 36(9): e74–76.

Ridker, P. M., et al. 2005. A randomized trial of low-dose aspirin in the primary prevention of cardiovascular disease in women. *New England Journal of Medicine* 352(13): 1293–1304.

Turhan, H., et al. 2005. High prevalence of metabolic syndrome among young women with premature coronary artery disease. *Coronary Artery Disease* 16(1): 37–40.

Willingham, S. A., and E. S. Kilpatrick. 2005. Evidence of gender bias when applying the new diagnostic criteria for myocardial infarction. *Heart* 91(2): 237–238.

Wittstein, I. S., et al. 2005. Neurohumoral features of myocardial stunning due to sudden emotional stress. *New England Journal of Medicine* 352(6): 539–548.

LAB 11.1 *Cardiovascular Health*

Part I   CVD Risk Assessment

Your chances of suffering a heart attack or stroke before age 55 depend on a variety of factors, many of which are under your control. To help identify your risk factors, circle the response for each risk category that best describes you.

1. Sex and Age
   - (0) Female age 55 or younger; male age 45 or younger
   - 2 Female over age 55; male over age 45

2. Heredity/Family History
   - (0) Neither parent suffered a heart attack or stroke before age 60.
   - 3 One parent suffered a heart attack or stroke before age 60.
   - 7 Both parents suffered a heart attack or stroke before age 60.

3. Smoking
   - 0 Never smoked
   - 3 Quit more than 2 years ago and lifetime smoking is less than 5 pack-years*
   - 6 Quit less than 2 years ago and/or lifetime smoking is greater than 5 pack-years*
   - (8) Smoke less than ½ pack per day
   - 13 Smoke more than ½ pack per day
   - 15 Smoke more than 1 pack per day

4. Environmental Tobacco Smoke
   - 0 Do not live or work with smokers
   - 2 Exposed to ETS at work
   - (3) Live with smoker
   - 4 Both live and work with smokers

5. Blood Pressure
   (If available, use the average of the last three readings.)
   - (0) 120/80 or below
   - 1 121/81–130/85
   - 3 Don't know blood pressure
   - 5 131/86–150/90
   - 9 151/91–170/100
   - 13 Above 170/100

6. Total Cholesterol
   - 0 Lower than 190
   - 1 190–210
   - (2) Don't know
   - 3 211–240
   - 4 241–270
   - 5 271–300
   - 6 Over 300

7. HDL Cholesterol
   - 0 Over 60 mg/dl
   - 1 55–60
   - (2) Don't know HDL
   - 3 45–54
   - 5 35–44
   - 7 25–34
   - 12 Lower than 25

8. Exercise
   - (0) Exercise three times a week
   - 1 Exercise once or twice a week
   - 2 Occasional exercise less than once a week
   - 7 Rarely exercise

9. Diabetes
   - (0) No personal or family history
   - 2 One parent with diabetes
   - 6 Two parents with diabetes
   - 9 Type 2 diabetes
   - 13 Type 1 diabetes

10. Body Mass Index (kg/m^2)
   - 0 <23.0
   - 1 23.0–24.9
   - 2 25.0–28.9
   - (3) 29.0–34.9
   - 5 35.0–39.9
   - 7 ≥40

11. Stress
   - 0 Relaxed most of the time
   - (1) Occasionally stressed and angry
   - 2 Frequently stressed and angry
   - 3 Usually stressed and angry

Scoring

Total your risk factor points. Refer to the list below to get an approximate rating of your risk of suffering an early heart attack or stroke.

Score	Estimated Risk
Less than 20	Low risk
20–29	Moderate risk
30–45	High risk
Over 45	Extremely high risk

Pack-years can be calculated by multiplying the number of packs you smoked per day by the number of years you smoked. For example, if you smoked a pack and a half a day for 5 years, you would have smoked the equivalent of 1.5 × 5 = 7.5 pack-years.

Part II   Hostility Assessment

Current research indicates that three aspects of hostility are particularly harmful to cardiovascular health: cynicism (a mistrusting attitude regarding other people's motives), anger (an emotional response to other people's "unacceptable" behavior), and aggression (behaviors in response to negative emotions such as anger and irritation). To get an idea of how hostile you are, check any of the following statements that are true for you.

_____ 1. Stuck in a long line at the express checkout in the grocery store, I often count the number of items the people in front of me have to see if anyone is over the limit.

__X__ 2. I am often irritated by other people's incompetence.

_____ 3. If a cashier gives me the wrong change, I assume he or she is probably trying to cheat me.

__X__ 4. I've been so angry at someone that I've thrown things or slammed a door.

_____ 5. If someone is late, I plan the angry words I'm going to say.

__X__ 6. I tend to remember irritating incidents and get mad all over again.

__X__ 7. If someone cuts me off in traffic, I honk my horn, flash my lights, pound the steering wheel, or shout.

_____ 8. Little annoyances have a way of adding up during the day, leaving me frustrated and impatient.

_____ 9. If the person who cuts my hair trims off more than I want, I fume about it for days afterward.

__X__ 10. When I get into an argument, I feel my jaw clench and my pulse and breathing rate climb.

__X__ 11. If someone mistreats me, I look for an opportunity to pay them back, just for the principle of the thing.

_____ 12. I find myself getting annoyed at little things my spouse or significant other does that get under my skin.

Add up the number of items you checked. A score of 3 or less indicates a generally cool head. A score between 4 and 8 indicates that your level of hostility could be raising your risk of heart disease. A score of 9 or more indicates a hothead—a level of cynicism, anger, and aggression high enough to endanger both heart health and interpersonal relationships.

Using Your Results

How did you score? (1) What is your CVD risk assessment score? Are you at all surprised by your score?

Are you satisfied with your CVD risk rating? If not, set a specific goal: _____

(2) What is your hostility assessment score? Are you at all surprised by the result?

Are you satisfied with your hostility rating? If not, set a specific goal: _____

What should you do next? Enter the results of this lab in the Preprogram Assessment column in Appendix D. (1) If you've set a goal for the overall CVD risk assessment score, identify a risk area that you can change, such as smoking, exercise, and stress. Then list three steps or strategies for changing the risk area you've chosen.

Risk area: _____

Strategies for change:

(2) If you've set a goal for the hostility assessment score, begin by keeping a log of your hostile responses as described in the box on p. 344. Review the anger management strategies in Chapter 10 (p. 323) and select several that you will try to use to manage your angry responses. Strategies for anger management:

Next, begin to put your strategies into action. After several weeks of a program to reduce CVD risk or hostility, do this lab again and enter the results in the Postprogram Assessment column of Appendix D. How do the results compare?

SOURCES: CVD risk assessment from Insel, P. M., and W. T. Roth. 2006. *Core Concepts in Health,* 10th ed. Copyright © 2006 The McGraw-Hill Companies, Inc. Reprinted with permission of The McGraw-Hill Companies, Inc.; Hostility quiz from *Anger Kills: 17 Strategies,* by Redford B. Williams, M.D., and Virginia Williams, Ph.D. Copyright © 1993 by Redford B. Williams, M.D., and Virginia Williams, Ph.D. Used by permission of Times Books, a division of Random House, Inc., and by Reid Boates Literary Agency.

Looking **AHEAD**

After reading this chapter, you should be able to

- Explain what cancer is and how it spreads
- List and describe common cancers—their risk factors, signs and symptoms, treatments, and approaches to prevention
- Discuss some of the causes of cancer and how they can be avoided or minimized
- Describe the signs and symptoms of cancer in its early stages
- List specific actions you can take to lower your risk of cancer

12

Cancer

Test Your Knowledge

1. **Eating which of these foods may help prevent cancer?**
   a. chili peppers
   b. broccoli
   c. oranges

2. **Use of full-body CT scans is recommended for routine cancer screening in healthy people.**
   True or false?

3. **The use of condoms during sexual intercourse can prevent cancer in women.**
   True or false?

ANSWERS

1. ALL THREE. These and many other fruits and vegetables are rich in phytochemicals, naturally occurring substances that may have anticancer effects.

2. FALSE. Such scans are expensive and may have false-positive findings that lead to unnecessary and invasive tests. Also, the amount of radiation used during a full-body CT scan—nearly 100 times that of a typical mammogram—may itself raise the risk of cancer.

3. TRUE. The primary cause of cervical cancer is infection with the human papillomavirus (HPV), a sexually transmitted pathogen. The use of condoms can prevent HPV infection.

W *Fit and Well* **Online Learning Center**   www.mhhe.com/fahey

Visit the *Fit and Well* Online Learning Center for study aids, online labs, additional information about cancer, links, Internet activities that explore the prevention of cancer, and much more.

359

C ancer is the second most common cause of death, after heart disease. Evidence indicates that more than half of all cancers in the United States could be prevented by simple changes in lifestyle. Tobacco use is responsible for about one-third of all cancer deaths (Figure 12.1). Diet and exercise, including their relationship with obesity, account for another large proportion of cancer deaths. Although cancer is primarily a disease of older adults, your behavior now will determine your cancer risk in the future. This chapter provides basic information about common types of cancer—risk factors, symptoms, and treatments—as well as concrete strategies for prevention.

WHAT IS CANCER?

Cancer is the abnormal, uncontrolled growth of cells, which, if left untreated, can ultimately cause death.

Benign Versus Malignant Tumors

Most cancers take the form of tumors, although not all tumors are cancerous. A tumor is simply a mass of tissue that serves no physiological purpose. It can be benign, like a wart, or malignant, like most lung cancers. The term **malignant tumor** (or *neoplasm*) is synonymous with cancer.

Benign tumors are made up of cells similar to the surrounding normal cells and are enclosed in a membrane that prevents them from penetrating neighboring tissues. They are dangerous only if their physical presence interferes with body functions. A malignant tumor, or cancer, is capable of invading surrounding structures, including blood vessels, the **lymphatic system,** and nerves. It can also spread to distant sites via the blood and lymphatic circulation. A few cancers, like leukemia, cancer of the blood, do not produce a mass but still have the fundamental property of rapid, uncontrolled growth of cells.

Every case of cancer begins as a change in a cell that allows it to grow and divide when it should not. A malignant cell divides without regard for normal control mechanisms and gradually produces a mass of abnormal cells, or a tumor. It takes about a billion cells to make a mass the size of a pea, so a single tumor cell must go through many divisions, often taking years, before the tumor grows to a noticeable size. Eventually a tumor produces a sign or symptom that is detected. In an accessible location, a tumor may be felt as a lump. In less accessible locations, a tumor may be noticed only after considerable growth has taken place and may then be detected only by an indirect symptom—for instance, a persistent cough or unexplained bleeding or pain.

How Cancer Spreads: Metastasis

Metastasis, the spreading of cancer cells, occurs because cancer cells do not stick to each other as strongly as normal

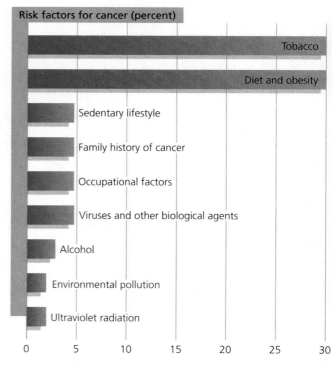

VITAL STATISTICS

Figure 12.1 Percentage of all cancer deaths linked to risk factors. SOURCE: Harvard Center for Cancer Prevention. 1996. Harvard Report on Cancer Prevention. Vol. 1: Causes of Human Cancer. *Cancer Causes and Control* 7(Suppl.).

cells do and therefore may not remain at the site of the *primary tumor,* the original location. They break away and can pass through the lining of lymph or blood vessels to invade nearby tissue. They can also drift to distant parts of the body, where they establish new colonies of cancer cells. This traveling and seeding process is called metastasizing, and the new tumors are called *secondary tumors,* or *metastases.*

This ability of cancer cells to metastasize makes early cancer detection critical. To control the cancer and prevent death, every cancerous cell must be removed. Once cancer cells enter either the lymphatic system or the bloodstream, it is extremely difficult to stop their spread.

COMMON CANCERS

Each year, about 1.4 million people are diagnosed with cancer, and more than 570,000 die (Figure 12.2). These statistics exclude the more than 1 million cases of the easily curable types of skin cancer. At current U.S. rates, nearly 1 in 2 men and more than 1 in 3 women will develop cancer at some point in their lives. There are now more than 10 million Americans alive who have a history of cancer.

A discussion of all types of cancer is beyond the scope of this book. In this section we look at the most common cancers and their causes, prevention, and treatment.

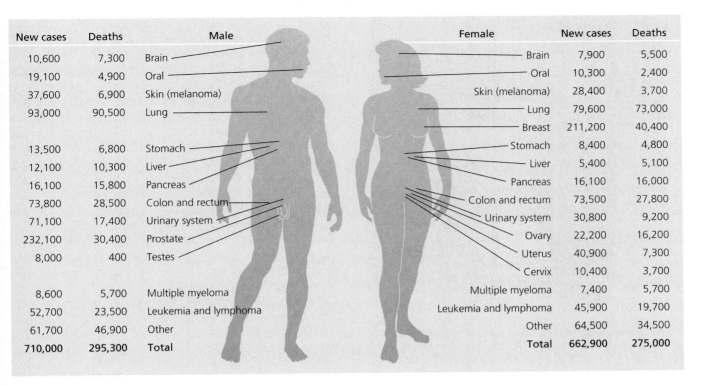

New cases	Deaths	Male	Female	New cases	Deaths
10,600	7,300	Brain	Brain	7,900	5,500
19,100	4,900	Oral	Oral	10,300	2,400
37,600	6,900	Skin (melanoma)	Skin (melanoma)	28,400	3,700
93,000	90,500	Lung	Lung	79,600	73,000
			Breast	211,200	40,400
13,500	6,800	Stomach	Stomach	8,400	4,800
12,100	10,300	Liver	Liver	5,400	5,100
16,100	15,800	Pancreas	Pancreas	16,100	16,000
73,800	28,500	Colon and rectum	Colon and rectum	73,500	27,800
71,100	17,400	Urinary system	Urinary system	30,800	9,200
232,100	30,400	Prostate	Ovary	22,200	16,200
8,000	400	Testes	Uterus	40,900	7,300
			Cervix	10,400	3,700
8,600	5,700	Multiple myeloma	Multiple myeloma	7,400	5,700
52,700	23,500	Leukemia and lymphoma	Leukemia and lymphoma	45,900	19,700
61,700	46,900	Other	Other	64,500	34,500
710,000	**295,300**	**Total**	**Total**	**662,900**	**275,000**

VITAL STATISTICS

Figure 12.2   Cancer cases and deaths by site and sex.   SOURCE: American Cancer Society. 2005.
Cancer Facts and Figures, 2005. Atlanta: American Cancer Society.

Lung Cancer

Lung cancer is the most common cause of cancer death in the United States; it is responsible for about 163,000 deaths each year. Breast cancer used to be the major cause of cancer death in women, but, since 1987, lung cancer has surpassed breast cancer as a killer of women.

The chief risk factor for lung cancer is tobacco smoke, which accounts for 87% of cancers. When smoking is combined with exposure to other environmental **carcinogens,** such as asbestos particles, the risk of cancer can be multiplied by a factor of 10 or more. Quitting substantially reduces risk, but ex-smokers remain at higher risk than those who never smoked. And the smoker is not the only one at risk. Long-term exposure to environmental tobacco smoke (ETS), or secondhand smoke, also increases risk for lung cancer. ETS causes about 3000 lung cancer deaths in nonsmokers each year.

Symptoms of lung cancer do not usually appear until the disease has advanced to the invasive stage. Signals such as a persistent cough, chest pain, or recurring bronchitis may be the first indication of a tumor's presence. Lung cancer is most often treated by some combination of surgery, radiation, and chemotherapy; if all the tumor cells can be removed or killed, a cure is possible. Unfortunately, lung cancer is usually detected only after it has begun to spread, and only about 15% of lung cancer patients are alive 5 years after diagnosis.

Colon and Rectal Cancer

Another common cancer in the United States is colon and rectal cancer (also called colorectal cancer). It is the second leading cause of cancer death, after lung cancer, for men and women combined. Age is a key risk factor, with more than 90% of cases diagnosed in people age 50 and older. Many cancers arise from preexisting polyps, small growths on the wall of the colon that may gradually develop into malignancies. The tendency to form colon polyps appears to be determined by specific genes, and about 15–30% of colon cancers may be due to inherited gene mutations.

Lifestyle also affects colon cancer risk. Regular physical activity reduces risk; obesity increases risk. Although the

Terms

cancer Abnormal, uncontrolled cellular growth.

malignant tumor A tumor that is cancerous and capable of spreading.

benign tumor A tumor that is not cancerous.

lymphatic system A system of vessels that returns proteins, lipids, and other substances from fluid in the tissues to the circulatory system.

metastasis The spread of cancer cells from one part of the body to another.

carcinogen Any substance that causes cancer.

Smoking is responsible for about 30% of all cancer deaths. The benefits of quitting are substantial. Smokers who quit before age 50 have half the risk of dying in the next 15 years as people who continue to smoke.

mechanisms are unclear, high intake of red meat, smoked meat and fish, or simple sugars appears to increase risk, as does excessive alcohol consumption and smoking. Protective lifestyle factors may include a diet rich in fruits, vegetables, and whole grains; adequate intake of folic acid, calcium, magnesium, and vitamin D; regular use of nonsteroidal anti-inflammatory drugs such as aspirin and ibuprofen; and, in women, use of oral contraceptives.

Because polyps may bleed as they progress, the standard warning signs of colon cancer are bleeding from the rectum or a change in bowel habits. A stool blood test, performed during a routine physical exam, can detect small amounts of blood in the stool long before obvious bleeding would be noticed. The American Cancer Society (ACS) recommends that this examination be performed annually after age 50 (earlier for people with a family history of the disease). A polyp may be directly detected and even removed with a sigmoidoscope, a flexible fiber-optic device inserted through the rectum. Surgery is the primary method of treatment. Colon and rectal cancer is more curable than lung cancer, particularly if caught before it spreads.

Breast Cancer

Breast cancer is the most common cancer in women and is second to lung cancer in the number of cancer deaths among women. In men, breast cancer occurs only rarely. In the United States, about 1 woman in 8 will develop breast cancer in her lifetime. There is a strong genetic factor in breast cancer. A woman who has two close relatives with breast cancer is four to six times more likely to develop the disease than a woman who has no close rela-

tives with breast cancer. However, only about 15% of cancers occur in women with a family history of it.

Other risk factors include early onset of menstruation; late onset of menopause, having no children or having a first child after age 30, current use of hormone replacement therapy, obesity, and alcohol use. The unifying factor for many of these risk factors may be the female sex hormone estrogen, which circulates in a woman's body in high concentrations between puberty and menopause. Fat cells also produce estrogen, and estrogen levels are higher in obese women. Alcohol can interfere with estrogen metabolism in the liver and increase estrogen levels in the blood. Estrogen promotes the growth of cells in responsive sites, including the breast and the uterus, so any factor that increases estrogen exposure may raise breast cancer risk. In addition, pregnancy and breastfeeding trigger changes in breast cells that make them less susceptible to cancerous changes.

Some studies indicate that certain types of dietary fat may be important in increasing or decreasing risk. Monounsaturated fats have been linked with reduced risk, while certain types of polyunsaturated fat may increase risk. A diet rich in vegetables may also have a protective effect. Regular exercise is extremely important. Vigorous exercise may reduce estrogen levels in the blood, and physical activity of all intensities helps control body weight. Smoking also increases risk. Although some of the risk factors for breast cancer cannot be changed, minimizing lifestyle risk factors reduces the chance of developing breast cancer, even for women at risk from family history or other factors.

The ACS stresses the early detection of breast cancer through a three-part approach:

1. *Mammography*: A **mammogram** (low-dose breast X-ray) is recommended every year for women over 40. Mammography is especially valuable because it can identify breast abnormalities that may be cancer at an early stage before physical symptoms develop. Digital mammography, which may be more accurate for premenopausal women and others with dense breast tissue, is becoming more widely available.

2. *Clinical breast exams*: Women between ages 20 and 39 should have a clinical breast exam about every 3 years, and women age 40 and over should have a breast exam by a health professional every year before their scheduled mammogram.

3. *Breast self-exams*: Breast self-exam (BSE) allows a woman to become familiar with her breasts, so she can alert her health care provider to any changes. Starting at age 20, women should consider BSE an option for early detection (see the box "Breast Self-Examination").

If a lump is detected, it may be scanned by **ultrasonography** and **biopsied** to see if it is cancerous. In 90%

The best time for a woman to examine her breasts is when the breasts are not tender or swollen. Women who are pregnant or breastfeeding or have breast implants can also choose to examine their breasts regularly. Women who examine their breasts should have their technique reviewed during their periodic health examinations by their health care professional. It is acceptable for women to choose not to do BSE or to do BSE occasionally. If you choose not to do BSE, you should still be familiar with your breasts and report any changes without delay to your doctor.

How to Examine Your Breasts

• Lie down and place your right arm behind your head. The exam is done while lying down, not standing up, because the breast tissue then spreads evenly over the chest wall and is as thin as possible, making it much easier to feel all the breast tissue.

• Use the finger pads of the three middle fingers on your left hand to feel for lumps in the right breast. Use overlapping dime-size circular motions of the finger pads to feel the breast tissue.

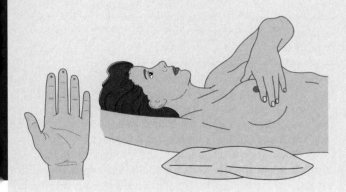

• Use three different levels of pressure to feel all the breast tissue. Light pressure is needed to feel the tissue closest to the skin; medium pressure to feel a little deeper; and firm pressure to feel the tissue closest to the chest and ribs. A firm ridge in the lower curve of each breast is normal. If you're not sure how hard to press, talk with your doctor or nurse. Use each pressure level to feel the breast tissue before moving on to the next spot.

• Move around the breast in an up-and-down pattern starting at an imaginary line drawn straight down your side from the underarm and moving across the breast to the middle of the chest bone (the sternum, or breastbone). Be sure to check the entire breast area, going down until you feel only ribs and going up to the neck or collar bone (clavicle).

• Repeat the exam on your left breast, using the finger pads of the right hand. Some evidence suggests that the up-and-down pattern (sometimes called the vertical pattern) is the most effective pattern for covering the entire breast, without missing any breast tissue.

• While standing in front of a mirror with your hands pressing firmly down on your hips, look at your breasts for any changes of size, shape, contour, or dimpling. (Pressing down on the hips contracts the chest wall muscles and enhances any breast changes.)

• Examine each underarm while sitting up or standing and with your arm only slightly raised so you can easily feel in this area. Raising your arm straight up tightens the tissue in this area and makes it difficult to examine.

SOURCE: American Cancer Society's Web site, www.cancer.org, 2005. Copyright © 2005 American Cancer Society, Inc. Reprinted with permission.

of cases, the lump is found to be a cyst or other harmless growth, and no further treatment is needed. If the lump does contain cancer cells, a variety of surgeries may be called for, ranging from a lumpectomy (removal of the lump and surrounding tissue) to a mastectomy (removal of the breast). Chemotherapy or radiation may also be used. Studies have shown that social support also can affect psychological and physical wellness of patients (see the box "Coping with Cancer," p. 364). If the tumor is discovered early, before it has spread to the adjacent lymph nodes, the patient has about a 97% chance of surviving more than 5 years.

Several drugs have been developed for the treatment or prevention of breast cancer. These include selective estrogen-receptor modulators, or SERMs, which act like estrogen in some tissues of the body but block estrogen's effects in others. The best-known of these is tamoxifen. Another therapy is trastuzumab (Herceptin), a special type of antibody that binds to a specific cancer-related target in the body; for women with cancers that respond to Herceptin, the drug significantly improves survival.

Prostate Cancer

The prostate gland is situated at the base of the bladder in men. It produces seminal fluid; if enlarged, it can block the flow of urine. Prostate cancer is the most common cancer in men and the second leading cause of cancer

Terms

mammogram A low-dose X-ray of the breasts used for the early detection of breast cancer.

ultrasonography An imaging method in which inaudible high-pitched sound (ultrasound) is bounced off body structures to create an image on a monitor.

biopsy The removal and examination of a small piece of body tissue for the purpose of diagnosis.

Visiting a Cancer Patient

- Before you visit, call ahead to ask if it's a good time. Surprise visits are often not welcome. Don't overstay your welcome.

- Be a good listener. Allow the person to express all his or her feelings and don't discount fears or minimize the seriousness of the situation. Let the patient decide whether the two of you talk about the illness. It's human to want to laugh and talk about other things sometimes.

- Ask "What can I get you?" or "How can I help?" instead of saying "Let me know if I can help." Make specific offers: to clean the bathroom, go grocery shopping, do laundry, or give caregivers a break.

- Refrain from offering advice. You may have heard about the latest treatment or hottest physician, but unless you are asked for suggestions, keep them to yourself.

- If you want to take food, ask about dietary restrictions ahead of time. Use a disposable container so the person doesn't have to worry about returning it.

- Don't be put off if your first visit gets a lukewarm reception. Many cancer victims are on an emotional roller coaster, and their feelings and needs will change over time.

If You Are the Patient

- Remember that cancer doesn't always mean death. Many cancers are curable or controllable for long periods, and survivors may return to a normal, healthy life. Hope and optimism can be important elements in cancer survival.

- Work toward having a positive attitude, but don't feel guilty if you can't keep a positive attitude all the time. Having cancer is difficult, and low moods will occur no matter how good you are at coping. If they become frequent or severe, seek help.

- Use any strategies that have helped you solve problems and manage your emotions in the past. Some people respond to information gathering, talking with others, and prayer or meditation. Physical activity, music, art, and sharing

personal stories may all help lessen stress.

- Find a physician you trust and with whom you can communicate well. Ask questions and be a partner in your treatment.

- Confide your worries to someone close to you. Don't bottle up your feelings to spare your loved ones. Ask someone you trust to accompany you on visits to your physician and treatment sessions.

- Explore groups that can help you get through this difficult time. There are many support groups for people who have cancer or who have survived it. Support group participation has been shown to reduce anxiety and depression and enhance quality of life.

SOURCES: National Cancer Institute. 2002. *Facing Forward Series: Life After Cancer Treatment* (http://www.cancer.gov/cancerinfo/life-after-treatment/page4; retrieved August 31, 2005). Life with cancer: How to provide support. 1996. *Women's Health Advocate.* September. Holland, J. C. 1996. Cancer's psychological challenges. *Scientific American,* September.

---

death in men. More than 230,000 new cases of prostate cancer are diagnosed in the United States each year.

Age is the strongest predictor of the risk of prostate cancer, with about 75% of cases diagnosed in men over age 65. Inherited genetic predisposition may be responsible for 5–10% of cases. African American men have the highest rate of prostate cancer of any group in the world; both genetic and lifestyle factors may be involved. Diets high in calories, dairy products, refined grains, and animal fats and low in plant foods (especially vegetable fiber) have been implicated as possible culprits, as have obesity, inactivity, and a history of sexually transmitted diseases. Compounds in soy foods, tomatoes, and cruciferous vegetables such as broccoli and cabbage are being investigated for their possible protective effects.

Some cases are first detected by rectal examination during a routine physical exam. The **PSA blood test**, which measures the amount of prostate-specific antigen (PSA) in the blood, can also be used to help diagnose prostate cancer. An elevated level or a rapid increase in PSA can signal trouble. A newer approach involves measuring the amount of PSA that is free-floating in the blood. Because PSA made by cancerous cells is more likely to circulate bound to other proteins, a low proportion of "free" PSA in the blood indicates a higher risk, whereas a high proportion of free PSA

indicates a lower risk. Ultrasound and biopsy may also be used to detect and diagnose prostate cancer.

If the tumor is malignant, the prostate is usually removed surgically. However, a small, slow-growing tumor in an older man may be treated with watchful waiting because he is more likely to die from another cause before his cancer becomes life-threatening. A less invasive treatment involves radiation of the tumor by surgically implanting radioactive seeds in the prostate gland. The 5-year survival rate for all stages of prostate cancer is about 98%.

Cancers of the Female Reproductive Tract

Because the uterus, cervix, and ovaries are subject to similar hormonal influences, the cancers of these organs can be discussed as a group.

Cervical Cancer Cervical cancer is at least in part a sexually transmitted disease. Probably more than 80% of cervical cancer stems from infection by the human papillomavirus (HPV), which causes genital warts and is transmitted during unprotected sex (see Chapter 14). Cervical cancer can be prevented by avoiding infection with HPV; sexual abstinence, mutually monogamous sex with an uninfected partner, or regular use of condoms can reduce the risk of HPV infection (see Chapter 14 for more on HPV and other STDs). Smoking and the STDs herpes and chlamydia are other possible risk factors.

Screening for the changes in cervical cells that precede cancer is done chiefly by means of the **Pap test.** During a pelvic exam, loose cells are scraped from the cervix, spread on a slide, stained for easier viewing, and examined under a microscope to see whether they are normal in size and shape. If cells are abnormal, a condition commonly referred to as *cervical dysplasia,* the Pap test is repeated at intervals. Sometimes cervical cells spontaneously return to normal, but, in about one-third of cases, the cellular changes progress toward malignancy. If this happens, the abnormal cells must be removed. Researchers are making good progress in developing a vaccine against HPV, which could prevent most cases of cervical cancer.

Uterine or Endometrial Cancer Cancer of the lining of the uterus, or endometrium, most often occurs after age 55. The risk factors are similar to those for breast cancer: prolonged exposure to estrogen, early onset of menstruation, late menopause, never having been pregnant, and other medical conditions, including obesity. The use of oral contraceptives, which combine estrogen and progestin, appears to provide protection. Endometrial cancer is usually detectable by pelvic examination. It is treated surgically, commonly by hysterectomy (removal of the uterus). Radiation and chemotherapy may be used as well. When the tumor is detected at an early stage, about 96% of patients are alive and disease-free 5 years later.

Ovarian Cancer Although ovarian cancer is rare compared with cervical or uterine cancer, it causes more deaths than the other two combined. It cannot be detected by Pap tests or any other simple screening method and is often diagnosed late in its development. The risk factors are similar to those for breast and endometrial cancer: increasing age, never having been pregnant, a family history of breast or ovarian cancer, and specific genetic mutations. Anything that lowers a woman's lifetime number of ovulation cycles—pregnancy, breastfeeding, or use of oral contraceptives—appears to reduce the risk of ovarian cancer. A diet rich in fruits and vegetables may also reduce risk. There are often no warning signs of ovarian cancer, but early clues may include increased abdominal size and bloating, urgency, and pelvic pain. Women with symptoms or at high risk should have thorough pelvic exams at regular intervals, perhaps with ultrasound imaging of the ovaries. Ovarian cancer is treated by surgical removal of one or both ovaries, the fallopian tubes, and the uterus.

Other Female Reproductive Tract Cancers Daughters born to women who took DES (diethylstilbestrol) to prevent miscarriage have an increased risk, about 1 in 1000, of a vaginal or cervical cancer called clear cell cancer. (There is also some risk to DES sons, who may have an increased risk of undescended testicles, a risk factor for testicular cancer.) A DES daughter should find a physician who is familiar with the problems of DES exposure; more frequent and more thorough pelvic exams may be recommended.

Skin Cancer

Skin cancer is the most common cancer of all when cases of the highly curable forms are included in the count. Treatments are usually simple and successful when the cancers are caught early. Almost all cases of skin cancer can be traced to excessive exposure to **ultraviolet (UV) radiation** from the sun, including longer-wavelength ultraviolet A (UVA) and shorter-wavelength ultraviolet B (UVB) radiation. UVB radiation causes sunburns and can damage the eyes and immune system. UVA is less likely to cause a sunburn, but it damages connective tissue and leads to premature aging of the skin. (Tanning lamps and tanning salon beds emit mostly UVA radiation.) Both solar and artificial sources of UVA and UVB radiation are human carcinogens that cause skin cancer.

Both severe, acute sun reactions (sunburns) and chronic low-level sun reactions (suntans) can lead to skin cancer. People with fair skin have less natural protection against skin damage from the sun and a higher risk of skin cancer than people with naturally dark skin. Severe sunburns in childhood have been linked to a greatly increased risk of skin cancer in later life, so children in particular should be protected. Other risk factors include having many moles, particularly large ones, spending time at high altitudes, and a family history of the disease.

There are three main types of skin cancer, named for the types of skin cell from which they develop. **Basal cell** and **squamous cell carcinomas** together account for about 95% of the skin cancers diagnosed each year. They are usually found in chronically sun-exposed areas, such as the face, neck, hands, and arms. They usually appear as pale, waxlike, pearly nodules, or red, scaly, sharply outlined patches. These cancers are often painless, although they may bleed, crust, and form an open sore.

Terms

PSA blood test A diagnostic test for prostate cancer that measures blood levels of prostate-specific antigen (PSA)

Pap test A scraping of cells from the cervix for examination under a microscope to detect cancer; also called *Pap smear.*

ultraviolet (UV) radiation Light rays of a specific wavelength, emitted by the sun; most UV rays are blocked by the ozone layer in the upper atmosphere.

basal cell carcinoma Cancer of the deepest layers of the skin.

squamous cell carcinoma Cancer of the surface layers of the skin.

The UVA radiation emitted by most tanning-salon beds doesn't usually cause an immediate sunburn, but it does cause premature wrinkling and aging of the skin and skin cancer.

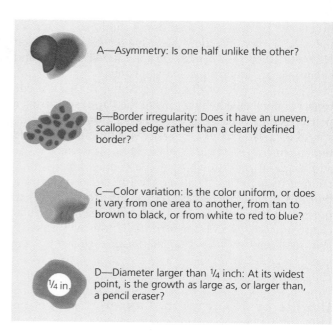

A—Asymmetry: Is one half unlike the other?

B—Border irregularity: Does it have an uneven, scalloped edge rather than a clearly defined border?

C—Color variation: Is the color uniform, or does it vary from one area to another, from tan to brown to black, or from white to red to blue?

D—Diameter larger than ¼ inch: At its widest point, is the growth as large as, or larger than, a pencil eraser?

¼ in.

Figure 12.3   The ABCD test for melanoma.   To see a variety of photos of melanoma and benign moles, visit the National Cancer Institute's Visuals Online site (http://visualsonline.cancer.gov).

Melanoma is by far the most dangerous skin cancer because it spreads so rapidly. It is the most common cancer among women age 25–29. It can occur anywhere on the body, but the most common sites are the back, chest, abdomen, and lower legs. A melanoma usually appears at the site of a preexisting mole. The mole may begin to enlarge, become mottled or varied in color (colors can include blue, pink, and white), or develop an irregular surface or irregular borders. Tissue invaded by melanoma may also itch, burn, or bleed easily.

One of the major steps you can take to protect yourself against all forms of skin cancer is to avoid lifelong overexposure to UV radiation. People of every age, including babies and children, need to be protected from the sun (see the box "Choosing and Using Sunscreens and Sun-Protective Clothing"). You can help with early detection by making it a habit to examine your skin regularly. Most of the spots, freckles, moles, and blemishes on your body are normal. But if you notice an unusual growth, discoloration, or sore that does not heal, see your physician or a dermatologist immediately. The characteristics that may signal that a skin lesion is a melanoma—asymmetry, border irregularity, color change, and a diameter greater than ¼ inch—are illustrated in Figure 12.3.

If you do have an unusual skin lesion, your physician will examine it and possibly perform a biopsy. If the lesion is cancerous, it is usually removed surgically, a procedure that can almost always be performed in the physician's office using a local anesthetic.

MOTIVATION FOR CHANGE!   Nearly half of all college students report having used tanning lamps within the past year, and more than 90% of tanning lamp users are aware that their use causes premature aging of the skin and skin cancer. These statistics illustrate that knowledge alone isn't enough to motivate people to change their behavior. If you find yourself lacking motivation to change, try to heighten your awareness of the short-term benefits of changing and the long-term costs of not changing. For example, place images of people with tan but aged, wrinkled, and leathery skin in a prominent location. (The same strategy of dramatic photos can work for other types of cancer prevention programs—for example, oral cancer photos for people who use spit tobacco.) You can also investigate other options for achieving your short-term goal with less long-term cost, such as using sunless tanning lotions and sprays.

Oral Cancer

Oral cancer—cancers of the lip, tongue, mouth, and throat—can be traced principally to cigarette, cigar, or pipe smoking; the use of smokeless (spit) tobacco; and excessive consumption of alcohol. These risk factors work together to multiply a person's risk of oral cancer. The incidence of oral cancer is more than twice as great in men as in women and most frequent in men over 40. Oral cancers are fairly easy to detect but often hard to cure. Treatment usually includes surgery and radiation.

Terms

VW

melanoma A malignant tumor of the skin that arises from pigmented cells, usually a mole.

With consistent use of the proper clothing, sunscreens, and common sense, you can lead an active outdoor life *and* protect your skin against most sun-induced damage. Clothing should be your first and best line of defense. Sun-protective clothing can effectively block nearly all UVA and UVB rays. Sunscreens do provide protection, but many allow considerable UVA radiation to pass through to your skin. And even the best sunscreens are effective only when applied properly and reapplied frequently—something most people fail to do.

Clothing

• Wear long-sleeved shirts and long pants. Dark-colored, tightly woven fabrics provide reasonable protection from the sun. Another good choice is clothing made from special sun-protective fabrics; these garments have an Ultraviolet Protection Factor (UPF) rating, similar to the SPF for sunscreens. For example, a fabric with a UPF rating of 20 allows only one-twentieth of the sun's UV radiation to pass through. There are three categories of UPF protection: A UPF of 15–24 provides "good" UV protection, a UPF of 25–39 provides "very good" protection, and a UPF of 40–50 provides "excellent" protection. By comparison, typical shirts provide a UPF of only 5–9, a value that drops when clothing is wet.

• Consider washing some extra sun protection into your current wardrobe. A new laundry additive adds UV protection to ordinary fabrics; it is recommended by the Skin Cancer Foundation.

• Put on a hat. Your face, ears, neck, and scalp are especially vulnerable to the sun's harmful effects, making hats an essential weapon in the battle against sun damage. Baseball caps are popular, but they don't protect the ears, the back of the neck, and the lower face. A better choice is a broad-brimmed hat or a legionnaire-style cap that covers the ears and neck. You still need to wear sunscreen on your face even if you are wearing a hat because sand, water, rocks, concrete, and snow all reflect the sun's rays back up into your face.

Sunscreen

• Use a sunscreen and lip balm with a sun protection factor (SPF) of 15 or higher. (An SPF rating refers to the amount of time you can stay out in the sun before you burn, compared with not using sunscreen; for example, a product with an SPF of 15 would allow you to remain in the sun without burning 15 times longer, on average, than if you didn't apply sunscreen.) If you're fair-skinned, have a family history of skin cancer, are at high altitude, or will be outdoors for many hours, use a sunscreen with a high SPF (30+).

• Choose a broad-spectrum sunscreen that protects against both UVA and UVB radiation. The SPF rating of a sunscreen currently applies only to UVB, but a number of ingredients, especially titanium dioxide and zinc oxide, are effective at blocking most UVA radiation. Use a water-resistant sunscreen if you swim or sweat quite a bit. If you have sensitive skin, you may need to try several brands before finding one that doesn't irritate your skin. If you have acne, look for a sunscreen that is labeled "noncomedogenic," which means that it will not cause pimples.

• Shake sunscreen before applying. Apply it 30 minutes before exposure to allow it time to penetrate the skin. Reapply sunscreen frequently and generously to all sun-exposed areas (many people overlook their temples, ears, and sides and backs of their necks). Most people use less than half as much as they would need to attain the full SPF rating. One ounce of sunscreen is about enough to cover an average-size adult in a swimsuit. Reapply sunscreen 15–30 minutes after sun exposure begins and then every few hours after that and/or following activities such as swimming or toweling that could remove sunscreen.

• If you're taking medications, ask your physician or pharmacist about possible reactions to sunlight or interactions with sunscreens. Medications for acne, allergies, and diabetes are just a few of the products that can trigger reactions. If you're using sunscreen and an insect repellent containing DEET, use extra sunscreen (DEET may decrease sunscreen effectiveness).

• Don't let sunscreens give you a false sense of security. Most of the sunscreens currently on the market allow considerable UVA radiation to penetrate the skin, with the potential for causing skin cancers (especially melanoma), as well as wrinkles and other forms of skin damage. Experts worry that our use of sunscreens may sometimes backfire by allowing us to spend many more hours in the sun than we would if we had to worry about getting a sunburn.

Time of Day and Location

• Avoid sun exposure between 10 A.M. and 4 P.M., when the sun's rays are most intense. Clouds allow as much as 80% of UV rays to reach your skin. Stay in the shade when you can.

• Consult the day's UV Index, which predicts UV levels on a 0–10+ scale, to get a sense of the amount of sun protection you'll need; take special care on days with a rating of 5 or above. UV Index ratings are available in local newspapers, from the weather bureau, or from certain Web sites. Also take special care in locations near the equator or at high altitudes, where the sun is more intense; use a stronger sunscreen and apply it more frequently.

• UV rays can penetrate at least 3 feet in water, so swimmers should wear water-resistant sunscreens. Snow reflects the sun's rays, so don't forget to apply sunscreen before skiing and other snow activities. Sand and water also reflect the sun's rays, so you still need to apply a sunscreen if you are under a beach umbrella. Concrete and white-painted surfaces are also highly reflective.

Tanning Salons

• Stay away from tanning salons! Despite advertising claims to the contrary, the lights used in tanning parlors are damaging to your skin. Tanning beds and lamps emit mostly UVA radiation, increasing your risk of premature skin aging (such as wrinkles) and skin cancer. If you *must* have a tan, consider using sunless self-tanning lotions. These can provide that bronzed look without the risks of UV radiation.

Testicle Self-Examination

The best time to perform a testicular self-exam is after a warm shower or bath, when the scrotum is relaxed. First, stand in front of a mirror and look for any swelling of the scrotum. Then, examine each testicle with both hands. Place the index and middle fingers under the testicle and the thumbs on top; roll the testicle gently between the fingers and thumbs. Don't worry if one testicle seems slightly larger than the other—that's common. Also, expect to feel the epididymis, the soft, sperm-carrying tube at the rear of the testicle.

Perform the self-exam each month. If you find a lump, swelling, or nodule, consult a physician right away. The abnormality may not be cancer, but only a physician can make a diagnosis. Other possible signs of testicular cancer include a change in the way a testicle feels, a sudden collection of fluid in the scrotum, a dull ache in the lower abdomen or groin, a feeling of heaviness in the scrotum, or pain in a testicle or the scrotum.

SOURCES: Testicular Cancer Resource Center. 2001. *How to Do a Testicular Self Examination* (http://www.acor.org/TCRC/ tcexam.html; retrieved February 14, 2001). National Cancer Institute. 2000. *Questions and Answers About Testicular Cancer* (http://cis.nci.nih.gov/fact/6_34.htm; retrieved February 14, 2001).

Testicular Cancer

Testicular cancer is relatively rare, accounting for only 1% of cancers in men, but it is the most common cancer in men age 20–35. Self-examination may help in the early detection of testicular cancer (see the box "Testicle Self-Examination"). Testicular cancer is much more common among white Americans than Latinos, Asian Americans, or African Americans. Men with undescended testicles are at increased risk for testicular cancer, and for this reason the condition should be corrected in early childhood. Tumors are treated by surgical removal of the testicle and, if the tumor has spread, by chemotherapy.

Other Cancers

Pancreatic cancer is the fifth leading cause of cancer death in the United States. The disease is usually well advanced before symptoms become noticeable, and no effective cure is available. About 3 out of 10 cases are linked to smoking. Other risk factors include being male, African American, or over age 60; having a family history of pancreatic cancer; having diabetes; being inactive and obese; and eating a diet high in fat and meat and low in vegetables.

Bladder cancer is twice as common in men as in women, and smoking is the key risk factor. The first symptoms are likely to be blood in the urine and/or increased frequency of urination. These symptoms can also signal a urinary infection but should trigger a visit to a physician, who can evaluate the possibility of cancer. With early detection, more than 90% of cases are curable.

Kidney cancer usually occurs in people over 50; smoking and obesity are mild risk factors, as is a family history of the disease. Symptoms may include fatigue, pain in the side, and blood in the urine. Kidney cancer has been difficult to treat, with a 5-year survival rate of only 64%.

One of the few established risk factors for brain cancer is ionizing radiation, such as X-rays of the head. Symptoms are often nonspecific and include headaches, fatigue, behavioral changes, and sometimes seizures. Some brain tumors are curable by surgery or by radiation and chemotherapy, but most are not. Survival time varies, depending on the type of the tumor, from 1 to 8 years.

Leukemia, cancer of the white blood cells, starts in the bone marrow but can then spread to the lymph nodes, spleen, liver, other organs, and central nervous system. Most people with leukemia have no known risk factors. About 20% of cases of adult leukemia are related to smoking; other possible risk factors include radiation and certain chemicals and infections. Most symptoms occur because leukemia cells crowd out the production of normal blood cells; the result can be fatigue, anemia, weight loss, and increased risk of infection. Treatment and survival rates vary, depending on the type and other factors.

Lymphoma is a form of cancer that begins in the lymph nodes and then may spread to almost any part of the body. There are two types—Hodgkin's disease and non-Hodgkin's lymphoma (NHL). NHL is the more common and more deadly form of the disease; risk factors for NHL are not well understood but may include genetic factors, radiation, and certain chemicals and infections. Rates of Hodgkin's disease have fallen by more than 50% since the early 1970s.

THE CAUSES OF CANCER

Although scientists do not know everything about what causes cancer, they have identified genetic, environmental, and lifestyle factors. Typically, these factors work together (see the box "Ethnicity, Poverty, and Cancer"). There are usually several steps in the transformation of a normal cell into a cancer cell, and different factors may work together in the development of cancer.

The Role of DNA

Almost daily, the mass media report on some new link between heredity and cancer. But how exactly do genes

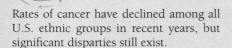

Rates of cancer have declined among all U.S. ethnic groups in recent years, but significant disparties still exist.

• Among U.S. ethnic groups, African Americans have the highest incidence of and death rates from cancer.

• White women have a higher incidence of breast cancer, but African American women have the highest death rate. Black women are less likely to receive regular mammograms and more likely to experience delays in follow-up.

• African American men have a higher rate of prostate cancer than any other U.S. group and more than twice the death rate of other groups. However, black men are less likely than white men to undergo PSA testing for prostate cancer.

• Latinas have the highest incidence of cervical cancer, but African American women have the highest death rate. Language and cultural barriers and problems accessing screening services are thought to particularly affect Latinas, who have relatively low rates of Pap testing.

• Asian Americans and Pacific Islander Americans have the highest rates of liver and stomach cancers. Recent immigration helps explain these higher rates, as these cancers are usually caused by infections that are more prevalent in the recent immigrant's country of origin.

Some disparities in cancer risks and rates may be influenced by genetic or cultural factors. For example, certain genetic/molecular features of aggressive breast cancer are more common among African American women; they are more likely to be diagnosed at a later stage and with more aggressive tumors. Genetic factors may also help explain the high rate of prostate cancer among black men. Women from cultures where early marriage and motherhood is common are likely to have a lower risk of breast cancer. People who don't smoke or who are vegetarians for religious or cultural reasons may have lower rates of many cancers.

Most of the differences in cancer rates and deaths, however, are thought to be the result of socioeconomic inequities, which influence the prevalence of many underlying cancer risk factors as well as access to early detection and quality treatment. People of low socioeconomic status are more likely to smoke, abuse alcohol, eat unhealthy foods, and be sedentary and overweight—all of which are associated with cancer. High levels of stress associated with poverty may impair the immune system, the body's first line of defense against cancer.

People with low incomes are more likely to live in unhealthy environments. For example, Latinos and Asian and Pacific Islander Americans are more likely than other groups to live in areas that do not meet federal air quality standards. Low-income people may also have jobs in which they come into daily contact with carcinogenic chemicals. They may face similar risks in their homes and schools, where they may be exposed to asbestos or other carcinogens.

People with low incomes also have less exposure to information about cancer, are less aware of the early warning signs of cancer, and are less likely to seek medical care when they have such symptoms.

Lack of health insurance is a key factor explaining higher death rates among people with low incomes. A study comparing low-income Americans and Canadians found that the Canadians were more likely to survive cancer, possibly due to Canada's system of universal health care, which ensures access to treatment regardless of income.

Public education campaigns that encourage healthy lifestyle habits, routine cancer screening, and participation in clinical trials may be one helpful strategy to reduce cancer disparities. But the effects of poverty are more difficult to overcome. Some medical scientists look to policymakers for solutions and maintain that living and working conditions in the inner cities must be improved and that access to quality health care must be assured for all Americans. Then, even without new miracle drugs or medical breakthroughs, the United States could see a real decrease in cancer rates in low-income populations.

SOURCES: American Cancer Society. 2005. *Cancer Facts and Figures 2005.* Atlanta: American Cancer Society. Chlebowski, R. T., et al. 2005. Ethnicity and breast cancer: Factors influencing differences in incidence and outcome. *Journal of the National Cancer Institute* 97(6): 439–448. CDC National Center for Chronic Disease Prevention and Health Promotion. 2005. *Health Disparities: Minority Cancer Awareness* (http://www.cdc.gov/cancer/minorityawareness/index.htm; retrieved January 26, 2005). CDC Office of Minority Health. 2004. *Eliminate Disparities in Cancer Screening and Management* (http://www.cdc.gov/omh/AMH/factsheets/cancer.htm; retrieved January 26, 2005). National Cancer Institute. 2003. *Cancer Health Disparities: Fact Sheet* (http://www.cancer.gov/newscenter/healthdisparities; retrieved January 26, 2005).

influence cancer? And what do these links mean for you and your risk of developing particular cancers?

DNA Basics   The nucleus of each cell in your body contains 23 pairs of **chromosomes,** which are made up of tightly packed coils of **DNA** (deoxyribonucleic acid). Each chromosome contains thousands of **genes;** you have about 25,000 genes in all. Each of your genes controls the production of a particular protein. By making different proteins at different times, genes can act as switches to alter the ways a cell works. Some genes are responsible for controlling the rate of cell division.

DNA Mutations and Cancer   A mutation is any change in the makeup of a gene. Some mutations are inherited; others are caused by environmental agents known as *mutagens*. Mutagens include radiation, certain viruses, and chemical substances in the air we breathe.

Terms

chromosomes The threadlike bodies in a cell nucleus that contain molecules of DNA; most human cells contain 23 pairs of chromosomes.

DNA Deoxyribonucleic acid, a chemical substance that carries genetic information.

gene A section of a chromosome that contains the instructions for making a particular protein; the basic unit of heredity.

(When a mutagen also causes cancer, it is called a carcinogen.) Some mutations are the result of copying errors that occur when DNA replicates itself as part of cell division.

A mutated gene no longer contains the proper code for producing its protein. It usually takes several mutational changes before a normal cell takes on the properties of a cancer cell. Genes in which mutations are associated with the conversion of a normal cell into a cancer cell are known as **oncogenes.** In their undamaged form, many oncogenes play a role in controlling or restricting cell growth; they are called suppressor genes. Mutational damage to suppressor genes releases the brake on growth and leads to rapid and uncontrolled cell division—a precondition for the development of cancer.

An example of an inherited mutated oncogene is an alteration in a suppressor gene vital for controlling the growth of colon cells. Children who inherit the altered gene are thought to face a 70–80% chance of developing the disease. Another example is BRCA1 (breast cancer gene 1): Women who inherit a damaged copy of this suppressor gene face a significantly increased risk of breast and ovarian cancer.

In most cases, however, mutational damage occurs after birth. For example, only about 5–10% of breast cancer cases can be traced to inherited copies of a damaged BRCA1 gene. In addition, lifestyle factors are important even for those who have inherited a damaged suppressor gene: Consuming a diet high in red meat may make colon cells divide more rapidly; increasing intake of fruits, vegetables, and calcium may reverse this effect. Testing and identification of hereditary cancer risks can be helpful for some people, especially if it leads to increased attention to controllable risk factors and better medical screening.

Cancer Promoters   Substances known as cancer promoters make up another important piece of the cancer puzzle. They don't directly produce DNA mutations, but they accelerate the growth of cells, which means less time for a cell to repair DNA damage caused by other factors. Estrogen, which stimulates cellular growth in the female reproductive organs, is an example of a cancer promoter. Although much still needs to be learned about the role of genetics in cancer, it's clear that minimizing mutation damage to our DNA will lower our risk of many cancers. Unfortunately, a great many substances produce cancer-causing mutations, and we can't escape them all. By identifying the important carcinogens and understanding how they produce their effects, we can help keep our DNA intact and avoid activating "sleeping" oncogenes.

Dietary Factors

Diet is one of the most important factors in cancer prevention, but it is also one of the most complex and controversial. Your food choices affect your cancer risk by both exposing you to potentially dangerous compounds and depriving you of potentially protective ones. Let's take a look at some of the dietary factors that may affect cancer risk, keeping in mind that it's the overall quality of your diet that is most important.

Dietary Fat and Meat   Diets high in fat and meat appear to contribute to certain cancers, including colon, stomach, and prostate. As is true with heart disease, certain types of fats may be riskier than others. Diets favoring omega-6 polyunsaturated fats are associated with a higher risk of certain cancers than are diets favoring the omega-3 forms commonly found in fish and canola oil. (See Chapter 8 for more information on types of fatty acids.)

Alcohol   Alcohol is a known human carcinogen and is associated with an increased incidence of several cancers. For example, an average alcohol intake of three drinks a day is associated with a doubling in the risk of breast cancer. Alcohol and tobacco interact as risk factors for oral cancer. Heavy users of both alcohol and tobacco have a risk for oral cancer up to 15 times greater than that of people who don't drink or use tobacco.

Fried Foods   Scientists have found high levels of the chemical acrylamide (a probable human carcinogen) in starch-based foods that have been fried or baked at high temperatures, including french fries and certain types of snack chips and crackers. Studies are ongoing, but, in 2005, WHO urged food companies to work to lower the acrylamide content of foods to reduce any risk to public health. Acrylamide levels vary widely in foods, and there are currently no warnings against eating specific foods. The wisest course may be to consume a variety of foods and avoid overindulging in any single class of foods, particularly things like french fries and potato chips, which may contain other unhealthy substances such as saturated and trans fats. You can also limit your exposure to

Terms

Ⓥ

oncogene A gene involved in the transformation of a normal cell into a cancer cell.

carotenoid Any of a group of yellow-to-red plant pigments; some can be converted to vitamin A by the liver, and many act as antioxidants or have other anticancer effects. The carotenoids include beta-carotene, lutein, lycopene, and zeaxanthin.

antioxidant A substance that can lessen the breakdown of food or body constituents; actions include binding oxygen and donating electrons to free radicals.

free radicals Electron-seeking compounds that can react with fats, proteins, and DNA, damaging cell membranes and mutating genes in their search for electrons; produced through chemical reactions in the body and through exposure to environmental factors such as sunlight and tobacco smoke.

phytochemical A naturally occurring substance found in plant foods that may help prevent chronic diseases such as cancer and heart disease; *phyto* means plant.

acrylamide by not smoking—you get much more of the chemical from smoking than from food.

Fiber Various potential cancer-fighting actions have been proposed for fiber, but none has been firmly established. Although further study is needed to clarify the relationship between fiber intake and cancer risk, experts still recommend a high-fiber diet for its overall positive effect on health.

Fruits and Vegetables A massive number of epidemiological studies provide evidence that high consumption of fruits and vegetables reduces the risk of many cancers. Exactly which constituents of fruits and vegetables are responsible for this reduction in risk is less certain. Some essential nutrients have been found to act against cancer. For example, vitamin C, vitamin E, selenium, and the **carotenoids** (vitamin A precursors) may help block the initiation of cancer by acting as **antioxidants.** Antioxidants prevent **free radicals** from damaging DNA. Vitamin C may also block the conversion of nitrates (food preservatives) into cancer-causing agents. Folic acid may inhibit the transformation of normal cells into malignant cells and strengthen immune function. Calcium inhibits the growth of cells in the colon and may slow the spread of potentially cancerous cells. Many other anticancer agents in the diet fall under the broader heading of **phytochemicals,** substances in plants that help protect against chronic diseases. One of the first to be identified was sulforaphane, a compound found in broccoli.

To increase your intake of potential cancer fighters, eat a wide variety of fruits, vegetables, legumes, and grains (see the box "Eating More Fruits and Vegetables" on p. 372). Don't rely on supplements. Isolated phytochemicals may be harmful if taken in high doses, and it is likely that the anticancer effects of many foods are the result of many chemical substances working in combination.

Eating for Cancer Prevention General dietary guidelines for reducing your risk of cancer include the following:

- Eat a varied plant-based diet.
- Eat 7–13 servings of fruits and vegetables each day, favoring foods from the following categories:
  - Cruciferous vegetables
  - Citrus fruits and berries
  - Dark green leafy vegetables
  - Dark yellow, orange, or red fruits or vegetables
- Eat other high-fiber foods, such as legumes and whole grains. Choose minimally processed complex carbohydrates and limit intake of simple sugars.
- Limit consumption of meat and total fat. Favor monounsaturated and omega-3 polyunsaturated fats over other types of fats.
- Limit consumption of meat and fish that has been grilled in a direct flame or is charred or blackened.

Your food choices significantly affect your risk of cancer. By consuming the recommended 7–13 servings of fruits and vegetables a day, this young man ensures that his diet is high in fiber and rich in cancer-fighting phytochemicals.

- Be moderate in your consumption of cured and smoked meats.
- Be moderate in your consumption of alcoholic beverages.

MOTIVATION FOR CHANGE! Healthier dietary choices are a key component of many health behavior change programs, but breaking long-standing habits relating to food choices can be challenging. To help make change easier and more enjoyable, look through the lists of strategies and recommended foods in this chapter and Lab 12.1, and make a list of ten foods that you really enjoy and that can help reduce your risk of cancer. Carry your list with you and get in the habit of referring to it when shopping for food and eating out. A list that serves as a reminder and a plan that includes many choices increase your chances of successful behavior change.

Inactivity and Obesity

Several common types of cancer are associated with an inactive lifestyle, and research has shown a relationship between increased physical activity and a reduction in cancer risk. There is good evidence that exercise reduces the risk of colon cancer, perhaps by speeding the movement of food through the digestive tract, strengthening immune function, and decreasing blood fat levels. Exercise

Take Charge

Breakfast

- Drink 100% juice every morning.
- Add raisins, berries, or sliced fruit to whole-grain cereal, pancakes, or waffles. Top bagels with tomato slices.
- Try a fruit smoothie made from fresh or frozen fruit and orange juice or low-fat yogurt.

Lunch

- Choose vegetable soup or salad with your meal.
- Replace potato chips or french fries with cut-up vegetables.
- Add extra chunks of fruits or vegetables to salads.
- Try adding vegetables such as roasted peppers, cucumber slices, shredded carrots, avocado, or salsa to sandwiches.
- Drink tomato or vegetable juice instead of soda.

Dinner

- Choose a vegetarian main course, such as stir-fry or vegetable stew. Have at least two servings of vegetables.

- Substitute vegetables for meat in casseroles and pasta and chili recipes.
- At the salad bar, pile your plate with healthy vegetables and use low-fat or nonfat dressing.

Snacks and On the Go

- Keep "grab and eat" fruits and vegetables on hand (apples, plums, pears, and carrots).
- Keep small packages of dried fruit in the car (try dried apricots, peaches, and pears and raisins).
- Make ice cubes from 100% fruit juice and drop them into regular or sparkling water.

SOURCES: National Cancer Institute. 2005. *Eat 5–9 a Day for Better Health* (http://www.5aday.gov; retrieved March 30, 2005). The produce prescription. 2000. *Consumer Reports on Health*, December. Welland, D. 1999. Fruits and vegetables: Easy ways to five-a-day. *Environmental Nutrition*, June.

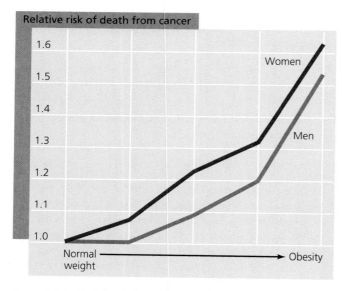

Figure 12.4 Body weight and cancer mortality. For both men and women, overweight and obesity are associated with significantly higher rates of death from cancer. SOURCE: Calle, E. E., et al. 2003. Overweight, obesity, and mortality from cancer in a prospectively studied cohort of U.S. adults. *New England Journal of Medicine* 348(17): 1625–1638.

is also important because it helps prevent obesity, an independent risk factor for cancers of the prostate, breast, female reproductive tract, and kidney, and possibly the colon and gallbladder (Figure 12.4).

Carcinogens in the Environment

Some carcinogens occur naturally in the environment, like the sun's UV rays. Others are synthetic substances that show up occasionally in the general environment but more often in the work environments of specific industries.

Ingested Chemicals   The food industry uses preservatives and other additives to prevent food from becoming spoiled or stale. Some of these compounds are antioxidants and may actually decrease any cancer-causing properties the food might have. Other compounds, like the nitrates and nitrites found in beer and ale, ham, bacon, hot dogs, and lunch meats, are potentially more dangerous. Although nitrates and nitrites are not themselves carcinogenic, they can combine with dietary substances in the stomach and be converted to nitrosamines, which are highly potent carcinogens. Foods cured with nitrites, as well as those cured by salt or smoke, have been linked to esophageal and stomach cancer, and they should be eaten only in modest amounts.

Environmental and Industrial Pollution   The best available data indicate that less than 2% of cancer deaths are caused by general environmental pollution, such as substances in our air and water. Exposure to carcinogenic materials in the workplace is a more serious problem. Occupational exposure to specific carcinogens may account for up to 5% of cancer deaths. With increasing industry and government regulations, industrial sources of cancer risk should continue to diminish.

Radiation   All sources of radiation are potentially carcinogenic, including medical X-rays, radioactive substances (radioisotopes), and UV radiation from the sun, sunlamps, and tanning beds. Most physicians and dentists are quite aware of the risk of radiation, and successful efforts have been made to reduce the amount of radiation needed for mammography, dental X-rays, and other necessary medical X-rays.

Another source of environmental radiation is radon gas. Radon is a radioactive decomposition product of radium, which is found in small quantities in some rocks and soils. Fortunately, in most of our homes and classrooms, radon is rapidly dissipated into the atmosphere, and very low levels of radon do not appear to significantly increase cancer risk. But in certain kinds of enclosed spaces, such as mines, some basements, and airtight buildings, it can rise to dangerous levels.

Microbes About 15% of the world's cancers are caused by microbes, including viruses, bacteria, and parasites, although the percentage is much lower in developed countries like the United States. As discussed earlier, certain types of HPV cause many cases of cervical cancer. Other microbes linked to cancer include the *Helicobacter pylori* bacterium, which can cause both stomach ulcers and stomach cancer. The Epstein-Barr virus, best known for causing mononucleosis, is also suspected of contributing to Hodgkin's disease, cancer of the pharynx, and some stomach cancers. Human herpesvirus 8 has been linked to Kaposi's sarcoma and certain types of lymphoma. Hepatitis virus B and C together cause as many as 80% of the world's liver cancers.

PREVENTING CANCER

Your lifestyle choices can radically lower your cancer risks, so you *can* take a practical approach to cancer prevention. Here are some guidelines:

- *Avoid tobacco.* Smoking is responsible for 80–90% of lung cancers and for about 30% of all cancer deaths. The carcinogenic chemicals in smoke are transported throughout the body in the bloodstream, making smoking a carcinogen for many forms of cancer other than lung cancer. The use of spit tobacco increases the risk of cancers of the mouth, larynx, throat, and esophagus. It's also important to avoid exposure to ETS.

- *Control diet and weight.* About one-third of all cancers are in some way linked to what we eat. Choose a low-fat, plant-based diet containing a wide variety of fruits, vegetables, and whole grains rich in phytochemicals. Drink alcohol only in moderation, if at all. Maintain a healthy weight.

- *Exercise regularly.* Regular exercise is linked to lower rates of colon and other cancers. It also helps control weight.

- *Protect skin from the sun.* Almost all cases of skin cancer are sun-related. Wear protective clothing when you're out in the sun and use a sunscreen with an SPF rating of 15 or higher. Don't go to tanning salons.

- *Avoid environmental and occupational carcinogens.* Try to avoid occupational exposure to carcinogens and

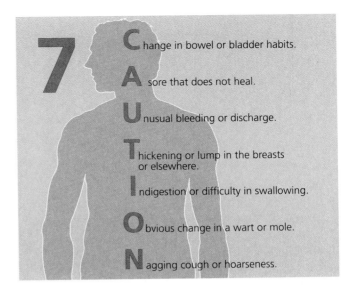

Figure 12.5   The seven major warning signs of cancer.

don't smoke; the cancer risks of many of these agents increase greatly when combined with smoking.

Your first line of defense against cancer involves the lifestyle changes described in this chapter. Your second line of defense against cancer is early detection. The American Cancer Society (ACS) recommends that you stay alert for any of the seven major warning signs illustrated in Figure 12.5; you can remember these with the acronym CAUTION. The appearance of any of these warning signs, although not a sure indication of cancer, should send you to your physician. The ACS also recommends routine tests to screen for common cancers. In addition to the screening guidelines listed in Table 12.1, some experts recommend regular skin self-exams and, for men, monthly testicular self-exams. Discuss appropriate screening tests with your physician.

Tips for Today

Our knowledge about the causes of cancer has grown exponentially in the past few decades, and research in biology and genetics offers the hope of better cancer therapies in the future. A growing body of research also suggests that we can take an active role in preventing many cancers by adopting a wellness lifestyle. Exercise, diet, and awareness are three important keys to cancer prevention.

Right now you can

- Do a breast self-exam, if you are a woman, or a testicular self-exam, if you are a man.

- Plan to have two vegetables with dinner tonight, one of them broccoli, cauliflower, brussels sprouts, or kale.

- Put your sunscreen by the front door so you'll remember to apply it the next time you go out in the sun, or put a brimmed hat by the door or in the car.

- Memorize the seven major warning signs of cancer represented by the acronym CAUTION.

Table 12.1 | Screening Guidelines for the Early Detection of Cancer in Asymptomatic People

Site	Recommendation
Breast	• Yearly mammograms are recommended starting at age 40. The age at which screening should be stopped should be individualized by considering the potential risks and benefits of screening in the context of overall health status and longevity. • Clinical breast exam should be part of a periodic health exam, about every 3 years for women age 20–39, and every year for women age 40 and older. • Women should know how their breasts normally feel and report any breast change promptly to their health care providers. Breast self-exam is an option for women starting at age 20. • Women at increased risk (e.g., family history, genetic tendency, past breast cancer) should talk with their doctors about the benefits and limitations of starting mammography screening earlier, having additional tests (i.e., breast ultrasound and MRI), or having more frequent exams.
Colon and Rectum	Beginning at age 50, men and women should begin screening with one of the examination schedules below. • A fecal occult blood test (FOBT) or fecal immunochemical test (FIT) every year • A flexible sigmoidoscopy (FSIG) every 5 years • Annual FOBT or FIT and flexible sigmoidoscopy every 5 years* • A double-contrast barium enema every 5 years • A colonoscopy every 10 years *Combined testing is preferred over either annual FOBT or FIT, or FSIG every 5 years, alone. People who are at moderate or high risk for colorectal cancer should talk with a doctor about a different testing schedule.*
Prostate	The PSA test and the digital rectal examination should be offered annually, beginning at age 50, to men who have a life expectancy of at least 10 years. Men at high risk (African American men and men with a strong family history of one or more first-degree relatives diagnosed with prostate cancer at an early age) should begin testing at age 45. For men at both average risk and high risk, information should be provided about what is known and what is uncertain about the benefits and limitations of early detection and treatment of prostate cancer so that they can make an informed decision about testing.
Uterus	**Cervix:** Screening should begin approximately 3 years after a woman begins having vaginal intercourse, but no later than age 21. Screening should be done every year with regular Pap tests or every 2 years using liquid-based tests. At or after age 30, women who have had three normal test results in a row may get screened every 2 to 3 years. Alternatively, cervical cancer screening with HPV DNA testing and conventional or liquid-based cytology could be performed every 3 years. However, doctors may suggest a woman get screened more often if she has certain risk factors, such as HIV infection or a weak immune system. Women age 70 and older who have had three or more consecutive normal Pap tests in the past 10 years may choose to stop cervical cancer screening. Screening after total hysterectomy (with removal of the cervix) is not necessary unless the surgery was done as a treatment for cervical cancer. **Endometrium:** The American Cancer Society recommends that at the time of menopause all women should be informed about the risks and symptoms of endometrial cancer and strongly encouraged to report any unexpected bleeding or spotting to their physicians. Annual screening for endometrial cancer with endometrial biopsy beginning at age 35 should be offered to women with or at risk for hereditary nonpolyposis colon cancer (HNPCC).
Cancer-Related Checkup	For individuals undergoing periodic health examinations, a cancer-related checkup should include health counseling and, depending on a person's age and gender, might include examinations for cancers of the thyroid, oral cavity, skin, lymph nodes, testes, and ovaries, as well as for some nonmalignant diseases.

SOURCE: American Cancer Society's *Cancer Facts and Figures 2005.* Copyright © 2005 American Cancer Society, Inc. www.cancer.org. Reprinted with permission.

SUMMARY

- Cancer is an abnormal and uncontrollable growth of cells or tissue; cancer cells can metastasize.

- Lung cancer kills more people than any other type of cancer; tobacco smoke is the primary cause.

- Colon and rectal cancer is linked to age, heredity, and a diet with low intake of fruits and vegetables.

- Breast cancer has a genetic component, but lifestyle and hormones are also factors. Prostate cancer is chiefly a disease of aging; diet, heredity, and ethnicity are other risk factors.

- Cancers of the female reproductive tract include cervical, uterine, and ovarian cancer. Cervical cancer is linked to HPV infection; the Pap test is an effective screening test.

- Melanoma is the most serious form of skin cancer; excessive exposure to UV radiation in sunlight is the primary cause.

What is a biopsy? A biopsy is the removal and examination of a small piece of body tissue. Biopsies enable cancer specialists to carefully examine cells that are suspected of having turned cancerous. Some biopsies are fairly simple to perform, such as those on tissue from moles or skin sores. Other biopsies may require the use of a needle or probe to remove tissue from inside the body, such as in the breast or stomach.

How is cancer treated? The ideal cancer therapy would kill or remove all cancer cells while leaving normal tissue untouched. Sometimes this is almost possible, as when a surgeon removes a small superficial tumor of the skin. Usually a tumor is less accessible, and some combination of treatments is necessary. Current treatments for cancer are based primarily on the following:

- *Surgery.* Sometimes the organ containing the tumor is not essential for life and can be partially or completely removed. Surgery is less effective when cancer involves widely distributed cells (such as in the case of leukemia) or when the cancer has already metastasized.

- *Chemotherapy.* Cancer cells can be killed by administering drugs that interfere chemically with their growth. Although chemotherapy is targeted at rapidly dividing cancer cells, it can also affect cells in normal tissue, leading to unpleasant side effects.

- *Radiation.* In radiation therapy, a beam of X-rays or gamma rays is directed at the tumor, killing the cancer cells. Radiation destroys both normal and cancerous cells but can usually be precisely directed at the tumor.

Some experimental techniques that show promise for some particular types of cancer include the following:

- *Bone marrow transplants,* in which healthy bone marrow cells from a compatible donor are transplanted following the elimination of the patient's bone marrow by radiation or chemotherapy. Transplants of *stem cells* may provide a solution to the problem of donor incompatibility. These unspecialized cells can divide and produce many specialized cell types, including bone marrow cells. Stem cells can be grown outside the body and then transplanted back into the cancer patient, allowing safe repopulation of bone marrow.

- *Vaccines and genetically modified immune cells,* which enhance the reaction of a patient's own immune system.

- *Anti-angiogenesis agents,* which starve tumors by blocking their blood supply.

- *Protease inhibitors,* which interfere with a tumor's ability to invade normal tissue and metastasize.

In the future, gene sequencing techniques may allow treatments to be targeted at specific cancer subtypes, much as specific antibiotics are now used to treat specific bacterial diseases.

Are genetic tests for cancer risk beneficial? Tests for hereditary mutations in genes are now available for some types of cancer, including breast cancer. However, such tests are not always beneficial for the individual. Good news from a genetic test is reassuring, but it doesn't guarantee freedom from cancer because most cancers are not due to inherited genetic mutations. For example, only 5–10% of all cases of breast cancer occur among women who inherit the most common genetic mutation associated with the disease. For people who do test positive for a genetic mutation, there aren't many good options beyond increased monitoring. And those who test positive can face problems in addition to an uncertain medical future. Health and life insurers may use results of a genetic test to refuse or cancel coverage; employers may use the information to screen current or prospective employees.

There is no simple answer to the question of who should undergo genetic testing for disease-related genes. If you think you are at high risk for a genetic abnormality because of your family or ethnic background, consider genetic counseling. A counselor can help you consider all the issues related to testing and can help you make the decision that is right for you.

Visit the Online Learning Center for answers to more common questions about cancer.

- Oral cancer is caused primarily by smoking, excess alcohol consumption, and use of spit tobacco.

- Testicular cancer can be detected early through self-examination.

- The genetic basis of some cancers appears to be mutational damage to suppressor genes, which normally limit cell division.

- Cancer-promoting dietary factors include meat, certain types of fat, and alcohol. Dietary elements that may protect against cancer include antioxidants and phytochemicals. An inactive lifestyle is associated with some cancers.

- Some carcinogens occur naturally in the environment; others are manufactured substances. Occupational exposure is a risk for some workers.

- All sources of radiation are potentially carcinogenic, including X-rays, UV rays of the sun, and radon gas.

- Strategies for preventing cancer include avoiding tobacco; eating a varied, moderate diet and controlling weight; exercising regularly; protecting skin from the sun; avoiding exposure to environmental and occupational carcinogens; staying alert for cancer warning signs; and getting recommended cancer-screening tests.

For Further Exploration

VW *Fit and Well* **Online Learning Center**
(www.mhhe.com/fahey)

Use the learning objectives, study guide questions, and glossary flashcards to review key terms and concepts and prepare for exams. You can extend your knowledge of cancer and gain experience in using the Internet as a resource by completing the activities and checking out the Web links for the topics in Chapter 12 marked with the World Wide Web icon. For this chapter, Internet activities explore cancer risk factors, UV index, major forms of cancer, and dietary factors; there are Web links for the Vital Statistics figures, the box on sunscreens, and the chapter as a whole.

Daily Fitness and Nutrition Journal

Engaging in regular physical activity and eating a healthy diet are two important strategies for preventing cancer. Continue to use your journal to monitor your exercise program and, if needed, to keep records of your diet. You may want to use the nutrition journal to focus on a specific dietary factor related to cancer, such as adequate intake of fruits and vegetables.

Books

American Cancer Society. 2003. *Cancer: What Causes It. What Doesn't.* Atlanta, Ga.: American Cancer Society. *Provides basic background information about cancer and its causes.*

American Institute for Cancer Research. 2005. *The New American Plate Cookbook.* Berkeley, Calif.: University of California Berkeley Press. *Provides guidelines and recipes for healthy eating to prevent cancer and other chronic diseases.*

Runkington, C., and J. J. Straus. 2005. *The Encyclopedia of Cancer.* New York: Facts on File. *Includes entries on a variety of topics relating to cancer causes, prevention, diagnosis, and treatment.*

WW Organizations, Hotlines, and Web Sites

American Academy of Dermatology. Provides information on skin cancer prevention.
888-462-DERM
http://www.aad.org

American Cancer Society. Provides a wide range of free materials on the prevention and treatment of cancer.
800-ACS-2345
http://www.cancer.org

American Institute for Cancer Research. Provides information on lifestyle and cancer prevention, especially nutrition.
800-843-8114
http://www.aicr.org

EPA/Sunwise. Provides information about the UV Index and the effects of sun exposure, with links to sites with daily UV Index ratings for U.S. and international cities.
http://www.epa.gov/sunwise/uvindex.html

Harvard Center for Cancer Prevention: Your Disease Risk. Includes interactive risk assessments as well as tips for preventing common cancers.
http://www.yourdiseaserisk.harvard.edu

MedlinePlus: Cancers. Provides links to reliable cancer information.
http://www.nlm.nih.gov/medlineplus/cancers.html

National Cancer Institute. Provides information on treatment options, screening, clinical trials, and newly approved drugs.
800-4-CANCER; 800-624-2511 (Cancer Fax)
http://www.cancer.gov
http://5aday.gov

Selected Bibliography

American Cancer Society. 2005. *Cancer Facts and Figures, 2005.* Atlanta, Ga.: American Cancer Society.

Brennan, P., et al. 2004. Secondhand smoke exposure in adulthood and risk of lung cancer among never smokers: A pooled analysis of two large studies. *International Journal of Cancer* 109(1): 125–131.

Brenner, D. J., et al. 2004. Estimated radiation risks potentially associated with full-body CT screening. *Radiology* 232(3): 735–738.

Centers for Disease Control and Prevention. 2005. Breast cancer screening and socioeconomic status. *Morbidity and Mortality Weekly Report* 54(39): 981–984.

Chan, J. M., F. Wang, and E. A. Holly. 2005. Vegetable and fruit intake and pancreatic cancer in a population-based case-control study in the San Francisco bay area. *Cancer, Epidemiology, Biomarkers and Prevention* 14(9): 2093–2097.

Chao, A., et al. 2005. Meat consumption and risk of colorectal cancer. *Journal of the American Medical Association* 293(2): 172–182.

Chia, K. S., et al. 2005. Profound changes in breast cancer incidence may reflect changes into a Westernized lifestyle: A comparative population-based study in Singapore and Sweden. *International Journal of Cancer* 113(2): 302–306.

Cho, E., et al. 2004. Alcohol intake and colorectal cancer: A pooled analysis of 8 cohort studies. *Annals of Internal Medicine* 140(8): 606–613.

Flood, A., et al. 2005. Calcium from diet and supplements is associated with reduced risk of colorectal cancer in a prospective cohort of women. *Cancer Epidemiology, Biomarkers and Prevention* 14(1): 126–132.

Food and Agriculture Organization and World Health Organization. 2005. *Joint FAO/WHO Expert Committee on Food Additives: Summary and Conclusions* (http://www.who.int/ipcs/food/jecfa/summaries/en; retrieved March 29, 2005).

Goff, B. A., et al. 2004. Frequency of symptoms of ovarian cancer in women presenting to primary care clinics. *Journal of the American Medical Association* 291(22): 2705–2712.

Knight, J. M., et al. 2002. Awareness of the risks of tanning lamps does not influence behavior among college students. *Archives of Dermatology* 138(10): 1311–1315.

Li, C. I., K. E. Malone, and J. R. Daling. 2005. The relationship between various measures of cigarette smoking and risk of breast cancer among older women 65–79 years of age (United States). *Cancer Causes Control* 16(8): 975–985.

Martinez, M. E. 2005. Primary prevention of colorectal cancer: Lifestyle, nutrition, exercise. *Recent Results in Cancer Research* 166: 177–211.

National Toxicology Program. 2005. *Report on Carcinogens,* 11th ed. Research Triangle Park, N.C.: National Toxicology Program.

Patel, J. D., P. B. Bach, and M. G. Kris. 2004. Lung cancer in U.S. women. *Journal of the American Medical Association* 291(14): 1763–1768.

Pelucchi, C., et al. 2004. Fibre intake and prostate cancer risk. *International Journal of Cancer* 109(2): 278–280.

Pisano, E. D., et al. 2005. Diagnostic performance of digital versus film mammography for breast-cancer screening. *New England Journal of Medicine* 353(17): 1773–1783.

Roden, R. B., et al. 2004. Vaccination to prevent and treat cervical cancer. *Human Pathology* 35(8): 971–982.

Romond, E. H., et al. 2005. Trastuzumab plus adjuvant chemotherapy for operable HER2-positive breast cancer. *New England Journal of Medicine* 353(16): 1673–1684.

Stein, C. J., and G. A. Colditz. 2004. Modifiable risk factors for cancer. *British Journal of Cancer* 90(2): 299–303.

Trimble, C. L., et al. 2005. Active and passive cigarette smoking and the risk of cervical neoplasia. *Obstetrics and Gynecology* 105(1): 174–181.

Van Gils, C. H., et al. 2005. Consumption of vegetables and fruits and risk of breast cancer. *Journal of the American Medical Association* 293(3): 183–193.

Walter, M., et al. 2005. Dietary patterns and risk of prostate cancer in Ontario, Canada. *International Journal of Cancer* 116(4): 592–598.

World Health Organization. 2005. *Cancer: Diet and Physical Activity's Impact* (http://www.who.int/dietphysicalactivity/publications/facts/cancer/en; retrieved January 20, 2005).

LAB 12.1 *Cancer Prevention*

This lab looks at two areas of cancer prevention over which you have a great deal of individual control—diet and sun exposure; additional self-assessments can be found on the Online Learning Center. For a detailed personal risk profile for many specific types of cancer, complete the assessments at the Harvard University Center for Cancer Prevention's "Your Disease Risk" site (http://www.yourdiseaserisk.harvard.edu).

Part I   Diet and Cancer

Track your diet for 3 days, recording the number of servings from each of the following groups that you consume.

Day 1	Day 2	Day 3	Potential Cancer Fighters
____	____	____	Orange, deep yellow, pink, and red vegetables and some fruits (for example, apricots, cantaloupe, carrots, corn, grapefruit, mangoes, nectarines, papayas, red and yellow bell peppers, sweet potatoes, pumpkin, tomatoes and tomato sauce, watermelon, winter squash such as acorn or butternut)
____	____	____	Dark green leafy vegetables (for example, broccoli rabe, chard, kale, romaine and other dark lettuces, spinach; beet, collard, dandelion, mustard, and turnip greens)
____	____	____	Cruciferous vegetables (bok choy, broccoli, brussels sprouts, cabbage, cauliflower, kohlrabi, turnips)
____	____	____	Citrus fruits (for example, grapefruit, lemons, limes, oranges, tangerines)
____	____	____	Whole grains (for example, whole-grain bread, cereal, and pasta; brown rice; oatmeal; whole-grain corn; barley; popcorn; bulgur)
____	____	____	Legumes (peas, lentils, and beans, including fava, navy, kidney, pinto, black, and lima beans)
____	____	____	Berries (for example, strawberries, raspberries, blackberries, blueberries)
____	____	____	Garlic and other allium vegetables (onions, leeks, chives, scallions, shallots)
____	____	____	Soy products (for example, tofu, tempeh, soy milk, miso, soybeans)
____	____	____	Other cancer-fighting fruits (apples, cherries, cranberries or juice, grapes, kiwifruit, pears, plums, prunes, raisins)
____	____	____	Other cancer-fighting vegetables (asparagus, beets, chili peppers, eggplant, green peppers, radishes)
____	____	____	**Daily Totals (Average for three days: _____)**

The goal is to eat at least 7 (women) or 9 (men) servings of cancer-fighting fruits and vegetables each day; the more servings, the better. (Research is ongoing, and this list of cancer fighters is not comprehensive. Remember, nearly all fruits, vegetables, and grains are healthy, disease-fighting dietary choices.)

Part II   Skin Cancer Risk Assessment

Your risk of skin cancer from the ultraviolet radiation in sunlight depends on several factors. Take the quiz that follows to see how sensitive you are. The higher your UV-risk score, the greater your risk of skin cancer—and the greater your need to take precautions against too much sun. Score 1 point for each true statement:

____ 1. I have blond or red hair.

____ 2. I have light-colored eyes (blue, gray, green).

____ 3. I freckle easily.

____ 4. I have many moles.

____ 5. I had two or more blistering sunburns as a child.

____ 6. I spent lots of time in a tropical climate as a child.

____ 7. I have a family history of skin cancer.

____ 8. I work outdoors.

____ 9. I spend a lot of time in outdoor activities.

____10. I like to spend as much time in the sun as I can.

____11. I sometimes go to a tanning parlor or use a sunlamp.

____ **Total Score**

Score	Risk of skin cancer from UV radiation
0	Low
1–3	Moderate
4–7	High
8–11	Very high

Using Your Results

How did you score? (1) How close did you come to the goal of eating 7–9 or more servings of cancer fighters each day? Are you at all surprised by your results?

Are you satisfied with your diet in terms of cancer prevention? If not, set a specific goal for a target number of servings of cancer-fighting fruits and vegetables: _____

(2) What is your skin cancer risk assessment score? Are you at all surprised by the result? Does it indicate that you are at high or very high risk? Do you feel you need to take action because of your risk level?

What should you do next? Enter the results of this lab in the Preprogram Assessment column in Appendix D. (1) If you've set a goal for the diet and cancer portion of the lab, select a target number of additional cancer fighters from the list to try over the next few days; list the foods below, along with your plan for incorporating them into your diet (as a side dish, as a snack, on a salad, as a substitute for another food, etc.).

Cancer fighter to try: Plan for trying:

_____   _____

_____   _____

_____   _____

_____   _____

(2) You cannot control all of your risk factors for skin cancer, but you can control your behavior with regard to sun exposure. Keep a journal to track your behavior on days when you are outdoors in the sun for a significant period of time. Compare your behavior with the recommendations for skin cancer prevention described in the chapter. Record such information as time of day, total duration of exposure, UV index for the day, clothing worn, type and amount of sunscreen used, frequency of sunscreen applications, and so on. From this record, identify ways to improve your behavior to lower your risk of skin cancer. Put together a behavior change plan.

Next, begin to put your strategies into action. After several weeks of a program to improve your diet or reduce your UV exposure, do this lab again and enter the results in the Postprogram Assessment column of Appendix D. How do the results compare?

SOURCE: Part II: Skin Cancer Risk Assessment adapted from Shear, N. 1996. "What's Your UV-risk Score?" Copyright © 1996 by the Consumers Union of the United States, Inc., Yonkers, NY 10703-1057, a nonprofit organization. Reprinted with permission from the author.

LABORATORY ACTIVITIES

Injury Prevention and Personal Safety

Unintentional injuries are the fifth leading cause of death among Americans overall and the leading killer of young people. Injuries affect all segments of the population, but they are particularly common among minorities and people with low incomes, primarily due to social, environmental, and economic factors. The economic cost of injuries in the United States is high, with more than $586 billion spent each year for medical care and rehabilitation of injured people, employer losses, vehicle-damage costs, and fire losses.

Injuries are generally classified into four categories, based on where they occur: motor vehicle injuries, home injuries, leisure injuries, and work injuries.

MOTOR VEHICLE INJURIES

Incidents involving motor vehicles are the leading cause of death for Americans between ages 1 and 34, the leading cause of paralysis due to spinal injury, and the leading cause of severe brain injury.

Factors in Motor Vehicle Injuries

Driving Habits Nearly two-thirds of motor vehicle injuries are caused by bad driving, especially speeding. As speed increases, momentum and force of impact increase and the time available for the driver to react decreases. Speed limits are posted to establish the safest *maximum* speed limit for a given area under *ideal* conditions. Aggressive driving, characterized by speeding, frequent and abrupt lane changes, tailgating, and passing on the shoulder, also increases the risk of crashes—both for the aggressive driver and for others (see p. A-2).

Anything that distracts a driver—sleepiness, bad mood, children or pets in the car, use of a cellular phone—can increase the risk of a crash. Sleepiness reduces reaction time, coordination, and speed of information processing and can be as dangerous as drug and alcohol use. Even mild sleep deprivation causes a deterioration in driving ability comparable to that caused by a 0.05% blood alcohol concentration.

Cell phone users respond to hazards about 20% slower and are about twice as likely to rear-end a braking car in front of them. Cell phone use reduces the reaction time of a 20-year-old to that of a 70-year-old not using a phone. Hands-free devices do not help significantly—it appears that the mental distraction of talking is the factor in crashes rather than holding a phone.

Safety Belts and Air Bags

Safety Belts and Air Bags A person who doesn't wear a safety belt is twice as likely to be injured in a crash as a person who does wear a safety belt. Safety belts not only prevent occupants from being thrown from the car at the time of the crash but also provide protection from the "second collision," which occurs when the occupant of the car hits something inside the car, such as the steering column or windshield. The safety belt also spreads the stopping force of a collision over the body.

Since 1998, all new cars have been equipped with dual air bags—one for the driver and one for the front passenger seat. Although air bags provide some supplemental protection in the event of a collision, most are useful only in head-on collisions. They also deflate immediately after inflating and so do not provide protection in collisions involving multiple impacts. To ensure that air bags work as intended, always follow these basic guidelines: Place infants in rear-facing infant seats in the backseat, transport children age 12 and under in the backseat, always use safety belts or appropriate safety seats, and keep 10 inches between the air bag cover and the breastbone of the driver or passenger. In the rare event that a person cannot comply with these guidelines, he or she can apply to the National Highway Traffic Safety Administration for permission to install an on-off switch that temporarily disables the air bag.

Although helpful, air bags are not a replacement for safety belts. Everyone in a vehicle should buckle up—wearing a safety belt is the single most effective way to reduce the risk of crash-related death.

Alcohol and Other Drugs Alcohol is involved in about half of all fatal crashes. Alcohol-impaired driving, defined by blood alcohol concentration (BAC), is illegal. The legal BAC limit is 0.08% in most states, but driving ability is impaired at much lower BACs. All psychoactive drugs have the potential to impair driving ability.

Preventing Motor Vehicle Injuries

About 75% of all motor vehicle collisions occur within 25 miles of home and at speeds lower than 40 mph. These crashes often occur because the driver believes safety measures are not necessary for short trips. Clearly, the statistics prove otherwise.

To prevent motor vehicle injuries:

- Obey the speed limit. If you have to speed to get to your destination on time, you're not allowing enough time. Try leaving 10–15 minutes earlier.

- Always wear a safety belt and ask passengers to do the same. Strap infants and toddlers into government-approved car seats in the backseat. Children who have outgrown child safety seats but who are still too small for adult safety belts alone (usually age 4–8) should be secured using booster seats. All children under 12 should ride in the backseat.

- Never drive under the influence of alcohol or other drugs. Never ride with a driver who has been drinking or using drugs.

- Do not drive when you are sleepy or have been awake for 18 or more hours.

- Avoid using your cell phone while driving—your primary obligation is to pay attention to the road. If you do make calls, follow laws set by your city or state. Place calls when you are at a stop and keep them short. Pull over if the conversation is stressful or emotional.

- Keep your car in good working order. Regularly inspect tires, oil and fluid levels, windshield wipers, spare tire, and so on.

- Always allow enough following distance. Follow the "3-second rule": When the vehicle ahead passes a reference point, count out 3 seconds. If you pass the reference point before you finish counting, drop back and allow more following distance.

- Always increase following distance and slow down if weather or road conditions are poor.

- Choose interstate highways rather than rural roads. Highways are much safer because of better visibility, wider lanes, fewer surprises, and other factors.

- Always signal before turning or changing lanes.

- Stop completely at stop signs. Follow all traffic laws.

- Take special care at intersections. Always look left, right, and then left again. Make sure you have plenty of time to complete your maneuver in the intersection.

- Don't pass on two-lane roads unless you're in a designated passing area and have a clear view ahead.

Motorcycles and Mopeds

About 1 out of every 10 traffic fatalities among people age 15–34 involves someone riding a motorcycle. Injuries from motorcycle collisions are generally more severe than those involving automobiles because motorcycles provide little, if any, protection. Moped riders face additional challenges. Mopeds usually have a maximum speed of 30–35 mph and have less power for maneuverability.

To prevent motorcycle and moped injuries:

- Make yourself easier to see by wearing light-colored clothing, driving with your headlights on, and correctly positioning yourself in traffic.

- Develop the necessary skills. Lack of skill, especially when evasive action is needed to avoid a collision, is a major factor in motorcycle and moped injuries. Skidding from improper braking is the most common cause of loss of control.

- Wear a close-fitting helmet, one marked with the symbol DOT (for Department of Transportation).

- Protect your eyes with goggles, a face shield, or a windshield.

- Drive defensively and never assume that other drivers see you.

Pedestrians and Bicycles

Injuries to pedestrians and bicyclists are considered motor vehicle related because they are usually caused by motor vehicles. About 1 in 7 motor vehicle deaths each year involves a pedestrian; more than 80,000 pedestrians are injured each year.

To prevent injuries when walking or jogging:

- Walk or jog in daylight.

- Make yourself easier to see by wearing light-colored, reflective clothing.

- Face traffic when walking or jogging along a roadway, and follow traffic laws.

- Avoid busy roads or roads with poor visibility.

- Cross only at marked crosswalks and intersections.

- Don't listen to a radio, tape, or CD on headphones while walking or jogging.

- Don't hitchhike; it places you in a potentially dangerous situation.

Bicycle injuries result primarily from not knowing or understanding the rules of the road, failing to follow traffic laws, and not having sufficient skill or experience to handle traffic conditions. Bicycles are considered vehicles; bicycle riders must obey all traffic laws that apply to automobile drivers, including stopping at traffic lights and stop signs.

To prevent injuries when riding a bike:

- Wear safety equipment, including a helmet, eye protection, gloves, and proper footwear. Secure the bottom of your pant legs with clips and secure your shoelaces so they don't get tangled in the chain.

- Make yourself easier to see by wearing light-colored, reflective clothing. Equip your bike with reflectors and use lights, especially at night or when riding in wooded or other dark areas.

- Ride with the flow of traffic, not against it, and follow traffic laws. Use bike paths when they are available.

- Ride defensively; never assume that drivers see you. Be especially careful when turning or crossing at corners and intersections. Watch for cars turning right.

- Stop at all traffic lights and stop signs. Know and use hand signals.

- Continue pedaling at all times when moving (don't coast) to help keep the bike stable and to maintain your balance.

- Properly maintain your bike in working condition.

Aggressive Driving

Aggressive driving, known as road rage, has increased more than 50% since 1990. Aggressive drivers increase the risk of crashes for themselves and others. They further increase the risk of injuries if they stop their vehicles and confront each other. Even if you are successful at controlling your own aggressive driving impulses, you may still encounter an aggressive driver.

To avoid being the victim of an aggressive driver:

- *Always keep distance between your car and others.* If you are behind a very slow driver and can't pass, slow down to increase distance in case that driver does something unexpected. If you are being tailgated, do not increase your speed; instead, let the other driver pass you. If you are in the left lane when being tailgated, signal and pull over to let the other driver go by, even if you are traveling at the speed limit. When you are merging, make sure you have plenty of room. If you are being cut off by a merging driver, slow down to make room.

- *Be courteous, even if the other driver is not.* Use your horn rarely, if ever. Avoid making gestures of irritation, even shaking your head. When parking, let the other driver have the space that you both found.

- *Refuse to join in a fight.* Avoid eye contact with an angry driver. If someone makes a rude gesture, ignore it. If you think another car is following you and you have a cell phone, call the police. Otherwise, drive to a public place and honk your horn to get someone's attention.

- *If you make a mistake while driving, apologize.* Raise or wave your hand or touch or knock your head with the palm of your hand to indicate "What was I thinking?" You can also mouth the words "I'm sorry."

HOME INJURIES

Contrary to popular belief, home is one of the most dangerous places to be. The most common fatal home injuries are caused by falls, poisoning, fires, suffocation and choking, and incidents involving firearms.

Falls

Falls are second only to motor vehicle injuries in terms of causing deaths. They are the fifth leading cause of unintentional death for people under age 25. Most deaths occurring from falls involve falling on stairs or steps or from one level to another. Falls also occur on the same level, from tripping, slipping, or stumbling. Alcohol is a contributing factor in many falls.

To prevent injuries from falls:

- Install handrails and nonslip applications in the shower and bathtub. Place skidproof backing on rugs and carpets.
- Keep floors clear of objects or conditions that could cause slipping or tripping, such as heavy wax coating, electrical cords, and toys.
- Put a light switch by the door of every room so that no one has to walk across a room to turn on a light. Use night-lights in bedrooms, halls, and bathrooms.
- Outside the house, clear dangerous surfaces created by ice, snow, fallen leaves, or rough ground.
- Install handrails on stairs. Keep stairs well lit and clear of objects.
- When climbing a ladder, use both hands. Never stand higher than the third step from the top. When using a stepladder, make sure the spreader brace is in the locked position. With straight ladders, set the base 1 foot out for every 4 feet of height. Don't stand on chairs to reach things.
- If there are small children in the home, place gates at the top and bottom of stairs. Never leave a baby unattended on a bed or table.

Poisoning

More than 2.2 million poisonings occur every year in the United States.

To prevent poisoning:

- Store all medicines out of the reach of children. Use medicines only as directed on the label or by a physician.
- Use cleaners, pesticides, and other dangerous substances only in areas with proper ventilation. Store them out of the reach of children.
- Never operate a vehicle in an enclosed space. Have your furnace inspected yearly. Use caution with any substance that produces potentially toxic fumes, such as kerosene. If appropriate, install carbon monoxide detectors.
- Keep poisonous plants out of the reach of children. These include azalea, oleander, rhododendron, wild mushrooms, daffodil and hyacinth bulbs, mistletoe berries, apple seeds, morning glory seeds, wisteria seeds, and the leaves and stems of potato, rhubarb, and tomato plants.

To be prepared in case of poisoning:

- Keep the number of the nearest Poison Control Center (or emergency room) in an accessible location. A call to the national poison control hotline (800-222-1222) will be routed to a local center.

Emergency first aid for poisonings:

1. Remove the poison from contact with eyes, skin, or mouth, or remove the victim from contact with poisonous fumes or gases.
2. Call the Poison Control Center immediately for instructions. Have the container with you.
3. Do not follow emergency instructions on labels. Some may be out-of-date and carry incorrect treatment information.
4. If you are instructed to go to an emergency room, take the poisonous substance or its container with you.

Guidelines for specific types of poisons:

- *Swallowed poisons.* If the person is awake and able to swallow, give water only; then call the Poison Control Center or a physician for advice.
- *Poisons on the skin.* Remove any affected clothing. Flood affected parts of the skin with warm water, wash with soap and water, and rinse. Then call for advice.
- *Poisons in the eye.* For children, flood the eye with lukewarm water poured from a pitcher held 3–4 inches above the eye for 15 minutes; alternatively, irrigate the eye under a faucet. For adults, get in the shower and flood the eye with a gentle stream of lukewarm water for 15 minutes. Then call for advice.
- *Inhaled poisons.* Immediately carry or drag the person to fresh air and, if necessary, give mouth-to-mouth resuscitation. If the victim is not breathing easily, call 911 for help. Ventilate the area. Then call for advice.

Fires

Each year about 80% of fire deaths and 65% of fire injuries occur in the home. Careless smoking is the leading cause of fire deaths.

To prevent fires:

- Dispose of all cigarettes in ashtrays. Never smoke in bed.
- Do not overload electrical outlets. Do not place extension cords under rugs or where people walk. Replace worn or frayed extension cords.
- Place a wire screen in front of fireplaces and woodstoves. Remove ashes carefully and store them in airtight metal containers, not paper bags.
- Properly maintain electrical appliances, kerosene heaters, and furnaces. Clean flues and chimneys annually.
- Keep portable heaters at least 3 feet away from curtains, bedding, towels, or anything that might catch fire. Never leave heaters on when you're out of the room or sleeping.

To be prepared for a fire:

- Plan at least two escape routes out of each room. Designate a location outside the home as a meeting place. Stage a home fire drill.
- Install a smoke-detection device on every level of your home. Clean the detectors and test batteries once a month and replace the batteries at least once a year.
- Keep a fire extinguisher in your home and know how to use it.

To prevent injuries from fire:

- Get out as quickly as possible and go to the designated meeting place. Don't stop for a keepsake or a pet. Never hide in a closet or under a bed. Once outside, count heads to see if everyone is out. If you think someone is still inside the burning building, tell the firefighters. Never go back inside a burning building.
- If you're trapped in a room, feel the door. If it is hot or if smoke is coming in through the cracks, don't open it; use the alternative escape route. If you can't get out of a room, go to the window and shout or wave for help.
- Smoke inhalation is the largest cause of death and injury in fires. To avoid inhaling smoke, crawl along the floor away from the heat and smoke. Cover your mouth and nose, ideally with a wet cloth, and take short, shallow breaths.
- If your clothes catch fire, don't run. Drop to the ground, cover your face, and roll back and forth to smother the flames. Remember: stop-drop-roll.

Suffocation and Choking

Suffocation accounts for about 3500 deaths annually in the United States. Young children account for nearly half of these deaths. Children can suffocate if they put small items in their mouths, get tangled in their crib bedding, or get trapped in airtight appliances like old refrigerators. Keep small objects out of reach of children under age 3, and don't give them raw carrots, hot dogs, popcorn, peanuts, or hard candy. Examine toys carefully for small parts that could come loose; don't give plastic bags or balloons to small children.

Adults can also become choking victims, especially if they fail to chew food properly, eat hurriedly, or try to talk and eat at the same time. Many choking victims can be saved with abdominal thrusts, also called the Heimlich maneuver (Figure A.1, p. A-5). Infants who are choking can be saved with blows to the upper back, followed by chest thrusts if necessary.

Incidents Involving Firearms

Firearms pose a significant threat of unintentional injury, especially to people between ages 15 and 24.

To prevent firearm injuries:

- Never point a loaded gun at something you do not intend to shoot.
- Store unloaded firearms under lock and key in a place separate from ammunition.
- Inspect firearms carefully before handling them.
- Follow the safety procedures advocated in firearm safety courses.

LEISURE INJURIES

Leisure injuries take place in public places (but do not involve motor vehicles) and include recreational, sports, and transportation injuries. Many injuries in this category involve such recreational activities as boating and swimming, playground activities, in-line skating, and sports.

Drowning and Boating Injuries

Although most drownings are reported in lakes, ponds, rivers, and oceans, more than half the drownings of young children take place in residential pools. Among adolescents and adults, alcohol plays a significant role in many boating injuries and drownings.

To prevent drowning and boating injuries:

- Develop adequate swimming skill and make sure children learn to swim.
- Make sure residential pools are fenced and that children are never allowed to swim without supervision.
- Don't swim alone or in unsupervised places.
- Use caution when swimming in unfamiliar surroundings or for an unusual length of time. To avoid being chilled, don't swim in water colder than 70°F.
- Don't swim or boat under the influence of alcohol or other drugs. Don't chew gum or eat while in the water.
- Check the depth of water before diving.
- When on a boat, use a life jacket (personal flotation device).

In-Line Skating and Scooter Injuries

Most in-line skating injuries occur because users are not familiar with the equipment and do not wear appropriate safety gear.

American Red Cross · **Steps for Choking Emergencies**

A

Check
✔ Check the scene for safety
✔ Check the victim for consciousness, breathing and signs of circulation

Call
✔ Dial 9-1-1 or local emergency number
✔ If alone and victim is under 8 years old, give 1 minute of care, then call 9-1-1

Care
✔ Care for conditions you find

INFANTS (birth to 1 year)

If conscious and choking...

Give 5 back blows   Then give 5 chest thrusts

Repeat back blows and chest thrusts until object comes out or victim becomes unconscious.

If infant becomes unconscious...

Look for and remove any foreign object seen in mouth   Give 1 rescue breath; if air does NOT go in—   Give 5 chest compressions

If air does NOT go in, repeat steps 1, 2 and 3. If air DOES go in, give another breath then check for signs of circulation.

CHILDREN (1 to 8 years old)

If conscious and choking...

Give abdominal thrusts until object comes out or victim is unconscious

If child becomes unconscious...

Look for and remove any foreign object seen in mouth   Give 1 rescue breath; if air does NOT go in—   Give 5 chest compressions

If air does NOT go in, repeat steps 1, 2 and 3. If air DOES go in, give another breath, then check for signs of circulation.

ADULTS

If conscious and choking...

Give abdominal thrusts until object comes out or victim is unconscious

If adult becomes unconscious...

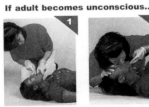

Look for and remove any foreign object seen in mouth   Give 2 rescue breaths; if air does NOT go in—   Give 15 chest compressions

If air does NOT go in, repeat steps 1, 2 and 3. If air DOES go in, check for signs of circulation.

THE SKILLS TO SAVE A LIFE...
American Red Cross lifesaving training can give you the skills and confidence to safely act in an emergency.

Don't Delay—Get Trained!
First aid, CPR and automated external defibrillation (AED) training can mean the difference between life and death. For more information, contact your local American Red Cross chapter or visit **www.redcross.org**

This poster should not be used as a substitute for training. If you do not have a breathing barrier or disposable gloves available, do not delay care.

American Red Cross

Together, we can save a life

Figure A.1   Rescue breathing and first aid for choking: procedures recommended by the American Red Cross.   SOURCE: Courtesy of the American Red Cross. All rights reserved in all countries.

Injuries to the wrist and head are the most common. To reduce your risk of being injured while skating, wear a helmet, elbow and knee pads, wrist guards, a long-sleeved shirt, and long pants.

Wearing a helmet and knee and elbow pads is also important for preventing scooter injuries. The rise in popularity of lightweight scooters has seen a corresponding increase in associated injuries. Scooters should not be viewed as toys, and young children should be closely supervised. Be sure that handlebars, steering column, and all nuts and bolts are securely fastened. Ride on smooth, paved surfaces away from motor vehicle traffic. Avoid streets and surfaces with water, sand, gravel, or dirt.

Sports Injuries

Since more people have begun exercising to improve their health, there has been an increase in sports-related injuries.

To prevent sports injuries:

- Develop the skills required for the activity. Recognize and guard against the hazards associated with it.
- Always warm up and cool down.
- Make sure facilities are safe.
- Follow the rules and practice good sportsmanship.
- Use proper safety equipment, including, where appropriate, helmets, eye protection, knee and elbow pads, and wrist guards. Wear correct footwear.
- When it is excessively hot and humid, avoid heat stress by following the guidelines given in the box "Exercising in Hot Weather" in Chapter 3.

WORK INJURIES

Many aspects of workplace safety are monitored by the Occupational Safety and Health Administration (OSHA), a federal agency. The highest rate of work-related injuries occurs among laborers, whose jobs usually involve extensive manual labor and lifting—two areas not addressed by OSHA safety standards. Back injuries are the most common work injury.

To protect your back when lifting:

- Don't try to lift beyond your strength. If you need it, get help.
- Get a firm footing, with your feet shoulder-width apart. Get a firm grip on the object.
- Keep your torso in a relatively upright position and crouch down, bending at the knees and hips. Avoid bending at the waist. To lift, stand up or push up with your leg muscles. Lift gradually, keeping your arms straight. Keep the object close to your body.
- Don't twist. If you have to turn with an object, change the position of your feet.
- Put the object down gently, reversing the rules for lifting.

Another type of work-related injury is damage to the musculoskeletal system from repeated strain on the hand, arm, wrist, or other part of the body. Such repetitive-strain injuries are proliferating due to increased use of computers. One type, carpal tunnel syndrome, is characterized by pain and swelling in the tendons of the wrists and sometimes numbness and weakness.

To prevent carpal tunnel syndrome:

- Maintain good posture at the computer. Use a chair that provides back support and place the feet flat on the floor or on a footrest.
- Position the screen at eye level and the keyboard so the hands and wrists are straight.
- Take breaks periodically to stretch and flex your wrists and hands to lessen the cumulative effects of stress.

VIOLENCE AND INTENTIONAL INJURIES

With more than 2 million Americans victims of violent injury each year, violence is a major public health concern. It includes assault, sexual assault, homicide, domestic violence, suicide, and child abuse. Compared with rates of violence in other industrialized countries, U.S. rates are abnormally high in two areas: homicide and firearm-related deaths.

Assault

Assault is the use of physical force to inflict injury or death on another person. Most assaults occur during arguments or in connection with another crime, such as robbery. Poverty, urban settings, and the use of alcohol and drugs are associated with higher rates of assault. Homicide is the sixteenth leading cause of death in the United States. Homicide victims are most likely to be male, between ages 19 and 24, and members of minority groups. Most homicides are committed with a firearm; the murderer and the victim usually know each other.

To protect yourself at home:

- Secure your home with good lighting and effective locks, preferably deadbolts. Make sure that all doors and windows are securely locked.
- Get a dog or post "Beware of Dog" signs.
- Don't hide keys in obvious places and don't give anyone the chance to duplicate your keys.
- Install a peephole in your front door. Don't open your door to people you don't know.
- If you or a family member owns a weapon, store it securely. Store guns and ammunition separately.
- If you are a woman living alone, use your initials rather than your full name in the phone directory. Don't use a greeting on your answering machine that implies you live alone or are not home.
- Teach everyone in the household how to obtain emergency assistance.
- Know your neighbors. Work out a system for alerting each other in case of an emergency.
- Establish a neighborhood watch program.

To protect yourself on the street:

- Avoid walking alone, especially at night. Stay where people can see and hear you.
- Walk on the outside of the sidewalk, facing traffic. Walk purposefully. Act alert and confident. If possible, keep at least two arm lengths between yourself and a stranger.

- Know where you are going. Appearing to be lost increases your vulnerability.
- Carry valuables in a fanny pack, pants pocket, or shoulder bag strapped diagonally across the chest.
- Always have your keys ready as you approach your vehicle or home.
- Carry a whistle to blow if you are attacked or harassed. If you feel threatened, run and/or yell. Go into a store or knock on the door of a home. If someone grabs you, yell "Help!" or "Fire!"

To protect yourself in your car:
- Keep your car in good working condition, carry emergency supplies, and keep the gas tank at least half full.
- When driving, keep doors locked and windows rolled up at least three-quarters of the way.
- Park your car in well-lighted areas or parking garages, preferably those with an attendant or a security guard.
- Lock your car when you leave it and check the interior before opening the door when you return.
- Don't pick up strangers. Don't stop for vehicles in distress; drive on and call for help.
- Note the location of emergency call boxes along highways and in public facilities. If you travel alone frequently, consider investing in a cell phone.
- If your car breaks, down, raise the hood and tie a white cloth to the antenna or door handle. Wait in the car with the doors locked and windows rolled up. If someone approaches to offer help, open a window only a crack and ask the person to call the police or a towing service.
- When you stop at a light or stop sign, leave enough room to maneuver if you need an escape route.
- If you are involved in a minor automobile crash and you think you have been bumped intentionally, don't leave your car. Motion to the other driver to follow you to the nearest police station. If confronted by a person with a weapon, give up your car.

To protect yourself on public transportation:
- While waiting, stand in a populated, well-lighted area.
- Make sure that the bus, subway, or train is bound for your destination before you board it. Sit near the driver or conductor in a single seat or an outside seat.
- If you flag down a taxi, make sure that it's from a legitimate service. When you reach your destination, ask the driver to wait until you are safely inside the building.

To protect yourself on campus:
- Make sure that door and window locks are secure and that halls and stairwells have adequate lighting.
- Don't give dorm or residence keys to anybody.
- Don't leave your door unlocked or allow strangers into your room.
- Avoid solitary late-night trips to the library or laundry room. Take advantage of on-campus escort services.
- Don't exercise outside alone at night. Don't take shortcuts across campus that are unfamiliar or seem unsafe.

- If security guards patrol the campus, know the areas they cover and stay where they can see or hear you.

Sexual Assault—Rape and Date Rape

The use of force and coercion in sexual relationships is one of the most serious problems in human interactions. The most extreme manifestation of sexual coercion—forcing a person to submit to another's sexual desires—is rape. Taking advantage of circumstances that render a person incapable of giving consent (such as when drunk) is also considered sexual assault or rape. Coerced sexual activity in which the victim knows or is dating the rapist is often referred to as date rape.

At least 3.5 million females are raped annually in the United States, and some males—perhaps 10,000 annually—are raped each year by other males. Rape victims suffer both physical and psychological injury. The psychological pain can be substantial and long-lasting.

To protect yourself against rape:
- Following the guidelines listed earlier for protecting yourself against assault.
- Trust your gut feeling. If you feel you are in danger, don't hesitate to run and scream.
- Think out in advance what you would do if you were threatened with rape. However, no one knows what he or she will do when scared to death. Trust that you will make the best decision at the time—whether to scream, run, fight, or give in to avoid being injured or killed.

To protect yourself against date rape:
- Believe in your right to control what you do. Set limits and communicate them clearly, firmly, and early. Be assertive; men often interpret passivity as permission.
- If you are unsure of a new acquaintance, go on a group date or double date. If possible, provide your own transportation.
- Remember that some men think flirtatious behavior or sexy clothing indicates an interest in having sex.
- Remember that alcohol and drugs interfere with judgment, perception, and communication about sex. In a bar or at a party, don't leave your drink unattended, and don't accept opened beverages; watch your drinks being poured. At a party or club, check on friends and ask them to check on you.
- Use the statement that has proven most effective in stopping date rape: "This is rape and I'm calling the cops!"

If you are raped:
- Tell what happened to the first friendly person you meet.
- Call the police. Tell them you were raped and give your location.
- Try to remember everything you can about your attacker and write it down.
- Don't wash or douche before the medical exam. Don't change your clothes, but bring a new set with you if you can.
- At the hospital you will have a complete exam. Show the physician any bruises or scratches.

- Tell the police exactly what happened. Be honest and stick to your story.
- If you do not want to report the rape to the police, see a physician as soon as possible. Be sure you are checked for pregnancy and STDs.
- Contact an organization with skilled counselors so you can talk about the experience. Look in the telephone directory under "Rape" or "Rape Crisis Center" for a hotline number.

Guidelines for men:

- Be aware of social pressure. It's OK not to score.
- Understand that "No" means "No." Stop making advances when your date says to stop. Remember that she has the right to refuse sex.
- Don't assume that flirtatious behavior or sexy clothing means a woman is interested in having sex, that previous permission for sex applies to the current situation, or that your date's relationships with other men constitute sexual permission for you.
- Remember that alcohol and drugs interfere with judgment, perception, and communication about sex.

Stalking and Cyberstalking

Stalking is characterized by harassing behaviors such as following or spying on a person and making verbal, written, or implied threats. It is estimated that 1 million U.S. women and 400,000 men are stalked each year; most stalkers are men. Cyberstalking, the use of electronic communications devices to stalk another person, is becoming more common. Cyberstalkers may send harassing or threatening e-mails or chat room messages to the victim, or they may encourage others to harass the victim by posting inflammatory messages and personal information on bulletin boards or chat rooms.

To protect yourself online:

- Never use your real name as an e-mail user name or chat room nickname. Select an age- and gender-neutral identity.
- Avoid filling out profiles for accounts related to e-mail use or chat room activities with information that could be used to identify you.
- Do not share personal information in public spaces anywhere online or give it to strangers.
- Learn how to filter unwanted e-mail messages.
- If you do experience harassment online, do not respond to the harasser. Log off or surf elsewhere. Save all communications for evidence. If harassment continues, report it to the harasser's Internet service provider, your Internet service provider, and the local police.
- Don't agree to meet someone you've met online face-to-face unless you feel completely comfortable about it. Schedule a series of phone conversations first. Meet initially in a very public place and bring along a friend to increase your safety.

Coping After Terrorism, Mass Violence, or Natural Disasters

Certain areas of the United States are prone to natural disasters such as hurricanes, tornadoes, flooding, and earthquakes. Less frequent in the United States are episodes of mass violence or terrorist events such as those that occurred in Oklahoma in April 1995 and on September 11, 2001. When such events occur, some people suffer direct physical harm and/or the loss of relatives, friends, or possessions; many others experience emotional distress and are robbed of their sense of security.

Each person reacts differently to traumatic disaster, and it is normal to experience a variety of responses. Reactions may include disbelief and shock, fear, anger and resentment, anxiety about the future, difficulty concentrating or making decisions, mood swings, irritability, sadness and depression, panic, guilt, apathy, feelings of isolation or powerlessness, and many of the behaviorial signs such as headaches or insomnia that are associated with excess stress (see Chapter 10). Reactions may occur immediately or may be delayed until weeks or months after the event.

Taking positive steps can help you cope with powerful emotions. Consider the following strategies:

- Share your experiences and emotions with friends and family members. Be a supportive listener. Reassure children and encourage them to talk about what they are feeling.
- Take care of your mind and body. Choose a healthy diet, exercise regularly, get plenty of sleep, and practice relaxation techniques. Don't turn to unhealthy coping techniques such as using alcohol or other drugs.
- Take a break from media reports and images, and try not to develop nightmare scenarios for possible future events.
- Reestablish your routines at home, school, and work.
- Find ways to help others. Donating money, blood, food, clothes, or time can ease difficult emotions and give you a greater sense of control.

Everyone copes with tragedy in a different way and recovers at a different pace. If you feel overwhelmed by your emotions, seek professional help. Additional information about coping with terrorism and violence is available from the Federal Emergency Management Agency (www.fema.gov), the U.S. Department of Justice (www.usdoj.gov), and the National Mental Health Association (www.nmha.org).

Emergency Preparedness

Most prevention and coping activities related to terrorism, mass violence, and natural disasters occur at the federal, state, and community levels. However, one step individuals can take is to put together an emergency plan and kit for their family or household that can serve for any type of emergency or disaster.

Emergency Supplies   Your kit of emergency supplies should include everything you'll need to make it on your own for at least 3 days. You'll need nonperishable food, water, first aid and sanitation supplies, a battery-powered radio, clothing, a flashlight, cash, keys, copies of important documents, and supplies for sleeping outdoors in any weather. Remember special-needs items for infants, seniors, and pets. Supplies for a basic emergency kit are listed in Figure A.2; add to your kit based on your family situation and the type of problems most likely to occur in your area.

In the case of certain types of terrorist attacks or natural disasters, you may also need supplies to "shelter in place"—to create a barrier between yourself and any dangerous airborne materials.

Basic emergency supplies

Map of the area for locating evacuation routes or shelters

Cash, coins, and credit cards

Copies of important documents stored in watertight container

Emergency contact list and phone numbers

Extra sets of house and car keys

Flashlights or lightsticks

Battery- or solar-powered radio

Battery-powered alarm clock

Extra batteries and bulbs

Cell phone or prepaid phone card

Signal flares

Fire extinguisher (small A-B-C type)

Whistle

Ladder

Tube tent and rope

Sleeping bags or warm blankets

Foam pads, pillows, baby bed

Complete change of warm clothing, footwear, outerware (jacket or coat, long pants, long-sleeved shirt, sturdy shoes, hat, gloves, raingear, extra socks and underwear, sunglasses)

Work gloves

Shut-off wrench for gas and water supplies

Shovel, hammer, pliers, screwdriver, and other tools

Compass

Matches in a waterproof container

Aluminum foil

Plastic storage containers, bucket

Duct tape, utility knife, and scissors

Paper, pens, pencils

Needles and thread

First aid kit

First aid manual

Thermometer

Scissors

Tweezers

Safety pins, safety razor blades

Needle

Latex or other sterile gloves

Sterile gauze pads

Cleansing agents (soap, isopropyl alcohol, antibiotic towelettes)

Sunscreen

Insect repellent

Antibiotic ointment

Burn ointment

Petroleum jelly or another lubricant

Sterile adhesive bandages, several sizes

Sterile rolled bandages and triangular bandages

Cotton balls

Eyewash solution

Chemical heat and cold packs

Aspirin or nonaspirin pain reliever

Anti-diarrhea medication

Laxative

Antacid

Activated charcoal (use if advised by Poison Control Center)

Potassium iodide (use following radiation exposure if advised by local health authorities)

Prescription medications and prescribed medical supplies

List of medications, dosages, and any allergies

Medicine dropper

Special needs items

Infant care needs (formula, bottles, diapers, powdered milk, diaper rash ointment)

Books or toys

Extra eyeglasses, contact lenses and supplies

Feminine hygiene supplies

Denture needs

Hearing aid or wheelchair batteries; other special equipment

Pet care supplies, including a leash, pet carrier, copy of vaccination history, and tie out stakes

Other (list)

Food and related supplies

Manual (non-electric) can opener

Utility knife

Paper towels

Eating utensils: Mess kits, or paper cups and plates and utensils

Plastic garbage bags and resealing bags

Small cooking stove and cooking fuel (if food must be cooked)

Water purification tablets

Water: Three-day-supply, at least 1 gallon of water per person per day, stored in plastic containers:

Number of people: _____ x <u>1 gallon</u> x <u>3 days</u> = _____ Total minimum gallons of water

Store additional water if you live in a hot climate or if your household includes infants, pregnant women, or people with special health needs. Don't forget to store water for pets. Containers can be sterilized by rinsing them with a diluted bleach solution (one part bleach to ten parts water). Replace your water supply every six months.

Food: At least a three-day supply of nonperishable foods—those requiring no refrigeration, preparation, or cooking and little or no water. Choose foods from the following list and add foods that members of your household will eat. Replace items in your food supply every six months.

Ready-to-eat canned meats, fruits, soups, and vegetables

Protein or fruit bars

Dry cereal or granola

Peanut butter

Sugar, salt, pepper

Dried fruit

Nuts

Crackers

Canned, powdered, or boxed juices

Non-perishable pasteurized milk or powered milk

Coffee, tea, sodas

High-energy foods

Comfort/stress foods

MREs (military rations)

Infant formula and baby foods

Pet foods

Sanitation

Plastic garbage bags (and ties)

Toilet paper

Moist towelettes or hand soap

Washcloth and towel

Personal hygiene items (toothbrush, shampoo, deodorant, comb, shaving cream, and so on)

Plastic bucket with tight lid

Household chlorine bleach, disinfectant

Powdered lime

Small shovel for digging a latrine

For a clean air supply

Face masks or several layers of dense-weave cotton material (handkerchiefs, t-shirts, towels) that fit snugly over your nose and mouth.

Shelter-in-place supplies, to be used in an interior room to create a barrier between you and potentially contaminated air outside: Heavyweight plastic garbage bags or plastic sheeting; duct tape; scissors; and if possible, a portable air purifier with a HEPA filter.

Family emergency plan

Plan places where your family will meet; choose one location near your home and one outside your neighborhood.

Local _____ Outside neighborhood _____

Have one local and one out-of-state contact person for family members to call if separated during a disaster. (It may be easier to make long-distance calls than local calls.)

Local _____ Out-of state _____

Figure A.2   Sample emergency preparedness kit and plan.

These supplies might include filter masks or folded cotton towels that can be placed over the mouth and nose. Plastic sheeting and duct tape can be used to seal windows and doors.

You may want to create several kinds of emergency kits. The primary one would contain supplies for home use. Put together a smaller, lightweight version that you can take with you if you are forced to evacuate your residence. Smaller kits for your car and your workplace are also recommended.

A Family or Household Plan You and your family or household members should have a plan about where to meet and how to communicate. Choose at least two potential meeting places—one in your neighborhood and one or more in other areas. Your community may also have set locations for community shelters. Where you go may depend on the circumstances of the emergency situation. Use your common sense, and listen to the radio or television to obtain instructions from emergency officials about whether to evacuate or stay in place. In addition, know all the transportation options in the vicinity of your home, school, and workplace; roadways and public transit may be affected, so a sturdy pair of walking shoes is a good item to keep in your emergency kit.

Everyone in the family or household should also have the same emergency contact person to call, preferably someone who lives outside the immediate area and won't be affected by the same local disaster. Local phone service may be significantly disrupted, so long-distance calls may be more likely to go through. Everyone should carry the relevant phone numbers and addresses at all times.

It is also important to check into the emergency plans at any location where you or family members spend time, including schools and workplaces. For each location, know the safest place to be for different types of emergencies—for example, load-bearing interior walls during an earthquake or the basement during a tornado. Also know how to turn off water, gas, and electricity in case of damaged utility lines; keep the needed tools next to the shutoff valves.

Other steps you can take to help prepare for emergencies include taking a first aid class and setting up an emergency response group in your neighborhood, residential building, or office. Talk with your neighbors: Who has specialized equipment (for example, a power generator) or expertise that might help in a crisis? Do older or disabled neighbors have someone to help them? More complete information about emergency preparedness is available from local government agencies and from the following:

American Academy of Pediatrics (www.aap.org)
American Red Cross (www.redcross.org)
Federal Emergency Management Agency (www.fema.gov)
U.S. Department of Homeland Security (www.ready.gov)

PROVIDING EMERGENCY CARE

You can improve someone else's chances of surviving if you are prepared to provide emergency help. A course in first aid offered by the American Red Cross and on many college campuses can teach you to respond appropriately when someone needs help. Emergency rescue techniques can save the lives of people who have stopped breathing, who are choking, or whose hearts have stopped beating. Pulmonary resuscitation (also known as rescue breathing, artificial respiration, or mouth-to-mouth resuscitation) is used when a person is not breathing (see Figure A.1). Cardiopulmonary resuscitation (CPR) is used when a pulse can't be found. Training is required before a person can perform CPR. Courses are offered by the American Red Cross and the American Heart Association.

When you have to provide emergency care:

Remain calm and act sensibly. The basic pattern for providing emergency care is *check-call-care*:

- *Check the situation.* Make sure the scene is safe for both you and the injured person. Don't put yourself in danger; if you get hurt too, you will be of little help to the injured person.

- *Check the victim.* Conduct a quick head-to-toe examination. Assess the victim's signs and symptoms, such as level of responsiveness, pulse, and breathing rate. Look for bleeding and any indications of broken bones or paralysis.

- *Call for help.* Call 911 or a local emergency number. Identify yourself and give as much information as you can about the condition of the victim and what happened.

- *Care for the victim.* If the situation requires immediate action (no pulse, shock, etc.), provide first aid if you are trained to do so (see Figure A.1).

SELECTED BIBLIOGRAPHY

AAA Foundation for Traffic Safety. 1997. *Road Rage: How to Avoid Aggressive Driving.* Washington, D.C.: AAA Foundation for Traffic Safety.

Bren, L. 2005. Prevent your child from choking. *FDA Consumer,* September/October.

Centers for Disease Control and Prevention. 2001. Surveillance for fatal and nonfatal firearm-related injuries. *CDC Surveillance Summaries* 50(SS2).

Cummings, P., and F. P. Rivara. 2004. Car occupant death according to the restraint use of other occupants. *Journal of the American Medical Association* 291(3): 343–349.

Federal Bureau of Investigation. 2004. *Crime in the United States: Uniform Crime Reports, 2003.* Washington, D.C.: U.S. Department of Justice.

Iudice, A., et al. 2005. Effects of prolonged wakefulness combined with alcohol and hands-free cell phone divided attention tasks on simulated driving. *Human Psychopharmacology* 20(2): 125–132.

National Institute on Drug Abuse. 2005. NIDA *InfoFacts: Drugged Driving* (http://www.nida.nih.gov/Infofacts/driving.html; retrieved August 5, 2005).

National Institutes of Health. 2001. Coping with terrorism. *Word on Health,* December.

National Mental Health Association. 2001. *Coping with Disaster: Tips for College Students* (http://www.nmha.org/reassurance/collegetips.cfm; retrieved April 30, 2002).

National Safety Council. 2004. *Injury Facts.* Itasca, Ill.: National Safety Council.

National Traffic Safety Administration. 2005. *Traffic Safety Facts Research Note: Driver Cell Phone Use in 2004—Overall Results.* Washington, D.C.: National Traffic Safety Administration.

Strayer, D. L., and F. A. Drews. 2004. Profiles in driver distraction: Effects of cell phone conversations on younger and older drivers. *Human Factors* 46(4): 640–649.

U.S. Department of Homeland Security. 2005. *Ready America* (www.ready.gov/index.html; retrieved March 4, 2005).

U.S. Department of Justice. 1999. *1999 Report on Cyberstalking: A New Challenge for Law Enforcement and Industry* (http://www.usdoj.gov:80/criminal/cybercrime/cyberstalking.htm; retrieved December 17, 2000).

Your preparedness guide for any emergency. 2004. *Consumer Reports,* September.

Nutritional Content of Common Foods

For this food composition table, foods are listed within the following groups, corresponding to MyPyramid: (1) breads, cereals, rice, and pasta; (2) vegetables; (3) fruit; (4) milk, yogurt, and cheese; (5) meat, poultry, fish, dry beans, eggs, and nuts; and (6) fats, oils, sweets, and alcoholic beverages.

Data are provided for a variety of nutrients. For planning and easy reference, complete the following chart with your approximate daily goals or limits; refer to Chapter 8 and the Nutrition Resources section that follows Chapter 8. Fill in the daily totals that apply to your approximate daily calorie intake, sex, and age.

TOTAL DAILY GOAL OR LIMIT			
Total energy	_____ calories	Cholesterol	_300_ mg
Protein	_____ grams	Sodium	_____ mg
Carbohydrate	_____ grams	Vitamin A	_____ RE
Dietary fiber	_____ grams	Vitamin C	_____ mg
Total fat	_____ grams	Calcium	_____ mg
Saturated fat	_____ grams	Iron	_____ mg

This appendix contains information on the same nutrients found on most food labels, so you can make easy comparisons. On food labels, percent Daily Values without corresponding units are usually provided for vitamins and minerals. For reference, the Daily Values are as follows: 5000 IU of vitamin A, 60 mg of vitamin C, 1000 mg of calcium, and 18 mg of iron.

BREADS, CEREALS, RICE, AND PASTA
MyPyramid recommends a range of daily servings of grains based on caloric intake; for someone consuming a 2000-calorie diet, 6 ounce-equivalents are recommended, half of them whole grains. Each of the following counts as 1 ounce-equivalent: a slice of bread, a small muffin, I cup ready-to-eat cereal flakes, or ½ cup cooked cereal, rice, grains, or pasta.

Name	Amount	Weight g	Energy calories	Protein g	Carb. g	Fiber g	Total fat g	Sat. fat g	Chol. mg	Sod. mg	Vit. A RE	Vit. C mg	Calc. mg	Iron mg
Bagel, plain	1 bagel, 4″ dia.	89	229	8.9	45.0	2.0	1.4	0.4	0	399	0	0	79	5.4
Barley, pearled, cooked	½ cup	79	97	1.8	22.2	3.0	0.4	0.1	0	2	0	0	9	1.0
Bulgur, cooked	½ cup	91	76	2.8	16.9	4.1	0.2	0	0	5	0	0	9	0.9
Biscuit	1 biscuit, 2½″ dia.	35	128	2.2	17.0	0.5	5.8	0.9	0	368	0	0	17	1.2
Bread, corn	1 piece	60	188	4.3	28.9	1.4	6.0	1.6	37	467	26	0	44	1.1
Bread, French	1 slice	64	175	5.6	33.2	1.9	1.9	0.4	0	390	0	0	48	1.6
Bread, mixed grain	1 slice, large	32	80	3.2	14.9	2.0	1.2	0.3	0	156	0	0.1	29	1.1
Bread, oatmeal	1 slice	27	73	2.3	13.1	1.1	1.2	0.2	0	162	1	0	18	0.73
Bread, pita, white	1 pita, 6½″ dia.	60	165	5.5	33.4	1.3	0.7	0.1	0	322	0	0	52	1.6
Bread, pita, whole wheat	1 pita, 6½″ dia.	64	170	6.3	35.2	4.7	1.7	0.3	0	340	0	0	10	2.0
Bread, pumpernickel	1 slice	26	65	2.3	12.4	1.7	0.8	0.1	0	174	0	0	18	0.8
Bread, raisin	1 slice	32	88	2.5	16.7	1.4	1.4	0.3	0	125	0	0	21	0.9
Bread, rye	1 slice	32	83	2.7	15.5	1.9	1.1	0.2	0	211	0	0.1	23	0.9
Bread sticks	2 sticks, 7⅝″ x ⅝″	20	82	2.4	13.7	0.6	1.9	0.3	0	131	0	0	4	0.9
Bread stuffing	½ cup	100	178	3.2	21.7	2.9	8.6	1.7	0	543	118	0	32	1.1

Name	Amount	Weight g	Energy calories	Protein g	Carb. g	Fiber g	Total fat g	Sat. fat g	Chol. mg	Sod. mg	Vit. A RE	Vit. C mg	Calc. mg	Iron mg
Bread, white	1 slice	30	80	2.3	15.2	0.7	1.0	0.2	0	204	0	0	45	1.1
Bread, whole wheat	1 slice	28	69	2.7	12.9	1.9	1.2	0.3	0	148	0	0	20	0.9
Buckwheat groats, cooked	½ cup	84	77	2.8	16.8	2.3	0.5	0.1	0	3	0	0	6	0.7
Bun, hamburger/hot dog	1 roll, plain	43	120	4.1	21.3	0.9	1.9	0.5	0	206	0	0	59	1.4
Cake, angelfood	1/12 of 10″ cake	50	128	3.1	29.4	0.1	0.2	0	0	254	0	0	42	0.1
Cake, chocolate w/frosting	⅛ of 18 oz cake	64	235	2.6	34.9	1.8	10.5	3.1	27	214	17	0.1	28	1.4
Cake, yellow w/frosting	⅛ of 18 oz cake	64	243	2.4	35.5	1.2	11.1	3.0	35	216	21	0	24	1.3
Cereal, All-Bran	⅓ cup	30	75	2.1	24.0	12.9	0.7	0.1	0	203	153	6.0	19	4.5
Cereal, Cheerios	1 cup	30	111	3.6	22.2	3.6	1.8	0.4	0	213	150	6.0	122	10.3
Cereal, corn flakes	1 cup	28	101	1.9	24.3	1.3	0	0	0	266	214	0	1	5.4
Cereal, Cream of Wheat	½ cup	120	65	1.8	13.4	0.6	0.2	0	0	69	0	0	25	5.1
Cereal, Frosted Flakes	¾ cup	31	114	1.0	28.0	1.0	0.2	0.1	0	148	160	6.2	2	4.5
Cereal, granola, low fat	⅔ cup	55	201	4.4	44.0	2.8	2.8	0.6	0	135	206	3.3	23	1.7
Cereal, raisin bran	1 cup	61	195	5.2	46.5	7.3	1.5	0.3	0	362	155	0.4	29	4.6
Cereal, Total	¾ cup	30	97	2.7	22.5	2.7	0.7	0.2	0	192	150	60.0	1104	22.4
Cereal, Wheat Chex	1 cup	30	104	3.0	24.3	3.3	0.6	0.1	0	267	90	3.6	60	8.7
Cereal, Wheaties	1 cup	30	106	3.0	24.3	3.0	1.0	0.2	0	218	150	6.0	0	8.1
Coffeecake w/topping	1 piece	56	178	3.1	30.0	0.7	5.4	1.0	27	236	20	0.1	76	0.8
Cookie, chocolate chip	1 medium cookie	16	78	0.9	9.3	0.4	4.5	1.3	5	58	23	0	6	0.4
Cookie, fig bar	1 cookie	16	56	0.6	11.3	0.7	1.2	0.2	0	56	1	0	10	0.5
Cookie, fortune	1 cookie	8	30	0.3	6.7	0.1	0.2	0.1	0	22	0	0	1	0.1
Cookie, oatmeal	1 large cookie	18	81	1.1	12.4	0.5	3.3	0.8	0	69	1	0.1	7	0.5
Cookie, sandwich	1 cookie	10	48	0.5	7.2	0.1	0.2	0.3	0	35	0	0	3	0.2
Corn meal, dry	¼ cup	35	126	2.9	26.8	2.6	0.6	0.1	0	1	0	0	2	1.4
Corn grits, cooked	½ cup	121	71	1.7	15.6	0.4	0.2	0	0	2	0	0	4	0.7
Couscous, cooked	½ cup	79	88	3.0	18.2	1.1	0.1	0	0	4	0	0	0	0.3
Cracker, crispbread, rye	3 crispbreads	30	110	2.4	24.7	5.0	0.4	0	0	79	0	0	9	0.7
Cracker, graham	3 squares	28	119	2.0	21.3	1.0	2.8	0.4	0	185	0	0	22	1.2
Cracker, matzo	1 matzo	28	111	2.8	23.4	0.8	0.4	0.1	0	1	0	0	4	0.9
Cracker, melba toast	6 pieces	30	117	3.6	23.0	1.9	1.0	0.1	0	249	0	0	28	1.1
Cracker, Ritz	5 crackers	16	79	1.2	10.3	0.3	3.7	0.6	0	124	0	0	24	0.6
Cracker, saltine	10 squares	30	130	2.8	21.5	0.9	3.5	0.9	0	230	0	0	36	1.6
Cracker, whole wheat	6 crackers	24	106	2.1	16.5	2.5	4.1	0.8	0	158	0	0	12	0.7
Croissant, butter	1 medium	57	231	4.7	26.1	1.5	12.0	6.6	38	424	117	0.1	21	1.2
Danish pastry, cheese	1 pastry	71	266	5.7	26.4	0.7	15.5	4.8	11	320	25	0.1	25	1.1
Doughnut, glazed	1 medium	45	192	2.3	22.9	0.7	10.3	2.7	14	181	1	0	27	0.5
English muffin, plain	½ muffin	29	67	2.2	13.1	0.8	0.5	0.1	0	132	0	0	50	0.3
French toast	1 slice	65	149	5.0	16.3	0	7.0	1.8	75	311	81	0.2	65	1.1
Macaroni, cooked	½ cup	70	111	4.1	21.6	1.3	0.7	0.1	0	1	0	0	5	1.0
Muffin, blueberry	2″ by 2¾″	57	162	3.71	23.2	0	6.2	1.2	21	251	22	0.9	108	1.3
Muffin, oat bran	1 small	66	178	4.6	31.9	3.0	4.9	0.7	0	259	0	0	42	2.8
Noodles, chow mein	½ cup	23	119	1.9	12.9	0.9	6.9	1.0	0	99	0	0	4	1.1
Noodles, egg, cooked	½ cup	80	110	3.6	20.0	1.0	1.7	0.3	23	4	5	0	10	1.2
Noodles, Japanese soba	½ cup	57	56	2.9	12.2	0	0.1	0	0	34	0	0	2	0.3
Oat bran, raw	¼ cup	24	58	4.1	15.6	3.6	1.7	0.3	0	1	0	0	14	1.3
Oatmeal, instant	1 packet	28	103	4.3	17.9	3.1	1.7	0.3	0	80	300	0	100	8.1
Pancake	4″ pancake	38	74	2.0	13.9	0.5	1.0	0.2	5	239	4	0.1	48	0.6
Pasta, cooked	2 oz.	57	75	2.9	14.2	0	0.6	0.1	19	3	3	0	3	0.7
Popcorn, air-popped	2 cups	16	62	2.0	12.4	2.3	0.7	0.1	0	1	2	0	1	0.5
Popcorn, oil-popped	2 cups	22	110	2.0	12.6	2.2	6.2	1.1	0	194	0	0.1	2	0.6
Pretzels, hard, salted	10 twists	60	229	5.5	47.5	1.7	2.1	0.5	0	1029	0	0	22	1.0
Quinoa, uncooked	¼ cup	43	159	5.6	29.3	2.5	2.5	0.3	0	9	0	0	26	3.9
Rice, brown, cooked	½ cup	98	108	2.5	22.4	1.8	0.9	0.2	0	5	0	0	10	0.4
Rice cake	1 cake	9	35	0.7	7.3	0.4	0.3	0	0	29	0	0	1	0.1
Rice, white, cooked	½ cup	79	103	2.1	22.3	0.3	0.2	0	0	1	0	0	8	0.9
Rice, wild, cooked	½ cup	82	83	3.3	17.5	1.5	0.3	0	0	3	0	0	2	0.5
Roll, dinner	1 roll, 2″ square	28	84	2.3	14.1	0.8	2.0	0.5	0	146	0	0	33	0.9
Spaghetti, cooked	½ cup	70	110	4.0	21.4	1.3	0.6	0.1	0	90	0	0	5	0.9
Taco shell	1 medium	13	62	1.0	8.3	1.0	3.0	0.4	0	49	0	0	21	0.3
Tortilla chips	1 oz.	28	136	2.2	18.5	1.5	6.6	0.7	0	119	1	0	49	0.7

Name	Amount	Weight g	Energy calories	Protein g	Carb. g	Fiber g	Total fat g	Sat. fat g	Chol. mg	Sod. mg	Vit. A RE	Vit. C mg	Calc. mg	Iron mg
Tortilla, corn	1 medium	24	52	1.4	10.7	1.5	0.6	0.1	0	11	0	0	19	0.3
Tortilla, flour	8″ tortilla	51	146	4.4	25.3	0	3.1	0.4	0	249	0	0	97	1.0
Wheat germ, toasted	¼ cup	28	108	8.3	14.1	4.3	3.0	0.5	0	1	1	1.7	13	2.6

VEGETABLES

VEGETABLES MyPyramid recommends a range of daily servings of vegetables based on caloric intake; for someone consuming a 2000-calorie diet, 2½ cups are recommended. Each of the following counts as ½ cup or equivalent: ½ cup raw or cooked vegetables, ½ cup vegetable juice, or 1 cup raw leafy salad greens.

Name	Amount	Weight g	Energy calories	Protein g	Carb. g	Fiber g	Total fat g	Sat. fat g	Chol. mg	Sod. mg	Vit. A RE	Vit. C mg	Calc. mg	Iron mg
Alfalfa sprouts	½ cup	17	5	0.7	0.6	0.4	0.1	0	0	1	1	1.4	5	0.2
Artichoke, cooked	1 medium	120	60	4.2	13.4	6.5	0.2	0	0	114	11	12.0	54	1.5
Arugula, raw	1 cup	20	5	0.5	0.7	0.3	0.1	0	0	5	24	3.0	32	0.3
Asparagus, cooked	6 spears	90	20	2.2	3.7	1.8	0.2	0.1	0	13	45	6.9	21	0.8
Bamboo shoots, canned	½ cup	66	12	1.1	2.1	0.9	0.3	0.1	0	5	1	0.7	5	0.2
*Beans, baked (plain)	½ cup	127	119	6.0	26.9	5.2	0.5	0.1	0	428	6	0	43	1.5
*Beans, black, cooked	½ cup	86	114	7.6	20.4	7.5	0.5	0.1	0	1	0	0	23	1.8
*Beans, fava, raw	½ cup	63	55	4.9	11.1	0	0.5	0.1	0	16	11	2.3	23	0.9
Beans, green snap, cooked	½ cup	63	22	1.2	4.9	2.0	0.2	0	0	1	22	6.1	28	0.4
*Beans, kidney, cooked	½ cup	89	112	7.7	20.2	5.7	0.4	0.1	0	1	0	1.1	31	2.0
*Beans, lentils, cooked	½ cup	99	115	8.9	19.9	7.8	0.4	0.1	0	2	0	1.5	19	3.3
*Beans, lima, cooked	½ cup	94	108	7.3	19.6	6.6	0.4	0.1	0	2	0	0	16	2.2
*Beans, navy, cooked	½ cup	91	127	7.5	23.7	9.6	0.5	0.1	0	0	0	0.8	63	2.2
*Beans, pinto, cooked	½ cup	85.5	122	7.7	22.4	7.7	0.6	0.1	0	1	0	0.7	39	1.8
*Beans, refried	½ cup	126	118	6.9	19.6	6.7	1.6	0.6	10	377	0	7.6	44	2.1
Beans, yellow snap, cooked	½ cup	63	22	1.2	4.9	2.1	0.2	0	0	2	2	6.1	29	0.8
Beet greens, cooked	½ cup	72	19	1.9	3.9	2.1	0.1	0	0	174	276	17.9	82	1.4
Beets, cooked	½ cup	85	37	1.4	8.5	1.7	0.2	0	0	65	2	3.1	14	0.7
Broccoli spears, cooked	2 spears	74	26	1.8	5.3	2.4	0.3	0.1	0	30	57	48.0	30	0.5
Brussels sprouts, cooked	4 sprouts	84	30	2.1	6.0	2.2	0.4	0.1	0	18	35	52.1	30	1.0
Cabbage, cooked	½ cup	75	16	0.8	3.3	1.4	0.3	0	0	6	5	15.1	23	0.1
Cabbage, raw	½ cup	45	11	0.6	2.4	1.0	0.1	0	0	8	4	14.3	21	0.3
Carrot, juice	¾ cup	177	71	1.7	16.4	1.4	0.3	0	0	51	1692	15.0	42	0.8
Carrots, cooked	½ cup	78	27	0.6	6.4	2.3	0.1	0	0	236	671	2.8	23	0.3
Carrots, raw	1 medium	61	25	0.6	5.8	1.7	0.2	0	0	42	513	3.6	20	0.2
Cauliflower, cooked	½ cup	62	14	1.1	2.5	1.7	0.3	0	0	9	1	27.5	10	0.2
Celery, raw	8 sticks	32	4	0.2	1.0	0.5	0	0	0	26	7	1.0	13	0.1
Chard, cooked	½ cup	88	18	1.6	3.6	1.8	0.1	0	0	157	268	15.8	51	2.0
Coleslaw, homemade	½ cup	60	41	0.8	7.4	0.9	1.6	0.2	5	14	32	19.6	27	0.4
Collards, cooked	½ cup	95	25	2.0	4.7	2.7	0.3	0	0	9	386	17.3	133	1.1
Corn, yellow, cooked	½ cup	82	89	2.7	20.6	2.3	1.1	0.2	0	14	11	5.1	2	0.5
Cucumber, raw	½ cup	52	8	0.3	1.9	0.3	0.1	0	0	1	3	1.5	8	0.2
Eggplant, cooked	½ cup	50	17	0.4	4.3	1.2	0.1	0	0	0	1	0.6	3	0.1
Endive, raw	½ cup	25	4	0.3	0.8	0.8	0.1	0	0	6	27	1.6	13	0.2
Hominy, canned	½ cup	83	59	1.2	11.8	2.1	0.7	0.1	0	173	0	0	8	0.5
Kale, cooked	½ cup	65	18	1.2	3.6	1.3	0.3	0	0	15	443	26.6	47	0.6
Kohlrabi, cooked	½ cup	83	24	1.5	5.5	0.9	0.1	0	0	17	2	44.5	21	0.3
Leeks, raw	½ cup	45	27	0.7	6.3	0.8	0.1	0	0	9	37	5.3	26	0.9
Lettuce, green leaf, shredded	1 cup	36	5	0.5	1.0	0.5	0.1	0	0	10	133	6.5	13	0.3
Lettuce, iceberg, shredded	1 cup	55	8	0.5	1.6	0.7	0.1	0	0	6	14	1.5	10	0.2
Lettuce, romaine, shredded	1 cup	47	8	0.6	1.5	1.0	0.1	0	0	4	136	11.3	16	0.5
Mushrooms, raw	½ cup	35	8	1.1	1.1	0.3	0.1	0	0	2	0	0.7	1	0.2
Mushrooms, cooked	½ cup	78	22	1.7	4.1	1.7	0.3	0	0	2	0	3.1	5	1.4
Mustard greens, cooked	½ cup	70	10	1.6	1.5	1.4	0.2	0	0	11	221	17.7	52	0.5
Okra, cooked	½ cup	80	18	1.5	3.6	2.0	0.1	0	0	5	11	13.0	62	0.2
Onion, raw	½ cup	80	34	0.7	8.5	1.1	0.6	0	0	2	0	5.1	18	0.2
Parsley, raw	2 tablespoons	8	3	0.2	0.5	0.3	0.1	0	0	4	32	10.1	10	0.5
Parsnip, raw	½ cup	67	50	0.8	12.0	3.3	0.2	0	0	7	0	11.3	24	0.4
*Peas, blackeye, cooked	½ cup	83	80	2.6	16.7	4.1	0.3	0.1	0	3	33	1.8	106	0.9
*Peas, chickpeas (garbanzos)	½ cup	82	134	7.3	22.5	6.2	2.1	0.2	0	6	1	1.1	40	2.4

Name	Amount	Weight g	Energy calories	Protein g	Carb. g	Fiber g	Total fat g	Sat. fat g	Chol. mg	Sod. mg	Vit. A RE	Vit. C mg	Calc. mg	Iron mg
Peas, edible, podded	10 pea pods	34	14	1.0	2.6	0.9	0.1	0	0	1	18	20.4	15	0.7
Peas, green	½ cup	80	62	4.1	11.4	4.4	0.2	0	0	58	84	7.9	19	1.2
*Peas, split, cooked	½ cup	98	116	8.2	20.6	8.1	0.4	0.1	0	2	0	0.4	14	1.3
Pepper, green chili, canned	½ cup	70	15	0.5	3.2	1.2	0.2	0	0	276	4	23.8	25	0.9
Pepper, sweet green, raw	1 small	74	15	0.6	3.4	1.3	0.1	0	0	2	13	59.5	7	0.3
Pepper, sweet red, raw	1 small	74	19	0.7	4.5	1.5	0.2	0	0	1	116	140.6	7	0.3
Pickle, dill	1 medium	65	12	0.4	2.7	0.8	0.1	0	0	833	6	1.2	6	0.3
Potato, mashed w/milk	½ cup	105	87	2.0	18.4	1.6	0.6	0.3	2	317	4	7.0	25	0.3
Potato salad	½ cup	125	179	3.4	14.0	1.6	10.3	1.8	85	661	40	12.5	24	0.8
Potato, baked w/skin	1 medium	173	163	3.6	36.5	3.6	0.2	0	0	12	2	21.8	17	1.1
Potato, boiled	1 potato, 2½″ dia.	136	118	2.5	27.4	2.4	0.1	0	0	5	0	17.7	7	0.4
Potato, french fries	10 fries	50	109	1.7	17.0	1.6	4.1	1.9	0	22	0	4.8	5	0.7
Pumpkin, canned	½ cup	123	42	1.3	9.9	3.6	0.3	0.2	0	6	953	5.1	32	1.7
Radish, raw	13 medium	59	9	0.4	2.0	0.9	0	0	0	23	0	8.7	15	0.2
Rutabaga, mashed	½ cup	120	47	1.5	10.5	2.2	0.3	0	0	24	0	22.6	58	0.6
Sauerkraut, canned	½ cup	71	13	0.6	3.0	1.8	0.1	0	0	469	1	10.4	21	1.0
Soybeans, green, boiled	½ cup	90	127	11.1	9.9	3.8	5.8	0.7	0	13	7	15.3	131	2.3
Spinach, raw	1 cup	30	7	0.9	1.1	0.7	0.1	0	0	24	141	8.4	30	0.8
Spinach, cooked	½ cup	90	21	2.7	3.4	2.2	0.2	0	0	63	472	8.8	122	3.2
Squash, summer, raw	½ small squash	59	9	0.7	2.0	0.6	0.1	0	0	1	6	10.0	9	0.2
Squash, summer, cooked	½ cup	90	18	0.8	3.9	1.3	0.3	0	0	1	10	5.0	24	0.3
Squash, winter	½ cup	103	38	0.9	9.1	2.9	0.4	0.1	0	1	268	9.8	23	0.5
Sweet potato, baked	½ cup	100	90	2.0	20.7	3.3	0.2	0	0	36	961	19.6	38	0.7
Sweet potato, canned w/syrup	½ cup	98	106	1.3	24.9	2.9	0.3	0.1	0	38	449	10.6	17	1.0
Tomato, red, raw	1 medium	123	22	1.1	4.8	1.8	0.2	0	0	13	21	16.0	17	0.9
Tomato sauce	½ cup	122	45	1.6	9.0	1.8	0.3	0	0	642	21	8.6	16	1.3
Tomato juice	¾ cup	182	31	1.4	7.7	0.7	0.1	0	0	18	42	33.4	18	0.8
Turnip, cooked, mashed	½ cup	115	25	0.8	5.8	2.3	0.1	0	0	118	0	13.3	38	0.2
Vegetable juice	¾ cup	182	34	1.1	8.3	1.5	0.2	0	0	490	142	50.3	20	0.8
Vegetables, mixed	½ cup	91	59	2.6	11.9	4.0	0.1	0	0	32	195	2.9	23	0.7
Vegetable soup	1 cup	241	72	2.1	12.0	0.5	1.9	0.3	0	822	116	1.4	22	1.1
Water chestnuts	½ cup	62	60	0.9	14.8	1.9	0.1	0	0	9	0	2.5	7	0

*Dry beans and peas (legumes) can be counted as servings of vegetables or as servings from the meat, poultry, fish, dry beans, eggs, and nuts group. They are listed here and marked with an asterisk.

FRUIT

MyPyramid recommends a range of daily servings of fruit based on caloric intake; for someone consuming a 2000-calorie diet, 2 cups are recommended. Each of the following counts as ½ cup or equivalent: ½ cup fresh, canned, or frozen fruit, ½ cup fruit juice, 1 small whole fruit, or ¼ cup dried fruit.

Name	Amount	Weight g	Energy calories	Protein g	Carb. g	Fiber g	Total fat g	Sat. fat g	Chol. mg	Sod. mg	Vit. A RE	Vit. C mg	Calc. mg	Iron mg
Apple, raw, w/skin	1 medium	138	72	0.4	19.1	3.3	0.2	0	0	1	4	6.3	8	0.2
Apple juice	¾ cup	179	84	0.3	20.7	0.2	0.2	0	0	13	0	44.8	11	0.5
Apple sauce, unsweetened	½ cup	122	52	0.2	13.8	1.5	0.1	0	0	2	1	25.9	4	0.1
Apricots	2 medium	70	34	1.0	7.8	1.4	0.3	0	0	1	67	7.0	10	0.3
Apricots, dried	9 halves	32	76	1.1	19.7	2.3	0.1	0	0	3	57	0.3	17	0.8
Avocado	1 medium	173	289	3.4	15.0	11.8	26.6	3.7	0	14	12	15.2	22	1.1
Banana	1 medium	118	105	1.3	27.0	3.1	0.4	0.1	0	1	4	10.3	6	0.3
Blackberries, raw	½ cup	72	31	1.0	6.9	3.8	0.4	0	0	1	8	15.1	21	0.5
Blueberries	½ cup	73	41	0.5	10.5	1.7	0.2	0	0	1	2	7.0	4	0.2
Cantaloupe	¼ melon, 5″ dia.	138	47	1.2	11.3	1.2	0.3	0.1	0	22	233	50.6	12	0.3
Carambola (starfruit)	1 small	70	22	0.7	4.7	1.2	0.2	0	0	1	2	24.1	2	0.1
Cherries, sweet, raw	11 cherries	75	47	0.8	12.0	1.6	0.2	0	0	0	2	5.2	10	0.3
Cherries, canned in syrup	½ cup	127	105	0.8	26.9	1.9	0.2	0	0	4	10	4.6	11	0.4
Cranberries, raw	½ cup	48	22	0.2	6.0	2.2	0.1	0	0	1	1	6.3	4	0.1
Cranberry juice cocktail	¾ cup	190	102	0	25.6	0	0.2	0	0	4	0	80.3	6	0.2
Cranberry sauce	¼ cup	69	105	0.1	26.9	0.7	0.1	0	0	20	1	1.4	3	0.2
Currants, dried	¼ cup	36	102	1.5	26.7	2.4	0.1	0	0	3	1	1.7	31	1.2
Dates, dried	¼ cup	45	125	1.1	33.4	3.6	0.2	0	0	1	0	0.2	17	0.5
Figs, raw	2 medium	100	74	0.8	19.2	2.9	0.3	0.1	0	1	7	2.0	35	0.4
Fruit cocktail, heavy syrup	½ cup	124	91	0.5	23.4	1.2	0.1	0	0	7	12	2.4	7	0.4

Name	Amount	Weight g	Energy calories	Protein g	Carb. g	Fiber g	Total fat g	Sat. fat g	Chol. mg	Sod. mg	Vit. A RE	Vit. C mg	Calc. mg	Iron mg
Fruit cocktail, light syrup	½ cup	121	69	0.5	18.1	1.2	0.1	0	0	7	12	2.3	7	0.4
Fruit cocktail, juice	½ cup	119	55	0.5	14.1	1.2	0	0	0	5	18	3.2	9	0.3
Grapefruit	½ medium	128	41	0.8	10.3	1.4	0.1	0	0	0	59	44.0	15	0.1
Grapefruit juice	¾ cup	185	72	1.0	17.0	0	0.2	0	0	2	41	70.4	17	0.4
Grapes	12 grapes	60	41	0.4	10.9	0.5	0.1	0	0	1	2	6.5	6	0.2
Guava	1 fruit	55	37	1.4	7.9	3.0	0.5	0.2	0	1	17	125.6	10	0.3
Honeydew	⅛ melon, 5¼" dia.	125	45	0.7	11.4	1.0	0.1	0	0	22	4	22.5	8	0.2
Kiwifruit	1 large	91	56	0.9	13.5	3.1	0.4	0	0	5	8	68.2	24	0.4
Kumquats	5 fruits	95	67	1.8	15.1	6.2	0.8	0.1	0	10	14	41.7	59	0.8
Lemon, with peel	1 fruit	108	22	1.3	11.6	5.1	0.3	0	0	3	2	83.2	66	0.8
Lemon juice	2 tablespoons	30	6	0.1	1.9	0.1	0.1	0	0	6	0	7.4	3	0
Mango	½ medium	103	67	0.5	17.0	1.9	0.3	0.1	0	2	39	28.7	10	0.1
Nectarine	1 fruit	136	60	1.4	14.4	2.3	0.4	0	0	0	23	7.3	8	0.4
Olives, ripe	10 large	44	51	0.3	2.8	1.4	4.7	0.6	0	384	9	0.4	39	1.5
Orange	1 medium	131	62	1.2	15.4	3.1	0.2	0	0	0	14	69.7	52	0.1
Orange juice	¾ cup	186	84	1.3	19.3	0.4	0.4	0	0	2	19	93	20	0.4
Papaya	½ medium	152	59	0.9	14.9	2.7	0.2	0.1	0	5	84	93.9	36	0.2
Passion fruit	½ cup	118	114	2.6	27.6	12.3	0.8	0.1	0	33	76	35.4	14	1.9
Peach, raw	1 medium	98	38	0.9	9.3	1.5	0.2	0	0	0	16	6.5	6	0.2
Peach, canned in juice	½ cup	124	55	0.8	14.3	1.6	0	0	0	5	24	4.5	7	0.3
Pear, raw	1 medium	166	96	0.6	25.6	5.1	0.2	0	0	2	2	7.0	15	0.3
Pear, canned	½ cup	124	52	0.4	15.0	2.0	0.1	0	0	12	0	2.5	9	0.2
Persimmon, raw	1 fruit	25	32	0.2	8.4	0	0.1	0	0	0	0	16.5	7	0.6
Pineapple, canned in juice	½ cup	125	75	0.5	19.5	1.0	0.1	0	0	1	2	11.8	17	0.3
Pineapple, raw	1 slice, 3½" x ¾"	84	40	0.5	10.6	1.2	0.1	0	0	1	3	30.4	11	0.2
Plantain, raw	1 medium	179	218	2.3	57.1	4.1	0.6	0.3	0	7	100	32.9	5	1.1
Plums	1½ medium	99	46	0.7	11.3	1.4	0.3	0	0	0	17	9.4	6	0.2
Prune juice	¾ cup	192	136	1.2	33.5	1.9	0.1	0	0	8	0	7.9	23	2.3
Prunes (dried plums)	5 prunes	42	101	0.9	26.8	3.0	0.2	0	0	1	16	0.3	18	0.4
Raisins	¼ cup	41	123	1.3	32.7	1.5	0.2	0	0	5	0	0.9	21	0.8
Raspberries	½ cup	62	32	0.7	7.3	4.0	0.4	0	0	1	1	16.1	15	0.4
Rhubarb, raw	1 stalk	51	11	0.5	2.3	0.9	0.1	0	0	2	3	4.1	44	0.1
Strawberries	5 large	90	29	0.6	6.9	2.1	0.3	0	0	1	1	52.9	14	0.4
Tangerine	1 medium	84	45	0.7	11.2	1.5	0.3	0	0	2	29	22.4	31	0.1
Watermelon	1/16 melon	284	85	1.7	21.5	1.1	0.4	0	0	3	80	23.1	20	0.7

MILK, YOGURT, AND CHEESE

MyPyramid recommends a range of daily servings of milk products based on caloric intake; for someone consuming a 2000-calorie diet, 3 cups of milk or the equivalent are recommended. Each of the following counts as 1 cup: 1 cup milk or yogurt, ½ cup ricotta cheese, 1½ ounces natural cheese, or 2 ounces processed cheese.

Name	Amount	Weight g	Energy calories	Protein g	Carb. g	Fiber g	Total fat g	Sat. fat g	Chol. mg	Sod. mg	Vit. A RE	Vit. C mg	Calc. mg	Iron mg
Buttermilk, lowfat	1 cup	245	98	8.1	11.7	0	2.2	1.3	10	257	17	2.5	284	0.1
Cheese, American	2 oz.	57	188	11.1	4.7	0	13.9	8.7	36	548	90	0	282	0.5
Cheese, blue	1½ oz.	43	150	9.1	1.0	0	12.2	7.9	32	593	84	0	225	0.1
Cheese, cheddar	1½ oz.	43	171	10.6	0.5	0	14.1	9.0	45	264	113	0	307	0.3
Cheese, cottage, creamed	1 cup	210	216	26.2	5.6	0	9.5	6.0	32	850	92	0	126	0.3
Cheese, cottage, lowfat (1%)	1 cup	226	163	28.0	6.1	0	2.3	1.5	9	918	25	0	138	0.3
Cheese, cottage, non-fat	1 cup	145	123	25.0	2.7	0	0.6	0.4	10	19	13	0	46	0.3
Cheese, cream	2 oz.	57	198	4.3	1.5	0	19.8	12.5	62	168	208	0	45	0.7
Cheese, cream, fat free	2 oz.	57	55	8.2	3.3	0	0.8	0.5	5	311	159	0	105	0.1
Cheese, feta	1½ oz.	43	112	6.0	1.7	0	9.0	6.4	38	475	53	0	210	0.3
Cheese, Mexican	1½ oz.	43	151	9.6	1.2	0	12.0	7.6	45	279	23	0	281	0.2
Cheese, Monterey	1½ oz.	43	159	10.4	0.3	0	12.9	8.1	38	228	84	0	317	0.3
Cheese, mozzarella (part skim)	1½ oz.	43	108	10.3	1.2	0	6.8	4.3	27	263	54	0	333	0.1
Cheese, Parmesan, grated	2 tablespoons	10	43	3.9	0.4	0	2.9	1.7	9	153	12	0	111	0.1
Cheese, process spread	2 oz.	56	170	9.1	5.5	0	12.3	8.1	45	839	100	0.1	261	0.1
Cheese, provolone	1½ oz.	43	149	10.9	0.9	0	11.3	7.3	29	373	100	0	321	0.2
Cheese, ricotta, part skim	½ cup	123	170	14.0	6.3	0	9.7	6.1	38	154	132	0	335	0.5
Cheese, Swiss	1½ oz.	43	162	11.5	2.3	0	11.8	7.6	39	82	94	0	336	0.1
Ice cream, chocolate	1 cup	132	285	5.0	37.2	1.6	14.2	9.0	45	100	156	0.9	144	1.2
Ice cream, vanilla, rich	1 cup	214	533	7.5	47.7	0	34.7	22.1	197	131	389	0	250	0.7

Name	Amount	Weight g	Energy calories	Protein g	Carb. g	Fiber g	Total fat g	Sat. fat g	Chol. mg	Sod. mg	Vit. A RE	Vit. C mg	Calc. mg	Iron mg
Ice cream, vanilla, light	1 cup	152	251	7.3	39.2	0.5	7.3	4.4	41	12	195	1.8	245	0.3
Ice cream, vanilla, soft-serve	1 cup	172	382	7.0	38.2	1.2	22.4	12.9	157	105	279	1.4	225	0.4
Milk, chocolate	1 cup	250	208	7.9	25.9	2.0	8.5	5.3	30	150	65	2.2	280	0.6
Milk, fat free (nonfat)	1 cup	245	83	8.3	12.1	0	0.2	0.3	5	103	149	0	306	0.1
Milk, lowfat (1%)	1 cup	244	102	8.2	12.2	0	2.4	1.6	12	107	142	0	290	0.1
Milk, reduced fat (2%)	1 cup	244	122	8.1	11.2	0	4.8	3.0	20	122	134	0.5	285	0.1
Milk, whole	1 cup	244	146	7.9	11.0	0	7.9	4.6	24	98	68	0	276	0.1
Pudding, chocolate	½ cup	147	163	4.6	27.6	1.5	4.6	2.7	16	417	38	1.3	150	0.4
Yogurt, frozen, vanilla	1 cup	144	235	5.8	34.9	0	8.1	4.9	3	125	85	1.2	206	0.4
Yogurt, lowfat, plain	8 oz. container	227	143	11.9	16.0	0	3.5	2.3	14	159	32	1.8	415	0.2
Yogurt, lowfat, with fruit	8 oz. container	227	238	11.0	42.2	0	3.2	2.1	14	132	36	1.6	345	0.2
Yogurt, nonfat, plain	8 oz. container	227	127	13.0	17.4	0	0.4	0.3	5	175	5	2.0	452	0.2

MEAT, POULTRY, FISH, DRY BEANS, EGGS, AND NUTS

MyPyramid recommends a range of daily servings of meat and beans based on caloric intake; for someone consuming a 2000-calorie diet, 5.5 ounce-equivalents are recommended. Each of the following counts as 1 ounce-equivalent: 1 ounce cooked lean meat, poultry, or fish; ¼ cup cooked dry beans or tofu; 1 egg; 1 tablespoon peanut butter; or ½ ounce nuts or seeds.

Name	Amount	Weight g	Energy calories	Protein g	Carb. g	Fiber g	Total fat g	Sat. fat g	Chol. mg	Sod. mg	Vit. A RE	Vit. C mg	Calc. mg	Iron mg
Bacon, Canadian	2 slices	47	87	11.3	0.6	0	3.9	1.3	27	727	0	0	5	0.4
Beef, ½" fat	3 oz.	85	332	22.1	0	0	26.3	10.8	84	49	0	0	8	2.5
Beef, lean, fat trimmed	3 oz.	85	179	25.4	0	0	7.9	3.0	73	56	0	0	7	2.5
Beef, corned	3 oz.	85	213	15.4	0	0	16.1	5.3	83	964	0	0	7	1.6
Beef, ground, 95% lean, broiled	3 oz.	85	145	22.4	0	0	5.6	2.5	65	55	0	0	6	2.4
Beef, ground, 85% lean, broiled	3 oz.	85	212	22.0	0	0	13.2	5.0	76	61	0	0	15	2.2
Beef, ground, 70% lean, broiled	3 oz.	85	232	21.6	0	0	15.5	6.3	70	69	0	0	30	1.9
Beef liver, braised	3 oz.	85	162	24.7	0	0	4.5	1.4	337	67	8026	1.6	5	5.6
Beef ribs, broiled	3 oz.	85	309	20.1	0	0	24.8	10.5	71	53	0	0	11	1.8
Chicken breast, w/skin, rst	½ breast	98	193	29.2	0	0	7.6	2.1	82	70	27	0	14	1.0
Chicken, dk mt, w/skin, rst	3 oz.	85	215	22.1	0	0	13.4	3.7	77	74	51	0	13	1.2
Chicken, dk mt, w/o skin, rst	3 oz.	85	205	27.4	0	0	9.7	2.7	93	93	22	0	15	1.3
Chicken, dk mt, w/skin, fried	3 oz.	85	253	18.6	8.0	0	15.8	4.2	76	251	26	0	18	1.2
Chicken, drumstick, w/skin, rst	1 drumstick	52	112	14.1	0	0	5.8	1.6	47	47	16	0	6	0.7
Chicken, lt mt, w/skin, rst	3 oz.	85	189	24.7	0	0	9.2	2.6	71	64	28	0	13	1.0
Chicken, lt mt, w/o skin, rst	3 oz.	85	147	26.3	0	0	3.8	1.1	72	65	8	0	13	0.9
Chicken, lt mt, w/skin, fried	3 oz.	85	235	20.0	8.1	0	13.1	3.5	71	244	20	0	17	1.1
Chicken, thigh, w/skin, rst	1 thigh	62	153	15.5	0	0	9.6	2.7	58	52	31	0	7	0.8
Chicken, wing, w/skin, rst	1 wing	34	99	9.1	0	0	6.6	1.9	29	28	16	0	5	0.4
Chicken liver, pan-fried	3 oz.	85	146	21.9	0.9	0	5.5	1.7	479	78	3652	2.3	8	11.0
Egg white, large	1 egg white	33	17	3.6	0.2	0	0	0	0	55	0	0	2	0
Egg, whole, large	1 egg	50	74	6.3	0.4	0	5.0	1.6	212	70	70	0	26	0.9
Egg yolk, large	1 yolk	17	55	2.7	0.6	0	4.5	1.6	210	8	65	0	22	0.5
Fish, catfish, baked/broiled	3 oz.	85	129	15.9	0	0	6.8	1.5	54	68	13	0.7	8	0.7
Fish, cod, baked/broiled	3 oz.	85	89	19.4	0	0	0.7	0.1	47	66	12	0.8	0.2	0.4
Fish, halibut, baked/broiled	3 oz.	85	119	22.7	0	0	2.5	0.4	35	59	46	0	51	0.9
Fish, salmon, baked/broiled	3 oz.	85	175	18.8	0	0	10.5	2.1	54	52	13	3.1	13	0.3
Fish, salmon, canned, w/o salt	3 oz.	85	130	17.4	0	0	6.2	1.4	37	64	45	0	203	0.9
Fish, salmon, smoked	3 oz.	85	99	15.5	0	0	3.7	0.8	20	666	22	0	9	0.7
Fish, sardine, canned in oil	1 can (3.75 oz.)	92	191	22.7	0	0	10.5	1.4	131	465	29	0	351	2.7
Fish, snapper, baked/broiled	3 oz.	85	109	22.3	0	0	1.5	0.3	40	48	30	1.4	34	0.2
Fish sticks	3 sticks	84	209	9.3	17.8	1.2	11.1	1.7	27	354	26	0	22	0.9
Fish, swordfish, baked/broiled	3 oz.	85	132	21.6	0	0	4.4	1.2	42	98	35	0.9	5	0.9
Fish, trout, baked/broiled	3 oz.	85	162	22.6	0	0	7.2	1.3	63	57	16	0.4	47	1.6
Fish, tuna, canned in oil	3 oz.	85	158	22.6	0	0	6.9	1.2	26	337	4	0	3	0.6
Fish, tuna, canned in water	3 oz.	85	109	20.1	0	0	2.5	0.7	36	320	5	0	12	0.8
Ham, extra lean	3 oz.	85	116	18.0	0.4	0	4.1	1.4	26	965	0	0	5	0.8
Ham, regular	3 oz.	85	137	13.9	3.2	1.1	7.2	2.5	48	1095	0	3.4	20	0.9
Lamb, trimmed	3 oz.	85	218	20.8	0	0	14.3	6.7	74	65	0	0	14	1.6
Lunch meat, beef pastrami, cured	3 oz.	85	125	18.5	0	0	5.0	2.8	58	752	28	1.1	8	1.9

Name	Amount	Weight g	Energy calories	Protein g	Carb. g	Fiber g	Total fat g	Sat. fat g	Chol. mg	Sod. mg	Vit. A RE	Vit. C mg	Calc. mg	Iron mg
Lunch meat, beef, sliced	3 oz.	85	127	16.2	0.8	0	6.0	2.5	60	1201	0	0	9	1.8
Lunch meat, bologna (beef)	3 slices	85	267	8.7	3.4	0	24.0	9.5	48	918	11	12.9	26	0.9
Lunch meat, bologna (turkey)	3 slices	85	178	9.7	4.0	0.4	13.6	3.7	64	1064	8	11.3	105	2.6
Lunch meat, chicken breast, fat-free	3 oz.	85	67	14.3	1.8	0	0.3	0.1	31	924	0	0	5	0.3
Lunch meat, franks (beef)	1 frank	56	162	7.0	1.2	0	14.4	5.9	38	557	2	11.2	8	1.0
Lunch meat, franks (chicken)	1 frank	45	116	5.8	3.1	0	8.8	2.5	45	616	18	0	43	0.9
Lunch meat, liverwurst	3 oz.	85	277	12.0	1.9	0	24.2	9.0	134	731	7066	0	22	5.4
Lunch meat, salami, dry	8 slices	80	326	18.1	1.2	0	27.0	9.5	63	1808	0	0	10	1.0
Lunch meat, turkey, smoked	3 oz.	85	85	15.0	2.0	0	2.0	0.5	36	781	0	0	8	0.6
Luncheon slices, meatless	3 oz.	85	161	15.1	3.8	0	9.4	1.1	0	604	0	0	35	1.5
Meatloaf (80% lean meat)	3 oz.	85	216	21.5	0	0	13.7	5.2	76	57	0	0	20	2.2
Nuts, almonds	⅓ cup	47	273	10.0	9.3	5.6	23.9	1.8	0	0	0	0	117	2.0
Nuts, cashews, dry roasted, w/o salt	⅓ cup	46	262	7.0	14.9	1.4	21.2	4.2	0	7	0	0	21	2.7
Nuts, chestnuts, roasted	⅓ cup	48	117	1.5	25.2	2.4	1.0	0.2	0	1	1	12.4	14	0.4
Nuts, macadamia, dry roasted	⅓ cup	45	321	3.5	6.0	3.6	34.0	5.3	0	2	0	0.3	31	1.2
Nuts, pecans	⅓ cup	36	249	3.3	5.0	3.5	25.9	2.2	0	0	1	0.4	25	0.9
Nuts, pine	⅓ cup	45	300	6.1	5.8	1.6	30.5	2.2	0	1	0	0.4	7	2.5
Nuts, pistachios, dry roasted	⅓ cup	41	234	8.8	11.3	4.2	18.9	2.3	0	4	5	0.9	45	1.7
Nuts, walnuts	⅓ cup	40	261	6.1	5.5	2.7	26.1	2.5	0	1	0	0.5	39	1.2
Peanut butter, chunky	2 tablespoons	32	190	8.3	5.7	1.8	16.5	3.2	0	117	375	0	17	5.6
Peanut butter, smooth	2 tablespoons	32	188	8.0	6.3	1.9	16.1	3.3	0	147	0	0	14	0.6
Peanuts, dry roasted	⅓ cup	48	282	11.4	10.4	3.9	23.9	3.3	0	3	0	0	26	1.1
Pork chop, pan fried	3 oz.	85	205	21.0	0	0	12.8	4.4	70	66	2	0.7	19	0.9
Pork ribs, braised	3 oz.	85	252	20.3	0	0	18.3	6.8	74	50	2	0.6	25	1.0
Pork roast	3 oz.	85	214	22.9	0	0	12.9	4.5	69	41	3	0	5	0.8
Pumpkin seeds, roasted	¼ cup	57	296	18.7	7.6	2.2	23.9	4.5	0	10	22	1.0	24	8.5
Sausage, beef	1 sausage	43	134	6.1	1.0	0	11.6	4.9	29	486	0	0	3	0.8
Sausage, pork	1 link	68	265	15.1	1.4	0	21.6	7.7	46	1020	0	1.4	20	0.8
Sausage, smoked links	3 2″ links	48	150	6.4	0.9	0	13.3	4.7	31	563	0	0	20	0.7
Shellfish, clams, canned	3 oz.	85	126	21.7	4.4	0	1.7	0.2	57	95	154	18.8	78	23.8
Shellfish, clams, steamed	10 clams	95	141	24.3	4.9	0	1.9	0.2	64	106	162	21.0	87	26.6
Shellfish, crab, steamed	3 oz.	85	82	16.4	0	0	1.3	0.1	45	911	8	6.5	50	0.6
Shellfish, oysters, fried	6 medium	88	173	7.7	10.2	0	11.1	2.8	71	367	80	3.3	55	6.1
Shellfish, shrimp, canned	3 oz.	85	85	17.4	0	0	1.2	0.2	214	660	0	3.5	123	1.8
Shellfish, shrimp, fried	4 large	30	73	6.4	3.4	0.1	3.7	0.6	53	103	17	0.5	20	0.4
Sunflower seeds, dry roasted	¼ cup	32	186	6.2	7.7	2.9	15.9	1.7	0	1	0	0.4	22	1.2
Tempeh	½ cup	83	160	15.4	7.8	0	9.0	1.8	0	7	0	0	92	2.2
Tofu, firm	½ cup	126	183	19.9	5.4	2.9	11.0	1.6	0	18	10	0.3	861	3.4
Turkey, dk mt, w/o skin, rst	3 oz.	85	138	24.5	0	0	3.7	1.2	95	67	0	0	22	2.0
Turkey, dk mt, w/skin, rst	3 oz.	85	155	23.5	0	0	6.0	1.8	99	65	0	0	23	2.0
Turkey, lt mt, w/o skin, rst	3 oz.	85	119	25.7	0	0	1.0	0.3	73	48	0	0	13	1.3
Turkey, lt mt, w/skin, rst	3 oz.	85	139	24.5	0	0	3.9	1.1	81	48	0	0	15	1.4
Veal, sirloin, roasted	3 oz.	85	172	21.4	0	0	8.9	3.8	87	71	0	0	11	0.8
Vegetarian bacon, cooked	1 oz.	16	50	1.7	1.0	0.4	4.7	0.7	0	234	1	0	4	0.4
Vegetarian franks	1 frank	70	163	13.7	5.4	2.7	9.6	1.4	0	330	0	0	23	1.0
Vegetarian patties (burger)	1 patty	70	124	11.0	10.0	3.4	4.4	0.4	4	398	0	3.1	95	1.7
Vegetarian sausage	1 patty	38	97	7.0	3.7	1.1	6.9	1.1	0	337	0	0	24	1.4

FATS, OILS, SWEETS, AND ALCOHOLIC BEVERAGES
If nutrient-dense forms are selected from each of the basic food groups in MyPyramid, a small amount of additional calories can be consumed from solid fats and added sugars (see Chapter 8). Foods in this category should not replace foods from the other groups because they tend to provide calories but few nutrients.

Name	Amount	Weight g	Energy calories	Protein g	Carb. g	Fiber g	Total fat g	Sat. fat g	Chol. mg	Sod. mg	Vit. A RE	Vit. C mg	Calc. mg	Iron mg
Alcoholic beverage, beer	1 can or bottle	356	153	1.6	12.6	0	0	0	0	14	0	0	14	0.1
Alcoholic beverage, liquor	1.5 oz. (80 proof)	42	97	0	0	0	0	0	0	0	0	0	0	0
Alcoholic beverage, wine	5 oz.	148	124	0.1	4.0	0	0	0	0	7	0	0	12	0.6
Bacon	3 slices	24	133	8.7	0.3	0	10.5	3.4	26	533	3	0	2	0.4
Beverage, fruit punch	1 cup	247	114	0	28.8	0.2	0	0	0	10	0	108.2	10	0.2

Name	Amount	Weight g	Energy calories	Protein g	Carb. g	Fiber g	Total fat g	Sat. fat g	Chol. mg	Sod. mg	Vit. A RE	Vit. C mg	Calc. mg	Iron mg
Beverage, cola	1 can	370	151	0	38.9	0	0	0	0	15	0	0	7	0.1
Beverage, lemon-lime soda	1 can	369	148	0.2	37.9	0	0.1	0	0	33	0	0	7	0.4
Beverage, tea, bottled, sweetened	1 bottle	518	186	0	47.1	0	0	0	0	109	0	0	16	0
Butter	1 tablespoon	14	102	0.1	0	0	11.5	7.3	31	82	97	0	3	0
Candy, caramels	1 piece	10	39	0.5	7.8	0	0.8	0.3	1	25	1	0	14	0
Candy, fudge	1 piece	17	70	0.4	13	0.3	1.8	1.0	2	8	7	0	8	0.3
Candy, jelly beans	10 large	28	105	0	26.4	0	0.1	0	0	14	0	0	1	0
Candy, milk chocolate	1 bar	44	235	3.4	26.1	1.5	13.1	6.3	10	35	22	0	83	1.0
Chocolate syrup	2 tablespoons	39	109	0.8	25.4	1.0	0.4	0.2	0	28	0	0.1	5	0.8
Cream, half and half	2 tablespoons	30	39	0.9	1.3	0	3.5	2.1	11	12	29	0.3	32	0
Cream, heavy, whipped	½ cup	60	207	1.2	1.7	0	22.2	13.8	82	23	247	0.4	39	0
Cream, sour	1 tablespoon	12	26	0.4	0.5	0	2.5	1.6	5	6	21	0.1	14	0
Frosting, chocolate	2 tablespoons	41	163	0.5	25.9	0.4	7.2	2.3	0	75	0	0	3	0.6
Honey	1 tablespoon	21	64	0.1	17.3	0	0	0	0	1	0	0.1	1	0.1
Jam/preserves	1 tablespoon	20	56	0.1	13.8	0.2	0	0	0	6	0	1.8	4	0.1
Juice bar	1 bar	92	80	1.1	18.6	0.9	0.1	0	0	4	1	8.7	5	0.2
Lard	1 tablespoon	13	115	0	0	0	12.8	5.0	12	0	0	0	0	0
Marmalade, orange	1 tablespoon	20	49	0.1	13.3	0	0	0	0	11	1	1.0	8	0
Margarine, regular stick	1 tablespoon	14	101	0.1	0.1	0	11.4	2.0	0	133	115	0	4	0
Margarine, liquid	1 tablespoon	14	102	0.3	0	0	11.4	1.9	0	111	116	0	9	0
Margarine-like spread (40% fat)	1 tablespoon	14	46	0.3	0.3	0	4.9	1.0	0	88	115	0	7	0
Mayonnaise, regular	1 tablespoon	15	57	0.1	3.5	0	4.9	0.7	4	105	3	0	2	0
Mayonnaise, fat free	1 tablespoon	16	11	0	2.0	0.3	0.4	0	2	120	1	0	1	0
Oil, canola	1 tablespoon	14	124	0	0	0	14.0	1.0	0	0	0	0	0	0
Oil, corn	1 tablespoon	14	120	0	0	0	13.6	1.7	0	0	0	0	0	0
Oil, olive	1 tablespoon	14	119	0	0	0	13.5	1.8	0	0	0	0	0	0.1
Salad dressing, blue cheese	2 tablespoons	30	151	1.4	2.2	0	15.7	3.0	5	328	20	0.6	24	0.1
Salad dressing, French	2 tablespoons	32	146	0.3	5.0	0	14.3	1.8	0	268	7	0	8	0.3
Salad dressing, Italian	2 tablespoons	29	86	0.1	3.1	0	8.3	1.3	0	486	1	0	2	0.2
Salad dressing, Italian, light	2 tablespoons	28	56	0.1	6.9	0.1	5.6	0.8	0	390	0	0.1	2	0
Sherbet	½ cup	74	107	0.8	22.5	0	1.5	0.9	0	34	7	2.3	40	0.1
Shortening, vegetable	1 tablespoon	13	115	0	0	0	12.8	7.0	0	0	0	0	0	0
Sugar, brown	1 tablespoon	14	52	0	13.4	0	0	0	0	5	0	0	12	0.3
Sugar, white	1 tablespoon	13	49	0	12.6	0	0	0	0	0	0	0	0	0
Syrup, corn	1 tablespoon	20	57	0	15.5	0	0	0	0	0	31	0	0	0.1
Syrup, maple	¼ cup	80	210	0	54.0	0	0.2	0	0	7	0	0	53	1.0

DATA SOURCE: U.S. Department of Agriculture, Agricultural Research Service. 2005. *USDA Nutrient Database for Standard Reference, Release 18* (http://www.nal.usda.gov/fnic/foodcomp).

Nutritional Content of Popular Items from Fast-Food Restaurants

Arby's

	Serving size (g)	Calories	Protein (g)	Total fat (g)	Saturated fat (g)	Total carbohydrate (g)	Sugars (g)	Fiber (g)	Cholesterol (mg)	Sodium (mg)	Vitamin A	Vitamin C	Calcium	Iron	% calories from fat
											% Daily Value				
Regular roast beef	154	320	21	13	6	34	5	2	45	950	0	0	6	20	34
Super roast beef	241	440	22	19	7	48	11	3	45	1130	2	2	8	25	39
Junior roast beef	125	270	16	9	4	34	5	2	30	740	0	0	6	15	33
Market Fresh® Ultimate BLT	293	780	23	46	9	75	18	6	50	1570	15	30	15	25	53
Market Fresh® Roast Turkey & Swiss	357	720	45	27	6	74	16	5	90	1790	8	4	35	30	35
Market Fresh® Low Carbys™ Southwest chicken wrap	259	550	35	30	9	45	1	30	75	1690	10	10	40	10	49
Chicken breast fillet	204	490	25	24	4	46	7	2	55	1220	2	2	8	15	44
Martha's Vineyard™ salad (w/o dressing)	291	250	26	8	4.5	23	23	4	60	490	60	40	20	10	28
Raspberry vinaigrette	57	172	0	12	1.5	16	14	0	0	344	0	4	0	0	63
Santa Fe™ salad (w/o dressing)	328	520	27	29	9	40	6	5	60	1120	130	45	25	20	50
Curly fries (medium)	128	410	5	22	3	47	N/A	5	0	950	8	10	6	10	49
Jalapeno Bites®, regular (5)	110	310	5	19	7	29	3	2	30	530	15	0	4	6	55
Chocolate shake, regular	397	510	13	13	0	83	81		35	360	8	10	50	2	23

SOURCE: Arby's © 2005, Arby's, Inc. (http://www.arbysrestaurant.com). Used with permission of Arby's, Inc.

Burger King

	Serving size (g)	Calories	Protein (g)	Total fat (g)	Saturated fat (g)	Trans fat (g)	Total carbohydrate (g)	Sugars (g)	Fiber (g)	Cholesterol (mg)	Sodium (mg)	Vitamin A	Vitamin C	Calcium	Iron	% calories from fat
												% Daily Value				
Whopper®	291	700	31	42	13	1	52	8	4	85	1020	20	15	10	30	54
Whopper® w/o mayonnaise	270	540	30	24	10	1	52	8	4	75	900	10	15	10	30	40
Double Whopper® w/cheese	399	1060	56	69	27	2.5	53	9	4	185	1540	25	15	30	45	59
Whopper Jr.®	158	390	17	22	7	0.5	31	5	2	45	550	10	6	8	15	51
BK Veggie® Burger*	215	420	23	16	3	0	46	7	7	10	1090	20	10	10	20	34
Original Chicken Sandwich	204	560	25	28	6	2	52	5	3	60	1270	8	0	6	15	45
Chicken Tenders® (8 pieces)	123	340	22	19	5	3.5	20	0	<1	50	840	2	0	2	4	50
French fries (medium, salted)	117	360	4	18	5	4.5	46	<1	4	0	640	0	15	2	4	45
Onion rings (medium)	91	320	4	16	4	3.5	40	5	3	0	460	0	0	10	0	45
Tendergrill™ Chicken Caesar Salad w/o dressing	299	220	31	7	3	0	7	1	2	60	710	80	40	20	10	29
Ken's ranch dressing (2 oz)	57	190	1	20	3	0	2	1	0	20	550	0	0	2	0	95
Croissan'wich® w/ bacon, egg & cheese	122	340	15	20	7	2	26	5	<1	155	890	8	0	15	10	53
Hershey®'s sundae pie	79	300	3	18	10	1.5	31	23	1	10	190	2	0	4	6	54
Chocolate shake (medium)	447	690	11	20	12	0	114	110	2	75	560	15	6	45	10	26

SOURCE: BURGER KING® nutritional information used with permission from Burger King Brands, Inc. (http://www.burgerking.com)

Domino's Pizza
(1 of 8 equal slices)

	Serving size	Calories	Protein	Total fat	Saturated fat	Total carbohydrate	Sugars	Fiber	Cholesterol	Sodium	Vitamin A	Vitamin C	Calcium	Iron	% calories from fat
	g		g	g	g	g	g	g	mg	mg	% Daily Value				
14-inch lg. hand tossed cheese	110	256	10	8	3	38	3	2	12	535.5	8	0	12	11	26
14-inch lg. thin crust cheese	68	188	7	10	3.5	19	2	1	13	408.5	8	4	12	4	40
14-inch lg. deep dish cheese	128	336	13	15	5	41	4	2	16	782	10	0	16	15	40
12-inch med. hand tossed cheese	79	186	7	5.5	2	28	2	1	9	385	6	0	9	8	26
12-inch med. thin crust cheese	49	137	5	7	2.5	14	2	1	10	292.5	6	3	9	3	40
12-inch med. deep dish cheese	90	238	9	11	3.5	28	3	2	11	555.5	7	0	11	11	41
14-inch lg. hand tossed pepperoni & sausage	130	350	14	16	6	39	3	2	31	863	9	0	14	13	41
14-inch lg. hand tossed ham & pineapple	130	275	12	8.5	3.5	40	5	2	17	653	8	2	12	12	28
14-inch lg. hand tossed ExtravaganZZa Feast®	165	388	17	18.5	7.5	40	3	3	37	1014	12	2	19	15	43
14-inch lg. hand tossed Hawaiian Feast®	141	309	14	11	4.5	41	5	2	23	765	11	2	18	13	32
14-inch lg. thin crust Vegi Feast®	97	231	10	13.5	5	21	3	2	19	550.5	11	5	18	6	53
14-inch lg. deep dish MeatZZa Feast®	167	458	19	25	9.5	42	4	3	40	1230	13	1	22	18	49
Barbecue buffalo wings (1 piece)	25	50	6	2.5	0.5	2	1	<1	26	175.5	1	0	1	2	36
Buffalo Chicken Kickers™ (1 piece)	24	47	4	2	0.5	3	0	0	9	162.5	0	0	0	0	38
Blue cheese sauce	43	223	1	23.5	4	2	2	0	20	417	1	0	2	0	93
Breadsticks (1 stick)	30	115	2	6.3	1.1	12	1	0	0	122.1	4	0	0	4	31
Cinna Stix® (1 stick)	30	123	2	6.1	1.1	15	3	1	0	111	4	0	0	4	45

SOURCE: Domino's Pizza, 2005 (http://www.dominos.com). © Domino's Pizza, 2004. Reproduced with permission from Domino's Pizza LLC.

KFC

	Serving size	Calories	Protein	Total fat	Saturated fat	Trans fat	Total carbohydrate	Sugars	Fiber	Cholesterol	Sodium	Vitamin A	Vitamin C	Calcium	Iron	% calories from fat
	g		g	g	g	g	g	g	g	mg	mg	% Daily Value				
Original Recipe® breast	161	380	40	19	6	2.5	11	0	0	145	1150	0	0	0	6	45
Original Recipe® thigh	126	360	22	25	7	1.5	12	0	0	165	1060	0	0	0	6	63
Extra Crispy™ breast	162	460	34	28	8	4.5	19	0	0	135	1230	0	0	0	8	55
Extra Crispy™ thigh	114	370	21	26	7	3	12	0	0	120	710	0	0	0	6	63
Tender Roast® sandwich w/ sauce	196	390	31	19	4	0.5	24	0	1	70	810	0	0	4	10	44
Tender Roast® sandwich w/o sauce	177	260	31	5	1.5	0.5	23	0	1	65	690	0	0	4	10	17
Tender Roast® Filet Meal	321	360	33	7	2	0.5	41	4	4	85	2010	20	6	6	15	18
Hot Wings™ (6 pieces)	134	450	24	29	6	4	23	1	1	145	1120	6	6	8	10	58
Popcorn chicken (large)	170	560	36	31	7	7	34	0	1	90	1790	4	0	4	15	50
Chicken pot pie	423	770	33	40	15	14	70	2	5	115	1680	200	0	0	20	47
Roasted Caesar Salad w/o dressing and croutons	301	220	29	9	4.5	0.5	6	4	3	75	850	45	35	25	10	37
KFC® creamy parmesan Caesar dressing	57	260	2	26	5	0.25	5	3	0	15	530	0	0	2	0	90
Corn on the cob (5.5 in.)	162	150	5	3	1	0	26	10	7	0	10	0	10	6	6	18
Mashed potatoes w/ gravy	136	120	2	4.5	1	0.5	18	<1	1	0	380	2	4	0	2	34
Baked beans	136	230	8	1	1	0.25	46	22	7	0	720	8	6	15	30	4
Cole slaw	130	190	1	11	2	0.25	22	13	3	5	300	25	40	4	0	52
Biscuit (1)	57	190	2	10	2	3.5	23	1	0	1.5	580	0	0	0	4	47
Potato salad	128	180	2	9	1.5	0.25	22	5	1	5	470	0	10	0	2	45

SOURCE: KFC Corporation, 2005. Nutritional information provided by KFC Corporation from its website www.kfc.com as of September 2005 and subject to the conditions listed therein. KFC and related marks are registered trademarks of KFC Corporation. Reproduced with permission from Kentucky Fried Chicken Corporation.

McDonald's

	Serving size	Calories	Protein	Total fat	Saturated fat	Trans fat	Total carbohydrate	Sugars	Fiber	Cholesterol	Sodium	Vitamin A	Vitamin C	Calcium	Iron	% calories from fat
	g		g	g	g	g	g	g	g	mg	mg	% Daily Value				
Hamburger	105	260	13	9	3.5	0.5	33	7	1	30	530	2	2	15	15	31
Quarter Pounder®	171	420	13	9	3.5	0.5	33	7	1	30	530	2	2	15	15	46
Quarter Pounder® w/ cheese	199	510	29	25	12	1.5	43	9	3	95	1150	10	2	30	25	43
Big Mac®	219	560	25	30	10	1.5	47	8	3	80	1010	8	2	25	25	48
Big N' Tasty®	232	470	24	23	8	1.5	41	9	3	80	790	8	8	15	25	50
Filet-O-Fish®	141	400	14	18	4	1	42	8	1	40	640	2	0	15	10	40
McChicken®	147	370	15	16	3.5	1	41	5	1	50	810	2	2	15	15	48
Medium French Fries	114	350	4	16	3	4	47	0	5	0	220	0	10	2	6	43
Chicken McNuggets® (6 pieces)	96	250	15	15	3	1.5	15	0	0	35	670	2	2	2	4	52
Chicken Select® Premium Breast Strips	221	630	39	33	6	4.5	46	0	0	90	1550	0	6	4	8	48
Tangy Honey Mustard Sauce	43	70	1	2	0	0	13	9	1	0	160	0	0	0	1	29
Bacon Ranch Salad w/ Grilled Chicken (w/o dressing)	320	260	33	9	4	0	12	5	3	90	1000	120	50	15	10	33
Caesar Salad w/Crispy Chicken (w/o dressing)	313	300	25	13	4	1.5	22	4	3	55	1020	120	50	20	10	40
California Cobb Salad (w/o chicken and dressing)	2374	160	11	9	4	0	9	5	4	85	410	120	50	15	8	53
Newman's Own® Ranch Dressing (2 oz)	59	170	1	15	2.5	0	9	4	0	20	530	0	0	4	0	76
Egg McMuffin®	138	290	17	11	4.5	0	30	2	2	235	850	10	2	30	14	34
Sausage Biscuit w/ Egg	162	500	18	32	10	5	36	2	1	250	1080	6	0	8	20	58
Hotcakes (2 pats margarine & syrup)	221	600	9	17	4	4	102	45	2	20	620	8	0	15	15	27
Fruit 'n Yogurt Parfait	149	160	4	2	1	0	31	21	<1	5	85	0	15	15	4	13
Chocolate Triple Thick® Shake (16 oz)	444	580	13	14	8	1	102	84	<1	50	250	20	0	45	10	21

SOURCE: McDonald's Corporation, 2005 (http://www.mcdonalds.com). Used with permission from McDonald's Corporation.

Subway
Based on standard formulas with 6-inch subs on Italian or wheat bread

	Serving size	Calories	Protein	Total fat	Saturated fat	Trans fat	Total carbohydrate	Sugars	Fiber	Cholesterol	Sodium	Vitamin A	Vitamin C	Calcium	Iron	% calories from fat
	g		g	g	g	g	g	g	g	mg	mg	% Daily Value				
Italian BMT®	242	450	23	21	8	0	47	8	4	55	1790	8	30	15	25	42
Meatball Marinara	377	560	24	24	11	1	63	13	7	45	1610	10	50	20	40	39
Subway® Seafood Sensation	250	450	16	22	6	0.5	51	8	5	25	1150	8	30	15	25	44
Cheese Steak	250	360	24	10	4.5	0	47	9	5	35	1100	8	30	15	45	25
Subway® Melt	254	380	25	12	5	0	48	8	4	45	1610	8	30	10	25	28
Tuna	250	530	22	31	7	0.5	45	7	4	45	1030	8	30	10	30	53
Sweet Onion Chicken Teriyaki	281	370	26	5	1.5	0	59	19	4	50	1220	6	40	8	25	12
Roast Beef	223	290	19	5	2	0	45	8	4	15	920	4	30	6	30	16
Turkey Breast	224	280	18	4.5	1.5	0	46	7	4	20	1020	4	30	4	25	14
Veggie Delite®	167	230	9	3	1	0	44	7	4	0	520	4	30	6	25	12
Turkey Breast Deli Style	152	210	13	3.5	1.5	0	36	4	3	15	730	4	15	6	25	15
Chicken & Bacon Ranch Wrap (w/ cheese)	256	440	41	27	10	0.5	18	1	9	90	1670	10	15	30	15	55
Turkey Breast Wrap	183	190	24	6	1	0	18	2	9	20	1290	4	10	10	15	28
Grilled Chicken & Baby Spinach Salad (w/o dressing)	300	140	20	3	1	0	11	4	4	50	450	200	80	10	20	19
Tuna (w/ cheese) Salad (w/o dressing)	404	360	16	29	6	0.5	12	5	4	45	600	70	50	15	15	73
New England Clam Chowder	240	110	5	3.5	0.5	0	16	1	1	10	990	2	2	10	4	29
Chili Con Carne	240	240	15	10	5	0	23	14	8	15	860	15	0	6	10	38
Sunrise Refresher (small)	341	120	1	0	0	0	29	28	1	0	20	4	210	2	0	0
Western Breakfast Sandwich w/ Cheese	211	400	27	14	7	0	46	6	4	40	1210	6	20	25	25	32
Chocolate Chip Cookie	45	210	2	10	4	1	30	18	1	15	160	4	0	0	6	43

SOURCE: Subway U.S. Nutrition Info as found on http://www.subway.com, 9/1/2005. Reprinted by permission of Subway.

Taco Bell

	Serving size (g)	Calories	Protein (g)	Total fat (g)	Saturated fat (g)	Trans fat (g)	Total carbohydrate (g)	Sugars (g)	Fiber (g)	Cholesterol (mg)	Sodium (mg)	Vitamin A (% DV)	Vitamin C (% DV)	Calcium (% DV)	Iron (% DV)	% calories from fat
Taco	92	150	7	7	2.5	0.5	14	1	2	20	360	4	4	2	6	53
Taco Supreme®	113	220	9	14	7	1	14	2	1	35	360	8	6	8	6	57
Soft taco, beef	99	210	10	10	4	1	21	2	1	25	620	4	0	10	8	43
Gordita Supreme®, steak	153	290	16	13	5	0.5	28	7	2	35	520	6	6	10	15	37
Gordita Baja®, chicken	153	320	17	15	3.5	0	29	7	2	40	690	6	6	10	10	42
Gordita Baja®, chicken, "Fresco Style"	153	230	15	6	1	0	29	7	2	25	570	6	10	6	10	23
Chalupa Supreme, beef	153	390	14	24	10	3	31	4	1	35	600	8	6	15	8	55
Chalupa Supreme, chicken	153	370	17	20	8	3	30	4	1	45	530	6	8	10	6	49
Bean burrito	198	370	14	10	3.5	2	55	4	8	10	1200	10	8	20	15	24
Burrito Supreme®, chicken	248	410	21	14	6	2	50	5	5	45	1270	15	15	20	15	31
Grilled stuffed burrito, beef	325	720	27	33	11	3.5	79	6	7	55	2090	15	6	35	25	41
Tostada	170	250	11	10	4	1.5	29	2	7	15	710	10	8	15	8	36
Zesty Chicken Border Bowl™ w/ dressing	418	730	23	42	9	4	65	5	12	45	1640	20	15	15	20	52
Fiesta taco salad	548	870	31	47	16	9	80	10	12	65	1780	20	20	40	35	49
Steak quesadilla	184	540	26	31	14	2	40	4	3	70	1370	15	2	50	15	52
Nachos Supreme	195	450	13	26	9	5	42	3	5	35	810	8	8	10	10	58
Nachos BellGrande®	308	780	20	43	13	10	80	5	11	35	1300	8	8	20	15	50
Pintos 'n cheese	128	180	10	7	3.5	1	20	1	6	15	700	10	6	15	6	35
Mexican rice	131	210	6	10	4	1.5	23	<1	3	15	740	20	8	10	10	43

SOURCE: Taco Bell Corporation, 2005 (http://www.tacobell.com). Reproduced courtesy of Taco Bell Corporation.

Wendy's

	Serving size (g)	Calories	Protein (g)	Total fat (g)	Saturated fat (g)	Trans fat (g)	Total carbohydrate (g)	Sugars (g)	Fiber (g)	Cholesterol (mg)	Sodium (mg)	Vitamin A (% DV)	Vitamin C (% DV)	Calcium (% DV)	Iron (% DV)	% calories from fat
Classic Single® w/ everything	218	430	25	20	7	1	37	8	2	65	890	8	10	4	25	42
Big Bacon Classic®	282	580	35	29	12	1.5	46	11	3	95	1390	20	20	15	30	45
Jr. Hamburger	117	280	15	9	3.5	0.5	34	7	1	30	600	2	2	2	20	30
Jr. Bacon Cheeseburger	165	380	20	18	7	0.5	34	6	2	55	810	10	10	10	20	45
Ultimate Chicken Grill Sandwich	225	360	31	7	1.5	0	44	10	2	75	1090	15	30	4	15	18
Spicy Chicken Fillet Sandwich	225	510	29	19	3.5	1.5	57	8	2	55	1480	15	10	4	20	34
Homestyle Chicken Fillet Sandwich	230	540	29	22	4	1.5	57	8	2	55	1320	15	15	4	20	37
Homestyle Chicken Strips (3)	159	410	28	18	3.5	3	33	0	0	60	1470	0	0	2	6	40
Caesar Side Salad (no toppings or dressing)	99	70	6	4.5	2	0	3	1	2	15	150	100	35	10	0	58
Mandarin Chicken® Salad (no toppings or dressing)	348	170	23	2	0.5	0	18	13	3	60	480	70	50	6	10	11
Taco Supremo salad (no toppings or dressing)	494	380	27	17	9	0.5	31	9	9	65	1000	70	35	35	20	40
Creamy ranch dressing	64	230	1	23	4	0.5	5	3	0	15	580	0	0	4	2	90
Reduced fat creamy ranch dressing	64	100	1	8	1.5	0	6	3	1	15	550	0	0	4	2	72
Biggie® fries	159	490	5	24	4	6	65	0	6	0	480	4	10	2	8	39
Broccoli & Cheese Baked Potato	397	340	10	3.5	1	0	69	6	9	10	430	10	110	20	20	9
Fresh Fruit Bowl	297	130	2	0	0	0	33	28	3	0	35	100	150	4	6	0
Chili, small, plain	227	220	17	6	2.5	0	23	6	5	35	780	4	4	8	15	23
Crispy Chicken Nuggets™ (5)	75	220	10	14	3	1.5	13	1	0	35	490	0	0	0	2	57
Barbecue sauce (1 packet)	28	40	1	0	0	0	11	5	0	0	160	0	0	0	4	0
Frosty,™ medium	298	430	10	11	7	0	74	55	0	45	200	20	0	40	20	23

SOURCE: Wendy's International, Inc., 2005 (http://www.wendys.com). Reproduced with permission from Wendy's International, Inc. The information contained in Wendy's International Information is effective as of August 2005. Wendy's International, Inc., its subsidiaries, affiliates, franchises, and employees do not assume responsibility for a particular sensitivity or allergy (including peanuts, nuts or other allergies) to any food product provided in our restaurants. We encourage anyone with food sensitivities, allergies, or special dietary needs to check on a regular basis with Wendy's Consumer Relations Department to obtain the most up-to-date information.

Information on additional foods and restaurants is available online; see the Web sites listed with the tables in this appendix and the following additional sites: **Hardees:** http://www.hardees.com; **Jack in the Box:** http://www.jackinthebox.com; **White Castle:** http://www.whitecastle.com

Name _____ Section _____ Date _____

As you completed the 14 labs listed below, you entered the results in the Preprogram Assessment column of this lab. Now that you have been involved in a fitness and wellness program for some time, do the labs again and enter your new results in the Postprogram Assessment column. You will probably notice improvement in several areas. Congratulations! If you are not satisfied with your progress thus far, refer to the tips for successful behavior change in Chapter 1 and throughout this book. Remember—fitness and wellness are forever. The time you invest now in developing a comprehensive, individualized program will pay off in a richer, more vital, life in the years to come.

	Preprogram Assessment	Postprogram Assessment
LAB 2.2 Activity Profile	Sleep: _____ hours Light activity: _____ hours Moderate activity: _____ hours Vigorous activity: _____ hours Stairs climbed: _____ flights	Sleep: _____ hours Light activity: _____ hours Moderate activity: _____ hours Vigorous activity: _____ hours Stairs climbed: _____ flights
LAB 2.4 Pedometer	Daily steps: _____	Daily steps: _____
LAB 3.1 Cardiorespiratory Endurance 1-mile walk test 3-minute step test 1.5-mile run-walk test	$\dot{V}O_{2max}$: _____ Rating: _____ $\dot{V}O_{2max}$: _____ Rating: _____ $\dot{V}O_{2max}$: _____ Rating: _____	$\dot{V}O_{2max}$: _____ Rating: _____ $\dot{V}O_{2max}$: _____ Rating: _____ $\dot{V}O_{2max}$: _____ Rating: _____
LAB 4.1 Muscular Strength Maximum bench press test Maximum leg press test Hand grip strength test	Weight: _____ lb Rating: _____ Weight: _____ lb Rating: _____ Weight: _____ kg Rating: _____	Weight: _____ lb Rating: _____ Weight: _____ lb Rating: _____ Weight: _____ kg Rating: _____
LAB 4.2 Muscular Endurance Curl-up test Push-up test	Number: _____ Rating: _____ Number: _____ Rating: _____	Number: _____ Rating: _____ Number: _____ Rating: _____
LAB 5.1 Flexibility Sit-and-reach test	Score: _____ cm Rating: _____	Score: _____ cm Rating: _____

	Preprogram Assessment	Postprogram Assessment
LAB 5.3 Low-Back Muscular Endurance Side bridge endurance test Trunk flexors endurance test Back extensors endurance test	Right: _____ sec Rating: _____ Left: _____ sec Rating: _____ Trunk flexors: _____ sec Rating: _____ Back extensors: _____ sec Rating: _____	Right: _____ sec Rating: _____ Left: _____ sec Rating: _____ Trunk flexors: _____ sec Rating: _____ Back extensors: _____ sec Rating: _____
LAB 6.1 Body Composition Body mass index Skinfold measurements (or other method for determining percent body fat) Waist circumference Waist-to-hip-circumference ratio	BMI: _____ kg/m^2 Rating: _____ Sum of 3 skinfolds: _____ mm % body fat: _____ % Rating: _____ Circumf.: _____ Rating: _____ Ratio: _____ Rating: _____	BMI: _____ kg/m^2 Rating: _____ Sum of 3 skinfolds: _____ mm % body fat: _____ % Rating: _____ Circumf.: _____ Rating: _____ Ratio: _____ Rating: _____
LAB 8.1 Daily Diet Number of oz-eq Number of cups Number of cups Number of cups Number of oz-eq Number of tsp Number of g Number of g or tsp	Grains: _____ Vegetables: _____ Fruits: _____ Milk: _____ Meat and beans: _____ Oils: _____ Solid fats: _____ Added sugars: _____	Grains: _____ Vegetables: _____ Fruits: _____ Milk: _____ Meat and beans: _____ Oils: _____ Solid fats: _____ Added sugars: _____
LAB 8.2 Dietary Analysis Percentage of calories Percentage of calories Percentage of calories Percentage of calories	From protein: _____% From fat: _____% From saturated fat: _____% From carbohydrate: _____%	From protein: _____% From fat: _____% From saturated fat: _____% From carbohydrate: _____%
LAB 9.1 Daily Energy Needs	Daily energy needs: _____ cal/day	Daily energy needs: _____ cal/day
LAB 10.1 Identifying Stressors	Average weekly stress score: _____	Average weekly stress score: _____
LAB 11.1 Cardiovascular Health CVD risk assessment Hostility assessment	Score: _____ Estimated risk: _____ Score: _____ Rating: _____	Score: _____ Estimated risk: _____ Score: _____ Rating: _____
LAB 12.1 Cancer Prevention Diet: Number of servings Skin cancer	Fruits/vegetables: _____ Score: _____ Risk: _____	Fruits/vegetables: _____ Score: _____ Risk: _____

D

Behavior Change Workbook

This workbook is designed to take you step by step through a behavioral change program. The first eight activities in the workbook will help you develop a successful plan—beginning with choosing a target behavior, moving through the planning steps described in Chapter 1, and completing and signing a behavior change contract. The final seven activities will help you work through common obstacles to behavior change and maximize your program's chances of success.

Part 1 Developing a Plan for Behavior Change and Completing a Contract
1. Choosing a Target Behavior
2. Gathering Information About Your Target Behavior
3. Monitoring Your Current Patterns of Behavior
4. Setting Goals
5. Examining Your Attitudes About Your Target Behavior
6. Choosing Rewards
7. Breaking Behavior Chains
8. Completing a Contract for Behavior Change

Part 2 Overcoming Obstacles to Behavior Change
9. Building Motivation and Commitment
10. Managing Your Time Successfully
11. Developing Realistic Self-Talk
12. Involving the People Around You
13. Dealing with Feelings
14. Overcoming Peer Pressure: Communicating Assertively
15. Maintaining Your Program over Time

ACTIVITY 1   CHOOSING A TARGET BEHAVIOR

Use your knowledge of yourself and the results of Lab 1.2 (Lifestyle Evaluation) to identify five behaviors that you could change to improve your level of wellness. Examples of target behaviors include smoking cigarettes, not exercising regularly, eating candy bars every night, not getting enough sleep, getting drunk frequently on weekends, and not wearing a safety belt when driving or riding in a car. List your five behaviors below.

1. _____
2. _____
3. _____
4. _____
5. _____

For successful behavior change, it's best to focus on one behavior at a time. Review your list of behaviors and select one to start with. Choose a behavior that is important to you and that you are strongly motivated to change. If this will be your first attempt at behavior change, start with a simple change, such as wearing your bicycle helmet regularly, before tackling a more difficult change, such as quitting smoking. Circle the behavior on your list that you've chosen to start with; this will be your target behavior throughout this workbook.

ACTIVITY 2   GATHERING INFORMATION ABOUT YOUR TARGET BEHAVIOR

Take a close look at what your target behavior means to your health, now and in the future. How is it affecting your level of wellness? What diseases or conditions does this behavior place you at risk for? What will changing this behavior mean to you? To evaluate your behavior, use information from this text, from the resources listed in the For Further Exploration section at the end of each chapter, and from other reliable sources.

Health behaviors have short-term and long-term benefits and costs associated with them. For example, in the short term, an inactive lifestyle allows for more time to watch TV and hang out with friends but leaves a person less able to participate in recreational activities. In the long term, it increases risk for cardiovascular disease, cancer, and premature death. Fill in the blanks below with the benefits and costs of continuing your current behavior and of changing to a new, healthier, behavior. Pay close attention to the short-term benefits of the new behavior—these are an important motivating force behind successful behavior change programs.

Target (current) behavior _____

| Benefits | *Short-Term* | *Long-Term* |

_____   _____

_____   _____

| Costs | *Short-Term* | *Long-Term* |

_____   _____

_____   _____

New behavior _____

| Benefits | *Short-Term* | *Long-Term* |

_____   _____

_____   _____

| Costs | *Short-Term* | *Long-Term* |

_____   _____

_____   _____

ACTIVITY 3   MONITORING YOUR CURRENT PATTERNS OF BEHAVIOR

To develop a successful behavior change program, you need detailed information about your current behavior patterns. You can obtain this information by developing a system of record keeping geared toward your target behavior. Depending on your target behavior, you may want to monitor a single behavior, such as your diet, or you may want to keep daily activity records to determine how you could make time for exercise or another new behavior. Consider tracking factors such as the following:

- The behavior
- When and for how long it occurs
- Where it occurs
- What else you were doing at the time
- What other people you were with and how they influenced you
- Your thoughts and feelings
- How strong your urge for the behavior was (for example, how hungry you were or how much you wanted to watch TV)

Figure 1.6 shows a sample log for tracking daily diet. Below, create a format for a sample daily log for monitoring the behavior patterns relating to your target behavior. Then use the log to monitor your behavior for a day. Evaluate your log as you use it. Ask yourself if you are tracking all the key factors that influence your behavior; make any necessary adjustments to the format of your log. Once you've developed an appropriate format, use a separate notebook (your health journal) to keep records of your behavior for a week or two. These records will provide solid information about your behavior that will help you develop a successful behavior change program. Later activities in this workbook will ask you to analyze your records.

ACTIVITY 4   SETTING GOALS

For your behavior change program to succeed, you must set meaningful, realistic goals. In addition to an ultimate goal, set some intermediate goals—milestones that you can strive for on the way to your final objective. For example, if your overall goal is to run a 5K road race, an intermediate goal might be to successfully complete 2 weeks of your fitness program. If you set a final goal of eating 7 servings of fruits and vegetables every day, an intermediate goal would be to increase your daily intake from 3 to 4 servings. List your intermediate and final goals below. Don't strive for immediate perfection. Allow an adequate amount of time to reach each of your goals.

Intermediate Goals   **Target Date**

_____   _____

_____   _____

_____   _____

_____   _____

_____   _____

Final Goal

_____   _____

ACTIVITY 5   EXAMINING YOUR ATTITUDES ABOUT YOUR TARGET BEHAVIOR

Your attitudes toward your target behavior can determine whether your behavior change program will be successful. Consider your attitudes carefully by completing the following statements about how you think and feel about your current behavior and your goal.

1. I like _____ because _____
            (current behavior)
_____

2. I don't like _____ because _____
              (current behavior)
_____

3. I like _____ because _____
            (behavior goal)
_____

4. I don't like _____ because _____
             (behavior goal)
_____

5. I don't _____ now because _____
           (behavior goal)
_____

6. I would be more likely to _____ if _____
               (behavior goal)
_____

If your statements indicate that you have major reservations about changing your behavior, work to build your motivation and commitment before you begin your program. Look carefully at your objections to changing your behavior. How valid and important are they? What can you do to overcome them? Can you adopt any of the strategies you listed under statement 6? Review the facts about your current behavior and your goals.

ACTIVITY 6   CHOOSING REWARDS

Make a list of objects, activities, and events you can use as rewards for achieving the goals of your behavior change program. Rewards should be special, relatively inexpensive, and preferably unrelated to food or alcohol: for example, tickets to a ball game, a CD, or a long-distance phone call to a family member or friend—whatever is meaningful for you. Write down a variety of rewards you can use when you reach milestones in your program and your final goal.

_____   _____

_____   _____

_____   _____

_____   _____

Many people also find it helpful to give themselves small rewards daily or weekly for sticking with their behavior change program. These could be things like a study break, a movie, or a Saturday morning bike ride. Make a list of rewards for maintaining your program in the short term.

_____   _____

_____   _____

_____   _____

_____   _____

And don't forget to congratulate yourself regularly during your behavior change program. Notice how much better you feel. Savor how far you've come and how you've gained control of your behavior.

ACTIVITY 7   BREAKING BEHAVIOR CHAINS

Use the records you collected about your target behavior in Activity 3 and in your health journal to identify what leads up to your target behavior and what follows it. By tracing these chains of events, you'll be able to identify points in the chain where you can make a change that will lead to your new behavior. The sample behavior chain on the next page shows a sequence of events for a person who wants to add exercise to her daily routine—but who winds up snacking and watching TV instead. By examining the chain carefully, one can identify ways to break it at every step. After you review the sample, go through the same process for a typical chain of events involving your target behavior. Use the blank behavior chain on the following page.

Some general strategies for breaking behavior chains include the following:

- *Control or eliminate environmental cues that provoke the behavior.* Stay out of the room where your television is located. Go out for an ice cream cone instead of keeping a half gallon of ice cream in your freezer.
- *Change behaviors or habits that are linked to your target behavior.* If you always smoke in your car when you drive to school, try taking public transportation instead.
- *Add new cues to your environment to trigger your new behavior.* Prepare easy-to-grab healthy snacks and carry them with you to class or work. Keep your exercise clothes and equipment in a visible location.

See also the suggestions in Chapter 1.

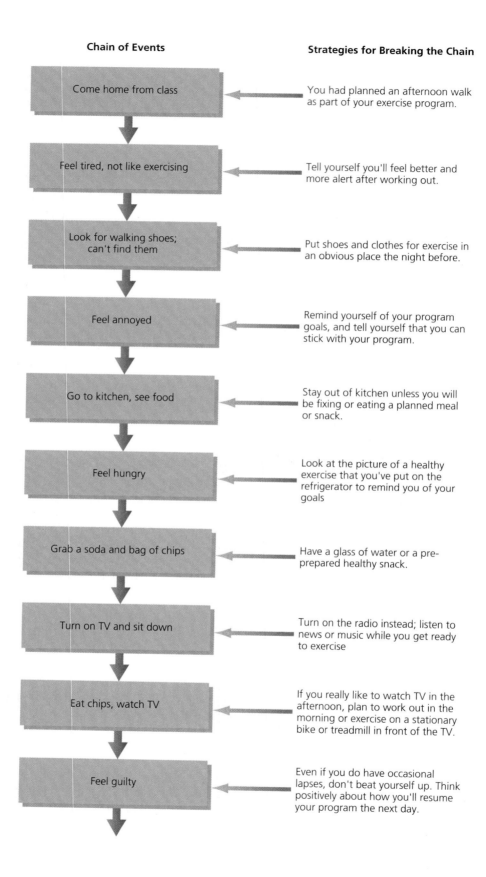

Chain of Events

Come home from class

Feel tired, not like exercising

Look for walking shoes; can't find them

Feel annoyed

Go to kitchen, see food

Feel hungry

Grab a soda and bag of chips

Turn on TV and sit down

Eat chips, watch TV

Feel guilty

Strategies for Breaking the Chain

You had planned an afternoon walk as part of your exercise program.

Tell yourself you'll feel better and more alert after working out.

Put shoes and clothes for exercise in an obvious place the night before.

Remind yourself of your program goals, and tell yourself that you can stick with your program.

Stay out of kitchen unless you will be fixing or eating a planned meal or snack.

Look at the picture of a healthy exercise that you've put on the refrigerator to remind you of your goals

Have a glass of water or a pre-prepared healthy snack.

Turn on the radio instead; listen to news or music while you get ready to exercise

If you really like to watch TV in the afternoon, plan to work out in the morning or exercise on a stationary bike or treadmill in front of the TV.

Even if you do have occasional lapses, don't beat yourself up. Think positively about how you'll resume your program the next day.

Chain of Events

Strategies for Breaking the Chain

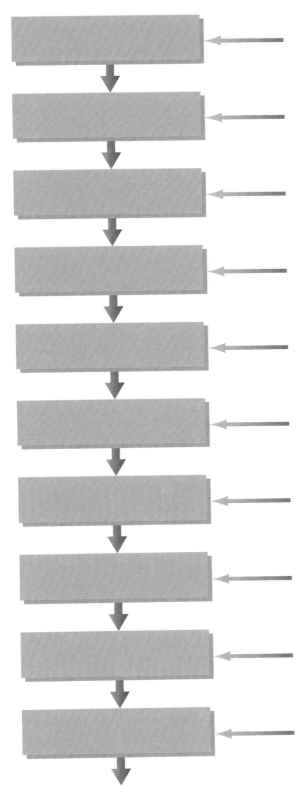

ACTIVITY 8   COMPLETING A CONTRACT FOR BEHAVIOR CHANGE

Your next step in creating a successful behavior change program is to complete and sign a behavior change contract. Your contract should include details of your program and indicate your commitment to changing your behavior. Use the information from previous activities in this workbook to complete the following contract. (If your target behavior relates to exercise, you may want to use the program plan and contract for a fitness program in Lab 7.1.)

1. I, _____ , agree to _____
   (name)   (specify behavior you want to change)

   _____

2. I will begin on _____ and plan to reach my goal of _____
   (start date)   (specify final goal)

   _____ by _____

3. To reach my final goal, I have devised the following schedule of mini-goals. For each step in my program, I will give myself the reward listed.

_____ (mini-goal 1)	_____ (target date)	_____ (reward)
_____ (mini-goal 2)	_____ (target date)	_____ (reward)
_____ (mini-goal 3)	_____ (target date)	_____ (reward)
_____ (mini-goal 4)	_____ (target date)	_____ (reward)
_____ (mini-goal 5)	_____ (target date)	_____ (reward)

   My overall reward for reaching my final goal will be _____

4. I have gathered and analyzed data on my target behavior and have identified the following strategies for changing my behavior: _____

   _____

   _____

5. I will use the following tools to monitor my progress toward reaching my final goal:

   _____
   (list any charts, graphs, or journals you plan to use)

   _____

   I sign this contract as an indication of my personal commitment to reach my goal.

   _____   _____
   (your signature)   (date)

   I have recruited a helper who will witness my contract and _____

   _____
   (list any way in which your helper will participate in your program)

   _____   _____
   (helper's signature)   (date)

Describe in detail any special strategies you will use to help change your behavior (refer to Activity 7).

Create a plan below for any charts, graphs, or journals you will use to monitor your progress. The log format you developed in Activity 3 may be appropriate, or you may need to develop a more detailed or specific record-keeping system. Examples of journal formats are included in Labs 3.2, 4.3, 5.2, 8.1, and 10.1. You might also want to develop a graph to show your progress; posting such a graph in a prominent location can help keep your motivation strong and your program on track. Depending on your target behavior, you could graph the number of push-ups you can do, the number of servings of vegetables you eat each day, or your average daily stress level.

BEHAVIOR CHANGE WORKBOOK

Complete the following checklist to determine whether you are motivated and committed to changing your behavior. Check the statements that are true for you.

_____ I feel responsible for my own behavior and capable of managing it.

_____ I am not easily discouraged.

_____ I enjoy setting goals and then working to achieve them.

_____ I am good at keeping promises to myself.

_____ I like having a structure and schedule for my activities.

_____ I view my new behavior as a necessity, not an optional activity.

_____ Compared with previous attempts to change my behavior, I am more motivated now.

_____ My goals are realistic.

_____ I have a positive mental picture of the new behavior.

_____ Considering the stresses in my life, I feel confident that I can stick to my program.

_____ I feel prepared for lapses and ups-and-downs in my behavior change program.

_____ I feel that my plan for behavior change is enjoyable.

_____ I feel comfortable telling other people about the change I am making in my behavior.

Did you check most of these statements? If not, you need to boost your motivation and commitment. Consider these strategies:

• Review the potential benefits of changing your behavior and the costs of not changing it (see Activity 2). Pay special attention to the short-term benefits of changing your behavior, including feelings of accomplishment and self-confidence. Post a list of these benefits in a prominent location.

• Visualize yourself achieving your goal and enjoying its benefits. For example, if you want to manage time more effectively, picture yourself as a confident, organized person who systematically tackles important tasks and sets aside time each day for relaxation, exercise, and friends. Practice this type of visualization regularly.

• Put aside obstacles and objections to change. Counter thoughts such as "I'll never have time to exercise" with thoughts like "Lots of other people do it and so can I."

• Bombard yourself with propaganda. Take a class dealing with the change you want to make. Read books and watch television shows on the subject. Post motivational phrases or pictures on your refrigerator or over your desk. Talk to people who have already made the change.

• Build up your confidence. Remind yourself of other goals you've achieved. At the end of each day, mentally review your good decisions and actions. See yourself as a capable person, as being in charge of your behavior.

List two strategies for boosting your motivation and commitment; choose from the list above or develop your own. Try each strategy, and then describe how well it worked for you.

Strategy 1: _____

How well it worked: _____

_____

Strategy 2: _____

How well it worked: _____

_____

"Too little time" is a common excuse for not exercising or engaging in other healthy behaviors. Learning to manage your time successfully is crucial if you are to maintain a wellness lifestyle. The first step is to examine how you are currently spending your time; use the following grid to track your activities.

Time	Activity	Time	Activity
6:00 A.M.		6:00 P.M.	
6:30 A.M.		6:30 P.M.	
7:00 A.M.		7:00 P.M.	
8:00 A.M.		8:00 P.M.	
9:00 A.M.		9:00 P.M.	
10:00 A.M.		10:00 P.M.	
11:00 A.M.		11:00 P.M.	
12:00 P.M.		12:00 A.M.	
1:00 P.M.		1:00 A.M.	
2:00 P.M.		2:00 A.M.	
3:00 P.M.		3:00 A.M.	
4:00 P.M.		4:00 A.M.	
5:00 P.M.		5:00 A.M.	

Next, list each type of activity and the total time you engaged in it on a given day in the chart below (for example, sleeping, 7 hours; eating, 1.5 hours; studying, 3 hours; working, 3 hours; and so on). Take a close look at your list of activities. Successful time management is based on prioritization. Assign a priority to each of your activities according to how important it is to you: essential (A), somewhat important (B), or not important (C). Based on these priority rankings, make changes in your schedule by adding and subtracting hours from different categories of activities; enter a duration goal for each activity. Add your new activities to the list and assign a priority and duration goal to each.

Activity	Current Total Duration	Priority (A, B, or C)	Goal Total Duration

Prioritizing in this manner will involve trade-offs. For example, you may choose to reduce the amount of time you spend watching television, listening to music, and chatting on the telephone while you increase the amount of time spent sleeping, studying, and exercising. Don't feel that you have to miss out on anything you enjoy. You can get more from less time by focusing on what you are doing. Strategies for managing time more productively and creatively are described in Chapter 10.

ACTIVITY 11   DEVELOPING REALISTIC SELF-TALK

Self-talk is the ongoing internal dialogue we have with ourselves throughout much of the day. Our thoughts can be accurate, positive, and supportive, or they can be exaggerated and negative. Self-talk is closely related to self-esteem and self-concept. Realistic self-talk can help maintain positive self-esteem, the belief that one is a good and competent person, worthy of friendship and love. A negative internal dialogue can reinforce negative self-esteem and can make behavior change difficult. Substituting realistic self-talk for negative self-talk can help you build and maintain self-esteem and cope better with the challenges in your life.

First, take a closer look at your current pattern of self-talk. Use your health journal to track self-talk, especially as it relates to your target behavior. Does any of your self-talk fall into the common patterns of distorted, negative self-talk shown in Chapter 10 (p. 324)? If so, use the examples of realistic self-talk from Chapter 10 to develop more accurate and rational responses. Write your current negative thoughts in the left-hand column, and then record more realistic thoughts in the right-hand column.

Current Self-Talk About Target Behavior

_____

_____

_____

_____

_____

_____

More Realistic Self-Talk

_____

_____

_____

_____

_____

_____

Your behavior change program will be more successful if the people around you are supportive and involved—or at least are not sabotaging your efforts. Use your health journal to track how other people influence your target behavior and your efforts to change it. For example, do you always skip exercising when you're with certain people? Do you always drink or eat too much when you socialize with certain friends? Are friends and family members offering you enthusiastic support for your efforts to change your behavior, or do they make jokes about your program? Have they even noticed your efforts? Summarize the reactions of those around you in the chart below.

Target behavior _____

Person	Typical Effect on Target Behavior	Involvement in/Reaction to Program

   It may be difficult to change the actions and reactions of the people who are close to you. For them to be involved in your program, you may need to develop new ways of interacting with them (for example, taking a walk rather than going out to dinner as a means of socializing). Most of your friends and family members will want to help you—if they know how. Ask for exactly the type of help or involvement you want. Do you want feedback, praise, or just cooperation? Would you like someone to witness your contract or to be involved more directly in your program? Do you want someone to stop sabotaging your efforts by inviting you to watch TV, eat rich desserts, and so on? Look for ways that the people who are close to you can share in your behavior change program. They can help to motivate you and to maintain your commitment to your program. Develop a way that each individual you listed above can become involved in your program in a positive way.

Person	Target Involvement in Behavior Change Program

   Choose one person on your list to tackle first. Talk to that person about her or his current behavior and how you would like her or him to be involved in your behavior change program. Below, describe this person's reaction to your talk and her or his subsequent behavior. Did this individual become a positive participant in your behavior change program?

_____

_____

_____

_____

Long-standing habits are difficult to change in part because many represent ways people have developed to cope with certain feelings. For example, people may overeat when bored, skip their exercise sessions when frustrated, or drink alcoholic beverages when anxious. Developing new ways to deal with feelings can help improve the chance that a behavior change program will succeed.

Review the records on your target behavior that you kept in your health journal. Identify the feelings that are interfering with the success of your program and develop new strategies for coping with them. Some common problematic feelings are listed below, along with one possible coping strategy for each. Put a check mark next to those that are influencing your target behavior and fill in additional strategies. Add the other feelings that are significant roadblocks in your program to the bottom of the chart, along with coping strategies for each.

✔	Feeling	Coping Strategies
	Stressed out	Go for a 10-minute walk.
	Anxious	Do one of the relaxation exercises described in Chapter 10.
	Bored	Call a friend for a chat.
	Tired	Take a 20-minute nap.
	Frustrated	Identify the source of the feeling and deal with it constructively.

- Julia is trying to give up smoking; her friend Marie continues to offer her cigarettes whenever they are together.
- Emilio is planning to exercise in the morning; his roommates tell him he's being antisocial by not having brunch with them.
- Tracy's boyfriend told her that in high school he once experimented with drugs and shared needles; she wants him to have an HIV test, but he says he's sure the people he shared needles with were not infected.

Peer pressure is the common ingredient in these situations. To successfully maintain your behavior change program, you must develop effective strategies for resisting peer pressure. Assertive communication is one such strategy. By communicating assertively—firmly, but not aggressively—you can stick with your program even in the face of pressure from others. Review your health journal to determine how other people affect your target behavior. If you find that you often do give in to peer pressure, try the following strategies for communicating more assertively:

- Collect your thoughts, and plan in advance what you will say. You might try out your response on a friend to get some feedback.
- State your case—how you feel and what you want—as clearly as you can.
- Use "I" messages—statements about how you feel—rather than "you" statements.
- Focus on the behavior rather than the person. Suggest a solution, such as asking the other person to change his or her behavior toward you. Avoid generalizations. Be specific about what you want.
- Make clear, constructive requests. Focus on your needs ("I would like . . .") rather than the mistakes of others ("You always . . .").
- Avoid blaming, accusing, and belittling. Treat others with the same respect you'd like to receive yourself.
- Ask for action ahead of time. Tell others what you would like to happen; don't wait for them to do the wrong thing and then get angry at them.
- Ask for a response to what you have proposed. Wait for an answer and listen carefully to it. Try to understand other people's points of view, just as you would hope that others would understand yours.

With these strategies in mind, review your health journal and identify three instances in which peer pressure interfered with your behavior change program. For each instance, write out what you might have said to deal with the situation more assertively. (If you can't find three situations from your experiences, choose one or more of the three scenarios described at the beginning of this activity.)

1. _____
   _____
   _____

2. _____
   _____
   _____

3. _____
   _____
   _____

Assertive communication can help you achieve your behavior change goals in a direct way by helping you keep your program on track. It can also provide a boost for your self-image and increase your confidence in your ability to successfully manage your behavior.

If you maintain your new behavior for at least 6 months, you've reached the maintenance stage and your chances of life-time success are greatly increased. However, you may find yourself sliding back into old habits at some point. If this happens, there are some things you can do to help maintain your new behavior.

- Remind yourself of the goals of your program (list them here).

_____

_____

_____

_____

_____

- Pay attention to how your new pattern of behavior has improved your wellness status. List the major benefits of changing your behavior, both now and in the future.

_____

_____

_____

_____

_____

- Consider the things you enjoy most about your new pattern of behavior. List your favorite aspects.

_____

_____

_____

_____

_____

- Think of yourself as a problem solver. If something begins to interfere with your program, devise strategies for dealing with it. Take time out now to list things that have the potential to derail your program and develop possible coping mechanisms.

Problem	**Solution**
_____	_____
	_____
_____	_____
	_____
_____	_____
	_____
_____	_____

- Remember the basics of behavior change. If your program runs into trouble, go back to keeping records of your behavior to pinpoint problem areas. Make adjustments in your program to deal with new disruptions. And don't feel defeated if you lapse. The best thing you can do is renew your commitment and continue with your program.

Index